UNDERSTANDING POETRY

Understanding Poetry

AN ANTHOLOGY FOR COLLEGE STUDENTS

REVISED

COMPLETE EDITION

CLEANTH BROOKS
Yale University

ROBERT PENN WARREN
University of Minnesota

New York
HENRY HOLT AND COMPANY

Printed in the United States of America
Designed by John King

June, 1952

COPYRIGHT ACKNOWLEDGMENTS

Brandt & Brandt
for E. E. Cummings, "Portrait" and "the season 'tis, my lovely lambs" from *Collected Poems,* published by Harcourt, Brace & Company, Inc. Copyright, 1926, by Horace Liveright.

Chatto and Windus
for Canadian rights for Richard Eberhart, "The Fury of Aerial Bombardment" from *Burr Oaks* and "The Groundhog" from *Reading the Spirit.*
for an extract from *Vulgarity in Literature* by Aldous Huxley, by permission of Chatto and Windus and the author.

The Clarendon Press, Oxford, England
for Robert Bridges, "Low Barometer" from *New Verse* and "Nightingales" from *The Shorter Poems by Robert Bridges* (1931). By permission of The Clarendon Press, Oxford.

Creative Age Press, Inc.
for Robert Graves, *The White Goddess,* p. 186; copyright, 1948, by Robert Graves. By permission of Creative Age Press, Inc.

The Dial Press, Inc.
for Randall Jarrell, "The Death of the Ball Turret Gunner" and "Losses." Reprinted from *Little Friend, Little Friend* by Randall Jarrell by permission of The Dial Press, Inc. Copyright 1945 by The Dial Press, Inc.

Doubleday & Company, Inc.
for Joyce Kilmer, "Trees" from *Trees and Other Poems* by Joyce Kilmer, copyright 1914 by Doubleday, Doran & Co., Inc.

Faber and Faber Limited
for Canadian rights for W. H. Auden, "As I Walked Out One Evening," "Doom Is Dark," "In Memory of W. B. Yeats," "Lay Your Sleeping Head, My Love," and "O Where Are You Going?" from *Collected Poems* of W. H. Auden.
for Canadian rights for T. S. Eliot, "Journey of the Magi," "The Love Song of J. Alfred Prufrock," "Preludes," and "The Waste Land" from *Collected Poems* of T. S. Eliot.
for Canadian rights for William Empson, "Just a Smack at Auden" and "Missing Dates" from *The Gathering Storm.*

Fearing, Kenneth
for permission to reprint "Portrait," copyright, 1938, by the author. Originally

Alfred A. Knopf, Inc.

for John Crowe Ransom, "Bells for John Whiteside's Daughter," "The Equilibrists," and "Winter Remembered" from *Selected Poems,* by John Crowe Ransom, by permission of Alfred A. Knopf, Inc. Copyright 1924, 1927, 1945, by Alfred A. Knopf, Inc.

for Wallace Stevens, "Peter Quince at the Clavier" from *Harmonium* by Wallace Stevens, by permission of Alfred A. Knopf, Inc. Copyright 1923, 1941, by Alfred A. Knopf, Inc. For "No Possum, No Sop, No Taters" from *Transport to Summer* by Wallace Stevens, by permission of Alfred A. Knopf, Inc. Copyright 1942, 1947, by Wallace Stevens.

Little, Brown and Company

for Emily Dickinson, "After Great Pain a Formal Feeling Comes," "Because I Could Not Stop for Death," and "The Soul Selects" from *The Poems of Emily Dickinson,* Centenary Edition, edited by Martha Dickinson Bianchi and Alfred Leete Hampson. Reprinted by permission of Little, Brown & Co.

for Ogden Nash, "Kind of an Ode to Duty," from *The Face Is Familiar,* copyright 1938, by Ogden Nash, by permission of Little, Brown & Co.

Liveright Publishing Corporation

for Hart Crane, "At Melville's Tomb," "Praise for an Urn," "Voyages, II," and "Voyages, VI" from *The Collected Poems of Hart Crane* by Hart Crane, published by Liveright Publishing Corp., New York. Copyright 1933, Liveright, Inc.

Macmillan & Co., Ltd., London

for Canadian rights for Thomas Hardy, "Channel Firing," "The Going," "In Tenebris, I," "The Man He Killed," and "Wessex Heights," from *Collected Poems* of Thomas Hardy. By permission of the Trustees of the Hardy Estate and Macmillan & Co., Ltd., publishers.

for Canadian rights for James Stephens, "The Goat Paths" and "The Main-Deep" from *Collected Poems of James Stephens.* By permission of the author and Macmillan & Co., Ltd., publishers.

The Macmillan Company

for Thomas Hardy, "Channel Firing," "The Going," "In Tenebris, I," "The Man He Killed," and "Wessex Heights" from Thomas Hardy *Collected Poems.* Copyright 1925 by The Macmillan Company and used with their permission.

for Marianne Moore, "In Distrust of Merits" from Marianne Moore *Nevertheless.* Copyright 1944 by Marianne Moore and used with the permission of The Macmillan Company.

for Edwin Arlington Robinson, "Mr. Flood's Party" from Edwin Arlington Robinson *Avon's Harvest.* Copyright 1921, 1949, by Edwin Arlington Robinson and used with the permission of The Macmillan Company.

for James Stephens, "The Goat Paths" from James Stephens *Songs from Clay.* Copyright 1915, 1943, by The Macmillan Company, and used with their permission. And for "The Main-Deep" from *Poetry Recital* by James Stephens. Copyright 1925 by The Macmillan Company and used with their permission.

for William Butler Yeats, "After Long Silence" from William Butler Yeats *Winding Stair.* Copyright 1933 by The Macmillan Company and used with their permission. For "Among School Children," "Sailing to Byzantium," and "Two Songs from a Play," from William Butler Yeats *The Tower.* Copyright 1928 by

pany, 1922 by John Peale Bishop, 1948 by Charles Scribner's Sons; used by permission of the publishers, Charles Scribner's Sons.

for Donald Davidson, "Lee in the Mountains," copyright 1926 by the Poetry Society of South Carolina, 1938 by Donald Davidson; from *Lee in the Mountains and Other Poems* (1949) by Donald Davidson. Reprinted by permission of the publishers, Charles Scribner's Sons.

for Edwin Arlington Robinson, "Luke Havergal." Reprinted from *The Children of the Night* by Edwin Arlington Robinson; published by Charles Scribner's Sons.

for Allen Tate, "The Last Days of Alice" and "Ode to the Confederate Dead." Reprinted from *Poems 1922–1947* by Allen Tate; copyright 1932, 1948, by Charles Scribner's Sons; used by permission of the publishers, Charles Scribner's Sons.

Shapiro, Karl

for permission, with *The Hopkins Review,* to reprint "Case History of 'The Minute' " and, with *The Nation,* to reprint "The Minute."

Simon and Schuster, Inc.

for Max Eastman, *Heroes I Have Known,* p. 177. Reprinted from *Heroes I Have Known* by permission of Simon and Schuster, publishers. Copyright, 1942, by Max Eastman.

The Society of Authors, London

for Canadian rights for A. E. Housman, "1887," "Epitaph on an Army of Mercenaries," "Farewell to Barn and Stack and Tree," "Hell Gate," "I Hoed and Trenched and Weeded," "The Immortal Part," "The Lads in Their Hundreds," and "To an Athlete Dying Young." By permission of the Society of Authors as the Literary Representative of the Trustees of the Estate of the late A. E. Housman, with reference to Jonathan Cape, Ltd., and Henry Holt and Company as British and United States publishers of A. E. Housman *Collected Poems.*

The Swallow Press

see William Morrow & Company, Inc.

Thomas, Helen (Mrs. Edward)

for permission to include Edward Thomas, "The Gallows," "The Owl," and "When First I Came Here."

The Viking Press, Inc.

for D. H. Lawrence, "Piano." From *The Portable D. H. Lawrence.* Copyright 1929 by Jonathan Cape and Harrison Smith, Inc. Reprinted by permission of The Viking Press, Inc., New York.

A. P. Watt & Son

for Canadian rights for Robert Graves, *The White Goddess,* p. 186, with the permission of Mr. Graves and Faber and Faber Limited; and for Canadian rights for Robert Graves, "Rocky Acres" from *Collected Poems 1914–47,* with the permission of Mr. Graves and Cassell and Company.

for Canadian rights for William Butler Yeats, "After Long Silence," "Among School Children," "A Deep-Sworn Vow," "Sailing to Byzantium," "The Second Coming," "Two Songs from a Play," and "Upon a Dying Lady." By permission of A. P. Watt & Son together with The Macmillan Company of Canada and Mrs. W. B. Yeats.

TO WILLIAM A. READ

Letter to the Teacher (1938)

With a Postscript (1950)

This book has been conceived on the assumption that if poetry is worth teaching at all it is worth teaching as poetry. The temptation to make a substitute for the poem as the object of study is usually overpowering. The substitutes are various, but the most common ones are:

1. Paraphrase of logical and narrative content;
2. Study of biographical and historical materials;
3. Inspirational and didactic interpretation.

Of course, paraphrase may be necessary as a preliminary step in the reading of a poem, and a study of the biographical and historical background may do much to clarify interpretation; but these things should be considered as means and not as ends. And though one may consider a poem as an instance of historical or ethical documentation, the poem in itself, if literature is to be studied as literature, remains finally the object for study. Moreover, even if the interest is in the poem as a historical or ethical document, there is a prior consideration: one must grasp the poem as a literary construct before it can offer any real illumination as a document.

When, as a matter of fact, an attempt is made to treat the poem as an object in itself, the result very often is, on the one hand, the vaguest sort of impressionistic comment, or on the other, the study of certain technical aspects of the poem, metrics for instance, *in isolation from other aspects and from the total intention.*

In illustration of these confused approaches to the study of poetry the editors submit the following quotations drawn almost at random from a group of current textbooks.

The sole critical comment on "Ode to a Nightingale" in one popular textbook is:

"The song of the nightingale brings sadness and exhilaration to the poet and makes him long to be lifted up and away from the limitations of life. The seventh stanza is particularly beautiful."

In the same textbook a typical exercise reads:

"What evidences of a love of beauty do you find in Keats's poems?"

But one is constrained to voice the following questions:

1. How is the paradox of "exhilaration" and "sadness" related to the theme of the poem? Surely, this is important. Yet the question of the theme of the poem is never raised in this textbook.

2. The seventh stanza is referred to as "beautiful," but on what grounds is the student to take any piece of poetry as "beautiful"?

3. Even if the exercise quoted is relevant, there is a real danger that the suggestion to the student to look for beautiful objects in the poem will tend to make him confuse with poetic excellence the mention of beautiful or agreeable objects.

Some of the same confusions reappear in another book: "These lyrics ["Ode to the West Wind" and "To a Skylark"] are characterized by a freshness and spontaneity, beautiful figures of speech in abundance, melody, and an unusually skillful adaptation of the form and movement of the verse to the word and the idea. Their melodiousness is sometimes compared with that of Schubert's music."

But in what, for example, does a beautiful comparison consist? The implication is that the beautiful comparison is one which makes use of beautiful objects. Again, when a student has been given no concrete exposition of the "adaptation of form and movement . . . to the word and the idea" of a poem, and has received no inkling of what the "idea" of a particular poem is, what is such a statement expected to mean to him?

Or again: "To the simplicity and exquisite melodiousness of these earlier songs, Blake added mysticism and the subtlest kind of symbolism." One is moved to comment: In the first place, the student can only be made to grasp the function of symbolism in poetry by the most careful investigation of particular instances; certainly, "the subtlest kind of symbolism" should not be flung at him with no further introduction than is provided by this sentence. In the second place, what can the sentence mean on any level? Is it proper to say that any poet "adds" mysticism to anything? And what sort of simplicity is it to which subtle symbolism can be added? Does the *mélange* remain simple? And what possible connection is implied here between the "exquisite melodiousness" and the mysticism and symbolism? In any case, the approach to poetry indicated in this sentence raises more problems than it solves.

To glean from another recent textbook: "Emily [Dickinson] the seer teases us into believing that she has dived into the depths where great truths lie and has brought up new and astounding specimens. Many of her bulletins from Immortality seem oracular. Shorn of her matchless imagery they turn out to be puritan platitudes or transcendental echoes. Her definitions of weighty abstractions are unphilosophical. They are quick fancies, created out of a fleeting mood, and are therefore frequently contradictory. But when Emily failed with logic, she succeeded with imagination." It is impossible, apparently, to determine from what principles of poetic criticism these remarks can be derived. The objection that Emily Dickinson's poetry when "shorn of its matchless imagery" would turn out to be platitudes could be raised with equal justification about the most celebrated passages of Shakespeare. The passage rests on a misconception of the relation of "truth" to poetry, and on a confused notion of what constitutes poetic originality. Certainly, to clarify the issue of "truth" and poetic excellence, or of originality and poetic excellence, would be a very ambitious undertaking; but that fact scarcely justifies a complete fogging of the issue.

Occasionally the writer of a textbook will attempt to deal with poetry as a thing in itself worthy of study; and apparently hoping to avoid the sort of vagueness found in the preceding quotation, will isolate certain aspects of poetry for special investigation. In its crudest manifestation this impulse leads to statistical surveys of one kind or another. The student, for instance, is exhorted to count or to classify the figures of speech in a poem; or to define metrical forms. A more sophisticated manifestation of the same impulse appears in the following classification of metrical effects:

"Some of the varied effects *produced by meter* are illustrated in the following stanzas:

Sweet softness—

Swiftly walk o'er the western wave,
  Spirit of Night!
Out of thy misty eastern cave,
Where all the long and lone daylight,
Thou wovest dreams of joy and fear, 5
Which makes thee terrible, and dear—
  Swift be thy flight!

—Shelley, 'To Night'

Stark simplicity—

Out of the night that covers me,
Black as the pit from pole to pole,
I thank whatever gods may be
For my unconquerable soul.
—Henley, 'Invictus' "

The author has said flatly concerning these quotations that the effects described are "produced by meter." The statement is completely misleading and rests upon an imperfect understanding of the relation of meter to the other factors in a poem. A clever student would immediately confute the author by pointing out that the line, "Out of thy misty eastern cave," the meter of which is supposed to communicate "soft sweetness," and the line, "Out of the night that covers me," the meter of which is supposed to communicate "stark simplicity," have *exactly* the same meter. In fact, he might point out that many metrical effects are common to selections which communicate very different emotional effects.

This is not to deny that meter is an important factor in poetry, but it is to deny that a specific emotional effect can be tied absolutely to a particular metrical instance. The selections cited do produce different emotional effects, but the basis for the effect can only be given accurately by a study of the relations existing among all the factors, of which meter is only one.

Another instance of the isolation of one technical feature without regard for the whole context and for the particular poet's method is the following observation in a recent textbook:

"Hamlet's 'take arms against a sea of troubles' is a classic instance of the poet's failure to visualize what he is saying. Longfellow's mariner, in 'A Psalm of Life' 'sailing o'er life's solemn main' and at the same time apparently examining 'footprints on the sands of time,' is another example of confused phrasing."

This passage might be taken as a classic example of the misapplication of an undigested critical principle. We frequently see in textbooks on poetry and in rhetorics the warning against the use of "mixed metaphor." But, of course, in applying this principle one must, in every case, examine the context of the instance, the psychological basis, and the poet's intention.[1] These factors are entirely

[1] This matter of mixed metaphor is discussed at length on pp. 274–85.

ignored in the present quotation. For instance, the dramatic situation in the passage from *Hamlet* and the relation of the style to it are dismissed by the high-handed and abstract application of this principle. Incidentally this method would eliminate the following well-known passages, among many, from the work of Shakespeare:

> Tomorrow and tomorrow and tomorrow
> Creeps in this petty pace from day to day
> To the last syllable. . . .
>
> *Macbeth*

> If the assassination
> Could trammel up the consequence and catch
> With his surcrease, success . . .
>
> *Macbeth*

> Was the hope drunk
> Wherein you dressed yourself? hath it slept since?
> And wakes it now, to look so green and pale . . .
>
> *Macbeth*

The critic in question would apparently be embarrassed by the imaginative agility required for reading much of Shakespeare's poetry, especially the poetry of his so-called "great period," simply because he places his reliance on the mechanical and legalistic application of a single principle without reference to context.

As a matter of ironical fact, the image involved in the speech quoted from *Hamlet* can be visualized. One has only to remember the stories of Xerxes and Cuchulain, one who punished and one who fought the sea, to grasp the point. Furthermore, in justice to "The Psalm of Life," which is on enough counts a very bad poem, one can indicate that a little more attentive reading will reveal the fact that the mariner who sees the footprints is not actually on the high seas at the moment, but is, as the poem specifically says, a "shipwrecked brother."

The editors of the present book hold that a satisfactory method of teaching poetry should embody the following principles.

1. Emphasis should be kept on the poem as a poem.

2. The treatment should be concrete and inductive.

3. A poem should always be treated as an organic system of relationships, and the poetic quality should never be understood as inhering in one or more factors taken in isolation.

With the hope of giving these principles some vitality the editors have undertaken this book.

This book must stand or fall by the *analyses* of individual poems which it contains. These *analyses* are intended to be discussions of the poet's adaptation of his means to his ends: that is, discussions of the relations of the various aspects of a poem to each other and to the total communication intended. The analyses presented in the early sections of this book are simple and very incomplete accounts of the problems involved. But the analyses become more difficult as the student is provided with more critical apparatus and becomes more accustomed to the method. The analyses, therefore, form parts of an ascending scale and should not be studied haphazardly.

The general organization of the book is, likewise, determined by this scale of ascending difficulty. The book has seven divisions.[1] Section I deals with poems in which the narrative element is relatively important. Poems of this general nature appear here because the narrative interest seems to afford the broadest and most unspecialized appeal to the ordinary student. The basic question behind the analyses in this section is: *What distinguishes the poetic treatment of a story from the more usual prose treatment?* Section II deals with poems in which the narrative is merely implied or is suppressed in favor of some such interest as that in psychology or character. Section III takes up another approach, that of the poet as observer rather than as narrator. The poems in this section range from those which are ostensibly simple, objective descriptions to those in which description emerges with a definite symbolic force.

Section IV takes up one of the more specialized technical problems, that of the nature of rhythm and meter as means of communication. The analyses in this section naturally emphasize the technical considerations of verse, but the attempt is constantly made to indicate the relation of these considerations to the others which the student has already studied. In Section V are considered some of the ways in which tone and attitude are communicated to the reader. The poems of Section VI present some special problems in the use of imagery as a device of communication, and those of Section VII raise questions concerning the function of idea and statement.

[1] For the organization of this revised edition, see the "Postscript" (p. xxv) and the *Table of Contents.*

Although the poems are arranged in these groups, it is not to be understood that the topics which determine the arrangement are treated in isolation. As a matter of fact, the analyses and questions which are appended to each poem aim at making the student aware of the organic relationship existing among these factors in poetic communication. Obviously, any poem whatsoever would, finally, raise the questions associated with all of these topics. Questions involving imagery, for example, occur even in Section I and are treated in the analyses. Pedagogical convenience, however, demands that special attention be focused on special problems; but, as has been said, it does not demand that those problems be treated in isolation. A poem, then, is placed in any given section because it may be used to emphasize a certain aspect of poetic method and offers an especially teachable example. But these classifications must be understood as classifications of convenience. Indeed, it might be a fruitful exercise for the students to return to poems in early sections after they have acquired more critical apparatus.

The poems, as has been pointed out, are arranged in a scale of increasing difficulty. Usually, poems of the simplest method and of the broadest general appeal appear in the early sections. But such a scale, of course, cannot be absolute. For example, a poem like "The Ancient Mariner," which appears in Section I,[1] is on absolute grounds more difficult than many poems appearing in later sections. But it does offer a strong narrative interest. Furthermore, the poems in each section offer a scale of ascending difficulty in regard to the particular problem under discussion. Since this is the case, if poems toward the end of each of the later sections prove too difficult, they may be omitted without impairing the general method.

Although the arrangement of poems adopted in this book is one of convenience, it is based on two considerations: first, on aspects of poetic communication, and second, on pedagogical expediency. Therefore, it is hoped that the present arrangement stands on a ground different from the arbitrary and irrational classifications frequently found in textbooks that depart from simple chronological order—classifications such as "lyrics of meditation," "religious lyrics," "poems of patriotism" or "the sonnet," the "Ode," the "song," etc.

If one accepts the principle that one must teach by a constant and

[1] This poem has been moved back to Section VII in this revised edition.

analytical use of concrete examples, then the nature of the *Introduction* will be readily understood. The *Introduction* does not attempt to arrive at a "definition" of poetry or to explain, for instance, the workings of imagery or meter. It attempts, instead, to dispose of a few of the basic misconceptions with which the teacher is usually confronted in the class room, and therefore to prepare the student to enter upon an unprejudiced study of the actual poems. Likewise, the *Glossary* of critical terms is based on the idea that the teaching of the book will be by concrete example. The *Glossary* does not provide a set of definitions to be memorized all at once by the student. Rather, it provides definitions and an index of cross references to concrete applications of definitions, which the student can consult as the occasion demands. Even the schematic presentation of metrical terms has been relegated to the *Glossary,* although there it is so organized that it may be studied, if desired, as a consecutive discussion. But even in the case of metrical study, the editors suggest that the general principle of the book be applied.

There are two objections to the method of the present book which may occur to a teacher at this point. It may be objected that this text by its number of analyses attempts to usurp the function of the teacher and to do by the written word what can better be done by the spoken word. Or, second, it may be objected that the judgments of literary value which are involved (and necessarily involved) in the analyses are dogmatic and perhaps often in error.

In answer to the first objection it may be urged that: first, the analyses, if they are at all effective, relieve the teacher of a certain amount of preliminary drudgery and free him for a critical and perhaps more advanced treatment of the unanalyzed poems in each section of the book; second, since no analyses here could pretend to final completeness, a certain amount of explanation and extension will be required even in treating poems which are analyzed; and third, the fact that a liberal number of analyses are in printed form gives the student an opportunity for a careful private study of the poems in question. With regard to the second objection—the objection that the judgments in the analyses are dogmatic—the editors can only say that no dogmatism is intended. Naturally, they hope that most of their judgments are reasonable, but even if a teacher disagrees with an individual analysis, an explanation of that disagreement should dramatize for the student the basic issues involved. And in fact, the editors feel that disagreement is to be encouraged in so far as pure impressionism can be eliminated from the debate.

Just as the editors feel that disagreement and debate may be healthful in sharpening the critical instinct of the student, so they feel that the study and analysis of bad and uneven poems will contribute to the same end. A reasonable number of such poems have been included, and a few have been analyzed. The great majority of the poems included in the book, however, represent positive achievement. The modern poems included have not been chosen at random, nor merely on the ground of current fashion. They are intended to represent some of the various lines taken in the development of poetic method in this century. In general, it is hoped that the juxtaposition of good and bad poems, and of new and old poems, will serve to place emphasis on the primary matter of critical reading and evaluation.

Although this book is based on a principle, and is not a casual anthology, and although it is organized in the light of that principle, the final effect, it is hoped, will be to liberate rather than restrict the initiative of the teacher. By positing a principle and a definite objective, the book allows the teacher a great deal of liberty in devising correlative approaches to the general end. Although the book does suggest a variety of exercises for the student, such as analyses modeled on those in the book, comparisons of the prose and poetic versions of the same material, comparisons of poems treating the same theme, etc., the possibility for development along this line is almost infinite and can be adapted to individual needs.[1]

[1] A particularly fruitful source for the development of further exercises will lie in the application of principles developed in later sections of the book to poems treated in earlier sections. For example, the teacher may wish to return, after a study of metrics and related matters, to a poem like "A Dirge" with such exercises as the following:

Discuss the substitutions, hovering accents, and defective feet in ll. 1–2, and l. 8.

For certain classes, the fact that this book has concentrated upon the interpretation and analysis of individual poems may provide an easy and suggestive approach to matters of literary theory and history. After the book has been completed, exercises may be framed, for instance, to relate Wordsworth's theories of diction to his actual practice in "Michael." The student may be

A last word: the editors of this book do not delude themselves that they have here provided, or could elsewhere provide, solutions for any of the fundamental problems of poetic criticism. Nor, least of all, have they provided in this book neat criteria which can be applied in rule-of-thumb fashion. Rather, they hope to present to the student, in proper context and after proper preparation, some of the basic critical problems—with the aim, not of making technical critics, but merely of making competent readers of poetry. At the least, they hope that this book will find some merit in the eyes of those who agree with Louis Cazamian: "that all students of literature should be regarded as historians is an exaggerated and a pernicious assumption. More important still, and much more fruitful than the problems of origins and development, are those of content and significance. What is the human matter, what the artistic value of the work?" So much for the general aim of this book. As for the general method, to quote again from this critic: "it is rightly felt that if the . . . student of literature is to be capable of an intelligent appreciation, he must go beyond the passive enjoyment of what he reads; he must be instructed, partly at least, in the mysteries of the art. . . ."

Postscript (1950)

In the twelve years that have elapsed since we wrote this *Letter to the Teacher,* our personal tastes have changed a little. In certain poets we have discovered values that we had earlier missed. In other poets we find a sad falling away, as inexplicable, perhaps, as the cooling of an old friendship. And some poetry that we had loved and lost has been restored again to us, sometimes the more preciously for the time of estrangement. Between ourselves we find new agreements and new disagreements. Such changes were to be expected, and are to be welcomed. It would be a mournful moment when a man discovered that his tastes were irrevocably fixed, for that would probably mean that his powers of growth had stopped. In that moment he would know that the frost of death was settling down. So we welcome what we like to think are enrichments of perception and expansions of critical sympathy. But at the same time we

asked to discuss lines 89, 169, and 434 in connection with the principle of the "language really used by men." And in this connection the tone of the entire poem may be analysed.

must confess that our fundamental approach to poetry remains the same. We still believe that poetry is worth serious study as poetry.

When we say that today, however, we say it in a situation different from that of twelve years ago. At that time the ordinary college course in poetry made little or no attempt to teach poetry except by paraphrase, by the study of biographical and historical material, or by didactic interpretation. The attempt to study poetry as poetry, if it was made at all, was usually made in an unsystematic or impressionistic way. There existed, of course, a large body of close criticism and of speculation about the relation of poetic method and poetic meaning, some of it new and some of it as old as Aristotle; but by and large this body of criticism was not often brought to the actual teaching of poetry. We wrote *Understanding Poetry* with the hope of bringing something of the critical attitude, even at a very simple level, into the classroom. We were not alone in that general intention. Other teachers were working in the same direction. But *Understanding Poetry* was the first textbook to embody, however imperfectly, that intention.

Today the critical attitude has entered into hundreds of classrooms. In this new context we are inclined, as we revise *Understanding Poetry,* to make certain shifts of emphasis, or if not shifts of emphasis, at least certain expansions in treatment. A decade ago the chief need was for a sharp focus on the poem itself. At that time it seemed expedient to provide that focus, and to leave to implication the relation of the poem to its historical background, to its place in the context of the poet's work, and to biographical and historical study generally. The years that have followed have indicated that these relationships could not safely be left to implication. Some teachers have felt that *Understanding Poetry* implied a disregard for historical and biographical study. Others, who did not misunderstand the editors on this point, nevertheless have indicated that the relation of criticism to other kinds of literary study needed to be spelled out rather than merely implied. They have quite rightly pointed out that this relationship is not simple but intricate and rich. In this revised edition, therefore, though we continue to insist upon the need for a sharp focus upon the poem itself, we have tried to relate criticism to other literary studies. Specifically, we have attempted to view the poem in relation to its historical situation and in relation to the body of the poet's work.

This is not to say that, feeling that there has been an over-emphasis on the study of the poem as a poem, we hasten to redress the balance. To think in that way is to falsify the whole issue. It is not a matter of putting in two pounds of biographical study or three slices of literary history to go with so much poem. *The problem is, rather, to see how history, literary and general, may be related to poetic meaning.* We have tried to illustrate the relation by extended discussions of Eliot's *The Waste Land* (pp. 645–67) and Marvell's *Horatian Ode* (pp. 667–82 of Section X). We are perfectly well aware that there is no *one* way in which history is related to poetic meaning. Every poem brings up new problems of this sort, and all the critical tact in the world and all the historical scholarship in the world will never render perfect solutions. The process is one of never-ending exploration. We do not profess to give models of procedure but modest examples. Needless to say, we are perfectly well aware that no intelligent teacher has ever presented poetry in a vacuum—that, on the contrary, he brings every resource he possesses to bear upon the poem.

As for the relation of the single poem to the whole body of the poet's work, we have tried to illustrate this in several ways. Several poems by Wordsworth are included in this edition of *Understanding Poetry,* scattered in different sections, but in Section X (pp. 631–44) we try, in an extended essay, to suggest the unity of style and theme. In the treatments of Frost (pp. 389–97) and of Eliot (pp. 433–44) we also try to give some indication of the continuity in the poet's work. Often the single poem may be profitably regarded as a mere stanza in the long developing and unfolding poem which is the whole work. For in the work of a serious poet we usually find not many themes but few. Even in a poet of great variety and complication, there is some central concern, some fundamental attitude, from which the richness exfoliates. Once we understand this, we find that one poem serves as a gloss upon the next.

In our own experience in the classroom (and out) we have frequently encountered something like the following remark: "How do you know that you aren't just reading your own ideas into the poem? He certainly couldn't have had all *that* in his mind when he was writing the poem." Perhaps the most effective way to get at this matter is to try to understand something of the process of poetic composition. Many readers, even readers who ought to know better, cannot break free from the notion that somehow the poem is a mechanical projection of an "intention"—that there is a fine plan, something like an architect's blueprint, existing in the poet's head before he begins to compose, and that the composition is the execution of this plan. Only by understanding that the creative process is deep and complicated, that it may manifest itself in many different ways, and that it is primarily a process of search for meanings and exploration of meanings—only by understanding all this, can we understand how ideas, themes, meanings get into poetry at all, and understand that, in the full sense, the poem is not a vehicle for its idea, but *is* its idea, its meaning. In Section IX (pp. 591–629), therefore, we have assembled and tried to interpret a body of material bearing on the question of the creative process. Some of this material, such as that from Wordsworth, Coleridge, Keats, Mozart, and Bonnard, is perfectly standard and readily accessible; but some, such as the work-sheets of A. E. Housman and the letters from Frost and Eliot, is made available here for the first time.

There is another kind of objection to analytic criticism, the objection that to analyze or interpret a poem destroys it. The objector protests that he wants to enjoy the poem, not to murder it by dissection. Such a protest commands one's respect. Certainly we should want to enjoy the poem, to confront it fully and appreciatively, to contemplate its qualities immediately and innocently. The trouble is that we may not even know what the qualities of the poem are until we have worked a little at the poem. Immediacy and innocence must sometimes be earned. Sometimes we cannot confront the poem fully and appreciatively until we understand the relation among the elements that make up the poem. This is not to deny that the intuitive grasp may precede exegesis. A poem that makes no direct appeal to anyone will never be studied. Criticism will never bother with it and there will never be any exegesis. But we must remember that the direct appeal is a direct appeal to *someone at some time.* Some people are never ready for the direct appeal of any poem, and the best of us progress only by gradual stages from *Mother Goose* to "Lycidas." We have to grow up to the level of a poem before we can experience the direct appeal, and criticism can sometimes help us in the process. Even our critical failures may help us if we can recognize them.

But we can never be sure that we have fully grown up to a rich poem like "Lycidas" or *Hamlet.* To assume that we can be sure is to imply that there is a fixed and proper relation between the reader and the poem, that there is, as it were, an official reading of the text. And to imply this is to falsify the whole matter. The good reader of poetry knows that there are no "official" readings. He knows that there is only a continuing and ever-renewing transaction between him and the poem, a perpetual dialectic. For this reason the process of criticism is a never-ending process. It cannot exhaust the good poem or the good poet. This means more criticism, not less. But it ought to mean a criticism constantly returning to the object and constantly refining itself by fresh appeals to intuition and perception.

Those who object to critical analysis may feel that they get some aid and comfort from the poets themselves. Many poets would sympathize with Frost in his fear of the reader who "stands at the end of a poem ready in waiting to catch you by both hands with enthusiasm and drag you off your balance over the last punctuation mark into more than you meant to say." Or with Yeats when he was reluctant to confirm a critic's interpretation of one of his poems because he thought that for a poet to accept the reading of a critic, or to interpret his own poem, would limit the poem. The poet's great aversion is for the abstract statement. He creates a poem because he wants meanings dramatized, embodied, developed through experience, realized in the medium of language. He tends to be suspicious of the critic on principle, for the critic must deal in abstraction and the critic is compelled to lay out discursively what the poet attempts to present massively. But the poet's suspicions should be allayed if the critic can assure him that he does not regard his analysis as a substitute for the poem itself or an account of the process by which the poem was composed, but merely as a preparation for the poem itself.

The poem itself. The phrase brings to mind another objection that has been raised against this book, the objection that it encourages "mere estheticism," that it makes no place for the human reference, the moral and social significance, of poetry. It would probably be fruitless to discuss this question with anyone who after a reasonably careful reading of this book repeated the objection, but for the sake of the record we shall speak briefly on the point.

A study of poetry that starts from the notion of the poem as a little drama can scarcely be said to ignore the human materials that enter into poetry, for the dramatic situation is dramatic only because it urgently involves human impulses. As the poem starts from an urgent situation, so it ends by making, directly or indirectly, a comment on human conduct and human values. And no good poem makes a merely trivial comment.

Granting this, where does what we may call poetic value come in? We believe that there is such a thing as intrinsic poetic value—else why would poetry have come to exist at all? Poetry is self-validating in that it fulfills some human need which cannot otherwise be fulfilled. *But this value can never exist in isolation.* What the relation is between this intrinsic value and other values is a most vexed and delicate question, one that can scarcely be settled here. Perhaps it can never be settled. Perhaps it is the fundamental kind of question that must be lived through, over and over again.

What we can and must say here, however, is that the various values that may attach to a poem are massively and organically involved together. In the final analysis, until the poem can be read as a poem we cannot discuss any of its values with confidence. The moral attitudes it embodies are, for instance, as deeply involved in the technical ordering of the poem as they are in any statement the poem may make. In fact, they are more deeply involved in the technical ordering. The meaning of the poem is, finally, in the kind of *being* the poem has and not in any particular statement (taken abstractly) that it may make. This is not to say that statements or ideas are not important in poetry. They are tremendously important; but they are important as elements entering into the total structure which is the poem and into the total experience of the poem.

If this is true, the study of what makes a poem a poem and not something else—the study of the nature of poetic expression—is essential for our apprehension of, not only the intrinsic value of the poetry, but also of the social and moral values. It is essential also for any serious study of poetry in relation to literary or general history. The historian who depends for his material upon the "statements" made by poetry is somewhat naïve. Ideas and attitudes work at a deeper level.

This *Postscript* has already run longer than we had intended, but at the risk of making the tail wag the dog, we shall say something about the new organization of the book and about the omissions and additions. In practice we found, as a significant number of other teachers have found, that the distinction between Sections I and II in the old edition—that is, between the poem of narrative and the poem of implied narrative—was unnecessary. Section I of the present edition, therefore, contains poems of both kinds. We also found that there were too many poems in the early sections of the book. At that stage most students are anxious to push on to new problems and new emphases. We decided, furthermore, that we had put into the section on metrics (the old Section IV) far too many poems and passages merely to illustrate a meter, a stanza, or something of the sort. Such illustrations are always available by reference to other sections of the book. We have, therefore, reduced this material to a minimum, and have retained in the new Section III only those items that seemed to have other values as well.

Experience in the classroom soon forced us to conclude that many of the exercises attached to the poems were perfunctory and superficial, and did not really offer a lead into fruitful discussion. In this edition we have thoroughly reworked the exercises. There can be, of course, no such thing as a completely satisfactory set of exercises for a poem—or at least there cannot be, within any reasonable space—but we are confident that the exercises in this new edition are an improvement on those in the old. The poems in the new Section VII, it should be noted, are printed *without exercises*. In this section are to be found simple as well as complex poems; and the teacher who wishes to put the student, from time to time, completely on his own may be grateful to have one section of poems without editorial apparatus.

This new edition of *Understanding Poetry* is greatly enlarged. We have added extended critical discussions in the section on special topics (Sections VIII, IX, and X) though not at the expense of the space devoted to poems. Feeling dissatisfied with the showing of the poetry of the eighteenth century, we have now included such works as *The Rape of the Lock* and the full text of *The Vanity of Human Wishes.* We have undertaken in particular to strengthen the representation of poetry from the present century. Not that we conceive this book to be a representative anthology of modern poetry. Some important names are omitted even now. But the book does give a fairly full showing of contemporary practice and of contemporary themes, enough to allow generalizations about various tendencies and to provide contrast and comparison with the past.

A casual examination may suggest that in expanding the book, we have rendered the teacher a dubious benefit, presenting him with far more material than he can possibly use. But the thoughtful teacher, we are confident, will be grateful for the enlargement. The greater variety of materials allows him a wider and more flexible choice of poems and problems which he may need for the particular class he faces. Furthermore, for use in more elementary courses, or in courses where the time available for the study of poetry is limited, there is a Shorter Edition of this book. This edition comprises the first six sections of the book—that is, all the poems which are accompanied by analyses or exercises—plus the indexes and the glossary.

In general we have tried to keep firmly in mind the principle that the teacher is central to the process of teaching. We know that the best book is ineffective without his mediation and that he can partially redeem even a bad book. We remind ourselves of this principle now as we commit this book to the press. We know that tomorrow, when the type has been cast for this edition, we shall have a hundred thoughts for revisions not now made. But we believe that we have made our book a more flexible instrument for the teacher to use. His revisions and modifications of it in his classroom practice are inevitable, and these we heartily welcome.

New Haven, Conn. C. B.
Minneapolis, Minn. R. P. W.
May 29, 1950

CONTENTS

[Asterisks (*) indicate poems that are analysed.]

SECTION VI—STATEMENT AND IDEA

SECTION VII—POEMS FOR STUDY: NEW AND OLD

[1] See pp. 645–67.

[2] See pp. 667–82. [3] See pp. 631–45.

INTRODUCTION

Poetry is a form of speech, or discourse, written or spoken. To the person who is not well acquainted with poetry the differences between poetic speech and other forms may seem to be more important than the similarities, but these differences should not be allowed to obscure the fundamental resemblances, for only by an understanding of the resemblances can one appreciate the meaning of the differences. In poetry, as in all other discourse, one person is saying something to another person. But what is that "something"? We usually identify it with information. As practical people going about our affairs, we ask directions, read road signs, order a dinner from a menu, study football scores or stock market reports. It is altogether natural, therefore, that we should tend to think the important and central matter in all discourse to be information. But, after all, we may do well to ask how much of the discourse of an average man in any given day is primarily concerned with information for the sake of information. After he has transacted his business, obeyed his road signs, ordered and eaten his dinner, and read the stock market reports, he might be surprised to reflect on the number of non-practical functions speech had fulfilled for him that day. He had told the office boy a joke; he had commented on the weather to the traffic officer, who could observe the weather as well as he; he had told an old friend that he was glad to see him again; he had chatted with his wife on some subject on which there was already full knowledge and agreement.

Even when he had been at lunch with some business associates, with whom the talk ran on informational topics, the trend in the stock market, for instance, he had not intended to use the information for buying or selling. The interest in the conversation had not been finally practical. This practical man might discover that a large part of the business of discourse had been concerned with matters which are not ordinarily thought of as really "practical," but with his relations to other people—that is, with such elusive matters as feelings and attitudes.

That "something," then, conveyed by discourse is not necessarily information to be used for practical purposes. Even when the man in question was concerned primarily with a matter of practical interest, his discourse was colored by other considerations. If he telephoned an associate to ask a price he probably prefaced his question by saying, "How are you?" and concluded his conversation by saying, "Thank you," and "Goodbye." For even the most practical man a large part of discourse is not prompted by purely practical considerations; another "something" is present.

Moreover, even when a man is using speech for the purpose of conveying information, it may prove surprising to see how little of such discourse is pure information, and how difficult it is to make speech deal only with pure and exact information. Almost always a speaker conveys not only the pure information but an attitude toward and a feeling about that information. For example, let us consider the case of a motorist who stops a man driving a hay wagon to ask about the condition of the road ahead. The man on the wagon says, "It's a tolerable good road, you won't have no trouble on it." The motorist drives on, encouraged. But after a mile or so, having experienced a few substantial jolts, he hails another motorist and asks the same question. This man says, "It's a devil of a road, it'll jerk your teeth out." Both the man on the hay wagon and the man in the second automobile think that they are telling the truth. Both intend to be helpful and to give exact information. And both feel that they know the road. But each man's language reflects his own experience with the road. For the man on the hay wagon the road *was* tolerably good, but for the second motorist, anxious to make time on his trip, the road was devilishly bad.

If this seems to be a fairly obvious example of confusion about information in ordinary speech, let us consider an example in which a trained scholar is trying to make an exact statement.

For sentimental pacifism is, after all, but a return to the method of the jungle. It is in the jungle that emotionalism alone determines conduct, and wherever that is true no other than the law of the jungle is possible. For the emotion of hate is sure sooner or later to follow on the emotion of love, and then there is a spring for the throat. It is altogether obvious that the only quality which really distinguishes man from the brutes is his reason.[1]

[1] "Science and Modern Life," *The Atlantic Monthly,* April, 1928.

The author of this statement is Robert Andrews Millikan, the internationally famous physicist and winner of the Nobel Prize. He is making a plea for the scientific attitude in political and international affairs, but when one inspects this statement carefully one finds some propositions about human beings that cannot be proved by Mr. Millikan, or by anyone else, in the same way that he can prove certain formulae of physics in his laboratory. Furthermore, waiving this question of whether the propositions stated and implied are really true or not, one finds that a very important part of the statement consists not in information about human beings but in appeals to the reader to take a certain attitude toward the statement. The comparisons concerning the jungle and the leap of one infuriated beast at the throat of another represent the sort of comparison one finds in poetry; for the comparisons are not based on scientific analogy—the resemblance is prompted by the emotional attitude of the speaker and is calculated to incite a corresponding attitude in the reader. But the coloring of the general statement—that is, the bringing in of an implied interpretation of the statement—extends beyond the mere use of a "poetic" comparison. In the first sentence, for example, the word *pacifism* is qualified by the word *sentimental*. Presumably it is a particular sort of pacifism here defined to which Mr. Millikan's objections apply; but does the adjective *sentimental* really set off a "bad kind of pacifism" from a good kind? Could the reader determine from Mr. Millikan's statement whether or not he would consider the pacifism of Jesus Christ, the Prince of Peace, a sentimental or a non-sentimental sort? Since the only kind of pacifism that Mr. Millikan sets over against his sentimental pacifism is a scientific pacifism operating through an organization of sociologists and economists, one might conceivably assume that Jesus Christ would fall into the former classification. Or, to state the matter otherwise: is the basic argument for peace to be found in the fact that war is unprofitable or is horrible, or in the belief that it is wrong to kill one's fellowman? As a matter of fact, the adjective *sentimental* is, on logical grounds, a bogus qualification: its real function is to set up an attitude in the reader that will forbid his inspection of the basis of the statement.

Whether or not the general statement is logically sound, Mr. Millikan has not stated it with scientific precision; in Mr. Millikan's defense it may be said that *the proposition is one that cannot be stated with scientific precision by anyone*. Mr. Millikan, a scientist trying to state the virtues of a scientific method in human relationships, is forced to resort to devices which we associate with poetry. We should never find him coloring a mathematical formula by referring to a "sentimental figure four," or describing a well-known chemical reaction by saying that two ferocious atoms of hydrogen spring at the throat of one defenseless atom of oxygen.

Limitations of Scientific Statement

The advantages of scientific statement are not to be had without the limitations of a scientific statement also. The primary advantage of the scientific statement is that of absolute precision. But we must remember that this precision is gained by using terms in special and previously defined senses. The scientist carefully cuts away from his technical terms all associations, emotional colorings and implications of judgment. He gives up, then, all attempts to influence the reader's attitude toward his statement. For this reason, only certain kinds of statement and certain kinds of meaning are possible to true science. Science tends, indeed, toward the condition of mathematics, and the really exact scientific statements can be expressed in mathematical formulae. The chemist describes water as H_2O—two atoms of hydrogen and one atom of oxygen. The formula, H_2O, differs tremendously from even the common word *water,* for the word water, neutral as it seems in connotation, still may possess all sorts of different associations—drinking, bathing, boating, the pull of the moon to create tides, the liquid from which the goddess Aphrodite rose, or, as Keats put it,

> The moving waters at their priestlike task
> Of pure ablution round earth's human shores.

As with the liquid itself, so with the word: the scientist needs a distilled product.

The language of science represents an extreme degree of specialization of language in the direction of a certain kind of precision. It is unnecessary, of course, to point out that in this specialization tremendous advantages inhere, and that the man of the twentieth century is rightly proud of this achievement. But it is more often necessary to point out that scientific precision can be brought to bear only on certain kinds of materials. Literature in general—poetry in particular—also represents a specialization of language for the purpose of precision; but it aims at treating kinds of materials different from those of science.

We have already seen that science has to forego, because of its method, matters of attitude and interpretation; or that, when it does not forego them, it is so much the less science. For better or worse, certain kinds of communication are not possible to scientific statement. To return to the question raised at the beginning of this discussion, what is the "something" which is conveyed by speech? We have already seen that it is not exclusively information in the ordinary sense, and even less exclusively information in the scientific sense. The speech of that ordinary citizen in an ordinary way conveys many things, attitudes, feelings, and interpretations, that fall outside of these restrictions. These things, though they fill a large part of the speech of that ordinary citizen, are never stated very clearly or precisely by him. The specialization of speech which we find in poetry aims at clarity and precision of statement in these matters.

That the communication of attitudes, feelings, and interpretations constitutes a real problem, and indeed, in one sense, a more difficult problem than that offered by the communication of mere information, may be clearly illustrated by such an example as the following. Suppose, for instance, that a student sitting on the front row in a classroom turns to his neighbor and whispers to him the information that it is ten minutes to eleven. This information might be passed from one person to another in the same manner through a whole class to the last man on the back row, and the probability is that the last man would receive correctly the message: it is ten minutes to eleven. The communication has been a relatively easy matter. But suppose that the first man on the first row, instead of whispering a mere bit of information, had made even a relatively simple statement involving a feeling or attitude: suppose he had said, for example, "John Jones is a fine fellow, but I feel sometimes that he is a little stuck-up." In all probability the last man who received the message would get an entirely different view of John's character from that intended by the original speaker. Indeed, anyone who is familiar with the distortions which often, and as a matter of fact, usually take place in the transmission of gossip will not be surprised at whatever the version has become by the time it has been transmitted through thirty people. One of the reasons for the error is simple. The original statement about John is an interpretation. The person who hears it, naturally, recognizes that it is an interpretation and not a statement of objective fact, and therefore, in turn, interprets the remark in his own fashion. For example, the last man makes an interpretation of an original interpretation which has been altered more or less by twenty-eight intervening interpretations. The "something" of the first piece of communication—that it is ten minutes to eleven—arrived safely at its destination. The "something" of the second piece of communication, unlike that of the first, involves feelings which each hearer has to define for himself. In ordinary life, a hearer unconsciously bases much of his definition of such pieces of communication, not on the words themselves, but on the gestures, tone of voice, and facial expression of the speaker, and on what he knows about the speaker. For instance, everyone understands how difficult it is to deal with a delicate personal matter in a letter, for the letter has nothing but words—that is, symbols written on paper and divorced from the tone of the voice, gestures, and facial expression.

Materials of Poetry

The basic problem of communication in poetry is, therefore, one of a totally different character from that involved in communication of matters of fact, and we shall merely confuse ourselves about the meaning of any poetry if we do not realize this distinction. The specialization of language in poetry is an attempt to deal with this problem.

By the very nature of the human being, the ordinary citizen in the ordinary day speaks much of what we might call incipient poetry—he attempts to communicate attitudes, feelings, and interpretations. (Unfortunately, most of this poetry is bad poetry.) And poetry in this sense is not confined to the speech of the ordinary citizen. It appears also in editorials, sermons, political speeches, magazine articles, and advertisements. We have seen that Mr. Millikan's essay can be discussed as poetry rather than as science. This, of course, is not apparent to everybody. Many a person would regard as mere poetry the Biblical statement

All they that take the sword shall perish by the sword.

But such a person might, during the next minute, regard Mr. Millikan's paragraph as a sober and verifiable scientific pronouncement. Or to take another case, this person might read an avowed poem:

The Man He Killed

THOMAS HARDY [1840–1928]

Had he and I but met
By some old ancient inn,
We should have sat us down to wet
Right many a nipperkin!

But ranged as infantry, 5
And staring face to face,
I shot at him as he at me,
And killed him in his place.

I shot him dead because—
Because he was my foe, 10
Just so: my foe of course he was;
That's clear enough; although

He thought he'd 'list, perhaps,
Off-hand like—just as I—
Was out of work—had sold his traps— 15
No other reason why.

Yes; quaint and curious war is!
You shoot a fellow down
You'd treat if met where any bar is,
Or help to half-a-crown. 20

He might dismiss this as mere literature, failing to see that Mr. Millikan's paragraph is "mere literature" also—and of course infinitely poorer literature. As has been indicated, Mr. Millikan's argument is not "science." And, as a matter of fact, it is possible that Hardy has, in his poem, put the case against war on a more solid basis than Mr. Millikan has done in his argument.

Mr. Millikan might or might not have been aware that he was using some of the methods of poetry to color the attitude of his readers and bring them to his own point of view; but any writer of advertising copy is perfectly aware of the fact that he is trying to persuade his readers to adopt a certain attitude.

Poetry as a Specialization of Ordinary Speech

From the examples already given we have seen that both the impulse of poetry—that is, the impulse to communicate feelings, attitudes and interpretations—and some of the methods of poetry —that is, comparisons, associations with words, etc.—appear in a great deal of our discourse that is not ordinarily considered as poetic at all. It is important to remember this fact because some people think of poetry as a thing entirely separate from ordinary life and of the matters with which poetry deals as matters with which the ordinary person is not concerned. More will have to be said about the special characteristics of formal poetry—characteristics which set it off from this "stuff of poetry" appearing in ordinary life; but it is highly important to see that both the impulse and methods of poetry are rooted very deep in human experience, and that formal poetry itself represents, not a distinction from, but a specialization of, thoroughly universal habits of human thinking and feeling.

Confusion between Scientific and Poetic Communication

The distinction earlier mentioned between the communication of science and the communication of poetry is also an extremely important one. People, as we have seen, are constantly confusing the two sorts of communication. They will, for example, often accept as sober scientific doctrine what is essentially a poetic statement, or they will judge formal poetry as if it were aiming at scientific truth.

An example of the first type of confusion has already been indicated in the quotation from Mr. Millikan. Mr. Millikan does not rest his case on scientifically verifiable facts but also makes an emotional appeal for a certain attitude concerning those facts. Mr. Millikan is speaking, not as a professional scientist, but as a man, and he is thoroughly justified in using this kind of speech; but it is important that the reader know exactly what Mr. Millikan is doing. Even to the person who thinks that he has no interest in formal poetry an awareness of this distinction is valuable, for he cannot move through the mass of conversation, sermons, editorials, historical and sociological writings, and advertisements without encountering situations in which this distinction is fundamental to an understanding of the actual meanings involved.

Advertising, of course, raises the question in an extreme form. Advertisers naturally are not content to rest on a statement of fact, whether such a statement is verifiable or not. They will attempt to associate the attitude toward a certain product with an attitude toward beautiful women, little children, or gray-haired mothers; they will appeal to snobbishness, vanity, patriotism, religion, and morality. In addition to these appeals to the consumer's most basic and powerful feelings, the advertiser often attempts to imply a scientific validity for his claims—a validity which may, or may not, be justified by the product—by pictures of white-robed surgeons and research experts, statements of abstruse scientific formulae, hints of recent discoveries, coy references to the research laboratories of the plant involved, and very frequent use of the phrase "science tells us." Even the man who is quite certain that he cares nothing for "literature" will find that he constantly has to deal with literary appeals and methods while living in the hardheaded, scientific, and practical twentieth century.

The second type of confusion mentioned above—the confusion that causes people to judge formal poetry as if it were science—is the source of most of the misunderstandings of poetry and of literature in general. It is highly necessary, if one is to understand poetry, to take up some of these typical misreadings.

1. "MESSAGE-HUNTING"

"Message-hunting"—the business of looking only for the statement of an idea which the reader thinks he can apply profitably in his own conduct—is one of the most ordinary forms of this general confusion. Here is a poem by Longfellow that has been greatly admired by many people who read poetry in this fashion:

A Psalm of Life

WHAT THE HEART OF THE YOUNG MAN SAID TO THE PSALMIST

HENRY WADSWORTH LONGFELLOW [1807–1882]

Tell me not, in mournful numbers,
  Life is but an empty dream!—
For the soul is dead that slumbers,
  And things are not what they seem.

Life is real! Life is earnest! 5
  And the grave is not its goal;
Dust thou art, to dust returnest,
  Was not spoken of the soul.

Not enjoyment, and not sorrow,
  Is our destined end or way; 10
But to act, that each tomorrow
  Find us farther than today.

Art is long, and Time is fleeting,
  And our hearts, though stout and brave,
Still, like muffled drums, are beating 15
  Funeral marches to the grave.

In the world's broad field of battle,
  In the bivouac of Life,
Be not like dumb, driven cattle!
  Be a hero in the strife! 20

Trust no Future, howe'er pleasant!
  Let the dead Past bury its dead!
Act,—act in the living Present!
  Heart within, and God o'erheard!

Lives of great men all remind us 25
  We can make our lives sublime,
And, departing, leave behind us
  Footprints on the sands of time;

Footprints, that perhaps another,
  Sailing o'er life's solemn main, 30
A forlorn and shipwrecked brother,
  Seeing, shall take heart again.

Let us, then, be up and doing,
  With a heart for any fate;
Still achieving, still pursuing, 35
  Learn to labor and to wait.

This poem seems to give a great deal of good advice. It tells the reader not to waste his time but to be up and doing; not to be discouraged by failures but to have a heart for any fate; not to judge life by temporary standards but to look to eternal reward. There are probably few people who would quarrel with the moral value of these statements. But granting that the advice is good advice, we can still ask whether or not the poem is a good poem. If the advice is what the poem has to offer us, then we can ask why a short prose statement of the advice itself is not as good as, or even better than, the poem, itself. But even the people who say they like the poem because of its "message" will usually prefer the poem to a plain prose statement. If such people would reject the prose summary in favor of the poem, they would also reject certain other versions of the poetic statement. For instance, let us alter one of the stanzas of the poem, taking care in the alteration, however, to preserve the idea. The original stanza is:

Lives of great men all remind us
  We can make our lives sublime,
And, departing, leave behind us
  Footprints on the sands of time.

An alteration might run:

Lives of all sorts of great men remind us
  That we ourselves can make our lives sublime,
And when we die we can leave behind us
  Noble recollections printed on the sands of time.

The fact that any admirer of the poem would unhesitatingly choose the first version proves that "something" aside from the mere value of the idea is involved in the choice.

The fact that we have just an idea in itself is not enough to make a poem, even when the idea may be a worthy one. The neglect of this principle causes frequent misunderstandings and misreadings of poems. But another type of misreading may result from the fact that the reader does not happen to agree with an idea expressed in a poem. We may treat this distinction by a concrete case: is an admirer of Longfellow's poem, even one who says that his admiration is based on the worth of the idea, disqualified from admiring the following poem, which states an idea rather opposed to some of the ideas in Longfellow's poem?

Expostulation and Reply

WILLIAM WORDSWORTH [1770–1850]

"Why, William, on that old gray stone,
  Thus for the length of half a day,
Why, William, sit you thus alone,
  And dream your time away?"

"Where are your books?—that light bequeathed 5
  To beings else forlorn and blind!
Up! up! and drink the spirit breathed
  From dead men to their kind.

"You look round on your Mother Earth,
  As if she for no purpose bore you; 10
As if you were her first-born birth,
  And none had lived before you."

One morning thus, by Esthwaite lake,
  When life was sweet, I knew not why,
To me my good friend Matthew spake, 15
  And thus I made reply:

"The eye—it cannot choose but see;
  We cannot bid the ear be still;
Our bodies feel, where'er they be,
  Against or with our will. 20

"Nor less I deem that there are Powers
  Which of themselves our minds impress;
That we can feed this mind of ours
  In a wise passiveness.

"Think you, 'mid all this mighty sum 25
  Of things forever speaking,
That nothing of itself will come,
  But we must still be seeking?

"—Then ask not wherefore, here, alone,
  Conversing as I may, 30
I sit upon this old gray stone,
  And dream my time away."

This poem seems to give the advice that one should neglect the "light bequeathed" by the great men of the past in favor of what one can only learn for himself; that one should not fritter away his time by being "up and doing" or by being a "hero in the strife"; and that one should learn in contemplation to cultivate that "wise passiveness" by which, only, one comes into harmony with the great powers of the universe. If the admirer of Longfellow's poem means literally what he says when he praises the poem for the "message," then he is absolutely disqualified from enjoying this poem, for its "message" is diametrically opposed to that of "The Psalm of Life." Of course, many people who describe their appreciation of poems in terms of the "messages" do not mean literally what they say; they are simply groping for some ground to justify the fact that they like poetry at all. Since they are accustomed to think of all communication as concerned with practical information, they try to put their liking on some "practical" or "scientific" basis.

As a matter of fact, the place of ideas in poetry and their relation to the goodness of a poem cannot be treated in such an over-simplified manner. We know, for example, that devout Protestants can accept the poetry of the Catholic poet Dante, or that Catholics can accept the poetry of the Protestant poet John Milton. The fact that the Protestant reader, who holds his religious beliefs seriously, may still accept the poetry of Dante does not mean that the reader regards poetry as merely trivial and unserious. This whole matter is one that cannot be dismissed in a few sentences, but requires for a satisfactory understanding the analysis of many special poems. It will suffice to say here that the "message-hunting" method of reading poetry breaks down even in the simplest cases.

2. "PURE REALIZATION"

Many readers and critics of poetry, realizing the insufficiency of the "message-hunting" approach to poetry, have adopted a view that poetry does not deal with any ideas or truths at all, but is an "expression of pure emotion," or "deals with emotion." This view is sometimes put in other terms, as when one critic says that a poem is the expression of "a moment of pure realization of being"—that is, it attempts merely to bring vividly to the reader some scene or sensation.

When a critic trying to point out the distinguishing marks of poetry says that poetry expresses an emotion or that poetry deals with emotion, exactly what does he mean? Does he mean that a poem, about grief, for instance, would "express" the grief a poet might feel, or have felt, in the same way as a burst of tears would express the emotion of grief? Or does he mean that the reading of a poem about grief would provoke in the reader an emotion of grief in the same way as would a personal bereavement? Quite obviously, the answer to both questions is "No." Certainly, writing of a poem would be no substitute for the relief of a burst of tears; nor would the response to the reading of a poem be as intense as the experience of a real bereavement. There is some difference. On the mere ground of emotional intensity the poem does not compete with the real experience. The justification of poetry as "pure realization," like its justification on the basis of "message-hunting," breaks down even in simple cases, for the pure realization of an experience is the experience at the moment it occurs. For instance, the taste or the smell of a real apple is always more intense than any poem describing the taste or smell of an apple. The following passage from "Ode to a Nightingale," by John Keats has sometimes been praised as a moment of "pure realization":

O for a draught of vintage! that hath been
 Cooled a long age in the deep-delvèd earth,
Tasting of Flora and the country-green,

Dance, and Provençal song, and sunburnt mirth!
O for a beaker full of the warm South, 5
Full of the true, the blushful Hippocrene,
With beaded bubbles winking at the brim,
And purple-stainèd mouth. . . .

Whatever "pure realization" there is here is certainly not the pure realization of wine as such. The stanza is obviously not a substitute for an actual glass of wine: not only does it fail to give the intensity of the sensation of actual wine-drinking but it gives an effect thoroughly different in kind from the experience of drinking a glass of wine. If there is a "pure realization" of anything it is of the poet's thinking about the wine as a thing which represents to him a certain kind of life—a warm, mirthful, carefree, healthy, pagan kind of life, which in the total context of the poem stands in contrast to his own troubled and fretful existence (see "Ode to a Nightingale" and analysis, pp. 340–41). As a matter of fact, when we inspect the passage we discover it is not so much a pictorial description of a beaker of wine, or a description of the sensation of drinking wine, as it is a cluster of associations with the wine—associations which suggest the kind of life we have mentioned. The poet is not saying, actually, that he is thirsty for a drink of wine but that he wants a certain kind of life, the qualities of which he implies.

We have seen that the attempt to conceive of poetry as the "expression of emotion" or as "pure realization" represents an attempt to get away from the "message-hunting" approach to poetry. But in the case which we have just examined we have seen that the experience which is "realized" or communicated to the reader is far different from the experience of a physical object (wine, in this instance), an emotional reaction, or a sensation. The experience, we have seen, really involves an interpretation by the poet, so that in so far as the term "realization" is used to imply an absence of interpretation it is thoroughly inaccurate.

3. "BEAUTIFUL STATEMENT OF SOME HIGH TRUTH"

There is another confused conception of poetry arising from the attempt to combine in a mechanical fashion the two false approaches which have just been discussed. This confused conception is variously stated. For instance, it may be expressed in a definition of poetry as "fine sentiments in fine language." Or as the "beautiful statement of some high truth." Whatever the precise manner of description may be, the basic idea may be stated as follows: poetry is a "truth" with "decorations," which may either be pleasant in themselves or dispose the reader to accept the truth.

Most often victims of this general misconception have treated poetry as a kind of "sugar-coated pill." They have justified the characteristics of poetry—rhythmical language, figures of speech, stories and dramatic situations, etc.—as a kind of bait that leads the reader to expose himself to the influence of the "truth" contained in a poem. They value these characteristics only in so far as the characteristics lead to the acceptance of the "truth." The final value of a poem for such people would depend on the value of the "truth" contained—which leads us back to the mistake of the "message hunters," which we examined with reference to Longfellow's poem.

But even if the person who regards poetry as "fine sentiments in fine language" says that he values the language as much as he values the sentiments, or "truth," he is still using a mistaken approach to poetry. For he is apparently committed to saying that the language, quite apart from its relation to some central idea or "truth," is valuable. He seems to be saying that certain words, or certain objects suggested by the words, are in themselves "poetic." He would be forced to consider a poem as simply a bundle of melodious word-combinations and pretty pictures. He would probably be embarrassed if we asked him what held these things together in any given poem, making it *a* poem rather than simply a collection of pleasing items. And he would probably be further embarrassed if we asked him to show us by what standard he would call a particular combination of sounds or a particular set of pictures poetically fine. If he should say that he took as a standard for poetical fitness the fact that any item—let us say, for instance, a rose—was pleasing in real life, he would be making a dangerous confusion. It is certainly true that in real life various combinations of word sounds and various objects and scenes, such as the rose, the moon, the ruins of a mediaeval tower, a maiden standing on a balcony, etc., are pleasing. But poetry does not consist merely in the use of objects of this sort or in the use of agreeable word combinations. Nor does the mere presence of these things make poetry. But the falsity of this conception can quickly be demonstrated by turning to great poetry from Shakespeare or Milton where we find material that in real life would be disagreeable or mean used for poetic effect. The image of a man grunting and sweating under a burden too heavy for him is not a poetic thing if judged by the above standard, but we will find it used in a passage of great poetry that is universally admired. In Hamlet's most famous speech we find these lines:

> For who would bear the whips and scorns of time,
> The oppressor's wrong, the proud man's contumely,
> The pangs of despised love, the law's delay,
> The insolence of office, and the spurns
> That patient merit of the unworthy takes, 5
> When he himself might his quietus make
> With a bare bodkin? who would fardels bear,
> To grunt and sweat under a weary life,
> But that the dread of something after death,
> The undiscovered country from whose bourn 10
> No traveller returns, puzzles the will. . . .

In fact, none of the things used in this passage would be thought of as being pleasing in itself in actual life. The passage does not give us a set of agreeable pictures that would be considered "poetic." Indeed, the more we examine good poetry the more difficult will appear the attempt to say that certain objects or situations or even ideas are in themselves poetic. *The poetic effect depends not on the things themselves but on the kind of use the poet makes of them.*

Organic Nature of Poetry

We have seen, then, that a poem is not to be thought of as merely a bundle of things which are "poetic" in themselves. Nor is it to be thought of, as the "message hunters" would seem to have it, as a kind of box, decorated or not, in which a "truth" or a "fine sentiment" is hidden. In order to avoid such difficulties, let us begin by thinking of a poem *as a piece of writing which gives us a certain effect in which, we discover, the "poetry" inheres.*

This is very different from thinking of a poem as a group of mechanically combined elements—meter, rime, figurative language, idea, etc.—which are put together to make a poem as bricks are put together to make a wall. We are not to be concerned, then, with whether any given element in a poem is in itself pleasing, or agreeable, or valuable, or "poetical," but with whether it works with the other elements to create the total effect. The relationship among the elements in a poem is all important; it is not a mechanical relationship but one which is far more intimate and fundamental. If we must compare a poem to the make-up of some physical object it ought not to be to a wall but to something organic like a plant.

We may investigate this general principle by looking at some particular examples. The following lines could scarcely be called melodious. Indeed, they may be thought to have a sibilant, hissing quality rather than that of melody.

> If it were done when 'tis done, then 'twere well
> It were done quickly: if the assassination
> Could trammel up the consequence, and catch,
> With his surcrease, success, that but this blow
> Might be the be-all and the end-all here, 5
> But here, upon this bank and shoal of time,
> We'd jump the life to come.

This is the speech of Macbeth at the moment when he is debating the murder of Duncan; the passage has been considered to be great poetry by innumerable critics and readers. We are not to consider that the passage is great poetry *in spite* of its lack of ordinary melodious effects; but rather we are to see that the broken rhythms and the tendency to harshness of sound are essential to the communication that Shakespeare wished. For instance, the piling up of the *s* sounds in the second, third, and fourth lines help give an impression of desperate haste and breathless excitement. The lines give the impression of a conspiratorial whisper. The rhythm and sound effects of the passage, then, are poetic in the only sense which we have seen to be legitimate: they are poetic because of a relation to the total effect of the passage.

Or we may approach the general problem in another way. Here are two lines by Robert Burns which have been greatly admired by the poet William Butler Yeats:

The white moon is setting behind the white wave,
And Time is setting with me, O!

Let us suppose that the lines had been written as follows:

The white moon is setting behind the white wave,
And Time, O! is setting with me.

Literally considered, the two versions say exactly the same thing: they describe a scene and give an exclamation provoked by it. If one will, however, read the two versions carefully with an ear for the rhythm he will discover that the transposition of the word *O* has made a great difference in the movement.

But this difference is not finally important *merely* because the first version may be in itself more melodious than the second. The movement of the first version is superior primarily because it contributes to the total effect, or to what we might call the total interpretation, of the scene. The placing of the cry at the emphatic position of a line-end implies that the speaker had scarcely realized the full force of his own statement until he had made it. The lingering rhythm caused by the position of the exclamation at the end of the second line coincides with the fact that the poet sees in the natural scene a representation of the pathos of the passing of Time and of his own life. By placing the exclamation anywhere else we impair this relationship between the rhythm and the other elements involved—the image of the moonset and the poet's statement about the passing of Time. Yeats has summarized the general effect of the passage and the relationship of the parts as follows:

Take from them [the lines] the whiteness of the moon and of the waves, whose relation to the setting of Time is too subtle for the intellect, and you take from them their beauty. But, when all are together, moon and wave and whiteness and setting Time and the last melancholy cry, they evoke an emotion which cannot be evoked by any other arrangement of colors and sounds and forms.[1]

The remarks by Yeats here apply, as we can see, to the elements of the scene itself as well as to the rhythm. He is not praising the

[1] From W. B. Yeats, "The Symbolism of Poetry," *Essays,* p. 191. Copyright, 1912, 1918, and used with the permission of The Macmillan Co.

lines merely because the scene of the white moon setting behind the white wave gives in itself a pretty picture. As a matter of fact, a white moon may not appear as beautiful as a golden moon, but if we rewrite the lines with a golden moon we have lost something from them:

> The gold moon is setting behind the gold wave,
> And Time is setting for me, O!

The "something" that has been lost obviously depends on the relationship of the color to the other elements in the general effect. The whiteness of the moon and the wave in connection with the idea of "setting" and then more specifically in connection with the idea of the irrevocable passage of Time, suggests, even though unconsciously to most readers, a connection with the paleness of something waning or dying. The connection is not a logical connection, as Yeats intimates when he says the "relation . . . is too subtle for the intellect," but it is nonetheless a powerful one. All of this merely means that Yeats is saying that the beauty—by which he means the total poetic effect—of the lines depends on the relationship of the parts to each other.

This last point may be amply proved, as we have already hinted in discussing the passage from *Hamlet,* by considering a passage of great poetry in which the pictures used, unlike that in the lines from Burns, would be considered in ordinary life as positively ugly or at least neutral.

> Time hath, my lord, a wallet at his back,
> Wherein he puts alms for oblivion,
> A great-sized monster of ingratitudes:
> Those scraps are good deeds past; which are devoured
> As fast as they are made, forgot as soon 5
> As done: perseverance, dear my lord,
> Keeps honor bright: to have done, is to hang
> Quite out of fashion, like a rusty mail
> In monumental mockery. . . .
>
> (From *Troilus and Cressida*)

This is a speech which Shakespeare puts into the mouth of a character, Ulysses, who is trying to persuade Achilles to take part again in the war against the Trojans and not to rest on the reputation for valor he has already made. The pictures given here are definitely unattractive: a beggar putting alms in his sack, a monster, scraps of food, a rusty suit of armor. The poetic effect of the passage, then, cannot depend on the intrinsic prettiness of any of the objects mentioned. If we speak of the beauty of the passage, as Yeats speaks of the beauty of the lines from Burns, we must mean the relation of the objects to each other and to the idea of the passage.

Let us try to see what these relationships are. Ulysses is saying that a reputation for good deeds is quickly forgotten. Good deeds are like alms given to an ungrateful beggar, or are like scraps of food which the beggar forgets as soon as he has satisfied his appetite. The picture is poetically good because it accurately indicates the *attitude* which Ulysses wishes Achilles to take toward his past achievements. If Ulysses had merely given Achilles the general statement that the public forgets good deeds, he could not have stirred the feelings which Achilles, the hero and aristocrat, must have felt toward beggars and broken scraps of food. He plays on this contempt and disgust. The images of the first five lines, as we have seen, are closely bound together to define a certain attitude. Then, after a general statement that perseverance is necessary to keep honor bright, the image of the coat of mail is introduced: a man who bases his claim to honor merely on a deed done in the past is like a suit of mail that, although it is hung up as a trophy of some great event, simply rusts. It is important to see that this is not a mere repetition of the general point made about perseverance, but that it also develops and adds to the idea, for it carries with it a special urgency to immediate action. There is not only the application, as it were, of the general idea in a concrete image that can be seen as a picture, but also an application appropriate to the special situation, the need for Achilles to arm and return to the battle.

The use of images in this passage, then, represents not only a close-knit organization because of the relation of the images to each other and to the intention of the passage, but also a psychological development, for the images lead from one attitude and state of mind to another. One can show the closeness of the organization of the passage even in the use of a single word. For example, take the word *monumental* in the last line. A great deal of the "meaning" of the passage is concentrated in this one word. The word *monumental* literally means, of course, the quality of something that stands as a monument. The coat of rusty mail which Ulysses uses in his comparison is one hung up as a trophy or monument to past achievement. But the word *monumental* is also used to indicate something tremendous in size. The word, then, as it appears in the present context suggests two applications to the reader: the mail is hung up as a monument and the mockery is monumental, or tremendous, in size. The fact that the word suggests to the reader these two applications gives a somewhat ironical, or sarcastic, effect to the passage—which is exactly what is intended by the speaker.

The purpose in giving the passages and comments above is to illustrate the principle that in judging the various elements of a poem or of a passage of poetry—rhythm, image, diction, etc.—one must consider not the elements taken in isolation but in relation to the total organization and intention. That is, the elements must play an organic part in the poem.

Dramatic Aspect of Poetry

It may be objected that most of the examples given above are drawn from plays and do not represent poetry as we more ordinarily find it. But the principle illustrated by these examples applies to all other poetry. It applies because all poetry, including even short lyrics or descriptive pieces (p. 75), involves a dramatic organization. This is clear when we reflect that every poem implies a speaker of the poem, either the poet writing in his own person or someone into whose mouth the poem is put, and that the poem represents the reaction of such a person to a situation, a scene, or an idea. In reading poetry it is well to remember this dramatic aspect and to be sure that one sees the part it plays in any given poem.

What Good Is Poetry?

But even if one understands the principles by which poetry is to be read, one may still ask, "What good is poetry?" The value of science we all know. But we have attempted in the preceding pages to show how different the organization of poetry is from that of

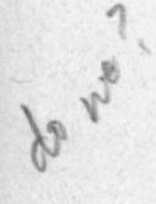

science, and how different are their objectives. It is only fair to admit that what makes science valuable cannot be held to make poetry valuable also. Science gives us a certain kind of description of the world—a description which is within its own terms verifiable—and gives us a basis for more effective practical achievement. Science is, as Bertrand Russell has called it, "power-knowledge."

> But scientific thought is . . . essentially power-thought—the sort of thought, that is to say, whose purpose, conscious or unconscious, is to give power to its possessor. Now power is a causal concept, and to obtain power over any given material one need only understand the causal laws to which it is subject. This is an essentially abstract matter, and the more irrelevant details we can omit from our purview, the more powerful our thoughts will become. The same sort of thing can be illustrated in the economic sphere. The cultivator, who knows every corner of his farm, has a concrete knowledge of wheat, and makes very little money; the railway which carries his wheat views it in a slightly more abstract way, and makes rather more money; the stock exchange manipulator, who knows it only in its purely abstract aspect of something which may go up or down, is, in his way, as remote from concrete reality as the physicist, and he, of all those concerned in the economic sphere, makes the most money and has the most power. So it is with science, though the power which the man of science seeks is more remote and impersonal than that which is sought on the stock exchange.[1]

But we have seen, and can see in real life every day, how much of our experience eludes the statements science can make; and how merely practical statements or statements that approximate a scientific form satisfy only a part of our interests. One does not have to look farther than the fact that this wide domain of human interests exists to find a justification for poetry. Most people are thoroughly satisfied to admit the value of any activity which satisfies a basic and healthy human interest. It may be well, however, to take a few moments to remind the reader that this interest exists, and to make plain that it is this interest which poetry seeks to satisfy.

We have already seen how often talk that is apparently practical really attempts to satisfy a non-practical interest. It is easy to point out many other aspects of our experience that testify to the fact

[1] *The Scientific Outlook*, p. 86. New York: W. W. Norton & Co.

that people—even people who think that they care nothing for poetry—really have interests which are the same as those satisfied by poetry. Very few people indeed depend for the satisfaction of these interests merely on their routine activities. Instead, they listen to speeches, go to church, listen to radio programs, read magazine stories or the gossip columns of newspapers. Such people do not see any relation between these activities and poetry, but poetry does concern the same impulses and the same interests. Why and how good poetry, and good literature in general, give a fuller satisfaction to these impulses and interests is a matter which can best be stated in connection with concrete examples before us, and the attempt in this book to state this matter will be gradually developed by the study of examples. But the fundamental point, namely, that poetry has a basis in common human interests, must not be forgotten at the beginning of any attempt to study poetry.

The question of the value of poetry, then, is to be answered by saying that it springs from a basic human impulse and fulfils a basic human interest. To answer the question finally, and not immediately, one would have to answer the question as to the value of those common impulses and interests. But that is a question which lies outside of the present concern. As we enter into a study of poetry it is only necessary to see that poetry is not an isolated and eccentric thing, but springs from the most fundamental interests which human beings have.

I

NARRATIVE POEMS

FOREWORD

We have said that the "stuff of poetry" is not something separate from the ordinary business of living, but itself inheres in that business. We hear some one say that a farm boy has suffered a fatal accident while cutting wood with a buzz-saw; or we read in the newspaper that a woman has shot her sweetheart; or we remember that there was once an outlaw from Missouri named Jesse James who was killed by treachery. This sort of thing, even though it may not at first strike us as beautiful, instructive, or elevating, appeals to the interest people have in other people. That interest, as we have indicated, is not scientific or practical but is simply the general interest we feel in people as human beings. Even though the account of a painful accident or a sordid murder seems almost as far removed as possible from poetry, it arouses the kind of interest which poetry attempts to satisfy, and, as we have already said, comprises the "stuff of poetry." In the case of the three incidents mentioned—the death of a farm boy, the murder of the sweetheart, and the betrayal of the outlaw—the "stuff of poetry" has actually been turned into poems. That is, the "human interest" has been put in a form that preserves it, even after the accidental and temporary curiosity has been satisfied.

The phrase, "put in a form that preserves it," can be misleading, if we are prone to think of poetic form as a kind of container, a kind of box, in which the stuff of poetry has been packed. Form is much more than that. The form does more than "contain" the poetic stuff: it organizes it; it shapes it; it defines its meaning. Much of our subsequent discussion will have to do with what form is and what it does.

Out, Out

ROBERT FROST [1875–]

The buzz-saw snarled and rattled in the yard
And made dust and dropped stove-length sticks of wood,
Sweet-scented stuff when the breeze drew across it.
And from there those that lifted eyes could count
Five mountain ranges one behind the other 5
Under the sunset far into Vermont.
And the saw snarled and rattled, snarled and rattled,
As it ran light, or had to bear a load.
And nothing happened: day was all but done.
Call it a day, I wish they might have said 10
To please the boy by giving him the half hour
That a boy counts so much when saved from work.
His sister stood beside them in her apron
To tell them "Supper." At the word, the saw,
As if to prove saws knew what supper meant, 15
Leaped out at the boy's hand, or seemed to leap—
He must have given the hand. However it was,
Neither refused the meeting. But the hand!
The boy's first outcry was a rueful laugh,
As he swung toward them holding up the hand 20
Half in appeal, but half as if to keep
The life from spilling. Then the boy saw all—
Since he was old enough to know, big boy
Doing a man's work, though a child at heart—
He saw all spoiled. "Don't let him cut my hand off— 25
The doctor, when he comes. Don't let him, sister!"
So. But the hand was gone already.
The doctor put him in the dark of ether.
He lay and puffed his lips out with his breath.
And then—the watcher at his pulse took fright. 30
No one believed. They listened at his heart.
Little—less—nothing!—and that ended it.
No more to build on there. And they, since they
Were not the one dead, turned to their affairs.

Frankie and Johnny

ANONYMOUS

Frankie and Johnny were lovers, O, how that couple could love.
Swore to be true to each other, true as the stars above.
He was her man, but he done her wrong.

Frankie she was his woman, everybody knows.
She spent one hundred dollars for a suit of Johnny's clothes. 5
He was her man, but he done her wrong.

Frankie and Johnny went walking, Johnny in his bran' new suit,
"O good Lawd," says Frankie, "but don't my Johnny look cute?"
He was her man, but he done her wrong.

Frankie went down to Memphis; she went on the evening train.
She paid one hundred dollars for Johnny a watch and chain. 11
He was her man, but he done her wrong.

Frankie went down to the corner, to buy a glass of beer;
She says to the fat bartender, "Has my loving man been here?
He was my man, but he done me wrong." 15

"Ain't going to tell you no story, ain't going to tell you no lie,
I seen your man 'bout an hour ago with a girl named Alice Fry.
If he's your man, he's doing you wrong."

Frankie went back to the hotel, she didn't go there for fun,
Under her long red kimono she toted a forty-four gun. 20
He was her man, but he done her wrong.

Frankie went down to the hotel, looked in the window so high,
There was her lovin' Johnny a-lovin' up Alice Fry;
He was her man, but he done her wrong.

Frankie threw back her kimono; took out the old forty-four; 25
Roota-toot-toot, three times she shot, right through that hotel door.
She shot her man, 'cause he done her wrong.

Johnny grabbed off his Stetson. "O good Lawd, Frankie, don't shoot."
But Frankie put her finger on the trigger, and the gun went roota-toot-toot.
He was her man, but she shot him down. 30

"Roll me over easy, roll me over slow,
Roll me over easy, boys, 'cause my wounds are hurting me so,
I was her man, but I done her wrong."

With the first shot Johnny staggered; with the second shot he fell;
When the third bullet hit him, there was a new man's face in hell.
He was her man, but he done her wrong. 36

Frankie heard a rumbling away down under the ground.
Maybe it was Johnny where she had shot him down.
He was her man, and she done him wrong.

"Oh, bring on your rubber-tired hearses, bring on your rubber-tired hacks, 40
They're takin' my Johnny to the buryin' groun' but they'll never bring him back.
He was my man, but he done me wrong."

The judge he said to the jury, "It's plain as plain can be.
This woman shot her man, so it's murder in the second degree.
He was her man, though he done her wrong." 45

Now it wasn't murder in the second degree, it wasn't murder in the third.
Frankie simply dropped her man, like a hunter drops a bird.
He was her man, but he done her wrong.

"Oh, put me in that dungeon. Oh, put me in that cell.
Put me where the northeast wind blows from the southeast corner of hell. 50
I shot my man 'cause he done me wrong."

Frankie walked up to the scaffold, as calm as a girl could be,
She turned her eyes to heaven and said, "Good Lord, I'm coming to thee.
He was my man, and I done him wrong."

Jesse James

ANONYMOUS

It was on a Wednesday night, the moon was shining bright,
  They robbed the Danville train.
And the people they did say, for many miles away,
  'Twas the outlaws Frank and Jesse James.

Jesse had a wife to mourn him all her life, 5
  The children they are brave.
'Twas a dirty little coward shot Mister Howard,
  And laid Jesse James in his grave.

Jesse was a man was a friend to the poor,
  He never left a friend in pain. 10
And with his brother Frank he robbed the Chicago bank
  And then held up the Glendale train.

It was Robert Ford, the dirty little coward,
  I wonder how he does feel,
For he ate of Jesse's bread and he slept in Jesse's bed, 15
  Then he laid Jesse James in his grave.

It was his brother Frank that robbed the Gallatin bank,
  And carried the money from the town.
It was in this very place that they had a little race,
  For they shot Captain Sheets to the ground. 20

They went to the crossing not very far from there,
  And there they did the same;
And the agent on his knees he delivered up the keys
  To the outlaws Frank and Jesse James.

It was on a Saturday night, Jesse was at home 25
  Talking to his family brave,
When the thief and the coward, little Robert Ford,
  Laid Jesse James in his grave.

How people held their breath when they heard of Jesse's death,
  And wondered how he ever came to die. 30

'Twas one of the gang, dirty Robert Ford,
  That shot Jesse James on the sly.

Jesse went to rest with his hand on his breast;
  He died with a smile on his face.
He was born one day in the county of Clay, 35
  And came from a solitary race.

The first of these poems was written by Robert Frost, a professional poet, who felt in the fatal accident to an obscure farm boy the pathos and horror of the unreasonable and unpredictable end that at any moment may come to life. We do not know who composed the other two poems, but certainly not professional poets. Apparently some ordinary person felt so strongly the force of an incident, the murder of Johnny or the betrayal of Jesse James, that he tried to express it in a song that would convey his own reactions to the event. And the songs did succeed in conveying something of the reactions of the unknown composers, for they have been passed down from mouth to mouth, probably being constantly altered in the process. Poems like "Frankie and Johnny" or "Jesse James," narratives to be sung that spring from unknown sources and are transmitted by word of mouth, and that may experience alteration in this process, are usually called *ballads* (*Glossary*).

The most ordinary way by which we express the interest we as human beings have in other human beings is by telling or attending to stories. Since poetry derives from this basic human interest we expect to find, and do find, many poems in which the element of story is large. As a matter of fact, the three poems we have just read, and all the poems in the first section of this book, give enough of the explicit action of a story to appeal to the usual curiosity we feel about how any situation will turn out. But this is not the only appeal the poems make to us, just as it is not the only appeal any good piece of fiction makes. We are interested not merely in getting the information about the conclusion, but in following the process by which the conclusion is reached. As a matter of fact, we do not even want all the details of the process, but just enough to make us experience the central feeling and grasp the central meaning of the events. But this is not all: we like a poem, not because it gives us satisfaction of our curiosity or because it gives us an idea we can "carry away with us," as people sometimes put it, but because the poem itself is an experience.

We can illustrate by a comparison with a football game. If a person listens to a radio report of a game, he may really have more accurate information about it than if he were present. And when the game is over, he will know the exact score. But if he has his choice he will probably take the trouble, and spend the money, to go to the game itself. He does this because the game is a richer experience. The score and the statistics of the game come to him, if he watches it, not as bare facts, but in terms of action.

This general principle is clear if we remember that the mere fact, as a fact, that a woman in the slums shot her sweetheart Johnny is of little interest to us. If we enjoy hearing "Frankie and Johnny" sung, we do so because of something more than the statistical importance of the subject. Furthermore, we do not merely enjoy it because it satisfies our curiosity about the outcome; for we enjoy the song for an indefinite length of time after we know the conclusion. It is obvious, then, that if we like it at all, we like it because of its particular nature as an experience—just as we like the football game.

The story element in a poem, then, whether it is prominent as in "Frankie and Johnny" or relatively unimportant as in "Out, Out," is only one of many elements which work together to give the total experience of the poem. We already know what some of these other elements are: rhythm, figurative language, etc. But in these poems, where the story element is prominent, we may proceed best by studying the way in which this one element is treated in concrete cases to give the effect we call poetry.

Johnie Armstrong

ANONYMOUS

There dwelt a man in faire Westmerland,
  Johnie Armstrong men did him call,
He had nither lands nor rents coming in,
  Yet he kept eight score men in his hall.

He had horse and harness for them all, 5
Goodly steeds were all milke-white;
O the golden bands an about their necks,
And their weapons, they were all alike.

Newes then was brought unto the king
That there was sicke [1] a won as hee, 10
That livèd lyke a bold out-law,
And robbèd all the north country.

The king he writt an a letter then,
A letter which was large and long;
He signed it with his owne hand; 15
And he promised to doe him no wrong.

When this letter came Johnie untill,[2]
His heart it was as blythe as birds on the tree:
"Never was I sent for before any king,
My father, my grandfather, nor none but mee. 20

"And if wee goe the king before,
I would we went most orderly;
Every man of you shall have his scarlet cloak,
Lacèd with silver laces three.

"Every won of you shall have his velvett coat, 25
Lacèd with sillver lace so white;
O the golden bands an about your necks,
Black hatts, white feathers, all alyke."

By the morrow morninge at ten of the clock,
Towards Edenburough gon was hee, 30
And with him all his eight score men;
Good Lord, it was a goodly sight for to see!

When Johnie came befower [3] the king,
He fell downe on his knee;
"O pardon, my soveraine leige," he said, 35
"O pardon my eight score men and mee!"

[1] such [2] unto [3] before

"Thou shalt have no pardon, thou traytor strong,
For thy eight score men nor thee;
For tomorrow morning by ten of the clock,
Both thou and them shall hang on the gallow-tree." 40

But Johnie looke'd over his left shoulder,
Good Lord, what a grevious look looked hee!
Saying, "Asking grace of a graceles face—
Why there is none for you nor me."

But Johnie had a bright sword by his side, 45
And it was made of the mettle so free,
That had not the king stept his foot aside,
He had smitten his head from his faire boddé.

Saying, "Fight on, my merry men all,
And see that none of you be taine; 50
For rather then men shall say we were hange'd,
Let them report how we were slaine."

Then, God wott, faire Eddenburrough rose,
And so besett poore Johnie rounde,
That fowerscore and tenn of Johnie's best men 55
Lay gasping all upon the ground.

Then like a mad man Johnie laide about,
And like a mad man then fought hee,
Untill a falce Scot came Johnie behinde,
And runn him through the faire boddee. 60

Saying, "Fight on, my merry men all,
And see that none of you be taine;
For I will stand by and bleed but awhile,
And then will I come and fight againe."

Newes then was brought to young Johnie Armstrong, 65
As he stood by his nurse's knee,
Who vowed if ere he live'd for to be a man,
On the treacherous Scots revengd hee'd be.

This poem treats the same kind of story as that treated by "Jesse James." In both cases there is the brave outlaw who is killed by treachery. In neither case do we know who composed the ballad, but both poems must have grown out of a fairly simple and illiterate society. In the case of this ballad, it was the society of the Scotch peasantry in the sixteenth century; in the case of "Jesse James" the ballad appeared in a frontier society in America. But the differences in time and in place do not conceal the fundamental likeness between the two ballads and, even, between the characters of the two heroes. The fact that human nature is very much the same at all times and places, makes it possible for us to read such poems with sympathy and understanding. In both cases, that of the outlaw Johnie Armstrong and the outlaw Jesse James, some one—we do not know who—was struck by the pathos of courage betrayed and was impelled to express his feeling by putting the incident that stirred him into a poem—or more accurately, into the song-poem which we call a ballad. In so far as the unknown composer did this successfully we can now grasp the meaning which the incident had for him.

The incident of Johnie Armstrong, like that of Jesse James, derives from historical fact. Johnie Armstrong was an outlaw lord of the Scotch border country, who was lured into the power of the Scotch king, James V—treacherously, according to the ballad—and was killed with his men. It is a simple story of violent action, such a story as might be expected to appeal strongly to the kind of people among whom the ballad arose.

The basic facts as given in the summary above are not in themselves interesting to us. The event described, for instance, is of no historical importance. But when the event appears to us in the form of the poem it immediately gains an interest. Perhaps we can do something toward defining the process that gives this added interest.

First, we may look at the way in which the story is organized in the ballad, a way characteristic of most ballads. The action is not presented in a straight narrative. The first two stanzas give us an identification of the hero, the *exposition* (*Glossary*), as one would say about ordinary fiction. The next two stanzas give a bit of narrative, but from that point on the action is handled by a succession of little scenes, presented much as in a play. There is the scene of Johnie Armstrong's reception of the letter, of the appearance of his company as it rides toward court, of the betrayal and the fight, and of the little son's vow of vengeance. The method, further, is dramatic in that much of the action is presented through dialogue and not indirectly by description. The characters speak up for themselves, and so we know them directly. By this selection of key scenes and by the emphasis on dialogue the reader or hearer gets an impression of speed and excitement and of nearness to the action.

In the second place, although the reader gets an impression of nearness, the story is not greatly elaborated. In a short story on the same subject one would expect a certain amount of description and detail that is absent in the poem. The only extended piece of description in the poem is that dealing with the appearance of the retainers of Armstrong as they get ready to go to court. But we can observe that this is not straight description. It is put in the mouth of Johnie Armstrong as he orders his men to make ready. And it serves a twofold purpose in the poem in addition to its value as a piece of *atmosphere* (*Glossary*) and setting. It indicates the joy the outlaw feels at the honor the king has done him, and it gives an *ironical* (*Glossary*) contrast to the betrayal that is to follow.

In ordinary prose fiction one would expect a certain amount of analysis and description of the thoughts and feelings of characters. But in this ballad there is very little of such material. For instance, only one line describes the feeling of a character:

> His heart it was as blythe as birds on the tree.

But at the climax of the situation, when Johnie Armstrong suddenly discovers that he has been betrayed, we are not told what he felt; we are given a glimpse of the way he looked, and so seize more imaginatively and directly on the meaning of the scene.

> But Johnie looke'd over his left shoulder,
> Good Lord, what a grevious look looked hee!
> Saying, "Asking grace of a graceles face—
> Why there is none for you nor me."

The ballad is moving as quickly as possible to its point, selecting such details as will most stimulate the imagination. With the sight of the betrayed outlaw's sudden glance over his shoulder (and notice how, to emphasize the scene and help us visualize it, the ballad specifies which shoulder), we can know as much about his reaction to the situation as a great deal of description would give us, and we know it in a way that makes us feel that our own imagination is participating in the poem. This is a detail that by the power of suggestion makes us see the whole picture and feel the effect.

The aim of this kind of treatment is to make as vivid and as *concrete* (*Glossary*) an effect as possible, in contrast with the general and purely factual summary of the event which we gave above. For instance, we are not told that the king is treacherous, and we are told nothing of his intentions. What we learn, we learn from the behavior of the king himself. We are never told that Johnie Armstrong is a proud and courageous man who feels an obligation to his followers, but we learn it from his own conduct and from what he says: when he discovers the king's treachery he thinks of his men as well as of himself; and there is a sort of exaltation rather than despair in his admonition to all of them to die fighting rather than be taken. "Let them report how we were slaine," he says. We are given a picture of Johnie Armstrong's character in action instead of a description of it. We know what his code is, even though it is not mentioned in the poem. It is a rather primitive one, a code of crude courage, and probably a very inadequate one for us, for he was a border outlaw living four hundred years ago, but he dies true to it. There is no moral given in the poem, no general statement of an idea, but an idea is suggested through the action itself: out of disaster a spiritual value that makes even disaster seem unimportant may be produced. All of these things are in the poem, but they are there by suggestion and implication of the action; we know them without being told, for we can discover them for ourselves.

What the poem does, in short, is to take some bare facts and treat them so that they have both an emotional and an intellectual interpretation. The sympathetic reader, or hearer, of the ballad might not analyze that interpretation but the effect would be there. He would react to the pathos of the betrayal of a strong, brave man, to the exaltation at Johnie Armstrong's courage and desire for an honorable death, to the ironical contrast between Johnie Armstrong's expectation as he goes to the court and his reception there, to the selection of imaginative detail, and to the suspense and speed of movement of the story. He might not analyze any of these items separately and might not try to understand the part they play in the poem; he might merely experience a certain pleasure in the poem, and simply attribute it, if asked, to the genius of the composer or composers. The genius is there, of course, but one's pleasure is enlarged by the attempt to understand as fully as possible the process by which that genius makes itself felt.

Sir Patrick Spence

ANONYMOUS

The king sits in Dumferling toune,
  Drinking the blude-reid wine:
"O whar will I get guid sailor,
  To sail this schip of mine?"

Up and spak an eldern knicht, 5
  Sat at the kings richt kne:
"Sir Patrick Spence is the best sailor,
  That sails upon the se."

The king has written a braid[1] letter,
  And signd it wi his hand, 10
And sent it to Sir Patrick Spence,
  Was walking on the sand.

The first line that Sir Patrick red,
  A loud lauch lauchèd[2] he;
The next line that Sir Patrick red, 15
  The teir blinded his ee.[3]

"O wha is this has don this deid,
  This ill deid don to me,
To send me out this time o' the yeir,
  To sail upon the se! 20

[1] broad [2] laughed [3] eye

"Mak hast, mak haste, my mirry men all
Our guid schip sails the morne:"
"O say na sae, my master deir,
For I feir a deadlie storme.

"Late, late yestreen I saw the new moone, 25
Wi the auld [1] moone in hir arme,
And I feir, I feir, my deir master,
That we will cum to harme."

O our Scots nobles wer richt laith [2]
To weet their cork-heild schoone; [3] 30
Bot lang owre [4] a' the play wer playd,
Thair hats they swam aboone.

O lang, lang may their ladies sit,
Wi thair fans into their hand,
Or eir they se Sir Patrick Spence 35
Cum sailing to the land.

O lang, lang may the ladies stand,
Wi thair gold kems [5] in their hair
Waiting for thar ain deir lords,
For they'll se thame na mair. 40

Haf owre,[6] haf owre to Aberdour,
It's fiftie fadom deip,
And thair lies guid Sir Patrick Spence,
Wi the Scots lords at his feit.

Exercise:

1. The poem begins with a scene at the royal court. Does the rest of the poem break up into scenes? What are they?

2. Discuss the use of concrete details such as "blude-reid wine," "richt kne," "cork-heild schoone," etc.

3. What are the ironical contrasts?

4. Though the shipwreck would seem to be the climax of the poem, the poem actually omits all direct description of the ship-

[1] old
[2] loath
[3] shoes
[4] ere
[5] combs
[6] over

wreck. Why? Does your answer to this question point to what the poem is "about"?

5. On p. 12 we observed that Johnie Armstrong lives by a code, and dies by his code. Does Sir Patrick live by a similar code?

6. What is the relation between the scene in the last stanza and that in the first?

The Wife of Usher's Well

ANONYMOUS

There lived a wife at Usher's Well,
  And a wealthy wife was she;
She had three stout and stalwart sons,
  And sent them oer the sea.

They hadna been a week from her, 5
  A week but barely ane,
Whan word came to the carline[1] wife
  That her three sons were gane.

They hadna been a week from her,
  A week but barely three, 10
Whan word came to the carlin wife
  That her sons she'd never see.

"I wish the wind may never cease,
  Nor fashes[2] in the flood,
Till my three sons come hame to me, 15
  In earthly flesh and blood."

It fell about the Martinmass,
  When nights are lang and mirk,
The carlin wife's three sons came hame,
  And their hats were o the birk.[3] 20

It neither grew in syke[4] nor ditch,
  Nor yet in ony sheugh;[5]
But at the gates o Paradise,
  That birk grew fair eneugh.

[1] peasant
[2] troubles
[3] birch
[4] trench
[5] furrow

"Blow up the fire, my maidens, 25
Bring water from the well;
For a' [1] my house shall feast this night,
Since my three sons are well."

And she has made to them a bed,
She's made it large and wide, 30
And she's taen her mantle her about,
Sat down at the bed-side.

Up then crew the red, red cock,
And up and crew the gray;
The eldest to the youngest said, 35
" 'T is time we were away."

The cock he hadna crawd but once,
And clappd his wings at a',
When the youngest to the eldest said,
"Brother, we must awa. 40

"The cock doth craw, the day doth daw,
The channerin [2] worm doth chide;
Gin we be mist out o our place,
A sair pain we maun bide.

"Fare ye weel, my mother dear! 45
Fareweel to barn and byre! [3]
And fare ye weel, the bonny lass
That kindles my mother's fire!"

This poem, too, is a ballad. A woman loses her three sons at sea, and in her grief, expresses the wish that she may see them again in flesh and blood. The three sons return to the woman one night, but since they are only ghosts, they have to leave again before dawn. The poem uses many more words to give this simple narrative than the two-sentence paraphrase which we have just given. Indeed, if we judge the poem's excellence in terms of the conciseness and the clearness with which it states the facts which it undertakes to give, then the prose paraphrase is much superior.

[1] all [2] devouring [3] cattle-shed

The difficulty which besets many people in reading poetry resides to a great extent in the fact that many people mistake the *concern* of poetry. Plainly in this poem, as we noticed in "Johnie Armstrong," the facts are *in themselves* unimportant. Furthermore, from one point of view, they are much less important than in "Johnie Armstrong," for here they are not even historically true.

With what is this poem concerned? And, judged in the light of that concern, in what ways is the poem superior to the prose paraphrase? If one considers the poem carefully, he notices that the poem, like so many ballads, breaks up into a number of little pictures, and that some of the detail (otherwise irrelevant) becomes justified when we realize that it has been employed to make the scenes vivid for us. The poem is not content merely to state certain things *abstractly* (*Glossary*): we must see the pictures. For example, consider the pictures given us in the seventh and eighth stanzas. The seventh conveys some sense of the bustling excitement with which the woman puts her maids to work when her sons unexpectedly arrive; the eighth conveys with a great deal of intensity the joy with which the mother receives her long-lost sons. She is anxious to make them comfortable; she has prepared the beds carefully for them. But she cannot tear herself away from them, even to let them go to sleep, and having thrown a shawl around her shoulders to keep warm as she sits up in the late chill night air, lingers for a little while by their beds. The poem does not *tell* us of her joy and relief at seeing them home again; it conveys a sense of this to us by showing the mother's joyful activity. In preferring the concrete form of statement to the abstract, "The Wife of Usher's Well" is typical of poetry in general. Consider also the last four stanzas. The poet might have merely stated that the sons regretted having to leave their home and having to go back to the grave. He wishes to do more than communicate the idea, however: he wishes us to share in their feeling of dread as well as to know that they had such a feeling. Which is the better means of doing this: to say, they dreaded leaving "very much," or "a great deal," or "bitterly,"—use whatever adverb you will; or to describe the scene itself? The latter method, the concrete method, is very properly the one chosen.

The crowing of the cocks announcing day is described, and the brief conversation between the brothers is given. Notice that the poem does not use words of great intensity in giving the conversation, but *understatement* (*Glossary*). The eldest brother merely says, "'T is time we were away"; the youngest brother, "Brother, we must awa." There is no shrieking of terror. And yet in this case the brief understatement conveys perhaps more of a feeling of horror and grief than exaggerated outcries would have conveyed. We can readily see why this use of understatement is particularly effective here. The poet has refrained throughout from making comments on the situation or from hinting to us what we ought to feel. The poem is *objective* (*Glossary*); the poet stands aside, and lets the poem do its work on us in its own way.

Notice too that this poem, like the previous ones considered, makes use of suggestion. People prefer suggestion to explicit statement in these matters—if for no other reason than that the person who feels the suggestion participates fully and immediately—he feels that he has made a discovery for himself, which is quite another thing than having some one tell him what he ought to feel. Moreover, suggestion is rich in that the reader's own imagination, aroused, goes on to enrich the whole subject with feeling. We have an excellent example of this power in the last stanza. After the dialogue between the brothers to the effect that they must go back to the grave, the youngest brother says,

> "Fare ye weel, my mother dear!
> Fareweel to barn and byre!
> And fare ye weel, the bonny lass
> That kindles my mother's fire!"

Was the youngest brother in love with the bonny lass before his death? We have received no earlier hint that he was. Perhaps he has been. But it is not necessary for an appreciation of the poem to read this interpretation into the passage. The stanza gives us all we need to have if we see the bonny lass as representing the warm, beautiful life of flesh and blood which the dead men have lost and which they now must leave. If the girl does stand for this, then one may perhaps find the reason for the effect which the last line gives—

> "That kindles my mother's fire!"

The description in its effect on us is not merely an identification of the girl; the association of the girl with the fire makes us think of her particularly in her contrast with the cold and desolate grave to which the dead brothers must return.[1]

One may raise the question at this point as to whether the average reader will feel that the line means this. Is the average reader expected to be able to make this interpretation? The answer must be, no; most readers do not make this interpretation consciously; and it is not necessary for them to make it consciously in order to enjoy the poem. Many of the details of poetry affect us *unconsciously*. We can not explain just how the effect was made. But if we are to enjoy poetry to its fullest we must be alert and sensitive to such details as this. In "The Wife of Usher's Well," the suggestiveness of the images works rather simply. In some poems, especially those in Section V and Section VI, the suggestions made by the images may have a much more complicated relationship to the general intention of the poem.

We have seen that this poem differs from the prose paraphrase in being concrete where the prose is abstract, in concerning itself with feelings as well as with mere ideas, and in making use of suggestions rather than depending merely on explicit statement. One more point may be worth making. The *structure* (*Glossary*) of the poem is based on an appeal to the reader's feelings. It is not merely logical or chronological. The poem takes advantage of a reader's natural curiosity. It employs suspense. (Though the end is foreshadowed when we are told where the birch grew which adorns the dead men's hats, we are not told that they are dead—only that the wife was told that she would never see them. The solution is held up to the end.) Furthermore, the poem builds to a climax. That climax lies in the contrast between the horrors of the grave and the warmth and friendliness of life. The channering worm is contrasted with the bonny lass in the last two stanzas, and the final crowing of the cock has been so prepared for that we feel it as a gruesome summons—we feel it as the dead men feel it.

[1] In order to accept this interpretation of the effect of the last stanza on the reader it is not necessary to assume that the effect was consciously planned by the poet. For a reference to the problem of the degree of self-consciousness in a poet's artistry, see pp. 599–610.

Moreover, the effectiveness is increased by an ironic contrast in the crowing itself. The scene is a farm-scene. The atmosphere of warmth and life has been developed in terms of the farmhouse setting. But the crowing of the birds, which have an integral part in this friendly setting—the crowing which is only one of the friendly noises associated with the boys' home—itself becomes the signal for departure from this comfortable and human world to the monstrous world to which the dead men must return.

The Demon Lover

ANONYMOUS

"O where have you been, my long, long love,
This long seven years and mair?"
"O I'm come to seek my former vows
Ye granted me before."

"O hold your tongue of your former vows, 5
For they will breed sad strife;
O hold your tongue of your former vows,
For I am become a wife."

He turned him right and round about,
And the tear blinded his ee: 10
"I wad never hae trodden on Irish ground,
If it had not been for thee.

"I might hae had a king's daughter,
Far, far beyond the sea;
I might have had a king's daughter, 15
Had it not been for love o thee."

"If ye might have had a king's daughter,
Yer sel ye had to blame;
Ye might have had taken the king's daughter,
For ye kend[1] that I was nane.[2] 20

"If I was to leave my husband dear,
And my two babes also,

[1] knew [2] none

O what have you to take me to,
  If with you I should go?"

"I hae seven ships upon the sea— 25
  The eighth brought me to land—
With four-and-twenty bold mariners,
  And music on every hand."

She has taken up her two little babes,
  Kissd them baith[1] cheek and chin: 30
"O fair ye weel, my ain[2] two babes,
  For I'll never see you again."

She set her foot upon the ship,
  No mariners could she behold;
But the sails were o the taffetie, 35
  And the masts o the beaten gold.

She had not sailed a league, a league,
  A league but barely three,
When dismal grew his countenance,
  And drumlie[3] grew his ee. 40

They had not saild a league, a league,
  A league but barely three,
Until she espied his cloven foot,
  And she wept right bitterlie.

"O hold your tongue of your weeping," says he, 45
  "Of your weeping now let me be;
I will shew you how the lilies grow
  On the banks of Italy."

"O what hills are yon, yon pleasant hills,
  That the sun shines sweetly on?" 50
"O yon are the hills of heaven," he said,
  "Where you will never win."

"O whaten a mountain is yon," she said,
  "All so dreary wi frost and snow?"

[1] both [2] own [3] dark

"O yon is the mountain of hell," he cried, 55
"Where you and I will go."

He strack the tap-mast wi his hand,
The fore-mast wi his knee,
And he brake that gallant ship in twain,
And sank her in the sea. 60

EXERCISE:

1. What finally motivates the woman to yield to the lover's entreaties?

2. What is the implication of the fact that the ship's sails are taffeta and the masts, gold? Is the ship too good to be true?

3. When the woman spies the "cloven foot"—the devils, for all their power to disguise themselves, are not permitted to conceal one mark of their deviltry—she knows that her supposed lover is a demon. How justify, then, the keeping up of the pretence until line 55? Is the portrayal of the woman and the demon from 43 to 55 acceptable? Is the psychology sound?

4. What actually happens in the last stanza? Read carefully, noting the details of the action, and describe the picture that emerges.

Farewell to Barn and Stack and Tree

A. E. HOUSMAN [1859–1936]

"Farewell to barn and stack and tree,
Farewell to Severn shore.
Terence, look your last at me,
For I come home no more.

"The sun burns on the half-mown hill, 5
By now the blood is dried;
And Maurice amongst the hay lies still
And my knife is in his side.

"My mother thinks us long away;
'Tis time the field were mown. 10
She had two sons at rising day,
To-night she'll be alone.

"And here's a bloody hand to shake,
  And oh, man, here's good-bye;
We'll sweat no more on scythe and rake, 15
  My bloody hands and I.

"I wish you strength to bring you pride,
  And a love to keep you clean,
And I wish you luck, come Lammastide,
  At racing on the green. 20

"Long for me the rick will wait,
  And long will wait the fold,
And long will stand the empty plate,
  And dinner will be cold."

EXERCISE:

1. It seems obvious that the poet here is modeling his work on the folk-ballad, several examples of which the student has read. (See pp. 7–20.) Has he managed to secure some of the qualities of the ballad such as starkness, concreteness, and direct presentation? How does his poem differ from the folk ballads that you have read?

2. Do we need to know more about the motive for the quarrel between the brothers? Why has the poet left out any account of it? On what is the poem focused?

3. Are the last two lines flat and anticlimactic? Can you justify the poem's ending on the presentation of this detail?

Michael

A PASTORAL [1] POEM

WILLIAM WORDSWORTH [1770–1850]

If from the public way you turn your steps
Up the tumultuous brook of Green-head Ghyll,
You will suppose that with an upright path
Your feet must struggle; in such bold ascent
The pastoral mountains front you face to face. 5

[1] (*Glossary*)

But courage! for around that boisterous brook
The mountains have all opened out themselves,
And made a hidden valley of their own.
No habitation can be seen; but they
Who journey thither find themselves alone 10
With a few sheep, with rocks and stones, and kites
That overhead are sailing in the sky.
It is in truth an utter solitude;
Nor should I have made mention of this Dell
But for one object which you might pass by, 15
Might see and notice not. Beside the brook
Appears a straggling heap of unhewn stones!
And to that simple object appertains,
A story—unenriched with strange events,
Yet not unfit, I deem, for the fireside, 20
Or for the summer shade. It was the first
Of those domestic tales that spake to me
Of Shepherds, dwellers in the valleys, men
Whom I already loved;—not verily
For their own sakes, but for the fields and hills 25
Where was their occupation and abode.
And hence this Tale, while I was yet a Boy
Careless of books, yet having felt the power
Of Nature, by the gentle agency
Of natural objects, led me on to feel 30
For passions that were not my own, and think
(At random and imperfectly indeed)
On man, the heart of man, and human life.
Therefore, although it be a history
Homely and rude, I will relate the same 35
For the delight of a few natural hearts;
And, with yet fonder feeling, for the sake
Of youthful Poets who among these hills
Will be my second self when I am gone.

Upon the forest-side in Grasmere Vale 40
There dwelt a Shepherd, Michael was his name;
An old man, stout of heart, and strong of limb.
His bodily frame had been from youth to age
Of an unusual strength: his mind was keen,
Intense, and frugal, apt for all affairs, 45

And in his shepherd's calling he was prompt
And watchful more than ordinary men.
Hence had he learned the meaning of all winds,
Of blasts of every tone; and, oftentimes,
When others heeded not, He heard the South 50
Make subterraneous music, like the noise
Of bagpipers on distant Highland hills.
The Shepherd, at such warning, of his flock
Bethought him, and he to himself would say,
'The winds are now devising work for me!' 55
And, truly, at all times, the storm, that drives
The traveler to a shelter, summoned him
Up to the mountains; he had been alone
Amid the heart of many thousand mists,
That came to him, and left him on the heights. 60
So lived he till his eightieth year was past.
And grossly that man errs, who should suppose
That the green valleys, and the streams and rocks,
Were things indifferent to the Shepherd's thoughts.
Fields, where with cheerful spirits he had breathed 65
The common air; hills, which with vigorous step
He had so often climbed; which had impressed
So many incidents upon his mind
Of hardship, skill or courage, joy or fear;
Which, like a book, preserved the memory 70
Of the dumb animals, whom he had saved,
Had fed or sheltered, linking to such acts
The certainty of honorable gain;
Those fields, those hills—what could they less?—had laid
Strong hold on his affections, were to him 75
A pleasurable feeling of blind love,
The pleasure which there is in life itself.

His days had not been passed in singleness.
His Helpmate was a comely matron, old—
Though younger than himself full twenty years. 80
She was a woman of a stirring life,
Whose heart was in her house: two wheels she had
Of antique form, this large for spinning wool,
That small for flax; and if one wheel had rest,
It was because the other was at work. 85

The Pair had but one inmate in their house,
An only Child, who had been born to them
When Michael, telling o'er his years, began
To deem that he was old,—in shepherd's phrase,
With one foot in the grave. This only Son, 90
With two brave sheep-dogs tried in many a storm,
The one of an inestimable worth,
Made all their household. I may truly say,
That they were as a proverb in the vale
For endless industry. When day was gone, 95
And from their occupations out of doors
The Son and Father were come home, even then,
Their labor did not cease; unless when all
Turned to the cleanly supper-board, and there,
Each with a mess of pottage and skimmed milk, 100
Sat round the basket piled with oaten cakes,
And their plain home-made cheese. Yet when the meal
Was ended, Luke (for so the Son was named)
And his old Father both betook themselves
To such convenient work as might employ 105
Their hands by the fire-side; perhaps to card
Wool for the Housewife's spindle, or repair
Some injury done to sickle, flail, or scythe,
Or other implement of house or field.

Down from the ceiling by the chimney's edge 110
That in our ancient uncouth country style
With huge and black projection overbrowed
Large space beneath, as duly as the light
Of day grew dim the Housewife hung a lamp;
An aged utensil, which had performed 115
Service beyond all others of its kind.
Early at evening did it burn—and late,
Surviving comrade of uncounted hours,
Which, going by from year to year, had found
And left the couple neither gay perhaps 120
Nor cheerful, yet with objects and with hopes,
Living a life of eager industry.
And now, when Luke had reached his eighteenth year
There by the light of this old lamp they sat,
Father and Son, while far into the night 125

The Housewife plied her own peculiar work,
Making the cottage through the silent hours
Murmur as with the sound of summer flies.
This light was famous in its neighborhood,
And was a public symbol of the life 130
That thrifty Pair had lived. For, as it chanced,
Their cottage on a plot of rising ground
Stood single, with large prospect, north and south,
High into Easedale, up to Dunmail-Raise,
And westward to the village near the lake; 135
And from this constant light, so regular
And so far seen, the House itself, by all
Who dwelt within the limits of the vale,
Both old and young, was named The Evening Star.

Thus living on through such a length of years, 140
The Shepherd, if he loved himself, must needs
Have loved his Helpmate; but to Michael's heart
This son of his old age was yet more dear—
Less from instinctive tenderness, the same
Fond spirit that blindly works in the blood of all— 145
Than that a child, more than all other gifts,
That earth can offer to declining man,
Brings hope with it, and forward looking thoughts,
And stirrings of inquietude, when they
By tendency of nature needs must fail. 150
Exceeding was the love he bare to him,
His heart and his heart's joy! For oftentimes
Old Michael, while he was a babe in arms,
Had done him female service, not alone
For pastime and delight, as is the use 155
Of fathers, but with patient mind enforced
To acts of tenderness; and he had rocked
His cradle as with a woman's gentle hand.

And, in a later time, ere yet the Boy
Had put on boy's attire, did Michael love, 160
Albeit of a stern unbending mind,
To have the Young one in his sight, when he
Wrought in the field, or on his shepherd's stool

Sat with a fettered sheep before him stretched,
Under the large old oak, that near his door, 165
Stood single, and, from matchless depth of shade,
Chosen for the Shearer's covert from the sun,
Thence in our rustic dialect was called
The Clipping Tree, a name which yet it bears.
There, while they two were sitting in the shade, 170
With others round them, earnest all and blithe,
Would Michael exercise his heart with looks
Of fond correction and reproof bestowed
Upon the Child, if he disturbed the sheep
By catching at their legs, or with his shouts 175
Scared them, while they lay still beneath the shears.

And when by Heaven's good grace the boy grew up
A healthy Lad, and carried in his cheek
Two steady roses that were five years old.
Then Michael from a winter coppice cut 180
With his own hand a sapling, which he hooped
With iron, making it throughout in all
Due requisites a perfect shepherd's staff,
And gave it to the Boy; wherewith equipt
He as a watchman oftentimes was placed 185
At gate or gap, to stem or turn the flock;
And, to his office prematurely called,
There stood the urchin, as you will divine,
Something between a hindrance and a help;
And for this course not always, I believe, 190
Receiving from his Father hire of praise;
Though nought was left undone which staff or voice,
Or looks, or threatening gestures could perform.

But soon as Luke, full ten years old, could stand
Against the mountain blasts; and to the heights, 195
Not fearing toil, nor length of weary ways,
He with his Father daily went, and they
Were as companions, why should I relate
That objects which the Shepherd loved before
Were dearer now? that from the Boy there came 200
Feelings and emanations—things which were

Light to the sun and music to the wind;
And that the old Man's heart seemed born again.

Thus in his Father's sight the Boy grew up;
And now when he had reached his eighteenth year, 205
He was his comfort and his daily hope.

While in this sort the simple household lived
From day to day, to Michael's ear there came
Distressful tidings. Long before the time
Of which I speak, the Shepherd had been bound 210
In surety for his brother's son, a man
Of an industrious life, and ample means—
But unforeseen misfortunes suddenly
Had pressed upon him,—and old Michael now
Was summoned to discharge the forfeiture, 215
A grievous penalty, but little less
Than half his substance. This unlooked-for claim,
At the first hearing, for a moment took
More hope out of his life than he supposed
That any old man ever could have lost. 220
As soon as he had armed himself with strength
To look his trouble in the face, it seemed
The Shepherd's sole resource to sell at once
A portion of his patrimonial fields.
Such was his first resolve; he thought again, 225
And his heart failed him. 'Isabel,' said he,
Two evenings after he had heard the news,
'I have been toiling more than seventy years,
And in the open sunshine of God's love
Have we all lived; yet if these fields of ours 230
Should pass into a stranger's hand, I think
That I could not lie quiet in my grave.
Our lot is a hard lot; the sun himself
Has scarcely been more diligent than I;
And I have lived to be a fool at last 235
To my own family. An evil man
That was, and made an evil choice, if he
Were false to us; and, if he were not false,
There are ten thousand to whom loss like this
Had been no sorrow. I forgive him—but 240

'T were better to be dumb, than to talk thus.
When I began, my purpose was to speak
Of remedies and of a cheerful hope.
Our Luke shall leave us, Isabel; the land
Shall not go from us, and it shall be free; 245
He shall possess it free as is the wind
That passes over it. We have, thou know'st,
Another kinsman—he will be our friend
In this distress. He is a prosperous man,
Thriving in trade—and Luke to him shall go, 250
And with his kinsman's help and his own thrift
He quickly will repair this loss, and then
He may return to us. If here he stay,
What can be done? Where every one is poor,
What can be gained?' At this the old Man paused, 255
And Isabel sat silent, for her mind
Was busy, looking back into past times.
There's Richard Bateman, thought she to herself,
He was a parish-boy—at the church-door
They made a gathering for him, shillings, pence, 260
And halfpennies, wherewith the neighbors bought
A basket, which they filled with pedlar's wares;
And with this basket on his arm, the lad
Went up to London, found a master there,
Who out of many chose the trusty boy 265
To go and overlook his merchandise
Beyond the seas: where he grew wondrous rich,
And left estates and monies to the poor,
And at his birthplace built a chapel floored
With marble, which he sent from foreign lands. 270
These thoughts, and many others of like sort,
Passed quickly through the mind of Isabel,
And her face brightened. The old Man was glad,
And thus resumed:—'Well, Isabel! this scheme
These two days has been meat and drink to me. 275
Far more than we have lost is left us yet.
We have enough—I wish indeed that I
Were younger,—but this hope is a good hope.
Make ready Luke's best garments, of the best
Buy for him more, and let us send him forth 280

Tomorrow, or the next day, or tonight:
If he *could* go, the Boy should go tonight.'

Here Michael ceased, and to the fields went forth
With a light heart. The Housewife for five days
Was restless morn and night, and all day long 285
Wrought on with her best fingers to prepare
Things needful for the journey of her son.
But Isabel was glad when Sunday came
To stop her in her work: for, when she lay
By Michael's side, she through the last two nights 290
Heard him, how he was troubled in his sleep:
And when they rose at morning she could see
That all his hopes were gone. That day at noon
She said to Luke, while they two by themselves
Were sitting at the door. 'Thou must not go: 295
We have no other Child but thee to lose,
None to remember—do not go away,
For if thou leave thy Father he will die.'
The Youth made answer with a jocund voice;
And Isabel, when she had told her fears, 300
Recovered heart. That evening her best fare
Did she bring forth, and all together sat
Like happy people round a Christmas fire.

With daylight Isabel resumed her work;
And all the ensuing week the house appeared 305
As cheerful as a grove in Spring: at length
The expected letter from their kinsman came,
With kind assurances that he would do
His utmost for the welfare of the Boy;
To which, requests were added, that forthwith 310
He might be sent to him. Ten times or more
The letter was read over; Isabel
Went forth to show it to the neighbors round;
Nor was there at that time on English land
A prouder heart than Luke's. When Isabel 315
Had to her house returned, the old Man said,
'He shall depart tomorrow.' To this word
The Housewife answered, talking much of things
Which, if at such short notice he should go,

Would surely be forgotten. But at length 320
She gave consent, and Michael was at ease.

Near the tumultuous brook of Green-head Ghyll,
In that deep valley, Michael had designed
To build a Sheep-fold; and, before he heard
The tidings of his melancholy loss, 325
For this same purpose he had gathered up
A heap of stones, which by the streamlet's edge
Lay thrown together, ready for the work.
With Luke that evening thitherward he walked;
And soon as they had reached the place he stopped, 330
And thus the old Man spake to him:—'My son,
Tomorrow thou wilt leave me: with full heart
I look upon thee, for thou art the same
That wert a promise to me ere thy birth,
And all thy life hast been my daily joy. 335
I will relate to thee some little part
Of our two histories; 't will do thee good
When thou art from me, even if I should touch
On things thou canst not know of.—After thou
First cam'st into the world—as oft befalls 340
To new-born infants—thou didst sleep away
Two days, and blessings from thy Father's tongue
Then fell upon thee. Day by day passed on,
And still I loved thee with increasing love.
Never to living ear came sweeter sounds 345
Than when I heard thee by our own fireside
First uttering, without words, a natural tune;
While thou, a feeding babe, didst in thy joy
Sing at thy Mother's breast. Month followed month,
And in the open fields my life was passed 350
And on the mountains, else I think that thou
Hadst been brought up upon thy Father's knees.
But we were playmates, Luke: among these hills,
As well thou know'st, in us the old and young
Have played together, nor with me didst thou 355
Lack any pleasure which a boy can know.'
Luke had a manly heart; but at these words
He sobbed aloud. The old Man grasped his hand
And said, 'Nay, do not take it so—I see

That these are things of which I need not speak. 360
Even to the utmost I have been to thee
A kind and a good Father: and herein
I but repay a gift which I myself
Received at others' hands; for, though now old
Beyond the common life of man, I still 365
Remember them who loved me in my youth.
Both of them sleep together: here they lived
As all their forefathers had done; and when
At length their time was come, they were not loath
To give their bodies to the family mold. 370
I wished that thou shouldst live the life they lived.
But 't is a long time to look back, my Son,
And see so little gain from threescore years.
These fields were burdened when they came to me;
Till I was forty years of age, not more 375
Than half of my inheritance was mine.
I toiled and toiled; God blessed me in my work,
And till these three weeks past the land was free.
It looks as if it never could endure
Another Master. Heaven forgive me, Luke, 380
If I judge ill for thee, but it seems good
That thou shouldst go.'

At this the old Man paused;
Then, pointing to the stones near which they stood,
Thus, after a short silence, he resumed:
'This was a work for us; and now, my Son, 385
It is a work for me. But, lay one stone—
Here, lay it for me, Luke, with thine own hands.
Nay, Boy, be of good hope;—we both may live
To see a better day. At eighty-four
I still am strong and hale;—do thou thy part, 390
I will do mine.—I will begin again
With many tasks that were resigned to thee:
Up to the heights, and in among the storms,
Will I without thee go again, and do
All works which I was wont to do alone, 395
Before I knew thy face.—Heaven bless thee, Boy!
Thy heart these two weeks has been beating fast
With many hopes; it should be so—yes—yes—
I knew that thou couldst never have a wish

To leave me, Luke: thou hast been bound to me 400
Only by links of love: when thou art gone,
What will be left to us!—But I forget
My purposes. Lay now the corner-stone,
As I requested; and hereafter, Luke,
When thou art gone away, should evil men 405
Be thy companions, think of me, my Son,
And of this moment; hither turn thy thoughts,
And God will strengthen thee: amid all fear
And all temptation, Luke, I pray that thou
Mayst bear in mind the life thy Fathers lived, 410
Who, being innocent, did for that cause
Bestir them in good deeds. Now, fare thee well—
When thou return'st, thou in this place wilt see
A work which is not here: a covenant
'T will be between us—but, whatever fate 415
Befall thee, I shall love thee to the last,
And bear thy memory with me to the grave.'

The Shepherd ended here; and Luke stooped down,
And, as his Father had requested, laid
The first stone of the Sheep-fold. At the sight 420
The old Man's grief broke from him; to his heart
He pressed his Son, he kissèd him and wept;
And to the house together they returned.
Hushed was that House in peace, or seeming peace,
Ere the night fell;—with morrow's dawn the Boy 425
Began his journey, and when he had reached
The public way, he put on a bold face;
And all the neighbors as he passed their doors
Came forth with wishes and with farewell prayers,
That followed him till he was out of sight. 430

A good report did from their Kinsman come,
Of Luke and his well doing: and the Boy
Wrote loving letters, full of wondrous news,
Which, as the Housewife phrased it, were throughout
'The prettiest letters that were ever seen.' 435
Both parents read them with rejoicing hearts.
So, many months passed on: and once again
The Shepherd went about his daily work

With confident and cheerful thoughts; and now
Sometimes when he could find a leisure hour 440
He to that valley took his way, and there
Wrought at the Sheep-fold. Meantime Luke began
To slacken in his duty; and at length
He in the dissolute city gave himself
To evil courses: ignominy and shame 445
Fell on him, so that he was driven at last
To seek a hiding-place beyond the seas.

There is a comfort in the strength of love;
'T will make a thing endurable, which else
Would overset the brain, or break the heart: 450
I have conversed with more than one who well
Remember the old Man, and what he was
Years after he had heard this heavy news.
His bodily frame had been from youth to age
Of an unusual strength. Among the rocks 455
He went, and still looked up to sun and cloud
And listened to the wind; and as before
Performed all kinds of labor for his sheep,
And for the land, his small inheritance.
And to that hollow dell from time to time 460
Did he repair, to build the fold of which
His flock had need. 'T is not forgotten yet
The pity which was then in every heart
For the old Man—and 't is believed by all
That many and many a day he thither went, 465
And never lifted up a single stone.

There, by the Sheep-fold, sometimes was he seen
Sitting alone, or with his faithful Dog,
Then old, beside him, lying at his feet.
The length of full seven years from time to time 470
He at the building of this Sheep-fold wrought,
And left the work unfinished when he died.
Three years, or little more, did Isabel
Survive her Husband: at her death the estate
Was sold, and went into a stranger's hand. 475
The cottage which was named the Evening Star
Is gone—the ploughshare has been through the ground

On which it stood; great changes have been wrought
In all the neighborhood:—yet the oak is left
That grew beside their door; and the remains 480
Of the unfinished Sheep-fold may be seen
Beside the boisterous brook of Green-head Ghyll.

This poem after the first forty lines, which serve as a sort of introduction to the story proper, is a direct and simple narrative. The poet is apparently not aiming at an effect of condensation or at a swift dramatic effect such as is aimed at, for example, in the ballads which have been analyzed. The effect is rather cumulative as the details of the story, piled up in chronological order, make their weight felt on the reader; the method is here effective, for the story deals with the whole life of a man and not with a single sharp, climactic incident.

Since the poem is so straightforward in its organization, the numerous details are really necessary for an appreciation of the story because the effect of the poem does not depend on the sharp imaginative flashes such as we have found in the preceding poems. It is no accident, then, that the poem is as long as it is. In fact, the method of this poem lies very close to that of prose fiction in its lack of condensation, just as that of the ballads we have read lies rather close to the method of drama.

But the reader may still be disposed to ask, "Have we not too many details? Are not some of the details really irrelevant?" For instance, he may ask, of what use in the poem is the statement that Michael's wife had a big wheel for spinning wool and a small one for spinning flax, and that the large oak by the cottage door was called the "Clipping Tree"? By way of reply, we could scarcely maintain that any specific detail is absolutely essential to the effect of the poem; but we can maintain that the effect of the total mass of detail is highly important if we are to understand the sort of life which Michael leads and is attached to. In the first place, the number of intimate details gives a sense of close observation and makes the reader feel that the scene and the incident that occurs in it are real. But in addition to giving an impression of *realism* (*Glossary*) this use of detail serves a second, and perhaps more important, purpose. Since the tragedy turns on the fact of Michael's attachment to the land and the way of life on it, it is necessary that the reader have some sense of the reason for his mastering desire to hold the land and pass it on to his son. The reader is led into an easy and familiar acquaintance with those objects that represent the kind of life on the land in much the same way as Michael himself would know them. The elaboration of details, then, serves to suggest the fundamental relationship on which the poem depends.

The poet, if he is to be successful in this poem, must make the reader feel as forcefully as possible the pathos of Michael's situation. But he cannot make the reader feel this merely by telling him that the situation is pathetic. As a matter of fact, mature people have a thoroughly justifiable suspicion of people who are prompt to weep over situations of pathos. Mature people do not like to be bullied into feeling something; they want, instead, to see the justification for the reaction. The poet, unless he is writing for an audience of *sentimentalists* (*Glossary*)—that is, people who enjoy any excuse for indulging their feelings—must really justify the reaction he wishes to provoke. How does Wordsworth do this? First, we can see what he does not do. He does not give sentimental comments himself. He merely presents the situation in an objective way. In the second place, he does not even have the characters themselves give way to violent grief. As a matter of fact, for Michael, who is presented as a sober and restrained person, to give violent expression to his disappointment and sorrow would seem to us false and out of character. How then is the poet to give us the impression of the depth of the grief when the character himself does not give way to it? Here the importance of the background which he has established—what Michael's life is, his attachment to the land, etc.—becomes clear. Because we have been given a vivid sense of this background through the use of detail early in the poem, the poet here can merely point out objectively the facts of the situation, and depend upon the imagination of his readers to do the rest. He does not insist on the pathos, but lets the reader discover it for himself. The old man does not die of heartbreak when the news of his son's running away comes to him. People do not often die of heartbreak; the poet does not test our credulity by making us believe that this one does; and moreover, the old man resting by the unfinished sheepfold is a more moving figure than is a person on a literal death-bed.

One further point should be mentioned in describing how the poem gets its effect. The poet has managed to find a concrete situation which stands for and concentrates the whole tragedy: it is, of course, the scene at the sheepfold, where Michael has his son lay the cornerstone so that the work may stand for the love and interest which unites them, and stand for the continuity of life which the old man is trying to preserve. The disappointment is made much more poignant by picturing the old man later at the fold, sometimes never lifting "up a single stone," than by the poet's own comment on the old man's sadness and disappointment.

One more word should be said about the general method which Wordsworth is using here. It has been pointed out that he does not concentrate his work by sudden flashes of the imagination but works by accumulation of details. Since this is so, he does not try for a strong dramatic conclusion at the end of this poem, such as we have, for example, in "The Wife of Usher's Well." Instead, he levels the poem off at the end by a description of the present appearance of Michael's farm, the cottage gone, but the oak remaining, and the ruins of the unfinished sheepfold still to be seen. It is an ending which accords with the general effect which the poet has been working for from the first—an effect of slow-moving forcefulness.

The Death of the Hired Man

ROBERT FROST [1875–]

Mary sat musing on the lamp-flame at the table
Waiting for Warren. When she heard his step,
She ran on tip-toe down the darkened passage
To meet him in the doorway with the news
And put him on his guard. "Silas is back." 5
She pushed him outward with her through the door
And shut it after her. "Be kind," she said.
She took the market things from Warren's arms
And set them on the porch, then drew him down
To sit beside her on the wooden steps. 10

"When was I ever anything but kind to him?
But I'll not have the fellow back," he said.
"I told him so last haying, didn't I?
'If he left then,' I said, 'that ended it.'
What good is he? Who else will harbor him 15
At his age for the little he can do?
What help he is there's no depending on.
Off he goes always when I need him most.
'He thinks he ought to earn a little pay,
Enough at least to buy tobacco with, 20
So he won't have to beg and be beholden.'
'All right,' I say, 'I can't afford to pay
Any fixed wages, though I wish I could.'
'Some one else can.' 'Then some one else will have to.'
I shouldn't mind his bettering himself 25
If that was what it was. You can be certain,
When he begins like that, there's some one at him
Trying to coax him off with pocket-money,—
In haying time, when any help is scarce.
In winter he comes back to us. I'm done." 30

"Sh! not so loud: he'll hear you," Mary said.

"I want him to: he'll have to soon or late."

"He's worn out. He's asleep beside the stove.
When I came up from Rowe's I found him here,
Huddled against the barn-door fast asleep, 35
A miserable sight, and frightening, too—
You needn't smile—I didn't recognize him—
I wasn't looking for him—and he's changed.
Wait till you see."

"Where did you say he'd been?"

"He didn't say. I dragged him to the house, 40
And gave him tea and tried to make him smoke.
I tried to make him talk about his travels.
Nothing would do: he just kept nodding off."

"What did he say? Did he say anything?"

"But little."

"Anything? Mary, confess 45
He said he'd come to ditch the meadow for me."

"Warren!"

"But did he? I just want to know."

"Of course he did. What would you have him say?
Surely you wouldn't grudge the poor old man
Some humble way to save his self-respect. 50
He added, if you really care to know,
He meant to clear the upper pasture, too.
That sounds like something you have heard before?
Warren, I wish you could have heard the way
He jumbled everything. I stopped to look 55
Two or three times—he made me feel so queer—
To see if he was talking in his sleep.
He ran on Harold Wilson—you remember—
The boy you had in haying four years since.
He's finished school, and teaching in his college. 60
Silas declares you'll have to get him back.
He says they two will make a team for work:
Between them they will lay this farm as smooth!
The way he mixed that in with other things.
He thinks young Wilson a likely lad, though daft 65
On education—you know how they fought
All through July under the blazing sun,
Silas up on the cart to build the load,
Harold along beside to pitch it on."

"Yes, I took care to keep well out of earshot." 70

"Well, those days trouble Silas like a dream.
You wouldn't think they would. How some things linger!
Harold's young college boy's assurance piqued him.
After so many years he still keeps finding
Good arguments he sees he might have used. 75
I sympathize. I know just how it feels
To think of the right thing to say too late.

Harold's associated in his mind with Latin.
He asked me what I thought of Harold's saying
He studied Latin like the violin 80
Because he liked it—that an argument!
He said he couldn't make the boy believe
He could find water with a hazel prong—
Which showed how much good school had ever done him.
He wanted to go over that. But most of all 85
He thinks if he could have another chance
To teach him how to build a load of hay—"

"I know, that's Silas' one accomplishment.
He bundles every forkful in its place,
And tags and numbers it for future reference, 90
So he can find and easily dislodge it
In the unloading. Silas does that well.
He takes it out in bunches like big birds' nests.
You never see him standing on the hay
He's trying to lift, straining to lift himself." 95

"He thinks if he could teach him that, he'd be
Some good perhaps to someone in the world.
He hates to see a boy the fool of books.
Poor Silas, so concerned for other folk,
And nothing to look backward to with pride, 100
And nothing to look forward to with hope,
So now and never any different."

Part of a moon was falling down the west,
Dragging the whole sky with it to the hills.
Its light poured softly in her lap. She saw 105
And spread her apron to it. She put out her hand
Among the harp-like morning-glory strings,
Taut with the dew from garden bed to eaves,
As if she played unheard the tenderness
That wrought on him beside her in the night. 110
"Warren," she said, "he has come home to die:
You needn't be afraid he'll leave you this time."

"Home," he mocked gently.

"Yes, what else but home?
It all depends on what you mean by home.
Of course he's nothing to us, any more 115
Than was the hound that came a stranger to us
Out of the woods, worn out upon the trail."

"Home is the place where, when you have to go there,
They have to take you in."

"I should have called it
Something you somehow haven't to deserve." 120

Warren leaned out and took a step or two,
Picked up a little stick, and brought it back
And broke it in his hand and tossed it by.
"Silas has better claim on us you think
Than on his brother? Thirteen little miles 125
As the road winds would bring him to his door.
Silas has walked that far no doubt today.
Why didn't he go there? His brother's rich,
A somebody—director in the bank."

"He never told us that."

"We know it though." 130

"I think his brother ought to help, of course.
I'll see to that if there is need. He ought of right
To take him in, and might be willing to—
He may be better than appearances.
But have some pity on Silas. Do you think 135
If he'd had any pride in claiming kin
Or anything he looked for from his brother,
He'd keep so still about him all this time?"

"I wonder what's between them."

"I can tell you.
Silas is what he is—we wouldn't mind him— 140
But just the kind that kinsfolk can't abide.
He never did a thing so very bad.

He don't know why he isn't quite as good
As anybody. Worthless though he is,
He won't be made ashamed to please his brother." 145

"*I* can't think Si ever hurt anyone."

"No, but he hurt my heart the way he lay
And rolled his old head on that sharp-edged chairback.
He wouldn't let me put him on the lounge.
You must go in and see what you can do. 150
I made the bed up for him there tonight.
You'll be surprised at him—how much he's broken.
His working days are done; I'm sure of it."

"I'd not be in a hurry to say that."

"I haven't been. Go, look, see for yourself. 155
But, Warren, please remember how it is:
He's come to help you ditch the meadow.
He has a plan. You mustn't laugh at him.
He may not speak of it, and then he may.
I'll sit and see if that small sailing cloud 160
Will hit or miss the moon."

It hit the moon.
Then there were three there, making a dim row,
The moon, the little silver cloud, and she.
Warren returned—too soon, it seemed to her,
Slipped to her side, caught up her hand and waited. 165

"Warren?" she questioned.

"Dead," was all he answered.

EXERCISE:

1. The problem in this poem, as in "Michael," is to present the pathos of the old man's condition, cleanly and sharply, without any mawkishness or too easy pity. Has the poet succeeded in doing this?

2. What is gained by keeping Silas off the stage? (All that we learn about him is through Mary or Warren.)

3. What is gained by having Mary and Warren take opposite

sides in discussing Silas? What, by the way, is Warren's basic attitude toward Silas?

4. What is gained by the use of realistic detail and natural and "unliterary" conversation?

5. Read carefully the description given in lines 103–10. Can you visualize the scene? Why is this bit of description put just here?

The Three Ravens

ANONYMOUS

There were three ravens sat on a tree,
  Downe a downe, hay downe, hay downe
There were three ravens sat on a tree,
  With a downe
There were three ravens sat on a tree, 5
They were as blacke as they might be.
  With a downe derrie, derrie, derrie,
    downe, downe.

The one of them said to his mate,
"Where shall we our breakefast take?"

"Downe in yonder greene field, 10
There lies a knight slain under his shield.

"His hounds they lie downe at his feete,
So well they can their master keepe.

"His haukes they flie so eagerly,
There's no fowle dare him come nie." 15

Downe there comes a fallow doe,
As great with yong as she might goe.

She lift up his bloudy hed,
And kist his wounds that were so red.

She got him up upon her backe, 20
And carried him to earthen lake.[1]

[1] pit

She buried him before the prime,
She was dead herselfe ere even-song time.

God send every gentleman,
Such haukes, such hounds, and such a leman.[1] 25

In this poem the narrative is largely implied. (Fullness of presentation of a narrative is, of course, a relative matter. One could argue that the story in "Sir Patrick Spence" is also largely "implied" —not fully presented. Even so, this poem, and most of the poems that are to follow in this section, tend to be, in a special sense, implied narratives.)

The story implied by this ballad may be stated as follows: A knight has been killed, but his hounds guard the body, and his hawks, waiting by their master, keep away the crows that would prey upon it. The knight's leman comes and with her own hands buries him, and then dies herself. But we know nothing more about the "story" as such. We do not know how the knight was killed, or why, or by whom. We simply have the scene by the body, and as elements of the scene, the picture of the ravens gathered in the tree, the picture of the knight with the hounds at his feet and his hawks flying above him. The only thing that happens is the coming of the woman and her death. The poet is not so much interested, then, in giving the reader the consecutive facts of the story as he is in creating a certain feeling about the scene.

What is the feeling which the poet is interested in giving the reader? What does he want the poem to mean to us? We can best answer these questions by examining the manner in which the poet has used the elements of the poem.

As we can quickly see, the details are chosen, not haphazardly, but for a particular effect. The hounds on guard are a type of loyalty, and so also are the vigilant hawks. And these two references prepare for the mention of the third and most important of those who are loyal to the dead knight, the woman herself. She is the *climactic* (*Glossary*) example of loyalty.

Why, then, does the poet mention the ravens? They have no affection for the dead man whatsoever; they consider him only as so

[1] loved one: wife or sweetheart

much food. The answer is that they form an effective contrast to what follows. They represent the cruelly impersonal background against which the various acts of loyalty are described. There is an ironic shock in passing from the ravens to the hounds, for we pass from a consideration of the knight as so much carrion to a consideration of him as master and friend, even in death master and friend still.

We may observe the cunning with which the poem presents this material. The poet does not depend on the kind of general statement which we have given in our prose paraphrase. The material is arranged so that we feel the effect intended without the direct statement. The mere fact that the poet allows the ravens themselves to describe the scene accomplishes two things that would otherwise be impossible. First, what would otherwise be flat description of a scene becomes dramatic action. The reader comes more directly to the central fact of the poem. Second, the ironic contrast is more pointed when the ravens themselves, examples of mere brute appetite, comment on the hawk and the hounds, examples of a fidelity that reaches beyond such appetite. Thus, the material is arranged in such a manner that a comment on the meaning of the situation is unnecessary: we grasp it immediately, even when we do not take the trouble to put it in the form of a general statement.

After the poet has set the scene directly and dramatically, the development of the action is given in terms of narrative. We are told how the "doe" comes down to the dead knight. But why is the leman of the dead knight called a doe?[1] The poet gains again a sort of dramatic shock by characterizing the woman as a deer. But we see that the characterization is "right," after all. The shyness and timidity of the deer provides a fitting description for the gentleness of the woman. But that is not all. A real doe would not come down among the hounds; she is the hunted animal, they are the hunters. Therefore the fact that the woman is described as a doe coming to the scene defines for us subtly but emphatically the strength of her fidelity and courage. In other words, the poet has made the comparison really tell us something that is essential for the meaning of

[1] For origin of this comparison see Wimberly: *Folklore in English and Scottish Ballads,* p. 55.

the poem. Furthermore, the comparison is the most concentrated way of giving us the meaning. But the comparison does not merely give us meaning in the sense of information about the situation; by appealing to our attitude toward the timidity and shyness of the doe, it creates our attitude toward the woman herself.

The line,

> As great with yong as she might goe

emphasizes further the pathos of the situation and the strength of the fidelity that brings the "doe" to the scene. It tells us that her action in burying her lover was most difficult, and helps account for her death. It has another effect. She is evidently great with the knight's child. The love has been consummated, and her grief is therefore all the more poignant.

In the body of the poem are given the various examples of loyalty in action. The poet himself refrains from any comment until the last stanza:

> God send every gentleman,
> Such haukes, such hounds, and such a leman.

But notice the form the comment takes. It does not insist on the loyalty. It does not exaggerate. It is, indeed, an understatement. But as such it employs a contrast which is more emphatic than fulsome praise would be. The form of the statement implies that there are few enough knights who have such hawks and hounds and such a lover. This implication is a clue to what might be called the *theme* (*Glossary*) of the poem. We may state the theme more largely somewhat as follows. The poem, taken as a whole, makes a contrast between two ways of looking at life. The ravens represent one way, the hawks, hounds, and "doe" the other. One view regards life in a purely materialistic way; the other finds an importance in life beyond mere material circumstance. The same theme appears in "Johnie Armstrong." Even though he knows he is going to be killed, he feels that the way in which he meets death is important. He says to his men,

> Let them report how we were slaine.

And a similar theme is found in "Sir Patrick Spence."

The statement of the theme of a poem must not be taken as equivalent to the poem itself. It is not to be taken as a "message." But the definition of the theme of a poem may help us to a fuller understanding of the entire poem, if we are careful never to think of it as a little moral comment or platitude which the poem has been written in order to give. We may put the matter in this way: the theme does not give the poem its force; the poem gives the theme its force.

Lord Randal

ANONYMOUS

"O where hae ye been, Lord Randal, my son?
O where hae ye been, my handsome young man?"
"I hae been to the wild wood; mother, make my bed soon,
For I'm weary wi hunting, and fain wald lie down."

"Where gat ye your dinner, Lord Randal, my son? 5
Where gat ye your dinner, my handsome young man?"
"I din'd wi my true-love; mother, make my bed soon,
For I'm weary wi hunting, and fain wald lie down."

"What gat ye to your dinner, Lord Randal, my son?
What gat ye to your dinner, my handsome young man?" 10
"I gat eels boiled in broo;[1] mother, make my bed soon,
For I'm weary wi hunting, and fain wald lie down."

"What became of your bloodhounds, Lord Randal, my son?
What became of your bloodhounds, my handsome young man?"
"O they swelld and they died; mother, make my bed soon, 15
For I'm weary wi hunting, and fain wald lie down."

"O I fear ye are poisond, Lord Randal, my son!
O I fear ye are poisond, my handsome young man!"
"O yes! I am poisond; mother, make my bed soon,
For I'm sick at the heart, and I fain wald lie down." 20

This ballad shows some devices that are not found in "Johnie Armstrong," for instance, but are characteristic of many folk ballads

[1] broth

—dialogue, as the only vehicle for narration, and repetition. The poem does not give a consecutive narrative, as does "Johnie Armstrong," but merely takes a single dramatic moment in an action and presents that in five questions and answers that are framed in the repetition. That is, the movement is defined by a series of leaps and pauses.

The action proper is suppressed, or only hinted at. But the treatment is extremely effective, moving, as it does, with increasing suspense from a simple question and apparently innocent answer in the first stanza to the tragic discovery in the last. In each stanza the refrain serves to focus this growing intensity, for with its recurrence the reader begins to realize that more and more is implied, until he discovers in the end that, not healthy weariness from the hunt, but death makes the young man fain to lie down.

The treatment is not the treatment of narrative. A more rigid selectivity has been brought to bear on the material than would apply in direct narrative. Just such details are used as will be essential and will suggest the rest of the story. The reader is not provided with the kind of information on which a newspaper account or even an ordinary piece of fiction would thrive. We know nothing about the relation between Lord Randal and his true-love except the fact that she poisoned him. The motivation is entirely lacking. Nor do we know anything about the relation between the mother and her son's true-love, although by reason of the mother's quick suspicion we may venture the surmise that the relation was not one of untroubled confidence, perhaps one of mutual jealousy. Just enough information is given to stimulate the imagination, to give the reader a sudden glimpse into the depth of the tragic and ironical situation in the lives of these three people. This sudden glimpse, if the details are properly chosen, may be more effective in provoking the emotional response of the reader than a careful elaboration of facts that might satisfy the full curiosity. Poetry frequently employs this kind of suggestiveness to gain its effects rather than a method of detailed analysis.

A further word might be said about the use of repetition here. We have said that the repetition frames the questions and answers on which the movement of the action depends. In Section III we shall discuss the function of meter, rime, and stanza—that is, the effect of rhythmical patterns. It is enough for our purpose here to notice the effect of a regular pattern in the form of the questions and answers—that is, the use of repetition and refrain. Repetition and refrain are devices a poet may use to bring the material of a poem under control. The repetition and refrain, like meter, rime, and stanza, help give the poem a *form* (*Glossary*).

If the material is deprived of a poetic form, we merely have left something like this: A young man named Lord Randal, on returning home from a hunt and a dinner with his true-love, asks his mother to make his bed because he is weary. After several questions about the meal and the disappearance of the son's dogs, which the son says died with mysterious suddenness, the mother comes to the conclusion that her son has been poisoned. The son, now desperately ill, says that this is true and that he must lie down. This account is flatter and less moving than the poem, not because it does not give the essential facts, but because it lacks the organization, the form, of the poem.

Perhaps it cannot finally be said why we are affected as we are by artistic and other forms. For the present, it is enough that the reader should be aware of the part certain things like meter or repetition, things he may have regarded merely as mechanical decorations, are playing in his total response. In this poem, the repetition, for instance, serves as a kind of binder for each stanza, the fixed item to which the new material is tied each time. But it serves a further purpose, as well. The request to make the bed soon because he is weary with hunting begins to affect us with a secondary and symbolic meaning which is gradually developed: he is going to die, he is weary of life not merely because of his sickness from the poison but because his own true-love has betrayed him, life has disappointed him and he returns to his mother as when a child, etc. All of this becomes involved in the repetition as the poem progresses, yet not explicitly; here again suggestiveness plays an important part. The poem does not state all that it has to say.

One may notice, in addition, the effect of the change from strict repetition in the last stanza of the poem. Instead of

> For I'm weary wi hunting, and fain wald lie down

there appears

For I'm sick at the heart, and I fain wald lie down.

The reader has come to expect the strict repetition, and when this variation comes, it comes with an effect of emphasis and climax. This is an example of expressive *variation* (*Glossary*) from a form that has been established in the poem. A reader should, in studying a poem, watch for variations of metrical and other patterns and should try to determine whether such variations are truly expressive or are arbitrary and accidental.

Edward

ANONYMOUS

'Why dois your brand sae drap[1] wi bluid,
Edward, Edward,
Why dois your brand sae drap wi bluid,
And why sae sad gang[2] yee O?"
'O I hae killed my hauke sae guid, 5
Mither, mither,
O I hae killed my hauke sae guid,
And I had nae mair bot hee O.'

'Your haukis bluid was nevir sae reid,
Edward, Edward, 10
Your haukis bluid was nevir sae reid,
My deir son I tell thee O.'
'O I hae killed my reid-roan steid,
Mither, mither,
O I hae killed my reid-roan steid, 15
That erst was sae fair and frie O.'

'Your steid was auld, and ye hae got mair,
Edward, Edward,
Your steid was auld, and ye hae got mair,
Sum other dule[3] ye drie[4] O.' 20
'O I hae killed my fadir deir,
Mither, mither,
O I hae killed my fadir deir,
Alas, and wae is mee O!'

[1] drop [2] go [3] grief [4] suffer

'And whatten penance wul ye drie for that, 25
Edward, Edward,
And whatten penance will ye drie for that?
My deir son, now tell me O.'
'Ile set my feit in yonder boat,
Mither, mither, 30
Ile set my feit in yonder boat,
And Ile fare ovir the sea O.'

'And what wul ye doe wi your towirs and your ha,[1]
Edward, Edward?
And what wul ye doe wi your towirs and your ha, 35
That were sae fair to see O?'
'Ile let thame stand tul they doun fa,[2]
Mither, mither,
Ile let thame stand tul they doun fa,
For here nevir mair maun[3] I bee O.' 40

'And what wul ye leive to your bairns[4] and your wife,
Edward, Edward?
And what wul ye leive to your bairns and your wife,
Whan ye gang ovir the sea O?'
'The warldis room, late them beg thrae[5] life, 45
Mither, mither,
The warldis room, late them beg thrae life,
For thame nevir mair wul I see O.'

'And what wul ye leive to your ain mither deir,
Edward, Edward? 50
And what wul ye leive to your ain mither deir?
My deir son, now tell me O.'
'The curse of hell frae me sall ye beir,
Mither, mither,
The curse of hell frae me sall ye beir, 55
Sic counseils ye gave to me O.'

EXERCISE:

1. The action of this poem is given, for the most part, by indirect rather than direct means. How do we know that Edward is a

[1] hall
[2] fall
[3] must
[4] children
[5] through

knight? What is the relation of the mother and father? What is the character of the mother?

2. How does this indirect method contribute to the suspense? How is it related to other effects of the poem?

3. What is Edward's attitude toward his wife and children? Is he cruel toward them or is what he says in line 45 susceptible of another interpretation?

4. Do the references to the hawk and to the steed "lead up" to the admission of the murder of the father? Why does not Edward come out immediately with the true explanation for the blood upon his sword? Is this good psychology which makes him put off stating the horrible fact as long as he can?

5. Is there any use of expressive variation (see p. 51) in this ballad?

Proud Maisie

SIR WALTER SCOTT [1771–1832]

Proud Maisie is in the wood,
  Walking so early;
Sweet Robin sits on the bush,
  Singing so rarely.

"Tell me, thou bonny bird, 5
  When shall I marry me?"
"When six braw[1] gentlemen,
  Kirkward shall carry ye."

Who makes the bridal bed,
  Birdie, say truly?"— 10
"The gray-headed sexton
  That delves the grave duly.

"The glow-worm o'er grave and stone
  Shall light thee steady;
The owl from the steeple sing, 15
  'Welcome, proud lady.'"

[1] brave

EXERCISE:

1. This poem evidently derives from the folk ballad. What are some of the specific ways in which it resembles the folk ballad?

2. The story is evidently a fantastic one: birds cannot speak, for example. But does the fairy-tale quality of the first stanza prevent the poem's becoming a thoroughly serious one?

3. Note that "carry" in line 8 may be used in the archaic sense of "escort," and does not necessarily mean "lift up and transport." Which interpretation does Maisie make (see line 9)?

4. Note that the funeral is consistently compared to a marriage, the six pall bearers becoming groomsmen, etc. What effect is gained by this device?

5. How heavily are we to weight the word "proud"? Is the rebuke given to Maisie's pride, harsh and bitter? What is the robin's attitude toward Maisie and her hopes? Jeering? Mocking? Playful? Or what? In trying to answer this question read the last stanza very carefully.

A Slumber Did My Spirit Seal

WILLIAM WORDSWORTH [1770–1850]

A slumber did my spirit seal;
  I had no human fears—
She seemed a thing that could not feel
  The touch of earthly years.

No motion has she now, no force; 5
  She neither hears nor sees;
Rolled round in earth's diurnal course,
  With rocks, and stones, and trees.

EXERCISE:

1. What is the story implied by this little poem?

2. Do lines 2–4 give the explanation for line 1: that is, is the speaker saying that his loved one seemed so thoroughly immortal that he simply was asleep to the possibility that she could ever die? If so, what has waked him up out of his sleep?

3. The loved one is now asleep and completely inert. How is her present inertness emphasized in the second stanza?

4. Actually, of course, the speaker, as a living man, is being whirled around by the motion of the earth just as rapidly as his dead sweetheart is being whirled around by that same earth. Yet does this last figure succeed in emphasizing her deadness? Try to indicate why.

Patterns

AMY LOWELL [1874–1925]

I walk down the garden paths,
And all the daffodils
Are blowing, and the bright blue squills.
I walk down the patterned garden paths
In my stiff, brocaded gown. 5
With my powdered hair and jewelled fan,
I too am a rare
Pattern. As I wander down
The garden paths.

My dress is richly figured, 10
And the train
Makes a pink and silver stain
On the gravel, and the thrift
Of the borders.
Just a plate of current fashion, 15
Tripping by in high-heeled, ribboned shoes.
Not a softness anywhere about me,
Only whale-bone and brocade.
And I sink on a seat in the shade
Of a lime tree. For my passion 20
Wars against the stiff brocade.
The daffodils and squills
Flutter in the breeze
As they please.
And I weep; 25
For the lime tree is in blossom
And one small flower has dropped upon my bosom.

And the plashing of waterdrops
In the marble fountain

Comes down the garden paths. 30
The dripping never stops.
Underneath my stiffened gown
Is the softness of a woman bathing in a marble basin,
A basin in the midst of hedges grown
So thick, she cannot see her lover hiding, 35
But she guesses he is near,
And the sliding of the water
Seems the stroking of a dear
Hand upon her.
What is Summer in a fine brocaded gown! 40
I should like to see it lying in a heap upon the ground,
All the pink and silver crumpled up on the ground.

I would be the pink and silver as I ran along the paths,
And he would stumble after
Bewildered by my laughter. 45
I should see the sun flashing from his sword hilt and the
  buckles on his shoes.
I would choose
To lead him in a maze along the patterned paths,
A bright and laughing maze for my heavy-booted lover,
Till he caught me in the shade, 50
And the buttons of his waistcoat bruised my body as he
  clasped me,
Aching, melting, unafraid,
With the shadows of the leaves and the sundrops,
And the plopping of the waterdrops,
All about us in the open afternoon— 55
I am very like to swoon
With the weight of this brocade,
For the sun sifts through the shade.

Underneath the fallen blossom
In my bosom, 60
Is a letter I have hid.
It was brought to me this morning by a rider from the Duke.
"Madam, we regret to inform you that Lord Hartwell
Died in action Thursday se'n-night."
As I read it in the white, morning sunlight, 65

The letters squirmed like snakes.
"Any answer, Madam," said my footman.
"No," I told him.
"See that the messenger takes some refreshment.
No, no answer." 70
And I walked into the garden,
Up and down the patterned paths,
In my stiff, correct brocade.
The blue and yellow flowers stood up proudly in the sun
Each one. 75
I stood upright too,
Held rigid to the pattern
By the stiffness of my gown.
Up and down I walked,
Up and down. 80

In a month he would have been my husband.
In a month, here, underneath this lime,
We would have broke the pattern;
He for me, and I for him,
He as Colonel, I as Lady, 85
On this shady seat.
He had a whim
That sunlight carried blessing.
And I answered, "It shall be as you have said."
Now he is dead. 90

In Summer and in Winter I shall walk
Up and down
The patterned garden paths
In my stiff, brocaded gown.
The squills and daffodils 95
Will give place to pillared roses, and to asters, and to snow.
I shall go
Up and down,
In my gown.
Gorgeously arrayed, 100
Boned and stayed.
And the softness of my body will be guarded from embrace
By each button, hook, and lace.

For the man who should loose me is dead,
Fighting with the Duke in Flanders, 105
In a pattern called a war.
Christ! What are patterns for?

The narrative, as such, does not compose the greater part of "Patterns," for it only takes a definite form in the second and third sections from the end of the poem. The content of the narrative is very simple. The heroine of the poem, of whose mind the poem is given as an expression, has been engaged to be married to a certain Lord Hartwell. On the morning of the action of the poem, she receives a letter from the Duke (whom, because of the eighteenth-century background and the line, "Fighting with the Duke in Flanders," we may take to be the Duke of Marlborough) to the effect that her lover has been killed in battle. On learning the news, she orders that the messenger be given some refreshment, and goes out to walk in the garden. There she thinks of her courtship and her present situation.

At least in one respect, then, this poem differs from those in the previous section. Like many other poems in this section, "Patterns" in only small part deals with direct narrative. Just enough narrative is given to make clear the present situation, to explain to the reader the basis in fact for the woman's state of mind: that is, to provide a dramatic context for the mood of the poem. The reader is concerned with the reaction of the woman after the narrative proper is over. In fact, the poem pretends to be a soliloquy, a monologue that the woman is carrying on alone in the garden. The fact that the course of the poem follows the workings of the mind of the grief-stricken woman accounts for the apparently illogical construction as compared with the rather straight chronological narrative of a poem like "Johnie Armstrong." In the present poem, for instance, we do not discover the cause of the situation, the death of Lord Hartwell, until the poem is two thirds over.

We have said that the method used to present the material of the poem is apparently illogical because it departs from the strict chronological order of events. But the poet is not merely interested in telling the story in as clear a way as possible. Giving the outline of the story in a quickly comprehensible form could, in any case, be done better in a prose summary, even in the summary in the first paragraph of this analysis. The reader must be in possession of the facts of the narrative before he can properly appreciate the poem, but he will quickly realize that a presentation of the facts of the narrative is not the aim of the poem; for, if it were, then the prose summary would be logically superior to the poem. The poem has another object, and understanding that object will probably make clear the method the poet has used.

We have seen from previous analyses that the poet has attempted not merely to give the facts of a story, but to give facts so selected and arranged and so expressed that the reader will adopt a certain attitude toward, and experience a certain emotion concerning, the story. Now, in "Patterns" the poet has decided that this kind of interest is best served by emphasizing the character and condition of the woman rather than the chain of events leading up to the scene in the garden on the morning when she receives news of the death of her lover. To accomplish this the poet has plunged us into the mind of the woman at the moment when she sees her past life and her future life in contrast, at the moment when she discovers that her life has definitely changed its course and will never be the same. We are not given this information all at once, but bit by bit, the poem following, as it were, the gradual growth of the conviction in the woman's mind on up to the climax when she cries out in protest. In other words, the poet has taken for the model of the organization of the poem, not the order in which a series of events occurred, historically speaking (the courtship, the death of Hartwell, etc.), but the sequence of thoughts and feelings the woman experiences as a result of those events.

But this cannot mean that the poet has organized the poem loosely and at random. First, the reader must feel that the progression from one thing to another is justified psychologically. He must feel that the woman in this condition might notice the beauty of the garden and her costume, and be aware of the fact that these things now have no meaning for her since her lover is dead; that her mind trying to escape from its grief might indulge in the fantasy of her lover's return to discover her bathing in the garden; that the stiffness of her dress and her suffocation might recall her to the miserable reality and to the letter in her bosom; that she might have a glimpse of what her future will be; and that as she cries out in protest, she might see herself and others as victims of the "patterns."

There is another aspect, however, of the organization of the poem, the organization of the parts in relation to a general idea, or what we have called a *theme*. "Patterns" is the title of the poem and indicates the theme, which we may state in its simplest and loosest terms as a contrast between the natural and the artificial. The theme appears almost casually in the first section with the observation that the garden has been patterned and that the woman is a pattern. In the second this is further developed:

> Not a softness anywhere about me,
> Only whale-bone and brocade.

Then the theme, having been hinted at, is given a more dramatic turn:

> For my passion
> Wars against the stiff brocade.

And again in the third section:

> What is summer in a fine brocaded gown!

In the fourth section the woman's self-control on receiving the letter means that she is conforming to another kind of pattern; then she goes out to walk along "the patterned paths" in her "stiff, correct brocade," being held rigid to the pattern. And in the last stanza the poem comes to its climax of theme as it comes to its psychological climax in the cry of protest. Not only are the gown, the paths, the whale-bone and stays, patterns, but a thing like war is a pattern too, something man has systematized to cut across the natural and happier development of life. Then, in the last cry of protest, the reader realizes that the "patterns" are all the systems and conventions that repress human development.

Two general principles will appear from the preceding discussion of the theme of "Patterns." First, one can see how the poem is held together, given *unity* (*Glossary*) by the fact that the various parts are connected, not only by reason of their reference to the workings of the mind of the grief-stricken woman, but by their reference to the theme of the poem. There is a *thematic development* (*Glossary*) of the poem and a psychological development, both working together. Second, one comes to realize, as the poem goes on, that the different things, such as the flower beds, the paths, the whale-bone and stays, the brocade, buttons and lace that appear again and again in the poem come to stand in the woman's mind for the idea of the patterns, the systems, and the restrictions against which she is protesting. In other words, they come to have the meaning of *symbols* (*Glossary*) in so far as they represent, not only themselves as particular objects, but an idea. Third, one may realize that the whole poem is a dramatization, the presentation of an idea, not abstractly, but concretely in a particular situation; the woman is like all people who are victims of the systems man has built up that sometimes react painfully on individual men just as the "pattern called a war" has robbed the woman of her lover, who was for her the one hope of full and happy development; and we therefore may feel that the poem has put in its special case an idea or theme that has at least a certain degree of general meaning. (At this point it may be added, however, that the bare statement in the form of a prose summary of the idea would not be equivalent to the poem, for the reader would not usually give much response to a general statement; the feeling is evoked only when one sympathizes with the pathos of the particular situation.)

Hell Gate

A. E. HOUSMAN [1859–1936]

Onward led the road again
Through the sad uncolored plain
Under twilight brooding dim,
And along the utmost rim
Wall and rampart risen to sight 5
Cast a shadow not of night,
And beyond them seemed to glow
Bonfires lighted long ago.
And my dark conductor broke
Silence at my side and spoke, 10

Saying, "You conjecture well:
Yonder is the gate of hell."

Ill as yet the eye could see
The eternal masonry,
But beneath it on the dark 15
To and fro there stirred a spark.
And again the somber guide
Knew my question and replied:
"At hell gate the damned in turn
Pace for sentinel and burn." 20

Dully at the leaden sky
Staring, and with idle eye
Measuring the listless plain,
I began to think again.
Many things I thought of then, 25
Battle, and the loves of men,
Cities entered, oceans crossed,
Knowledge gained and virtue lost,
Cureless folly done and said,
And the lovely way that led 30
To the slimepit and the mire
And the everlasting fire.
And against a smolder dun
And a dawn without a sun
Did the nearing bastion loom, 35
And across the gate of gloom
Still one saw the sentry go,
Trim and burning, to and fro,
One for women to admire
In his finery of fire. 40
Something, as I watched him pace,
Minded me of time and place,
Soldiers of another corps
And a sentry known before.

Ever darker hell on high 45
Reared its strength upon the sky,

And our footfall on the track
Fetched the daunting echo back.
But the soldier pacing still
The insuperable sill, 50
Nursing his tormented pride,
Turned his head to neither side,
Sunk into himself apart
And the hell-fire of his heart.
But against our entering in 55
From the drawbridge Death and Sin
Rose to render key and sword
To their father and their lord.
And the portress foul to see
Lifted up her eyes on me 60
Smiling, and I made reply:
"Met again, my lass," said I.
Then the sentry turned his head,
Looked, and knew me, and was Ned.

Once he looked, and halted straight, 65
Set his back against the gate,
Caught his musket to his chin,
While the hive of hell within
Sent abroad a seething hum
As of towns whose king is come 70
Leading conquest home from far
And the captives of his war,
And the car of triumph waits,
And they open wide the gates.
But across the entry barred 75
Straddled the revolted guard,
Weaponed and accoutred well
From the arsenals of hell;
And beside him, sick and white,
Sin to left and Death to right 80
Turned a countenance of fear
On the flaming mutineer.
Over us the darkness bowed,
And the anger in the cloud

Clenched the lightning for the stroke; 85
But the traitor musket spoke.

And the hollowness of hell
Sounded as its master fell,
And the mourning echo rolled
Ruin through his kingdom old. 90
Tyranny and terror flown
Left a pair of friends alone,
And beneath the nether sky
All that stirred was he and I.

Silent, nothing found to say, 95
We began the backward way;
And the ebbing luster died
From the soldier at my side,
As in all his spruce attire
Failed the everlasting fire. 100
Midmost of the homeward track
Once we listened, and looked back;
But the city, dusk, and mute,
Slept, and there was no pursuit.

EXERCISE:

1. What is the story? Admitting that the story is a fantastic one, is the poem merely playful and absurd, or does it have a more serious level of meaning?

2. The story depends upon the fact that the damned souls have to take turns walking sentry beat in front of the gate of hell. This would seem to be poor policy on the devil's part. Can you justify the poet in using this detail?

3. By what "code" does the speaker live? How do you know? By what code does Ned live?

4. Note carefully the imagery in lines 36–40. What does it tell us about Ned's character? Is the imagery justified?

5. Does this poem have a message? Is the poem offensively "moralizing," making its point too patly? If not, try to indicate as specifically as you can what keeps the poem from appearing solemnly moralistic.

Lucy Gray; or, Solitude

WILLIAM WORDSWORTH [1770–1850]

Oft I had heard of Lucy Gray:
And, when I crossed the wild,
I chanced to see at break of day
The solitary child.

No mate, no comrade Lucy knew; 5
She dwelt on a wide moor,
—The sweetest thing that ever grew
Beside a human door!

You yet may spy the fawn at play,
The hare upon the green; 10
But the sweet face of Lucy Gray
Will never more be seen.

"To-night will be a stormy night—
You to the town must go;
And take a lantern, Child, to light 15
Your mother through the snow."

"That, Father! will I gladly do:
'Tis scarcely afternoon—
The minster-clock has just struck two,
And yonder is the moon!" 20

At this the father raised his hook,
And snapped a faggot-band;
He plied his work;—and Lucy took
The lantern in her hand.

Not blither is the mountain roe: 25
With many a wanton stroke
Her feet disperse the powdery snow,
That rises up like smoke.

The storm came on before its time:
She wandered up and down; 30

And many a hill did Lucy climb:
But never reached the town.

The wretched parents all that night
Went shouting far and wide;
But there was neither sound nor sight 35
To serve them for a guide.

At daybreak on a hill they stood
That overlooked the moor;
And thence they saw the bridge of wood,
A furlong from their door. 40

They wept—and, turning homeward, cried,
"In heaven we all shall meet";
—When in the snow the mother spied
The print of Lucy's feet.

Then downwards from the steep hill's edge 45
They tracked the footmarks small;
And through the broken hawthorn hedge,
And by the long stone wall;

And then an open field they crossed:
The marks were still the same; 50
They tracked them on, nor ever lost;
And to the bridge they came.

They followed from the snowy bank
Those footmarks, one by one,
Into the middle of the plank; 55
And further there were none!

—Yet some maintain that to this day
She is a living child;
That you may see sweet Lucy Gray
Upon the lonesome wild. 60

O'er rough and smooth she trips along,
And never looks behind;
And sings a solitary song
That whistles in the wind.

EXERCISE:

1. Omit the first three stanzas and the last two, and see how flat the little story becomes.
2. What does this "frame" do then for the story?
3. What is the effect of saying that Lucy was the "sweetest thing that ever grew/Beside a human door"? Of saying that you yet may see the fawn and the hare, but not Lucy?
4. Does the speaker believe in ghosts? Does he ask that we believe in them?
5. Why "And never looks behind"? What is a "solitary song"?
6. Does the last line help to provide some sort of basis for the illusion that Lucy still walks the moors?

Ulysses

ALFRED, LORD TENNYSON [1809–1892]

It little profits that an idle king,
By this still hearth, among these barren crags,
Matched with an agèd wife, I mete and dole
Unequal laws unto a savage race,
That hoard, and sleep, and feed, and know not me. 5
I cannot rest from travel; I will drink
Life to the lees. All times I have enjoyed
Greatly, have suffered greatly, both with those
That loved me, and alone; on shore, and when
Through scudding drifts the rainy Hyades 10
Vext the dim sea. I am become a name;
For always roaming with a hungry heart
Much have I seen and known,—cities of men
And manners, climates, councils, governments,
Myself not least, but honored of them all; 15
And drunk delight of battle with my peers,
Far on the ringing plains of windy Troy.
I am a part of all that I have met;
Yet all experience is an arch wherethro'
Gleams that untraveled world, whose margin fades 20
For ever and for ever when I move.
How dull it is to pause, to make an end,

To rust unburnished, not to shine in use!
As though to breathe were life! Life piled on life
Were all too little, and of one to me 25
Little remains; but every hour is saved
From that eternal silence, something more,
A bringer of new things; and vile it were
For some three suns to store and hoard myself,
And this gray spirit yearning in desire 30
To follow knowledge like a sinking star,
Beyond the utmost bound of human thought.

This is my son, mine own Telemachus,
To whom I leave the scepter and the isle—
Well-loved of me, discerning to fulfil 35
This labor, by slow prudence to make mild
A rugged people, and through soft degrees
Subdue them to the useful and the good.
Most blameless is he, centered in the sphere
Of common duties, decent not to fail 40
In offices of tenderness, and pay
Meet adoration to my household gods,
When I am gone. He works his work, I mine.

There lies the port; the vessel puffs her sail:
There gloom the dark, broad seas. My mariners, 45
Souls that have toiled, and wrought, and thought with me—
That ever with a frolic welcome took
The thunder and the sunshine, and opposed
Free hearts, free foreheads—you and I are old;
Old age hath yet his honor and his toil. 50
Death closes all; but something ere the end,
Some work of noble note, may yet be done,
Not unbecoming men that strove with Gods.
The lights begin to twinkle from the rocks;
The long day wanes; the slow moon climbs; the deep 55
Moans round with many voices. Come, my friends,
'T is not too late to seek a newer world.
Push off, and sitting well in order smite
The sounding furrows; for my purpose holds
To sail beyond the sunset, and the baths 60
Of all the western stars, until I die.

It may be that the gulfs will wash us down;
It may be we shall touch the Happy Isles,
And see the great Achilles, whom we knew.
Though much is taken, much abides; and though 65
We are not now that strength which in old days
Moved earth and heaven, that which we are, we are;
One equal temper of heroic hearts,
Made weak by time and fate, but strong in will
To strive, to seek, to find, and not to yield. 70

EXERCISE:

1. Ulysses, the hero of Homer's *Odyssey,* has returned home from the siege of Troy after ten years of wandering and adventure. (Consult the library for a full account.) He is here picturing the prospect of old age. The poet uses this situation for dramatizing what general attitude and feeling?

2. Compare the mood of this poem with that established in "Michael."

3. What distinguishes Ulysses' yearning for travel from mere wanderlust—from mere distaste for responsibility and hunger for new sensations? For one thing, the poet has tried to connect Ulysses' yearning for travel with a yearning for knowledge. Has he been successful?

4. Does the Ulysses of this poem patronize his wife ("an aged wife")? Does he patronize his son, Telemachus? If you feel that he does not, try to indicate, by reference to the text, why you feel he does not.

Epitaph on an Army of Mercenaries

A. E. HOUSMAN [1859–1936]

These, in the day when heaven was falling,
  The hour when earth's foundations fled,
Followed their mercenary calling
  And took their wages and are dead.

Their shoulders held the sky suspended; 5
  They stood, and earth's foundations stay;

What God abandoned, these defended,
And saved the sum of things for pay.

Exercise:

1. These "mercenaries" are not named, nor is the battle in which they fell. Has the poet given enough information about them to allow you to identify them? What sort of people are they?

2. Their motives are not ostensibly patriotic or religious or idealistic. If they are "mercenaries," they fight for pay. But can a man be hired to die? What are their real motives for holding firm?

3. Even if it should turn out that the poet had in mind an actual group of soldiers in a particular war (the British professional soldiers in World War I), could it be argued that this poem has a more general reference—that it makes a penetrating comment upon courage and honor as they are actually met with in human beings? Is the poet contrasting a religious and a naturalistic view of the world—and dramatizing the values to be found in the latter?

AFTERWORD

In the section just completed we have been considering poems in which the narrative element is relatively prominent. In opening this section, we decided to use our interest in narrative as a device for leading into the study of poetry, because narrative presents the most obvious form which our interest in the stuff of literature takes. As we pointed out there, however, and as the analyses of various poems have indicated, narrative is only one element among several which the poet may use to gain his effect. The poet is not content with the narrative as such, even in the poems of the first group, which have a direct and prominent use of narrative. He is primarily interested in provoking a certain reaction toward the narrative. He wants to present the material of the narrative so that the reader will have a certain feeling toward it and will grasp a certain interpretation of it.

But this is also true of the writers of novels or short stories in prose, for such writers, like the poet, are more than reporters giving us a bare statement of facts and events. Indeed, it is not easy, except in regard to the use of verse, to make an absolute distinction between poetry and prose fiction, but it is possible on the basis of the poems we have already analyzed to state a difference in the following terms. Poetry *tends* toward *concentration* (*Glossary*). A poem treating, let us say, the story of Johnie Armstrong is a great deal shorter than a piece of prose fiction on the same subject would be. In general, it may be said that the writer of prose fiction tries to convince his reader by the accumulation of detail, and that the poet tries to convince his reader by the sharpness of selected detail. The distinction, as we have suggested, is not absolute, but the analyses which have already been studied will provide instances of the use which poetry makes of details. The poet tries to make a direct appeal to the imagination. The suggestiveness, which we have already commented on in several analyses, is an example of this. This method may be described as a short cut to the effect desired, as compared with the more roundabout method which prose fiction is forced to use. In the poems that follow we shall discover other methods whereby the poet can condense his material far more than the writer of prose fiction is able to do.

The effect of this condensation in poetry is a sense of greater *intensity* (*Glossary*) than is usually found in prose fiction. If poetry employs fewer details than prose fiction, then it stands to reason that to gain a comparable result the details must (1) be more effective in themselves than those in prose fiction—that is, they must be very carefully selected—and/or (2) they must be so arranged that they will have the greatest effect on the reader. The arrangement or *form* (*Glossary*) of a poem, then, is a most important matter and is directly connected with the concentration and intensity of poetry. In the analyses previously presented we have touched on certain aspects of the form of various poems, for the form of a poem must obviously differ from case to case according to the effect given. It is enough at this point, however, if we see that the form of poetry in general as contrasted with the form of prose fiction is more closely organized. For instance, in poetry even the rhythms are usually put into more definite form—into a pattern which we call meter. In Section III we shall discuss this matter at length, but for the present it is only necessary to be aware of the contribution meter makes to the concentration and intensity of poetry.

II

DESCRIPTIVE POEMS

FOREWORD

Most of the poems in this section would be called descriptive. For example, the poems "The Main-Deep," "Pear Tree," and "Heat," which will be presented early in this section, apparently give, as accurately as the poet could manage, a direct impression received through the poet's senses. In the poems we have read in Section I the element of narrative is relatively prominent, but, as we have seen, these poems do more than merely tell a story. In the same way, the poems in the present section do more than merely give a picture or a description. But what is the meaning of such a poem as "The Main-Deep," which appears merely to give an impression of the sea?

The Main-Deep

JAMES STEPHENS [1882–]

The long, rolling,
Steady-pouring,
Deep-trenchèd
Green billow:

The wide-topped, 5
Unbroken,
Green-glacid,
Slow-sliding,

Cold-flushing,
On—on—on— 10

Chill-rushing,
Hush-hushing,

Hush—hushing . . .

When we read this poem, although our imagination may call up a picture of the sea, we are having an experience different from the experience of looking at the real sea. In other words the poem does not attempt to provide us with a substitute for a trip to the seashore. If providing such a substitute were the purpose of a poem, then the poem would have very slight justification for being, for it can provide only a very inferior substitute for the real object in nature. The interest and pleasure one takes in the poem is of a different kind from the interest and pleasure one would take in the real object in nature. This can easily be proved if a reader studies his reaction to a poetic treatment of an object that in real nature would be unpleasant to look at. A pair of bloody hands would, in reality, be a disgusting rather than a pleasant sight. Let us take a passage from Shakespeare's *Macbeth,* however, that treats such a sight. Macbeth has just killed the king, Duncan, and is shocked at the sight of the blood on his hands:

What hands are here! Ha! they pluck out mine eyes.
Will all great Neptune's ocean wash this blood
Clean from my hand? No, this my hand will rather
The multitudinous seas incarnadine,
Making the green one red.

The passage does not disgust us. Rather, it stirs our imagination so that we really grasp Macbeth's own feeling that nothing in the world can remove the guilt from him. The blood has become an expression of a psychological fact.

But one might argue that a poem like "The Main-Deep" is different, because the passage from *Macbeth* comes in a play which provides us with a situation giving a basis for the interpretation of the expressive quality of the passage. This is true to a certain extent. We know nothing about the situation of "The Main-Deep" except that a human being, the poet, is looking at the sea. We know nothing about the circumstances leading up to the event and nothing about the spectator except what we can read by implication from the poem. Indeed the presence of a human being is not even mentioned in the poem, but we feel, nevertheless, that the poem is an expression of a human being; it involves an ordering and therefore an *interpretation* (*Glossary*).

How is this true?

First, we know that the poet has assumed a particular view of the sea to the exclusion of other possible views. For instance, the sea in "The Main-Deep" is not a stormy one. The poet, then, has selected the particular view that will suit his purpose.

Second, his selectivity has been exercised further in regard to the details from the particular view. We know that it is obviously impossible for the poet to put into a poem the enormous body of real detail in his view of the sea. He must select details to build up the poem. But the selection is not performed at random. It must be directed by some principle if the finished poem is to appear coherent in its organization and unified in its effect. Both types of selection mentioned show that the poem is expressive of the action of a human mind contemplating the sea. The sea that comes over to our imagination from the poem is not the sea that we might chance upon in a walk along the coast. Such a chance view might provoke any of a number of different feelings and reactions in us, or perhaps none at all; but the sea in the poem has been arranged by the poet so as to cause the reaction he wished to communicate. That reaction communicated by the poet is his interpretation of the material—the material being in this case a special and particular view of the sea.

Let us try to analyze the way in which the present poem, which seems at first glance so purely descriptive and *objective* (*Glossary*), embodies, after all, an interpretation.

The poet has chosen, as it were, one billow on which the attention can be directed and which can give a kind of focus for the poem. The concentration on the single billow has another advantage, for while the sea as a whole, though agitated, does not progress, the single billow does seem to move forward. The eyes of the reader seem to be directed to a single billow advancing toward him, as though he were on a ship at sea. Only those qualities of the billow are singled out for comment that will not distract him from a concentrated gaze at the billow itself; the poet does not comment on the general scene. There is no direct reference, even, to the fact that the billow approaches the spectator but we gather this from the nature of the billow's movement. In the third stanza with the line

On—on—on—

we get an impression of increased speed, an impression not only from the words but from the additional accent in the line (no other line has more than two accents) that implies the hurry and piling up as the billow approaches. Further, this stanza gives a reference to the temperature of the billow, "cold-flushing," and "chill-rushing," as though on its nearer approach the spectator could almost tell the coldness of the water, something one could not think of in connection with a distant wave. Then with the last rush the billow passes and there is only the thin line of receding foam. This effect is supported by the repetition of the line

Hush—hushing . . .

We have here a process working itself out to a natural fulfilment. Out of the beautiful and splendid tumult of the billow comes the moment of poise when the process is completed. The idea is not stated—the poem seems quite objectively descriptive—but the poem has been so arranged that the effect is communicated to the reader. Even less does the poet present an application of his idea, as is the case in some poems; he does not moralize. He does not say, for instance, that the billow is like man's life, or that the billow shows us the process of struggle and fulfilment, or that nature always holds out a promise of peace, or anything of that sort. It might be possible to write a poem about the sea that would say these things and that would not necessarily be better or worse than "The Main-Deep," but it would be a different kind of poem. James Stephens, however, leaves the reader, apparently, as close to the simple experience of looking at the sea as possible; but he has given an interpretation because, by his management of the materials, he has made the sea give the reader one feeling, the feeling of peace and fulfilment, and not any of the almost innumerable other feelings which the sea might be used by a poet to suggest. The reader may or may not take the step himself of attributing a specific application to the poem. The poem may be richer and more exciting if the reader does not fix on one specific application of the feeling and idea; for if he does leave it so, the poem has potential in it an attitude one might take toward many different experiences of life.

The following poems obviously bear a close resemblance to "The Main-Deep" in their method of objective presentation.

Pear Tree

H. D. [1886–]

Silver dust
lifted from the earth,
higher than my arms reach,
you have mounted.
O silver, 5
higher than my arms reach
you front us with great mass;
no flower ever opened
so staunch a white leaf,
no flower ever parted silver 10
from such rare silver;

O white pear,
your flower-tufts,
thick on the branch,
bring summer and ripe fruits 15
in their purple hearts.

Heat

H. D. [1886–]

O wind, rend open the heat,
cut apart the heat,
rend it to tatters.

Fruit cannot drop
through this thick air— 5

fruit cannot fall into heat
that presses up and blunts
the points of pears
and rounds the grapes.

Cut through the heat— 10
plow through it,
turning it on either side
of your path.

In a Station of the Metro

EZRA POUND [1885–]

The apparition of these faces in the crowd;
Petals on a wet, black bough.

These poems by H. D. (Hilda Doolittle) and Ezra Pound obviously bear a close resemblance to "The Main-Deep" in their objective and descriptive quality. But, as we have said, no poem is ever purely objective, for the fact of the poem involves an observer who necessarily has some attitude toward the material, since, otherwise, he would not write the poem at all. And further, the selection of details of the material for a poem means in itself that the poet is controlling the effect on the reader; if the reader himself should see a pear tree in bloom the chances are that he would have a reaction somewhat different from that of H. D. That is, the poem, like all poems, embodies an interpretation.

Both H. D. and Ezra Pound belonged at one time to a group of poets who called themselves "Imagists" (*Glossary*), a group that also included Amy Lowell and John Gould Fletcher. One of the theories of this group was that poetry should concern itself with presenting to the reader a very sharp, clear picture, or image, and should not attempt to discuss ideas or give applications of the meanings of the images presented. The poems here are very good examples of "imagist poetry," but as we have seen, they involve interpretation on the part of the poet. Let us take Pound's poem describing the faces of people in a subway station.

The apparition of these faces in the crowd;
Petals on a wet, black bough.

Suppose he had written:

The apparition of these faces in the crowd;
Dead leaves caught in the gutter's stream.

Or:

The apparition of these faces in the crowd;
Dry leaves blown down the dry gutter.

The revised versions and the original version make very different interpretations of exactly the same sight, the faces in the subway. In the original version the reader catches a glimpse of something beautiful and fresh in the most unlikely place, and therefore grasps an interpretation that is potentially applicable to a great deal of experience. The poem is similar in this respect to the one which follows.

Dust of Snow

ROBERT FROST [1875–]

The way a crow
Shook down on me
The dust of snow
From a hemlock tree

Has given my heart 5
A change of mood
And saved some part
Of a day I had rued.

But Frost makes his poem much more explicit than does Pound in that he presents his poem in the form of a little incident and also defines the effect of the incident on the poet himself.

But to return to the comparison of the revised versions with the original version of Pound's poem. The comparison of the faces to leaves caught on the water in a gutter or blown down a dry gutter by a gust of wind has just as much basis in common sense or logic as does the comparison of the faces to white petals on a bough. The subway station does bear a certain resemblance to a gutter; the stream of people hurrying down bears likewise a resemblance to a stream of water, as the ordinary use of the word "stream" in such a connection in ordinary speech indicates; or we might say that the roar of the subway train and the gust of its passing reminds one of the wind; and the comparison of faces to leaves is probably as valid as the comparison to petals. As we inspect the different implications of the sets of comparisons, however, we see that the interpretations are different. The revised versions give an impression of the confusion of the crowd, the people seem lost and dead, going from one place to another driven by forces over which they have no control. Even if a reader does not analyze a poem at all he is affected by the poem; we usually say that one poem has a certain mood, and another poem has another mood. But this mood that an apparently objective poem gives is the thing the poet communicates; it is what he has used the material of the poem for, and it is the result of the way he has handled the material.

But poems that merely give us one or a few "images" or aim at a single mood are usually short, for such poems have no narrative, no incident, no presentation of character, and no progression of interpretation, that is, no thinking about the various different ways in which an idea or interpretation might be applied to life. Such poems, therefore, have a more limited range of interest. (It is quite significant that most of the poets in the Imagist group soon gave up the writing of poetry that would strictly fit their theory. The theory of Imagism limited them too much. For instance, "Patterns," by Amy Lowell, which has already been studied, is not an Imagist poem, although Amy Lowell was very prominent among that group of poets. And James Stephens, who was not a member of the Imagist group, has written very few poems similar to his "The Main-Deep.")

The sharp presentation of images and the use of description that appeals clearly to the imagination are important factors, however, in all good poetry, both in poetry that aims at creating mood, and in poetry that offers very complicated interpretations.

Spring

WILLIAM SHAKESPEARE [1564–1616]

When daisies pied and violets blue
  And lady-smocks all silver-white
And cuckoo-buds of yellow hue
  Do paint the meadows with delight,
The cuckoo then, on every tree, 5
Mocks married men; for thus sings he,
          "Cuckoo;
Cuckoo, cuckoo": O, word of fear,
Unpleasing to a married ear!

When shepherds pipe on oaten straws, 10
  And merry larks are ploughmen's clocks,
When turtles tread, and rooks, and daws,
  And maidens bleach their summer smocks,
The cuckoo then, on every tree,
Mocks married men; for thus sings he, 15
          "Cuckoo;
Cuckoo, cuckoo": O, word of fear,
Unpleasing to a married ear!

Winter

WILLIAM SHAKESPEARE [1564–1616]

When icicles hang by the wall,
  And Dick the shepherd blows his nail,
And Tom bears logs into the hall,
  And milk come frozen home in pail,
When blood is nipped and ways be foul, 5
Then nightly sings the staring owl,
          "Tu-whit, tu-who!"
A merry note,
While greasy Joan doth keel[1] the pot.

[1] skim

When all aloud the wind doth blow,
And coughing drowns the parson's saw, 10
And birds sit brooding in the snow,
And Marian's nose looks red and raw,
When roasted crabs [2] hiss in the bowl,
Then nightly sings the staring owl,
"Tu-whit, tu-who!"
A merry note, 15
While greasy Joan doth keel the pot.

(From *Love's Labour's Lost*)

EXERCISE:

"Spring" presents a pleasant world of birds and flowers—a world in which the very meadows are painted "with delight." "Winter," on the contrary, gives us a world of ice and snow, of frost-bitten fingers and greasy kitchen-maids. We can see that the descriptive details have been selected in terms of this basic contrast. We can elaborate the contrast further: in addition to the general opposition of spring and winter, there are more particular contrasts. Outdoor scenes dominate one poem; indoor, the other. Youthful merry-making balances humdrum piety and domesticity; the beautiful and romantic are set over against the drab and comfortable.

1. In view of this general pattern, why has the poet introduced the cuckoo's song into the one poem; the owl's, into the other? (The cuckoo's song is "unpleasing to a married ear" because the Elizabethans associated its call with the taunting of cuckolds.)

2. Does the poet really think that the hooting of the owl is merry? (*Cf.* "Proud Maisie," p. 53.)

3. Granting that the two little poems are quite "objective," and do not pretend to present any explicit interpretation of life, still do they not suggest an attitude toward the world of our experience? Could you suggest what this attitude is?

To Spring

WILLIAM BLAKE [1757–1827]

O thou with dewy locks, who lookest down
Through the clear windows of the morning, turn

[2] crab-apples

Thine angel eyes upon our western isle,
Which in full choir hails thy approach, O Spring!

The hills tell one another, and the listening 5
Valleys hear; all our longing eyes are turned
Up to thy bright pavilions: issue forth,
And let thy holy feet visit our clime.

Come o'er the eastern hills, and let our winds
Kiss thy perfumèd garments; let us taste 10
Thy morn and evening breath; scatter thy pearls
Upon our love-sick land that mourns for thee.

O deck her forth with thy fair fingers; pour
Thy soft kisses on her bosom; and put
Thy golden crown upon her languished head, 15
Whose modest tresses were bound up for thee.

EXERCISE:

1. A consideration of the diction of this poem will indicate that Spring is addressed, not only as a godlike being, but more specifically under the guise of an oriental prince coming in state to visit his betrothed. Is this implied comparison adopted merely for prettification and decoration? Or does it have any more significant justification?

2. Compare the language used in this poem with that of the *Song of Solomon* in the King James version of the Bible.

3. Does the poem have something of the quality of a prayer? Why is the head of the "western isle" languished? What is meant by "Whose modest tresses were bound up for thee"?

A Dirge

JOHN WEBSTER [1580?–1625?]

Call for the robin-redbreast and the wren,
Since o'er shady groves they hover,
And with leaves and flowers do cover
The friendless bodies of unburied men.
  Call unto his funeral dole 5
  The ant, the field-mouse, and the mole,

To rear him hillocks that shall keep him warm,
And, when gay tombs are robbed, sustain no harm;
But keep the wolf far thence, that's foe to men,
For with his nails he'll dig them up again. 10

EXERCISE:

1. The robin was fabled to do this office for the dead—compare the old ballad of "The Babes Lost in the Wood." But can you account for the wren? Is the wren an appropriate bird for this poem?

2. The poem seems to be saying that nature is kindly toward man, and buries the bodies of men who have been abandoned by humankind. But the wolf is a part of nature too. Why has the poet selected the birds and animals that he has? And why has he included in this poem the warning against the wolf?

3. Is "gay" a proper adjective to use with "tombs"? What is a *gay* tomb? Can you defend the use of the phrase here?

4. What is this poem "about"—if it is about anything?

All But Blind

WALTER DE LA MARE [1873–]

All but blind
  In his chambered hole
Gropes for worms
  The four-clawed Mole.

All but blind 5
  In the evening sky,
The hooded Bat
  Twirls softly by.

All but blind
  In the burning day 10
The Barn-Owl blunders
  On her way.

And blind as are
  These three to me,
So, blind to Someone 15
  I must be.

Exercise:

What function do the following words fulfil in the poem: *four-clawed, twirls,* and *blunders?* They give a sense of sharp perception to the description. But do they have a further function?

To a Waterfowl

WILLIAM CULLEN BRYANT [1794–1878]

Whither, midst falling dew,
While glow the heavens with the last steps of day,
Far, through their rosy depths, dost thou pursue
Thy solitary way?

Vainly the fowler's eye 5
Might mark thy distant flight to do thee wrong,
As, darkly seen against the crimson sky,
Thy figure floats along.

Seek'st thou the plashy brink
Of weedy lake, or marge of river wide, 10
Or where the rocking billows rise and sink
On the chafed ocean-side?

There is a Power whose care
Teaches thy way along that pathless coast—
The desert and illimitable air— 15
Lone wandering, but not lost.

All day thy wings have fanned,
At that far height, the cold thin atmosphere,
Yet stoop not, weary, to the welcome land,
Though the dark night is near. 20

And soon that toil shall end;
Soon shalt thou find a summer home, and rest,
And scream among thy fellows; reeds shall bend
Soon, o'er thy sheltered nest.

Thou'rt gone, the abyss of heaven 25
Hath swallowed up thy form; yet, on my heart

Deeply has sunk the lesson thou hast given,
And shall not soon depart.

He who, from zone to zone,
Guides through the boundless sky thy certain flight, 30
In the long way that I must tread alone,
Will lead my steps aright.

EXERCISE:

1. Ostensibly the speaker in this poem is addressing the bird. He asks the bird where it is going, and tells it that its journey soon shall end. But is the fourth stanza properly addressed to the bird? Or the seventh and eighth stanzas?

2. Some of the descriptive detail in this poem is very sharp and good. Indicate that which most vividly appeals to your imagination.

3. Is the "lesson" that the bird impresses upon the man's heart presented to the reader dramatically, so that the reader, participating imaginatively in the man's experience, also participates in the meaning of the experience? Or is the lesson "preached" to the reader? (Note that the matter at issue is not whether the message is or is not a true one, nor is it whether a poet may not properly make use of bold and direct statement; it is rather whether the method of presentation used here is effective and appropriate in this particular poem.)

Desert Places

ROBERT FROST [1875–]

Snow falling and night falling fast oh fast
In a field I looked into going past,
And the ground almost covered smooth in snow,
But a few weeds and stubble showing last.

The woods around it have it—it is theirs. 5
All animals are smothered in their lairs.
I am too absent-spirited to count;
The loneliness includes me unawares.

And lonely as it is that loneliness
Will be more lonely ere it will be less— 10

A blanker whiteness of benighted snow
With no expression, nothing to express.

They cannot scare me with their empty spaces
Between stars—on stars where no human race is.
I have it in me so much nearer home 15
To scare myself with my own desert places.

Let us assume that the poem had been written without the last stanza. It would still be a poem, and a good one, but a very different one from the poem we know. Such a poem would differ from "The Main-Deep," for instance, in several particulars. In the first place, the reader knows who the observer is. A man, at dusk, is passing an open field where snow is falling. The poem is quickly defined as *his* observation. In the second place, the man, in the second stanza, indicates a relation between himself and the empty field on which the snow falls, although he does not definitely state it. The field, with its desolation, stands as a kind of symbol for the man's own loneliness. And since this relation is established for us in the second stanza, what follows in the third, though it is stated only in application to the field, comes to us as having application to the loneliness of the man who is observing. Then follow the lines:

A blanker whiteness of benighted snow
With no expression, nothing to express.

As implied here, it does not matter what happens to the man now or what he does, for nothing can have any further meaning.

If the poem be taken as ending there, the process used by the poet to give his effect is very easily defined: the observer describes a natural scene which becomes for the reader a *symbol (Glossary)* of the observer's own despairing state of mind. The scene in nature has been presented so that it serves to communicate a human meaning.

But the poem in reality does not end with the third stanza, and the last stanza introduces a new element into the poem, that is, the poet's own analysis and statement, an element that is almost wholly lacking from previous poems in this section.

The last stanza is not introduced with a transition from the earlier part; the observer does not say that, after looking at the empty field he lifted his eyes to the sky and remembered what he had been told about the great emptiness of the stars and the interstellar spaces. But the reader understands that, and by the very abruptness of the shift gets a more dramatic effect, as though the man had jerked himself from his musing on the field to look at the sky and then make his comment. This comment, in summary, says this: a man who has known the desolation possible to human experience cannot be frightened or depressed by mere desolation in nature. And though this comment emphasizes the loneliness of the man, it gives us a different impression of him and gives a different total impression of the poem. It is not an impression of mere despair, for the man, we feel, has not been overcome by his own "desert places," but has mastered them.

He does not make this statement in so many words, but his attitude is implied. A reader analyzing the poem can almost base this implication of the man's attitude on the use of the single word *scare*. The man says,

They cannot scare me with their empty spaces.

He does not use *terrify,* or *horrify,* or *astound*—any word that would indicate the full significance of human loneliness and despair. Instead, he uses the word *scare,* which is an understatement, a common, colloquial word. One "scares" children by telling them ghost stories, by jumping at them from behind corners, etc. But by the use of the word in the poem the man is made to imply that he is not a child to be so easily affected. Knowledge of the infinite emptiness of space, which astronomers may give him, cannot affect him, for he knows, being a grown man, that the loneliness of spirit can be greater than the loneliness of external nature. But in the last line the word *scare* is repeated, and its *connotations* (*Glossary*) are brought into play in the new connection:

To scare myself with my own desert places.

That is, the man has had so much experience of life, is so truly mature, that even that greater loneliness of the spirit cannot make him behave like a child who is afraid of the dark or of ghost stories. Even in his loneliness of spirit he can still find strength enough in himself.

After Apple-Picking

ROBERT FROST [1875–]

My long two-pointed ladder's sticking through a tree
Toward heaven still,
And there's a barrel that I didn't fill
Beside it, and there may be two or three
Apples I didn't pick upon some bough. 5
But I am done with apple-picking now.
Essence of winter sleep is on the night,
The scent of apples: I am drowsing off.
I cannot rub the strangeness from my sight
I got from looking through a pane of glass 10
I skimmed this morning from the drinking trough
And held against the world of hoary grass.
It melted, and I let it fall and break.
But I was well
Upon my way to sleep before it fell, 15
And I could tell
What form my dreaming was about to take.
Magnified apples appear and disappear,
Stemend and blossomend,
And every fleck of russet showing clear. 20
My instep arch not only keeps the ache,
It keeps the pressure of a ladder-round.
I feel the ladder sway as the boughs bend.
And I keep hearing from the cellar bin
The rumbling sound 25
Of load on load of apples coming in.
For I have had too much
Of apple-picking: I am overtired
Of the great harvest I myself desired.
There were ten thousand thousand fruit to touch, 30
Cherish in hand, lift down, and not let fall.
For all
That struck the earth,
No matter if not bruised or spiked with stubble,
Went surely to the cider-apple heap 35
As of no worth.

One can see what will trouble
This sleep of mine, whatever sleep it is.
Were he not gone,
The woodchuck could say whether it's like his 40
Long sleep, as I describe its coming on,
Or just some human sleep.

EXERCISE:

1. What specific details are effective in giving a sense of the autumn scene? In giving the sense of a man's weariness after a day in the apple orchard?

2. Try to define the character of the speaker. How old a man is he? Does he have a sense of humor? Is he tough-minded? Is he sensitive and perceptive?

3. What is the function of the reference to the woodchuck? Why would the speaker like to compare notes with the woodchuck? Does this bit of whimsy make the poem more serious or less serious?

On a Drop of Dew

ANDREW MARVELL [1621–1678]

See how the orient dew,
  Shed from the bosom of the morn
  Into the blowing roses,
Yet careless of its mansion new;
For the clear region where 'twas born 5
  Round in itself encloses:
  And in its little globe's extent,
Frames as it can its native element.
  How it the purple flower does slight,
    Scarce touching where it lies, 10
  But gazing back upon the skies,
    Shines with a mournful light;
      Like its own tear,
Because so long divided from the sphere.
  Restless it rolls and unsecure, 15
    Trembling lest it grow impure:
  Till the warm sun pity its pain,
And to the skies exhale it back again.

So the soul, that drop, that ray
Of the clear fountain of eternal day, 20
Could it within the human flower be seen,
Rememb'ring still its former height,
Shuns the sweet leaves and blossoms green;
And, recollecting its own light,
Does, in its pure and circling thoughts, express 25
The greater heaven in a heaven less.
In how coy a figure wound,
Every way it turns away:
So the world excluding round,
Yet receiving in the day. 30
Dark beneath, but bright above:
Here disdaining, there in love.
How loose and easy hence to go:
How girt and ready to ascend.
Moving but on a point below, 35
It all about does upwards bend.
Such did the manna's sacred dew distill;
White, and entire, though congealed and chill.
Congealed on earth: but does, dissolving, run
Into the glories of the almighty sun. 40

EXERCISE:

1. Analyze carefully the points of resemblance which the poet establishes between the dewdrop and the soul. Has the poet overdone this matter of parallels? Does the poem become too mathematically exact? Or does the very disparity between the little globule of moisture and an abstract entity like the soul make the careful elaboration of the figure necessary?

2. Does the poem make its point too explicitly? Compare it in this regard with "To a Waterfowl" (p. 85). Does Marvell's poem avoid any note of oversolemn moralizing? If so, how?

3. What is the meaning of "orient" in line 1; of "recollecting" in line 24; of "manna" in line 37 (see *Exodus:* Chapter 36, and particularly verse 21)?

To Autumn

JOHN KEATS [1795–1821]

Season of mists and mellow fruitfulness,
  Close bosom-friend of the maturing sun:
Conspiring with him how to load and bless
  With fruit the vines that round the thatch-eaves run;
To bend with apples the mossed cottage-trees, 5
  And fill all fruit with ripeness to the core;
    To swell the gourd, and plump the hazel shells
With a sweet kernel; to set budding more,
  And still more, later flowers for the bees,
  Until they think warm days will never cease, 10
    For Summer has o'er-brimmed their clammy cells.

Who hath not seen thee oft amid thy store?
  Sometimes whoever seeks abroad may find
Thee sitting careless on a granary floor,
  Thy hair soft-lifted by the winnowing wind; 15
Or on a half-reaped furrow sound asleep,
  Drowsed with the fume of poppies, while thy hook
    Spares the next swath and all its twinèd flowers:
And sometimes like a gleaner thou dost keep,
  Steady thy laden head across a brook; 20
  Or by a cider-press, with patient look,
    Thou watchest the last oozings hours by hours.

Where are the songs of Spring? Ay, where are they?
  Think not of them, thou hast thy music too,—
While barrèd clouds bloom the soft-dying day, 25
  And touch the stubble-plains with rosy hue;
Then in a wailful choir the small gnats mourn
  Among the river sallows, borne aloft
    Or sinking as the light wind lives or dies;
And full-grown lambs loud bleat from hilly bourn; 30
  Hedge-crickets sing: and now with treble soft
  The red-breast whistles from a garden-croft;
    And gathering swallows twitter in the skies.

EXERCISE:

1. Compare and contrast the mood of this poem with Frost's "After Apple-Picking" (p. 89).

2. Note that after the predominantly visual imagery of the first two stanzas, the last stanza emphasizes auditory imagery. Why is this shift of emphasis especially appropriate? What does it contribute to the mood of the poem?

3. In this poem autumn is personified—treated as if she were a person. Does autumn remain an abstraction, or does she acquire in the poem a personality? What does the descriptive detail in each of the three stanzas contribute to the definition of that personality?

4. Compare the theme of this poem with the theme of "The Main-Deep" (p. 72).

Rocky Acres

ROBERT GRAVES [1895–]

This is a wild land, country of my choice,
  With harsh craggy mountain, moor ample and bare.
Seldom in these acres is heard any voice
  But voice of cold water that runs here and there
  Through rocks and lank heather growing without care. 5
No mice in the heath run nor no birds cry
For fear of the dark speck that floats in the sky.

He soars and he hovers, rocking on his wings,
  He scans his wide parish with a sharp eye,
He catcnes the trembling of small hidden things, 10
  He tears them in pieces, dropping from the sky:
  Tenderness and pity the land will deny
Where life is but nourished from water and rock,
A hardy adventure, full of fear and shock.

Time has never journeyed to this lost land, 15
  Crakeberries and heather bloom out of date,
The rocks jut, the streams flow singing on either hand,
  Careless if the season be early or late.
  The skies wander overhead, now blue, now slate:
Winter would be known by his cold cutting snow 20
If June did not borrow his armor also.

Yet this is my country beloved by me best,
The first land that rose from Chaos and the Flood,
Nursing no fat valleys for comfort and rest,
Trampled by no hard hooves, stained with no blood. 25
Bold immortal country whose hill-tops have stood
Strongholds for the proud gods when on earth they go,
Terror for fat burghers in far plains below.

EXERCISE:

1. Does the description indicate why this land is the country of the speaker's "choice" and why it is the "country beloved by [him] best"? What kind of man is the speaker?

2. In what sense is it a "bold immortal country"? Is this fact merely asserted, or is it given meaning by the descriptive detail?

Nightingales

ROBERT BRIDGES [1844–1930]

Beautiful must be the mountains whence ye come,
And bright in the fruitful valleys the streams wherefrom
Ye learn your song:
Where are those starry woods? O might I wander there,
Among the flowers, which in that heavenly air 5
Bloom the year long!

Nay, barren are those mountains and spent the streams:
Our song is the voice of desire, that haunts our dreams,
A throe of the heart,
Whose pining visions dim, forbidden hopes profound, 10
No dying cadence nor long sigh can sound,
For all our art.

Alone, aloud in the raptured ear of men
We pour our dark nocturnal secret; and then,
As night is withdrawn 15
From these sweet-springing meads and bursting boughs of May,
Dream, while the innumerable choir of day
Welcome the dawn.

The idea of this poem might be stated somewhat crudely as follows: the greatest beauty does not spring from pleasure but from pain, not from happiness but from sorrow, not from satisfaction, but from desire. It is, we might say, a kind of conquest of pain and sorrow and desire. But how does the idea become incorporated into a poem? The poet does not say in so many words that this is his idea or theme; instead, he has put it in a form that appeals to our imagination.

First, we observe that the poem is composed of two parts, a statement to the nightingales by the poet (the first stanza) and the reply of the nightingales (the second and third stanzas). Given as a prose paraphrase the poem might be stated in this way: The poet says that, since the song of the nightingales is so beautiful, they must come from a place where the beauty of the mountains and the music of streams in the fruitful valleys instructs them; and that he, who lives in a far less beautiful place, longs to wander where the flowers in that heavenly air never wither and where there is no change from perfect beauty. But the birds reply to him that the land from which they come is a harsh place with spent streams, and that the beauty of their song comes, not from satisfaction, but from desire which is so great and so hopeless that it can never be fully expressed even in their song. At night, they add, they pour their song into the ears of men, and then with the coming of dawn on the spring landscape, dream while the birds of the day sing with pleasure.

Obviously, this paraphrase does not exhaust even the meaning of the poem that can be reduced to statement. (It is entirely lacking, of course, in the kind of meaning that comes to us from the nature of the poetic form. See "Afterword" to Section I.) One might even add to this paraphrase a statement of the theme of the poem, and the description would remain incomplete. It may repay us in understanding the method a poet uses in communicating his meaning to try to define some of the things that are absent from the paraphrase and the general statement of the idea.

First, this poem, like many poems, carries with it an allusion to a special piece of information, the Greek myth concerning the woman who, after a tragic experience, was turned into the nightingale. Tereus raped Philomela and then cut out her tongue and cut off her hands lest she tell her sister Procne, Tereus's wife, what had happened to her. But Philomela managed to weave the story into a tapestry and showed it to Procne. The sisters revenged themselves upon Tereus by killing his son and serving his body to Tereus as food. Philomela was turned into a nightingale; Procne, into a swallow; and Tereus, into the hawk who pursues them.

The poem would still make sense to a person who was unacquainted with the suppressed reference to the myth, but a knowledge of the myth does support the meaning of the poem.

But dismissing the implied allusion, we can strike on other implications in the poem that are necessary to a full appreciation. In the first stanza an important instance is involved. Why does the poet in addressing the nightingales express a wish to wander in the beautiful land from which he assumes they have come? There is the answer that anyone likes agreeable surroundings. Then we realize that this land is a kind of mythical paradise where there is no decay or change, a static perfection, such a place as men in a world of change, struggle, and decay dream of. This land of the nightingales implies, then, all men's longing for a kind of otherworldly peace and happiness. But something more is implied here. The speaker evidently is a poet and in the present world is compelled to create his imperfect beauty by effort; he feels that if he inhabited that other land his poems might be as perfect and as spontaneous as the song of the nightingales.

The implications of the second stanza depend on these of the first, and merely involve a correction of the mistaken beliefs implied in the first stanza. But the third stanza raises some new issues, and becomes richer as we contemplate it. First, what is the "dark nocturnal secret"? It is of course the song of the nightingales. The bird sings at night and the use of "dark" seems merely to support and emphasize the use of "nocturnal." The bird also sings from some hidden or secret place, and not in the open. So far the phrase seems only a very good poetic statement about the song. But it carries further a truth about life, that beauty comes from desire, struggle, and pain and not from easy perfection. It is a dark truth, a truth usually hidden, and it may be a depressing truth. But—and this takes us back to the "raptured ear" of the previous line—it is a paradoxical fact that the statement of this dark secret does not depress but exalts the hearer more than the merely pleasant songs of the "innumerable choir of day" can do.

The poet, then, has made the nightingales serve as a symbol to express his idea. He has developed the implications of the image so that it is unnecessary for him to argue his point; we seize on it in seizing on the image itself. The poet is not merely describing his own pleasure in the song of nightingales, or merely trying to make the reader who has no acquaintance with nightingales appreciate the poem fully; he is, instead, using the image of the nightingale to make us respond, emotionally and intellectually, to an interpretation of human experience.

EXERCISE:

Compare the theme of this poem with that of "Rocky Acres" (p. 93).

Slow, Slow, Fresh Fount

BEN JONSON [1573–1637]

Slow, slow, fresh fount, keep time with my salt tears;
  Yet slower, yet, O faintly gentle springs:
List to the heavy part the music bears,
  Woe weeps out her division, when she sings.
    Droop herbs, and flowers; 5
    Fall grief in showers;
    Our beauties are not ours:
      O, I could still
(Like melting snow upon some craggy hill,)
      Drop, drop, drop, drop, 10
Since nature's pride is, now, a withered daffodil.

(From *Cynthia's Revels*)

EXERCISE:

1. What is the meaning of "division" in line 4? (See the dictionary.)

2. What is the meaning of the last line? How is your interpretation of the meaning supported by the preceding lines?

Ode to the West Wind

PERCY BYSSHE SHELLEY [1792–1822]

terza rima

I

O, wild West Wind, thou breath of Autumn's being,
Thou, from whose unseen presence the leaves dead
Are driven, like ghosts from an enchanter fleeing,

Yellow, and black, and pale, and hectic red,
Pestilence-stricken multitudes: O, thou, 5
Who chariotest to their dark wintry bed

leaf

The wingèd seeds, where they lie cold and low,
Each like a corpse within its grave, until
Thine azure sister of the spring shall blow

Her clarion o'er the dreaming earth, and fill 10
(Driving sweet buds like flocks to feed in air)
With living hues and odors plain and hill:

Wild Spirit, which art moving everywhere;
Destroyer and preserver; hear, O, hear!

II

Thou on whose stream, 'mid the steep sky's commotion, 15
Loose clouds like earth's decaying leaves are shed,
Shook from the tangled boughs of Heaven and Ocean,

Angels of rain and lightning: there are spread
On the blue surface of thine airy surge,
Like the bright hair uplifted from the head 20

Of some fierce Mænad, even from the dim verge
Of the horizon to the zenith's height,
The locks of the approaching storm. Thou dirge

Of the dying year, to which this closing night
Will be the dome of a vast sepulcher, 25
Vaulted with all thy congregated might

Of vapors, from whose solid atmosphere
Black rain, and fire, and hail will burst: O hear!

III

Thou who didst waken from his summer dreams
The blue Mediterranean, where he lay, 30
Lulled by the coil of his crystalline streams,

Beside a pumice isle in Baiæ's bay,
And saw in sleep old palaces and towers
Quivering within the wave's intenser day,

All overgrown with azure moss, and flowers 35
So sweet, the sense faints picturing them! Thou
For whose path the Atlantic's level powers

Cleave themselves into chasms, while far below
The sea-blooms and the oozy woods which wear
The sapless foliage of the ocean, know 40

Thy voice, and suddenly grow gray with fear,
And tremble and despoil themselves: O hear!

IV

If I were a dead leaf thou mightest bear;
If I were a swift cloud to fly with thee;
A wave to pant beneath thy power, and share 45

The impulse of thy strength, only less free
Than thou, O, uncontrollable! If even
I were as in my boyhood, and could be

The comrade of thy wanderings over heaven,
As then, when to outstrip thy skiey speed 50
Scarce seemed a vision; I would ne'er have striven

As thus with thee in prayer in my sore need.
Oh! lift me as a wave, a leaf, a cloud!
I fall upon the thorns of life! I bleed!

A heavy weight of hours has chained and bowed 55
One too like thee: tameless, and swift, and proud.

V

Make me thy lyre, even as the forest is:
What if my leaves are falling like its own!
The tumult of thy mighty harmonies

Will take from both a deep, autumnal tone, 60
Sweet though in sadness. Be thou, spirit fierce,
My spirit! Be thou me, impetuous one!

Drive my dead thoughts over the universe
Like withered leaves, to quicken a new birth!
And, by the incantation of this verse, 65

Scatter, as from an unextinguished hearth
Ashes and sparks, my words among mankind!
Be through my lips to unawakened earth

The trumpet of a prophecy! O, wind,
If Winter comes, can Spring be far behind? 70

EXERCISE:

1. Relate the general structure of this poem to the leaf-cloud-wave imagery.

2. It is easy to relate the leaf imagery to the role of the west wind as "destroyer and preserver" (line 14). The dead leaves must be blown away if the new leaves are to come, and the same wind that scatters the old leaves scatters the "winged seeds." Can you relate the cloud and wave imagery to the destroyer-preserver pattern? In this connection consider the comparison of clouds to leaves (line 16 ff. and the despoiling of the "sapless foliage" of the ocean (line 40).

3. What does section four tell us about the speaker? Does the poem sufficiently present his situation? Or do you need to consult a life of Shelley in order for the passage to gain full significance?

4. In section five, the poet refers to "my dead thoughts." Are they really dead, or does he mean that they are only apparently dead like the "ashes and sparks" of line 67?

5. What does the west wind come to symbolize in this poem?

Composed upon Westminster Bridge Sept. 3 1802

WILLIAM WORDSWORTH [1770–1850]

Earth has not anything to show more fair:
Dull would he be of soul who could pass by
A sight so touching in its majesty:
This city now doth like a garment wear
The beauty of the morning; silent, bare, 5
Ships, towers, domes, theaters, and temples lie
Open unto the fields, and to the sky;
All bright and glittering in the smokeless air.
Never did sun more beautifully steep
In his first splendor valley, rock, or hill; 10
Ne'er saw I, never felt, a calm so deep!
The river glideth at his own sweet will:
Dear God! the very houses seem asleep;
And all that mighty heart is lying still!

EXERCISE:

The description of the city given in this poem is general rather than particular—we are presented with a panorama rather than with a detailed scene. The description does not abound in bold comparisons or in striking realistic details. Yet many readers have testified to the power and excitement of the poem. Try to determine why the poem is successful. The following questions may be helpful in this enterprise.

1. Does the spectator seem to manifest surprise? Why?

2. What is the point in his saying that the city is "open" unto the fields and to the sky? Is it not always "open"?

3. Does the river not always glide "at his own sweet will"? Why is the spectator struck with this fact? What are the implications of the fact?

4. What is the point in comparing the city to scenes of natural beauty?

5. If the city were less quiet, would it seem to the spectator less "alive" or more "alive"?

6. In the light of your answer to Question 5, can you justify the last two lines? Ordinarily, the comparisons made in these lines ("houses . . . asleep" and the city as a "mighty heart") might seem trite.

Preludes

T. S. ELIOT [1888–]

I

The winter evening settles down
With smell of steaks in passageways.
Six o'clock.
The burnt-out ends of smoky days.
And now a gusty shower wraps 5
The grimy scraps
Of withered leaves about your feet
And newspapers from vacant lots;
The showers beat
On broken blinds and chimney-pots, 10
And at the corner of the street
A lonely cab-horse steams and stamps.
And then the lighting of the lamps.

II

The morning comes to consciousness
Of faint stale smells of beer 15
From the sawdust-trampled street
With all its muddy feet that press
To early coffee-stands.
With the other masquerades
That time resumes, 20
One thinks of all the hands
That are raising dingy shades
In a thousand furnished rooms.

III

You tossed a blanket from the bed,
You lay upon your back, and waited; 25
You dozed, and watched the night revealing

The thousand sordid images
Of which your soul was constituted;
They flickered against the ceiling.
And when all the world came back 30
And the light crept up between the shutters
And you heard the sparrows in the gutters,
You had such a vision of the street
As the street hardly understands;
Sitting along the bed's edge, where 35
You curled the papers from your hair,
Or clasped the yellow soles of feet
In the palms of both soiled hands.

IV

His soul stretched tight across the skies
That fade behind a city block, 40
Or trampled by insistent feet
At four and five and six o'clock;
And short square fingers stuffing pipes,
And evening newspapers, and eyes
Assured of certain certainties, 45
The conscience of a blackened street
Impatient to assume the world.

I am moved by fancies that are curled
Around these images, and cling:
The notion of some infinitely gentle 50
Infinitely suffering thing.

Wipe your hand across your mouth, and laugh;
The worlds revolve like ancient women
Gathering fuel in vacant lots.

EXERCISE:

1. The first two sections of this poem describe a winter evening and a winter morning in a city. The description in these sections is objective, but it establishes a mood and attitude. Discuss the mood and attitude. What effect do the last three lines of the second section give?

2. In the third section, one of the people whose hand will raise dingy shades is addressed. Out of her own misery she has "a vision of the street"—an awareness of the general loneliness and defeat. Why does the poet say that the street hardly understands this vision?

3. In the fourth section another character is referred to, a man who is sensitive enough to be constantly affected by the life he sees around him—a life which appears to be dominated by a meaningless routine of satisfying animal requirements, the "certain certainties." Ironically, the poet calls this assurance of these certainties the only "conscience" that the street has; and the street seems to impose its own standards on the entire world. Then (in line 48) the poet announces himself as a commentator on the scenes he has presented. What attitude does he take? Whom is he addressing in the last three lines? How do the last two lines serve as a symbolic summary of the poem? Is the poet ready to wipe his own hand across his mouth—the gross gesture of satisfied appetite—and laugh at human suffering?

4. Before attempting to answer the last question, it may be well to consider carefully the comparison that dominates the last three lines. Is there a realistic basis for the comparison? Does an old woman gathering chips—or anyone, for that matter, who keeps his eyes fixed on the ground—tend to move in circles? What are the "worlds" referred to? May they be the planets revolving in the solar system? If so, what is implied? Is the poet prepared to say that man is merely a trivial mechanism in a mechanistic universe?

III

METRICS

FOREWORD

We have said ("Afterword," Section I, p. 70) that concentration and intensity are two of the qualities that tend to distinguish the poetic treatment of a subject from the prose treatment; and we related these qualities to the emphasis on form in poetry. The form of poetry, we said, is more closely organized than is the form of prose. As an example of this principle we indicated the greater selectivity in use of detail, the emphasis on suggestiveness, and the importance in the placing of details in relation to the central intention of a poem. For example, we indicated the importance of the line, "That kindles my mother's fire" in "The Wife of Usher's Well" (p. 18); the accumulation of descriptive detail in "Michael" as a basis for the final presentation of the pathos of the poem (p. 37); and the implications of the phrase "our dark nocturnal secret" in "Nightingales" (p. 96). All of these things indicate the close-knit organization of various elements which one finds in poetry. Some of the same types of organization are to be found in prose as well as in poetry; but we have pointed out that poetry *tends* toward a higher degree of formal organization than does prose. For example, the poor choice of words on the basis of connotation is much less damaging to a novel than to a poem. The damaged novel may still give some satisfaction, but the poem in which the writer has given little attention to connotation would certainly be a complete failure.

This tendency toward a high degree of organization in poetry is most obvious in the use of *rhythmical* language (*Glossary*). Some people, in fact, are accustomed to think that the use of rhythmical language is what chiefly distinguishes poetry from prose. But the distinction made on this basis can in the end only be one of degree and not of kind. This is obviously true when we reflect that any use of language in prose or poetry involves rhythm. In any prose whatsoever we feel a rise and fall of emphasis: we do not pronounce each syllable with precisely the same emphasis. We may say, however, that even if there is not an absolute difference between prose and poetry on the basis of rhythm, there is still a very important relative difference. A consideration of the following extracts from essays, stories, and poems may make clear what the relative difference is:

(1)

As a sample of popular interest it may be noted that a single talk last spring by Professor MacMurry on psychology brought 17,000 requests for the supplementary aid-to-study pamphlet, and one by Professor Burt on the study of the mind brought 26,000.

("The Level of Thirteen-Year-Olds," William Orton)

(2)

But verse, you say, circumscribes a quick and luxuriant fancy, which would extend itself too far on every subject, did not the labor which is required to well-turned and polished rime, set bounds to it. Yet this argument, if granted, would only prove that we may write better in verse, but not more naturally.

("An Essay of Dramatic Poesy," John Dryden)

(3)

If there be any truth in astrology, I may outlive a jubilee; as yet I have not seen one revolution of Saturn, nor hath my pulse beat thirty years, and yet, excepting one, have seen the ashes of, and left underground, all the kings of Europe; have been contemporary to three emperors, four grand signiors, and as many popes: methinks I have outlived myself, and begin to be weary of the sun; I have shaken hands with delight in my warm blood and canicular days; I perceive I do anticipate the vices of age; the world to me is but a dream or mock-show, and we all therein but pantaloons and antics, to my severer contemplations.

(*Religio Medici,* Sir Thomas Browne)

(4)

These and all else were to me the same as they are to you,
I loved well those cities, loved well the stately and rapid river,
The men and women I saw were all near to me,
Others the same—others who look back on me because I looked forward to them
(The time will come, though I stop here today and tonight).
("Crossing Brooklyn Ferry," Walt Whitman)

(5)

These our actors,
As I foretold you, were all spirits, and
Are melted into air, into thin air:
And, like the baseless fabric of this vision,
The cloud-capped towers, the gorgeous palaces, 5
The solemn temples, the great globe itself,
Yea, all which it inherit, shall dissolve,
And, like this insubstantial pageant faded,
Leave not a wrack behind.
(*The Tempest,* William Shakespeare)

(6)

The gale, it plies the saplings double,
It blows so hard, 'twill soon be gone:
Today the Roman and his trouble
Are ashes under Uricon.
("On Wenlock Edge," A. E. Housman)

If one will read, preferably aloud, the specimens given above, it will be clear that all of them possess the quality of rhythm—even the first one with its dull, flat, matter-of-fact statement. Indeed, if we read carefully we can see that the specimens form, roughly speaking, a sort of ascending scale in regard to the regularity of the rhythm. If one hears specimen 1 and 6 read aloud he can easily detect the difference in the regularity and emphasis of the rhythm. In the case of specimen 1 the rhythm is almost completely unsystematized and chaotic; in the case of specimen 6 the rhythm is systematized and regularized—that is, it takes the form of *verse* (*Glossary*).

But if specimens 1 and 6 represent extremes of regularity and irregularity, what of a comparison between specimens 3 and 4 or between 4 and 5? Specimen 3 is taken from a work in *prose,* specimen 4 from a *poem;* yet a person hearing the two read aloud might not very easily distinguish them on this basis. Evidently there are degrees, as we have said, of regularization of rhythm, and the distinction between verse (regularized rhythm) and prose (unregularized rhythm) is not an absolute one.

The systematic ordering of rhythm we call verse. In most poetry, verse is so obvious that a body of special terms has been developed to describe its various elements. For instance, by the term *meter* we mean the measure of the verse according to the line. The unit of measure is called the *foot,* a unit composed, in English verse, of one accented syllable and one or more unaccented syllables. And we have given names to the various types of foot. (For full discussion of the general subject, see *Glossary.*) For instance, the most common foot in English poetry is called the *iambic foot;* it is composed of one unaccented and one accented syllable. The following line is composed of iambic feet:

Is this the face that launched a thousand ships

We can mark the divisions into feet and the accents as follows:

Ĭs thís | thĕ fáce | thăt láunched | ă thóu | sănd shíps

The line may be described as *iambic pentameter;* that is, it is composed of five iambic feet (*Glossary*).

Because of the prominence of rhythmical system in poetry and perhaps because of the amount of attention which is usually given to the technique of *versification* (*Glossary*), people sometimes tend to confuse verse with poetry, forgetting that *verse is only one of the instruments which the poet uses to gain his effect* (*Introduction* pp. l–li). This confusion is avoided if we realize that it is entirely possible to have verse without having a poetic effect. To illustrate the fact that verse, as such, does not give the poetic effect and is not to be confused with poetry, we can point to the following line, which provides an example of iambic pentameter:

A Mr. Wilkerson, a clergyman

We can scan it as follows:

A Mist | er Wilk | er son | a clerg | y man

Or it would be possible to construct a pattern of pure nonsense that could be accurately scanned.

Investigation sad or verbally
Reveal unvision here this house no cat
Divest warm compromise imperially
What yes untold unwicked hiss nor that.

These lines are in regular iambic pentameter. They are arranged, furthermore, in the form of a simple stanza, the quatrain (*Glossary* under *stanza*). No one would care to maintain that the mere fact that these unrelated words are put into a metrical pattern creates poetry. To have poetry the words must be related in other ways as well. Verse is simply one of many instruments—narrative, dramatic incident, figurative language, logical sense of words, associations of words, etc.—at the poet's disposal. Our present interest is, then, to see some of the ways in which this element of verse works in making its contribution to the poetic effect, and to see some of its relations to the other elements used by the poet; for one must always remember that poetry is the result of a combination of relationships among the elements and does not inhere specially in any one of them (*Introduction,* pp. l–li).

We have said that verse represents a specialization of rhythm in language, and that it is one aspect of the greater formality, or of the closer organization, of poetry as contrasted with other literary modes. Form in poetry, as in anything else, is simply the arrangement of the various elements for a given effect. Verse is a means for controlling the use of language. One of the functions of this control is to focus attention. The pattern of accents, once we have grasped it as a pattern, sets up the unconscious expectation in us that the pattern will continue. Variations from the pattern register forcibly as our expectations are confirmed or momentarily disappointed. The skilful poet finds in verse a most subtle instrument for binding parts of the poem together, for regulating emphasis, for underlining the connection between words, etc. Verse is an adjunct of meaning. Indeed, in great poetry the movement of the verse seems indivisible from the movement of the thought and feeling, and the verse seems to be an embodiment of the meaning.

Very diverse claims have been made for the functions performed by verse, ranging from the intrinsic beauty that verse confers on the poem to the hypnotic power that verse exerts upon the reader. Writers who stress the hypnotic power are thinking, it should be pointed out, not of the apparent sluggishness and dullness of the hypnoidal state, but of the increased concentration of attention and suggestibility. The person who is in such a condition hangs upon every word of the hypnotist and attends to, and accepts, even the slightest suggestion. One of the most interesting statements about this aspect of verse comes from Coleridge who says that meter tends "to increase the vivacity and susceptibility both of the general feelings and of the attention. . . . As a medicated atmosphere, or as a wine during animated conversation, they [the anticipations set up by the meter] act powerfully, though themselves unnoticed."[1]

Verse may be also examined, however, not in terms of its effect upon the reader or hearer, but in terms of its origin. Intense states of emotion do seem, quite naturally and instinctively, to tend toward a rhythmical expression. Investigation of the life of primitive peoples or of the habits of children or of the nature of religious rituals—all testify to this psychological fact. And we know how the moans of a person in great grief or pain tend to assume a rhythmical pattern. Considerations of this sort may help to indicate why verse has become traditionally associated with poetry. For poetry, though it is not *merely* emotional nor to be defined as the "expression of pure emotion" (*Introduction,* pp. xlvi–xlvii), does attempt to do justice to the emotional elements in experience, and poetry often treats experiences of great intensity.

But having noted the variety of speculations on the nature of verse and the justifications of verse that may be drawn from its origin and from its effect upon the reader, we shall probably do well to rest in our earlier statement on the matter—verse, we have said, is an adjunct of meaning, and is best discussed in relation to the meaning of the poem as a whole. What the verse does in a spe-

[1] *Biographia Literaria,* Ch. XVIII.

cific context—how the verse is related to the other elements in this particular poem or that—we shall take up in the pages that follow. For in this textbook, our primary interest is in learning how to deal with particular poems, and our principal concern will be with the poem as a unified structure of meanings. This, of course, is not to say that psychological theories which attempt to account in general for the effect of verse are not interesting and important. They are interesting and important, but they bear in only a general way upon the kinds of problems with which we shall be concerned. For example, if verse does exercise an hypnotic effect, we have still to confront the fact that of many poems using verse, some are "good" and some are "bad"; that the hypnotic spell "works" in some instances and does not in others—or if we maintain that it always works, we must recognize that its working does not automatically insure the success of the poem, but that we must take into account the other elements of the poem and their relationship to each other.

The modest generalization that verse is an adjunct of meaning does, however, yield one general working principle—the verse must be in some sort of harmony with the rest of the poem. A poem on a serious subject, for example, will hardly prove successful if the poet has chosen a light, tripping verse—that is, if he has chosen a verse which works at cross purposes to the other elements in the poem. The following poem, especially the first two stanzas, is often used to illustrate the choice of a wrong type of rhythm for a subject:

Death

PERCY BYSSHE SHELLEY [1792–1822]

Death is here, and death is there,
Death is busy everywhere,
All around, within, beneath,
Above is death—and we are death.

Death has set his mark and seal
On all we are and all we feel,
On all we know and all we fear,

. . .

First our pleasures die—and then
Our hopes, and then our fears—and when
These are dead, the debt is due, 10
Dust claims dust—and we die too.

All things that we love and cherish,
Like ourselves must fade and perish;
Such is our rude mortal lot—
Love itself would, did they not. 15

Here, in "Death," then, we have a case in which the specific feeling stimulated by the jigging rhythm tends to contradict the response suggested by the ideas, images, etc., of the poem. The poem is an unsuccessful poem because the parts do not work together—they are not properly related. Let us examine, then, a somewhat longer poem in terms of this general principle.

The Bells of Shandon

FRANCIS MAHONY [1805–1866]

With deep affection,
And recollection,
I often think of
    Those Shandon bells,
Whose sounds so wild would, 5
In the days of childhood,
Fling around my cradle
    Their magic spells:
On this I ponder
Where'er I wander, 10
And thus grow fonder,
    Sweet Cork, of thee;
With thy bells of Shandon,
That sound so grand on
The pleasant waters 15
    Of the River Lee.

I've heard bells chiming
Full many a clime in,

Tolling sublime in
    Cathedral shrine, 20
While at a glib rate
Brass tongues would vibrate—
But all their music
    Spoke naught like thine;
For memory, dwelling 25
On each proud swelling
Of the belfry knelling
    Its bold notes free,
Made the bells of Shandon
Sound far more grand on 30
The pleasant waters
    Of the River Lee.

I've heard bells tolling
Old Adrian's Mole in,
Their thunder rolling 35
    From the Vatican,
And cymbals glorious
Swinging uproarious
In the gorgeous turrets
    Of Notre Dame; 40
But thy sounds were sweeter
Than the dome of Peter
Flings o'er the Tiber,
    Pealing solemnly—
O, the bells of Shandon 45
Sound far more grand on
The pleasant waters
    Of the River Lee.

There's a bell in Moscow,
While on tower and kiosk O 50
In Saint Sophia
    The Turkman gets,
And loud in air
Calls men to prayer
From the tapering summits 55
    Of tall minarets.

Such empty phantom
I freely grant them;
But there's an anthem
    More dear to me,— 60
'Tis the bells of Shandon,
That sound so grand on
The pleasant waters
    Of the River Lee.

This poem is apparently a serious attempt to deal with an experience which is familiar enough in everyday life: the superior beauty possessed by things which are endeared to us by memory or some personal tie. The bells of Shandon, because they were heard by the poet in his childhood, always sound sweeter to him than any other bells which he has ever heard.

The first two stanzas embody this statement. The rest of the poem is taken up with naming the various famous bells which the poet has heard and which have less meaning for him than do the bells of Shandon. The experience in its general terms, we have already said, is one which people often have, and it might form the basis of a fine poem. Has the poet made "The Bells of Shandon" a fine poem? An adverse criticism of the poem does not *question* the fact that in actuality the bells of Shandon may have had a very profound meaning for Francis Mahony, the man. The criticism to follow is occupied rather with this question: Has Francis Mahony, the artist, succeeded in constructing a poem which will really suggest to us the quality and meaning of such an experience?

A really thoughtful consideration of the poem will reveal that we can take the experience only on our faith in the sincerity of Mahony, the man. He does not re-create the experience for us at all. Perhaps the most obvious reason for the failure of the poem is the lack of any real dramatic quality (*Introduction,* p. liv). Notice how little development there is. The poem gives nothing more than the statement that the bells have such and such effect, and a statement of their superiority to a whole list of other bells. The statement is mere repetition, the list of bells merely a catalogue which lengthens the poem without developing the experience. The whole experience is vague and undramatic, and the statement of it is rambling and monotonous. This deficiency in structure is matched by a comparable deficiency in the monotonous and inexpressive meter.

One notices that the meter (which is elaborate and emphatic enough to call attention to itself) is mechanical and inflexible. We continue at the same trot whether the subject is the bells of Shandon or those of Notre Dame or—not bells at all—the cry of the muezzin. If the meter were a little more self-effacing, the lack of appropriateness in the movement of the verse in various parts of the poem would not be so sharply indicated as it is. But in spite of some few variations, the tripping speed of the rhythm sweeps away any effect of contrast or development. Instead of being co-ordinated with the other elements in the poem, the meter has broken loose from the other elements and dominates the poem; the jog-trot metrical pattern is emphasized, apparently, as an end in itself.

But the domination by the meter goes to even greater extremes. The inversions of grammar which occur in the poem can hardly be defended as giving force or emphasis: they rather plainly evidence the fact that this poet could not control his meter. The meter in this poem—far from being one of the instruments used by the poet to get certain effects—actually twists the sense into distortion.

An examination of the riming will corroborate this judgment. The poet establishes a pattern of *feminine rimes* (*Glossary*)—perhaps from some vague notion of achieving melodious effects suitable to a poem on the music of the bells. But very soon we see that the feminine rimes have become as merciless a taskmaster to the poet as the meter. The poet gives us such rimes as: *wild would*, with *childhood; Shandon*, with *grand on; Mole in*, with *tolling;* and finally such an absurdity as *Moscow*, with *kiosk O*. Such rimes as these, which impress the reader as having been consciously striven for and violently forced, tend to give a comic effect. Forced rimes are quite appropriate in the plays of Gilbert and Sullivan, but in this poem the ludicrous effect of the forced rimes is completely at variance with that suggested by the other elements in the poem.

Why is it that more people have not been aware of these discordant comic effects? Why should the poem have been so popular as it has been? (It is included in the *Oxford Book of English*

Verse.) One may best explain perhaps in this way: many people in reading a poem lay aside the critical habit of mind, doing so out of deference to the poet, though of course this is a very poor compliment to the poet. Such a person, however, seizing on the statement about fond recollection and the beauty of the bells so recollected, might easily be seduced into feeling that the poem was good. He would probably consider the elaborate metrics as contributing beauty to the poem, for he would hardly inspect it closely enough to see the discrepancies between what the meter does and what the other elements in the poem do. But as we have already seen, meter is only one of several means which the poet may use and must use in securing certain effects. The meter and these other means must pull together—not apart, as in this poem. As a matter of fact, monotony of meter is one of the surest symptoms of the fact that the materials of a poem have not been focused sharply and clearly by the poet. The poet has not mastered his subject. The impulse behind the poem is apparently weak, and the elaborate metrics and riming have probably been used to disguise this very fact. In "The Bells of Shandon" this failure to master the subject is indicated by the dependence on mere prosy statement and by the failure to develop dramatically the quality of the feelings actually referred to the bells.

After Long Silence

WILLIAM BUTLER YEATS [1865–1939]

Speech after long silence; it is right,
All other lovers being estranged or dead,
Unfriendly lamplight hid under its shade,
The curtains drawn upon unfriendly night,
That we descant and yet again descant 5
Upon the supreme theme of Art and Song:
Bodily decrepitude is wisdom; young
We loved each other and were ignorant.

The dramatic situation implied by the poem is easily defined. The two lovers are in a shadowed room alone, the lamplight being almost hidden by the shade. One of the lovers is speaking to the other, and before we comment on what he says, several points may be rehearsed. The lovers are evidently old. The relationship has not been a constant one, for we are told that all other lovers are "estranged or dead." The first line suggests that there has been a long silence after they have "descanted" upon the "supreme theme of Art and Song." (The nature of this theme will be discussed later.) This silence has been broken by more talk on the same subject, apparently now the only subject left to them, and one of the lovers makes the comment which constitutes the poem itself.

The speaker says, in effect, this: one lover can no longer take pleasure in the physical beauty of the other (for the lamplight, which would reveal the decay of age, is described as "unfriendly"). Furthermore, the outside world has no more use for them (for the world outside their drawn curtains is likewise "unfriendly"). It is right that, having passed through the other phases of their lives, they should now talk of the "theme of Art and Song," which is "supreme" because it involves the interpretation of their own previous experience. Wisdom, the power to reach an interpretation, comes only as the body decays. The poet sees the wisdom as a positive gain, but at the same time he can regret the time of beauty and youth when the lovers could dispense with wisdom. The basic point of the poem is the recognition, with its attendant pathos, of the fact that man cannot ever be complete—cannot, that is, possess beauty and wisdom together.

Why is the poem so much richer and more moving than the bare statement in our summary? The reader would say immediately that the poet has dramatized the general statement—that is, he has made us feel that the idea as given through the incident has the weight of experience belonging to real people. The reader would also point out the suggestiveness of the images used in the first four lines. Such comments would be incomplete as an account of any poem, but would be particularly incomplete for a poem like the present one. For it will be possible in this poem to show how the use made of the verse is especially important in making the poem achieve its intended effect. But this will require a detailed examination of the versification.

∧Speech | after long | silence; |∧it | is right,
All o | ther lo | vers be | ing estranged | or dead,
Unfriend | ly lamp | light hid | under | its shade,
The cur | tains drawn | upon | unfriend | ly night,
That we | descant | and yet | again | descant 5
Upon | the supreme |∧theme | of Art | and Song:
Bodily | decre | pitude | is wis | dom; young
We loved | each o | ther and | were ig | norant.

The reader will observe that the basic metrical pattern is that of iambic pentameter. He will also observe, however, that there are a number of variations from the basic pattern. What are they, and do they play any part in giving the poem its effect?

Consider the first line. The line does not set the regular metrical pattern of the poem. The irregularity here supports, with dramatic appropriateness, the effect of informal conversation. This is the general effect of the line, but let us analyze the particular details. Instead of the normal iambic opening, we find an accent falling on the first syllable, *speech,* which may be regarded as a *defective foot* (*Glossary*), with the missing syllable marked thus ∧. The second foot, *after long,* may be regarded as an anapest, in which the syllable added to the iambic norm is a *compensation* (*Glossary*) for the defect in the first foot.[1] The foot, *silence,* represents a trochaic *substitution* (*Glossary*) for the normal iambic foot. Let us pause here to see what effect these variations have on the movement of the line. *Speech* is accented emphatically, as it should be for dramatic reasons: the abrupt beginning is appropriate to the idea of speech suddenly breaking upon silence. The fact that the reader must hurry over the two unaccented syllables of *after* before he can rest on the accent of *long* makes the emphasis on *long* greater than it would otherwise be; and this heavy emphasis on *long* fortifies the meaning of

[1] Some students may prefer to scan the first line thus:

Speech af | ter long | silence; |∧it | is right.

Even if one takes such a view, the system of accents and pauses is not altered.

the word. This emphasis is further increased by the fact that the accented syllable *si-* of the trochaic foot *silence* follows the accented *long* without an intervening unaccented syllable. But when two accented syllables are thrust together in this way, the reader is forced to take a slight pause between them. The effect of such a condition is to increase the emphasis on the accented syllables, because the reader has lingered at that point in the verse.

To proceed with the analysis of the line, we may say that the word *it* is an imperfect foot, with the pause dictated by the end of the previous phrase (marked by the semicolon) standing as the missing unaccented syllable. This is followed by a regular iambic foot. The heavy pause after *silence* (a pause dictated by rhetorical construction) gives the effect of the speaker's meditating a moment after making his initial statement as though in order to explore its full meaning before he commits himself to a conclusion. The words that follow, then, come to us with the weight of this meditation. But in addition to this there is a more special effect. The word *it* receives, by reason of the weak syllable (the second syllable of *si-lence*) and the pause which precede it, more than its ordinary emphasis. This emphasis, again, is dramatically right, for the word *it,* usually a fairly unimportant word and lightly stressed, in this context is important. When the word occurs we do not yet know what the *it* refers to; and what it does refer to—what the speaker says is "right"—constitutes the basic statement of the poem. Explaining the *it* gives us the body of the poem.

To summarize, we can say that the first line is characterized by several daring departures from what we discover to be the metrical norm of the poem as a whole; and yet each of these variations, as we have seen, operates to support the intention of the line. (The division into feet used here may seem to some readers arbitrary. There are perhaps other possible interpretations. But in any case, the accented syllables and the pauses are definitely fixed. The important matter is to understand the function of the variations in making the line expressive.)

After the very irregular first line, the basic pattern is asserted in the second line with only one slight and usual variation (the fourth foot, *-ing estranged,* is anapaestic rather than iambic, and tends to accelerate the line and emphasize the word *estranged*).

The third line offers two slight variations from the norm. There is a strong *secondary accent* (*Glossary*) [1] on the syllable *-light,* for in the compound word *lamplight,* as is true of most such compounds (*midnight, bookcase*), there is a marked secondary accent. (Contrast, for example, *lamplight* with a word like *truly.*) The result is to give the accent in the foot *-light hid* a hovering effect rather than that of a decisive fixing on one of the two syllables.[2] The use of a hovering accent gives a lingering rhythm—a dwelling on the statement of the central idea of light being hidden. After this retardation, the trochaic substitution of *under* again accelerates the line to its conclusion, because of the grouping together of the weak syllables (*-der its*), so that the reader hastens to the accented syllable at the end.

The next metrical variation occurs in line 6. The second foot, *the supreme,* is anapaestic; this means that the syllable *-preme* receives a more than normally emphatic pronunciation.[3] The next foot is imperfect, containing only the syllable *theme;* a lingering on the syllable *-preme* and a pause compensate for the missing syllable in the next foot. This situation, as we have already seen from line 1, gives unusual emphasis. The emphasis at this point is further increased by the unusual device of the rime of the two accented syllables.

[1] Some readers will find other instances of secondary accents in this poem; for instance, in the first foot of the second line,

All o-,

or the first foot of the third line,

Unfriend-,

and elsewhere.

[2] The foot might be marked *-light hid* rather than *-light hid.* The latter marking emphasizes that the secondary accent is practically of the same weight as the primary, but this is a nuance that the student need not observe.

[3] Some students may prefer to scan the line as follows:

Upon | the su | preme theme | of Art | and Song

though this alternate scansion is somewhat arbitrary in that it gives a primary accent to *su-* and thus suggests that it is on something of the same stress level as *-preme,* a syllable actually much more heavily accented. In this connection, see pp. 129–31.

Early in line 7 we have the rather unusual situation of three unaccented syllables in succession between two accented syllables, the first of the line, *Bod-* and the fifth *cre-*. (This situation may be described as a dactylic followed by an iambic foot.) [1] The reader is forced, as it were, to accelerate the pace to reach the second accent. In this part of the line he is somewhat like a man running off balance. When he reaches the pause after *wisdom,* the metrical structure of the line is still undefined, even though the iambic movement has begun to reassert itself. After the pause, therefore, the reader is forced to stress, and linger on, the syllable *young,* for only by this accent does the line achieve any metrical system. So much for the metrical stress on *young*. But how does this relate to the meaning intended? *Young* is, obviously, a very important word here. It is set over against everything that has come before it in the poem, for the preceding part of the poem gives the picture of age. Indeed, the single adjective *young* serves as a condensation for some such statement as "But when we were young, etc." The word serves, therefore, as a kind of pivot for the poem. The unusual emphasis forced on it by the metrical arrangement of the line fortifies the whole meaning of the word in the poem.

Before discussing the last line, which completes the contrast suggested in the word *young,* it may be well to summarize the general metrical situation in the first seven lines of the poem. We have seen that these seven lines are characterized by a great deal of variation, only lines 4 and 5 being perfectly systematic. The poet has used variation, sometimes extreme variation, to stress certain words and to give to the whole poem a flexible movement suggestive of conversation. The reader unconsciously has been waiting for an emphatic assertion of the pattern, which is built toward in lines 1, 2, and 3, and finally stated in lines 4 and 5, but which is rather violently broken again in lines 6 and 7. Consequently, when the pattern is strongly and regularly reaffirmed in the last line, the reader has a sense of a statement uttered with positiveness and finality. This is the general effect of the line, but there is a special effect in the line which is worthy of some comment. We observe that the

[1] Or the opening of this line may be scanned as a trochaic foot followed by an anapaestic foot.

conjunction *and,* which ordinarily is an unimportant word, receives an accent. But here *and* is a highly important word, for it serves as more than a mere casual connective. We have said earlier that the point of the poem—the theme on which the lovers descant—is that man cannot be complete, cannot possess beauty and wisdom at the same time; and the emphatic connective here condenses and asserts this meaning. The metrical accent falling on *and* gives a clue to, and a reenforcement of, the interpretation of the line and of the poem.

We began the discussion of the meter of this poem by asking why it is so much more rich and moving than the bare statement of content which we had given; and we had just pointed out that, whereas in part this is due to the dramatization and the use of imagery, the meter is largely responsible for the richness and concreteness which the poem has. More specifically, this richness and concreteness is gained in three ways: (1) The handling of the meter is flexible enough to give the dramatic impression of speech without violating the impression of a metrical pattern. (The poet, of course, does not undertake to give a transcript of conversation; he merely gives, as we have said, an impression, by moving away from a fixed pattern.) (2) The metrical variations are never arbitrary but are used to secure the proper degree of emphasis on words where the meaning is focused. (3) The development of the idea of the poem is made alive and significant by being underscored by the metrical contrast between lines 7 and 8.

People sometimes make the mistake of supposing that very particular effects are attached to particular metrical situations. They will identify a special emotion or idea with a special movement of verse, and perhaps assume the movement of the verse to be *the* cause. That is, they assume that a particular metrical situation would convey the effect even to a person who did not understand the language in which the poem was written. In opposition to this view I. A. Richards writes as follows:

. . . if the meaning of the words is irrelevant to the form of the verse, and if this independent form possesses aesthetic virtue [can transmit the effect without regard to actual meaning of the words involved], as not a few have maintained . . . , it should be possible to take some recognised masterpiece of poetic rhythm and compose, with nonsense syllables, a double or dummy which at least comes recognisably near to possessing the same virtue.

> J. Drootan-Sussting Benn
> Mill-down Leduren N.
>   Telamba-taras oderwainto weiring
> Awersey zet bidreen
> Ownd istellester sween
>   Lithabian tweet ablissood owdswown stiering
> Apleven aswetsen sestinal
> Yintomen I adaits afurf I gallas Ball.

If the reader has any difficulty in scanning these verses, reference to Milton, *On the Morning of Christ's Nativity* [ll. 113–20, p. 317] will prove of assistance, and the attempt to divine the movement of the original before looking it up will at least show how much the sense, syntax, and feeling of verse may serve as an introduction to its form. But the illustration will also support a subtler argument against anyone who affirms that the mere sound of verse has *independently* any considerable aesthetic virtue. For he will *either* have to say that this verse is valuable (when he may be implored to take up his pen at once and enrich the world with many more such verses, for nothing could be easier), *or* he will have to say that it is the differences *in sound* between this purified dummy and the original which deprive the dummy of poetic merit. In which case he will have to account for the curious fact that just those transformations which redeem it as sound, should also give it the sense and feeling we find in Milton. A staggering coincidence, unless the meaning were highly relevant to the effect of the form.

Such arguments (which might be elaborated) do not tend to diminish the power of the sound (the inherent rhythm) *when it works in conjunction with sense and feeling*. . . . In fact the close co-operation of the form with the meaning—modifying it and being modified by it in ways that though subtle are, in general, perfectly intelligible—is the chief secret of Style in poetry. But so much mystery and obscurity has been raised around this relation by talk about the *identity* of Form and Content, or about the extirpation of the Matter in the Form, that we are in danger of forgetting how natural and inevitable their co-operation must be.[1]

The real point is this: the meter, no more than any other single element in a poem, gives absolute effects; that is, the particular poetic effect in any case does not inhere in the meter alone. But the meter, as our analysis of "After Long Silence" has shown, can be used by the poet as a highly important element to combine with the other elements in order to give the total result which is the poem.

The impression that metrical and other technical analysis is valuable as an end in itself is sometimes given in handbooks on poetry, and may have been suggested by the relative length of the analyses of poems in this section. A confusion of the length of discussion and the importance is, however, to be avoided. Metrical analysis, in the very nature of the case, requires detailed and consistent study of specific instances. The question of meter and other technical factors is, of course, extremely important; but, as has been said repeatedly in this section, these are but a few of the contributing elements among many, and finally should be considered only in relation to the other elements.

The great value of exercise in scansion and other technical analysis is that it makes us really attend to elements in poetry that are sometimes neglected. Ordinarily we are so conditioned to the use of language as a sign on a page that we forget sound as an essential part of it. Poetry (as well as good prose) uses language in its fullness. Even when we read poetry or prose silently, if we are trained and sensitive readers, we are aware sub-vocally of the rhythm and texture of the language and are affected by them. If we do not have this ability naturally, we can cultivate it by exercise and study that make us focus our attention upon that aspect of language.

This is not to say that any system of indicating scansion, certainly not the rather rudimentary system suggested in this book, will render the enormous subtlety, the complication and shading, of rhythm and texture in language when it is well used. We must depend

[1] *Practical Criticism,* New York: Harcourt, Brace and Company, Inc., pp. 232–233.

upon the tact and discrimination of our ear to do that. But the use of a system will help us. It will give us a sort of standard, however crude, to which we can refer the actual language. And it is to the actual language that we always want to come back. That is where the poetry exists.

Absent Yet Present

EDWARD BULWER-LYTTON, LORD LYTTON [1803–1873]

As the flight of a river
  That flows to the sea
My soul rushes ever
  In tumult to thee.

A twofold existence 5
  I am where thou art;
My heart in the distance
  Beats close to thy heart.

Look up, I am near thee,
  I gaze on thy face; 10
I see thee, I hear thee,
  I feel thine embrace.

As a magnet's control on
  The steel it draws to it,
Is the charm of thy soul on 15
  The thoughts that pursue it.

And absence but brightens
  The eyes that I miss,
And custom but heightens
  The spell of thy kiss. 20

It is not from duty,
  Though that may be owed,—
It is not from beauty,
  Though that be bestowed;

But all that I care for, 25
  And all that I know,
Is that, without wherefore,
  I worship thee so.

Through granite it breaketh
  A tree to the ray; 30
As a dreamer forsaketh
  The grief of the day,

My soul in its fever
  Escapes unto thee;
O dream to the griever! 35
  O light to the tree!

A twofold existence
  I am where thou art;
Hark, hear in the distance
  The beat of my heart! 40

Exercise:

The first stanza of this poem may be scanned as follows:

As the flight | of a ri | ver
  That flows | to the sea
My soul | rushes e | ver
  In tu | mult to thee.

As with most anapaestic poems in English, there are many iambic substitutions. The first and third lines have *feminine endings* (*Glossary*), which may be indicated as in the scansion above.

1. Scan the next three stanzas.

2. Is the verse happily chosen for this poem? See the analysis of "The Bells of Shandon" (pp. 114–16). Note that "I" in line 9, "thee" in line 11, and "thou" in line 38 are important rhetorically and deserve emphasis. Does the metrical pattern throw emphasis upon them? Do the metrical pattern and the rhetorical pattern in this poem pull against each other or in harmony with each other?

Absence

JOHN HOSKINS [1566–1638]

Absence, hear my protestation
  Against thy strength,
  Distance and length,
Do what thou canst for alteration:
  For hearts of truest metal 5
  Absence doth join, and time doth settle.

Who loves a mistress of right quality,
  His mind hath found
  Affection's ground
Beyond time, place, and all mortality: 10
  To hearts that cannot vary
  Absence is present, time doth tarry.

My senses want their outward motion
  Which now within
  Reason doth win, 15
Redoubled by her secret notion:
  Like rich men that take pleasure
  In hiding more than handling treasure.

By absence this good means I gain
  That I can catch her 20
  Where none can watch her
In some close corner of my brain:
  There I embrace and kiss her,
  And so enjoy her, and so miss her.

EXERCISE:

1. Scan the last stanza of this poem. (First try to determine the *normal* foot and the *normal* line. In doing this, it is wise to read a number of lines of the poem. The first line (or any other line) of a poem may be highly irregular.)

2. Is the meter in this poem too irregular? Too regular? What is the relation between the metrical pattern and the rhetorical pattern? Compare and contrast this poem on this score with "Absent Yet Present."

3. Can you defend the disposition of substitutions and strong secondary accents in this poem? Do they work against the other patterns of the poem or with them?

To Heaven

BEN JONSON [1573–1637]

Good and great God! can I not think of thee,
But it must straight my melancholy be?
Is it interpreted in me disease,
That, laden with my sins, I seek for ease?
O be thou witness, that the reins dost know 5
And hearts of all, if I be sad for show;
And judge me after, if I dare pretend
To aught but grace, or aim at other end.
As thou art all, so be thou all to me,
First, midst, and last, converted One and Three! 10
My faith, my hope, my love; and, in this state,
My judge, my witness, and my advocate!
Where have I been this while exiled from thee,
And whither rapt, now thou but stoop'st to me?
Dwell, dwell here still! O, being everywhere, 15
How can I doubt to find thee ever here?
I know my state, both full of shame and scorn,
Conceived in sin, and unto labor born,
Standing with fear, and must with horror fall,
And destined unto judgment, after all. 20
I feel my griefs too, and there scarce is ground
Upon my flesh t' inflict another wound;
Yet dare I not complain or wish for death
With holy Paul, lest it be thought the breath
Of discontent; or that these prayers be 25
For weariness of life, not love of thee.

Exercise:

1. Discuss the metrical situation in the first four lines and in line 15.

2. Are the substitutions of trochees for iambs defensible in terms of the dramatically appropriate rhetorical stress?

3. Do hovering accents occur? Have they been used meaningfully or capriciously in this poem?

Ah, Sunflower

WILLIAM BLAKE [1757–1827]

Ah, Sunflower, weary of time,
  Who countest the steps of the sun;
Seeking after that sweet golden clime
  Where the traveller's journey is done;

Where the Youth pined away with desire, 5
  And the pale virgin shrouded in snow,
Arise from their graves, and aspire
  Where my Sunflower wishes to go!

EXERCISE:

This poem is prevailingly anapaestic in meter. Such poems often tend to give a mechanical rhythm. (See pp. 115, 126.) But this poem does not give such an effect, and, as a matter of fact, is characterized by its delicate and lingering rhythm. We can notice that the first foot in lines 1, 2, and 7 constitute iambic substitutions. Relate these substitutions to the context. But the most important item in securing the characteristic rhythm of this poem is the use of what might be called the secondary accent on the first syllable of the anapaest. For example, the following line might be scanned:

Seeking aft | er that sweet | golden clime

The first and the third feet are obviously different in effect from the second foot, which is a normal anapaest. The effect of this situation in the anapaest corresponds to that hovering effect given by the secondary accent in an iambic foot. Work out the scansion of the entire poem.

RHETORICAL VARIATION

It has probably already occurred to the careful reader of poetry that the rhythm of any individual line, as actually experienced by the reader, is determined by other factors than the formal metrical scheme or shifts of metrical accent in that scheme. It should be clear to anyone that no line of verse, however accurately it can be scanned, has a purely mechanical regularity—such a regularity, for instance, as is given by the beat of a metronome. Let us look at the following line:

Not marble, nor the gilded monuments
(Shakespeare, Sonnet 55)

This line can be scanned as iambic pentameter with absolute metrical regularity;

N˘ot már | b˘le nór | t˘he gíld | ˘ed món | ˘u mérnts

The meter would seem to demand an equal accent on each of the syllables indicated. This might be graphed as follows:

Not mar | ble nor | the gild | ed mon | u ments

But obviously some accented syllables are more important than others, and no one would ever read the line as a purely mechanical sing-song. In earlier comments on meter the student has undoubtedly realized that the marking of accents did not mean the same stress, in practice, would be given to each syllable so indicated. The degree of emphasis dictated by the *sense* would also have to be taken into account. For instance, in the line given above, the word *nor* as a conjunction would not receive as much emphasis as some other syllables. Or, to take another case, *-ments* in the word *monuments* cannot receive an emphasis equal to that on *mon-* because the word *monuments* is, as a matter of fact, accented on the first syllable. To sum up, any but a purely mechanical reading of the line must take into account such variations as these we have described. On this basis the emphatic syllables in the line are *mar-, gild-,* and *mon-*. Variation from a fixed degree of emphasis for the accented syllables because of the requirements of sense may be called *rhetorical variation*. Thus:

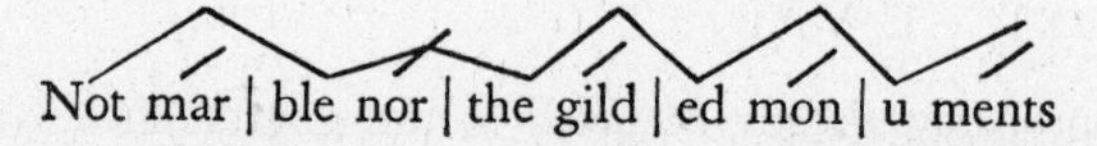

We may describe the situation above by saying that we have three rhetorical accents (first, third, and fourth feet), or by saying that we have three major and two minor accents. That is, we want to indicate some difference in level, as it were, between the accent on the first foot, for example, and that on the second. There is no absolute line of demarcation between the major and minor; it is a distinction that may in some instances be debatable. But in general the ear has no great difficulty in making the distinction.[1]

Once the distinction is made we see that the placing of the major accents in relation to the minor accents has some effect on the verse. If the major accents fall in the same position in every line, we get a monotonous effect. In certain instances this repetition may be appropriate, it may give the effect the poet wishes, a weightiness, an emphasis, the pointing up of a parallel construction, or something of the sort. But by and large the poet aims at a variety in the placing of the major accents to give the verse flexibility and vibration.

This factor of rhetorical variation appears in all verse, because it exists by the very nature of language; and this factor is one which the competent poet attempts to control. Francis Mahony in "The Bells of Shandon" has so neglected the relation of the rhetorical pattern to the metrical pattern that one has to read certain parts of the poem as mechanical singsong, distorting the sense, or has to read them according to sense, distorting the metrical pattern past recognition. For instance:

> There's a bell | in Mos | cow,
> While on tow | er and kiosk | O!
> In Saint | Sophi | a
>   The Turk | man gets,
> And loud | in air
> Calls men | to pray | er
> From tap | ering sum | mits
>   Of tall | minarets

[1] Just as accented syllables do not have the same level, neither do the unaccented syllables. Differences in level among the unaccented syllables, their relative lightness and heaviness, modify the quality of the verse. There is no system for indicating such subtle distinctions, but the ear is aware of them if we really attend to the verse.

Here we may see that the exclamation *O* in the second line, which by all sense, or rhetorical, requirements should be heavily accented, is treated according to the metrical pattern as a weak syllable. For an example of very effective co-ordination of metrical and rhetorical factors we may return to "After Long Silence" (p. 116). Let us inspect the relation of the pause which marks the rhetorical units in line 1 to the meaning.

‸Speech | after long | silence; || ‸it | is right

Such a pause is usually called a *caesura* (*Glossary*). The caesura in line 1 falls after the word *silence*. That is, one word group is completed at that point and another word group is begun. The pause here contributes to the weight of the accent on *it,* and we also have a metrical situation which, as we have said in our previous discussion (p. 119), is dramatically right. Or for another example, let us look at line 6. The line may be scanned and the caesura marked as follows:

Upon | the supreme |‸theme || of Art | and Song

The sense division gives us two word groups which are marked by the caesura. But we see the significant metrical pause between *supreme* and *theme,* which we have discussed earlier (p. 120). The caesura and the metrical pause before *theme* isolate, as it were, and emphasize that word; and the rime with *supreme* also contributes to the emphasis. And it can be easily observed that *theme* also takes the greatest rhetorical emphasis, with *supreme,* which is also emphasized heavily on metrical grounds, next in importance. A general consideration of this poem in contrast with "The Bells of Shandon" will show that the meter, the rhetorical variations, and the other factors, such as imagery, supplement and corroborate each other. That is, we have a real coherence and unity.

We have been discussing the relation of the various aspects of meter and variations from strict metrical regularity to what is being said in a given poem. Here is a famous passage of verse written to illustrate some of the principles which we have been discussing. The student should attempt to see how fully the poet justifies his statement that the sound should echo the sense, and to ascertain the means which he employs.

Sound and Sense

ALEXANDER POPE [1688–1744]

True ease in writing comes from art, not chance,
As those move easiest who have learned to dance.
'T is not enough no harshness gives offense,
The sound must seem an echo to the sense:
Soft is the strain when Zephyr gently blows, 5
And the smooth stream in smoother numbers flows:
But when loud surges lash the sounding shore,
The hoarse, rough verse should like the torrent roar:
When Ajax strives some rock's vast weight to throw,
The line too labors, and the words move slow; 10
Not so, when swift Camilla scours the plain,
Flies o'er th' unbending corn, and skims along the main.
Hear how Timotheus' varied lays surprise,
And bid alternate passions fall and rise! 15

(From "An Essay on Criticism")

EXERCISE:

Though this passage is written in iambic pentameter couplets, there is actually a great deal of variety in the verse. Moreover, Pope is practicing in this passage what he is preaching: he is making the sound "seem an echo to the sense."

1. Indicate the instances of hovering accents.

2. Note that Pope sometimes uses clusters of consonants difficult to pronounce rapidly (see *Glossary* for *cacophonous effects*). Where do these clusters occur? What use is the poet making of them?

3. Note that one line has twelve syllables rather than the normal ten. Is this an instance of clumsiness on the poet's part, or is it calculation?

FURTHER EXERCISES:

1. Scan lines 25–34 of "Out, Out" (p. 2). What substitutions do you find? What instances of rhetorical variation? Can you justify them in terms of the meaning of the poem?

2. Note the hovering accents in the fourth stanza of "Proud Maisie" (p. 53). What effect do they give? Is the effect dramatically justified?

3. Scan "A Slumber Did My Spirit Seal" (p. 54). Note that the last line of this poem is probably the least varied line in it—

With rócks | and stónes | and trées.

Why has Wordsworth insisted upon the regularity of the meter here? What effect is produced?

4. Study the "Ode to the West Wind" (p. 98) as an instance of the principle of rhetorical variation.

5. In many of the lines of "Westminster Bridge" (p. 101), the first syllable of the line is heavily accented (the first foot being a trochee substituted for the expected iamb, or else having a heavily stressed secondary accent). Why has the poet handled his meter in this fashion? Can you justify him?

6. Scan lines 11–30 of "The Death of the Hired Man" (p. 39). Study the poet's variations from the iambic pentameter norm, and relate his handling of the metrical factors to the other elements in the poem.

7. Scan lines 45–52 of "Lucy Gray" (p. 66). Is the metrical pattern in these lines used effectively to support the rhetorical pattern? The word "by," for example, usually receives light stress. Here it is heavily stressed, and appropriately so. How does the metrical pattern affect the emphasis on certain other words of this sort?

QUANTITATIVE VARIATION AND ONOMATOPOEIA

There remains to be considered one more important kind of variation from the regularity that would be dictated by meter. This variation involves the question of time. Some syllables require a relatively longer time than others for pronunciation. Syllables containing long vowels or syllables containing several consonants, for example, require a longer time than other syllables. This means that, for example, one iambic foot may be really longer than another iambic foot, or one iambic pentameter line longer than another. For instance, both of the following lines are iambic pentameter:

'Mid hushed, cool-rooted flowers fragrant-eyed
("Ode to Psyche," John Keats)

How soon they find fit instruments of ill
("Rape of the Lock," Alexander Pope)

By the very nature of language what we may call the *quantitative aspect* (*Glossary*) will vary from line to line. From syllable to syllable different lengths of time are required for pronunciation. This factor is constantly interplaying with the strictly metrical factor. For instance, a syllable that is long in quantity may or may not receive a metrical accent. In the line by Keats given above, the foot, *cool-root-*, is composed of two very long syllables; there is a hovering effect in the accentuation, but the foot fits the iambic pattern. The mere fact of the interplay of the quantitative with the strictly metrical factor gives a vitality to verse. But, further, the quantitative factor may sometimes be adjusted to special effects, as in the line by Keats which is quoted above.

In regard to the relation of verse effects to the meaning, it may be well to comment on the special relation which is called *onomatopoeia* (*Glossary*). The word means properly *name-making*. Words that are imitative of their own literal meanings are *onomatopoeic*. For example: *bang, fizz, hiss, crackle, murmur, moan, whisper, roar*. We may observe that all of the words listed here denote special sounds. *The sound of a word can only be truly imitative of a sound, and only to such words can the term onomatopoeia be strictly applied*. Obviously, onomatopoeia can be only occasional in poetry. An example often given is found in the following lines from Tennyson's "Princess":

The moan of doves in immemorial elms,
And murmuring of innumerable bees.

We have two strictly onomatopoeic words in these lines, *moan* and *murmuring*. The poet, in each line, supports and extends the particular onomatopoeic effect by repeating the sounds found in the onomatopoeic word. For instance, in the first line, the *m* and *o* are repeated in "i*mm*e*mo*rial el*m*s." Since the particular sound association has been already established by the denotation of *moan*, the repetitions of the sounds become part of the onomatopoeic effect.

The same principle is at work in the next line. But if, for example, the line were not introduced by the specific meaning of *moan* it is highly improbable that anyone would discover onomatopoeia in the line.

It is important to insist upon at least a relatively strict interpretation of the term onomatopoeia and of onomatopoeic effects, for it is very easy for an unwary critic to attribute to onomatopeia effects which arise from other causes. Such critics attribute a particular imitative meaning to the sound of a word, when at best only a general suitability, usually arising from causes which we have been discussing in this section, can actually be observed. For example, here is what one critic has written of a certain line of Edna St. Vincent Millay's poetry:

"But she gets many different effects with clusters of unaccented syllables. With the many *f*'s and *r*'s and *th*'s a fine feeling of fluffiness is given to one line by the many unaccented syllables:

Cómfort, sófter than the féathers of its bréast,

sounds as soft as the bird's downy breast feels."

But another critic challenges this interpretation, as follows: ". . . the effect [is said to be] a fine feeling of fluffiness and a softness as of the bird's downy breast, while the cause is said to be the many unaccented syllables, assisted by the many *f*'s, *r*'s and *th*'s. But I will substitute a line which preserves all these factors and departs from the given line mainly by rearrangement:

Crumpets for the foster-fathers of the brats.

Here I miss fluffiness and the downiness." [1]

In the same way, one might imagine a critic stating that the following line by Keats is onomatopoeic, and identifying the suggestion of coolness and repose with the presence of certain vowel and consonant sounds:

'Mid hushed, cool-rooted flowers fragrant-eyed.

The line may give an effect of coolness and repose, *but the effect is not to be identified with specific vowels or consonants, nor are*

[1] John Crowe Ransom, "The Poet as Woman," *The World's Body,* New York: Charles Scribner's Sons, 1938, pp. 96–97.

specific vowels and consonants to be defined as the cause of the impression. What one can say of the sound effect of the line is this. The hovering accent on the foot, *cool-root-,* and the length and sonority of the vowels repeated in the foot, emphasize these words, which with the accented word *hushed* just preceding, set the whole impression of coolness and repose; but the words set this impression primarily by their literal meanings. The function of the verse as such is highly important, but important in supporting and stressing the meaning. Close analysis of the elements of verse is extremely valuable for any reader of poetry. But such analysis runs into absurdity when the reader begins to forget the cardinal principle which has already been stated several times: poetry is a result of a relationship among various elements and does not ever inhere specially in any single element.

The Blindness of Samson

JOHN MILTON [1608–1674]

O loss of sight, of thee I most complain!
Blind among enemies, O worse than chains,
Dungeon, or beggary, or decrepit age!
Light, the prime work of God, to me is extinct,
And all her various objects of delight 5
Annulled, which might in part my grief have eased,
Inferior to the vilest now become
Of man or worm; the vilest here excel me,
They creep, yet see, I dark in light exposed
To daily fraud, contempt, abuse and wrong, 10
Within doors, or without, still as a fool,
In power of others, never in my own;
Scarce half I seem to live, dead more than half.
O dark, dark, dark, amid the blaze of noon,
Irrecoverably dark, total eclipse 15
Without all hope of day!
O first created beam, and thou great Word,
Let there be light, and light was over all;
Why am I thus bereaved Thy prime decree?
The sun to me is dark 20
And silent as the moon.

When she deserts the night
Hid in her vacant interlunar cave.
Since light so necessary is to life,
And almost life itself, if it be true 25
That light is in the soul,
She all in every part; why was the sight
To such a tender ball as th' eye confined?
So obvious and so easy to be quenched,
And not as feeling through all parts diffused, 30
That she might look at will through every pore?
Then had I not been thus exiled from light;
As in the land of darkness yet in light,
To live a life half dead, a living death,
And buried; but O yet more miserable! 35
Myself, my sepulcher, a moving grave.

(From *Samson Agonistes*)

Exercise:

In Milton's play, Samson speaks this passage under the following circumstances: he has been betrayed by his wife Delilah to his enemies the Philistines, who have blinded him and chained him to the mill as a slave. See *Judges:* Chapter 16.

1. Discuss metrical variation in the first five lines of this passage and in line 14.

2. What is the reason for the unusual grammatical construction in lines 17 and 18?

3. Why, in lines 20 and 21, does Samson say that the sun is silent as the moon? Since the sun is, of course, silent, what is served by this statement?

4. Comment on metrical variation in line 35.

Further Exercises:

1. Note the onomatopoeic and quasi-onomatopoeic effects in the "Ode to the West Wind" (p. 98). How are these related to the development of the poem?

2. Scan lines 39–42 of "Preludes" (p. 103). How does the metrical effect support the meaning here? What part is played by the alliteration? Does the meter of lines 53–55 seem to "go to pieces"? Is this the result of clumsiness or ineptitude on the part of the poet? What is the approximate effect? And how is it related to the theme of the poem?

3. Are there any instances of onomatopoeia in the last stanza of "To Autumn" (p. 92)? Are the metrical variations in the last stanza mere metrical tricks or are they closely related to the meaning of the poem? How are they related?

4. Are there any instances of onomatopoeia in "Sound and Sense" (p. 133)? Where? How is the onomatopoeic effect supported by other elements in the line?

RIME

All of our previous discussion in this section of the book has been concerned with aspects of rhythm. We have pointed out that rhythm is a constant factor in all use of language, and that its use in verse is a special adaptation. But there are other factors that tend to shape and bind poetry, factors that are not ever-present in the use of language. These are *alliteration, assonance, consonance,* and *rime* (*Glossary*). All of these involve the element of repetition of identical or of related sounds; and it is this repetition that gives the impression of a binding of the words together.

In poetry written during the Old English period the device of alliteration was used regularly for the purpose of defining a poetic scheme. The following lines illustrate, in modern English, the way alliteration was used to give lines unity, just as meter tends to unify a line:

> Now *B*eowulf *b*ode in the *b*urg of the Scyldings,
> *l*eader be*l*ovèd, and *l*ong he ruled
> in *f*ame with all *f*olk, since his *f*ather had gone
> a*w*ay from the *w*orld, till a*w*oke an heir . . .
>
> (From *Beowulf,* translated by Francis B. Gummere)

But now alliteration is not used in verse according to any regular scheme. Where it occurs frequently, as in the work of Swinburne, it often impresses the reader as a mechanical and monotonous mannerism or a too gaudy decoration. Most poets use it with discretion to give a line or a group of lines a greater unity or to emphasize the words alliterated. In the following lines we can see how alliteration is used to emphasize and support the contrast in the second line and to relate the contrast to the word, *forgot:*

Hast thou *f*orgot me then, and do I seem
Now in thine eye so *f*oul, once deemed so *f*air
(From *Paradise Lost,* Book II)

Assonance may sometimes serve the same purposes of binding or emphasis. In the following line from Keats, one already given for other illustration, we can see a good example of assonance used for emphasis:

'Mid hushed, c*oo*l-r*oo*ted flowers fragrant-eyed

We have already pointed out the effect of the hovering accent in the foot c*oo*l-r*oo*t- and of the length and sonority of the vowel sound (p. 136). The repetition of this vowel sound, that is, the assonance, lends even greater emphasis. Let us examine another example:

Or Alum st*y*ptics w*i*th contract*i*ng pow'r
Shr*i*nk h*i*s th*i*n essence like a r*i*veled flow'r;
Or, as *I*xion f*i*xed, the wretch shall feel
The g*i*dd*y* motion of the whirl*i*ng M*i*ll . . .
(From *The Rape of the Lock,* Canto II)

Here it is obvious that the sustained assonance, involving both accented and unaccented syllables, gives a high degree of unification. We can also see that emphasis is secured by the repetition in new combinations of the vowel sounds of the more important syllables. But the quality of the particular "run" here is of some significance, for the tight frontal sound is appropriate to, and supports, the general idea of the passage. (See also L. C. Knights on "Be No More Grieved," pp. 152–53; and the analysis of "Lucifer in Starlight," pp. 367–73.)

Consonance occurs much more rarely than assonance, but is sometimes used much more systematically. In the following lines we see consonance serving to link lines in the same way as rime:

You are the one whose part it is to *lean,*
For whom it is not good to be *alone.*
Laugh warmly turning shyly in the *hall*
Or climb with bare knees the volcanic *hill.* . . .
(From "III," *Poems,* by W. H. Auden)

Consonance is not confined, however, to such cases, but may occur internally in a single line or in several lines to serve the same general function as assonance. This use, however, is much rarer than the use of mere alliteration or assonance.

Rime is the most emphatic binder used in English verse. Alliteration, assonance, and consonance may be regarded as types of rime; that is, they derive from sound resemblances. But it is customary to confine the use of the term *rime* to instances of end-rime. There are several types of rime, *masculine, feminine, weak*, etc. (*Glossary*).

Rime serves usually, as we have already said, to bind lines together into larger units of composition. We have already seen that the metrical scheme of a single line does its work by setting up in the mind of the hearer or reader an anticipation of regular recurrence. In the same way a fixed pattern of riming, a *rime scheme*, will, in conjunction with a fixed pattern of line lengths, a *stanza* (*Glossary*), define a group of lines as a unit. In stanzas where rime is employed the rime emphasizes the nature of the stanza pattern by marking the end of each line unit. But rime is sometimes used irregularly; in such cases, it still exerts a binding and unifying effect, though much less forcefully. In addition, irregular rime may appear as a device of emphasis, in so far as it has not been used consistently in the poem or passage. The basic function of rime, however, has already been described: the unifying and "forming" function, which is most positively exhibited in the reinforcing of the line pattern of stanzas.[1]

FURTHER EXERCISES:

1. Is the alliteration used in "Proud Maisie" (p. 53) merely decorative? Or is it functional?

2. What use of alliteration does Pope make in "Sound and Sense" (p. 133)? Note particularly the effect of the alliteration in lines 5-6.

3. Can you justify the irregular riming in "Patterns" (p. 55)? Note that certain passages are much more fully interlaced with rime than others. Compare lines 61–73 (2 words rimed) with lines 91–107 (12 words rimed) or with lines 10–27 (12 words rimed).

[1] Although the function of rime as a structural factor is emphasized here, there is, of course, a pleasure intrinsic in rime itself. Children, for example, delight even in nonsense rimes. But the functional use of rime is much more important than the "decorative" use (*Glossary* under *rime*).

4. In "After Apple-Picking" (p. 89) all the lines are rimed. Is the arrangement of the rimes purely haphazard and capricious? Or can you find any sort of justification for it?

STANZA FORMS

There are many different stanza forms in use in English poetry. A student may consult the *Glossary* for systematic definitions of them. A knowledge of the stanza types is important, of course; but *any given type of stanza must be regarded as an instrument at the poet's disposal and not as a thing important in itself.* The same instrument may be used for widely different purposes. Any given type of stanza is used in conjunction with so many other poetic factors that a reader must be very wary of attributing special effects to special stanza forms. Only the most general principles may be arrived at concerning stanza forms considered in isolation from other poetic factors. For instance, it is fair to say that complicated stanza forms such as the *Spenserian stanza* (*Glossary*) offer disadvantages for use in long narrative poems because the involved form may become monotonous and may impede the movement of the action. But the folly of asserting, as many people have, that the *sonnet* (*Glossary*) is especially adapted for love poetry will be demonstrated by the following pair of sonnets:

How Do I Love Thee?

ELIZABETH BARRETT BROWNING [1809–1861]

How do I love thee? Let me count the ways.
I love thee to the depth and breadth and height
My soul can reach, when feeling out of sight
For the ends of Being and ideal Grace.
I love thee to the level of everyday's 5
Most quiet need, by sun and candle-light.
I love thee freely, as men strive for Right;
I love thee purely, as they turn from Praise.
I love thee with the passion put to use
In my old griefs, and with my childhood's faith. 10

I love thee with a love I seemed to lose
With my lost saints,—I love thee with the breath,
Smiles, tears, of all my life!—and, if God choose,
I shall but love thee better after death.
(From *Sonnets from the Portuguese*)

On the Late Massacre in Piedmont

JOHN MILTON [1608–1674]

Avenge, O Lord, thy slaughtered saints, whose bones
Lie scattered on the Alpine mountains cold;
Ev'n them who kept thy truth so pure of old,
When all our fathers worshipped stocks and stones,
Forget not: in thy book record their groans 5
Who were thy sheep, and in their ancient fold
Slain by the bloody Piedmontese, that rolled
Mother with infant down the rocks. Their moans
The vales redoubled to the hills, and they
To heav'n. Their martyred blood and ashes sow 10
O'er all th' Italian fields, where still doth sway
The triple Tyrant that from these may grow
A hundredfold, who, having learnt thy way,
Early may fly the Babylonian woe.

These sonnets have precisely the same rime scheme, both being examples of what is called the *Italian sonnet* (*Glossary*). But the difference in subject matter and treatment is obvious, and this simple example should indicate why one should be extremely cautious in assuming that any effect or subject matter is absolutely associated with a particular stanza form. The proper approach to the study of the significance of stanza form may be through this question: *How does the poet use his stanza form in any given poem to produce the special effect of that poem?*

In answering this question in any instance, one must bring into play all the principles which have been previously discussed in this section. But there are still other principles which must be taken into consideration in answering this question. In particular, there is the consideration of the relation of the rhetorical structure, not only to the metrical pattern within the line, which we have already discussed (pp. 130–31) but also to the stanza pattern itself. Obviously the distribution of pauses within the lines (p. 132) and of pauses at the ends of lines will have an important bearing on the general effect of any stanza form. Stanzas that have a large number of marked pauses at the ends of lines tend to be strongly defined; stanzas that have many run-over lines, or *enjambments* (*Glossary*), tend to give an impression of fluidity and speed. But the effects of the distribution of pauses at the ends of lines are constantly conditioned by the rhythms used within the lines themselves and by the distribution and emphasis of pauses within the lines.

The student has already encountered a number of rime schemes and stanza forms in the earlier pages of this book—blank verse, for example, in "Out, Out" (p. 2), "Michael" (p. 23), and "The Death of the Hired Man" (p. 38); octosyllabic couplets in "Hell Gate" (p. 61); pentameter (or heroic) couplets in "To Heaven" (p. 128) and "Sound and Sense" (p. 133); terza rima in "Ode to the West Wind" (p. 98); and various kinds of quatrains in "Dust of Snow" (p. 79), "Ah, Sunflower" (p. 129), "Lord Randal" (p. 48), "Desert Places" (p. 86), "Proud Maisie" (p. 53), etc. For definitions of some of the more important stanza forms in English, the student should consult the *Glossary;* for a systematic account of the various rime schemes and stanza forms to be found in this book, he should consult the "Index of Stanza Forms." But it cannot be too much emphasized that a mere knowledge of stanza forms as abstract and mechanical patterns has little to do with the reading of poetry. The student's aim should be to see what the poet has been able to do with the particular form that he has chosen.

Rose Aylmer

WALTER SAVAGE LANDOR [1775–1864]

Ah, what avails the sceptred race,
  Ah, what the form divine!
What every virtue, every grace!
  Rose Aylmer, all were thine.

Rose Aylmer, whom these wakeful eyes 5
May weep, but never see,
A night of memories and of sighs
I consecrate to thee.

Like "After Long Silence," this poem seems perfectly straightforward in its statement. But the statement alone does not give us the poem—that is, other factors are required to make the statement come alive for us. One thing that serves very obviously to convert the bare statement into poetry is the use made of the various elements which we have previously discussed in this general section. As a preliminary to analysis we may mark the accents:

Ah, what | avails | the scep | tred race,
Ah, what | the form | divine!
What ev | ery vir | tue, ev | ery grace!
Rose Ayl | mer, all | were thine.

Rose Ayl | mer, whom | these wake | ful eyes 5
May weep, | but nev | er see,
A night | of mem | ories and | of sighs
I con | secrate | to thee.

In the first stanza, in the first foot of every line, we may note the hovering accent, and the length of the first syllable of the foot. These factors tend to give an unusual emphasis to those feet, especially since the remainder of each line is characterized by a very positive difference between accented and unaccented syllables; and those feet, by the repetitions, set the basic attitude of questioning. The marked regularity of the metrical pattern of each line, the definite stop at the end of each line, and the repetition involved in the first three lines—all of these factors contribute to a formal and elevated tone. (We can notice the formal tone supported, further, by the repetitive balance of the first and second lines, which is repeated by the balance within the third line. "What every virtue" is balanced against "[what] every grace." And we can notice how the distinction between the first and second parts of the line is marked by the pause, which tends to cause greater emphasis to fall on the first syllable of *every*.)

The first line of the second stanza, with the repetition of the name *Rose Aylmer,* picks up the metrical pattern characteristic of the first stanza, providing a kind of transition between the rhythm characteristic of the first stanza and that characteristic of the second. The difference in the rhythm of the second stanza is caused chiefly by the run-on lines, the absence of the hovering accents on the initial syllables of the last three lines, and the metrical accenting of syllables not usually accented. We may try to relate some of these special details to the meaning of the poem.

The first run-on line serves to emphasize the word *weep:* since the sense unit is so radically divided by the line end, when we do pick up the rest of the clause at the beginning of the second line, it comes with a feeling of emphatic fulfilment, which is further supported by the marked pause after the word *weep*. The emphasis on the word *weep* is, of course, rhetorically right because it is set over in contrast with the word *see* at the end of the second line. And we may also observe how the alliteration of the word *weep* with the word *wakeful* in the preceding line helps to mark the association of the two ideas: it is not merely weeping which is to be contrasted with seeing, but the lonely weeping at night when the sense of loss becomes most acute.

The third line is also a run-on line, giving a kind of balance to the structure of the stanza, which functions as do the various balances of structure in the first stanza. Although neither the first line nor the third line of the second stanza is punctuated at the end, we can see that the tendency to run on into the next line is not so strong in the third line as in the first; we can see that the phrase "whom these wakeful eyes" strikes us with a more marked sense of incompleteness than does the phrase "A night of memories and of sighs." This is especially true because the first of the two phrases, coming early in the stanza, is less supported by a context, by the sense of things preceding it. But, even though the tendency to run on is not so strong in the third line as in the first, the tendency is still marked; and such a tendency to enjambment fixes our attention on the clause, "I consecrate," which begins the last line, and forces a pause after that clause.

The word *consecrate,* which is thereby emphasized, is very important. We can see how important it is, and how effective it is in avoiding a sentimental or stereotyped effect, by substituting other words which convey approximately the same meaning. For instance, the lines might be re-written:

> A night of memories and of sighs
> I now will give to thee.

We immediately see a great difference. The re-written passage tends toward sentimentality. The word *consecrate* means "to set apart perpetually for sacred uses"; it implies the formality and impersonality of a ceremony. This implication in conjunction with the formality of tone, which has already been discussed in connection with the technique of the first stanza, helps to prevent any suggestion of self-pity.

Another technical feature appears in the use of the word *consecrate,* which does not appear in the re-written line

> I now will give to thee.

The word *consecrate* is accented in ordinary usage on the first syllable. But when the word is used in this poem, meter dictates an additional accent on the last syllable, for the line is to be scanned as follows:

> I˘ cón | se˘cráte | to˘ thée.

Thus the metrical situation tends to give the word an emphasis which it would not possess in ordinary prose usage; and this is appropriate because of the importance of the word in the poem.

Exercise:

1. What would have been the difference in effect if the poet had written, in the next to the last line, "an age" instead of "a night"?

2. Discuss the effect of the accent on the ordinarily unimportant word *and* in the same line.

A Deep-Sworn Vow

WILLIAM BUTLER YEATS [1865–1939]

Others because you did not keep
That deep-sworn vow have been friends of mine;
Yet always when I look death in the face,
When I clamber to the heights of sleep,
Or when I grow excited with wine, 5
Suddenly I meet your face.

The theme of this poem is the lasting impression made by a love-affair which has been broken off, apparently long ago, and which has been superseded by other friendships. On the conscious level of the mind, the loved one has been forgotten, but the image is still carried indelibly imprinted on the deeper, unconscious mind.

When we come to consider how this theme is made concrete and forceful in its statement in the poem, we must consider of course such matters as tone, imagery, structure of incidents, etc. For example, there is the contrast of the almost casual tone of the opening of the poem and the tone of excitement with which the poem ends. One notices also the arrangement of the three instances which the lover gives of the moments when the face suddenly appears to him: at moments of great danger, in sleep when the subconscious is released, and in moments of intoxication. The last item balances the first: the poet does not intend to falsify the experience by saying, "Only when I look death in the face, I remember you." The memory comes also when the occasion is one of no seriousness at all—merely one of conviviality. And yet the three classes of occasions, though they contrast with each other in their associations, all reinforce one particular idea: the face appears when concern for the immediate, self-conscious everyday existence has been let down—for whatever reason.

One needs to inspect the imagery too, though this poem is relatively bare of imagery. One notices, however, that the image in the line

When I clamber to the heights of sleep

supports the theme. Sleep, we usually think of as completely passive, yet the image is one of difficult action, and of attainment after such action—as if her face lay over a mountain ridge and as if sleep were a sort of search in which the poet managed (the implication is "with difficulty and not often") to reach the top and be granted the vision.

Yet important as are all the details of this sort which have been mentioned, we shall have to examine the metrical arrangement and rime scheme of this poem before we can account for its effectiveness. The poem may be scanned as follows:

> Others | because | you did | not keep |
> That deep | sworn vow | have been friends | of mine; |
> Yet al | ways when | I look | death | in the face, |
> When I clam | ber to | the heights | of sleep, |
> Or when | I grow | exci | ted with wine, | 5
> Suddenly | I meet | your face. |

The poem is highly irregular. There is a considerable variation in the kinds of lines, trimeter, tetrameter, and pentameter; though the basic foot is of two syllables, some feet are defective and others have three syllables—that is, are anapaestic or dactylic. Moreover, there are, one notices, a number of hovering accents. But the irregularity in this poem is far from a haphazard matter. If we examine the poem carefully we shall see that the irregularity supports the meaning of the poem.

The tone of the first lines, we have already pointed out, is that of calm, unexcited statement. There is no anger or bitterness toward the woman who did not keep her vow. And this tone is supported by the casual rhythm of the line. One notices that the poet does not emphasize the word, *you,* but the word, *others*. The accent is thrown on the first syllable of *others,* and the word, *you,* does not receive a metrical accent at all, though rhetorical considerations throw some emphasis on it, and there is, because of the competition here between rhetoric and meter, a slight hover on the foot, *you did,* and on the foot, *not keep.*[1] This hovering accent in each case retards the movement; and the substitution of the trochaic foot, *others,* for the normal iamb forces a slight pause before the word, *because*—a pause which is justified by the rhetorical emphasis: there is a contrast between the conduct of the "others" and that of the loved one.

The second line is highly irregular. There is a decided hovering accent on the foot, *sworn vow,* and the long syllables here, plus the foregoing accented long syllable, *deep,* urge the reader to give all three syllables decided emphasis, and force him to pause before going on with the rest of the line. One notices, also, that the sense unit does not terminate with the end of the first line but runs on rapidly to the second. The important phrase, "deep-sworn vow," is thus isolated, as it were, for emphasis.

The attempt to reassert the metrical pattern at the end of the second line causes a rather heavy accent to be placed on the words, *friends* and *mine.* This is proper, for the word, *friends,* is important. The speaker has carefully chosen this word rather than some other word, such as, say, *lovers.* The quieter, more guarded word is important for the tone which the poet wishes to establish in the opening lines of the poem. The word, *friends,* stands as a correlative of the word, *others.*

The next three lines of the poem are more regular, and in the three instances of memory which the poet gives, the basic pattern is more clearly affirmed and established in the reader's mind. One notices, however, that in the third line, the syllable, *-ways,* receives a rather definite secondary accent. The word, *always,* is, thus, emphasized and dwelt upon—quite properly, for it is the important

[1] Some readers will prefer to mark these feet thus:

you did not keep,

feeling that *you* and *not* are quite as heavily accented as *did* and *keep.* Some readers will prefer to mark the first foot of the third line as regular:

Yet al-.

The important thing to remember is that the scansion is simply a pointer to variations of which we should be aware but cannot hope to define adequately short of a very elaborate system of notation.

word here. In this same line there is also a rather marked pause between the words, *look* and *death,* because both words are accented.[1] The defect in the foot, *death,* is compensated for by the substitution of an anapaest for an iamb in the following foot, and by the pause after the word *look*.

The fourth line, with the exception of one detail, the substitution of an anapaest for an iamb in the first foot, is regular, and asserts the pattern which has been obscured to some extent by the variations of lines 2 and 3.

The fifth line has a rapid movement which is consonant with the sense of the line and with the effect of rapid, casual, even careless excitement. The movement may be accounted for in its metrical aspect as follows: The last foot of the line represents an anapaestic substitution for the expected iamb, and the extra syllable speeds up the end of the line. This added speed results from the following special situation. The fact that the first syllable of the last foot, *-ted,* is an integral part of the word, *excited,* demands that the anapaest be given unusual speed if the syllable, *-ted,* is to be drawn into the last foot at all. (Contrast the situation in this anapaest with the situation in the anapaest at the beginning of the fourth line. See Exercise on "Ah, Sunflower," p. 129.)

Moreover, this last substitution helps to bring into sharper focus the substitution made in the last line of the poem, where a dactyl is substituted for the iamb in the first foot. The abrupt shock given by this substitution (the accent on the syllable, *sud-,* follows immediately after the heavy accent on the word, *wine*) and the pause after *suddenly* prepare us for the climax of the poem, which appears in the phrase, "I meet your face." Other factors in the last line tend to underscore the climax. The line has only three accents, two less than line three, and one less than any other line. The reader, conditioned to the longer line, is prompted to take this line more slowly. The reader is further encouraged to do this by the fact that the word *your,* from rhetorical considerations, demands a rather strong accent. This provides a hovering effect on the last foot. The pause after *suddenly,* the strong accent on *meet,* and the

[1] In connection with this pause, see also the Exercise on "In Tenebris, I," p. 154.

definite hover on the phrase *your face,* give an effect of reserved and solemn statement.

One observes that the rime scheme is a, b, c, a, b, c. But *c* is a repetition, and not a rime. The repetition suggests that death's face, at moment of crisis when the speaker meets it, is somehow equated for him with the face of the lost love. The reader expects the rime, and the repetition, therefore, comes with an appropriate shock. The face is, as it were, echoed, and echoed at the climactic point of the poem, where the meter has helped to prepare us to receive the whole implication.

No More Be Grieved

WILLIAM SHAKESPEARE [1564–1616]

No more be grieved at that which thou hast done,
Roses have thorns, and silver fountains mud,
Clouds and eclipses stain both Moon and Sun,
And loathsome canker lives in sweetest bud.
All men make faults, and even I in this, 5
Authorizing thy trespass with compare,
My self corrupting salving thy amiss,
Excusing thy sins more than thy sins are:
For to thy sensual fault I bring in sense,
Thy adverse party is thy Advocate, 10
And 'gainst myself a lawful plea commence,
Such civil war is in my love and hate,
That I an accessory needs must be,
To that sweet thief which sourly robs from me.

The following analysis of this poem has been made by a modern critic:

The first four lines we may say, both in movement and imagery, are . . . straightforward. The fifth line begins by continuing the excuses, 'All men make faults,' but with an abrupt change of rhythm Shakespeare turns the generalization against himself: 'All men make faults, and even I in this,' *i.e.* in wasting my time finding romantic parallels for your sins, as though intellectual analogies ('sense') were relevant to your sensual fault. The painful complexity of feeling (Shakespeare is at the same time tender towards the sinner and infuriated by his own tenderness) is evident in the seventh line, which means both, 'I corrupt myself when I find excuses for you' (or 'when I comfort myself in this way') and 'I'm afraid I myself make you worse by excusing your faults'; and although there is a fresh change of tone towards the end (the twelfth line is virtually a sigh as he gives up hope of resolving the conflict), the equivocal 'needs must' and the sweet-sour opposition show the continued civil war of the emotions.

Some such comment as this was unavoidable, but it is upon the simplest and most obvious of technical devices that I wish to direct attention. In the first quatrain the play upon the letters *s* and *l* is mainly musical and decorative, but with the change of tone and direction the alliterative *s* becomes a hiss of half-impotent venom:

> All men make faults, and even I in thi*s*,
> Authori*z*ing thy tre*s*pa*ss* with compare,
> My *s*elf corrupting *s*alving thy ami*ss*,
> E*x*cu*s*ing thy *s*in*s* more than thy *s*ins are:
> For to thy *s*en*s*ual fault I bring in *s*en*s*e . . .

The scorn is moderated here, but it is still heard in the slightly rasping note of the last line,

> To that sweet thief which sourly robs from me.

From the fifth line, then, the alliteration is functional: by playing off against the comparative regularity of the rhythm it expresses an important part of the meaning, and helps to carry the experience alive into the mind of the reader.[1]

In Tenebris, I

THOMAS HARDY [1840–1928]

> Wintertime nighs;
> But my bereavement pain
> It cannot bring again:
> Twice no one dies.

[1] L. C. Knights, "Shakespeare's Sonnets." From *Explorations,* New York: George W. Stewart, Inc., 1947, p. 65.

Flower-petals flee; 5
But since it once hath been,
No more that severing scene
Can harrow me.

Birds faint in dread:
I shall not lose old strength 10
In the lone frost's black length:
Strength long since fled!

Leaves freeze to dun;
But friends cannot turn cold
This season as of old 15
For him with none.

Tempests may scath;
But love cannot make smart
Again this year his heart
Who no heart hath. 20

Black is night's cope;
But death will not appall
One who, past doubtings all,
Waits in unhope.

Exercise:

This poem, unlike "Slow, Slow, Fresh Fount" (p. 97), would not be regarded as euphonious. As a matter of fact, there are a number of pauses forced by *cacophonous combinations* (*Glossary*). Are such pauses functional in this poem or are they an indication of inferior craftsmanship? Write a complete analysis of the poem which will deal with this problem.

Further Exercises:

1. Try to justify the poet's choice of a stanza form in "Nightingales" (p. 94), particularly the use of the short third and sixth lines of the stanza.

2. Line 39 of "On a Drop of Dew" (p. 91) is a run-on line. What is the effect? Why is the effect particularly appropriate here?

3. Using Knights's discussion of "No More Be Grieved" (pp. 152–53) as a general model, write an account of Milton's use of metrical factors in "On the Late Massacre in Piedmont" (p. 143). Take particular account of substituted feet, hovering accents, alliteration, consonance, and quantitative variation.

IV

TONE AND ATTITUDE

FOREWORD

The *tone* of a poem indicates the poet's *attitude* toward his subject and toward his audience. In conversation we often imply our attitude by the tone of voice which we use. We are respectful or contemptuous, mocking or reverent. In a poem the poet must of course indicate this tone by his treatment of the material itself; he must so choose and arrange his words that the proper tone will be dictated to the reader of the poem by the poem itself.

Obviously, tone is very important. As we have emphasized again and again, in poetry the important thing is not the intrinsic value of the facts as such; it is rather the value of the poem as an experience, and since this is true, so important an element of the experience as the attitude of the writer toward subject and audience needs careful examination. We praise a poet for being able to set and sustain a tone without breaking it by ineptitude, or we praise him for his ability to shift effectively from one tone to another.

In some of the poems already analyzed, particularly in poems which have a strong dramatic element, such as "Patterns" (p. 55) or "After Long Silence" (p. 116), we have really considered without using the term many questions of tone. In poems with a marked dramatic framework, the tone is usually more easily grasped than in other poems, because the identity of the speaker and his attitude toward the listener (who in cases like "After Long Silence" or "Rose Aylmer" is usually, as it were, a kind of silent character in the little drama) is rather clearly implied or even stated. But all poems involve questions of tone, for all poems, as we have said (*Introduction,* p. liv), are fundamentally dramatic.

In taking up the question of tone, therefore, the student is not approaching a new element. But the poems that follow in this section allow him to inspect more closely the relationship of tone to other elements that go to create the poetic effect. Furthermore, the student can see in these poems illustrations of certain technical devices whereby a poet may define his tone.

Portrait

E. E. CUMMINGS [1894–]

Buffalo Bill's
defunct
who used to
ride a watersmooth-silver
stallion
and break onetwothreefourfive pigeonsjustlikethat
Jesus
he was a handsome man
and what i want to know is
how do you like your blueeyed boy
Mister Death

This poem deals with what is a rather common theme, and treats that theme simply. Death claims all men, even the strongest and most glamorous. How does the poet in treating such a common theme manage to give a fresh and strong impression of it? He might have achieved this effect of course in a number of different ways, and as a matter of fact, the general device which he employs is not simply one device: it is complex. In this case, however, the most prominent element is the unconventional attitude which he takes toward a conventional subject, and in this particular poem, the matter of tone is isolated sufficiently for us to examine it rather easily (though we must not forget either that there are other matters to be examined in this poem or that tone is a factor in every poem).

In the first place, what is the difference between writing

Buffalo Bill's
defunct

and

Buffalo Bill's
dead?

The first carries something of a tone of conscious irreverence. The poet here does not approach the idea of death with the usual and expected respect for the dead. He is matter-of-fact, unawed, and even somewhat flippant and joking. But the things which he picks out to comment on in Buffalo Bill make a strong contrast with the idea of death. The picture called up is one of tremendous vitality and speed: for example, the stallion is mentioned and is described as "watersmooth-silver." The adjective contains not only a visual description of the horse which Buffalo Bill rode but a kinetic description is implied too. How was the horse "watersmooth"? Smooth, graceful, in action. (The poet by running the words together in the next line is perhaps telling us how to read the line, running the words together to give the effect of speed. The way the poem is printed on the page is designed probably to serve the same purpose, the line divisions being intended as a kind of arrangement for punctuation and emphasis. But the odd typography is not of fundamental importance.) The "portrait" of Buffalo Bill given here after the statement that he is "defunct" is a glimpse of him in action breaking five claypigeons in rapid succession as he flashes by on his stallion—the sort of glimpse which one might remember from the performance of the Wild West show in which Buffalo Bill used to star. The exclamation which follows is exactly the sort of burst of boyish approval which might be struck from a boy seeing him in action or remembering him as he saw him. And the quality of "handsome" applies, one feels, not merely to his face but to his whole figure in action.

The next lines carry on the tone of unabashed, unawed, slangy irreverence toward death. Death becomes "Mister Death." The implied figure of the spectator at a performance of the Wild West show helps justify the language and manner of expression used here, making us feel that it is in character. But the question as asked here strikes us on another level. It is a question which no boy would ask; it is indeed one of the old unanswerable questions. But here it is transformed by the tone into something fresh and startling. Moreover, the dashing, glamorous character of the old Indian fighter gets a sharp emphasis. The question may be paraphrased like this: Death, you don't get lads like him every day, do you? The way the question is put implies several things. First, it implies the pathos at the fact that even a man who had such enormous vitality and unfailing youthfulness, had to die. But this pathos is not insisted upon; rather, it is presented indirectly and ironically because of the bantering and flippant attitude given in the question, especially in the phrases "Mister Death" and "blueeyed boy." And in the question, which sums up the whole poem, we also are given the impression that death is not terrible for Buffalo Bill—it is "Mister Death" who stands in some sort of fatherly and prideful relation to the "blueeyed boy."

In attempting to state what the tone is here we have, in trying to state it specifically, perhaps distorted it somewhat. Moreover, we have certainly not given an exhaustive account of the tone of this poem. But what has been said above is perhaps nearly enough complete to let us see how important an element the tone of the poem is. In this case—a case as we have already noted in which it is easy to deal with the tone in some isolation—it is the *tone* which transforms what might be easily a hackneyed and dead poem into something fresh and startling.

Little Trotty Wagtail

JOHN CLARE [1793–1864]

Little trotty wagtail, he went in the rain,
And tittering, tottering sideways he ne'er got straight again,
He stooped to get a worm, and looked up to get a fly,
And then he flew away ere his feathers they were dry.

Little trotty wagtail, he waddled in the mud, 5
And left his little footmarks, trample where he would.
He waddled in the water-pudge, and waggle went his tail,
And chirrupt up his wings to dry upon the garden rail.

Little trotty wagtail, you nimble all about,
And in the dimpling water-pudge you waddle in and out; 10

Your home is nigh at hand, and in the warm pigsty,
So, little Master Wagtail, I'll bid you a good-bye.

EXERCISE:

1. Does the poet manage to give a vivid sense of the bird? What details seem particularly effective?

2. What is the poet's attitude toward the bird? Does he think it cute, charming, funny, foolish, or what? In defining this attitude, what part is played by the realistic details in the description? By the humorous details in the description?

Two Butterflies Went Out at Noon

EMILY DICKINSON [1830–1886]

Two butterflies went out at noon
And waltzed upon a farm,
And then espied circumference
And caught a ride with him;

Then lost themselves and found themselves 5
In eddies of the sun,
Till rapture missed her footing
And both were wrecked in noon.

To all surviving butterflies
Be this biography, 10
Example, and monition
To entomology.

EXERCISE:

Try to define the difference in tone between this and the preceding poem. What is the difference, for example, in the kind of vocabulary used? How seriously intended is the moralizing in the last stanza?

His Prayer to Ben Jonson

ROBERT HERRICK [1591–1674]

When I a verse shall make,
Know I have prayed thee,

For old religion's sake,
Saint Ben, to aid me.

Make the way smooth for me, 5
When I, thy Herrick,
Honoring thee, on my knee
Offer my lyric.

Candles I'll give to thee,
And a new altar; 10
And thou, Saint Ben, shalt be
Writ in my psalter.

An Ode for Ben Jonson

ROBERT HERRICK [1591–1674]

Ah, Ben!
Say how or when
Shall we, thy guests,
Meet at those lyric feasts,
Made at the Sun, 5
The Dog, the Triple Tun;
Where we such clusters had,
As made us nobly wild, not mad?
And yet each verse of thine
Out-did the meat, out-did the frolic wine. 10

My Ben!
Or come again,
Or send to us
Thy wit's great overplus;
But teach us yet 15
Wisely to husband it,
Lest we that talent spend;
And having once brought to an end
That precious stock, the store
Of such a wit the world should have no more. 20

EXERCISE:

Both "His Prayer to Ben Jonson" and "An Ode for Ben Jonson" were written by Herrick to the poet whom he regarded as his friend and master. (Consult the library for information concerning the relationship between the two poets.) In one of these poems the poet adopts a half-playful attitude and in the other an attitude of serious tribute.

1. Attempt to define this difference more closely and more fully; and relate the difference to metrical and other technical factors.

2. Note that in "His Prayer," Ben Jonson is addressed as if he were a saint (in whose honor candles are to be burned, etc.). Is the poet making fun of Jonson? Teasing him? Is the effect to destroy any sense of reverence for Jonson?

3. Which of the two poems indicates the deeper homage to Jonson? Which, the warmer affection? How do you distinguish the two poems as to tone?

Channel Firing

THOMAS HARDY [1840–1928]

That night your great guns, unawares,
Shook all our coffins as we lay,
And broke the chancel window-squares,
We thought it was the Judgment-day

And sat upright. While drearisome 5
Arose the howl of wakened hounds:
The mouse let fall the altar-crumb,
The worms drew back into the mounds,

The glebe cow drooled. Till God called, "No;
It's gunnery practice out at sea 10
Just as before you went below;
The world is as it used to be:

"All nations striving strong to make
Red war yet redder. Mad as hatters
They do no more for Christés sake 15
Than you who are helpless in such matters.

"That this is not the judgment-hour
For some of them's a blessed thing,

For if it were they'd have to scour
Hell's floor for so much threatening . . . 20

"Ha, ha. It will be warmer when
I blow the trumpet (if indeed
I ever do; for you are men,
And rest eternal sorely need)."

So down we lay again. "I wonder, 25
Will the world ever saner be,"
Said one, "than when He sent us under
In our indifferent century!"

And many a skeleton shook his head.
"Instead of preaching forty year," 30
My neighbor Parson Thirdly said,
"I wish I had stuck to pipes and beer."

Again the guns disturbed the hour,
Roaring their readiness to avenge,
As far inland as Stourton Tower, 35
And Camelot, and starlit Stonehenge.

The situation in this poem is a fantastic one. The practice firing of battleships at night in the English Channel (and ironically enough this poem is dated by Hardy in April, 1914) disturbs the sleep of the dead at a church near the coast, and even frightens the church mouse that has been stealing crumbs left from the sacrament, and the worms that have crept out of the mounds. Then God speaks to the dead, telling them that the noise isn't the clap of doom, as they had thought, that it's just the world going about the same old business, with the same old disregard for the teachings of Christ. Then a preacher buried there, thinking how little good his forty years of work had accomplished, says that he regrets not having spent his time in worldly pleasure. Meanwhile the guns continue the firing. To make the situation even more fantastic, the person who speaks the poem is one of the skeletons of the churchyard.

If the situation is fantastic, at what sort of reality is the poet aiming? He is aiming to dramatize a theme, a certain view of human life, a fatalistic and somewhat ironical view of the persistence of evil in human life. The situation, then, is a little fable, or parable.

But what attitude does the poet expect us to take to the unreality of the situation? And how does he define the attitude that he does desire? He approaches the whole matter very casually, playing down rather than up the weird and ghostly element of the situation. A poorer poet, or even a good poet with a very different intention from that of Hardy, might have emphasized the horror of the scene. But Hardy domesticates that horror, as it were, for he puts the poem in the mouth of one of the skeletons; to the skeleton there is naturally nothing unusual and shocking in the surroundings. A poor poet would have emphasized the conventional devices for giving a weird effect, for instance, the dolorous howling of the hounds and the crawling of the grave worms, things that are the stage-properties of horror. Hardy uses these things, but he mixes them with the hungry little church mouse and the cow that is drooling over its cud in the meadow. There is, then, a casual and perhaps slightly ironical approach to the horror.

This casual tone is emphasized by the conversational quality. For instance, observe the effect of the running over of the first stanza into the second, and of the second into the third. This spilling over of a stanza to a full pause in the middle of the first line of the next stanza, breaks up the regular and stately movement of the verse, with a kind of tag. The content of each of these tags that spills over supports the same impression. In the first instance, we would get a much more serious effect if the statement should end with the line

We thought it was the Judgment-day.

But, no. Hardy makes the spill-over tag a kind of anti-climax, almost comic in its effect. The dead do not rise to the sound of the Judgment, filled with hope and terror. They merely sit up in their coffins, a little irritated at being bothered, like people who have been disturbed in their beds at night. The same kind of effect is attained in the tag that spills over into the third stanza,

The glebe cow drooled.

The effect here again is that of a kind of anti-climax and ironical contrast, for the drooling cow follows the grave worms, conventional creatures of horror.

When God speaks, the effect is still conversational and simple. He says: "The world is as it used to be"—a line that might be spoken by any one in ordinary talk. And He uses such a phrase as "Mad as hatters." He even makes a kind of sardonic joke about scouring the floors of hell, and another one, at which He himself laughs, about the time when the trumpet will be blown. And the same tone is held in the following stanzas of dialogue among the skeletons. The whole effect, thus far, is a mixture of the grotesque and the horrible with the comic and of the serious with the ironical.

But the tone of the last stanza changes abruptly. The movement becomes emphatic and stately,[1] and the imagination is presented with a sudden panoramic vision of the whole English countryside at night with the sound of the great guns dying inland. All of this elevated poetic effect is more emphatic because of the contrast in abrupt juxtaposition with the earlier section of the poem.

Perhaps further details are worthy of some comment. In the first section of the poem there is no such use of conventional poetic suggestiveness as in the second with "Camelot" and "Stonehenge." The effectiveness of this suggestion is increased by the contrast. But we may ask ourselves how the aura of poetic suggestion about these names really works in the poem. Is it merely decoration, as it were, or does it have a direct reference to the meaning of the poem? On the slightest reflection, we see that the use of these place names, with their poetic associations, is really necessary and functional. The meaning is this: Even though the sound of modern heavy guns is contrasted with the medieval associations of Arthurian chivalry, with Camelot and the prehistoric Stonehenge, man's nature does not change. The starlit scene with the guns roaring in the distance becomes a kind of symbolic conclusion for the poem.

[1] How do the devices of alliteration, assonance, quantitative emphasis, and hovering accents function in this stanza?

The Fury of Aerial Bombardment

RICHARD EBERHART [1904–]

You would think the fury of aerial bombardment
Would rouse God to relent; the infinite spaces
Are still silent. He looks on shock-pried faces.
History, even, does not know what is meant.

You would feel that after so many centuries 5
God would give man to repent; yet he can kill
As Cain could, but with multitudinous will,
No farther advanced than in his ancient furies.

Was man made stupid to see his own stupidity?
Is God by definition indifferent, beyond us all? 10
Is the eternal truth man's fighting soul
Wherein the Beast ravens in its own avidity?

Of Van Wettering I speak, and Averill,
Names on a list, whose faces I do not recall
But they are gone to early death, who late in school 15
Distinguished the belt feed lever from the belt holding pawl.

EXERCISE:

1. This poem invites comparison with Hardy's "Channel Firing." Compare and contrast the poems in their attitudes toward war, in their attitudes toward God, and in their attitudes toward ordinary men.

2. In the last stanza, the "belt feed lever" and the "belt holding pawl" evidently refer to parts of a machine gun. What effect does this technical precision give? What is the effect on the tone of the poet's calling two particular names? What is the speaker's relation to these men? How does this relationship relate to the theme of the poem?

The Leg

KARL SHAPIRO [1913–]

Among the iodoform, in twilight-sleep,
What have I lost? he first inquires,
Peers in the middle distance where a pain,
Ghost of a nurse, hastily moves, and day,
Her blinding presence pressing in his eyes 5
And now his ears. They are handling him
With rubber hands. He wants to get up.

One day beside some flowers near his nose
He will be thinking, *When will I look at it?*
And pain, still in the middle distance, will reply, 10
At what? and he will know it's gone,
O where! and begin to tremble and cry.
He will begin to cry as a child cries
Whose puppy is mangled under a screaming wheel.

Later, as if deliberately, his fingers 15
Begin to explore the stump. He learns a shape
That is comfortable and tucked in like a sock.
This has a sense of humor, this can despise
The finest surgical limb, the dignity of limping,
The nonsense of wheel-chairs. Now he smiles to the wall: 20
The amputation becomes an acquisition.

For the leg is wondering where he is (all is not lost)
And surely he has a duty to the leg;
He is its injury, the leg is his orphan,
He must cultivate the mind of the leg, 25
Pray for the part that is missing, pray for peace
In the image of man, pray, pray for its safety,
And after a little it will die quietly.

The body, what is it, Father, but a sign
To love the force that grows us, to give back 30
What in Thy palm is senselessness and mud?
Knead, knead the substance of our understanding
Which must be beautiful in flesh to walk,

That if Thou take me angrily in hand
And hurl me to the shark, I shall not die! 35

EXERCISE:

1. The first three stanzas describe the amputation and the convalesence with a studied restraint and understatement. What of the tone of the fourth stanza? Does the reasoning in the fourth stanza —"the leg is his orphan"—become fantastic? What is the function of the fourth stanza?

2. What is the tone of the fifth stanza? Does it have the tone of a prayer? How is it prepared for by the preceding stanzas? How does it complete the poem?

Stopping by Woods on a Snowy Evening

ROBERT FROST [1875–]

Whose woods these are I think I know
His house is in the village though;
He will not see me stopping here
To watch his woods fill up with snow.

My little horse must think it queer 5
To stop without a farmhouse near
Between the woods and frozen lake
The darkest evening of the year.

He gives his harness bells a shake
To ask if there is some mistake. 10
The only other sound's the sweep
Of easy wind and downy flake.

The woods are lovely, dark and deep.
But I have promises to keep,
And miles to go before I sleep, 15
And miles to go before I sleep.

EXERCISE:

1. Why does the speaker stop by the woods? (The horse thinks it queer that he stops; the owner of the woods, it is implied, would also think it queer if he could see him.)

2. Does the speaker drive on with reluctance? What does this implied reluctance tell us about the motive for stopping?

3. What attitude toward nature is implied in this little poem?

Bells for John Whiteside's Daughter

JOHN CROWE RANSOM [1888–]

There was such speed in her little body,
And such lightness in her footfall,
It is no wonder her brown study
Astonishes us all.

Her wars were bruited in our high window. 5
We looked among orchard trees and beyond,
Where she took arms against her shadow,
Or harried unto the pond

The lazy geese, like a snow cloud
Dripping their snow on the green grass, 10
Tricking and stopping, sleepy and proud,
Who cried in goose, Alas,

For the tireless heart within the little
Lady with rod that made them rise
From their noon apple-dreams, and scuttle 15
Goose-fashion under the skies!

But now go the bells, and we are ready;
In one house we are sternly stopped
To say we are vexed at her brown study,
Lying so primly propped. 20

EXERCISE:

As one of the editors has put the matter elsewhere, "the first stanza of this poem is based on two time-honored clichés—first, 'Heavens, won't that child ever be still; she is driving me distracted'; and second, 'She was such an active, healthy-looking child, would you've ever thought she would just up and die?' "

1. Can the poem be said to be a working out of the ironic contrast between these two clichés?

2. If the poem makes use of ironic contrast, may it also be said to make use of a general method of understatement? In this connection consider the effect of such phrases as "sternly stopped," "brown study," and "primly propped."

3. Is the whimsical and playful allusion to the geese in stanza three out of place in this poem of grief? Can you justify it?

Mr. Flood's Party

EDWIN ARLINGTON ROBINSON [1869–1935]

Old Eben Flood, climbing alone one night
Over the hill between the town below
And the forsaken upland hermitage
That held as much as he should ever know
On earth again of home, paused warily. 5
The road was his with not a native near;
And Eben, having leisure, said aloud,
For no man else in Tilbury Town to hear:

"Well, Mr. Flood, we have the harvest moon
Again, and we may not have many more; 10
The bird is on the wing, the poet says,
And you and I have said it here before.
Drink to the bird." He raised up to the light
The jug that he had gone so far to fill,
And answered huskily: "Well, Mr. Flood, 15
Since you propose it, I believe I will."

Alone, as if enduring to the end
A valiant armor of scarred hopes outworn,
He stood there in the middle of the road
Like Roland's ghost winding a silent horn. 20
Below him, in the town among the trees,
Where friends of other days had honored him,
A phantom salutation of the dead
Rang thinly till old Eben's eyes were dim.

Then, as a mother lays her sleeping child 25
Down tenderly, fearing it may awake,

He set the jug down slowly at his feet
With trembling care, knowing that most things break;
And only when assured that on firm earth
It stood, as the uncertain lives of men 30
Assuredly did not, he paced away,
And with his hand extended paused again:

"Well, Mr. Flood, we have not met like this
In a long time; and many a change has come
To both of us, I fear, since last it was 35
We had a drop together. Welcome home!"
Convivially returning with himself,
Again he raised the jug up to the light;
And with an acquiescent quaver said:
"Well, Mr. Flood, if you insist, I might. 40

"Only a very little, Mr. Flood—
For auld lang syne. No more, sir; that will do."
So, for the time, apparently it did,
And Eben evidently thought so too;
For soon amid the silver loneliness 45
Of night he lifted up his voice and sang,
Secure, with only two moons listening,
Until the whole harmonious landscape rang—

"For auld lang syne." The weary throat gave out,
The last word wavered; and the song being done, 50
He raised again the jug regretfully
And shook his head, and was again alone.
There was not much that was ahead of him,
And there was nothing in the town below—
Where strangers would have shut the many doors 55
That many friends had opened long ago.

EXERCISE:

This poem is about an old drunken derelict, a disgrace to his community. The poet intends to evoke sympathy for the old man, but he wants to do justice to the several aspects of the situation. Mr. Flood is not only pitiful, he is also comic. Furthermore, he has a kind of gallantry.

1. How is the poet's desire to do justice to the whole situation reflected in the details of the poem? For instance, what has Roland to do with the poem? Who was Roland? How is the jug like a horn? (We know that the jug lifted to the lips might factually resemble a horn, but is that all involved here?)

2. What is implied in the comparison of the jug to a sleeping child? What is the poet "smuggling" into the poem with this image? Why is the idea "knowing that most things break," expressed almost incidentally in a subordinate construction?

3. What complications of tone do you find in the next to the last stanza?

The Indian Serenade

cf. comment p. 294

PERCY BYSSHE SHELLEY [1792–1822]

I arise from dreams of thee
In the first sweet sleep of night,
When the winds are breathing low,
And the stars are shining bright:
I arise from dreams of thee, 5
And a spirit in my feet
Hath led me—who knows how?
To thy chamber window, Sweet!

The wandering airs they faint
On the dark, the silent stream— 10
The Champak odors fail
Like sweet thoughts in a dream;
The nightingale's complaint,
It dies upon her heart;—
As I must on thine, 15
Oh! belovèd as thou art!

Oh lift me from the grass!
I die! I faint! I fail!
Let thy love in kisses rain
On my lips and eyelids pale. 20
My cheek is cold and white, alas!
My heart beats loud and fast;—
Oh! press it to thine own again,
Where it will break at last.

The lover is speaking to his mistress. He has been dreaming of her and, awaking, finds himself at her window. He describes the night scene. The winds are lulled, the stars shining brightly overhead, and the air perfumed faintly with the odor of the champak tree. The nightingale has just ceased her singing. Quite overcome by his passion, he half swoons away, and appeals to his mistress to revive him, or at least (though the poem is not too clear here) to allow him to die upon her breast.

The *atmosphere* (*Glossary*) of the poem is that of the love swoon: the hushed, perfumed air, starlight, and the dying echoes of the nightingale. Her song and the breezes themselves seem to faint in sympathy with the lover.

The poet is attempting then to convey to the reader the experience of a very intense love, and love in a very remote and romantic setting. Moreover his method is a direct method. He might conceivably have conveyed the intensity of his love to the reader by hints and implications merely, allowing the reader to infer for himself the intensity. Or he might have given emphasis by understatement. But he has chosen to state the intensity directly and to the full. The poet using the method of understatement runs the risk of falling into dullness and flatness; the characteristic danger of the method Shelley has chosen, on the other hand, is that the reader may feel that the statements are overstatements—merely absurd exaggerations.

Is the method chosen successful? Perhaps we can answer this question more clearly by approaching the matter in this way. The poet tells us outright that his love is so intense that he is dying of it. But some people die very easily—they are always dying over this or that—always thinking that they are dying. Has the poet taken his lover out of this class? Has he made his reader feel that the lover's statement that he is dying is meant literally and is justified by the intensity of his love? Or does the statement seem to be a glib and easy exaggeration?

What is implied then about the character of the lover in the poem? There is little to keep us from feeling that he is a confirmed sentimentalist, ready to faint and fail whenever the proper stimulus is applied. We know nothing of the lover except that he has lost control over himself. If he is usually poised and restrained, overpowered here only because of tremendous emotions, we have no hint of it. We see him in this poem only at the moment of romantic ecstasy. The poet, as a matter of fact, makes no attempt to supply a context which would give a background for this particular experience. Instead, he merely tries to give an exotic and remote atmosphere to the scene by assembling the conventional exhibits of a "prettified" love affair, and by removing it to a far-off and romantic scene.

The student should notice that the question at issue here is not whether Shelley felt "sincere" when he wrote the poem, or whether Shelley ever had such an experience. Even if Shelley had had in real life just the experience described, that fact would have no relevance for the problem before us here. For what we have to determine is this question: Are the statements made by the lover in this poem convincing to the reader? They are unconvincing and the poem, for the mature reader, is a sentimental one. Sentimentality we may define as the display of more emotion than the situation warrants. The poet has not in this case properly prepared for the outburst of emotion. We also use the term *sentimentalist* occasionally to indicate a person whose emotions are on hair-trigger. And we also use it to indicate a person who likes to indulge in emotion for its own sake. The last two meanings are obviously closely related to the first one. And this poem will, as a matter of fact, illustrate all three meanings. For the lover in this poem seems to the reader to go into an ecstasy under very little stimulus indeed, and, furthermore, he certainly seems to revel in the emotions without much concern for their occasion or for their specific quality or for anything else than their thrilling sweetness.

An almost inevitable accompaniment of sentimentality is this obsession with one's own emotions—an exclusive interest which blinds the person involved to everything except the sweet intensity of the emotion in question. It is symptomatic of this sentimental attitude that there is nowhere in this poem a sharp and definite image. The poet apparently does not perceive anything sharply and compellingly and he does not cause the reader to perceive anything very compellingly. This obsession with the sweet thrill is so strong here that the mistress herself is not described—even by implication. But the poet does describe himself and his own feelings—in detail. The whole of the last stanza is devoted to a description of his "symptoms."

And having seen that this blindness to the context is characteristic of the sentimental attitude, we are better able to understand the reason for the remote, vague, exotic setting of the poem. Sentimentality, since it is an emotional one-sidedness, has to be posed in a special light. Under anything like critical inspection it is seen to be one-sided. It is this critical inspection which the poet wishes to avoid—or rather it does not occur to him to inspect his experience critically. Hence, the vague, romantic setting. If the reader can be induced to yield himself to the dreamy sweetness of the setting, and if his intellect can be lulled to sleep, he feels that the poem is fine. Good love poetry, on the other hand, does not need to resort to such devices. The poet achieves an effect of intensity without violating our sense of reality and without asking us to stop thinking so that we can exclusively and uninterruptedly "emote." Compare with this poem such love poems as "A Litany," by Philip Sidney (p. 205), "Rose Aylmer," by Walter Savage Landor (p. 144).

When Love Meets Love

THOMAS EDWARD BROWN [1830–1897]

When love meets love, breast urged to breast,
God interposes,
An unacknowledged guest,
And leaves a little child among our roses.

We love, God makes: in our sweet mirth 5
God spies occasion for a birth.
Then is it His, or is it ours?
I know not—He is fond of flowers.

O, gentle hap!
O, sacred lap! 10
O, brooding dove!
But when he grows
Himself to be a rose,

God takes him—where is then our love?
O, where is all our love? 15

EXERCISE:

1. In this little poem does God become a "guest," though entertained unawares, or does the poet seem to make of God a Peeping Tom?

2. What is the effect of "spies" (line 6)? What is the effect of line 8?

3. Conceding that the idea behind the poem is a serious and profound idea (the idea that love is a sacramental act), does the poem render the idea worthily? Or is it a sentimental poem?

On Lucretia Borgia's Hair

WALTER SAVAGE LANDOR [1775–1864]

Borgia, thou once wert almost too august
And high for adoration; now thou'rt dust;
All that remains of thee these plaits unfold,
Calm hair meandering in pellucid gold.

EXERCISE:

Lucretia Borgia was a beautiful and cruel lady who belonged to one of the powerful families of the Italian Renaissance.

1. What is the dramatic situation in this poem?
2. What is the speaker's attitude toward the dead woman?
3. Why "calm hair"? Isn't hair always calm?
4. Look up the word *meander*. Why is *meandering* peculiarly appropriate here?

Western Wind

ANONYMOUS

Western wind, when will thou blow,
The small rain down can rain?
Christ, if my love were in my arms
And I in my bed again!

At first glance this poem seems very simple, a single cry of loneliness for the absent beloved. We may notice, however, a contrast in tone between the first two lines and the fourth line, with the third line as a kind of transition between them. The first two lines give the romantic cry, the cry that the wind and the rain come to relieve, alleviating the deadness and aridity of the lover's loneliness. This is expansive; it involves all nature in the lover's plight. And even the third line continues something of this expansive treatment. The exclamation, "Christ," continues the excitement of the earlier part. And the phrase, "in my arms," has a general romantic implication. But with the last line a change occurs. The generalized romantic excitement is all at once brought down to the literal and realistic. The tone of the last works to make the whole poem more credible and acceptable. It gives a context for the romantic cry.

EXERCISE:

1. Do the realistic details ("small rain," "in my bed") negate the romantic quality or do they reinforce it? How does the last line affect the tone?

2. In what sense is this a simple poem? A "direct" poem? Is it a sentimental poem? Compare and contrast it with "The Indian Serenade" (p. 173).

O, Wert Thou in the Cauld Blast

ROBERT BURNS [1759–1796]

O, wert thou in the cauld blast
  On yonder lea, on yonder lea,
My plaidie to the angry airt,
  I'd shelter thee, I'd shelter thee.
Or did misfortune's bitter storms 5
  Around thee blaw, around thee blaw,
Thy bield should be my bosom,
  To share it a', to share it a'.

Or were I in the wildest waste,
  Sae black and bare, sae black and bare, 10
The desert were a paradise,
  If thou wert there, if thou wert there.

Or were I monarch of the globe,
  Wi' thee to reign, wi' thee to reign,
The brightest jewel in my crown 15
  Wad be my queen, wad be my queen.

EXERCISE:

1. Is this a sentimental poem or not? If not, how has the poet avoided sentimentality?

2. The speaker does not claim that he can take the loved one out of the storm. He will merely wrap his plaid about her. He does not say that he can prevent misfortune. He promises merely "to share it all." Does this give an effect of realism and understatement? Do such devices apply to the second stanza of the poem? Which is the more successful stanza?

Piano

D. H. LAWRENCE [1885–1930]

Softly, in the dusk, a woman is singing to me;
Taking me back down the vista of years, till I see
A child sitting under the piano, in the boom of the tingling strings
And pressing the small, poised feet of a mother who smiles as she
  sings.

In spite of myself, the insidious mastery of song 5
Betrays me back, till the heart of me weeps to belong
To the old Sunday evenings at home, with winter outside
And hymns in the cozy parlor, the tinkling piano our guide.

So now it is vain for the singer to burst into clamor
With the great black piano appassionato. The glamor 10
Of childish days is upon me, my manhood is cast
Down in the flood of remembrance, I weep like a child for the past.

EXERCISE:

Suppose the poem ran as follows:

Softly, in dusk a woman is singing to me;
Taking me back down the vista of years, till I see
Myself as a happy child in the old Sunday evenings at home,
Singing hymns in the pleasant parlor inside
With the tinkling piano our guide 5

While outside the wind raised its clamor—
Outside in the wintry gloom.
I am taken back down the years. The glamor
Of childish days is upon me, my manhood is cast 9
Down in the flood of remembrance, I weep like a child for the past.

What would be lost? What difference in tone can you see?

Summer Night

ALFRED, LORD TENNYSON [1809–1892]

Now sleeps the crimson petal, now the white;
Nor waves the cypress in the palace walk;
Nor winks the gold fin in the porphyry font:—
The firefly wakens: waken thou with me.

Now droops the milk-white peacock like a ghost, 5
And like a ghost she glimmers on to me.

Now lies the Earth all Danaë to the stars,
And all thy heart lies open unto me.

Now slides the silent meteor on, and leaves
A shining furrow, as thy thought in me. 10

Now folds the lily all her sweetness up,
And slips into the bosom of the lake:
So fold thyself, my dearest, thou, and slip
Into my bosom and be lost in me.

EXERCISE:

Write an analysis of this poem, making sure that you take into account such matters as:

a. The function of the nature imagery;

b. The function of the sleep-wake formula;

c. The attitude of the lover toward his sweetheart.

1. Does the tone of this poem resemble that of "The Indian Serenade"? Or does it differ? If so, how?

2. What does the lover mean by telling his sweetheart to "be lost in me"? Is he protective? Patronizing? Or what?

The Pilgrims

ADELAIDE ANNE PROCTER [1825–1864]

The way is long and dreary,
The path is bleak and bare;
Our feet are worn and weary,
But we will not despair;
More heavy was Thy burden, 5
More desolate Thy way;—
O Lamb of God who takest
The sin of the world away,
Have mercy on us.

The snows lie thick around us 10
In the dark and gloomy night;
And the tempest wails above us,
And the stars have hid their light;
But blacker was the darkness
Round Calvary's Cross that day:— 15
O Lamb of God who takest
The sin of the world away,
Have mercy on us.

Our hearts are faint with sorrow,
Heavy and hard to bear; 20
For we dread the bitter morrow,
But we will not despair:
Thou knowest all our anguish,
And Thou wilt bid it cease,—
O Lamb of God who takest 25
The sin of the world away,
Give us Thy peace!

Even though the work of Adelaide Procter, who is known now only as the author of "The Lost Chord," was once greatly admired by Charles Dickens, most modern readers of poetry would find this poem bad. Most readers who admire it probably do so because they approve of the pious sentiment expressed in it. Such readers go to poetry merely to have their own beliefs and feelings flattered or to find what they would call "great truths" or "worth-while ideas" expressed in an agreeable form. Such readers do not go to poetry for anything that poetry, as poetry, can give them, but for something that they might get, though in not so compact and pleasant a form, in a sermon or a collection of adages.

"The Pilgrims" can be appreciated only because of something the reader may bring to it (an uncritical and sentimental piety) and not because of anything it brings to the reader. A truly pious person who was also an experienced reader of poetry might, as a matter of fact, have his piety offended rather than sustained by this poem. He might feel it as stupid, trivial, and not worthy of the subject.

He might feel this because the business of a poem is to sharpen and renew the experience of the subject. But the present poem does nothing to accomplish that purpose. It is composed of worn-out materials, stereotyped images and phrases. The trouble is not that the basic idea of salvation through the Christ has been used in poetry before. Basic ideas, or themes, of poetry are relatively limited in number and occur again and again. Numerous fine poems (several in this book) have been written on this theme, and others in all probability will be written. But if a poem is successful, the reader feels it as a new experience; it is again proved, as it were, by the fact that the poem provokes a new response to it, by new devices of dramatization, new images and combinations of images, new shades of feeling in expression, new phrasing, new combinations of rhythm.

"The Pilgrims" has a serious theme and one about which a body of emotional response might easily gather. But if that response is stereotyped, if the theme merely appeals to what is called the *stock response* (*Glossary*) the seriousness or interest of the theme loses all value. Now Adelaide Procter, apparently, responded to her theme in a perfectly stereotyped way. The attitude developed in the poem is *conventional* (*Glossary*) in a bad sense.

This failure to bring any freshness to the theme, to make it into something the reader could experience as new, is indicated by the numerous *clichés* (*Glossary*) in the poem. A *cliché* is a trite expression, an expression that has become so worn-out that it no longer can impress the reader with a fresh and sharp perception. The poem is built up of such phrases: the way is *long and dreary;* the path *bleak and bare;* the snows *lie thick;* the tempest *wails;* the stars *hide* their *light;* hearts are *faint with sorrow,* etc. In every instance the poet has used a phrase that dulls the reader's perception of the scene rather than stimulates it. In other words, the poet has made no real attempt to visualize, or make the reader visualize, the objects. Nothing strikes the reader with the force of a new perception, and the total effect is vague. (By the very nature of language every poem must employ certain stereotyped expressions; the poet may even deliberately use clichés to set a certain tone (see "A Litany," p. 208). The question is to see how the clichés relate to the general intention in each case.)

This defect in the use of detail is paralleled by a similar defect in the general dramatic framework of the poem. Life is presented as a journey over difficult country in bad weather. This basic comparison has been used innumerable times, and does not in itself bring any poetic or dramatic freshness to the theme. It could only be effective if the detail work were adequate. But that is not the case. The clichés, the poorly visualized imagery, and the mechanical rhythms all help to dull the reader's response.

After the Burial

JAMES RUSSELL LOWELL [1819–1891]

Yes, faith is a goodly anchor;
  When skies are sweet as a psalm,
At the bows it lolls so stalwart,
  In its bluff, broad-shouldered calm.

And when over breakers to leeward 5
  The tattered surges are hurled,
It may keep our head to the tempest,
  With its grip on the base of the world.

But, after the shipwreck, tell me
  What help in its iron thews, 10
Still true to the broken hawser,
  Deep down among sea-weed and ooze?

In the breaking gulfs of sorrow,
When the helpless feet stretch out
And find in the deeps of darkness 15
No footing so solid as doubt,

Then better one spar of Memory,
One broken plank of the Past,
That our human heart may cling to,
Though hopeless of shore at last! 20

To the spirit its splendid conjectures,
To the flesh its sweet despair,
Its tears o'er the thin-worn locket
With its anguish of deathless hair!

Immortal? I feel it and know it, 25
Who doubts it of such as she?
But that is the pang's very secret—
Immortal away from me.

There's a narrow ridge in the graveyard
Would scarce stay a child in his race, 30
But to me and my thought it is wider
Than the star-sown vague of Space.

Your logic, my friend, is perfect,
Your moral most drearily true;
But, since the earth clashed on *her* coffin, 35
I keep hearing that, and not you.

Console if you will, I can bear it;
'T is a well-meant alms of breath;
But not all the preaching since Adam
Has made Death other than Death. 40

It is pagan; but wait till you feel it,—
That jar of our earth, that dull shock
When the ploughshare of deeper passion
Tears down to our primitive rock.

Communion in spirit! Forgive me, 45
But I, who am earthly and weak,
Would give all my incomes from dreamland
For a touch of her hand on my cheek.

That little shoe in the corner,
So worn and wrinkled and brown, 50
With its emptiness confutes you,
And argues your wisdom down.

EXERCISE:

1. We know that this poem was written by Lowell as an expression of personal grief. But this does not mean that the poem is necessarily a good one. Why are the third and eleventh stanzas better than the rest of the poem? Why are stanzas ten and twelve especially poor?

2. Is this poem sentimental in its effect? Does such a poem as this suggest that we have to distinguish between the sincerity of the writer as a *man* and the integrity of the poem as a *work of art?*

3. This poem, like "Ah, Sunflower" (p. 129), employs an anapaestic meter. Try to determine why the rhythm of this poem is mechanical and monotonous and that of "Ah, Sunflower" flexible.

On His Blindness

JOHN MILTON [1608–1674]

When I consider how my light is spent
Ere half my days in this dark world and wide,
And that one talent which is death to hide
Lodged with me useless, though my soul more bent
To serve therewith my Maker, and present 5
My true account, lest he returning chide,
"Doth God exact day-labor, light denied?"
I fondly ask. But Patience, to prevent
That murmur, soon replies, "God doth not need
Either man's work or his own gifts. Who best 10
Bear his mild yoke, they serve him best. His state
Is kingly: thousands at his bidding speed,
And post o'er land and ocean without rest;
They also serve who only stand and wait."

EXERCISE:

1. Here Milton seems to take quite as direct an approach to the subject of his own blindness as Lowell does to the subject of his own grief in "After the Burial." Try to define the difference in attitude and tone. Why is one poem sentimental and the other not?

2. The sonnet obviously alludes to the Parable of the Talents (see Matthew 25:14–30). What is meant by "that one talent which is death to hide"?

3. Does Patience answer his question, or does Patience show that the question is badly asked?

Poor Soul, the Center of My Sinful Earth

WILLIAM SHAKESPEARE [1564–1616]

Poor soul, the center of my sinful earth,
Thrall to these rebel powers that thee array,
Why dost thou pine within and suffer dearth,
Painting thy outward walls so costly gay?
Why so large cost, having so short a lease, 5
Dost thou upon thy fading mansion spend?
Shall worms, inheritors of this excess,
Eat up thy charge? Is this thy body's end?
Then, soul, live thou upon thy servant's loss,
And let that pine to aggravate thy store; 10
Buy terms divine in selling hours of dross;
Within be fed, without be rich no more:
So shalt thou feed on Death, that feeds on men,
And Death once dead, there's no more dying then.

EXERCISE:

1. What effect does the dominant business metaphor have upon the tone of this poem? Is the soul being chided for making a poor investment in spending its income upon a house which is not owned but merely leased?

2. Does the dominance of this metaphor rob the poem of its effect by seeming to make prosaic and matter-of-fact what ought to be solemn and momentous? Or is the effect of the metaphor to revitalize a subject often made merely conventionally solemn?

Blame Not My Cheeks

THOMAS CAMPION [1567–1620]

Blame not my cheeks, though pale with love they be;
The kindly heat unto my heart is flown,
To cherish it that is dismaid by thee,
Who art so cruel and unsteadfast grown:
For nature, called for by distressèd hearts, 5
Neglects and quite forsakes the outward parts.

But they whose cheeks with careless blood are stained,
Nurse not one spark of love within their hearts,
And, when they woo, they speak with passion feigned,
For their fat love lies in their outward parts: 10
But in their breasts, where love his court should hold,
Poor Cupid sits and blows his nails for cold.

EXERCISE:

1. To whom is this poem addressed?

2. How seriously does the speaker take his proposed formula for distinguishing sincerity in love: outward warmth means inward cold and outward coldness means inner fervor?

3. What is the force of "careless" blood and "fat" love?

4. How is the speaker's attitude reflected in the closing image of the poem? Is the picture of a little naked Cupid shivering beside a fireless hearth supposed to be pathetic? Ridiculous? Or what?

5. Scan lines 4 and 8. How many hovering accents are there? Are these hovering accents justified in terms of the meaning of the poem?

6. Using "The Indian Serenade" and "Cupid and Campaspe" as points of comparison, try to fix the tone of this poem. Is it sentimental? Playful? Serious? Or what?

Delight in Disorder

ROBERT HERRICK [1591–1674]

A sweet disorder in the dress
Kindles in clothes a wantonness:

A lawn about the shoulders thrown
Into a fine distraction:
An erring lace, which here and there 5
Enthralls the crimson stomacher:
A cuff neglectful, and thereby
Ribbands to flow confusedly:
A winning wave (deserving note)
In the tempestuous petticoat: 10
A careless shoe-string, in whose tie
I see a wild civility:
Do more bewitch me, than when art
Is too precise in every part.

EXERCISE:

F. W. Bateson has analyzed as follows the attitudes implicit in this poem:—"The impression of a surprising richness, and almost grandeur (as of a painting by Titian), with a certain tantalizing quality, that Herrick's poem leaves, is primarily due to the skill with which he has exploited the ambiguous associations of the epithets. On the surface his subject is the 'Delight in the Disorder' of the title—a disorder, that is, of costume. But a second subject is hinted at, though not protruded: a delight in disorder, not of costume but of manners and morals. It is not only the clothes but their wearers too whom he would have *sweet, wanton, distracted, erring, neglectful, winning, tempestuous, wild,* and *bewitching* rather than *precise.* The poem, in fact, instead of being the mere *jeu d'esprit* that it would seem to be, is essentially a plea for paganism. There are three themes: (1) untidiness is becoming; (2) the clothes are the woman; (3) anti-Puritanism. But the success of the poem depends upon the fact that the themes are not isolated and contrasted but grow out of and into each other. The suspension between the various meanings produces a range of reference that none of them would have alone." [1]

Indicate other words and phrases in the poem which would support Bateson's view.

[1] *English Poetry and the English Language,* Oxford: Oxford University Press, pp. 42–43.

Cupid and Campaspe

JOHN LYLY [1554–1606]

Cupid and my Campaspe played
At cards for kisses; Cupid paid.
He stakes his quiver, bow, and arrows,
His mother's doves and team of sparrows;
Loses them too; then down he throws 5
The coral of his lip, the rose
Growing on's cheek (but none knows how);
With these the crystal of his brow,
And then the dimple of his chin;
All these did my Campaspe win. 10
At last he set her both his eyes;
She won, and Cupid blind did rise.
O Love, has she done this to thee?
What shall, alas! become of me?

EXERCISE:

1. Here the poet presents a fanciful picture of a game at cards between Cupid and the poet's mistress, Campaspe; at the end Cupid has wagered ("set") and lost even his eyes. How does this incident define the tone of the compliment? (See *Glossary* under *vers de société.*)

2. The obvious playfulness of this little poem effectually precludes any danger of our feeling that the speaker takes himself "too seriously"; i.e., that he falls into sentimentality. The poem is obviously not the expression of a "deep" or "serious" love. Is it thereby worthless? Is there any trace of seriousness?

Why So Pale and Wan?

SIR JOHN SUCKLING [1609–1642]

Why so pale and wan, fond lover?
  Prithee, why so pale?
Will, when looking well can't move her,
  Looking ill prevail?
  Prithee, why so pale? 5

Why so dull and mute, young sinner?
  Prithee, why so mute?
Will, when speaking well can't win her,
  Saying nothing do't?
  Prithee, why so mute? 10

Quit, quit for shame! This will not move;
  This cannot take her.
If of herself she will not love,
  Nothing can make her:
  The devil take her! 15

EXERCISE:

1. In this poem the *Petrarchan* (*Glossary*) attitude is exposed to the acid of common sense. Compare and contrast it with "Blame Not My Cheeks" (p. 187).

2. Is the tone that of matter-of-fact rationality? Indignation? Light-hearted gaiety? Try to define the attitude as clearly as you can and indicate the devices used to define the tone.

To Roses in the Bosom of Castara

WILLIAM HABINGTON [1605–1654]

Ye blushing virgins happy are
In the chaste nunn'ry of her breasts,
For he'd profane so chaste a fair
Whoe'er should call them Cupid's nests.

Transplanted thus, how bright ye grow, 5
How rich a perfume do ye yield!
In some close garden, cowslips so
Are sweeter than i' th' open field.

In those white cloisters live secure
From the rude blasts of wanton breath, 10
Each hour more innocent and pure,
Till you shall wither into death.

Then that which living gave you room,
Your glorious sepulcher shall be.

There wants no marble for a tomb, 15
Whose breast hath marble been to me.

EXERCISE:

1. Ostensibly the speaker addresses the poem to the roses; but is he indirectly addressing it to his mistress? What does he mean by "Whose breast hath marble been to me"?

2. Is this poem an example of *vers de société* (see p. 189), courtly, graceful, adroitly complimentary? Or does it reflect any deeper emotion? On this point, compare this poem with "Cupid and Campaspe" (p. 189) and "Blame Not My Cheeks" (p. 187).

Winter Remembered

JOHN CROWE RANSOM [1888–]

Two evils, monstrous either one apart,
Possessed me, and were long and loath at going:
A cry of Absence, Absence, in the heart,
And in the wood the furious winter blowing.

Think not, when fire was bright upon my bricks, 5
And past the tight boards hardly a wind could enter,
I glowed like them, the simple burning sticks,
Far from my cause, my proper heat and center.

Better to walk forth in the murderous air
And wash my wound in the snows; that would be healing;
Because my heart would throb less painful there, 11
Being caked with cold, and past the smart of feeling.

And where I went, the hugest winter blast
Would have this body bowed, these eyeballs streaming,
And though I think this heart's blood froze not fast 15
It ran too small to spare one drop for dreaming.

Dear love, these fingers that had known your touch,
And tied our separate forces first together,
Were ten poor idiot fingers not worth much,
Ten frozen parsnips hanging in the weather. 20

Exercise:

1. What is the dramatic situation implied in this poem? Who is speaking to whom, and under what circumstances?

2. Literally, the speaker is saying that he did *not* spend the winter of his absence in thinking of his loved one. How can this fact become a proof of the intensity of his love?

3. Is there any justification for the comparison of his fingers to ten frozen parsnips?

4. How would you define the tone of this poem? Are these shifts of tone?

Song

EDMUND WALLER [1606–1687]

Go, lovely Rose,
Tell her that wastes her time and me,
That now she knows,
When I resemble her to thee,
How sweet and fair she seems to be. 5

Tell her that's young,
And shuns to have her graces spied,
That hadst thou sprung
In deserts where no men abide,
Thou must have uncommended died. 10

Small is the worth
Of beauty from the light retir'd:
Bid her come forth,
Suffer herself to be desir'd,
And not blush so to be admir'd. 15

Then die, that she
The common fate of all things rare
May read in thee,
How small a part of time they share,
That are so wondrous sweet and fair. 20

Exercise:

1. In line 2, why does the poet write "wastes her time and me"? How does this differ from "wastes her time and mine"?

2. What is the force of the word "suffer" in line 14?

3. Compare the tone of this poem with that of "To Roses in the Bosom of Castara" (p. 190).

Envoi (1919)

EZRA POUND [1885–]

Go, dumb-born book,
Tell her that sang me once that song of Lawes:
Hadst thou but song
As thou hast subjects known,
Then were there cause in thee that should condone 5
Even my faults that heavy upon me lie,
And build her glories their longevity.

Tell her that sheds
Such treasure in the air,
Recking naught else but that her graces give 10
Life to the moment,
I would bid them live
As roses might, in magic amber laid,
Red overwrought with orange and all made
One substance and one color 15
Braving time.

Tell her that goes
With song upon her lips
But sings not out the song, nor knows
The maker of it, some other mouth, 20
May be as fair as hers,
Might, in new ages, gain her worshippers,
When our two dusts with Waller's shall be laid,
Siftings on siftings in oblivion,
Till change hath broken down 25
All things save Beauty alone.

EXERCISE:

Waller's "Song" (see above) was set to music by Henry Lawes, seventeenth-century musician and friend of Milton.

1. Compare the theme of this poem with that of Waller's "Song."

2. What is the speaker's attitude toward the girl "that sang me once that song of Lawes"?

3. Does Pound's poem gain from a knowledge of Waller's poem? How does it differ from it in tone?

Ulalume—A Ballad

EDGAR ALLAN POE [1809–1849]

The skies they were ashen and sober;
  The leaves they were crispéd and sere—
  The leaves they were withering and sere.
It was night, in the lonesome October
  Of my most immemorial year: 5
It was hard by the dim lake of Auber,
  In the misty mid region of Weir:
It was down by the dank tarn of Auber,
  In the ghoul-haunted woodland of Weir.

Here once, through an alley Titanic, 10
  Of cypress, I roamed with my Soul—
  Of cypress, with Psyche, my Soul.
These were days when my heart was volcanic
  As the scoriac rivers that roll—
  As the lavas that restlessly roll 15
Their sulphurous currents down Yaanek
  In the realms of the Boreal Pole.

Our talk had been serious and sober,
  But our thoughts they were palsied and sere—
  Our memories were treacherous and sere; 20
For we knew not the month was October,
  And we marked not the night of the year
  (Ah, night of all nights in the year!)
We noted not the dim lake of Auber
  (Though once we had journeyed down here)— 25
We remembered not the dank tarn of Auber,
  Nor the ghoul-haunted woodland of Weir.

And now, as the night was senescent
  And star-dials pointed to morn—
  As the star-dials hinted of morn— 30
At the end of our path a liquescent
  And nebulous luster was born,
Out of which a miraculous crescent
  Arose with a duplicate horn—
Astarte's bediamonded crescent 35
  Distinct with its duplicate horn.

And I said—"She is warmer than Dian;
  She rolls through an ether of sighs—
  She revels in a region of sighs.
She has seen that the tears are not dry on 40
  These cheeks, where the worm never dies,
And has come past the stars of the Lion,
  To point us the path to the skies—
  To the Lethean peace of the skies—
Come up, in despite of the Lion, 45
  To shine on us with her bright eyes—
Come up through the lair of the Lion,
  With love in her luminous eyes."

But Psyche, uplifting her finger,
  Said—"Sadly this star I mistrust— 50
  Her pallor I strangely mistrust:
Ah, hasten!—ah, let us not linger!
  Ah, fly!—let us fly!—for we must."
In terror she spoke, letting sink her
  Wings till they trailed in the dust— 55
In agony sobbed, letting sink her
  Plumes till they trailed in the dust—
  Till they sorrowfully trailed in the dust.

I replied—"This is nothing but dreaming:
  Let us on by this tremulous light! 60
  Let us bathe in this crystalline light!
Its Sibyllic splendor is beaming
  With Hope and in Beauty to-night:—
  See!—it flickers up the sky through the night!

Ah, we safely may trust to its gleaming, 65
And be sure it will lead as aright—
We surely may trust to a gleaming,
That cannot but guide us aright,
Since it flickers up to Heaven through the night."

Thus I pacified Psyche and kissed her, 70
And tempted her out of her gloom—
And conquered her scruples and gloom;
And we passed to the end of the vista,
But were stopped by the door of a tomb—
By the door of a legended tomb: 75
And I said—"What is written, sweet sister,
On the door of this legended tomb?"
She replied—"Ulalume—Ulalume!—
'Tis the vault of thy lost Ulalume!"

Then my heart it grew ashen and sober 80
As the leaves that were crispéd and sere—
As the leaves that were withering and sere;
And I cried—"It was surely October
On *this* very night of last year
That I journeyed—I journeyed down here!— 85
That I brought a dread burden down here—
On this night of all nights in the year,
Ah, what demon hath tempted me here?
Well I know, now, this dim lake of Auber—
This misty mid region of Weir— 90
Well I know, now, this dank tarn of Auber,
This ghoul-haunted woodland of Weir."

Said *we,* then—the two, then—"Ah, can it
Have been that the woodlandish ghouls—
The pitiful, the merciful ghouls— 95
To bar up our way and to ban it
From the secret that lies in these wolds
From the thing that lies hidden in the wolds
Have drawn up the specter of a planet
From the limbo of lunary souls— 100
This sinfully scintillant planet
From the Hell of the planetary souls?"

"Ulalume," by Edgar Allan Poe, raises some questions about suggestiveness and atmosphere in poetry. Poe is sometimes praised because of an ability to create a mood, an atmosphere, by suggestion and association. All poetry in one sense shares this quality with the work of Poe. But why do admirers of Poe usually connect these things especially with him? Perhaps the best way to approach this particular matter will be to try to analyze the poem as a whole.

What is it about? The element of incident may be summarized as follows: A man, engaged in conversation with Psyche, his soul, walks through a mysterious landscape. He and his soul are so preoccupied that they do not notice the setting nor do they even know what month of the year it is, even though, as it is pointed out, they have been here before and this night marks a mysterious and important anniversary. Then a light appears, which the man takes to be Astarte, and not Diana, that is, love and not chastity. Psyche is terrified by this and wishes to flee, but the man overcomes her scruples and persuades her to follow the light. They stumble upon a tomb, which, Psyche tells the man, is the tomb of his lost love, Ulalume. Then the man remembers that, precisely a year before, he had brought the body to the tomb. This discovery being made, both the man and Psyche simultaneously say that the sight of Astarte's crescent has been conjured up, perhaps, by the merciful ghouls to prevent them from stumbling on the tomb. But they had failed to heed the warning.

This is, apparently, an *allegorical* (*Glossary*) way of saying that love (or the semblance of love, for the crescent is defined as "the specter of a planet") only leads him to the door of the tomb where Ulalume is buried.

But all of this leaves a great many questions, even questions that should have factual answers, without answer. For instance, what significance, if any, is possessed by the following lines:

> It was hard by the dim lake of Auber,
> In the misty mid region of Weir:
> It was down by the dank tarn of Auber,
> In the ghoul-haunted woodland of Weir.

The poet returns to similar descriptions during the course of the poem and evidently attaches considerable importance to them. He is trying to give an unreal, mysterious atmosphere to the poem. These places have no historical or geographical existence; the reference to them is supposed to tease the reader with mysterious implications in the same way as do the later references to Mount Yaanek and "the stars of the Lion." The details of the first description are directed to the same end: "the ghoul-haunted woodland." It is the kind of suggestiveness used in romantic ghost stories, a kind of atmosphere that we can accept only if we do not inspect its occasion too closely—for dank tarns and ghoul-haunted woodlands are stage-sets, we might say, that are merely good for frightening children. We accept them only if we happen to be willing to forego our maturity and make a temporary concession. The process whereby the poet has created his atmosphere is too transparent, too obvious; we feel that we humor him by accepting it. The process whereby the atmosphere of mystery and foreboding is created here is similar to that whereby the atmosphere of exotic romance is created in "The Indian Serenade," by Shelley (p. 173).

One might justify the general atmosphere of the poem, perhaps, by saying that the whole poem is unrealistic, is a kind of fable (though this justification would not necessarily excuse the poet for the particular manner by which the atmosphere is given, the stale devices of mystification). But even in such a poem as this the reader can expect that the parts all contribute something directly to the poem, that they be consistent among themselves, and that the devices of mystification bear some relation to the business of the poem and do more than indicate a love of mystification merely for its own sake (see "Channel Firing," p. 163). What, then, about the ghouls that haunt the woodland of Weir? A ghoul, according to the dictionary, is a "demon who robs graves and feeds on corpses." But these are pitiful ghouls that summon up ghosts of planets from "the Hell of the planetary souls," in order to save the man from finding the tomb. The situation might be something like this: The poet could not let the planet of Astarte appear as a fact in itself; it was a ghost of a planet. He felt that he had to account for its presence. Arbitrarily he chose ghouls to serve this purpose. He had used the word *ghoul-haunted* earlier in the poem and so had some preparation for the reference; ghouls may provoke in the reader a kind of shudder of supernatural mystery and horror. But the reader feels that this has little or no real reference to the meaning of the poem. It may be said to contribute to the atmosphere of the poem, but otherwise it does not connect with the meaning of the poem; it simply does not pull its weight in the boat.

One might compare this rather disorderly use of suggestion in "Ulalume," the use of the place names, the ghouls, etc., with the use made in other poems in this collection. For instance, one can see how the suggestions of the names Camelot, Stourton Tower, and Stonehenge in "Channel Firing," by Hardy, directly contribute to the meaning of the poem itself. (See p. 166.) Or one can see how, in a similar fashion, suggestion is employed in poems like "Ode on a Grecian Urn" (p. 474) and "Ode to a Nightingale" (p. 336), by Keats, to develop and present the actual theme of a poem as well as to create an atmosphere. We feel that in the poems by Hardy and Keats, who are poets with great differences between them, the atmosphere is not only appropriate to the poem in question, but that the suggestion actually helps us to the meaning of the experience in the poem; the devices used by the poet will stand a logical definition and inspection. It is no surprise, after studying "Ulalume" in this respect, to discover that Poe could make the following remark about poetry in general: "Poetry, above all things, is a beautiful painting whose tints, to minute inspection, are confusion worse confounded, but start boldly out to the cursory glance of the connoisseur." (Letter to Mr. Elam Bliss, Preface to the *Poems* of 1831.) That is, Poe expected poetry to stand little analysis, and to affect only the person who gave it a "cursory glance," a superficial reading. It is no wonder, then, that much of Poe's work is very vague and confused, for he said that poetry has for its "object an *indefinite* instead of a *definite* pleasure." But really good poetry will stand a great deal of close inspection, even poetry that is simple and unambitious. We feel that the parts all contribute definitely to the total meaning of the poem.

We may apply the same line of reasoning to another feature of "Ulalume," the rhythm. In this connection we may quote again from Poe: ". . . presenting perceptible images with definite, poetry with *indefinite* sensations, to which music is an *essential,* since the comprehension of sweet sound is our most indefinite conception."

Poe, then, holds that the function of the rhythms of poetry is to lull the reader; to increase the indefiniteness of the impression; to prevent him, in fact, from having the impulse to analyze the poem closely; to contribute to the general atmosphere; to have a hypnotic effect on the reader. One may notice that in "Ulalume," by consequence, there is an emphatic beat of rhythm that becomes monotonous, that there is a lack of variation in the rhythmic effects of the poem.

Aldous Huxley, in *Vulgarity in Literature,* has this to say about Poe's handling of his meter in this poem:

These lines protest too much (and with what a variety of voices!) that they are poetical, and, protesting, are therefore vulgar. To start with, the walloping dactylic meter is all too musical. Poetry ought to be musical, but musical with tact, subtly and variously. Meters whose rhythms, as in this case, are strong, insistent and practically invariable offer the poet a kind of short cut to musicality. They provide him (my subject calls for a mixture of metaphors) with a ready-made, reach-me-down music. He does not have to create a music appropriately modulated to his meaning; all he has to do is to shovel the meaning into the moving stream of the meter and allow the current to carry it along on waves that, like those of the best hairdressers, are guaranteed permanent. . . . A quotation and a parody will illustrate the difference between ready-made music and music made to measure. I remember (I trust correctly) a simile of Milton's:—

Like that fair field
Of Enna, where Proserpine gathering flowers,
Herself a fairer flower, by gloomy Dis
Was gathered, which cost Ceres all that pain
To seek her through the world. 5

Rearranged according to their musical phrasing, these lines would have to be written thus:—

Like that fair field of Enna,
where Proserpine gathering flowers,
Herself a fairer flower,
by gloomy Dis was gathered,
Which cost Ceres all that pain
To seek her through the world.

The contrast between the lyrical swiftness of the first four phrases, with that row of limping spondees which tells of Ceres' pain, is thrillingly appropriate. Bespoke, the music fits the sense like a glove.

How would Poe have written on the same theme? I have ventured to invent his opening stanza.

It was noon in the fair field of Enna,
  When Proserpina gathering flowers—
  Herself the most fragrant of flowers,
Was gathered away to Gehenna
  By the Prince of Plutonian powers; 5
Was borne down the windings of Brenner
  To the gloom of his amorous bowers—
Down the tortuous highway of Brenner
  To the god's agapemonous bowers.

The parody is not too outrageous to be critically beside the point; and anyhow the music is genuine Poe. That permanent wave is unquestionably an *ondulation de chez Edgar*. The much too musical meter is (to change the metaphor once more) like a rich chasuble, so stiff with gold and gems that it stands unsupported, a carapace of jewelled sound, into which the sense, like some snotty little seminarist, irrelevantly creeps and is lost. This music of Poe's —how much less really musical it is than that which, out of his nearly neutral decasyllables, Milton fashioned on purpose to fit the slender beauty of Proserpine, the strength and swiftness of the ravisher and her mother's heavy, despairing sorrow!

The Sleeper

EDGAR ALLAN POE [1809–1849]

At midnight in the month of June,
I stand beneath the mystic moon.
An opiate vapor, dewy, dim,
Exhales from out her golden rim,
And, softly dripping, drop by drop, 5
Upon the quiet mountain top,
Steals drowsily and musically
Into the universal valley.

The rosemary nods upon the grave;
The lily lolls upon the wave; 10
Wrapping the fog about its breast,
The ruin moulders into rest;
Looking like Lethe, see! the lake
A conscious slumber seems to take,
And would not, for the world, awake. 15
All Beauty sleeps!—and lo! where lies
Irene, with her Destinies!

Oh, lady bright! can it be right—
This window open to the night?
The wanton airs, from the tree-top, 20
Laughingly through the lattice drop—
The bodiless airs, a wizard rout,
Flit through thy chamber in and out,
And wave the curtain canopy
So fitfully—so fearfully— 25
Above the closed and fringed lid
'Neath which thy slumb'ring soul lies hid,
That, o'er the floor and down the wall,
Like ghosts the shadows rise and fall!
Oh, lady dear, hast thou no fear? 30
Why and what art thou dreaming here?
Sure thou art come o'er far-off seas,
A wonder to these garden trees!
Strange is thy pallor! strange thy dress!
Strange, above all, thy length of tress, 35
And this all solemn silentness!

The lady sleeps! Oh, may her sleep,
Which is enduring, so be deep!
Heaven have her in its sacred keep!
This chamber changed for one more holy, 40
This bed for one more melancholy,
I pray to God that she may lie
Forever with unopened eye,
While the pale sheeted ghosts go by!

My love, she sleeps! Oh, may her sleep, 45
As it is lasting, so be deep!

Soft may the worms about her creep!
Far in the forest, dim and old,
For her may some tall vault unfold—
Some vault that oft hath flung its black 50
And winged panels fluttering back,
Triumphant, o'er the crested palls,
Of her grand family funerals—
Some sepulchre, remote, alone,
Against whose portal she hath thrown, 55
In childhood, many an idle stone—
Some tomb from out whose sounding door
She ne'er shall force an echo more,
Thrilling to think, poor child of sin!
It was the dead who groaned within. 60

EXERCISE:

1. Discuss the appropriateness of the poet's handling of meter and rime in lines 18–19 and in lines 30–31.

2. Line 35 presumably refers to the belief that the hair continues to grow after death. But would Irene's hair have grown noticeably longer in some two or three days after her death?

3. Consider the wish expressed in line 47. Even if the worms were not very considerate, and flung themselves about in a noisy, rowdy manner, how much noise would they make?

4. The picture of the naughty, mischievous little girl (lines 54–60), throwing pebbles at the funeral vault is convincing. But how well does it accord with the tone of the rest of the poem?

Luke Havergal

EDWIN ARLINGTON ROBINSON [1869–1935]

Go to the western gate, Luke Havergal,
There where the vines cling crimson on the wall,
And in the twilight wait for what will come.
The leaves will whisper there of her, and some,
Like flying words, will strike you as they fall; 5
But go, and if you listen, she will call.
Go to the western gate, Luke Havergal—
Luke Havergal.

No, there is not a dawn in eastern skies
To rift the fiery night that's in your eyes; 10
But there, where western glooms are gathering,
The dark will end the dark, if anything:
God slays Himself with every leaf that flies,
And hell is more than half of paradise.
No, there is not a dawn in eastern skies— 15
In eastern skies.

Out of a grave I come to tell you this,
Out of a grave I come to quench the kiss
That flames upon your forehead with a glow
That blinds you to the way that you must go. 20
Yes, there is yet one way to where she is,
Bitter, but one that faith may never miss.
Out of a grave I come to tell you this—
To tell you this.

There is the western gate, Luke Havergal, 25
There are the crimson leaves upon the wall.
Go, for the winds are tearing them away,—
Nor think to riddle the dead words they say,
Nor any more to feel them as they fall;
But go, and if you trust her she will call. 30
There is the western gate, Luke Havergal—
Luke Havergal.

Exercise:

1. Compare and contrast this poem with "Ulalume" (p. 194).

2. What paradoxes does the poet use? What is their effect upon the tone of the poem?

3. Discuss the rhythm of the poem. Does it suggest an incantation? Is the rhythm used to conceal weaknesses in the poem? Or does it strengthen the poem by emphasizing and enforcing the meaning of the poem?

Voices

WALTER DE LA MARE [1873–]

Who is it calling by the darkened river
  Where the moss lies smooth and deep,

And the dark trees lean unmoving arms,
  Silent and vague in sleep,
And the bright-heeled constellations pass 5
  In splendour through the gloom;
Who is it calling o'er the darkened river
    In music, "Come!"?

Who is it wandering in the summer meadows
  Where the children stoop and play 10
In the green faint-scented flowers, spinning
  The guileless hours away?
Who touches their bright hair? who puts
  A wind-shell to each cheek,
Whispering betwixt its breathing silences, 15
    "Seek! seek!"?

Who is it watching in the gathering twilight
  When the curfew bird hath flown
On eager wings, from song to silence,
  To its darkened nest alone? 20
Who takes for brightening eyes the stars,
  For locks the still moonbeam,
Sighs through the dews of evening peacefully
    Falling, "Dream!"?

EXERCISE:

1. Compare and contrast this poem with "Luke Havergal" (p. 203) and with "Ulalume" (p. 194).

2. Does this poem attempt to work up an indefinite and vague "poetic" mood? Or does the poem have a definite and meaningful structure?

A Litany

SIR PHILIP SIDNEY [1554–1586]

Ring out your bells, let mourning shows be spread; } solemnity
For Love is dead.
  All Love is dead, infected
With plague of deep disdain;
  Worth, as nought worth, rejected, 5

And Faith fair scorn doth gain.
From so ungrateful fancy,
From such a female franzy,
From them that use men thus,
Good Lord, deliver us! 10

Weep, neighbors, weep! do you not hear it said
That Love is dead?
His death-bed, peacock's folly;
His winding-sheet is shame;
His will, false-seeming holy; 15
His sole executor, blame.
From so ungrateful fancy,
From such a female franzy,
From them that use men thus,
Good Lord, deliver us! 20

Let dirge be sung and trentals rightly read,
For Love is dead.
Sir Wrong his tomb ordaineth
My mistress Marble-heart,
Which epitaph containeth, 25
"Her eyes were once his dart."
From so ungrateful fancy,
From such a female franzy,
From them that use men thus,
Good Lord, deliver us! 30

Alas! I lie, rage hath this error bred;
Love is not dead.
Love is not dead, but sleepeth
In her unmatchèd mind,
Where she his counsel keepeth, 35
Till due desert she find.
Therefore from so vile fancy,
To call such wit a franzy,
Who Love can temper thus,
Good Lord, deliver us! 40

What is the tone of the first stanza of this poem? The title tells us that the poem is a litany, that is, a prayer connected with religious ritual; and we find that the last line of the refrain is actually taken from the liturgy of the Church. Moreover, the poet asks that the bells be rung. The death of love is described as if it were the death of a person, a person who has died of the plague. Disdain, like a disease, has infected the love of the lady for the speaker, and that love is now dead, altogether dead.

By describing the death of love in terms of a funeral, the poet achieves a certain solemnity. He refrains from comment on the situation, or rather he defers his comment on the situation until the last line, and this last line of comment is not mere bold comment—it is part of the imagery of the church service already prepared for above.

The first stanza has then the tone of a solemn announcement. The word *fancy,* by the way, means "love." It is used here in the sense which it has still in our phrase "fancy free"—a meaning which is otherwise obsolete today.

But the tone of the poem, already shifted a little in the refrain with the phrase "female franzy," alters radically in the second stanza. The change is indicated in the very first line in calling on the neighbors to weep. It is as if the poet querulously and in self-mockery should nudge the people next to him and say, Why don't you do something about it? The movement of the first two lines helps to convey this sense of mocking impatience. In the first stanza there is a heavy pause after the long first line, so that the short line

For Love is dead

comes as a solemn announcement. In the second stanza, in the first line, a heavy pause occurs after the second *weep* so that we hurry on rapidly through the sense-unit: "Do you not hear it said that Love is dead?"

But in his self-mockery the poet does not abandon his original figure. He retains it, for ironical effect, exaggerating it somewhat, for the purpose of making it a vehicle for his bitter scorn. The little allegory of the death of love is thus made a piece of conscious frippery for the poet to exhibit ironically for laughter. He pictures love on a death bed made of peacock feathers and the gorgeousness of the bed itself increases the irony. The peacock, incidentally, is a stock figure of overweening pride. It is appropriate therefore that its feathers should furnish forth love's death bed. The poet goes on to elaborate for the purposes of mockery all the other appurtenances of a human death—the winding-sheet, the will, the executor.

The third stanza, which carries on this elaboration, contains several elliptical constructions which the reader must be aware of if he is to understand the grammar: "Sir Wrong ordaineth (that is, solemnly proclaims) my mistress's Marble-heart as his (love's) tomb which containeth (the) epitaph 'Her (the mistress's) eyes were once his (love's) dart.'" The irony of this last clause would be more apparent to a reader of Sidney's own time than perhaps to a modern reader, for in Elizabethan time certain mannerisms of love poetry were flourishing. These mannerisms grew from the tradition of Petrarch, the Italian poet of the fourteenth century who first popularized the love sonnet. In what came to be known as the Petrarchan tradition, the lover's mistress was often ridiculously idolized; her beauty was superlative; her eyes gave death-dealing glances, etc.; the devotion of the lover could only be described in extravagant terms. The imagery, used here in the description of Love's tomb, is Petrarchan; princely tombs were made of marble, and the hardness of the lady's heart, its marblelike quality, makes it appropriate that it should be Love's tomb. She once furnished Love with his darts, supplying him with the bright beams of her eyes (with an allusion to the belief that love flashed from a beautiful woman's eyes). But the imagery here is plainly *mock-heroic* (*Glossary*). Sidney has used these clichés ironically, expecting the reader to recognize their stereotyped quality. They help define the appropriate tone. (See "The Pilgrims," p. 181.)

But with the fourth stanza the tone is abruptly changed again. The poet suddenly tells us in the first line that he has been lying. The meter of the first four lines of this stanza reflects the change in tone. Consider the system of pauses. There is a definite pause after *lie*. The sense demands it, but in addition the meter supports it. Sidney has substituted a trochee for the expected iamb in the third foot. Compare for example

Alas! | I lie, | rage hath | this er | ror bred

with

Alas! | I lie, | for rage | this er | ror bred.

The first demands more than usual stress on *rage* and it demands a heavy pause after *I lie.* (See analysis of "After Long Silence," pp. 116–22.)

There is, of course, a heavy pause after *bred,* but the poet has done something else to throw emphasis on the statement that "Love is not dead." In the three earlier stanzas the second line reads, "For Love is dead," "That Love is dead," and "For Love is dead." All of these are regular iambic lines, and we have become accustomed to expect that pattern at this point in each stanza. But in this stanza the poet makes a trochaic substitution in the first foot and writes:

Love is not dead.

The result is a slight shock—the other pattern having been established in our minds—and a slowing down of the line: this is appropriate because the poem turns here. The poet has used still another device. He repeats in the next line "Love is not dead" and the statement is emphasized only to be swept along with the full line: "Love is not dead, but sleepeth."

The flow of the verse through this part of the stanza with the run-on line and the volume given to *unmatchèd* by pronouncing it as a trisyllable, gives a sense of triumphant assurance after the halting pauses of the first part of the stanza.

The tone is that which a man might use who has come to himself and finds that the precious thing which he has believed lost is not lost at all. This tone is supported not only by the movement of the verse but also by the contrast of the imagery of the last stanza with the Petrarchan frippery of the two preceding stanzas.

Moreover, the refrain which has been used to castigate his mistress is now turned on himself and the belief to which he has been previously giving expression. We have already pointed out that the word *fancy* as used earlier in the poem means "love" though it also bears the meaning of "whim" associated as it is with "female franzy." But in this last stanza its meaning is clearly defined. It is merely an imagination and it is a vile imagination "To call such wit a franzy."

The poem then shows several changes of tone: the solemn pronouncement of the first lines, the mock-heroic ironic tone of the middle section, and the tone of the last section just described. The changes of tone correspond to a very definite psychological structure. It is as if a lover stated to himself the fact that his love was dead; then went on to parade his grief in scorn of it and revulsion; and finally, having vented his irony—his anger having spent itself and cleared the air—turned suddenly to see that love was not dead at all, and that his mistress, far from being whimsical and cruel, was justified, his temporary revulsion having the effect of letting him see her real nature better. We do not of course have to read this dramatic interpretation into the poem. But the development of tone in a poem always conforms, in so far as the work is successful, to a psychological structure; for, as we have said, every poem is a little drama (*Introduction,* p. liv). It is easy to isolate, in a poem like "A Litany," the matter of tone for discussion, but it must be remembered that tone is a factor in all poetry.

Cynara

ERNEST DOWSON [1867–1900]

Last night, ah, yesternight, betwixt her lips and mine
There fell thy shadow, Cynara! thy breath was shed
Upon my soul between the kisses and the wine;
And I was desolate and sick of an old passion,
  Yea, I was desolate and bowed my head: 5
I have been faithful to thee, Cynara! in my fashion.

All night upon mine heart I felt her warm heart beat,
Night-long within mine arms in love and sleep she lay;
Surely the kisses of her bought red mouth were sweet;
But I was desolate and sick of an old passion, 10
  When I awoke and found the dawn was gray:
I have been faithful to thee, Cynara! in my fashion.

I have forgot much, Cynara! gone with the wind,
Flung roses, roses, riotously with the throng,
Dancing, to put thy pale, lost lilies out of mind; 15
But I was desolate and sick of an old passion,
  Yea, all the time, because the dance was long:
I have been faithful to thee, Cynara! in my fashion.

I cried for madder music and for stronger wine,
But when the feast is finished and the lamps expire, 20
Then falls thy shadow, Cynara! the night is thine;
And I am desolate and sick of an old passion,
  Yea, hungry for the lips of my desire:
I have been faithful to thee, Cynara! in my fashion.

EXERCISE:

This poem, like "A Litany," by Sidney (p. 205), deals with the subject of lost love. Dowson centers his poem on a paradox: "I have been faithful to thee, Cynara! in my fashion." Presumably, he felt that the use of this paradox would lend a sharpness, a sense of precise statement, and a toughness that would help him to avoid the sentimental and trite in treating his subject.

1. Assuming that there is an element of truth in the paradox, and that a successful poem might be based upon it, the question remains: Is this a successful poem?

2. Does the speaker seem to enjoy feeling sorry for himself? Does he enjoy recalling what a sad dog he has been? In this connection, consider how much of the poem is taken up with recounting his past exploits.

3. How well (or ill) do the "pale, lost lilies" (in contrast with the riotous roses) suggest the personality of Cynara?

4. Does the paradox develop as the poem proceeds? Does repetition enrich its meaning or weaken it? (Suppose that we reversed the order of the last three stanzas. Would transposing them make any difference?)

Lay Your Sleeping Head, My Love

W. H. AUDEN [1907–]

Lay your sleeping head, my love,
Human on my faithless arm;
Time and fevers burn away
Individual beauty from
Thoughtful children, and the grave 5
Proves the child ephemeral:
But in my arms till break of day

Let the living creature lie,
Mortal, guilty, but to me
The entirely beautiful. 10

Soul and body have no bounds:
To lovers as they lie upon
Her tolerant enchanted slope
In their ordinary swoon,
Grave the vision Venus sends 15
Of supernatural sympathy,
Universal love and hope;
While an abstract insight wakes
Among the glaciers and the rocks
The hermit's sensual ecstasy. 20

Certainty, fidelity
On the stroke of midnight pass
Like vibrations of a bell,
And fashionable madmen raise
Their pedantic boring cry: 25
Every farthing of the cost,
All the dreaded cards foretell,
Shall be paid, but from this night
Not a whisper, not a thought,
Not a kiss nor look be lost. 30

Beauty, midnight, vision dies:
Let the winds of dawn that blow
Softly round your dreaming head
Such a day of sweetness show
Eye and knocking heart may bless, 35
Find the mortal world enough;
Noons of dryness see you fed
By the involuntary powers,
Nights of insult let you pass
Watched by every human love. 40

EXERCISE:

1. In this poem the speaker attempts to account for the facts which the illusion of love does not alter, and yet attempts to do justice to the intensity of the illusion itself. Is he successful or not?

If successful, what sort of tone does he gain by his manner of procedure?

2. Why does he call his arm (line 2) "faithless"? Does this acknowledgment deny seriousness to his protestation of love, or does it intensify the seriousness?

3. What is the meaning of "Find the mortal world enough" (line 36)? May this line be said to summarize the theme of the poem?

A Fine Old Ballad

JOHN CLARE [1793–1864]

Fare you well, my own true love,
And fare you well for a while;
And I will be sure to return back again
If I go ten thousand miles, my dear,
  If I go ten thousand miles. 5

Ten thousand mile's a long, long way,
When from me you are gone;
You'll leave me here to lament and sigh
But never shall hear me moan, my dear,
  But never shall hear me moan. 10

To hear you moan I cannot bear,
Or cure you of your disease;
I shall be sure to return back again
When all your friends are pleased, my dear,
  When all your friends are pleased. 15

If my friends should never be pleased—
They're grown so lofty and high—
I will never prove false to the girl I love
Till the stars they fall from the sky, my love,
  Till the stars they fall from the sky. 20

Oh, if the stars never fall from the sky
Nor the rocks never melt in the sun,
I never will prove false to the girl I love
Till all these things are done, my dear,
  Till all these things are done. 25

Don't you see yon little turtle-dove
That sits on yonder tree,
Making a moan for the loss of her love
As I will do for thee, my dear,
As I will do for thee? 30

The blackest crow that ever flies
Shall change his color white,
And if ever I prove false to thee, my love,
The day shall turn to night, my dear,
The day shall turn to night. 35

But if these things ne'er come to pass
So long as we both do live,
I ne'er will prove false, my love, to thee
Till we're both laid in one grave, my dear,
Till we're both laid in one grave. 40

EXERCISE:

As the title indicates, this poem makes use of certain ballad conventions, including extravagant promises of faithfulness.

1. Is the poem intended as a parody of the ballad conventions? Or does it use them for its own purpose? What is that purpose?

2. Consider the poem as a love poem. Does it manage to convey any sense of tenderness? What is the effect of line 36 on the tone of the poem?

3. Compare the use of extravagant statement in this poem with that in "Lay Your Sleeping Head, My Love." With the use of extravagant statement in "The Definition of Love" (p. 293).

The Going

THOMAS HARDY [1840–1928]

Why did you give no hint that night
That quickly after the morrow's dawn,
And calmly, as if indifferent quite,
You would close your term here, up and be gone
Where I could not follow 5
With wing of swallow
To gain one glimpse of you ever anon!

Never to bid good-bye,
Or lip me the softest call,
Or utter a wish for a word, while I 10
Saw morning harden upon the wall,
Unmoved, unknowing
That your great going
Had place that moment, and altered all.

Why do you make me leave the house 15
And think for a breath it is you I see
At the end of the alley of bending boughs
Where so often at dusk you used to be;
Till in darkening dankness
The yawning blankness 20
Of the perspective sickens me!

You were she who abode
By those red-veined rocks far West,
You were the swan-necked one who rode
Along the beetling Beeny Crest, 25
And, reining nigh me,
Would muse and eye me,
While Life unrolled us its very best.

Why, then, latterly did we not speak,
Did we not think of those days long dead, 30
And ere your vanishing strive to seek
That time's renewal? We might have said,
"In this bright spring weather
We'll visit together
Those places that once we visited." 35

Well, well! All's past amend,
Unchangeable. It must go.
I seem but a dead man held on end
To sink down soon. . . . O you could not know
That such swift fleeing 40
No soul foreseeing—
Not even I—would undo me so!

Exercise:

Hardy wrote this poem to his wife, who had died at night from a heart attack. One other piece of information may be useful: there had been some estrangement between the poet and his wife and for some years she had been accustomed to take trips away from home without previously telling her husband of her intention. So her dying without warning becomes a kind of extension of the ordinary habit of leaving unexpectedly.

1. Discuss contrast and shifts of tone in the poem. In doing so, the following considerations may be useful. The word *term,* as it appears in line 3, has some sense of the term of a lease or some other formal or legal arrangement. The phrase "great going" in the next to the last line of the second stanza has a Shakespearian or Elizabethan flavor—the sort of phrase that might have been used, say, of a royal progress. In the last line of the third stanza, the word *perspective* is precise and semi-technical.

2. The phrase "Not even I" in the last line of the poem comes in parenthetically, almost casually. How important, however, is this for the poem? What does it imply about the poet's attitude in the past toward his wife?

3. "Undo" (line 42) might seem too flat and tame a word to describe the change in him. Can you justify the choice of this word here?

4. How is the poem kept restrained and yet powerful in its effect? Consider in this connection, among other things, line 36. How would you describe the tone of this poem?

5. Compare this poem with "Rose Aylmer" (p. 144) and with "Luke Havergal" (p. 203).

Shadwell

JOHN DRYDEN [1631–1700]

Now stop your noses, readers, all and some,
For here's a tun of midnight work to come,
Og, from a treason-tavern rolling home.
Round as a globe, and liquor'd ev'ry chink,
Goodly and great he sails behind his link; 5

With all this bulk there's nothing lost in Og,
For ev'ry inch that is not fool is rogue:
A monstrous mass of foul corrupted matter,
As all the devils had spew'd to make the batter.
When wine has given him courage to blaspheme, 10
He curses God, but God before curs'd him;
And if man could have reason, none has more,
That made his paunch so rich, and him so poor.
With wealth he was not trusted, for Heav'n knew
What 'twas of old to pamper up a Jew; 15
To what would he on quail and pheasant swell,
That ev'n on tripe and carrion could rebel?
But tho' Heav'n made him poor, (with rev'rence speaking,)
He never was a poet of God's making;
The midwife laid her hand on his thick skull, 20
With this prophetic blessing: *Be thou dull;*
Drink, swear, and roar, forbear no lewd delight
Fit for thy bulk, do anything but write.
Thou art of lasting make, like thoughtless men,
A strong nativity—but for the pen; 25
Eat opium, mingle arsenic in thy drink,
Still you mayst live, avoiding pen and ink.
I see, I see, 'tis counsel given in vain,
For treason botch'd in rhyme will be thy bane;
Rhyme is the rock on which thou art to wreck, 30
'Tis fatal to thy fame and to thy neck.
Why should thy metre good King David blast,
A psalm of his will surely be thy last.
Dar'st thou presume in verse to meet thy foes,
Thou whom the penny pamphlet foil'd in prose? 35
Doeg, whom God for mankind's mirth has made,
O'ertops thy talent in thy very trade;
Doeg to thee, thy paintings are so coarse,
A poet is, tho' he's the poets' horse.
A double noose thou on thy neck dost pull 40
For writing treason, and for writing dull;
To die for faction is a common evil,
But to be hang'd for nonsense is the devil.
Hadst thou the glories of thy king express'd,
Thy praises had been satire at the best; 45

But thou in clumsy verse, unlick'd, unpointed,
Hast shamefully defied the Lord's anointed:
I will not rake the dunghill of thy crimes,
For who would read thy life that reads thy rhymes?
But of King David's foes, be this the doom, 50
May all be like the young man Absalom;
And for my foes may this their blessing be,
To talk like Doeg, and to write like thee.

EXERCISE:

Og is Thomas Shadwell and Doeg is Elkanah Settle, two Whig poets who had attacked Dryden in a verse pamphlet. King David represents Charles II, and Absalom his illegitimate son, the Duke of Monmouth, whom the Whigs hoped to have legitimized so that he might succeed his father instead of the unpopular brother of the King, the Duke of York. Dryden suggests that Shadwell was involved in treasonous plots against the king.

1. Does Dryden hate Shadwell? Does he feel righteous indignation? Or does he refuse to take seriously either his poetry or his treason?

2. How is Doeg used to point the satire?

3. Dryden does not hesitate to jibe at personal defects (Og's corpulence) or at his poverty. Can you justify these personal references? Is there a sense in which the tone remains "good-natured" in spite of these? Characterize the tone of this satire as precisely as you can.

The Season 'Tis, My Lovely Lambs

E. E. CUMMINGS [1894–]

the season 'tis, my lovely lambs,

of Sumner Volstead Christ and Co.
the epoch of Mann's righteousness
the age of dollars and no sense.
Which being quite beyond dispute 5

as prove from Troy (N. Y.) to Cairo
(Egypt) the luminous dithyrambs

of large immaculate unmute
antibolshevistic gents
(each manufacturing word by word 10
his own unrivalled brand of pyro
-technic blurb anent the (hic)
hero dead that gladly (sic)
in far lands perished of unheard
of maladies including flu) 15

my little darlings, let us now
passionately remember how—
braving the worst, of peril heedless,
each braver than the other, each
(a typewriter within his reach) 20
upon his fearless derrière
sturdily seated—Colonel Needless
To Name and General You know who
a string of pretty medals drew

(while messrs jack james john and jim 25
in token of their country's love
received my dears theorder of
The Artificial Arm and Limb)

—or, since bloodshed and kindred questions
inhibit unprepared digestions, 30
come: let us mildly contemplate
beginning with his wellfilled pants
earth's biggest grafter, nothing less;
the Honorable Mr. (guess)
who, breathing on the ear of fate, 35
landed a seat in the legislat-
ure whereas tommy so and so
(an erring child of circumstance
whom the bulls nabbed at 33rd)

pulled six months for selling snow 40

Exercise:

1. What is the tone of this poem? Relate to the tone the poet's puns, forced rimes, slang expressions, and irreverently used clichés.

2. Does the poet merely delight in disfiguring whatever stuffed shirts conveniently present themselves? Is his satire briskly irresponsible? Or does it stem from a positive set of values? How would you justify the satiric method used here?

Kind of an Ode to Duty

OGDEN NASH [1903–]

O Duty,
Why hast thou not the visage of a sweetie or a cutie?
Why glitter thy spectacles so ominously?
Why art thou clad so abominously?
Why art thou so different from Venus 5
And why do thou and I have so few interests mutually in common between us?
Why art thou fifty per cent martyr
And fifty-one per cent Tartar?

Why is it thy unfortunate wont
To try to attract people by calling on them either to leave undone the deeds they like, or to do the deeds they don't? 10
Why art thou so like an April post-mortem
On something that died in the ortumn?
Above all, why dost thou continue to hound me?
Why art thou always albatrossly hanging around me?

Thou so ubiquitous, 15
And I so iniquitous.
I seem to be the one person in the world thou art perpetually preaching at who or to who;
Whatever looks like fun, there art thou standing between me and it, calling yoo-hoo.
O Duty, Duty!
How noble a man should I be hadst thou the visage of a sweetie or a cutie! 20
But as it is thou art so much forbiddinger than a Wodehouse hero's forbiddingest aunt
That in the words of the poet, When Duty whispers low, Thou must, this erstwhile youth replies, I just can't.

EXERCISE:

How does the varied line length affect the tone?

The Death of the Ball Turret Gunner

RANDALL JARRELL [1914–]

From my mother's sleep I fell into the State
And I hunched in its belly till my wet fur froze.
Six miles from earth, loosed from its dream of life,
I woke to black flak and the nightmare fighters.
When I died they washed me out of the turret with a hose. 5

EXERCISE:

1. How is the brevity of the gunner's life emphasized by the imagery? How is its "unreality" emphasized? Is it suggested that he remains an embryo?

2. Comment upon the use of understatement and irony in this poem. Try to characterize the tone. Does it seem ragingly bitter? Or coldly bitter? Or what?

Departmental

ROBERT FROST [1875–]

An ant on the table cloth
Ran into a dormant moth
Of many times his size.
He showed not the least surprise.
His business wasn't with such. 5
He gave it scarcely a touch,
And was off on his duty run.
Yet if he encountered one
Of the hive's enquiry squad
Whose work is to find out God 10
And the nature of time and space,
He would put him onto the case.
Ants are a curious race;

One crossing with hurried tread
The body of one of their dead 1
Isn't given a moment's arrest—
Seems not even impressed.
But he no doubt reports to any
With whom he crosses antennae,
And they no doubt report 2
To the higher up at court.
Then word goes forth in Formic:
"Death's come to Jerry McCormic,
Our selfless forager Jerry.
Will the special Janizary 25
Whose office it is to bury
The dead of the commissary
Go bring him home to his people.
Lay him in state on a sepal.
Wrap him for shroud in a petal. 30
Embalm him with ichor of nettle.
This is the word of your Queen."
And presently on the scene
Appears a solemn mortician;
And taking formal position 35
With feelers calmly atwiddle,
Seizes the dead by the middle,
And heaving him high in air,
Carries him out of there.
No one stands round to stare. 40
It is nobody else's affair.

It couldn't be called ungentle.
But how thoroughly departmental.

EXERCISE:

1. What is being satirized in this poem?

2. What is the quality of the irony? Compare and contrast it with that of "The Death of the Ball Turret Gunner" (p. 221).

3. How does the handling of the meter and the use of forced rimes contribute to the special tone? What is the tone?

The Rape of the Lock

ALEXANDER POPE [1688–1744]

CANTO I

What dire offense from am'rous causes springs,
What mighty contests rise from trivial things,
I sing—This verse to Caryl,[1] Muse! is due:
This, e'en Belinda may vouchsafe to view:
Slight is the subject, but not so the praise, 5
If She inspire, and He approve my lays.
  Say what strange motive, Goddess! could compel
A well-bred Lord t' assault a gentle Belle?
O say what stranger cause, yet unexplored,
Could make a gentle Belle reject a Lord? 10
In tasks so bold, can little men engage,
And in soft bosoms dwells such mighty Rage?
  Sol through white curtains shot a tim'rous ray,
And oped those eyes that must eclipse the day:
Now lap-dogs give themselves the rousing shake, 15
And sleepless lovers, just at twelve, awake:
Thrice rung the bell, the slipper knocked the ground,
And the pressed watch returned a silver sound.
Belinda still her downy pillow pressed,
Her guardian Sylph prolonged the balmy rest: 20
'T was He had summoned to her silent bed
The morning-dream that hovered o'er her head;
A Youth more glitt'ring than a Birth-night Beau
(That e'en in slumber caused her cheek to glow),
Seemed to her ear his winning lips to lay, 25
And thus in whispers said, or seemed to say:
  'Fairest of mortals, thou distinguished care
Of thousand bright Inhabitants of Air!
If e'er one vision touched thy infant thought,
Of all the Nurse and all the Priest have taught; 30
Of airy Elves by moonlight shadows seen,
The silver token, and the circled green,
Or virgins visited by Angel-pow'rs,
With golden crowns and wreaths of heav'nly flow'rs;

[1] a friend of Pope, who suggested the subject

Hear and believe! thy own importance know, 35
Nor bound thy narrow views to things below.
Some secret truths, from learnèd pride concealed,
To Maids alone and Children are revealed:
What though no credit doubting Wits may give?
The Fair and Innocent shall still believe. 40
Know, then, unnumbered Spirits round thee fly,
The light Militia of the lower sky:
These, though unseen, are ever on the wing,
Hang o'er the Box, and hover round the Ring.[1]
Think what an equipage thou hast in Air, 45
And view with scorn two Pages and a Chair.
As now your own, our beings were of old,
And once enclosed in Woman's beauteous mold;
Thence, by a soft transition, we repair
From earthly Vehicles to these of air. 50
Think not, when Woman's transient breath is fled,
That all her vanities at once are dead;
Succeeding vanities she still regards,
And though she plays no more, o'erlooks the cards.
Her joy in gilded Chariots, when alive, 55
And love of Ombre,[2] after death survive.
For when the Fair in all their pride expire,
To their first Elements their Souls retire:
The Sprites of fiery Termagants in Flame
Mount up, and take a Salamander's name. 60
Soft yielding minds to Water glide away,
And sip, with Nymphs, their elemental Tea.
The graver Prude sinks downward to a Gnome,
In search of mischief still on Earth to roam.
The light Coquettes in Sylphs aloft repair, 65
And sport and flutter in the fields of Air.
'Know further yet; whoever fair and chaste
Rejects mankind, is by some Sylph embraced:
For Spirits, freed from mortal laws, with ease
Assume what sexes and what shapes they please. 70
What guards the purity of melting Maids,
In courtly balls, and midnight masquerades,
Safe from the treach'rous friend, the daring spark,
The glance by day, the whisper in the dark,

[1] a circular drive in Hyde Park [2] a game of cards

When kind occasion prompts their warm desires, 75
When music softens, and when dancing fires?
'T is but their Sylph, the wise Celestials know,
Though Honor is the word with Men below.
'Some nymphs there are, too conscious of their face,
For life predestined to the Gnomes' embrace. 80
These swell their prospects and exalt their pride,
When offers are disdained, and love denied:
Then gay Ideas crowd the vacant brain,
While Peers, and Dukes, and all their sweeping train,
And Garters, Stars, and Coronets appear, 85
And in soft sounds, Your Grace salutes their ear.
'T is these that early taint the female soul,
Instruct the eyes of young Coquettes to roll,
Teach Infant-cheeks a bidden blush to know,
And little hearts to flutter at a Beau. 90
'Oft, when the world imagine women stray,
The Sylphs through mystic mazes guide their way,
Through all the giddy circle they pursue,
And old impertinence expel by new.
What tender maid but must a victim fall 95
To one man's treat, but for another's ball?
When Florio speaks what virgin could withstand,
If gentle Damon did not squeeze her hand?
With varying vanities, from ev'ry part,
They shift the moving Toyshop of their heart; 100
Where wigs with wigs, with sword-knots sword-knots strive,
Beaux banish beaux, and coaches coaches drive.
This erring mortals Levity may call;
Oh blind to truth! the Sylphs contrive it all.
'Of these am I, who thy protection claim, 105
A watchful sprite, and Ariel is my name.
Late, as I ranged the crystal wilds of air,
In the clear Mirror of thy ruling Star
I saw, alas! some dread event impend,
Ere to the main this morning sun descend, 110
But heav'n reveals not what, or how, or where:
Warned by the Sylph, oh pious maid, beware!
This to disclose is all thy guardian can:
Beware of all, but most beware of Man!'

He said; when Shock, who thought she slept too long, 115
Leaped up, and waked his mistress with his tongue.
'T was then, Belinda, if report say true,
Thy eyes first opened on a Billet-doux;
Wounds, Charms, and Ardors were no sooner read,
But all the Vision vanished from thy head. 120
And now, unveiled, the Toilet stands displayed,
Each silver Vase in mystic order laid.
First, robed in white, the Nymph intent adores,
With head uncovered, the Cosmetic pow'rs.
A heav'nly image in the glass appears, 125
To that she bends, to that her eyes she rears;
Th' inferior Priestess, at her altar's side,
Trembling begins the sacred rites of Pride.
Unnumbered treasures ope at once, and here
The various off'rings of the world appear; 130
From each she nicely culls with curious toil,
And decks the Goddess with the glitt'ring spoil.
This casket India's glowing gems unlocks,
And all Arabia breathes from yonder box.
The Tortoise here and Elephant unite, 135
Transformed to combs, the speckled, and the white.
Here files of pins extend their shining rows,
Puffs, Powders, Patches, Bibles, Billet-doux.
Now awful Beauty puts on all its arms;
The fair each moment rises in her charms, 140
Repairs her smiles, awakens ev'ry grace,
And calls forth all the wonders of her face;
Sees by degrees a purer blush arise,
And keener lightnings quicken in her eyes.
The busy Sylphs surround their darling care, 145
These set the head, and those divide the hair,
Some fold the sleeve, whilst others plait the gown;
And Betty's praised for labors not her own.

CANTO II

Not with more glories, in th' etherial plain,
The Sun first rises o'er the purpled main,
Than, issuing forth, the rival of his beams
Launched on the bosom of the silver Thames.

Fair Nymphs, and well-dressed Youths around her shone, 5
But ev'ry eye was fixed on her alone.
On her white breast a sparkling Cross she wore,
Which Jews might kiss, and Infidels adore.
Her lively looks a sprightly mind disclose,
Quick as her eyes, and as unfixed as those: 10
Favors to none, to all she smiles extends;
Oft she rejects, but never once offends.
Bright as the sun, her eyes the gazers strike,
And, like the sun, they shine on all alike.
Yet graceful ease, and sweetness void of pride, 15
Might hide her faults, if Belles had faults to hide:
If to her share some female errors fall,
Look on her face, and you'll forget 'em all.
This Nymph, to the destruction of mankind,
Nourished two Locks which graceful hung behind 20
In equal curls, and well conspired to deck
With shining ringlets the smooth iv'ry neck.
Love in these labyrinths his slaves detains,
And mighty hearts are held in slender chains.
With hairy springes we the birds betray, 25
Slight lines of hair surprise the finny prey,
Fair tresses man's imperial race ensnare,
And beauty draws us with a single hair.
Th' advent'rous Baron the bright locks admired;
He saw, he wished, and to the prize aspired. 30
Resolved to win, he meditates the way,
By force to ravish, or by fraud betray;
For when success a Lover's toil attends,
Few ask, if fraud or force attained his ends.
For this, ere Phœbus rose, he had implored 35
Propitious heav'n, and every pow'r adored,
But chiefly Love—to Love an Altar built,
Of twelve vast French Romances, neatly gilt.
There lay three garters, half a pair of gloves;
And all the trophies of his former loves; 40
With tender Billet-doux he lights the pyre,
And breathes three am'rous sighs to raise the fire.
Then prostrate falls, and begs with ardent eyes
Soon to obtain, and long possess the prize:

The pow'rs gave ear, and granted half his pray'r, 45
The rest, the winds dispersed in empty air.
  But now secure the painted vessel glides,
The sun-beams trembling on the floating tides:
While melting music steals upon the sky,
And softened sounds along the waters die; 50
Smooth flow the waves, the Zephyrs gently play,
Belinda smiled, and all the world was gay.
All but the Sylph—with careful thoughts oppressed,
Th' impending woe sat heavy on his breast.
He summons straight his Denizens of air; 55
The lucid squadrons round the sails repair:
Soft o'er the shrouds aërial whispers breathe,
That seemed but Zephyrs to the train beneath.
Some to the sun their insect-wings unfold,
Waft on the breeze, or sink in clouds of gold; 60
Transparent forms, too fine for mortal sight,
Their fluid bodies half dissolved in light,
Loose to the wind their airy garments flew,
Thin glitt'ring textures of the filmy dew,
Dipped in the richest tincture of the skies, 65
Where light disports in ever-mingling dyes,
While ev'ry beam new transient colors flings,
Colors that change whene'er they wave their wings.
Amid the circle, on the gilded mast,
Superior by the head, was Ariel placed; 70
His purple pinions op'ning to the sun,
He raised his azure wand, and thus begun:
  'Ye Sylphs and Sylphids, to your chief give ear!
Fays, Fairies, Genii, Elves, and Demons, hear!
Ye know the spheres and various tasks assigned 75
By laws eternal to th' aërial kind.
Some in the fields of purest ether play,
And bask and whiten in the blaze of day.
Some guide the course of wand'ring orbs on high,
Or roll the planets through the boundless sky. 80
Some less refined, beneath the moon's pale light
Pursue the stars that shoot athwart the night,
Or suck the mists in grosser air below,
Or dip their pinions in the painted bow,

Or brew fierce tempests on the wintry main, 85
Or o'er the glebe distil the kindly rain.
Others on earth o'er human race preside,
Watch all their ways, and all their actions guide:
Of these the chief the care of Nations own,
And guard with Arms divine the British Throne. 90
'Our humbler province is to tend the Fair,
Not a less pleasing, though less glorious care;
To save the powder from too rude a gale,
Nor let th' imprisoned essences exhale;
To draw fresh colors from the vernal flow'rs; 95
To steal from rainbows e'er they drop in show'rs
A brighter wash; to curl their waving hairs,
Assist their blushes, and inspire their airs;
Nay oft, in dreams, invention we bestow,
To change a Flounce, or add a Furbelow. 100
'This day, black Omens threat the brightest Fair,
That e'er deserved a watchful spirit's care;
Some dire disaster, or by force, or slight;
But what, or where, the fates have wrapped in night.
Whether the nymph shall break Diana's law, 105
Or some frail China jar receive a flaw;
Or stain her honor, or her new brocade;
Forget her pray'rs, or miss a masquerade;
Or lose her heart, or necklace, at a ball;
Or whether Heav'n has doomed that Shock must fall. 110
Haste, then, ye spirits! to your charge repair:
The flutt'ring fan be Zephyretta's care;
The drops to thee, Brillante, we consign;
And, Momentilla, let the watch be thine;
Do thou, Crispissa, tend her fav'rite Lock; 115
Ariel himself shall be the guard of Shock.
'To fifty chosen Sylphs, of special note,
We trust th' important charge, the Petticoat:
Oft have we known that seven-fold fence to fail,
Though stiff with hoops, and armed with ribs of whale; 120
Form a strong line about the silver bound,
And guard the wide circumference around.
'Whatever spirit, careless of his charge,
His post neglects, or leaves the fair at large,

Shall feel sharp vengeance soon o'ertake his sins, 125
Be stopped in vials, or transfixed with pins;
Or plunged in lakes of bitter washes lie,
Or wedged whole ages in a bodkin's eye:
Gums and Pomatums shall his flight restrain,
While clogged he beats his silken wings in vain; 130
Or Alum styptics with contracting pow'r
Shrink his thin essence like a riveled flow'r:
Or, as Ixion fixed, the wretch shall feel
The giddy motion of the whirling Mill,
In fumes of burning Chocolate shall glow, 135
And tremble at the sea that froths below!'
He spoke; the spirits from the sails descend;
Some, orb in orb, around the nymph extend;
Some thread the mazy ringlets of her hair;
Some hang upon the pendants of her ear: 140
With beating hearts the dire event they wait,
Anxious, and trembling for the birth of Fate.

CANTO III

Close by those meads, for ever crowned with flow'rs,
Where Thames with pride surveys his rising tow'rs,
There stands a structure of majestic frame,
Which from the neighb'ring Hampton takes its name.
Here Britain's statesmen oft the fall foredoom 5
Of foreign Tyrants and of Nymphs at home;
Here thou, great Anna! whom three realms obey,
Dost sometimes counsel take—and sometimes Tea.
Hither the heroes and the nymphs resort,
To taste awhile the pleasures of a Court; 10
In various talk th' instructive hours they passed,
Who gave the ball, or paid the visit last;
One speaks the glory of the British Queen,
And one describes a charming Indian screen;
A third interprets motions, looks, and eyes; 15
At ev'ry word a reputation dies.
Snuff, or the fan, supply each pause of chat,
With singing, laughing, ogling, *and all that.*
Meanwhile, declining from the noon of day,
The sun obliquely shoots his burning ray; 20

The hungry Judges soon the sentence sign,
And wretches hang that jurymen may dine;
The merchant from th' Exchange returns in peace,
And the long labors of the Toilet cease.
Belinda now, whom thirst of fame invites, 25
Burns to encounter two advent'rous Knights,
At Ombre singly to decide their doom;
And swells her breast with conquests yet to come.
Straight the three bands prepare in arms to join,
Each band the number of the sacred nine. 30
Soon as she spreads her hand, th' aërial guard
Descend, and sit on each important card:
First Ariel perched upon a Matadore,[1]
Then each, according to the rank they bore;
For Sylphs, yet mindful of their ancient race, 35
Are, as when women, wondrous fond of place.
  Behold, four Kings in majesty revered,
With hoary whiskers and a forky beard;
And four fair Queens whose hands sustain a flow'r,
Th' expressive emblem of their softer pow'r; 40
Four Knaves in garbs succinct, a trusty band,
Caps on their heads, and halberts in their hand;
And particolored troops, a shining train,
Draw forth to combat on the velvet plain.
  The skillful Nymph reviews her force with care: 45
'Let Spades be trumps!' she said, and trumps they were.
  Now move to war her sable Matadores,
In show like leaders of the swarthy Moors.
Spadillio[2] first, unconquerable Lord!
Led off two captive trumps, and swept the board. 50
As many more Manillio[3] forced to yield,
And marched a victor from the verdant field.
Him Basto[4] followed, but his fate more hard
Gained but one trump and one plebeian card.
With his broad saber next, a chief in years, 55
The hoary Majesty of Spades appears,

[1] one of the three highest cards at ombre
[2] the ace of spades
[3] the two of a black, the seven of a red trump
[4] the ace of clubs

Puts forth one manly leg, to sight revealed,
The rest, his many-colored robe concealed.
The rebel Knave, who dares his prince engage,
Proves the just victim of his royal rage. 60
E'en mighty Pam,[1] that Kings and Queens o'erthrew
And mowed down armies in the fights of Lu,
Sad chance of war! now destitute of aid,
Falls undistinguished by the victor spade!
  Thus far both armies to Belinda yield; 65
Now to the Baron fate inclines the field.
His warlike Amazon her host invades,
Th' imperial consort of the crown of Spades.
The Club's black Tyrant first her victim died,
Spite of his haughty mien, and barb'rous pride: 70
What boots the regal circle on his head,
His giant limbs, in state unwieldy spread;
That long behind he trails his pompous robe,
And, of all monarchs, only grasps the globe?
  The Baron now his Diamonds pours apace; 75
Th' embroidered King who shows but half his face,
And his refulgent Queen, with pow'rs combined
Of broken troops an easy conquest find.
Clubs, Diamonds, Hearts, in wild disorder seen,
With throngs promiscuous strew the level green. 80
Thus when dispersed a routed army runs,
Of Asia's troops, and Afric's sable sons,
With like confusion different nations fly,
Of various habit, and of various dye,
The pierced battalions dis-united fall, 85
In heaps on heaps; one fate o'erwhelms them all.
  The Knave of Diamonds tries his wily arts,
And wins (oh shameful chance!) the Queen of Hearts.
At this, the blood the virgin's cheek forsook,
A livid paleness spreads o'er all her look; 90
She sees, and trembles at th' approaching ill,
Just in the jaws of ruin, and Codille.[2]
And now (as oft in some distempered State)
On one nice Trick depends the gen'ral fate.

[1] the knave of clubs, the highest card in the game of loo
[2] failure of the player to take the requisite number of tricks

An Ace of Hearts steps forth: The King unseen 95
Lurked in her hand, and mourned his captive Queen:
He springs to Vengeance with an eager pace,
And falls like thunder on the prostrate Ace.
The nymph exulting fills with shouts the sky;
The walls, the woods, and long canals reply. 100
O thoughtless mortals! ever blind to fate,
Too soon dejected, and too soon elate.
Sudden, these honors shall be snatched away,
And cursed for ever this victorious day.
For lo! the board with cups and spoons is crowned, 105
The berries crackle, and the mill turns round;
On shining Altars of Japan they raise
The silver lamp; the fiery spirits blaze:
From silver spouts the grateful liquors glide,
While China's earth receives the smoking tide: 110
At once they gratify their scent and taste,
And frequent cups prolong the rich repast.
Straight hover round the Fair her airy band;
Some, as she sipped, the fuming liquor fanned,
Some o'er her lap their careful plumes displayed, 115
Trembling, and conscious of the rich brocade.
Coffee (which makes the politician wise,
And see through all things with his half-shut eyes),
Sent up in vapors to the Baron's brain
New Stratagems, the radiant Lock to gain. 120
Ah cease, rash youth! desist ere 't is too late,
Fear the just Gods, and think of Scylla's Fate!
Changed to a bird, and sent to flit in air,
She dearly pays for Nisus' injured hair!
But when to mischief mortals bend their will, 125
How soon they find fit instruments of ill!
Just then, Clarissa drew with tempting grace
A two-edged weapon from her shining case:
So Ladies in Romance assist their Knight,
Present the spear, and arm him for the fight. 130
He takes the gift with rev'rence, and extends
The little engine on his fingers' ends;
This just behind Belinda's neck he spread,
As o'er the fragrant steams she bends her head.

Swift to the Lock a thousand Sprites repair, 135
A thousand wings, by turns, blow back the hair;
And thrice they twitched the diamond in her ear;
Thrice she looked back, and thrice the foe drew near.
Just in that instant, anxious Ariel sought
The close recesses of the Virgin's thought; 140
As on the nosegay in her breast reclined,
He watched th' Ideas rising in her mind,
Sudden he viewed, in spite of all her art,
An earthly Lover lurking at her heart.
Amazed, confused, he found his pow'r expired, 145
Resigned to fate, and with a sigh retired.
The Peer now spreads the glitt'ring Forfex wide,
T' enclose the Lock; now joins it, to divide.
E'en then, before the fatal engine closed,
A wretched Sylph too fondly interposed; 150
Fate urged the shears, and cut the Sylph in twain,
(But airy substance soon unites again)
The meeting points the sacred hair dissever
From the fair head, for ever, and for ever!
Then flashed the living lightning from her eyes, 155
And screams of horror rend th' affrighted skies.
Not louder shrieks to pitying heav'n are cast,
When husbands, or when lapdogs breathe their last;
Or when rich China vessels fall'n from high,
In glitt'ring dust and painted fragments lie! 160
Let wreaths of triumph now my temples twine
(The victor cried) the glorious Prize is mine!
While fish in streams, or birds delight in air,
Or in a coach and six the British Fair,
As long as Atalantis [1] shall be read, 165
Or the small pillow grace a Lady's bed,
While visits shall be paid on solemn days,
When num'rous wax-lights in bright order blaze,
While nymphs take treats, or assignations give,
So long my honor, name, and praise shall live! 170
What Time would spare, from Steel receives its date,
And monuments, like men, submit to fate!
Steel could the labor of the Gods destroy,
And strike to dust th' imperial towers of Troy;

[1] a popular book by Mrs. Manley

Steel could the works of mortal pride confound, 175
And hew triumphal arches to the ground.
What wonder then, fair nymph! thy hairs should feel
The conqu'ring force of unresisted steel?

CANTO IV

But anxious cares the pensive nymph oppressed,
And secret passions labored in her breast.
Not youthful kings in battle seized alive,
Not scornful virgins who their charms survive,
Not ardent lovers robbed of all their bliss, 5
Not ancient ladies when refused a kiss,
Not tyrants fierce that unrepenting die,
Not Cynthia when her manteau's pinned awry,
E'er felt such rage, resentment, and despair,
As thou, sad Virgin! for thy ravished Hair. 10
For, that sad moment, when the Sylphs withdrew
And Ariel weeping from Belinda flew,
Umbriel, a dusky, melancholy sprite,
As ever sullied the fair face of light,
Down to the central earth, his proper scene, 15
Repaired to search the gloomy Cave of Spleen.
Swift on his sooty pinions flits the Gnome,
And in a vapor reached the dismal dome.
No cheerful breeze this sullen region knows,
The dreaded East is all the wind that blows. 20
Here in a grotto, sheltered close from air,
And screened in shades from day's detested glare,
She sighs for ever on her pensive bed,
Pain at her side, and Megrim at her head.
Two handmaids wait the throne: alike in place, 25
But diff'ring far in figure and in face.
Here stood Ill-nature like an ancient maid,
Her wrinkled form in black and white arrayed;
With store of pray'rs, for mornings, nights, and noons,
Her hand is filled; her bosom with lampoons. 30
There Affectation, with a sickly mien,
Shows in her cheek the roses of eighteen,
Practised to lisp, and hang the head aside,
Faints into airs, and languishes with pride,

On the rich quilt sinks with becoming woe, 35
Wrapped in a gown, for sickness, and for show.
The fair ones feel such maladies as these,
When each new night-dress gives a new disease.
A constant Vapor o'er the palace flies;
Strange phantoms rising as the mists arise; 40
Dreadful, as hermit's dreams in haunted shades,
Or bright, as visions of expiring maids.
Now glaring fiends, and snakes on rolling spires,
Pale specters, gaping tombs, and purple fires:
Now lakes of liquid gold, Elysian scenes, 45
And crystal domes, and angels in machines.
Unnumbered throngs on every side are seen,
Of bodies changed to various forms by Spleen.
Here living Tea-pots stand, one arm held out,
One bent; the handle this, and that the spout: 50
A Pipkin there, like Homer's Tripod walks;
Here sighs a Jar, and there a Goose-pie talks;
Men prove with child, as powerful fancy works,
And maids turned bottles, call aloud for corks.
Safe passed the Gnome through this fantastic band, 55
A branch of healing Spleenwort in his hand.
Then thus addressed the pow'r: 'Hail, wayward Queen!
Who rule the sex to fifty from fifteen:
Parent of vapors and of female wit,
Who give th' hysteric, or poetic fit, 60
On various tempers act by various ways,
Make some take physic, others scribble plays;
Who cause the proud their visits to delay,
And send the godly in a pet to pray.
A nymph there is, that all thy pow'r disdains, 65
And thousands more in equal mirth maintains.
But oh! if e'er thy Gnome could spoil a grace,
Or raise a pimple on a beauteous face,
Like Citron-waters matrons' cheeks inflame,
Or change complexions at a losing game; 70
If e'er with airy horns I planted heads,
Or rumpled petticoats, or tumbled beds,
Or caused suspicion when no soul was rude,
Or discomposed the head-dress of a Prude,

Or e'er to costive lap-dog gave disease, 75
Which not the tears of brightest eyes could ease:
Hear me, and touch Belinda with chagrin,
That single act gives half the world the spleen.'
The Goddess with a discontented air
Seems to reject him, though she grants his pray'r. 80
A wondrous Bag with both her hands she binds,
Like that where once Ulysses held the winds;
There she collects the force of female lungs,
Sighs, sobs, and passions, and the war of tongues.
A Vial next she fills with fainting fears, 85
Soft sorrows, melting griefs, and flowing tears.
The Gnome rejoicing bears her gifts away,
Spreads his black wings, and slowly mounts to day.
Sunk in Thalestris' arms the nymph he found,
Her eyes dejected and her hair unbound. 90
Full o'er their heads the swelling bag he rent,
And all the Furies issued at the vent.
Belinda burns with more than mortal ire,
And fierce Thalestris fans the rising fire.
'O wretched maid!' she spread her hands, and cried 95
(While Hampton's echoes, 'Wretched maid!' replied),
'Was it for this you took such constant care
The bodkin, comb, and essence to prepare?
For this your locks in paper durance bound,
For this with tort'ring irons wreathed around? 100
For this with fillets strained your tender head,
And bravely bore the double loads of lead?
Gods! shall the ravisher display your hair,
While the Fops envy, and the Ladies stare!
Honor forbid! at whose unrivaled shrine 105
Ease, pleasure, virtue, all our sex resign.
Methinks already I your tears survey,
Already hear the horrid things they say,
Already see you a degraded toast,
And all your honor in a whisper lost! 110
How shall I, then, your helpless fame defend?
'T will then be infamy to seem your friend!
And shall this prize, th' inestimable prize,
Exposed through crystal to the gazing eyes,

And heightened by the diamond's circling rays, 115
On that rapacious hand for ever blaze?
Sooner shall grass in Hyde-park Circus grow,
And wits take lodgings in the sound of Bow;
Sooner let earth, air, sea, to Chaos fall,
Men, monkeys, lap-dogs, parrots, perish all!' 120
  She said; then raging to Sir Plume repairs,
And bids her Beau demand the precious hairs:
(Sir Plume of amber snuff-box justly vain,
And the nice conduct of a clouded cane)
With earnest eyes, and round unthinking face, 125
He first the snuff-box opened, then the case,
And thus broke out—'My Lord, why, what the devil?
Z—ds! damn the lock! 'fore Gad, you must be civil!
Plague on 't! 't is past a jest—nay prithee, pox!
Give her the hair'—he spoke, and rapped his box. 130
  'It grieves me much' (replied the Peer again)
'Who speaks so well should ever speak in vain.
But by this Lock, this sacred Lock I swear
(Which never more shall join its parted hair;
Which never more its honors shall renew, 135
Clipped from the lovely head where late it grew),
That while my nostrils draw the vital air,
This hand, which won it, shall for ever wear.'
He spoke, and speaking, in proud triumph spread
The long-contended honors of her head. 140
  But Umbriel, hateful Gnome! forbears not so;
He breaks the Vial whence the sorrows flow.
Then see! the nymph in beauteous grief appears,
Her eyes half-languishing, half-drowned in tears;
On her heaved bosom hung her drooping head, 145
Which, with a sigh, she raised; and thus she said:
  'For ever cursed be this detested day,
Which snatched my best, my fav'rite curl away!
Happy! ah, ten times happy had I been,
If Hampton Court these eyes had never seen! 150
Yet am not I the first mistaken maid,
By love of Courts to num'rous ills betrayed.
O had I rather un-admired remained
In some lone isle, or distant Northern land;

Where the gilt Chariot never marks the way, 155
Where none learn Ombre, none e'er taste Bohea!
There kept my charms concealed from mortal eye,
Like roses, that in deserts bloom and die.
What moved my mind with youthful Lords to roam?
O had I stayed, and said my pray'rs at home! 160
'T was this, the morning omens seemed to tell:
Thrice from my trembling hand the patchbox fell;
The tott'ring China shook without a wind,
Nay, Poll sat mute, and Shock was most unkind!
A Sylph too warned me of the threats of fate, 165
In mystic visions, now believed too late!
See the poor remnants of these slighted hairs!
My hands shall rend what e'en thy rapine spares:
These in two sable ringlets taught to break,
Once gave new beauties to the snowy neck; 170
The sister-lock now sits uncouth, alone,
And in its fellow's fate foresees its own;
Uncurled it hangs, the fatal shears demands
And tempts once more thy sacrilegious hands.
O hadst thou, cruel! been content to seize 175
Hairs less in sight, or any hairs but these!'

CANTO V

She said: the pitying audience melt in tears.
But Fate and Jove had stopped the Baron's ears.
In vain Thalestris with reproach assails,
For who can move when fair Belinda fails?
Not half so fixed the Trojan [1] could remain, 5
While Anna begged and Dido raged in vain.
Then grave Clarissa graceful waved her fan;
Silence ensued, and thus the nymph began:
'Say why are Beauties praised and honored most,
The wise man's passion, and the vain man's toast? 10
Why decked with all that land and sea afford,
Why Angels called, and Angel-like adored?
Why round our coaches crowd the white-gloved Beaux,
Why bows the side-box from its inmost rows;

[1] Æneas

How vain are all these glories, all our pains, 15
Unless good sense preserve what beauty gains;
That men may say, when we the front-box grace:
"Behold the first in virtue as in face!"
Oh! if to dance all night, and dress all day,
Charmed the small-pox, or chased old age away; 20
Who would not scorn what housewife's cares produce,
Or who would learn one earthly thing of use?
To patch, nay ogle, might become a Saint,
Nor could it sure be such a sin to paint.
But since, alas! frail beauty must decay, 25
Curled or uncurled, since Locks will turn to gray;
Since painted, or not painted, all shall fade,
And she who scorns a man, must die a maid;
What then remains but well our pow'r to use,
And keep good-humor still whate'er we lose? 30
And trust me, dear! good-humor can prevail,
When airs, and flights, and screams, and scolding fail.
Beauties in vain their pretty eyes may roll;
Charms strike the sight, but merit wins the soul.'
  So spoke the Dame, but no applause ensued; 35
Belinda frowned, Thalestris called her Prude.
'To arms, to arms!' the fierce Virago cries,
And swift as lightning to the combat flies.
All side in parties, and begin th' attack;
Fans clap, silks rustle, and tough whalebones crack; 40
Heroes' and Heroines' shouts confus'dly rise,
And bass and treble voices strike the skies.
No common weapons in their hands are found,
Like Gods they fight, nor dread a mortal wound.
  So when bold Homer makes the Gods engage, 45
And heav'nly breasts with human passions rage;
'Gainst Pallas, Mars; Latona, Hermes arms;
And all Olympus rings with loud alarms:
Jove's thunder roars, heav'n trembles all around,
Blue Neptune storms, the bellowing deeps resound: 50
Earth shakes her nodding tow'rs, the ground gives way,
And the pale ghosts start at the flash of day!
  Triumphant Umbriel on a sconce's height
Clapped his glad wings, and sat to view the fight:

Propped on their bodkin spears, the Sprites survey 55
The growing combat, or assist the fray.
While through the press enraged Thalestris flies,
And scatters death around from both her eyes,
A Beau and Witling perished in the throng,
One died in metaphor, and one in song. 60
'O cruel nymph! a living death I bear,'
Cried Dapperwit, and sunk beside his chair.
A mournful glance Sir Fopling upwards cast,
'Those eyes are made so killing'—was his last.
Thus on Mæander's flowery margin lies 65
Th' expiring Swan, and as he sings he dies.
When bold Sir Plume had drawn Clarissa down,
Chloe stepped in, and killed him with a frown;
She smiled to see the doughty hero slain,
But, at her smile, the Beau revived again. 70
Now Jove suspends his golden scales in air,
Weighs the Men's wits against the Lady's hair;
The doubtful beam long nods from side to side;
At length the wits mount up, the hairs subside.
See, fierce Belinda on the Baron flies, 75
With more than usual lightning in her eyes:
Nor feared the Chief th' unequal fight to try,
Who sought no more than on his foe to die.
But this bold Lord with manly strength endued,
She with one finger and a thumb subdued: 80
Just where the breath of life his nostrils drew,
A charge of Snuff the wily virgin threw;
The Gnomes direct, to ev'ry atom just,
The pungent grains of titillating dust.
Sudden, with starting tears each eye o'erflows, 85
And the high dome re-echoes to his nose.
'Now meet thy fate,' incensed Belinda cried,
And drew a deadly bodkin from her side.
(The same, his ancient personage to deck,
Her great great grandsire wore about his neck, 90
In three seal-rings; which after, melted down,
Formed a vast buckle for his widow's gown:
Her infant grandame's whistle next it grew,
The bells she jingled, and the whistle blew;

Then in a bodkin graced her mother's hairs, 95
Which long she wore, and now Belinda wears.)
'Boast not my fall' (he cried) 'insulting foe!
Thou by some other shalt be laid as low,
Nor think, to die dejects my lofty mind:
All that I dread is leaving you behind! 100
Rather than so, ah, let me still survive,
And burn in Cupid's flames—but burn alive.'
'Restore the Lock!' she cries; and all around
'Restore the Lock!' the vaulted roofs rebound.
Not fierce Othello in so loud a strain 105
Roared for the handkerchief that caused his pain.
But see how oft ambitious aims are crossed,
And chiefs contend 'till all the prize is lost!
The Lock, obtained with guilt, and kept with pain,
In every place is sought, but sought in vain: 110
With such a prize no mortal must be bless'd,
So heav'n decrees! with heav'n who can contest?
Some thought it mounted to the Lunar sphere,
Since all things lost on earth are treasured there.
There Heroes' wits are kept in pond'rous vases, 115
And beaux' in snuff-boxes and tweezer-cases.
There broken vows and death-bed alms are found,
And lovers' hearts with ends of riband bound,
The courtier's promises, and sick man's pray'rs,
The smiles of harlots, and the tears of heirs, 120
Cages for gnats, and chains to yoke a flea,
Dried butterflies, and tomes of casuistry.
But trust the Muse—she saw it upward rise,
Though marked by none but quick, poetic eyes
(So Rome's great founder to the heav'ns withdrew, 125
To Proculus alone confessed in view);
A sudden Star, it shot through liquid air,
And drew behind a radiant trail of hair.
Not Berenice's Locks first rose so bright,
The heav'ns bespangling with disheveled light. 130
The Sylphs behold it kindling as it flies,
And pleased pursue its progress through the skies.
This the Beau monde shall from the Mall survey,
And hail with music its propitious ray.

This the bless'd Lover shall for Venus take, 135
And send up vows from Rosamonda's lake.
This Partridge[1] soon shall view in cloudless skies,
When next he looks through Galileo's eyes;
And hence th' egregious wizard shall foredoom
The fate of Louis, and the fall of Rome. 140
Then cease, bright Nymph! to mourn thy ravished hair,
Which adds new glory to the shining sphere!
Not all the tresses that fair head can boast,
Shall draw such envy as the Lock you lost.
For, after all the murders of your eye, 145
When, after millions slain, yourself shall die:
When those fair suns shall set, as set they must,
And all those tresses shall be laid in dust,
This Lock, the Muse shall consecrate to fame,
And 'midst the stars inscribe Belinda's name. 150

EXERCISE:

To say that this poem is a *mock-epic* (*Glossary*) in itself gives a general indication of the tone and of Pope's attitude toward his characters. A trivial event (the clipping of a lock of hair from Belinda's head) is mockingly treated as if it were an event of cosmic importance. But if we are to enjoy the poem fully, we need to grasp more precisely still Pope's attitude toward Belinda, toward society, toward the war of the sexes, etc.

1. One of the sources of Pope's humor is the juxtaposition of incongruities: e.g., "Or stain her honor, or her new brocade" (Canto II, line 107), "Dost sometimes counsel take—and sometimes Tea" (III, 8). Collect other examples.

2. What is Pope's attitude toward the sylphs? Does he believe in them? Does he expect us to believe in them? What do they represent?

3. What is Pope's attitude toward Belinda? Does he find her charming? Does he expect her to take Clarissa's advice? Is she guilty of vanity? Does he think of her as a pretty, spoiled child? Or as a goddess? How is our attitude toward Belinda qualified?

4. Pope compares Belinda's glances to the sun (I, 14; II, 1–14; V, 147). Is the comparison wholly and simply complimentary? What are some of the implications of the sun comparison?

[1] an almanac-maker of the period

5. Belinda at her dressing table (I, 121–48) is described as a priestess officiating at a rite—"the rites of pride." Her maid is referred to as the "inferior Priestess" (I, 127). What is Belinda? The high priestess? Or the goddess? Is there a contradiction here, or not?

6. The poem ends in a mock-epic combat between the beaux and the belles. How has Pope prepared for this battle earlier in the poem? Collect the various instances of war and battle images in the first four cantos.

7. What attitude toward the rape of the lock does the poet expect us to take? It is an act of rudeness, granted, and Belinda properly resents it. But are there any indications in the poem that Belinda is in some sense the aggressor? She "nourishes" her locks "to the destruction of mankind" (II, 19; II, 24–28; V, 145–6). What is the significance of the rape of the lock with reference to the war between the sexes? Can it be said that Pope can reduce the incident to its proper insignificance because he realizes fully its true significance?

To Blossoms

ROBERT HERRICK [1591–1674]

Fair pledges of a fruitful tree,
  Why do ye fall so fast?
  Your date is not so past;
But you may stay yet here a while,
  To blush and gently smile; 5
    And go at last.

What, were ye born to be
  An hour or half's delight;
  And so to bid goodnight?
'Twas pity Nature brought ye forth 10
  Merely to show your worth,
    And lose you quite.

But you are lovely leaves, where we
  May read how soon things have
  Their end, though ne'er so brave: 15

And after they have shown their pride,
Like you a while: they glide
Into the grave.

The Blossom

JOHN DONNE [1573–1631]

Little think'st thou, poor flower,
Whom I have watched six or seven days,
And seen thy birth, and seen what every hour
Gave to thy growth, thee to this height to raise,
And now dost laugh and triumph on this bough, 5
Little think'st thou
That it will freeze anon, and that I shall
Tomorrow find thee fallen, or not at all.

Little think'st thou poor heart
That labor'st yet to nestle thee, 10
And think'st by hovering here to get a part
In a forbidden or forbidding tree,
And hop'st her stiffness by long siege to bow:
Little think'st thou,
That thou tomorrow, ere that sun doth wake, 15
Must with this sun, and me a journey take.

But thou which lov'st to be
Subtle to plague thy self, wilt say,
Alas, if you must go, what's that to me?
Here lies my business, and here I will stay: 20
You go to friends, whose love and means present
Various content
To your eyes, ears, and tongue, and every part.
If then your body go, what need you a heart?

Well then, stay here; but know, 25
When thou hast stayed and done thy most;
A naked thinking heart, that makes no show,
Is to a woman, but a kind of Ghost;
How shall she know my heart; or having none,
Know thee for one? 30

Practise may make her know some other part,
But take my word, she doth not know a Heart.

Meet me at London, then,
Twenty days hence, and thou shalt see
Me fresher, and more fat, by being with men, 35
Than if I had stayed still with her and thee.
For God's sake, if you can, be you so too:
I would give you
There, to another friend, whom we shall find
As glad to have my body, as my mind. 40

Here are two poems which are similar in title and similar in other regards. Both poems make use of an object drawn from nature as a symbol for the fragility of all life and of all earthly beauty. The generalization, as such, is a conventional one, and the symbol used is also a conventional one. What raises such a poem from a commonplace utterance is the *tone* of the poem. The tone of a poem, as we have already seen, is one indication of the poet's attitude toward his subject and toward his audience. What is Herrick's attitude toward the blossoms? And how does he indicate the attitude to his readers?

Herrick's attitude is one of tenderness and regret. He establishes this, in part, by dramatizing the scene and personifying the flowers, speaking to them first in a tone of surprise that they are already falling. He pretends that they are leaving of their own will and might be persuaded to stay. With the beginning of the second stanza, he implies that not until this moment has he realized that the flowers have no power to remain. The point is made dramatic by the exclamation of surprise, "What, were ye born to be," at the beginning of the second stanza. And this dramatic device gives renewed emphasis to what would otherwise be a merely commonplace generalization. The reader feels with something of renewed surprise what he has known on the level of abstract generalization all along.

This renewed sense of the fragility of all temporal beauty prepares for and justifies the application to the universal which he makes in the last stanza. The flowers he says are leaves, and we see in a moment that he means, not merely leaves of a plant but leaves of a book, wherein one may read what is true of all that lives.

It is most important to notice, however, that the poet does not overemphasize his personification nor does he unduly insist on the beauty of the flowers. He uses hint and implication instead. For example, the blossoms are addressed first as "Fair pledges of a fruitful tree." The poets of Herrick's time and later often refer to children as fair pledges and this much of personification is implied at once. Notice that the poet also merely implies the beauty of the blossoms. One gathers that they are beautiful from their effect on the poet. He does not develop this point. His references to the flowers are altogether in terms of their innocence and brevity of life: "To blush and gently smile." But the sense of their beauty is stronger because of the fact that it is merely to be inferred from what the poet says; and the point of the poem is enforced from the fact that all of the references are directed to this one end.

The use of the word *glide* at the end of the last stanza is effective and gives just the amount of emphasis required at the end of the poem. It is the exact word to describe the easy descent of blossoms falling through the air, and so supports the actual picture; but it also implies the easy, quiet descent into the grave which the poet is emphasizing in the poem. It is therefore thoroughly appropriate to the tone and atmosphere of the poem.

Here one may well call attention to the stanza form. The pattern of the stanza, one notices, is of lines of four feet, three, three, four, three, and *two*. The pattern is not quite symmetrical: the last line has one less foot than we might expect, and this fact gives the line an especial emphasis. We read it more slowly than the others. We can notice how at the end of each stanza the idea of finality and loss appears in this line of retarded movement.

When we look at the first stanza of Donne's "The Blossom" we find that it has a tone very similar to that of Herrick's poem. If we analyze carefully, of course, we shall see that it is not exactly the same. It could hardly be exactly the same any more than the personalities of two different people could be exactly the same or the features of two men, even men who resembled each other strongly. But there is in Donne's poem something of the same tenderness and regret which we find in Herrick's, though Donne's attitude toward the flower has in it a more prominent note of patronage: he speaks out of a knowledge which the flower cannot have. He knows the fate which is in store for it. The patronage is far from a supercilious one, however. He is tender in his attitude toward the blossom, and we feel already that what he says about the fate of the blossom is no more than the general fate which he knows is in store for everything, including himself. We sense even in this first stanza the application to his own heart which he is going to make in the second stanza.

Even the second stanza does not depart altogether from the tone of Herrick's poem. The application of the flowers' innocence and ignorance to his heart parallels Herrick's application of the transient beauty of the blossoms to all temporal beauty. Donne, of course, is making the comparison for a different effect: he is telling his heart, pretending that it is as ignorantly innocent as the blossom, that it little realizes how soon he must leave his mistress and that its freezing time (lack of love) will soon be upon it.

With the third stanza a new attitude is taken toward the subject, and the poem exhibits a radical shift in tone. The poet no longer considers the heart a passive thing like the blossom but lets it state its own reply to him; or rather he himself states what the heart's reply will be, for he implies that he knows the arguments of old. The attitude changes, therefore, from pitying tenderness to amused tolerance such as one might have for a stubborn but charming child who argues brightly but unreasonably for something on which it has set its heart.

The turn at the beginning of the third stanza, one may notice, is supported by a metrical shift. The first line of the first stanza may be scanned as follows:

Little | think'st thou, | poor flower.

In both the second and third foot of the line we have an instance of a hovering accent; and in the third foot with the syllable *poor* we have the hovering effect further supported by the quantitative factor. The differences between non-accented and accented syllables tend to be reduced. The whole line gives a lingering, retarded effect. The same is true of the first line of the second stanza. But the first line of the third stanza is sharply defined metrically, with positive differences between non-accented and accented syllables, and furthermore, falls into a precise iambic pattern:

But thou | which lov'st | to be.

The change in tone is supported by the change from the characteristic rhythm of the initial lines of the two preceding stanzas.

With the fourth stanza the poet abruptly changes his tone, a shift which again reflects itself in the meter, and the poet turns suddenly and says to his heart, "Well then, stay here." He decides to humor his heart in its folly; but he assures it that it is remaining in vain. A heart deprived of a body cannot express itself. Women are too sensual to be able to perceive a "naked thinking heart"—something of pure spirit.

And in the last stanza the poet, accepting the heart's decision and addressing it as if it were another man, a friend, tells it to meet him in London "twenty days hence," and prophesies that it will find him "fresher, and more fat, by being with men." The poet advises the heart to be so too, if it can. He does not wish it ill: he merely knows, and knows positively, that there is no chance that the heart will prosper.

The poem ends with an explicit statement of the point up to which the whole poem has been moving: a protest against an absurd idealizing of love:

I would give you
There, to another friend, whom we shall find
As glad to have my body, as my mind.

The absurd idealizing of love which ignores its realistic elements, and ignores the fact that the human being is made of many elements, body and soul, flesh and spirit, etc., is in this particular case the idealizing attitude of the Petrarchan tradition, to which we have already referred in our discussion of "A Litany," by Philip Sidney (pp. 208). But the poet here, especially in the third stanza and after, employs many of the devices of the Petrarchan tradition in order to upset them. He makes use of all the Petrarchan machinery—the heart speaking as a separate person, for example—in his protest; and he has his own heart maintain the Petrarchan argument. In answering the heart, the attitude, as we have indicated, is ironical, but the irony is not bitter or heavily sarcastic; there is a certain tolerance and understanding mixed with the irony. The poem on the surface seems almost as artificial and as trifling as the kind of poetry which it really attacks; but this is only true superficially because the reader who gets a sense of the whole poem sees that the trifling, which is conscious and ironical here, is a way of presenting the positive theme of the poem: love (or any other experience) that is to be real and meaningful must involve the entire nature of man.

The shifts in tone in the poem, as we have seen, are brilliant and complex, and a close comparison of Donne's poem with Herrick's will readily illustrate the degree of this complexity. For the first two stanzas of Donne's poem form the only part that is as consistent in tone as the poem by Herrick. Had Donne cared to end his poem at this point he would have given us a poem remarkably similar to Herrick's (though we can observe that the tone of Donne's poem, even in the first two stanzas, is more conversational and informal). Instead, Donne is merely using his first two stanzas as an introduction, and with the third stanza begins to develop his real theme and to turn the imagery, which in Herrick is direct, into a kind of teasing travesty of the Petrarchan tradition.

One more point needs to be made. Are we to conclude that Donne's poem is better than Herrick's? Herrick's poem, within its limits (which are narrower than Donne's) is splendid. But the study of the two poems in conjunction with one another may illustrate for us the relation of a good poem which is rather simple to a good poem which is far more complex.

The Fairies' Farewell

RICHARD CORBET [1582–1635]

"Farewell rewards and fairies,"
  Good housewives now may say,
For now foul sluts in dairies
  Do fare as well as they.
And though they sweep their hearths no less 5
  Than maids were wont to do,
Yet who of late for cleanliness,
  Finds sixpence in her shoe?

Lament, lament, old abbeys,
  The fairies lost command; 10
They did but change priests' babies,
  But some have changed your land;
And all your children sprung from thence
  Are now grown Puritanes;
Who live as changelings ever since 15
  For love of your domains.

At morning and at evening both
  You merry were and glad,
So little care of sleep or sloth
  These pretty ladies had; 20
When Tom came home from labor,
  Or Cisse to milking rose,
Then merrily, merrily went their tabor,
  And nimbly went their toes.

Witness those rings and roundelays 25
  Of theirs, which yet remain,
Were footed in Queen Mary's days
  On many a grassy plain;
But since of late, Elizabeth,
  And later, James came in, 30
They never danced on any heath
  As when the time hath been.

By which we note the fairies
  Were of the old profession;
Their songs were Ave-Marys, 35
  Their dances were procession:
But now, alas! they all are dead
  Or gone beyond the seas,
Or farther for religion fled,
  Or else they take their ease. 40

A tell-tale in their company
  They never could endure,
And who so kept not secretly
  Their mirth was punished sure.

It was a just and Christian deed 45
  To pinch such black and blue.
Oh how the commonwealth doth want
  Such justices as you!

Now they have left our quarters,
  A register they have, 50
Who looketh to their charters,
  A man both wise and grave.
An hundred of their merry pranks
  By one that I could name
Are kept in store; conn twenty thanks 55
  To William for the same.

I marvel who his cloak would turn
  When Puck had led him round;
Or where those walking fires would burn,
  Where Cureton would be found; 60
How Broker would appear to be
  For whom this age doth mourn
But that their spirits live in thee,
  In thee, old William Churne.

To William Churne of Staffordshire 65
  Give laud and praises due,
Who every meal can mend your cheer
  With tales both old and true;
To William all give audience
  And pray ye for his noddle, 70
For all the fairies' evidence
  Were lost, if that were addle.

Exercise:

The "rings" referred to in line 25 are the circles of darker grass sometimes found in pastures (the effect of a certain kind of mold) and once regarded by the superstitious as marking a place where the fairies had danced. The "old profession" (line 34) is the Roman Catholicism of pre-Reformation England. The reference to the abbeys in the second stanza alludes to the destruction of monasteries at the time of the Reformation. Thus, the poem, in spite of the fact that it is playful in spirit and ends with a mock-serious compliment to William Churne, a servant of Corbet's father-in-law, actually glances at very serious issues: at religious changes in England and changes in the national spirit and temper. Corbet himself, by the way, was later to become a Bishop in the Church of England.

1. What is his attitude toward Roman Catholicism? Toward Puritanism? Toward the native paganism (the belief in the fairies)?

2. Corbet argues that the fairies left England at the time of the Reformation and that they were actually Roman Catholics (lines 33–40). If this is to be taken as a jibe at the Catholics for countenancing "paganism," what are we to make of Corbet's attitude toward those who were for extirpating all that smacked of superstition—the Puritans (lines 9–16)?

3. Corbet's total attitude is obviously rather complex. Can you suggest what it is? How would you relate it to the general lightness of touch with which he takes notice of these fundamentally serious matters?

4. What is Corbet's attitude toward old William Churne, the "register" of the fairies and the expert on fairy lore? Is he scornful? teasing? patronizing? or what?

Affliction

GEORGE HERBERT [1593–1632]

When first Thou didst entice to Thee my heart,
        I thought the service brave:
So many joys I writ down for my part,
        Besides what I might have
Out of my stock of natural delights, 5
Augmented with Thy gracious benefits.

I lookéd on Thy furniture so fine,
        And made it fine to me;
Thy glorious household-stuff did me entwine,
        And 'tice me unto Thee. 10
Such stars I counted mine: both heaven and earth
Paid me my wages in a world of mirth.

What pleasures could I want, whose King I served,
Where joys my fellows were?
Thus argued into hopes, my thoughts reserved 15
No place for grief or fear;
Therefore my sudden soul caught at the place,
And made her youth and fierceness seek Thy face.

At first Thou gav'st me milk and sweetnesses;
I had my wish and way: 20
My days were strew'd with flowers and happiness;
There was no month but May.
But with my years sorrow did twist and grow,
And made a party unawares for woe.

My flesh began unto my soul in pain, 25
Sicknesses cleave my bones,
Consuming agues dwell in every vein,
And tune my breath to groans:
Sorrow was all my soul; I scarce believed,
Till grief did tell me roundly, that I lived. 30

When I got health, Thou took'st away my life,
And more; for my friends die:
My mirth and edge was lost; a blunted knife
Was of more use than I.
Thus thin and lean without a fence or friend, 35
I was blown through with every storm and wind.

Whereas my birth and spirit rather took
The way that takes the town;
Thou didst betray me to a ling'ring book,
And wrap me in a gown. 40
I was entangled in the world of strife,
Before I had the power to change my life.

Yet, for I threaten'd oft the siege to raise,
Not simp'ring all mine age,
Thou often didst with academic praise 45
Melt and dissolve my rage.
I took Thy sweeten'd pill, till I came near;
I could not go away, nor persevere.

Yet lest perchance I should too happy be
In my unhappiness, 50
Turning my purge to food, Thou throwest me
Into more sicknesses.
Thus doth Thy power cross-bias me, not making
Thine own gift good, yet me from my ways taking.

Now I am here, what Thou wilt do with me 55
None of my books will show:
I read and sigh, and wish I were a tree;
For sure then I should grow
To fruit or shade: at least some bird would trust
Her household to me, and I should be just. 60

Yet, though Thou troublest me, I must be meek;
In weakness must be stout;
Well, I will change the service, and go seek
Some other master out.
Ah, my dear God! though I am clean forgot, 65
Let me not love Thee, if I love Thee not.

EXERCISE:

This poem begins by chiding God for having "enticed" the speaker into his service and then proving a harsh and unfair master.

1. What shift in the tone occurs at line 55? Attempt to characterize the tone of this stanza (lines 55–60).

2. Characterize the tone of lines 61–64. What does he mean by lines 61–62: (1) "In spite of everything, however, I ought to be meek"? Or (2) "In terms of this deceitful bargain, it is actually insisted that the more I am afflicted, the more meek I am supposed to be"?

3. What shift in tone occurs at line 65? Is line 66 repetitious nonsense, or is it meaningful? If meaningful, what does it mean?

Wessex Heights

THOMAS HARDY [1840–1928]

There are some heights in Wessex, shaped as if by a kindly hand
For thinking, dreaming, dying on, and at crises when I stand,

Say, on Ingpen Beacon eastward, or on Wylls-Neck westwardly,
I seem where I was before my birth, and after death may be.

In the lowlands I have no comrade, not even the lone man's friend—
Her who suffereth long and is kind; accepts what he is too weak to
mend: 6
Down there they are dubious and askance; there nobody thinks as I,
But mind-chains do not clank where one's next neighbor is the sky.

In the towns I am tracked by phantoms having weird detective
ways—
Shadows of beings who fellowed with myself of earlier days: 10
They hang about at places, and they say harsh heavy things—
Men with a frigid sneer, and women with tart disparagings.

Down there I seem to be false to myself, my simple self that was,
And is not now, and I see him watching, wondering what crass
cause
Can have merged him into such a strange continuator as this, 15
Who yet has something in common with himself, my chrysalis.

I cannot go to the great gray Plain; there's a figure against the
moon,
Nobody sees it but I, and it makes my breast beat out of tune;
I cannot go to the tall-spired town, being barred by the forms now
passed
For everybody but me, in whose long vision they stand there fast.

There's a ghost at Yell'ham Bottom chiding loud at the fall of the
night, 21
There's a ghost in Froom-side Vale, thin lipped and vague, in a
shroud of white,
There is one in the railway-train whenever I do not want it near,
I see its profile against the pane, saying what I would not hear.

As for one rare fair woman, I am now but a thought of hers, 25
I enter her mind and another thought succeeds me that she prefers;
Yet my love for her in its fulness she herself even did not know;
Well, time cures hearts of tenderness, and now I can let her go.

So I am found on Ingpen Beacon, or on Wylls-Neck to the west,
Or else on homely Bulbarrow, or little Pilsdon Crest, 30

Where men have never cared to haunt, nor women have walked
  with me,
And ghosts then keep their distance; and I know some liberty.

EXERCISE:

1. What is the speaker's attitude toward the past? He is obviously a man haunted by the past: what does he gain by expressing his haunted condition in *spatial* terms (Wylls-Neck, Ingpen Beacon, etc.)?

2. Does Hardy make his ghosts dramatically convincing? Notice that side by side with the conventional ghost "in a shroud of white," he gives us "one in the railway-train." Does he manage actually to get the ghost into the train—so that we see it there?

3. The reader is likely to feel (1) that this is a clumsy poem, marred by a number of lapses of tone (lines 8, 9, 23, 26, 32, etc.) or (2) that it is a remarkably fine poem, characterized by a brilliant handling of tone. Consider the poem carefully, and then try to justify your answer.

Missing Dates

WILLIAM EMPSON [1906–]

Slowly the poison the whole blood stream fills.
It is not the effort nor the failure tires.
The waste remains, the waste remains and kills.

It is not your system or clear sight that mills
Down small to the consequence a life requires; 5
Slowly the poison the whole blood stream fills.

They bled an old dog dry yet the exchange rills
Of young dog blood gave but a month's desires;
The waste remains, the waste remains and kills.

It is the Chinese tombs and the slag hills 10
Usurp the soil, and not the soil retires.
Slowly the poison the whole blood stream fills.

Not to have fire is to be a skin that shrills.
The complete fire is death. From partial fires
The waste remains, the waste remains and kills. 15

It is the poems you have lost, the ills
From missing dates, at which the heart expires.
Slowly the poison the whole blood stream fills.
The waste remains, the waste remains and kills.

EXERCISE:

1. This poem is a villanelle (a poem written in tercets, usually five, plus a final quatrain, making use of two rimes). We associate the villanelle with love poetry, often of the courtly sort. Is the villanelle a good choice for this rather unexpected subject matter? Does the contrast between the stanzaic form and the content have its effect on the tone of the poem? Does the fact that the villanelle allows for a great deal of repetition make for the effect of this particular poem?

2. Note the variety of instances of the "waste [that] remains." Does the variety of instances help secure conviction for the reiterated thesis?

Portrait

KENNETH FEARING [1902–]

The clear brown eyes, kindly and alert, with 12-20 vision, give confident regard to the passing world through R. K. Lampert & Company lenses framed in gold;
His soul, however, is all his own;
Arndt Brothers necktie and hat (with feather) supply a touch of youth.

With his soul his own, he drives, drives, chats and drives,
The first and second bicuspids, lower right, replaced by bridge-work, while two incisors have porcelain crowns; 5

(Render unto Federal, state and city Caesar, but not unto time;
Render nothing unto time until Amalgamated Death serves final notice, in proper form;

The vault is ready;
The will has been drawn by Clagget, Clagget, Clagget & Brown;
The policies are adequate, Confidential's best, reimbursing for disability, partial or complete, with double indemnity should the end be a pure and simple accident) 10

Nothing unto time,
Nothing unto change, nothing unto fate,
Nothing unto you, and nothing unto me, or to any other known or unknown party or parties, living or deceased;

But Mercury shoes, with special arch supports, take much of the wear and tear;
On the course, a custombuilt driver corrects a tendency to slice; 15
Love's ravages have been repaired (it was a textbook case) by Drs. Schultz, Lightner, Mannheim, and Goode,
While all of it is enclosed in excellent tweed, with Mr. Baumer's personal attention to the shoulders and the waist;

And all of it now roving, chatting amiably through space in a Plymouth 6,
With his soul (his own) at peace, soothed by Walter Lippmann, and sustained by Haig & Haig.

Exercise:

1. Is the description of the eyes in line 1 ("kindly and alert") merely sarcastic? Or is there any sense in which the adjectives are "meant"?

2. Does the tone shift in the development of the poem? How would you characterize the tone?

3. What is the meaning of "The vault is ready" (line 8)? Is the meaning developed and enriched by the lines that follow?

No Possum, No Sop, No Taters

WALLACE STEVENS [1879–]

He is not here, the old sun,
As absent as if we were asleep.

The field is frozen. The leaves are dry.
Bad is final in this light.

In this bleak air the broken stalks 5
Have arms without hands. They have trunks

Without legs or, for that, without heads.
They have heads in which a captive cry

Is merely the moving of a tongue.
Snow sparkles like eyesight falling to earth, 10

Like seeing fallen brightly away.
The leaves hop, scraping on the ground.

It is deep January. The sky is hard.
The stalks are firmly rooted in ice.

It is in this solitude, a syllable, 15
Out of these gawky flitterings,

Intones its single emptiness,
The savagest hollow of winter-sound.

It is here, in this bad, that we reach
The last purity of the knowledge of good. 20

The crow looks rusty as he rises up.
Bright is the malice in his eye . . .

One joins him there for company,
But at a distance, in another tree.

Exercise:

On the surface, this poem simply presents the scene beneath the January sky. But the descriptive detail is not only sharp and vivid. It defines an attitude as well.

1. What is the poem "about"? Can you relate to your answer lines 4 and 19–20?

2. Why is so much of the descriptive detail given a human reference ("Snow sparkles like eyesight," etc.)?

3. Why has the poet ended the poem as he has (lines 21–24)? What effect do these last details have upon the tone?

The Equilibrists

JOHN CROWE RANSOM [1888–]

Full of her long white arms and milky skin
He had a thousand times remembered sin.
Alone in the press of people traveled he,
Minding her jacinth and myrrh and ivory.

Mouth he remembered: the quaint orifice 5
From which came heat that flamed upon the kiss,
Till cold words came down spiral from the head,
Gray doves from the officious tower illsped.

Body: it was a white field ready for love.
On her body's field, with the gaunt tower above, 10
The lilies grew, beseeching him to take,
If he would pluck and wear them, bruise and break.

Eyes talking: Never mind the cruel words,
Embrace my flowers but not embrace the swords.
But what they said, the doves came straightway flying 15
And unsaid: Honor, Honor, they came crying.

Importunate her doves. Too pure, too wise,
Clambering on his shoulder, saying, Arise,
Leave me now, and never let us meet,
Eternal distance now command thy feet. 20

Predicament indeed, which thus discovers
Honor among thieves, Honor between lovers.
O such a little word is Honor, they feel!
But the gray word is between them cold as steel.

At length I saw these lovers fully were come 25
Into their torture of equilibrium:
Dreadfully had forsworn each other, and yet
They were bound each to each, and they did not forget.

And rigid as two painful stars, and twirled
About the clustered night their prison world, 30
They burned with fierce love always to come near,
But Honor beat them back and kept them clear.

Ah, the strict lovers, they are ruined now!
I cried in anger. But with puddled brow
Devising for those gibbeted and brave 35
Came I descanting: Man, what would you have?

For spin your period out, and draw your breath,
A kinder saeculum begins with Death.
Would you ascend to Heaven and bodiless dwell?
Or take your bodies honorless to Hell? 40

In Heaven you have heard no marriage is,
No white flesh tinder to your lecheries,
Your male and female tissue sweetly shaped
Sublimed away, and furious blood escaped.

Great lovers lie in Hell, the stubborn ones 45
Infatuate of the flesh upon the bones;
Stuprate, they rend each other when they kiss;
The pieces kiss again—no end to this.

But still I watched them spinning, orbited nice.
Their flames were not more radiant than their ice. 50
I dug in the quiet earth and wrought the tomb
And made these lines to memorize their doom:—

Equilibrists lie here; stranger, tread light;
Close, but untouching in each other's sight;
Mouldered the lips and ashy the tall skull, 55
Let them lie perilous and beautiful.

Exercise:

1. What is the meaning of the title? What is the principal image by which the mutual attraction and repulsion of the lovers is expressed?

2. Consider carefully the diction of the poem. (Some of it has an

archaic flavor; some of it, a technical.) How does the diction help determine the tone?

3. What is the attitude of the speaker toward the lovers? Toward honor? Toward the lovers' predicament? He cries out against their fate "in anger" (line 34). What attitude does the speaker go on to adopt? What attitude does the *poet* seem to adopt?

V

IMAGERY

FOREWORD

In many of the poems read thus far we have commented on various functions of imagery, and we have seen how important these are. The poems in this section raise no new principles concerning the fundamental nature of poetic imagery, but they have been chosen because they offer the student an opportunity for further analysis. Some poems, more than others, rely on imagery for conveying their meanings. The following analysis of two lines from Shakespeare's *Venus and Adonis* is made by Samuel Taylor Coleridge, the poet and critic, and has been further expanded by I. A. Richards, a psychologist and critic. This analysis indicates some of the ways in which imagery does its work.

> Look! how a bright star shooteth from the sky
> So glides he in the night from Venus' eye.

How many images and feelings are here brought together without effort and without discord—the beauty of Adonis—the rapidity of his flight—the yearning yet helplessness of the enamoured gazer—and a shadowy ideal character thrown over the whole (Raysor, I, 213).

Here, in contrast to the other case, the more the image is followed up, the more links of relevance between the units are discovered. As Adonis to Venus, so these lines to the reader seem to linger in the eye like the after-images that make the trail of the meteor. Here Shakespeare is realizing, and making the reader realize—not by any intensity of effort, but by the fulness and self-completing growth of the response—Adonis' flight as it was to Venus, and the sense of loss, of increased darkness, that invades her. The separable meanings of each word, *Look!* (our surprise at the meteor, hers at his flight), *star* (a light-giver, an influence, a remote and uncontrollable thing) *shooteth* (the sudden, irremediable, portentous fall or death of what had been a guide, a destiny), *the sky* (the source of light and now of ruin), *glides* (not rapidity only, but fatal ease too), *in the night* (the darkness of the scene and of Venus' world now)—all these separable meanings are here brought into one. And as they come together, as the reader's mind finds cross-connexion after cross-connexion between them, he seems, in becoming more aware of them, to be discovering not only Shakespeare's meaning, but something which he, the reader, is himself making. His understanding of Shakespeare is sanctioned by his own activity in it. As Coleridge says: "You feel him to be a poet, inasmuch as for a time he has made you one—an active creative being."[1]

The reader should be on the alert for the implications the imagery in any poem may have and for the relation of imagery to the full meaning of the poem.

To an Athlete Dying Young

A. E. HOUSMAN [1859–1936]

The time you won your town the race
We chaired you through the market-place;
Man and boy stood cheering by,
And home we brought you shoulder-high.

Today, the road all runners come, 5
Shoulder-high we bring you home,
And set you at your threshold down,
Townsman of a stiller town.

Smart lad, to slip betimes away
From fields where glory does not stay 10
And early though the laurel grows
It withers quicker than the rose.

Eyes the shady night has shut
Cannot see the record cut,

[1] *Coleridge on the Imagination,* New York: Harcourt, Brace and Company, Inc., pp. 82–84.

And silence sounds no worse than cheers 15
After earth has stopped the ears:

Now you will not swell the rout
Of lads that wore their honors out,
Runners whom renown outran
And the name died before the man. 20

So set, before its echoes fade,
The fleet foot on the sill of shade,
And hold to the low lintel up
The still-defended challenge-cup.

And round that early-laureled head 25
Will flock to gaze the strengthless dead,
And find unwithered on its curls
The garland briefer than a girl's.

In this poem the poet states a paradox: namely, that the early death of the young athlete is a matter for congratulation rather than for sorrow. This is the real theme of the poem. But we should hardly be impressed with the bare statement that it is better to die young rather than old, and even the startling quality of the statement would awaken interest for only a moment. The poet has known better than to state the matter baldly, therefore. He has arranged a little dramatic framework for the statement. In a familiar, almost conversational tone—"Smart lad"—he addresses his congratulations to the young man who is dead; and more than that, he uses the images which are associated with the young man's athletic achievements to describe his death. Indeed, the statement implied by the imagery of the poem is that the young runner has, in dying, won his race again—he has beaten his competitors to the final goal of all of them, death.

Notice, for example, that the funeral is treated exactly as if it were a triumph for the young runner celebrated by his friends. On the day on which he won the race for his town, his friends made a chair for him of their hands and carried him home shoulder-high in triumph. Now on the day of his funeral, they carry him "shoulder-high" again, and they bring him "home." "Smart lad," the poet then calls him, as if he had just finished running a heady race.

The reasons for saying this follow: it is better to die at the prime than to witness one's records broken by some one else. But the poet does not relax his hold on concrete details in making this statement. The laurel, symbol of fame, withers even quicker than does the rose, emblem of beauty. Eyes closed in death cannot see the record broken; to ears stopped with earth, the silence rings as loud as the air filled with cheering. And now the poet returns to the dominant figure of the race. Fame has a habit of outrunning the fastest runner and leaving him behind; the young athlete has not been outrun by his renown.

The figure is developed further in the sixth stanza. The brink of the grave is "the sill of shade" on which the young man has just placed his fleet foot, and the edge of the grave is the "low lintel" up to which the boy holds the "still defended challenge cup." The paradoxes here are especially rich. We think of death as being opposed in every regard to fleetness, and its inertia as incapable of defending anything. Yet by the reasoning which has preceded this stanza, the foot of the dead youth *is* fleet in death—only in death can he hold his challenge-cup still defended. Others will not be able to wrest it from him. The passage is a fine example of the poet's ability to put things which we ordinarily think of as quite unrelated, or even opposed to each other, into a pattern which gives a meaningful relation where one had not been seen before.

The last stanza exhibits also a fine effect which the poet has prepared for. The stanza catches up the contrast between the laurel and the rose already made in the third stanza. The connection is hinted at in the phrase "early-laureled head." Fame perishes even more quickly than beauty—the garland of laurel withers even faster than the garland of roses which a girl might be supposed to wear. We think of a young girl dead in the first flush of her beauty as an object of pathos, and at the same time think of her as having achieved a sort of triumph at having brought all her beauty untarnished with her into the grave. The poet wishes to get, and does get, something of the same effect for the athlete, and he gets it by suggesting the comparison.

Does he overplay his hand? Does he appear to be trying to extract the last degree of pathos from the situation? The mature reader will feel that the effect of pathos has been secured legitimately, and that the poet is not guilty of sentimentality; that is, that the emotion evoked in the poem is really inherent in the situation and has been developed by the poet for the reader by no unfair means. The pathos is a clean pathos therefore, revealed by a sudden insight but not lingered over for its own sake. One may observe how the firmness of the rhythm of the poem and the familiar tone of the opening stanzas help to avoid a sentimental effect.

The use of paradox in this poem is also important in this regard, for a paradox tends to provoke a certain mental alertness, a certain awareness which in this case prevents the tone of the poem from becoming too soft. In the same way, and important for the same effect, is the use of symbol (laurel and rose), the use of the particular detail and image, and the use of suggestion rather than flat statement. All of these means are *indirect* as opposed to the direct prose statement; and this means that the reader must to some extent discover the meaning and the pathos for himself. The reader responds to the situation with force, but legitimately, because he feels that he has been merely helped by the poet to see the real character of the experience.

Days

RALPH WALDO EMERSON [1803–1882]

Daughters of Time, the hypocritic Days,
Muffled and dumb like barefoot dervishes,
And marching single in an endless file,
Bring diadems and faggots in their hands.
To each they offer gifts after his will, 5
Bread, kingdoms, stars, and sky that holds them all.
I, in my pleachèd garden, watched the pomp,
Forgot my morning wishes, hastily
Took a few herbs and apples, and the Day
Turned and departed silent. I, too late, 10
Under her solemn fillet saw the scorn.

EXERCISE:

1. What is the meaning of the word "pomp"? Is the word well chosen? (Look up the word in the dictionary, noting the meaning of Latin *pompa* from which it derives.)

2. Why are the days called "hypocritic"?

3. What keeps the poem from seeming a heavy-handed moralization? Is the imagery simply a transparent screen for the moral? Or does it constitute a means for defining and shaping the meaning of the poem?

I Wandered Lonely as a Cloud

WILLIAM WORDSWORTH [1770–1850]

I wandered lonely as a cloud
That floats on high o'er vales and hills,
When all at once I saw a crowd,
A host of golden daffodils;
Beside the lake, beneath the trees, 5
Fluttering and dancing in the breeze.

Continuous as the stars that shine
And twinkle on the milky way,
They stretched in never-ending line
Along the margin of a bay: 10
Ten thousand saw I at a glance,
Tossing their heads in sprightly dance.

The waves beside them danced, but they
Outdid the sparkling waves in glee:—
A poet could not but be gay 15
In such a jocund company:
I gazed—and gazed—but little thought
What wealth the show to me had brought.

For oft when on my couch I lie
In vacant or in pensive mood, 20
They flash upon that inward eye
Which is the bliss of solitude,
And then my heart with pleasure fills,
And dances with the daffodils.

EXERCISE:

1. What is the importance of the cloud comparison in line 1? What does it suggest about the speaker's purpose or lack of pur-

pose? What does it suggest of his mood? Would the experience which the rest of the poem relates have occurred to a man possessed by another mood?

2. Does the poet succeed in dramatizing the suggestion that the daffodils accept the speaker as a companion—overcome his loneliness? If so, what are the devices important in gaining the reader's acceptance?

Lucifer

JOHN MILTON [1608–1674]

. . . as when the sun new-risen
Looks through the horizontal misty air
Shorn of his beams, or from behind the moon,
In dim eclipse, disastrous twilight sheds
On half the nations, and with fear of change 5
Perplexes monarchs. Darkened so, yet shone
Above them all the Archangel; but his face
Deep scars of thunder had intrenched, and care
Sat on his faded cheek, but under brows
Of dauntless courage, and considerate pride 10
Waiting revenge. Cruel his eye, but cast
Signs of remorse and passion, to behold
The fellows of his crime, the followers rather
(Far other once beheld in bliss), condemned
Forever now to have their lot in pain; 15
Millions of Spirits for his fault amerced
Of Heaven, and from eternal splendors flung
For his revolt; yet faithful how they stood,
Their glory withered: as, when Heaven's fire
Hath scathed the forest oaks or mountain pines, 20
With singèd top their stately growth, though bare,
Stands on the blasted heath.

(From *Paradise Lost,* Book I)

Exercise:

This passage describes Lucifer as he surveys his defeated army which has been driven out of Heaven into Hell by the thunderbolts of the Almighty.

1. It is easy to see why the poet compares Lucifer to a sun dimmed and darkened. But what, if anything, is gained by the poet's sug-

gesting *two* situations in which the sun is dimmed? Is the poet simply interested in enriching the pictorial effect? (Look up the original meaning of "disastrous.") Can you connect the implications of this double figure with Lucifer's plot to seduce mankind from God?

2. Work out the implications of the figure which compares the army of fallen angels to a noble forest destroyed by fire.

The Solitary Reaper

WILLIAM WORDSWORTH [1770–1850]

Behold her, single in the field,
Yon solitary Highland Lass!
Reaping and singing by herself;
Stop here, or gently pass!
Alone she cuts and binds the grain, 5
And sings a melancholy strain;
O listen! for the Vale profound
Is overflowing with the sound.

No Nightingale did ever chaunt
More welcome notes to weary bands 10
Of travelers in some shady haunt,
Among Arabian sands:
A voice so thrilling ne'er was heard
In spring-time from the Cuckoo-bird,
Breaking the silence of the seas 15
Among the farthest Hebrides.

Will no one tell me what she sings?—
Perhaps the plaintive numbers flow
For old, unhappy, far-off things,
And battles long ago: 20
Or is it some more humble lay,
Familiar matter of today?
Some natural sorrow, loss, or pain,
That has been, and may be again?

Whate'er the theme, the Maiden sang 25
As if her song could have no ending;

I saw her singing at her work,
And o'er the sickle bending;—
I listened, motionless and still;
And, as I mounted up the hill, 30
The music in my heart I bore,
Long after it was heard no more.

Exercise:

1. If we omit the second stanza, we are given an account of the situation and of the effect of the girl's song upon the traveler. What, then, would be lost—if anything—had the poet decided to cancel the second stanza?

2. Consider as carefully as you can the meaning of the girl-bird comparison. In what specific ways does the song of the girl resemble the song of the birds? Is the poet simply suggesting that the girl's song is beautiful? Or is he defining its special quality and significance for the traveler who overhears it?

Like as to Make Our Appetites

WILLIAM SHAKESPEARE [1564–1616]

Like as, to make our appetites more keen,
With eager compounds we our palate urge;
As, to prevent our maladies unseen,
We sicken to shun sickness when we purge;
Even so, being full of your ne'er-cloying sweetness, 5
To bitter sauces did I frame my feeding;
And, sick of welfare, found a kind of meetness
To be diseased, ere that there was true needing.
Thus policy in love, to anticipate
The ills that were not, grew to faults assured, 10
And brought to medicine a healthful state,
Which, rank of goodness, would by ill be cured;
But thence I learn, and find the lesson true,
Drugs poison him that so fell sick of you.

Exercise:

1. Work out the argument of lines 1–8. Try to state abstractly what the speaker proposed to do. What is gained by the poet's making his statement in terms of metaphor?

2. Some of the comparisons used here would be regarded, taken in isolation, as unpleasant. Why are such details chosen? What effect do they have upon the tone of the poem.

3. Having looked back at Knights's short analysis of "No More Be Grieved" (pp. 152–53), comment upon the use of alliteration in this poem.

Trees

JOYCE KILMER [1886–1918]

I think that I shall never see
A poem lovely as a tree.

A tree whose hungry mouth is pressed
Against the earth's sweet flowing breast;

A tree that looks to God all day, 5
And lifts her leafy arms to pray;

A tree that may in summer wear
A nest of robins in her hair;

Upon whose bosom snow has lain;
Who intimately lives with rain. 10

Poems are made by fools like me,
But only God can make a tree.

This poem has been very greatly admired by a large number of people. The fact that it has been popular does not necessarily condemn it as a bad poem. But it is a bad poem.

First, let us look at it merely on the technical side, especially in regard to the use Kilmer makes of his imagery. Now the poet, in a poem of twelve lines, only makes one fundamental comparison on which the other comparisons are based; this is the same method used by Housman in "To an Athlete Dying Young." In "Trees" this fundamental comparison is not definitely stated but is constantly implied. The comparison is that of the tree to a human being. If the tree is compared to a human being, the reader has a right to expect a consistent use to be made of the aspects of the human being which appear in the poem. But look at stanza two:

> A tree whose hungry mouth is pressed
> Against the earth's sweet flowing breast.

Here the tree is *metaphorically* (*Glossary*) treated as a sucking babe and the earth, therefore, as the mother—a perfectly good comparison that has been made for centuries—the earth as the "great mother," the "giver of life," etc.

But the third stanza introduces a confusion:

> A tree that looks to God all day,
> And lifts her leafy arms to pray.

Here the tree is no longer a sucking babe, but, without warning, is old enough to indulge in religious devotions. But that is not the worst part of the confusion. Remember that the tree is a human being and that in the first stanza the *mouth* of that human being was the *root* of the tree. But now if the branches are "leafy arms," the tree is a strangely deformed human being.

The fourth and fifth stanzas maintain the same anatomical arrangement for the tree as does the third, but they make other unexpected changes: the tree that wears a "nest of robins in her hair" must be a grown-up person, a girl with jewels in her hair; the tree with snow on its bosom is a chaste and pure girl, for so the *associations* of snow with purity and chastity tell the reader; and the tree that "lives with rain" is a chaste and pure young woman who, although vain enough to wear jewels, is yet withdrawn from the complications of human relationships and lives alone with "nature," i.e., rain, or might be said to be nun-like, an implication consonant with the religious tone of the poem.

Now it would be quite legitimate for the poet to use any one of the thoughts he wishes to convey about the tree (1. the tree as a babe nursed by mother earth, 2. the tree as a devout person praying all day, 3. the tree as a girl with jewels in her hair, or 4. the tree as a chaste woman alone with nature and God) and to create a metaphor for it, but the trouble is that he tries to convey all of these features by a single basic comparison to a person, and therefore presents a picture thoroughly confused.

It is possible to try to defend the poem by appealing to the title, "Trees," pointing out that no over-all consistency is called for: one tree is like the babe nursing at its mother's breast; another tree is a girl lifting her arms to pray, etc. But this defense is probably more damaging than the charge it seeks to meet; for the poem provides no real basis for seeing one tree as babe and another as a devout young woman. Furthermore, such a defense calls attention to the general shallowness and superficiality of the imagery: the various comparisons reveal themselves as so many fanciful analogies, grounded in nothing deeper than a vague approval of the general loveliness of trees. (The student can easily determine how loosely decorative the images are by shifting some of the couplets about: the poem is so formless that its "structure" is not in the least disturbed thereby.)

In stressing the inconsistency in Kilmer's use of imagery, we do not mean to imply, however, that a poet must take a single comparison and develop it *fully* and *consistently,* or that there must be a strict *transition* from one comparison or image to the next. For instance:

> O my love's like a red, red rose,
>   That's newly sprung in June;
> O my love's like the melody
>   That's sweetly played in tune.

Although this stanza seems to have in it the same abrupt change in the comparison, there is really a very important difference. Burns does not say that his love is like a rose in the same way that Kilmer says that the tree is like a person; Burns merely implies that his love is beautiful, fragrant, etc., like a rose, or affects him like a rose, but he does not insist on a consistent development of the comparison; he merely wanted to point out the effective part of the comparison, not even thinking, for instance, of the thorns which are not pretty and are painful and which would have caused trouble if he had started a consistent development of the image, as Kilmer does.

Kilmer jumps from a sucking babe to a grown person without warning and thereby creates a confusion in the reader's mind. Burns, also without warning, leaps to the mention of the melody, but he creates no confusion. Why? Because Burns makes an absolute leap from rose to melody with reference to his "love" as the only connecting link, while Kilmer is maintaining a false consistency by a continued reference to a human being. Poets are constantly jumping from one comparison to another quite successfully because they treat each comparison in terms of its own special contribution to the poet's intention. (For another example of a poet's ability to move from image to image without confusion, see "The Hound of Heaven," p. 278.)

But in "Trees" there are other difficulties on the technical side. The rhythm is not well chosen. It is monotonous. Each stanza has the same rhythm, with a full pause at the end of a couplet and no pauses within the lines. The effect is sharp and pert, with no impression of thoughtfulness or of competent control on the part of the poet. This is especially inappropriate for a poem which pretends to treat a serious subject. Compare the rhythm of "Trees" with this passage from another poem in the same meter and rime scheme:

> Accept, thou shrine of my dead Saint,
> Instead of dirges this complaint;
> And for sweet flowers to crown thy hearse,
> Receive a strew of weeping verse
> From thy grieved friend, whom thou might'st see 5
> Quite melted into tears for thee.

(From "The Exequy," by Henry King)

But how seriously does Kilmer treat his "serious subject"?

The rhythm does not contribute to a serious approach; nor does the confusion of the treatment of imagery. But let us try to consider his *meaning* or *thought* as such.

The poet is expressing a highly romantic mood in which he pretends that the works of man's mind are not comparable in "loveliness" to the works of nature. What he wants to say is that he is tired of the works of man and takes refuge in the works of nature, which is quite different from comparing the two things on the basis of "loveliness." (See "The Garden," by Marvell, p. 354, or "Expostulation and Reply," by Wordsworth, p. xliv.) But the two kinds of loveliness, that of art and that of nature, are not comparable; and in the second place "loveliness" is not the word to apply to *Hamlet,* by Shakespeare, "Lycidas," by Milton, "The Canterbury Tales," by Chaucer, etc. And the tree, as opposed to the poem, is lacking in *meaning* and *expressiveness;* it has those things only in so far as a man can give them to it. Kilmer writes:

> Poems are made by fools like me,
> But only God can make a tree.

That is perfectly true, but by the same line of reasoning God makes the poems too, through his agency in man. Or reversing the argument: Bad poems are made by bad poets like Kilmer and good poems are made by good poets like Yeats, Shakespeare, Landor, Milton, etc. Furthermore the paradox created by Kilmer breaks down, because it isn't justified in terms given in the poem; it will not stand inspection. Housman uses a paradox successfully in "To an Athlete Dying Young," because in the poem he limits the application and illustrates the precise ways in which it contains a truth.

But why has the poem been popular, if so bad? It appeals, as does "The Pilgrims" (p. 181), to a stock response which has nothing to do, as such, with poetry. It praises God and appeals to a religious sentiment. Therefore people who do not stop to look at the poem itself or to study the images in the poem and think about what the poem really says, are inclined to accept the poem because of the pious sentiment, the prettified little pictures (which in themselves appeal to stock responses), and the mechanical rhythm.

The Hound of Heaven

FRANCIS THOMPSON [1859–1907]

I fled Him, down the nights and down the days;
  I fled Him, down the arches of the years;
I fled Him, down the labyrinthine ways
  Of my own mind; and in the mist of tears
I hid from Him, and under running laughter. 5
    Up vistaed hopes, I sped;
    And shot, precipitated,

Adown Titanic glooms of chasmèd fears,
From those strong Feet that followed, followed after.
But with unhurrying chase, 10
And unperturbèd pace,
Deliberate speed, majestic instancy,
They beat—and a Voice beat
More instant than the Feet—
"All things betray thee, who betrayest Me." 15

I pleaded, outlaw-wise,
By many a hearted casement, curtained red,
Trellised with intertwining charities;
(For, though I knew His love Who followèd,
Yet was I sore adread 20
Lest, having Him, I must have naught beside.)
But, if one little casement parted wide,
The gust of His approach would clash it to.
Fear wist not to evade as Love wist to pursue.
Across the margent of the world I fled, 25
And troubled the gold gateways of the stars,
Smiting for shelter on their clangèd bars;
Fretted to dulcet jars
And silvern chatter the pale ports o' the moon.
I said to dawn: Be sudden; to eve: Be soon— 30
With thy young skyey blossoms heap me over
From this tremendous Lover!
Float thy vague veil about me, lest He see!
I tempted all His servitors, but to find
My own betrayal in their constancy, 35
In faith to Him their fickleness to me,
Their traitorous trueness, and their loyal deceit.
To all swift things for swiftness did I sue;
Clung to the whistling mane of every wind.
But whether they swept, smoothly fleet, 40
The long savannahs of the blue;
Or whether, Thunder-driven,
They clanged His chariot 'thwart a heaven,
Plashy with flying lightnings round the spurn o' their feet:—
Fear wist not to evade as Love wist to pursue. 45
Still with unhurrying chase,
And unperturbèd pace,

Deliberate speed, majestic instancy,
Came on the following Feet,
And a Voice above their beat— 50
"Naught shelters thee, who wilt not shelter Me."

I sought no more that after which I strayed
In face of man or maid;
But still within the little children's eyes
Seems something, something that replies, 55
They at least are for me, surely for me!
I turned me to them very wistfully;
But just as their young eyes grew sudden fair
With dawning answers there,
Their angel plucked them from me by the hair. 60
"Come then, ye other children, Nature's—share
With me" (said I) "your delicate fellowship;
Let me greet you lip to lip,
Let me twine with you caresses,
Wantoning 65
With our Lady-Mother's vagrant tresses,
Banqueting
With her in her wind-walled palace,
Underneath her azured daïs,
Quaffing, as your taintless way is, 70
From a chalice
Lucent-weeping out of the dayspring."
So it was done:
I in their delicate fellowship was one—
Drew the bolt of Nature's secrecies. 75
I knew all the swift importings
On the wilful face of skies;
I knew how the clouds arise,
Spumèd of the wild sea-snortings;
All that's born or dies 80
Rose and drooped with; made them shapers
Of mine own moods, or wailful or divine—
With them joyed and was bereaven.
I was heavy with the even,
When she lit her glimmering tapers 85
Round the day's dead sanctities.
I laughed in the morning's eyes.

I triumphed and I saddened with all weather,
Heaven and I wept together,
And its sweet tears were salt with mortal mine; 90
Against the red throb of its sunset-heart
I laid my own to beat,
And share commingling heat;
But not by that, by that, was eased my human smart.
In vain my tears were wet on Heaven's gray cheek. 95
For ah! we know not what each other says,
These things and I; in sound *I* speak—
Their sound is but their stir, they speak by silences.
Nature, poor stepdame, cannot slake my drouth;
Let her, if she would owe me, 100
Drop yon blue bosom-veil of sky, and show me
The breasts o' her tenderness:
Never did any milk of hers once bless
My thirsting mouth.
Nigh and nigh draws the chase, 105
With unperturbèd pace,
Deliberate speed, majestic instancy,
And past those noisèd Feet
A Voice comes yet more fleet—
"Lo! naught contents thee, who content'st not Me." 110

Naked I wait Thy love's uplifted stroke!
My harness piece by piece Thou hast hewn from me,
And smitten me to my knee;
I am defenseless utterly.
I slept, methinks, and woke, 115
And, slowly gazing, find me stripped in sleep.
In the rash lustihead of my young powers,
I shook the pillaring hours
And pulled my life upon me; grimed with smears,
I stand amid the dust o' the mounded years— 120
My mangled youth lies dead beneath the heap.
My days have crackled and gone up in smoke,
Have puffed and burst as sun-starts on a stream.
Yea, faileth now even dream
The dreamer, and the lute the lutanist; 125
Even the linkèd fantasies, in whose blossomy twist
I swung the earth a trinket at my wrist,

Are yielding; cords of all too weak account
For earth, with heavy griefs so overplussed.
        Ah! is Thy love indeed 130
A weed, albeit an amaranthine weed,
Suffering no flowers except its own to mount?
        Ah! must—
        Designer infinite!—
Ah! must Thou char the wood ere Thou canst limn with it?
My freshness spent its wavering shower i' the dust; 136
And now my heart is as a broken fount,
Wherein tear-drippings stagnate, spilt down ever
    From the dank thoughts that shiver
Upon the sighful branches of my mind. 140
    Such is; what is to be?
The pulp so bitter, how shall taste the rind?
I dimly guess what Time in mists confounds;
Yet ever and anon a trumpet sounds
From the hid battlements of Eternity: 145
Those shaken mists a space unsettle, then
Round the half-glimpsèd turrets slowly wash again;
    But not ere him who summoneth
    I first have seen, enwound
With glooming robes purpureal, cypress-crowned; 150
His name I know, and what his trumpet saith.
Whether man's heart or life it be which yields
    Thee harvest, must Thy harvest fields
    Be dunged with rotten death?

      Now of that long pursuit 155
      Comes on at hand the bruit;
  That Voice is round me like a bursting sea:
      "And is thy earth so marred,
      Shattered in shard on shard?
  Lo, all things fly thee, for thou fliest Me! 160
    Strange, piteous, futile thing!
Wherefore should any set thee love apart?
Seeing none but I makes much of naught"
        (He said),
"And human love needs human meriting:
    How hast thou merited— 165

Of all man's clotted clay the dingiest clot?
    Alack, thou knowest not
How little worthy of any love thou art!
Whom wilt thou find to love ignoble thee,
    Save Me, save only Me? 170
All which I took from thee I did but take,
    Not for thy harms,
But just that thou might'st seek it in My arms,
  All which thy child's mistake
Fancies as lost, I have stored for thee at home: 175
  Rise, clasp My hand, and come!"
    Halts by me that footfall:
    Is my gloom, after all,
Shade of His hand, outstretched caressingly?
    "Ah, fondest, blindest, weakest, 180
    I am He Whom thou seekest!
Thou dravest love from thee, who dravest Me."

This poem, like "Trees," is a religious poem, and one which makes use of a profusion of images, many of them highly complicated. Furthermore, it is a poem in which the reader is forced to shift rapidly from image to image. Has Thompson succeeded in avoiding the kind of absurdity which we found in "Trees"?

Lines 111 to 135 furnish a particularly interesting succession of images. The passage begins with a figure that suggests a knight beaten to his knees and prepared to receive the death stroke from his opponent. "Harness" suggests armor; the armor has been "hewn" from him. He says at line 114, "I am defenseless utterly." The statement serves as a conclusion to the three lines that precede it; but as we read on, we see that it points forward to the next image suggested in the next two lines, that of a man who has waked to find himself "stripped in sleep."

Notice that neither figure is developed explicitly: neither that of the defeated warrior, nor that of the traveler who falls asleep by the wayside and is robbed. And this fact may have something to do with the ease with which we move through the statement "I am defenseless utterly" from one implied figure to the other. For the poet is merely drawing upon the concrete strength of the implied images; their relation to the line of development is kept perfectly clear.

This process carries right on through the passage. The first implied image suggests that his defenses have been cut from him by an opponent; the second emphasizes the suddenness with which this has been done; and a third implied image (lines 119–21) suggests that the injury has been finally of his own doing. For the third implied image is that of a Samson who has destroyed himself—destroyed, that is, his youth and now contemplates the "mounded years" beneath which it lies.

Images of the suddenness with which a dried field goes up in smoke, or with which a sparkling bubble on a stream suddenly bursts and becomes nothing, follow in the next two lines. Both images emphasize the abrupt vanishing of his former days. ("Puffed," which can apply to either image, acts as an internal link between them.) How those youthful days were spent is suggested by the reference to the dream and the lute. We have a statement that neither now avail, but the poet goes on to develop through a rather complex figure his reference to the dream. His "linkèd fantasies" were like a clover chain or daisy chain by which a child might swing a trinket about his wrist. In his youth the world seemed so light that it could be swung nonchalantly in this fashion, but now it has become the heavy, weighted earth, and breaks through the "blossomy twist" which once sufficed to hold it.

The image now shifts sharply once more, though "blossomy twist" may suggest the new figure of the "weed." The speaker protests that the divine love has the jealousy of a weed which chokes out all flowers but its own. The bitter protest carries forward through the next lines, but shifts to another figure as it does so: a figure taken from the artist's studio—designs sketched in charcoal. It seems that God as the great artist must burn and char the wood before he can use it to portray his design.

What Thompson is doing in this passage is shifting his imagery constantly and sometimes quite shockingly, but the images, for all their variety, are related to a definite psychological "line." The images do not beget confusion. They do not tumble over each other. Through them the poem moves forward, not, however, as an abstract statement, but with a great deal of concreteness and dramatic power. The passage will illustrate one very important way in which a poem may shift from image to image without confusion.

EXERCISE:

1. Analyze the flow of imagery from lines 136 through 154, paying special attention to the transitions from image to image.

2. What is the dominant metaphor of the poem as a whole? How is it related to the incidental imagery? Can you justify the shift at the end in which the "Hound of Heaven," having brought his quarry to bay, speaks with tenderness?

Tomorrow and Tomorrow

I.

WILLIAM SHAKESPEARE [1564–1616]

Tomorrow, and tomorrow, and tomorrow,
Creeps in this petty pace from day to day,
To the last syllable of recorded time;
And all our yesterdays have lighted fools
The way to dusty death. Out, out, brief candle; 5
Life's but a walking shadow; a poor player,
That struts and frets his hour upon the stage,
And then is heard no more: it is a tale
Told by an idiot, full of sound and fury,
Signifying nothing. 10

(From *Macbeth*)

II.

SIR WILLIAM DAVENANT [1606–1668]

Tomorrow and tomorrow and tomorrow
Creeps in a stealing pace from day to day,
To the last minute of recorded time,
And all our yesterdays have lighted fools
To their eternal homes; out, out, that candle! 5
Life's but a walking shadow, a poor player

That struts and frets his hour upon the stage,
And then is heard no more. It is a tale
Told by an idiot, full of sound and fury,
Signifying nothing. 10

(From *Macbeth*)

Exercise:

The second version of this passage is a rewriting of the first. The intention of Sir William Davenant was to remove certain defects, offenses against what he considered "correctness" and "reasonableness."

1. Analyze the passage from Shakespeare. Can you justify the transition from image to image? (Is an actor in any sense "a walking shadow"?)

2. Write a detailed comparison of the two passages.

Cleopatra's Lament

WILLIAM SHAKESPEARE [1564–1616]

Cleopatra. I dreamed there was an Emperor Antony:
O! such another sleep, that I might see
But such another man.
Dolabella. If it might please ye,—
Cleopatra. His face was as the heavens, and therein stuck 5
A sun and moon, which kept their course, and lighted
The little O, the earth.
Dolabella. Most sovereign creature,—
Cleopatra. His legs bestrid the ocean; his reared arm
Crested the world; his voice was propertied 10
As all the tunèd spheres, and that to friends;
But when he meant to quail and shake the orb,
He was as rattling thunder. For his bounty,
There was no winter in 't, an autumn 'twas
That grew the more by reaping; his delights 15
Were dolphin-like, they showed his back above
The element they lived in; in his livery
Walked crowns and crownets, realms and islands were
As plates dropped from his pocket.
Dolabella. Cleopatra,— 20

Cleopatra. Think you there was, or might be, such a man
As this I dreamed of?
Dolabella. Gentle madam, no.
(From *Antony and Cleopatra*)

EXERCISE:

This selection is a section of the conversation between Cleopatra and the emissary of Octavius Caesar, who has just defeated the forces of Antony and Cleopatra. Antony is now dead, and Cleopatra is speaking from the memory of his grandeur and generosity. Some of the comparisons here may, at first glance, seem exaggerated and far-fetched. Can they be justified? (With reference to the dolphin-image, what would have been the effect if Cleopatra had said that Antony was immersed in his delights—drowned in pleasure?) Furthermore, the relations among the various images are not specifically stated. Is there a confusion on this ground?

Crossing the Bar

ALFRED, LORD TENNYSON [1809–1892]

Sunset and evening star,
And one clear call for me!
And may there be no moaning of the bar,
When I put out to sea,

But such a tide as moving seems asleep, 5
Too full for sound and foam,
When that which drew from out the boundless deep
Turns again home.

Twilight and evening bell,
And after that the dark! 10
And may there be no sadness of farewell,
When I embark;

For though from out our bourne of Time and Place
The flood may bear me far,
I hope to see my Pilot face to face 15
When I have crossed the bar.

Exercise:

Much of the force of this poem comes from the fact that the poet has built his poem upon one elaborate image: that of a ship putting out at eventide from the harbor. The bar that lies across the harbor-mouth, a peril to navigation except at high tide, is obviously death. The sea is the sea of eternity. The soul puts out across this sea to go home to God. Who is the pilot? Are there any inconsistencies or lapses in the imagery?

To Helen

EDGAR ALLAN POE [1809–1849]

Helen, thy beauty is to me
  Like those Nicèan barks of yore
That gently, o'er a perfumed sea,
  The weary way-worn wanderer bore
  To his own native shore. 5

On desperate seas long wont to roam,
  Thy hyacinth hair, thy classic face,
Thy Naiad airs have brought me home
  To the glory that was Greece,
And the grandeur that was Rome. 10

Lo, in yon brilliant window-niche
  How statue-like I see thee stand,
  The agate lamp within thy hand,
Ah! Psyche, from the regions which
  Are holy land! 15

Exercise:

1. The poet says that the woman addressed has a "classic face." How does the imagery support this statement?

2. The first stanza refers to Ulysses brought home at the end of his wanderings. How has the speaker been brought "home"? Where is his home?

3. Another poem by Poe, "Ulalume" (p. 194), has been unfavor-

ably analyzed. Try to define the reasons why "To Helen" is more successful.

Follow Thy Fair Sun, Unhappy Shadow

THOMAS CAMPION [1567–1620]

Follow thy fair sun, unhappy shadow,
Though thou be black as night,
And she made all of light,
Yet follow thy fair sun, unhappy shadow.

Follow her whose light thy light depriveth, 5
Though here thou liv'st disgraced,
And she in heaven is placed,
Yet follow her whose light the world reviveth.

Follow those pure beams whose beauty burneth,
That so have scorchèd thee, 10
As thou still black must be,
Till her kind beams thy black to brightness turneth.

Follow her while yet her glory shineth:
There comes a luckless night,
That will dim all her light; 15
And this the black unhappy shade divineth.

Follow still since so thy fates ordainèd;
The sun must have his shade,
Till both at once do fade,
The sun still proud, the shadow still disdainèd. 20

EXERCISE:

1. How does the sun-shadow figure exemplify the relation between the lover and his cruel mistress? For example, his blackness is an effect of being scorched by the sun. What other aspects of their relationship are treated through this figure?

2. How does the figure help determine the tone of the poem? What is the tone?

When the Lamp Is Shattered

PERCY BYSSHE SHELLEY [1792–1822]

When the lamp is shattered
The light in the dust lies dead—
When the cloud is scattered
The rainbow's glory is shed.
When the lute is broken, 5
Sweet tones are remembered not;
When the lips have spoken,
Loved accents are soon forgot.

As music and splendor
Survive not the lamp and the lute, 10
The heart's echoes render
No song when the spirit is mute:—
No song but sad dirges,
Like the wind through a ruined cell,
Or the mournful surges 15
That ring the dead seaman's knell.

When hearts have once mingled
Love first leaves the well-built nest,
The weak one is singled
To endure what it once possessed. 20
O Love! who bewailest
The frailty of all things here,
Why choose you the frailest
For your cradle, your home, and your bier?

Its passions will rock thee 25
As the storms rock the ravens on high:
Bright reason will mock thee,
Like the sun from a wintry sky.
From thy nest every rafter
Will rot, and thine eagle home 30
Leave thee naked to laughter,
When leaves fall and cold winds come.

Exercise:

1. The images of this poem fall into two general groupings: the first two stanzas are dominated by sound images; the last two by the images connected with the bird's nest. What is the poet saying by means of these images?

2. Can you justify the shift from one basic pattern of imagery to another? What transitional devices if any are used?

3. What is the antecedent of *its* in line 25?

The Night

HENRY VAUGHAN [1622–1695]

Through that pure virgin-shrine,
That sacred veil drawn o'er thy glorious noon
That men might look and live as glow-worms shine,
And face the moon:
Wise Nicodemus saw such light 5
As made him know his God by night.

Most blest believer he!
Who in that land of darkness and blind eyes
Thy long-expected healing wings could see,
When thou didst rise, 10
And what can never more be done,
Did at midnight speak with the Sun!

O who will tell me, where
He found thee at that dead and silent hour!
What hallowed solitary ground did bear 15
So rare a flower,
Within whose sacred leaves did lie
The fullness of the Deity.

No mercy-seat of gold,
No dead and dusty cherub, nor carved stone, 20
But his own living works did my Lord hold
And lodge alone;
Where trees and herbs did watch and peep
And wonder, while the Jews did sleep.

Dear night! this world's defeat; 25
The stop to busy fools; care's check and curb;
The day of spirits; my soul's calm retreat
Which none disturb!
Christ's progress, and his prayer time;
The hours to which high heaven doth chime. 30

God's silent, searching flight:
When my Lord's head is filled with dew, and all
His locks are wet with the clear drops of night;
His still, soft call;
His knocking time; the soul's dumb watch, 35
When spirits their fair kindred catch.

Were all my loud, evil days
Calm and unhaunted as is thy dark tent,
Whose peace but by some angel's wing or voice
Is seldom rent; 40
Then I in heaven all the long year
Would keep, and never wander here.

But living where the sun
Doth all things wake, and where all mix and tire
Themselves and others, I consent and run 45
To every mire,
And by this world's ill-guiding light,
Err more than I can do by night.

There is in God (some say)
A deep, but dazzling darkness; as men here 50
Say it is late and dusky, because they
See not all clear;
O for that night! where I in Him
Might live invisible and dim.

Exercise:

1. Is a cherub carved in stone a "dead" cherub? Why "dusty"? What are the usual associations of "cherub"? What is the meaning of "living works" (line 21)?

2. Compare and contrast "the Sun" (line 12) and "this world's

ill-guiding light" (line 47). Does "light" come to have a double meaning in this poem? Does "darkness" have a double meaning?

3. In the last stanza, the poet boldly associates darkness with God himself. Does he make the notion dramatically convincing? How? Comment on the *d-* alliteration in the last stanza. Could it be termed "functional alliteration"?

The Definition of Love

ANDREW MARVELL [1621–1678]

My love is of a birth as rare
As 'tis for object strange and high:
It was begotten by Despair
Upon Impossibility.

Magnanimous Despair alone 5
Could show me so divine a thing,
Where feeble Hope could ne'er have flown
But vainly flapped its tinsel wing.

And yet I quickly might arrive
Where my extended soul is fixed, 10
But Fate does iron wedges drive,
And always crowds itself betwixt.

For Fate with jealous eye does see
Two perfect loves, nor lets them close:
Their union would her ruin be, 15
And her tyrannic power depose.

And therefore her decrees of steel
Us as the distant poles have placed,
(Though love's whole world on us doth wheel)
Not by themselves to be embraced, 20

Unless the giddy heaven fall,
And earth some new convulsion tear,
And, us to join, the world should all
Be cramped into a planisphere.

As lines, so loves oblique may well 25
Themselves in every angle greet;
But ours, so truly parallel,
Though infinite, can never meet.

Therefore the love which us doth bind,
But fate so enviously debars, 30
Is the conjunction of the mind,
And opposition of the stars.

This poem deals with a subject which may seem at first glance too narrow to afford very much scope, and which would seem to afford little opportunity to say anything very fresh and new. The intensity of one's love is surely a conventional enough theme. The poet might easily, in handling such a subject, fail to convey the sense of the intensity, or, in attempting to convey it, might easily overwrite his poem and find himself betrayed into hollow sounding exaggeration or embarrassing sentimentality, as in the case of "The Indian Serenade" (p. 173). This is the problem which the poet faces here. The solution which he makes is not the only solution, of course. It is only one of the many possible solutions, as the great number of fine poems on the same theme will indicate, but a close examination of it may tell us a great deal about the use of imagery. For it is largely in terms of his imagery that this poet presents the complex and rich experience which the poem embodies.

The poet begins by stating the matter in terms of a paradox, and the shock of this paradox—the sharp break which it makes with the stale and conventional in general—allows him to state with no sense of overfacile, glib exaggeration that

My love is of a birth as rare
As 'tis for object strange and high.

The first word of the second stanza enforces the paradox. It lets us know that the poet is going to stand by his paradox. Despair is not *grim* or *harsh* or *cruel,* as one would anticipate, but *magnanimous*. His love is too divine to have been hoped for—it could only have been shown to him by Despair itself. Already the paradox has done something more than startle us out of an accustomed attitude;

but the startling paradox is only a device to lead one to grasp the poet's attitude which is an attitude complex enough to perceive a magnanimity in the very hopelessness of attaining his love since only that hopelessness allows him to see the true and ideal character of his love.

The poet now proceeds to develop this paradox through the remainder of the poem. The development is made largely in terms of images.

It is nothing less than fate that separates him from his love—but again the poet provides us with a concrete image: Fate drives iron wedges between them. And the poet, having personified fate—having turned it into a person—provides the person with a motive. Fate itself would cease to exist if any complete perfection might be attained. Their love is so perfect that its consummation would be incompatible with a world ruled over by fate. That this should be prevented from happening is therefore not the result of one of fate's malicious caprices—the character of the love itself determines the "fate."

Notice at this point that the poet's attitude toward fate is not that of hysterical outrage. There is a calm reasoned tone here such as we have already found in the ability to see despair as "magnanimous." And yet this sense of reasonableness has been achieved *in the process* of making statements which ordinarily would seem the most outrageous exaggerations! His love is the highest possible; his love is too divine to be even hoped for. The result is that the statements are felt, not as outrageous statements to be immediately discounted, but as having the weight of reasoned truth.

In the fifth stanza the major paradox is given a particularly rich statement by means of the use of an unusually fine figure. Fate has placed the two lovers as far apart as the poles. "As far apart as the poles" seems at first merely the conventional expression which we use to indicate great distance apart. But the poet immediately seizes on the implied figure and develops it for us. The two lovers are, like the poles of the earth, unable to touch each other; but though they are separated by the distance of the entire globe, they are the focal points in determining the rotation of the earth. Thus, the lovers, though separated, define the ideal nature of love. The world of love, like a globe, turns on the axis of their relationship. The exactness of the comparison gives force to his statement, and Marvell further stresses the exactness of the relationship between his own situation and the figure which he uses to illustrate it, by going on to state the only condition on which the poles might be united. The poles might be united only if the earth were suddenly compressed into a two-dimensional disc which would have no thickness at all—that is, into a *planisphere*. The associations of a technical word again support the sense of exact, calculated statement in the poem. The poet continues to expound the incredible nature of his love with the poise of a mathematician. Therefore we are more readily inclined to accept the statement.

The technical word also prepares somewhat perhaps for the figure which the poet uses in the seventh stanza. Loves "oblique," the loves of those who are not in perfect accord, are like lines which cross each other at an angle. Their very lack of parallelism forms the possibility of their meeting. His own love and that of his mistress accord with each other so perfectly that, though stretched to infinity, they could draw no nearer together. In this image, then, the poet finds exactly the illustration of the paradoxical relationship of which he is writing. The application of this image is made easier by the ordinary association of the idea of infinity with the idea of love; it is a conventional association in love poetry. But Marvell has taken the conventional association and, by developing it, has derived a renewed life and freshness.

The poem closes with another paradox, this time drawn from astrology. We say that stars are in *conjunction* when they are seen in the sky very close together; that they are in *opposition* when they are situated in opposite parts of the sky. According to astrology, moreover, planets in conjunction unite their influences. In opposition they fight against each other. Here the lovers' minds are in conjunction. They are united, but their stars (fate) are against them. This concluding comparison, then, combines the idea of the third and fourth stanza with that of the fifth and sixth. In a way, it epitomizes the whole poem.

Is the poem merely an ingenious bundle of paradoxes? Some readers may dislike the very active play of the mind here, and will dislike also the exactness of the diction, and the imagery drawn from mathematics and kindred subjects. But does this ingenuity and exactness make the poem insincere? Does it not have indeed the opposite effect? The lover protesting his love is too often vague and rhetorical. He gives a sense of glibness and effusiveness. The effect of Marvell's imagery is not only one of freshness as opposed to stale conventionality—it is also one of calculation as opposed to one of unthinking excitement.

My Springs

SIDNEY LANIER [1842–1881]

In the heart of the Hills of Life, I know
Two springs that with unbroken flow
Forever pour their lucent streams
Into my soul's far Lake of Dreams.

Not larger than two eyes, they lie 5
Beneath the many-changing sky
And mirror all of life and time,
—Serene and dainty pantomime.

Shot through with lights of stars and dawns,
And shadowed sweet by ferns and fawns, 10
—Thus heaven and earth together vie
Their shining depths to sanctify.

Always when the large Form of Love
Is hid by storms that rage above,
I gaze in my two springs and see 15
Love in his very verity.

Always when Faith with stifling stress
Of grief hath died in bitterness,
I gaze in my two springs and see
A faith that smiles immortally. 20

Always when Charity and Hope,
In darkness bounden, feebly grope,

I gaze in my two springs and see
A Light that sets my captives free.

Always when Art on perverse wing 25
Flies where I cannot hear him sing,
I gaze in my two springs and see
A charm that brings him back to me.

When Labor faints, and Glory fails,
And coy Reward in sighs exhales, 30
I gaze in my two springs and see
Attainment full and heavenly.

O Love, O Wife, thine eyes are they,
—My springs from out whose shining gray
Issue the sweet celestial streams 35
That feed my life's bright Lake of Dreams.

Oval and large and passion-pure
And gray and wise and honor-sure;
Soft as a dying violet-breath
Yet calmly unafraid of death; 40

Thronged, like two dove-cotes of gray doves,
With wife's and mother's and poor-folk's loves,
And home-loves and high glory-loves
And science-loves and story-loves,

And loves for all that God and man 45
In art and nature make or plan,
And lady-loves for spidery lace
And broideries and supple grace

And diamonds and the whole sweet round
Of littles that large life compound, 50
And loves for God and God's bare truth,
And loves for Magdalen and Ruth,

Dear eyes, dear eyes and rare complete—
Being heavenly-sweet and earthly-sweet,
—I marvel that God made you mine, 55
For when He frowns, 'tis then ye shine!

This poem by Sidney Lanier would probably be regarded as a sentimental poem by most experienced readers of poetry. It appears sentimental because it insists on more response than the reader feels is justified by the occasion as presented in the poem. The poem is, therefore, extravagant. We know that, as a matter of fact, a very great devotion existed between Sidney Lanier and his wife, and that she was a constant source of comfort to him in his struggles against poverty and illness. *But the mere fact that we know of this relationship between the poet and his wife does not necessarily redeem the poem from the charge of sentimentality, for a poem must be able to achieve its effect without reference to the biographical facts behind its composition.*

Sentimentality often makes itself felt as a kind of strain, a strain on the part of the writer to convince the reader that he should respond in such and such a way. In this poem the strain most clearly manifests itself in the use the poet makes of imagery. In the discussion of "The Pilgrims" (p. 181), it was said that the clichés of phrase and idea indicate a sentimental approach, the lack of any attempt on the part of the poet to investigate the real possibilities of the subject, the poet's unconscious dependence on some sort of stock response in the reader. Both of these defects may indicate sentimentality, for both imply an attempt to get a response not justified in the poem itself. But let us try to study the nature of the imagery in Lanier's poem.

The first nine stanzas are constructed about one basic image, that of the springs, and the next four about another, that of the doves in a dove-cote. Now the image of the eyes as springs is given a kind of geographical location in an imaginary landscape. The springs (the eyes) are located, says the poet, in the midst of the Hills of Life, and by their overflow keep full the Lake of Dreams of the poet's soul. Is there any basis for what we might call the construction of this little piece of poetic landscape? Does anything really bind its parts together? The poet apparently means by the Hills of Life the difficulties that beset him. He has taken an abstraction, the general idea of difficulties, and has in his poem made it equivalent to the concrete objects, hills. This is really a cliché, but the poet has tried to save the comparison by giving it a relationship to the Springs. The comparison of eyes to pools or springs, however, is another cliché, equally dull. These two worn-out images could be given new strength only if the relationship established between them were really expressive and imaginatively justifiable. (We have seen how Marvell succeeded in such an attempt in "The Definition of Love.")

But first we may observe that the two images are not arrived at by the same process. That of the hills is an identification of an abstraction (difficulties) with a concrete object (hills); that of the springs is an identification of one concrete object (eyes) with another concrete object (springs). The image of the Lake of Dreams is arrived at by the former process. Yet all of these three images are parts of the same landscape: the springs in the hills overflow into the lake. The reader feels that the poet has arbitrarily put these things together and that they do not really represent an imaginative insight.

There is no particular reason why, for instance, the Dreams should be represented by a lake rather than by any of a dozen other objects except that a lake fits the landscape better. As a matter of fact, as the poem goes on, we discover that the Lake of Dreams is not at all what we presume the poet to mean. In plain prose, the eyes of his wife encourage him in Love, Faith, Charity, Hope, Art, and Ambition. Yet we know that the poet does not mean to say that the things by which he lives, for instance, love, faith, and art, are illusions; he would maintain that they are realities. Or perhaps the poet does not mean the image in this sense; he may mean that the eyes of his wife encourage him to dream of worth-while things. This is more consistent with the general temper of the poem, but it bears no specific connection with the image itself.

Further, the poet was not really willing to stand by his identification of the eyes with springs, and he proceeds without dealing at all with one important inconsistency implied in the image. The springs, we remember, overflow. The springs are eyes. The most emphatic implication here is that of weeping, which is inconsistent with the meaning the poet has in mind. The poet should have solved this difficulty of implication for the reader or should have abandoned the image. Instead, he ignored the matter, which seems to argue that he himself really was not paying much attention to the full implication of what he was doing. In other words, there is a kind of vagueness here, and a kind of strain.

The personifications, the "Form of Love," "Faith," "Charity," and "Hope," bear no real relation to the scene in which they are put. For instance, how much close investigation can the relation between Charity and the basic scene of the springs, etc., be made to bear? In what darkness are Charity and Hope, personified as real persons, bound? Is there a dungeon or a cave near by? No provision has been made for this in the scene. And how can the Light that the poet sees in the spring set the "captives free"? It would have been perfectly possible for the poet to leap from one image to another in pursuit of his idea, *if he had not insisted on the formal connection between the two images.* For example, in the following passage by Shakespeare there is no attempt to make the series of images logically consistent with each other, and yet the reader's imagination can make the leap from one to the next because each in itself is appropriate:

> To be, or not to be: that is the question:
> Whether 'tis nobler in the mind to suffer
> The slings and arrows of outrageous fortune,
> Or to take arms against a sea of troubles,
> And by opposing end them? To die: to sleep;
> No more; and by a sleep to say we end
> The heart-ache and the thousand natural shocks
> That flesh is heir to. 'Tis a consummation
> Devoutly to be wished.
>
> (From *Hamlet*)

But Lanier does insist on the consistency between the image of Charity and Hope as captives in darkness and that of the springs, etc., because the latter provides the location, as it were, of the former. Therefore, since this consistency is not really inherent in the images employed, we have an effect of strain and artificiality.

The basic image of the eleventh, twelfth, and thirteenth stanzas, the image of the dove-cote and doves, shares the same quality of strain and artificiality. On what basis can we conceive of the love of science ("science-loves") or the love of fine lace ("lady-loves for spidery lace") or the love of fiction and poetry ("story-loves") as gray doves? It is a purely arbitrary equating of the two things. And the image becomes even more arbitrary and more complicated when we conceive, or try to conceive, of those doves in two dove-cotes which are a lady's eyes. If a reader will compare the imagery of this poem with the imagery in most other poems in this collection, he will see that the present poem lacks imagery that is truly functional and expressive, and that the poet by his use of imagery is trying to force a reaction on the reader that is not justified by the material.

The Tear

RICHARD CRASHAW [1613?–1649]

What bright soft thing is this,
  Sweet Mary, thy fair eyes' expense?
A moist spark it is,
  A wat'ry diamond; from whence
The very term, I think, was found, 5
The water of a diamond.

Oh! 'tis not a tear,
  'Tis a star about to drop
From thine eye, its sphere;
  The Sun will stoop and take it up. 10
Proud will his sister be to wear
This thine eye's jewel in her ear.

Oh! 'tis a tear,
  Too true a tear; for no sad eyne,[1]
How sad soe'er, 15
  Rain so true a tear as thine;
Each drop, leaving a place so dear,
Weeps for itself, is its own tear.

Such a pearl as this is,
  (Slipped from Aurora's dewy breast) 20
The rose-bud's sweet lip kisses;
  And such the rose itself, when vexed
With ungentle flames, does shed,
Sweating in too warm a bed.

[1] eyes

Such the maiden gem 25
By the wanton Spring put on,
Peeps from her parent stem,
And blushes on the manly Sun:
This wat'ry blossom of thy eyne,
Ripe, will make the richer wine. 30

Fair drop, why quak'st thou so?
'Cause thou straight must lay thy head
In the dust? Oh no;
The dust shall never be thy bed:
A pillow for thee will I bring, 35
Stuffed with down of angel's wing.

Thus carried up on high,
(For to heaven thou must go)
Sweetly shalt thou lie,
And in soft slumbers bathe thy woe; 40
Till the singing orbs awake thee,
And one of their bright chorus make thee.

There thyself shalt be
An eye, but not a weeping one;
Yet I doubt of thee, 45
Whither th'hadst rather there have shone
An eye of Heaven; or still shine here
In th' Heaven of Mary's eye, a tear.

Exercise:

1. The images of this poem are usually condemned because they are too "far-fetched." But is this the point? Are the images any "farther fetched" than those in many poems that we have judged to be good? See "The Hound of Heaven" (p. 278) or "Cleopatra's Lament" (p. 286).

2. Can it be argued that these comparisons are essentially "decorative"—that they do not develop the poem but merely say over and over that Mary Magdalene's tears are very precious?

3. Does the poem have any development in theme or attitude? Could the order of the stanzas be rearranged without affecting the poem? If so, what, if anything, does this tell us about the poem?

A Valediction: Forbidding Mourning

JOHN DONNE [1573–1631]

As virtuous men pass mildly away,
  And whisper to their souls, to go,
Whilst some of their sad friends do say,
  The breath goes now, and some say, no:

So let us melt, and make no noise, 5
  No tear-floods, nor sigh-tempests move,
'Twere profanation of our joys
  To tell the laity our love.

Moving of th' earth brings harms and fears,
  Men reckon what it did and meant, 10
But trepidation of the spheres,
  Though greater far, is innocent.

Dull sublunary lovers' love
  (Whose soul is sense) cannot admit
Absence, because it doth remove 15
  Those things which elemented it.

But we by a love, so much refined,
  That our selves know not what it is,
Inter-assurèd of the mind,
  Care less, eyes, lips, and hands to miss. 20

Our two souls therefore, which are one,
  Though I must go, endure not yet
A breach, but an expansion,
  Like gold to airy thinness beat.

If they be two, they are two so 25
  As stiff twin compasses are two,
Thy soul the fixed foot, makes no show
  To move, but doth, if th' other do.

And though it in the center sit,
  Yet when the other far doth roam, 30

It leans, and hearkens after it,
  And grows erect, as that comes home.

Such wilt thou be to me, who must
  Like th' other foot, obliquely run;
Thy firmness makes my circle just, 35
  And makes me end, where I begun.

EXERCISE:

Write an analysis of this poem, taking into account the following topics:

1. The tone of the first two stanzas.
2. The implications of the imagery in the last four stanzas. (For instance, how do the associations one ordinarily has with compasses tend to give an impression of accuracy and conviction to the conclusion of the poem?)
3. The use of enjambment.
4. The use of alliteration and repetition.
5. The metrical situation in the first line of the seventh stanza.
6. The relationship of the various images to each other.

Shadows in the Water

THOMAS TRAHERNE [1637?–1674]

In unexperienced infancy
Many a sweet mistake doth lie:
Mistake though false, intending true;
A seeming somewhat more than view,
  That doth instruct the mind 5
  In things that lie behind,
And many secrets to us show
Which afterwards we come to know.

Thus did I by the water's brink
Another world beneath me think; 10
And while the lofty spacious skies
Reversèd there abused mine eyes,
  I fancied other feet
  Came mine to touch or meet;

As by some puddle I did play 15
Another world within it lay.

Beneath the water people drowned,
Yet with another heaven crowned,
In spacious regions seemed to go
As freely moving to and fro: 20
In bright and open space
I saw their very face;
Eyes, hands, and feet they had like mine;
Another sun did with them shine.

'Twas strange that people there should walk, 25
And yet I could not hear them talk:
That through a little wat'ry chink,
Which one dry ox or horse might drink,
We other worlds should see,
Yet not admitted be; 30
And other confines there behold
Of light and darkness, heat and cold.

I called them oft, but called in vain;
No speeches we could entertain:
Yet did I there expect to find 35
Some other world, to please my mind.
I plainly saw by these
A new Antipodes,
Whom, though they were so plainly seen,
A film kept off that stood between. 40

By walking men's reversèd feet
I chanced another world to meet;
Though it did not to view exceed
A phantasm, 'tis a world indeed,
Where skies beneath us shine, 45
And earth by art divine
Another face presents below,
Where people's feet against ours go.

Within the regions of the air,
Compassed about with heavens fair, 50

Great tracts of land there may be found
Enriched with fields and fertile ground;
  Where many numerous hosts,
  In those far distant coasts,
For other great and glorious ends, 55
Inhabit, my yet unknown friends.

O ye that stand upon the brink,
Whom I so near me, through the chink,
With wonder see: what faces there,
Whose feet, whose bodies, do ye wear? 60
  I my companions see
  In you, another me.
They seemed others, but are we;
Our second selves those shadows be.

Look how far off those lower skies 65
Extend themselves! scarce with mine eyes
I can them reach, O ye my friends,
What secret borders on those ends?
  Are lofty heavens hurled
  'Bout your inferior world? 70
Are ye the representatives
Of other people's distant lives?

Of all the playmates which I knew
That here I do the image view
In other selves; what can it mean 75
But that below the purling stream
  Some unknown joys there be
  Laid up in store for me;
To which I shall, when that thin skin
Is broken, be admitted in. 80

EXERCISE:

1. This poem elaborates a child's misconception about the reality of the world he sees mirrored in the water. Why is the misconception called a "sweet mistake" (line 2)?

2. What realistic details are given? What is the effect of these upon the tone of the poem?

3. Does the elaboration of the childhood incident become monotonous? Discuss this question in relation to the tone of the poem.

The Last Days of Alice

ALLEN TATE [1899–]

Alice grown lazy, mammoth but not fat,
Declines upon her lost and twilight age,
Above in the dozing leaves the grinning cat
Quivers forever with his abstract rage;

Whatever light swayed on the perilous gate 5
Forever sways, nor will the arching grass
Caught when the world clattered undulate
In the deep suspension of the looking-glass.

Bright Alice! always pondering to gloze
The spoiled cruelty she had meant to say 10
Gazes learnedly down her airy nose
At nothing, nothing thinking all the day:

Turned absent-minded by infinity
She cannot move unless her double move,
The All-Alice of the world's entity 15
Smashed in the anger of her hopeless love,

Love for herself who as an earthly twain
Pouted to join her two in a sweet one:
No more the second lips to kiss in vain
The first she broke, plunged through the glass alone— 20

Alone to the weight of impassivity
Incest of spirit, theorem of desire
Without will as chalky cliffs by the sea
Empty as the bodiless flesh of fire;

All space that heaven is a dayless night 25
A nightless day driven by perfect lust
For vacancy, in which her bored eyesight
Stares at the drowsy cubes of human dust.

We, too, back to the world shall never pass
Through the shattered door, a dumb shade-harried crowd, 30

Being all infinite, function, depth and mass
Without figure; a mathematical shroud

Hurled at the air—blessèd without sin!
O God of our flesh, return us to Your wrath
Let us be evil could we enter in 35
Your grace, and falter on the stony path!

Exercise:

1. The "Alice" referred to in this poem is the heroine of *Alice in Wonderland* and *Alice Through the Looking-Glass*. How much of the imagery of the first five stanzas is derived from these two books?

2. What does Alice stand for in this poem? What does the absurdly but inhumanly logical world of the Looking-Glass (or of her Wonderland) stand for? Why is *our* plight (see line 29) like that of Alice? (Note how many figures suggest that the Alice of this poem has hypnotized herself—has locked herself into the world spun out of her own head.)

3. Comment on the meaning of such phrases as "Incest of spirit," "mathematical shroud," and "blessèd without sin." What is this poem about? The poem may be said to end with a prayer. How is the prayer related to the rest of the poem?

In the Holy Nativity of Our Lord God

A Hymn Sung as by the Shepherds

RICHARD CRASHAW [1613?–1649]

Chorus

Come, we shepherds, whose blest sight
Hath met Love's noon in Nature's night;
Come, lift we up our loftier song
And wake the sun that lies too long.

To all our world of well-stol'n joy 5
He slept, and dreamt of no such thing;
While we found out heaven's fairer eye
And kissed the cradle of our King.

Tell him he rises now, too late
To show us aught worth looking at. 10

Tell him we now can show him more
Than he e'er showed to mortal sight;
Than he himself e'er saw before;
Which to be seen needs not his light.
Tell him, Tityrus, where th' hast been, 15
Tell him, Thyrsis, what th' hast seen.

TITYRUS. Gloomy night embraced the place
Where the noble infant lay,
The babe looked up and showed his face;
In spite of darkness, it was day. 20
It was thy day, sweet! and did rise
Not from the east, but from thine eyes.

CHORUS. It was thy day, sweet, etc.

THYRSIS. Winter chid aloud; and sent
The angry North to wage his wars. 25
The North forgot his fierce intent;
And left perfumes instead of scars..
By those sweet eyes' persuasive powers,
Where he meant frost he scattered flowers.

CHO. By those sweet eyes', etc. 30

BOTH. We saw thee in thy balmy nest,
Young dawn of our Eternal Day!
We saw thine eyes break from their east
And chase the trembling shades away.
We saw thee, and we blest the sight, 35
We saw thee by thine own sweet light.

TIT. Poor World, said I, what wilt thou do
To entertain this starry stranger?
Is this the best thou canst bestow?
A cold, and not too cleanly, manger? 40
Contend, ye powers of heaven and earth,
To fit a bed for this huge birth!

CHO. Contend ye powers, etc.

THYR. Proud World, said I; cease your contest
    And let the mighty babe alone; 45
      The phœnix builds the phœnix' nest,
    Love's architecture is his own;
      The babe whose birth embraves this morn,
    Made his own bed e'er he was born.

CHO. The babe whose, etc. 50

TIT. I saw the curled drops, soft and slow,
    Come hovering o'er the place's head;
      Off'ring their whitest sheets of snow
    To furnish the fair infant's bed.
      Forbear, said I; be not too bold. 55
    Your fleece is white, but 't is too cold.

CHO. Forbear, said I, etc.

THYR. I saw the obsequious seraphim
    Their rosy fleece of fire bestow,
      For well they now can spare their wings, 60
    Since heaven itself lies here below.
      Well done, said I; but are you sure
    Your down so warm, will pass for pure?

CHO. Well done, said I, etc.

TIT. No, no, your king's not yet to seek 65
    Where to repose his royal head;
      See, see how soon his new-bloomed cheek
    'Twixt's mother's breasts is gone to bed!
      Sweet choice, said we! no way but so
    Not to lie cold, yet sleep in snow. 70

CHO. Sweet choice, said we, etc.

BOTH. We saw thee in thy balmy nest,
    Bright dawn of our Eternal Day!
      We saw thine eyes break from their east
    And chase the trembling shades away. 75

We saw thee, and we blessed the sight,
We saw thee by thine own sweet light.

CHO. We saw thee, etc.

FULL CHORUS

Welcome all wonders in one sight!
Eternity shut in a span, 80
Summer in winter, day in night,
Heaven in earth, and God in man.
Great Little One, whose all-embracing birth
Lifts earth to heaven, stoops heaven to earth!

Welcome, though nor to gold nor silk, 85
To more than Cæsar's birthright is;
Two sister-seas of virgin-milk
With many a rarely-tempered kiss
That breathes at once both maid and mother,
Warms in the one, cools in the other. 90

Welcome, though not to those gay flies
Gilded i' th' beams of earthly kings,
Slippery souls in smiling eyes,
But to poor shepherds, homespun things,
Whose wealth's their flock, whose wit's to be 95
Well read in their simplicity.

Yet when young April's husband showers
Shall bless the fruitful Maia's bed,
We'll bring the first-born of her flowers
To kiss thy feet and crown thy head. 100
To thee, dread Lamb! Whose love must keep
The shepherds, more than they the sheep.

To Thee, meek Majesty! soft King
Of simple graces and sweet loves!
Each of us his lamb will bring, 105
Each his pair of silver doves!
Till burnt at last in fire of thy fair eyes,
Ourselves become our own best sacrifice!

EXERCISE:

1. This poem is a tissue of paradoxes: the birth of Christ is the noon of love though it occurs in "Nature's night"; the true sun has arisen, though the earthly sun is still asleep, etc. Are the paradoxes used in this poem merely as extravagant compliments, or are they used actually to state accurately the meaning of the Incarnation, of the Virgin Birth, etc.? In this connection, compare and contrast this poem with Crashaw's poem "The Tear" (p. 302).

2. What is the meaning of "starry stranger" (line 38)? Why is the phoenix comparison appropriate here? In terms of Christian theology can it be said that lines 48–49 are literally true?

3. Lines 51–70 pay what may appear to some a high compliment to the Virgin Mary: she alone offers an appropriate place for the Christ Child's repose—transcendant purity which is yet humanly warm. How is this worked out in the imagery? Is the imagery merely decorative or does it have its own accuracy and precision in defining the doctrinal meaning?

On the Morning of Christ's Nativity

JOHN MILTON [1608–1674]

This is the month, and this the happy morn,
Wherein the Son of Heaven's eternal King,
Of wedded maid and virgin mother born,
Our great redemption from above did bring;
For so the holy sages once did sing, 5
  That he our deadly forfeit should release,
And with his Father work us a perpetual peace.

That glorious form, that light unsufferable,
And that far-beaming blaze of majesty,
Wherewith he wont at Heaven's high council-table 10
To sit the midst of Trinal Unity,
He laid aside, and, here with us to be,
  Forsook the courts of everlasting day,
And chose with us a darksome house of mortal clay.

Say, Heavenly Muse, shall not thy sacred vein 15
Afford a present to the Infant God?

Hast thou no verse, no hymn, or solemn strain,
To welcome him to this his new abode,
Now while the heaven, by the Sun's team untrod,
Hath took no print of the approaching light, 20
And all the spangled host keep watch in squadrons bright?

See how from far upon the eastern road
The star-led wizards haste with odors sweet!
Oh! run; prevent them with thy humble ode,
And lay it lowly at his blessèd feet; 25
Have thou the honor first thy Lord to greet,
And join thy voice unto the Angel Quire,
From out his secret altar touched with hallowed fire.

THE HYMN

It was the winter wild,
While the heaven-born child
All meanly wrapt in the rude manger lies;
Nature, in awe to him,
Had doffed her gaudy trim, 5
With her great Master so to sympathize:
It was no season then for her
To wanton with the Sun, her lusty paramour.

Only with speeches fair
She woos the gentle air 10
To hide her guilty front with innocent snow,
And on her naked shame,
Pollute with sinful blame,
The saintly veil of maiden white to throw;
Confounded, that her Maker's eyes 15
Should look so near upon her foul deformities.

But he, her fears to cease,
Sent down the meek-eyed Peace:
She, crowned with olive green, came softly sliding
Down through the turning sphere, 20
His ready harbinger,
With turtle wing the amorous clouds dividing;

And, waving wide her myrtle wand,
She strikes a universal peace through sea and land.

No war, or battle's sound, 25
Was heard the world around;
The idle spear and shield were high uphung;
The hookèd chariot stood,
Unstained with hostile blood;
The trumpet spake not to the armèd throng; 30
And kings sat still with awful eye,
As if they surely knew their sovran Lord was by.

But peaceful was the night
Wherein the Prince of Light
His reign of peace upon the earth began. 35
The winds, with wonder whist,
Smoothly the waters kissed,
Whispering new joys to the mild Ocean,
Who now hath quite forgot to rave,
While birds of calm sit brooding on the charmèd wave. 40

The stars, with deep amaze,
Stand fixed in steadfast gaze,
Bending one way their precious influence,
And will not take their flight,
For all the morning light, 45
Or Lucifer that often warned them thence;
But in their glimmering orbs did glow,
Until their Lord himself bespake, and bid them go.

And, though the shady gloom
Had given day her room, 50
The Sun himself withheld his wonted speed,
And hid his head for shame,
As his inferior flame
The new-enlightened world no more should need:
He saw a greater Sun appear 55
Than his bright throne or burning axletree could bear.

The shepherds on the lawn,
Or ere the point of dawn,

Sat simply chatting in a rustic row;
Full little thought they than 60
That the mighty Pan
Was kindly come to live with them below:
Perhaps their loves, or else their sheep,
Was all that did their silly thoughts so busy keep.

When such music sweet 65
Their hearts and ears did greet
As never was by mortal finger struck,
Divinely-warbled voice
Answering the stringed noise,
As all their souls in blissful rapture took: 70
The air, such pleasure loth to lose,
With thousand echoes still prolongs each heavenly close.

Nature, that heard such sound
Beneath the hollow round
Of Cynthia's seat the airy region thrilling, 75
Now was almost won
To think her part was done,
And that her reign had here its last fulfilling:
She knew such harmony alone
Could hold all Heaven and Earth in happier union. 80

At last surrounds their sight
A globe of circular light,
That with long beams the shamefaced Night arrayed;
The helmèd cherubim
And sworded seraphim 85
Are seen in glittering ranks with wings displayed,
Harping in loud and solemn quire,
With unexpressive notes, to Heaven's new-born Heir.

Such music (as 'tis said)
Before was never made, 90
But when of old the Sons of Morning sung,
While the Creator great
His constellations set,
And the well-balanced World on hinges hung,
And cast the dark foundations deep, 95
And bid the weltering waves their oozy channel keep.

Ring out, ye crystal spheres!
Once bless our human ears,
If ye have power to touch our senses so;
And let your silver chime 100
Move in melodious time;
And let the bass of heaven's deep organ blow;
And with your ninefold harmony
Make up full consort to th' angelic symphony.

For, if such holy song 105
Enwrap our fancy long,
Time will run back and fetch the Age of Gold;
And speckled Vanity
Will sicken soon and die,
And leprous Sin will melt from earthly mould; 110
And Hell itself will pass away,
And leave her dolorous mansions to the peering day.

Yea, Truth and Justice then
Will down return to men,
Orbed in a rainbow; and, like glories wearing, 115
Mercy will sit between,
Throned in celestial sheen,
With radiant feet the tissued clouds down steering;
And Heaven, as at some festival,
Will open wide the gates of her high palace-hall. 120

But wisest Fate says No,
This must not yet be so;
The Babe lies yet in smiling infancy
That on the bitter cross
Must redeem our loss, 125
So both himself and us to glorify:
Yet first, to those ychained in sleep,
The wakeful trump of doom must thunder through the deep,

With such a horrid clang
As on Mount Sinai rang, 130
While the red fire and smouldering clouds outbrake:
The aged Earth, aghast
With terror of that blast,
Shall from the surface to the center shake,

When, at the world's last session, 135
The dreadful Judge in middle air shall spread his throne.

And then at last our bliss
Full and perfect is,
But now begins; for from this happy day
Th' Old Dragon under ground, 140
In straiter limits bound,
Not half so far casts his usurpèd sway;
And, wroth to see his Kingdom fail,
Swinges the scaly horror of his folded tail.

The Oracles are dumb; 145
No voice or hideous hum
Runs through the archèd roof in words deceiving.
Apollo from his shrine
Can no more divine,
With hollow shriek the steep of Delphos leaving. 150
No nightly trance, or breathèd spell,
Inspires the pale-eyed priest from the prophetic cell.

The lonely mountains o'er,
And the resounding shore,
A voice of weeping heard, and loud lament; 155
From haunted spring, and dale
Edged with poplar pale,
The parting genius is with sighing sent,
With flower-inwov'n tresses torn
The nymphs in twilight shade of tangled thickets mourn. 160

In consecrated earth,
And on the holy hearth,
The Lars and Lemurs moan with midnight plaint,
In urns and altars round,
A drear and dying sound 165
Affrights the flamens at their service quaint;
And the chill marble seems to sweat,
While each peculiar power forgoes his wonted seat.

Peor and Baalim
Forsake their temples dim, 170

With that twice-battered god of Palestine,
And moonèd Ashtaroth,
Heav'n's queen and mother both,
Now sits not girt with tapers' holy shine,
The Lybic Hammon shrinks his horn; 175
In vain the Tyrian maids their wounded Thammuz mourn.

And sullen Moloch, fled,
Hath left in shadows dread
His burning idol all of blackest hue;
In vain with cymbals' ring 180
They call the grisly king,
In dismal dance about the furnace blue;
The brutish gods of Nile, as fast,
Isis and Orus and the dog Anubis, haste.

Nor is Osiris seen 185
In Memphian grove or green,
Trampling the unshowered grass with lowings loud;
Nor can he be at rest
Within his sacred chest;
Naught but profoundest Hell can be his shroud; 190
In vain, with timbrelled anthems dark,
The sable-stolèd sorcerers bear his worshipped ark.

He feels from Juda's land
The dreaded infant's hand;
The rays of Bethlehem blind his dusky eyn; 195
Nor all the gods beside
Longer dare abide,
Not Typhon huge ending in snaky twine:
Our Babe, to show his Godhead true,
Can in his swaddling bands control the damnèd crew. 200

So when the sun in bed,
Curtained with cloudy red,
Pillows his chin upon an orient wave,
The flocking shadows pale
Troop to th' infernal jail, 205
Each fettered ghost slips to his several grave,
And the yellow-skirted fays
Fly after the night-steeds, leaving their moon-loved maze.

But see! the Virgin blest
Hath laid her Babe to rest. 210
Time is our tedious song should here have ending:
Heaven's youngest-teemed star
Hath fixed her polished car,
Her sleeping Lord with handmaid lamp attending;
And all about the courtly stable 215
Bright-harnessed angels sit in order serviceable.

EXERCISE:

1. Compare and contrast Milton's hymn with that by Crashaw (p. 309).

2. Note the way in which the hymn proper breaks into two principal parts: (1) an account of the harmony of earth and heaven which attends the event, and (2) an account of the immediate influence of Christ's entry into the world upon pagan beliefs. How does Milton manage the transition between these parts of the hymn?

3. Note the panoramic quality of the description. It is as if the whole world were laid out before us and we saw it from some height and some distance. How does the imagery work to give us this sense of perspective and wide panorama?

4. Has the stanza form been well chosen for the effect which Milton is attempting to give?

5. Can you justify the ending of the poem?

To His Coy Mistress

ANDREW MARVELL [1621–1678]

Had we but world enough, and time,
This coyness, Lady, were no crime.
We would sit down and think which way
To walk and pass our long love's day.
Thou by the Indian Ganges' side 5
Shouldst rubies find; I by the tide
Of Humber would complain. I would
Love you ten years before the Flood,
And you should, if you please, refuse
Till the conversion of the Jews. 10
My vegetable love should grow

Vaster than empires, and more slow;
An hundred years should go to praise
Thine eyes and on thy forehead gaze;
Two hundred to adore each breast, 15
But thirty thousand to the rest;
An age at least to every part,
And the last age should show your heart.
For, Lady, you deserve this state,
Nor would I love at lower rate. 20
  But at my back I always hear
Time's wingèd chariot hurrying near;
And yonder all before us lie
Deserts of vast eternity.
Thy beauty shall no more be found, 25
Nor, in thy marble vault, shall sound
My echoing song; then worms shall try
That long preserved virginity,
And your quaint honor turn to dust,
And into ashes all my lust: 30
The grave's a fine and private place,
But none, I think, do there embrace.
  Now therefore, while the youthful hue
Sits on thy skin like morning lew [1]
And while thy willing soul transpires 35
At every pore with instant fires,
Now let us sport us while we may,
And now, like amorous birds of prey,
Rather at once our time devour
Than languish in his slow-chapt power. 40
Let us roll all our strength and all
Our sweetness up into one ball,
And tear our pleasures with rough strife
Thorough the iron gates of life:
Thus, though we cannot make our sun 45
Stand still, yet we will make him run.

EXERCISE:

1. Distinguish the three divisions of the logical structure of the poem. Comment upon the tone of each division.

2. Someone has said that the imagery in the first part of the poem is playful, conversational, and absurd; that of the second section,

[1] Warmth. Conjectured by H. M. Margoliouth. The 1681 text reads *glew*. Other conjectured readings are "dew" and "glow."

grand; and that of the third section, exciting. Can you justify this characterization? Or is there too much interpenetration among the parts to justify the remark?

3. What does the poet mean by "amorous birds of prey"? Does this figure carry over into "tear our pleasures" (line 43)?

4. Define the attitude presented in the passage comprising lines 25 to 32.

Corinna's Going A-Maying

ROBERT HERRICK [1591–1674]

Get up, get up for shame, the blooming morn
Upon her wings presents the god unshorn.
See how Aurora throws her fair
Fresh-quilted colors through the air:
Get up, sweet slug-a-bed, and see 5
The dew bespangling herb and tree.
Each flower has wept and bow'd toward the east
Above an hour since: yet you not dressed;
Nay; not so much as out of bed?
When all the birds have matins said 10
And sung their thankful hymns, 't is sin,
Nay, profanation, to keep in,
Whenas a thousand virgins on this day
Spring, sooner than the lark, to fetch in May.

Rise, and put on your foliage, and be seen 15
To come forth, like the spring-time, fresh and green,
And sweet as Flora. Take no care
For jewels for your gown or hair:
Fear not; the leaves will strew
Gems in abundance upon you: 20
Besides, the childhood of the day has kept,
Against you come, some orient pearls unwept;
Come and receive them while the light
Hangs on the dew-locks of the night:
And Titan on the eastern hill 25
Retires himself, or else stands still
Till you come forth. Wash, dress, be brief in praying:
Few beads are best when once we go a-Maying.

Come, my Corinna, come; and, coming, mark
How each field turns a street, each street a park 30
Made green and trimmed with trees; see how
Devotion gives each house a bough
Or branch: each porch, each door ere this
An ark, a tabernacle is,
Made up of white-thorn, neatly interwove; 35
As if here were those cooler shades of love.
Can such delights be in the street
And open fields and we not see't?
Come, we'll abroad; and let's obey
The proclamation made for May: 40
And sin no more, as we have done, by staying;
But, my Corinna, come, let's go a-Maying.

There's not a budding boy or girl this day
But is got up, and gone to bring in May.
A deal of youth, ere this, is come 45
Back, and with white-thorn laden home.
Some have despatched their cakes and cream
Before that we have left to dream:
And some have wept, and wooed, and plighted troth,
And chose their priest, ere we can cast off sloth: 50
Many a green-gown has been given;
Many a kiss, both odd and even:
Many a glance too has been sent
From out the eye, love's firmament;
Many a jest told of the keys betraying 55
This night, and locks picked, yet we're not a-Maying.

Come, let us go while we are in our prime;
And take the harmless folly of the time.
We shall grow old apace, and die
Before we know our liberty. 60
Our life is short, and our days run
As fast away as does the sun;
And, as a vapor or a drop of rain,
Once lost, can ne'er be found again,
So when or you or I are made 65
A fable, song, or fleeting shade,
All love, all liking, all delight
Lies drowned with us in endless night.

Then while time serves, and we are but decaying,
Come, my Corinna, come, let's go a-Maying. 7(

EXERCISE:

1. Compare and contrast this poem with "To His Coy Mistress' in terms of theme, tone, and method of presentation.

2. Is Corinna being compared to a plant? Where? What are the implications of the comparison with reference to the theme of the poem? Is the speaker suggesting that Corinna, like the birds and the flowers, is a part of nature and should celebrate the return of the god of springtime?

3. What elements in the imagery suggest that this May Day rite is a religious celebration? Is the rite described in a parody of Christian religious terms? Is it seen at any point as a rival religion to Christianity?

4. Does the conflict between the claims of Christianity and paganism find any satisfactory resolution in the poem? Characterize as carefully as you can the tone of the last stanza.

After Great Pain a Formal Feeling Comes

EMILY DICKINSON [1830–1886]

After great pain a formal feeling comes—
The nerves sit ceremonious like tombs;
The stiff Heart questions—was it He that bore?
And yesterday—or centuries before?

The feet mechanical go round 5
A wooden way
Of ground or air or Ought,
Regardless grown,
A quartz contentment like a stone.

This is the hour of lead 10
Remembered if outlived
As freezing persons recollect
The snow—
First chill, then stupor, then
The letting go. 15

In this poem the imagery may seem mixed. (See analysis of "My Springs," pp. 299–302.) The poet uses the figure of the tombs and then immediately drops it to state that the stiff heart questions. Other images like the "hour of lead" are only mentioned, not developed. Indeed, the only rather fully developed figure is that of the person dying in the snow. Are the figures, then, tightly enough related, or are they vague and confused? If they are related, what is it that binds them together? A comparison with the imagery of a poem like "The Definition of Love," for example, sharply emphasizes the questions. Obviously, the figures used by Emily Dickinson here are not related in the same fashion as are those of Marvell's poem. Are they, then, no more unified than those of "My Springs"? Or are we to conclude that the present poem is successful, but that the figures are related in some other fashion?

The poem is obviously an attempt to communicate to the reader the nature of the experience which comes "after great pain." The poet is using the imagery for this purpose, and the first line of the poem, which states the subject of the poem, is the only abstract statement in the poem. The pain is obviously not a physical pain; it is some great sorrow or mental pain which leaves the mind numbed. The nerves, she says, "sit ceremonious like tombs." The word *sit* is very important here. The nerves, it is implied, are like a group of people after a funeral sitting in the parlor in a formal hush. Then the poet changes the image slightly by adding "like tombs." The nerves are thus compared to two different things, but these two comparisons contribute to the same effect, and indeed are closely related: people dressed in black sitting around a room after a funeral may be said to be like tombs. And why does the reference to "tombs" seem such a good symbol for a person who has just suffered great pain (whether it be a real person or the nerves personified)? Because a tomb has to a supreme degree the qualities of deadness (quietness, stillness) and of formality (ceremony, stiffness).

Notice that the imagery (through the first line of the last stanza) is characterized by a common quality, the quality of *stiff lifelessness*. For instance, the heart is "stiff," the feet walk a "wooden" way, the contentment is a "quartz" contentment, the hour is that of "lead." The insistence on this type of imagery is very important in confirming the sense of numbed consciousness which is made more explicit by the statement that the feet move mechanically and are "regardless" of where they go. Notice too that the lines are bound together, not only by the constant reference of the imagery to the result of grief, but also by the fact that the poet is stating in series what happens to the parts of the body: nerves, heart, feet.

Two special passages in the first two stanzas deserve additional comment before we pass on to the third stanza. The heart obsessed with pain has lost the sense of time and even of its own identity. The question it asks is abrupt and elliptic as if the speaker were half dazed. The other passage to be noted, "A quartz contentment like a stone," is particularly interesting. The comparison involves two things. First, we see an extension of the common association of stoniness with the numbness of grief, as in such phrases as "stony-eyed" or "heart like a stone," etc. But why does the poet use "quartz"? There are several reasons. The name of the stone helps to particularize the figure and prevent the effect of a cliché. Moreover, quartz is a very hard stone. And, for one who knows that quartz is a crystal, a "quartz contentment" is a contentment crystallized, as it were, out of the pain. This brings us to the second general aspect involved by the comparison. This aspect is ironical. The contentment arising after the shock of great pain is a contentment because of the inability to respond any longer, rather than the ability to respond satisfactorily and agreeably.

To summarize, the poet has developed up to this point an effect of inanimate lifelessness, a stony, or wooden, or leaden stiffness; now, she proceeds to use a new figure, that of the freezing person, which epitomizes the effect of those which have preceded it, but which also gives a fresh and powerful statement.

The line "Remembered if outlived" is particularly forceful. The implication is that few outlive the experience to be able to remember it and recount it to others. This experience of grief is like a death by freezing: there is the chill, then the stupor as the body becomes numbed, and then the last state in which the body finally gives up the fight against the cold, and relaxes and dies. The correspondence of the stages of death by freezing to the effect of the shock of deep grief on the mind is close enough to make the passage very powerful. But there is another reason for the effect which this last figure has on us. The imagery of the first two stanzas corresponds to the "stupor." The last line of the poem presents a new idea, one which supplies a context for the preceding imagery and which by explaining it, makes it more meaningful. The formality, the stiffness, the numbness of the first two stanzas is accounted for: it is an attempt to hold in, the fight of the mind against letting go; it is the mind's unconscious gesture of defense.

Mystery

ELIZABETH BARRETT BROWNING [1806–1861]

We sow the glebe, we reap the corn,
  We build the house where we may rest,
And then, at moments, suddenly,
We look up to the great wide sky,
Inquiring wherefore we were born . . . 5
  For earnest, or for jest?

The senses folding thick and dark
  About the stifled soul within,
We guess diviner things beyond,
And yearn to them with yearning fond; 10
We strike out blindly to a mark
  Believed in, but not seen.

We vibrate to the pant and thrill
  Wherewith Eternity has curled
In serpent-twine about God's seat; 15
While, freshening upward to his feet,
In gradual growth his full-leaved will
  Expands from world to world.

And, in the tumult and excess
  Of act and passion under sun, 20
We sometimes hear—oh, soft and far,

As silver star did touch with star,
The kiss of Peace and Righteousness
  Through all things that are done.

God keeps His holy mysteries 25
  Just on the outside of man's dream.
In diapason slow, we think
To hear their pinions rise and sink,
While they float pure beneath His eyes,
  Like swans adown a stream. 30

And, sometimes, horror chills our blood
  To be so near such mystic Things,
And we wrap round us, for defence,
Our purple manners, moods of sense—
As angels, from the face of God, 35
  Stand hidden in their wings.

And, sometimes, through life's heavy swound
  We grope for them!—with strangled breath
We stretch out hands abroad and try
To reach them in our agony,— 40
And widen, so, the broad life-wound
  Which soon is large enough for death.

EXERCISE:

With close attention to the analyses of "The Definition of Love" (pp. 294–97) and "My Springs" (pp. 299–302), write a comparison of this poem with "The Night" (p. 291), which also treats the mystery of man's relation to God. In this connection consider the following topics:

1. The inferiority of the imagery in the first part of the third stanza to that in the second part.

2. The confusion of imagery in the fifth stanza.

3. The credibility of the statement that "horror chills our blood. . . ." (Does the word *horror* have any accurate application here? Or does it merely represent an attempt to gain dramatic force?)

4. The relation of the rhythm to the other elements in the poem.

On First Looking into Chapman's Homer

JOHN KEATS [1795–1821]

Much have I traveled in the realms of gold,
And many goodly states and kingdoms seen;
Round many western islands have I been
Which bards in fealty to Apollo hold.
Oft of one wide expanse had I been told 5
That deep-browed Homer ruled as his demesne;
Yet did I never breathe its pure serene
Till I heard Chapman speak out loud and bold:
Then felt I like some watcher of the skies
When a new planet swims into his ken; 10
Or like stout Cortez when with eagle eyes
He stared at the Pacific—and all his men
Looked at each other with a wild surmise—
Silent, upon a peak in Darien.

EXERCISE:

1. Keats is here attempting to describe the effect made upon him by his first reading of the translation of Homer by Chapman, the Elizabethan poet and dramatist. How is this effect summarized in the two concluding images?

2. Justify the term "swims" in line 10.

3. It was Balboa, not Cortez, who discovered the Pacific. Does Keats's mistake here make any difference in the value of the poem? If not, why not?

4. Is the tableau presented in the last four lines of the poem effective? In this connection can you justify line 13 as presenting a realistic and telling detail?

The Soul Selects

EMILY DICKINSON [1830–1886]

The soul selects her own society,
Then shuts the door;

On her divine majority
Obtrude no more.

Unmoved, she notes the chariot's pausing 5
At her low gate;
Unmoved, an emperor is kneeling
Upon her mat.

I've known her from an ample nation
Choose one; 10
Then close the valves of her attention
Like stone.

EXERCISE:

1. What images are suggested in stanza two by "chariot's," by "emperor," and by "mat"? Is the collocation of the emperor and the door-mat absurd, or is it justified?

2. What images are suggested by the last two lines of the poem? What does "valves" mean here? Can the term be justified? Does it clash too much with the rest of the imagery?

3. Attempt to define the tone of this poem. In answering this question take into account, not only the imagery, but the stanza form that has been chosen.

Doom Is Dark

W. H. AUDEN [1907–]

Doom is dark and deeper than any sea-dingle.
Upon what man it fall
In spring, day-wishing flowers appearing,
Avalanche sliding, white snow from rock-face,
That he should leave his house, 5
No cloud-soft hand can hold him, restraint by women;
But ever that man goes
Through place-keepers, through forest trees,
A stranger to strangers over undried sea,
Houses for fishes, suffocating water, 10
Or lonely on fell as chat,
By pot-holed becks
A bird stone-haunting, an unquiet bird.

There head falls forward, fatigued at evening,
And dreams of home, 15
Waving from window, spread of welcome,
Kissing of wife under single sheet;
But waking sees
Bird-flocks nameless to him, through doorway voices
Of new men making another love. 20

Save him from hostile capture,
From sudden tiger's spring at corner;
Protect his house,
His anxious house where days are counted
From thunderbolt protect, 25
From gradual ruin spreading like a stain;
Converting number from vague to certain,
Bring joy, bring day of his returning,
Lucky with day approaching, with leaning dawn.

EXERCISE:

This poem gets much of its effect through its imagery which, though carefully general in its reference to the fate of all men, is at the same time very concrete and even shockingly particular. For example, "day-wishing flowers," "place-keepers" (i.e., things which are immobile), "houses for fishes," etc.

1. The imagery of the first section suggests a primitive life in an upland glacial country—"pot-holed becks," etc. On the other hand, at line 22 there is the image of the tiger, and the phrase "tiger's spring at corner" suggests the tropical animal encountered at the end of a city block. Is the imagery a meaningless jumble, or can you justify it?

2. What is the tone of the poem? (The last section sounds like a prayer.) What effect does the imagery have upon the tone? What effect does the rhythm have upon the tone?

Let Me Not to the Marriage of True Minds

WILLIAM SHAKESPEARE [1564–1616]

Let me not to the marriage of true minds
Admit impediments. Love is not love

Which alters when it alteration finds,
Or bends with the remover to remove:
O, no! it is an ever-fixèd mark 5
That looks on tempests and is never shaken;
It is the star to every wandering bark,
Whose worth's unknown, although his height be taken.
Love's not Time's fool, though rosy lips and cheeks
Within his bending sickle's compass come; 10
Love alters not with his brief hours and weeks,
But bears it out even to the edge of doom.
If this be error and upon me proved,
I never writ, nor no man ever loved.

EXERCISE:

1. Work out in detail the implied as well as the developed images. What is the relation among the various images? Is the imagery inconsistent or confused?

2. What is the meaning of "Love's not Time's fool"? And of "bending sickle's compass"?

3. What is the tone of the poem? How does the poet avoid a tone of extravagant protestation?

At Melville's Tomb

HART CRANE [1899–1932]

Often beneath the wave, wide from this ledge
The dice of drowned men's bones he saw bequeath
An embassy. Their numbers as he watched,
Beat on the dusty shore and were obscured.

And wrecks passed without sound of bells, 5
The calyx of death's bounty giving back
A scattered chapter, livid hieroglyph,
The portent wound in corridors of shells.

Then in the circuit calm of one vast coil,
Its lashings charmed and malice reconciled, 10
Frosted eyes there were that lifted altars;
And silent answers crept across the stars.

Compass, quadrant and sextant contrive
No farther tides . . . High in the azure steeps
Monody shall not wake the mariner. 15
This fabulous shadow only the sea keeps.

This poem is a little elegy upon Herman Melville, the author of *Moby Dick,* the great American novel of the sea and whaling. The general meaning of the poem is easy enough. The poet says that the spirit of the writer whose imagination was so vividly engaged by the sea, and who saw such grandeur in man's struggle with it, though his body might be buried on land, would find its real abiding place in the sea:

This fabulous shadow only the sea keeps.

The imagery of the poem, however, provoked the editor who first published the poem to write the poet to ask several questions concerning the detailed meanings:

Take me for a hard-boiled unimaginative unpoetic reader, and tell me how *dice* can *bequeath an embassy* (or anything else); and how a calyx (*of death's bounty* or anything else) can give back a *scattered chapter, livid hieroglyph;* and how, if it does, such a *portent* can be *wound in corridors* (of shells or anything else).

And so on. I find your image of *frosted eyes lifting altars* difficult to visualize. Nor do compass, quadrant and sextant *contrive* tides, they merely record them, I believe.

All this may seem impertinent, but is not so intended. Your ideas and rhythms interest me, and I am wondering by what process of reasoning you would justify this poem's succession of champion mixed metaphors, of which you must be conscious. The packed line should pack its phrases in orderly relation, it seems to me, in a manner tending to clear confusion instead of making it worse confounded.

The first part of the poet's reply to the editor's letter containing these questions was concerned with the general justification of comparisons which are not scientifically and logically exact. This general consideration has already been raised in some degree in dealing with various poems analyzed in this section (pp. 274–78, 299–302, and particularly the analysis of "After Great Pain," pp. 324–27). The poet then undertook to analyze the implied points of reference behind his own use of imagery:

. . . I'll . . . come at once to the explanations you requested on the Melville poem:

> "The dice of drowned men's bones he saw bequeath
> An embassy."

Dice bequeath an embassy, in the first place, by being ground (in this connection only, of course) in little cubes from the bones of drowned men by the action of the sea, and are finally thrown up on the sand, having "numbers" but no identification. These being the bones of dead men who never completed their voyage, it seems legitimate to refer to them as the only surviving evidence of certain messages undelivered, mute evidence of certain things, experiences that the dead mariners might have had to deliver. Dice as a symbol of chance and circumstance is also implied.

> "The calyx of death's bounty giving back," etc.

This calyx refers in a double ironic sense both to a cornucopia and the vortex made by a sinking vessel. As soon as the water has closed over a ship this whirlpool sends up broken spars, wreckage, etc., which can be alluded to as *livid hieroglyphs,* making a *scattered chapter* so far as any complete record of the recent ship and her crew is concerned. In fact, about as much definite knowledge might come from all this as anyone might gain from the roar of his own veins, which is easily heard (haven't you ever done it?) by holding a shell close to one's ear.

> "Frosted eyes lift altars"

refers simply to a conviction that a man, not knowing perhaps a definite god yet being endowed with a reverence for deity—such a man naturally postulates a deity somehow, and the altar of that deity by the very *action* of the eyes *lifted* in searching.

> "Compass, quadrant and sextant contrive no farther tides."

Hasn't it often occurred that instruments originally invented for record and computation have inadvertently so extended the concepts of the entity they were invented to measure (concepts of space, etc.) in the mind and imagination that employed them, that they may metaphorically be said to have extended the original boundaries of the entity measured? This little bit of "relativity" ought not to be discredited in poetry now that scientists are proceeding to measure the universe on principles of pure *ratio,* quite as metaphorical, so far as previous standards of scientific methods extended. . . .

This correspondence raises in concrete form some very interesting questions that frequently appear in connection not only with the analysis of poems of the type of this one by Hart Crane, but also with the analysis of all other types of poems. People sometimes say: "But the poet couldn't have been thinking of all this when he wrote the poem." And in the sense in which they are using the term "thinking" they are right. The poet certainly did not draw up an analysis of his intention, a kind of blueprint, and then write the poem to specification. But it is only a very superficial view of the way the mind works that would cast the question into those terms. Does a finely trained pole-vaulter in the act of making his leap think specifically of each of the different muscles he is employing; or does a boxer in the middle of a round think of the details of his boxing form? Probably not, even though the vaulter or boxer may have acquired his form by conscious practice which involved detail after detail. Furthermore, at the moment of action, a competent coach would be able to analyze and criticize the performance in detail. In the same way, one might say that a poet, in his role as craftsman in the process of making a poem, does not work by blueprint specifications, but toward a sort of general objective which is conditioned by his "training"—by his previous study of his own responses and by his study of the detailed methods and effects in the work of other poets. The poet, we can say, usually knows what general effect and meaning he intends a poem to have. The process of composing the poem is a process of exploring the full implications of the intended meaning and of finding a suitable structure. The process is probably one of movement by trial and error, governed by self-criticism.[1]

But to return to the matter of Crane's analysis of his own poem: in attempting to answer questions about his poem, Crane is ob-

[1] See "How Poems Come About" (p. 591).

viously acting in the rôle of observer or critic, and one is not to confuse the process of analysis with the process that probably occurred in the actual composition. Moreover, one is not to suppose that the reader necessarily must duplicate the process of analysis in experiencing the force of the poem. Many people who enjoy the work of Emily Dickinson have never, for instance, actually analyzed the meanings of the phrase "A quartz contentment," but they have felt that the phrase is rich in its meaning and "right" in its application. But as the preliminary discipline of the poet extends and enriches his capacity for creation, so the process of analysis extends the reader's capacity for appreciation.

Ode to a Nightingale

JOHN KEATS [1795–1821]

My heart aches, and a drowsy numbness pains
  My sense, as though of hemlock I had drunk,
Or emptied some dull opiate to the drains
  One minute past, and Lethe wards had sunk:
'Tis not through envy of thy happy lot, 5
  But being too happy in thy happiness,—
    That thou, light-wingèd Dryad of the trees,
      In some melodious plot
  Of beechen green, and shadows numberless,
    Singest of summer in full-throated ease. 10

O for a draught of vintage! that hath been
  Cooled a long age in the deep-delvèd earth,
Tasting of Flora and the country-green,
  Dance, and Provençal song, and sunburnt mirth!
O for a beaker full of the warm South, 15
  Full of the true, the blushful Hippocrene,
    With beaded bubbles winking at the brim,
      And purple-stainèd mouth;
  That I might drink, and leave the world unseen,
    And with thee fade away into the forest dim: 20

Fade far away, dissolve, and quite forget
  What thou among the leaves hast never known,

The weariness, the fever, and the fret
  Here, where men sit and hear each other groan;
Where palsy shakes a few, sad, last gray hairs, 25
  Where youth grows pale, and spectre-thin, and dies;
    Where but to think is to be full of sorrow
      And leaden-eyed despairs,
  Where Beauty cannot keep her lustrous eyes,
    Or new Love pine at them beyond tomorrow. 30

Away! away! for I will fly to thee,
  Not charioted by Bacchus and his pards,
But on the viewless wings of Poesy,
  Though the dull brain perplexes and retards:
Already with thee! tender is the night, 35
  And haply the Queen-Moon is on her throne,
    Clustered around by all her starry Fays;
      But here there is no light,
  Save what from heaven is with the breezes blown
    Through verdurous glooms and winding mossy ways. 40

I cannot see what flowers are at my feet,
  Nor what soft incense hangs upon the boughs,
But, in embalmèd darkness, guess each sweet
  Wherewith the seasonable month endows
The grass, the thicket, and the fruit-tree wild; 45
  White hawthorn, and the pastoral eglantine;
  Fast-fading violets covered up in leaves;
      And mid-May's eldest child,
  The coming musk-rose, full of dewy wine,
    The murmurous haunt of flies on summer eves. 50

Darkling I listen; and, for many a time
  I have been half in love with easeful Death,
Called him soft names in many a musèd rhyme,
  To take into the air my quiet breath;
Now more than ever seems it rich to die, 55
  To cease upon the midnight with no pain,
    While thou art pouring forth thy soul abroad
      In such an ecstasy!
  Still wouldst thou sing, and I have ears in vain—
    To thy high requiem become a sod. 60

Thou wast not born for death, immortal Bird!
No hungry generations tread thee down;
The voice I hear this passing night was heard
In ancient days by emperor and clown:
Perhaps the self-same song that found a path 65
Through the sad heart of Ruth, when, sick for home,
She stood in tears amid the alien corn;
The same that oft-times hath
Charmed magic casements, opening on the foam
Of perilous seas, in faery lands forlorn. 70

Forlorn! the very word is like a bell
To toll me back from thee to my sole self!
Adieu! the fancy cannot cheat so well
As she is famed to do, deceiving elf.
Adieu! adieu! thy plaintive anthem fades 75
Past the near meadows, over the still stream,
Up the hill-side; and now 'tis buried deep
In the next valley-glades:
Was it a vision, or a waking dream?
Fled is that music:—Do I wake or sleep? 80

I

This poem is essentially a reverie induced by the poet's listening to the song of the nightingale. In the first stanza the poet is just sinking into the reverie; in the last stanza, he comes out of the reverie and back to a consciousness of the actual world in which he and all other human beings live. The first lines of the poem and the last, therefore, constitute a sort of frame for the reverie proper.

The poet has chosen to present his reverie largely in terms of imagery—imagery drawn from nature—the flowers and leaves, etc., associated with the bird actually, or imaginatively in myth and story. The images are elaborate and decorative and the poet dwells upon them lovingly and leisurely, developing them in some detail as pictures. It is not the sort of method which would suit a poem exhibiting a rapid and dramatic play of thought such as one finds in the passage from Shakespeare's *Antony and Cleopatra* (p. 286). But one remembers the general character of the poem. The loving elaboration and slowed movement resemble the slowed movement of meditative trance, or dream, and therefore is appropriate to the general mood of this poem. The imagery, then, in its elaboration is not merely beautifully decorative but has a relation to the general temper of the whole poem.

The poet, with his desire to escape from the world of actuality, calls for a drink of wine

> That I might drink, and leave the world unseen.

But the wish for the draught of wine is half fancy. The poet lingers over the description of the wine, making it an idealized and lovingly elaborated thing too. We know that it is not a serious and compelling request. The grammar of the passage itself tells us this: after "O for a draught of vintage" the poet interposes seven lines of rich description identifying the wine with the spirit of summer and pastoral joys and with the romantic associations of Provençe, and finally gives a concrete picture of a bubbling glass of the wine itself before he goes on to tell us why he wishes the draught of wine. (*Introduction,* pp. xlvi–xlvii.)

The third stanza amplifies the desire to get away from the world of actuality. The word *fade* in the last line of the second stanza is echoed in the next stanza in "Fade far away, dissolve . . ." The implication is that the poet wishes for a dissolution of himself; a wish which later in the poem becomes an explicit pondering on death as something attractive and desirable. The principal aspects of the actual world which the poet would like to escape are just those aspects of it which seem opposed to the world conjured up by the bird's song: its feverish hurry, the fact that in it youth dies and beauty fades. The world which the nightingale seems to inhabit is one of deathless youth and beauty. This idea too is to be developed explicitly by the poet in the seventh stanza.

In the fourth stanza the poet apparently makes a sudden decision to attempt to leave actual life and penetrate to the world of the imagination. The apparent suddenness of the decision is reflected in the movement of the first line of the stanza,

> Away! away! for I will fly to thee.

But he will fly to it by exciting his mind, not with wine, but with poetry. And in line 35 the poet has apparently been successful:

"Already with thee," he says. There follows down to the opening of the sixth stanza a very rich description of the flowery, darkened thicket in which the nightingale is singing.

The poet's wish for dissolution, which he expresses in the third stanza, becomes in the sixth, a wish for death itself, an utter dissolution. But the idea as repeated receives an additional twist. Earlier, his wish to fade away was a desire to escape the sorrow and sordidness of the real world. Now even death itself seems to the poet an easy and attractive thing; and, more than that, it seems even a sort of positive fulfillment to die to the sound of the nightingale's high requiem.

But the nightingale at the height of its singing does not seem to be subject to death. The poet describes the effect of the nightingale's song by two incidents drawn from the remote past as if he believed that the nightingale which he now hears had literally lived forever. The two incidents are chosen also to illustrate two different aspects of the bird's song. The first, the song as heard by Ruth, is an incident taken from Biblical literature, and gives the effect of the song as it reminded the home-sick girl of her native land. The second, hinting at some unnamed romance of the Middle Ages, gives the unearthly magic of the song.

With the first word of the last stanza, the poet breaks out of his reverie. He catches up the word "forlorn," which he has just used in describing one of the imagined scenes induced by his reverie, and suddenly realizes that it applies all too accurately to himself. The effect is almost that of an abrupt stumbling: the chance employment of a particular word in one of the richly imaginative scenes induced by the bird's song suddenly comes home to him—with altered weight and tone, of course—to remind him that it is he who is forlorn—whose plight is hopeless. With the new and chilling meaning of "forlorn," the song of the nightingale itself alters: what had a moment before been an ecstatic "high requiem" becomes a "plaintive anthem." The song becomes fainter: what had had power to make the sorrowing man "fade . . . away" from a harsh and bitter world, now itself "fades" (line 75) and the speaker is left alone in the silence.

The vitality of the poem, of course, lies in its imagery. The imagery is so rich and resonant, taken line by line, that it is a temptation to treat it as amazingly rich decoration. Consider, for example, the description of the wine in the second stanza. The poet uses the term *vintage* rather than *wine* because of the associations of vintage with age and excellence. It tastes of Flora (goddess of flowers) and the country green (a land predominantly fruitful and rich) and of dance and Provençal song (associations with the merry country of the Troubadours and associations with the period of the Troubadours) and sunburnt mirth. Mirth cannot, of course, be literally sunburnt, but the sensitive reader will not be troubled by this. The phrase is a condensation of the fuller phrase: mirth of hearty folk who live close to nature and to the earth and whose sunburnt faces and arms indicate that they live close to nature. These associations of the wine with Provence and with all that Provence implies are caught up and corroborated by another bold and condensed phrase: "full of the warm South." For the word, *South,* not only carries its associations of warmth but also of the particular South which the poet has just been describing: the south of France.

This for a rather inadequate account of only one item of the sort of description which fills the poem. The student might attempt to analyze in the same way certain other passages. In making such an examination, he will notice that Keats does not sacrifice sharpness of perception to mere prettiness. Again and again it is the sharp and accurate observation which gives the richness a validity. For example,

> The coming musk-rose, full of dewy wine,
> The murmurous haunt of flies on summer eves.

The passage is not merely beautiful and rich. It embodies acute observation. We feel that the poet knows what he is talking about. A poorer poet would try only for the decorative effect and would fail. Moreover, much of the suggestiveness resides also in the choice of precise details. Many a poet feels that, because the stimulus to the imagination makes for an indefinite richness of association, this indefiniteness is aroused by vague, general description. On the contrary, the force of association is greatest when it is aroused by precise detail. For example, consider the passage most famous for its suggestiveness.

> Charmed magic casements, opening on the foam
> Of perilous seas, in faery lands forlorn.

After all, these lines present a scene that is precisely visualized. If the casements opening on the seas and framing the scene were omitted, the general, vague words, *perilous, faery,* and *forlorn,* would not be sufficient to give the effect actually transmitted.

II

One may, however, read the "Ode to a Nightingale" at a deeper level. Indeed, if we are to do full justice to the general architecture of the poem and to the intensity of many of the individual passages, one must read it at this deeper level.

A basic problem—already hinted at in earlier paragraphs of this analysis—has to do with the speaker's attitude toward death. If he wishes to escape from a world overshadowed by death, why then does he go on to conceive of that escape as a kind of death? The nightingale's song makes him yearn to leave a world where "youth grows pale . . . and dies," yet, as we remember, the highest rapture that he can conceive of is to die—"To cease upon the midnight with no pain." The last phrase ("with no pain") offers only a superficial resolution of our problem. We shall not find our answer in distinguishing between the "easeful Death" of line 52 and some agonizing death. The speaker in this poem is not saying merely that he would like to die if he could be sure that his death would be painless.

The death with which he falls "half in love" is not a negative thing, but is conceived of as a rich and positive experience. To see how Keats brings this about will require a reexamination of the whole poem. We might well begin with the beginning of the poem, for the ambiguous relationship between life and death, joy and pain, intensity of feeling and numb lack of feeling, runs through the poem, and is to be found even in the opening lines.

The song of the nightingale has a curious double effect. The speaker's "heart aches" through the very intensity of pleasure—by "being too happy in thy happiness." But the song also acts as an opiate, making the listener feel drowsy and numbed. Now an opiate is used to deaden pain, and the song of the bird does deaden (see stanzas three and four) the pain of the mortal world in which "to think is to be full of sorrow." A reader may be tempted therefore to say that the nightingale's song gives to the sorrowing man a little surcease from his unhappiness. But the experience is more complex than this: the song itself causes the pain. Thus, though the song means to the hearer life, freedom, and ease, its effect is to deaden him and render him drowsy.

Are we to say, then, that the poet is confused in this first stanza? No, because the apparent contradictions are meaningful and justified in terms of the poem as a whole. First, as to the realistic basis of the opiate metaphor: the initial effect of a heavy opiate may be painfully numbing. Second, as to the psychological basis: what is pleasurable, if carried to an extreme degree, becomes painful. The nightingale's song which suggests a world beyond mortality gives the hearer happiness, but by reminding him of his own mortal state, gives him pain. But the full implications of this paradox of pleasure-pain, life-death, immortal-mortal require the whole of the poem for their full development.

We have commented upon what the speaker wishes to escape from; he has himself made clear the primary obstacle to his escape. It is the "dull brain" that "perplexes and retards." The opiate, the draught of vintage for which the speaker has called, the free play of the imagination—all have this in common: they release one from the tyranny of the "dull brain." The brain insists upon clarity and rigid order; it is an order that must be "dissolved" if the speaker is to escape into, and merge with, the richer world for which he longs.

But the word which the speaker uses to describe this process is "fade," and his entry into this world of the imagination is symbolized by a fading into the rich darkness out of which the nightingale sings. We associate darkness with death, but this darkness is instinct with the most intense life. How is the darkness insisted upon —and thus defined? The nightingale sings in a plot of "shadows numberless"; the speaker would leave the world "unseen" and join the bird in "the forest dim"; he would "fade far away"—would "dissolve"; and when he feels that he is actually with the nightingale, he is in a place of "verdurous glooms."

Having attained to that place, he "cannot see." Though the poem abounds in sensuous detail, and appeals so powerfully to all the senses, most of the images of sight are *fancied* by the speaker. He does not actually see the Queen-Moon or the stars. He "guess[es]" at what flowers are at his feet. He has found his way into a warm "embalmèd darkness." The last adjective means primarily "filled with incense," "sweet with balm," but it must also have suggested death—in Keats's day as well as in ours. In finding his way imaginatively into the dark covert from which the bird is singing, the speaker has approached death. He has wished to fade far away, "dissolve, and quite forget"; but the final dissolution and the ultimate forgetting is death. True, death here is apprehended in a quite different fashion from the death depicted in stanza three: here the balm is the natural perfume of growing flowers and the gloom is "verdurous," with suggestions of rich organic growth. But the fading has been complete—he is completely encompassed with darkness.

It is worth remarking that Keats has described the flowery covert with full honesty. If his primary emphasis is on fertility and growth, still he recognizes that death and change have their place here too: the violets, for instance, are thought of as "fast-fading." But the atmosphere of this world of nature is very different, to be sure, from that of the human world haunted by death, where "men sit and hear each other groan." The world of nature is a world of cyclic change (the "seasonable month," "the coming musk-rose," etc.) and consequently can seem fresh and immortal, like the bird whose song seems to be its spirit.

The poem, then, is not only about death and deathlessness, or about the actual and the ideal; it is also about alienation and wholeness. It is man's necessary alienation from nature that invests death with its characteristic horror. To "dissolve"—to "fade"—into the warm darkness is to merge into the eternal pattern of nature. Death itself becomes something positive—a flowering—a fulfilment. Keats has underlined this suggestion very cunningly in the sixth stanza. The ancients thought that at death, a man's soul was breathed out with his last breath. Here the nightingale is pouring forth its "soul" and at this high moment the man listening in the darkness would be glad to die. Soul and breath become interchangeable. The most intense expression of life (the nightingale's ecstatic song) invites the listener to breathe forth his soul (death).

The foregoing paragraphs may suggest the sense in which the speaker calls the nightingale immortal. The nightingale symbolizes the immortality of nature which, harmonious with itself, remains through all its myriad changes, unwearied and beautiful. We need not suppose that the speaker, even in his tranced reverie, thinks of the particular biological mechanism of flesh and bone and feathers as deathless—any more than he thinks of the "fast-fading violets" and the "coming musk-rose" as unwithering. Keats has clearly specified the sense in which the bird is immortal: it is in harmony with its world—not, as man is, in competition with his ("No hungry generations tread thee down"); and the bird cannot even conceive of its separation from the world which it knows and expresses and of which it is a part ("Thou wast not born for death"). Man knows that he was born to die—"What thou among the leaves hast never known"—and that knowledge overshadows man's life, and necessarily all his songs.

That knowledge overshadows this song, and gives it its special poignance. As the poem ends, the speaker's attempt to enter the world of the nightingale breaks down. The music by means of which he hoped to flee from his mortal world has itself fled—"Fled is that music." The music which almost succeeded in making him "fade far away" now itself "fades / Past the near meadows" and in a moment is "buried deep / In the next valley-glades." The word "buried" here suggests a view of death very different from that conjured up by "embalmèd darkness" in the fifth stanza. Death here is bleak and negative. The poem has come full circle.

Exercise:

1. The phrase "alien corn" (line 67) comes with special poignance. Why would "alien trees" or "alien hills"—the loss of the rime apart—be less poignant?

2. Justify "Do I wake or sleep?" as the proper conclusion to the poem. How is the question related to the rest of the stanza and to the rest of the poem?

3. Can it be said that this poem is, among other things, about the imagination? About the world as seen through the imagination contrasted with the world as apprehended by the analytical mind?

Ode to Psyche

JOHN KEATS [1795–1821]

O Goddess! hear these tuneless numbers, wrung
By sweet enforcement and remembrance dear,
And pardon that thy secrets should be sung
Even into thine own soft-conchèd ear:
Surely I dreamt today, or did I see, 5
The wingèd Psyche with awaken'd eyes?
I wander'd in a forest thoughtlessly,
And, on the sudden, fainting with surprise,
Saw two fair creatures, couchèd side by side
In deepest grass, beneath the whisp'ring roof 10
Of leaves and trembled blossoms, where there ran
A brooklet, scarce espied:

'Mid hush'd, cool-rootèd flowers fragrant-eyed,
Blue, silver-white, and budded Tyrian,
They lay calm-breathing on the bedded grass; 15
Their arms embracèd, and their pinions too;
Their lips touch'd not, but had not bade adieu,
As if disjoinèd by soft-handed slumber,
And ready still past kisses to outnumber
At tender eye-dawn of aurorean love: 20
The wingèd boy I knew;
But who wast thou, O happy, happy dove?
His Psyche true!

O latest-born and loveliest vision far
Of all Olympus' faded hierarchy! 25
Fairer than Phoebe's sapphire-region'd star,
Or Vesper, amorous glowworm of the sky;
Fairer than these, though temple thou hast none,
Nor altar heap'd with flowers;
Nor virgin-choir to make delicious moan 30
Upon the midnight hours;

No voice, no lute, no pipe, no incense sweet
From chain-swung censer teeming;
No shrine, no grove, no oracle, no heat
Of pale-mouth'd prophet dreaming. 35

O brightest! though too late for antique vows,
Too, too late for the fond believing lyre,
When holy were the haunted forest boughs,
Holy the air, the water, and the fire;
Yet even in these days so far retir'd 40
From happy pieties, thy lucent fans,
Fluttering among the faint Olympians,
I see, and sing, by my own eyes inspir'd.
So let me be thy choir, and make a moan
Upon the midnight hours; 45
Thy voice, thy lute, thy pipe, thy incense sweet
From swingèd censer teeming;
Thy shrine, thy grove, thy oracle, thy heat
Of pale-mouth'd prophet dreaming.

Yes, I will be thy priest, and build a fane 50
In some untrodden region of my mind,
Where branchèd thoughts, new grown with pleasant pain,
Instead of pines shall murmur in the wind;
Far, far around shall those dark-cluster'd trees
Fledge the wild-ridgèd mountains steep by steep; 55
And there by zephyrs, streams, and birds, and bees,
The moss-lain Dryads shall be lull'd to sleep;
And in the midst of this wide quietness
A rosy sanctuary will I dress
With the wreath'd trellis of a working brain, 60
With buds, and bells, and stars without a name,
With all the gardener Fancy e'er could feign,
Who, breeding flowers, will never breed the same:
And there shall be for thee all soft delight
That shadowy thought can win, 65
A bright torch, and a casement ope at night,
To let the warm Love in!

EXERCISE:

One of the most attractive myths of the Greeks had to do with the love between Psyche (the soul) and Cupid, the god of love.

Cupid, because of his mother's hostility, visited Psyche secretly at night, and was unseen by Psyche until Psyche was urged by her jealous sisters to break her promise to him and look at him as he slept. As she leaned over him, a drop of burning oil fell on the sleeping god, and he awakened and disappeared. Then followed Psyche's search for Cupid and the various trials imposed upon her by Cupid's mother, Venus, until the pair were finally united. But the story of Psyche was developed too late for Psyche to be worshipped as a goddess, and the poet here promises to erect her a temple and be her priest.

1. How important is it that Keats should write with a consciousness that the Greek gods are dead? How does this consciousness qualify his attitude toward myth and toward Psyche herself? Does it keep his tribute to Psyche from seeming too easy and his praise of her too languidly sweet?

2. Is this poem "about" Psyche? Or is it about an unbelieving world which has banished the myths as mere daydreams? How does the imagery bear upon this point?

3. Consider the imagery for its sharpness and particularity. What details, if any, possess this quality? Relate to the problem of possible over-lushness of imagery.

4. How has Keats worked in the details of the Psyche legend? Can it be said that his motive for building Psyche's fame "in some untrodden region of [his] mind" parallels Cupid's motive in placing Psyche in a place remote and secret? Who is the jealous Venus whom Keats is trying to outwit by this maneuver?

Come into the Garden, Maud

ALFRED, LORD TENNYSON [1809–1892]

Come into the garden, Maud,
  For the black bat, Night, has flown.
Come into the garden, Maud,
  I am here at the gate alone;
And the woodbine spices are wafted abroad, 5
  And the musk of the roses is blown.

For a breeze of morning moves,
  And the planet of Love is on high,
Beginning to faint in the light that she loves
  On a bed of daffodil sky, 10
To faint in the light of the sun she loves,
  To faint in his light and to die.

All night have the roses heard
  The flute, violin, bassoon;
All night has the casement jessamine stirred 15
  To the dancers dancing in tune;
Till a silence fell with the waking bird,
  And a hush with the setting moon.

I said to the lily, "There is but one
  With whom she has heart to be gay. 20
When will the dancers leave her alone?
  She is weary of dance and play."
Now half to the setting moon are gone,
  And half to the rising day;
Low on the sand and loud on the stone 25
  The last wheel echoes away.

I said to the rose, "The brief night goes
  In babble and revel and wine.
O young lord-lover, what sighs are those
  For one that will never be thine? 30
But mine, but mine," so I sware to the rose,
  "For ever and ever, mine."

And the soul of the rose went into my blood,
  As the music clashed in the hall;
And long by the garden lake I stood, 35
  For I heard your rivulet fall
From the lake to the meadow and on to the wood,
  Our wood, that is dearer than all;

From the meadow your walks have left so sweet
  That whenever a March-wind sighs 40
He sets the jewel-print of your feet
  In violets blue as your eyes,

To the woody hollows in which we meet
  And the valleys of Paradise.

The slender acacia would not shake 45
  One long milk-bloom on the tree;
The white lake-blossom fell into the lake,
  As the pimpernel dozed on the lea;
But the rose was awake all night for your sake,
  Knowing your promise to me; 50
The lilies and roses were all awake,
  They sigh'd for the dawn and thee.

Queen rose of the rosebud garden of girls,
  Come hither, the dances are done,
In gloss of satin and glimmer of pearls, 55
  Queen lily and rose in one;
Shine out, little head, sunning over with curls,
  To the flowers, and be their sun.

There has fallen a splendid tear
  From the passion-flower at the gate. 60
She is coming, my dove, my dear;
  She is coming, my life, my fate;
The red rose cries, "She is near, she is near;"
  And the white rose weeps, "She is late;"
The larkspur listens, "I hear, I hear;" 65
  And the lily whispers, "I wait."

She is coming, my own, my sweet;
  Were it ever so airy a tread,
My heart would hear her and beat,
  Were it earth in an earthy bed; 70
My dust would hear her and beat,
  Had I lain for a century dead;
Would start and tremble under her feet,
  And blossom in purple and red.

(From *Maud*)

Exercise:

1. Compare this poem with "The Indian Serenade" (p. 173). Both are love poems and in both nature itself seems to sympathize with the lover as he waits for his mistress to appear.

2. Among the brilliant passages of description in this poem are stanzas two and four. The fading of the morning star indicates the coming of dawn, and in stanza four the sound of the carriages rolling away indicates that the ball is over. Note the precise development of the images in both of these stanzas.

3. The student should consider very carefully, however, the success or lack of success of the description in the last four stanzas. Granting that it is possible to convince the reader that the flowers share the lover's anticipation, has the poet been successful here? For example, is there any justification for the white rose weeping at the sweetheart's lateness when the red rose does not? Has the poet endowed the various flowers with enough dramatic particularity to make their various kinds of behavior convincing?

4. Lines 53–58 suggest that his sweetheart is a kind of nature goddess whom both he and the flowers properly worship. But does one patronize a goddess (*cf.* "Shine out, little head")?

5. Does the poem avoid sentimentality?

Tears, Idle Tears

ALFRED, LORD TENNYSON [1809–1892]

Tears, idle tears, I know not what they mean,
Tears from the depth of some divine despair
Rise in the heart, and gather to the eyes,
In looking on the happy Autumn-fields,
And thinking of the days that are no more. 5

Fresh as the first beam glittering on a sail,
That brings our friends up from the underworld,
Sad as the last which reddens over one
That sinks with all we love below the verge;
So sad, so fresh, the days that are no more. 10

Ah, sad and strange as in dark summer dawns
The earliest pipe of half-awakened birds
To dying ears, when unto dying eyes
The casement slowly grows a glimmering square;
So sad, so strange, the days that are no more. 15

Dear as remembered kisses after death,
And sweet as those by hopeless fancy feigned
On lips that are for others; deep as love,
Deep as first love, and wild with all regret;
O Death in Life, the days that are no more! 20
(From *The Princess*)

EXERCISE:

1. The subject of this poem, like that of "Ulalume" (p. 194), is vague. Why is it more "successful" than "Ulalume"?

2. Are the tears idle (i.e., meaningless) or are they the most meaningful of tears? What occasion prompts them? Does the speaker himself know?

3. The days that are no more are called "sad" and "fresh" in stanza two; and in stanza three, "sad" and "strange." Why are they *fresh* and *strange?* Does the imagery of stanzas two and three throw any light on their freshness and strangeness? On their "wildness" (see line 19)?

4. What do the tears mean? Is this a weepy, sentimental poem or is it something quite different?

As I Walked Out One Evening

W. H. AUDEN [1907–]

As I walked out one evening,
Walking down Bristol Street,
The crowds upon the pavement
Were fields of harvest wheat.

And down by the brimming river 5
I heard a lover sing
Under an arch of the railway:
"Love has no ending.

I'll love you, dear, I'll love you
Till China and Africa meet, 10
And the river jumps over the mountain
And the salmon sing in the street.

I'll love you till the ocean
Is folded and hung up to dry,

And the seven stars go squawking 15
  Like geese about the sky.

The years shall run like rabbits,
  For in my arms I hold
The Flower of the Ages,
  And the first love of the world." 20

But all the clocks in the city
  Began to whirr and chime:
"O let not Time deceive you,
  You cannot conquer Time.

In the burrows of the Nightmare 25
  Where Justice naked is,
Time watches from the shadow
  And coughs when you would kiss.

In headaches and in worry
  Vaguely life leaks away, 30
And Time will have his fancy
  Tomorrow or today.

Into many a green valley
  Drifts the appalling snow;
Time breaks the threaded dances 35
  And the diver's brilliant bow.

O plunge your hands in water,
  Plunge them in up to the wrist;
Stare, stare in the basin
  And wonder what you've missed. 40

The glacier knocks in the cupboard,
  The desert sighs in the bed,
And the crack in the tea-cup opens
  A lane to the land of the dead.

Where the beggars raffle the banknotes 45
  And the Giant is enchanting to Jack,
And the Lily-white Boy is a Roarer,
  And Jill goes down on her back.

O look, look in the mirror,
  O look in your distress; 50
Life remains a blessing
  Although you cannot bless.

O stand, stand at the window
  As the tears scald and start;
You shall love your crooked neighbor 55
  With your crooked heart."

It was late, late in the evening,
  The lovers they were gone;
The clocks had ceased their chiming,
  And the deep river ran on. 60

EXERCISE:

1. Compare and contrast the tone of this poem with "A Fine Old Ballad" (p. 213). Is Auden using the ballad conventions (the lover's promise, etc.) for the same effect that Clare used them?

2. In one sense, the imagery used in the latter half of the poem is quite as extravagant as that used in the lover's declaration in the earlier part of the poem. What is the difference in effect? Give special attention to the images in lines 25–26 and in lines 41–44.

3. What is the tone of this poem? The clocks, the voice of time, confront the lover's illusion with a statement of reality. Is the tone of the poem, then, one of quiet moralizing, or of bitter mockery, or of cynical disillusionment? Or what? How is the last stanza related to the tone?

The Garden

ANDREW MARVELL [1621–1678]

How vainly men themselves amaze,
To win the palm, the oak, or bays,
And their uncessant labors see
Crowned from some single herb or tree
Whose short and narrow-vergèd shade
Does prudently their toils upbraid,
While all the flowers and trees do close
To weave the garlands of repose!

Fair Quiet, have I found thee here,
And Innocence, thy sister dear? 10
Mistaken long, I sought you then
In busy companies of men.
Your sacred plants, if here below,
Only among the plants will grow;
Society is all but rude 15
To this delicious solitude.

No white nor red was ever seen
So amorous as this lovely green.
Fond lovers, cruel as their flame,
Cut in these trees their mistress' name. 20
Little, alas! they know or heed,
How far these beauties hers exceed!
Fair trees! wheres'e'r your barks I wound
No name shall but your own be found.

When we have run our passion's heat, 25
Love hither makes his best retreat.
The gods, that mortal beauty chase,
Still in a tree did end their race;
Apollo hunted Daphne so,
Only that she might laurel grow; 30
And Pan did after Syrinx speed,
Not as a nymph, but for a reed.

What wondrous life in this I lead!
Ripe apples drop about my head;
The luscious clusters of the vine 35
Upon my mouth do crush their wine;
The nectarine, and curious peach,
Into my hands themselves do reach;
Stumbling on melons, as I pass,
Ensnared with flowers, I fall on grass. 40

Meanwhile the mind, from pleasure less,
Withdraws into its happiness;—
The mind, that ocean where each kind
Does straight its own resemblance find;
Yet it creates, transcending these, 45
Far other worlds, and other seas,

Annihilating all that's made
To a green thought in a green shade.

Here at the fountain's sliding foot,
Or at some fruit-tree's mossy root, 50
Casting the body's vest aside,
My soul into the boughs does glide:
There, like a bird, it sits and sings,
Then whets and combs its silver wings,
And, till prepared for longer flight, 55
Waves in its plumes the various light.

Such was that happy garden-state,
While man there walked without a mate
After a place so pure and sweet.
What other help could yet be meet! 60
But 't was beyond a mortal's share
To wander solitary there:
Two paradises 't were in one,
To live in paradise alone.

How well the skilful gardener drew 65
Of flowers, and herbs, this dial new;
Where, from above, the milder sun
Does through a fragrant zodiac run,
And, as it works, th' industrious bee
Computes its time as well as we! 70
How could such sweet and wholesome hours
Be reckoned but with herbs and flowers?

Exercise:

In the first stanza, the poet says that men labor incessantly for the few inches of shade meagerly yielded by a chaplet of victory woven from the leaves of one tree, when they might have effortlessly the wide shade spontaneously woven by the overarching boughs of all the trees. The palm, the oak, and bays were used to crown victors. The poet pretends that men strive to win the "narrow-vergèd shade," of the chaplet—not what it symbolizes. Why does the poet do this? Is he describing a garden? Or is he commenting on the life of action as compared with the life of contemplation? Or is he doing both—describing his experience in a garden, but through his description, commenting upon the meaning of life and man's values? Note that "vainly" may mean "fruitlessly" or "in vanity," and that "upbraid" may mean to "reproach" as well as "to braid up." Note the way in which the crown of victory is set over against "the garlands of repose." Most important of all, note that the tone here is not matter-of-fact nor solemn, but witty and playful. This first stanza is a fair sample of the richness of the poem. Try to work out the rest of the poem in this fashion, taking particular account of the imagery and what it does, and of the various shifts in tone. Here are a few of the topics into which the student will want to inquire:

1. In lines 29–32, Marvell has the gods chase the nymphs in order that they may turn into plants. Why? Compare lines 61–64 where the Genesis story is reversed: Eve is created, not to help Adam, but to trouble him.

2. Stanza five treats of the delights of the senses; stanza six, those of the mind; stanza seven, those of the soul. How are these delights related to the garden? How, to each other?

3. What is a "green thought" (line 48)? How can the mind *create* other worlds by *annihilating* everything created ("all that's made")?

4. For what flight is the soul (as bird) preparing itself? What is the tone of this seventh stanza? Is there a shift in tone in the next stanza?

5. A sun-dial consists of a vane, set at the proper angle, which shows the time by throwing a shadow upon the proper numeral. In the sun-dial in the garden, the numbers are worked out in beds of living flowers. What does "fragrant zodiac" mean? What is the meaning of lines 69–70?

Among School Children

WILLIAM BUTLER YEATS [1865–1939]

I

I walk through the long schoolroom questioning;
A kind old nun in a white hood replies;
The children learn to cipher and to sing,

To study reading-books and history,
To cut and sew, be neat in everything 5
In the best modern way—the children's eyes
In momentary wonder stare upon
A sixty-year-old smiling public man.

II

I dream of a Ledaean body, bent
Above a sinking fire, a tale that she 10
Told of a harsh reproof, or trivial event
That changed some childish day to tragedy—
Told, and it seemed that our two natures blent
Into a sphere from youthful sympathy,
Or else, to alter Plato's parable, 15
Into the yolk and white of the one shell.

III

And thinking of that fit of grief or rage
I look upon one child or t'other there
And wonder if she stood so at that age—
For even daughters of the swan can share 20
Something of every paddler's heritage—
And had that color upon cheek or hair,
And thereupon my heart is driven wild:
She stands before me as a living child.

IV

Her present image floats into the mind— 25
Did Quattrocento finger fashion it
Hollow of cheek as though it drank the wind
And took a mess of shadows for its meat?
And I though never of Ledaean kind
Had pretty plumage once—enough of that, 30
Better to smile on all that smile, and show
There is a comfortable kind of old scarecrow.

V

What youthful mother, a shape upon her lap
Honey of generation had betrayed,

And that must sleep, shriek, struggle to escape 35
As recollection or the drug decide,
Would think her son, did she but see that shape
With sixty or more winters on its head,
A compensation for the pang of his birth,
Or the uncertainty of his setting forth? 40

VI

Plato thought nature but a spume that plays
Upon a ghostly paradigm of things;
Solider Aristotle played the taws
Upon the bottom of a king of kings;
World-famous golden-thighed Pythagoras 45
Fingered upon a fiddle-stick or strings
What a star sang and careless Muses heard:
Old clothes upon old sticks to scare a bird.

VII

Both nuns and mothers worship images,
But those the candles light are not as those 50
That animate a mother's reveries,
But keep a marble or a bronze repose.
And yet they too break hearts—O Presences
That passion, piety or affection knows,
And that all heavenly glory symbolize— 55
O self-born mockers of man's enterprise;

VIII

Labor is blossoming or dancing where
The body is not bruised to pleasure soul,
Nor beauty born out of its own despair,
Nor blear-eyed wisdom out of midnight oil. 60
O chestnut tree, great rooted blossomer,
Are you the leaf, the blossom or the bole?
O body swayed to music, O brightening glance,
How can we know the dancer from the dance?

EXERCISE:

1. The structure of the poem may be sketched briefly as follows: Stanza I gives the situation which stimulates the speaker to his rev-

erie. Stanzas II, III, and IV present the relation of childhood to maturity and of maturity to age with reference to the speaker himself and to the woman he loves. Stanzas V and VI extend the personal comment to a general one: would any mother, if she could see the old age of her child, feel that her own love and sacrifice had been justified; for even the greatest men, Plato, Aristotle, and Pythagoras, were, in old age, little better than scarecrows? Stanza VII goes on to comment that the images which people hold in affection and reverence always mock man's inability to realize them. Stanza VIII presents the idea that when the mind and body are in harmony, there is no distinction between the real and the ideal; the image and the actuality are one. Investigate the ways by which the imagery serves to present these ideas. (Consult the library for information concerning Leda, Quattrocento, Plato, Aristotle, Alexander the Great, who is referred to here as "king of kings," the meaning of the word *taws,* and Pythagoras.)

2. What are the interrelations among the images? Observe, for instance, that the story of Leda and the swan is alluded to in line 20.

3. Is it suggested that man should do away with cruel idealisms of every kind, since none can ever be attained and all bruise man in his struggle to attain them? What does the speaker say on this point? In attempting an answer here, consider the evidence of imagery.

4. Why does the speaker refer to both nuns and mothers? How do the nuns and mothers complement each other in this poem?

5. What does the speaker mean by his last two questions (lines 61–64)? Is there a sense in which we literally cannot know the dancer apart from the dance?

Voyages

HART CRANE [1899–1932]

II

And yet this great wink of eternity,
Of rimless floods, unfettered leewardings,
Samite sheeted and processioned where

Her undinal vast belly moonward bends,
Laughing the wrapt inflections of our love; 5

Take this Sea, whose diapason knells
On scrolls of silver snowy sentences,
The sceptered terror of whose sessions rends
As her demeanors motion well or ill,
All but the pieties of lovers' hands. 10

And onward, as bells off San Salvador
Salute the crocus lusters of the stars,
In these poinsettia meadows of her tides,—
Adagios of islands, O my Prodigal,
Complete the dark confessions her veins spell. 15

Mark how her turning shoulders wind the hours,
And hasten while her penniless rich palms
Pass superscription of bent foam and wave,—
Hasten, while they are true,—sleep, death, desire,
Close round one instant in one floating flower. 20

Bind us in time, O seasons clear, and awe.
O minstrel galleons of Carib fire,
Bequeath us to no earthly shore until
Is answered in the vortex of our grave
The seal's wide spindrift gaze toward paradise. 25

VI

Where icy and bright dungeons lift
Of swimmers their lost morning eyes,
And ocean rivers, churning, shift
Green borders under stranger skies,

Steadily as a shell secretes 5
Its beating leagues of monotone,
Or as many waters trough the sun's
Red kelson past the cape's wet stone;

O rivers mingling toward the sky
And harbor of the phoenix' breast— 10

My eyes pressed black against the prow,
—Thy derelict and blinded guest

Waiting, afire, what name, unspoke,
I cannot claim: let thy waves rear
More savage than the death of kings, 15
Some splintered garland for the seer.

Beyond siroccos harvesting
The solstice thunders, crept away,
Like a cliff swinging or a sail
Flung into April's inmost day— 20

Creation's blithe and petaled word
To the lounged goddess when she rose
Conceding dialogue with eyes
That smile unsearchable repose—

Still fervid convenant, Belle Isle, 25
—Unfolded floating dais before
Which rainbows twine continual hair—
Belle Isle, white echo of the oar!

The imaged word, it is, that holds
Hushed willows anchored in its glow. 30
It is the unbetrayable reply
Whose accent no farewell can know.

EXERCISE:

These two poems make use of a very rich and perhaps tangled imagery. The student ought to try to determine whether the imagery is confused, or whether it hangs together; and if so, on what principle the images are interrelated. Before beginning this examination, he might well reread what Crane has to say about the imagery used in "At Melville's Tomb" (p. 332).

1. What aspects of the sea are pictured by the imagery? Suggested by the imagery?

2. In the first poem the sea is referred to as if it were a goddess; in the second, the goddess Aphrodite (who was born of the sea-foam), is referred to. What does the sea come to symbolize in these poems?

VI

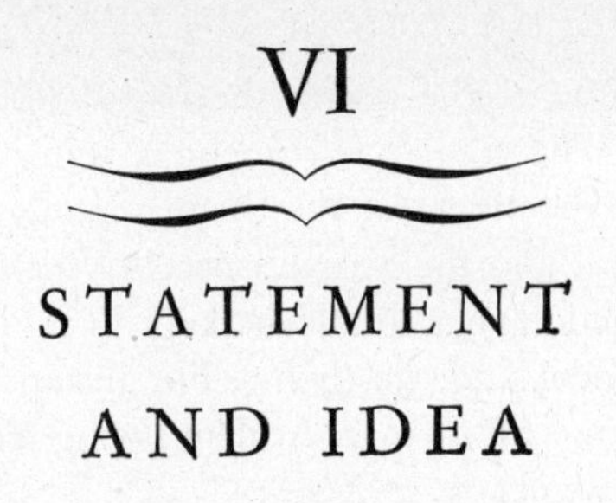

STATEMENT AND IDEA

FOREWORD

In examining the poems in this section, the reader will find special opportunities for considering some of the ways in which an idea appears in poetry. But, of course, the idea of any poem, in so far as the poem is being read as poetry, can only be considered in relation to the various other factors which we have previously discussed—narrative, meter, imagery, etc. Just as the student should continually take these factors into account, he should remember that in stressing theme in these poems he is dealing with an aspect of all poetry ("Foreword" to Section II, p. 75) and a topic which has often been discussed in previous pages (pp. 12, 60, 117). That is, every poem involves an idea, for a poem represents an interpretation of its materials. Obviously, the method of presenting theme will vary from poem to poem, as we have already seen. The method will vary according to the special combinations of imagery, rhythm, statement, etc. Each case must be treated on its own merits, for no poem is exactly like any other. But one may, however, offer this basic principle: the real poet in presenting his theme never depends *merely* on general statement. The poem itself is the dramatizing of the theme in terms of situation, character, imagery, rhythm, tone, etc.

We have said that a theme in poetry manifests itself in constantly varying ways. Among these manifestations, of course, we find the use of explicit statement as one possible means. For instance, in the "Ode to a Nightingale," which we have already analyzed (pp. 338–45), Keats makes the explicit statement,

> Now more than ever seems it rich to die,
> To cease upon the midnight with no pain.

Certainly, the theme of the poem, the basic idea, is not the desirability of suicide. The explicit statement is being used here merely as a step in the development of the theme: man's inability to correlate finally the ideal and the actual aspects of his experience.

A further distinction that should be kept in mind is that between the subject of a poem and the theme. For instance, let us compare the following poem with "To an Athlete Dying Young," which has already been discussed (pp. 267–69):

The Lads in Their Hundreds

A. E. HOUSMAN [1859–1936]

The lads in their hundreds to Ludlow come in for the fair,
  There's men from the barn and the forge and the mill and the fold,
The lads for the girls and the lads for the liquor are there,
  And there with the rest are the lads that will never be old.

There's chaps from the town and the field and the till and the cart, 5
  And many to count are the stalwart, and many the brave,
And many the handsome of face and the handsome of heart,
  And few that will carry their looks or their truth to the grave.

I wish one could know them, I wish there were tokens to tell
  The fortunate fellows that now you can never discern; 10
And then one could talk with them friendly and wish them farewell
  And watch them depart on the way that they will not return.

But now you may stare as you like and there's nothing to scan;
  And brushing your elbow unguessed-at and not to be told
They carry back bright to the coiner the mintage of man, 15
  The lads that will die in their glory and never be old.

It should be clear that both of these have the same general theme, but the *subject* of the first, as the title states, is the death of a young athlete, and the subject of the other is a scene at Ludlow Fair. In the same way, a little study of the "Ode on a Grecian Urn," by Keats

(p. 474), will show that it has the same basic theme as the "Ode to a Nightingale." The ideal life pictured on the urn, perfect beyond change and time, is brought into contrast with the actual world where desire pushes on to its fulfilment and to the "burning forehead, and a parching tongue." But the subjects are very different, one subject being the reactions of a man to the song of the bird, and the other being the reactions of a modern man to an ancient Greek vase.

A further question may have presented itself to the student in this general regard: what is the importance of "truth" in poetry? This question has been raised earlier in the *Introduction* (pp. xlii–xlvi). It was there pointed out that the goodness of a poem could never be based on the *mere* fact that it said something true or instructive. It was also pointed out that a person can admire poems that contradict each other or express views that are not in agreement with the reader's own views. This general question of the "truth" of poetry is answered if we reflect for a moment on the impulses which take us to poetry. We do not read poetry for the scientific truth of particular statements. We do not read poetry for specific moral instructions. Statements that, taken in isolation, would seem to raise issues of scientific truth or falsity, and statements that would seem to embody specific moral judgments are not, as we have seen, to be taken by themselves, but as factors contributing to the development of the total experience and the total meaning which the poet is trying to develop for us. A reading which selects such statements out of context for either praise or blame springs from the "message-hunting" impulse (*Introduction,* pp. xlii–xlvi). A reader should constantly remember that such detailed statements should be interpreted in the light of the total effect.

But suppose the reader does master the poem as a whole and does see the relation of any detailed statement in the poem to the total intention. There still remains the question of the reader's judgment of the general attitude toward life, the interpretation of life made or implied, in the poem. Suppose the reader does not agree with the interpretation involved? Can he still accept the poem?

Let us approach this question somewhat indirectly. Obviously, a silly or superficial or childish attitude cannot result in a good poem

This is true even if the writer has a skill in the use of certain technical devices. For instance, we can look back to "The Indian Serenade," by Shelley (p. 173), and see that the rhythms of the poem are not handled crudely and amateurishly. But, as has been pointed out, the poem as a whole is sentimental, and if we care to isolate the conception of love implied in the poem, we can see that it is very superficial and immature when contrasted with that implied in poems like "Rose Aylmer" (p. 144), "A Deep-Sworn Vow" (p. 148), "A Litany" (p. 205), or a sonnet by Shakespeare (p. 331).

Indeed, any attitude or interpretation, whether or not the reader habitually adopts it himself, will not invalidate a poem, provided that the attitude or interpretation is one that could conceivably be held by a serious and intelligent person in the dramatic situation implied or stated in the poem. (Obviously words like *serious* and *intelligent* do not mean absolutely the same thing to different people, and consequently there is a margin here for disagreement in estimating poetry. But such disagreements, taken by and large over a long period of time, after contemporary prejudices have died, are rather infrequent when really first-rate work is concerned.)

It is easy to see why a considerable difference may exist between the habitual attitudes of a reader and the attitudes inherent in poems which he, nevertheless, appreciates. No matter how strongly a person may hold to certain attitudes and interpretations, he is aware, unless he is fanatical or stupid, that human experience is infinitely complicated and various. Poetry demands, on this ground, to be approached with a certain humility. And human nature is such that the reader will usually approach a poem without raising too immediately the question of his agreement or disagreement in attitude; because poetry is about human experience it appeals to his interests. This postponement of the question of agreement or disagreement—even the reader's feeling that the question may be irrelevant—arises from the fact that the attitude involved in a poem does not come merely as a bare general statement; it comes as part of a complex experience arising from the relation to each other of many different elements. The successful poem is a set of organized and controlled relations.

It is only when the attitude involved in the poem comes as an oversimplified generalization or when the response which the poem insists on seems not warranted by the dramatic situation which is presented or implied—it is only in these cases that the ordinary reader will reject a poem on the basis of his disagreement with its implied "view of life." For in so far as he appreciates the poem he has a sense of the conquest over the disorder and meaninglessness of experience. Perhaps this sense may be the very basis for his exhilaration in the poem—just as it may be the basis for the pleasure one takes in watching the clean drive of an expert golfer or the swoop of a bird in the air, as contrasted with the accidental tumbling of a stone down a hillside. It is this same sense of order and control given by a successful poem that confirms us in the faith that the experiences of life itself may have meaning.

Lucifer in Starlight

GEORGE MEREDITH [1828–1909]

On a starred night Prince Lucifer uprose.
Tired of his dark dominion, swung the fiend
Above the rolling ball in cloud part screened,
Where sinners hugged their specter of repose.
Poor prey to his hot fit of pride were those. 5
And now upon his western wing he leaned,
Now his huge bulk o'er Afric's sands careened,
Now the black planet shadowed Arctic snows.
Soaring through wider zones that pricked his scars
With memory of the old revolt from Awe, 10
He reached a middle height, and at the stars,
Which are the brain of heaven, he looked, and sank.
Around the ancient track marched, rank on rank,
The army of unalterable law.

Some of the ways in which an idea finds expression in poetry have been treated more or less fully in many of the earlier discussions, especially in the section dealing with imagery. But the ways in which this process occurs are innumerable and, in fact, vary from poem to poem. In the present instance, "Lucifer in Starlight," the process is a fairly simple one.

An understanding of the poem depends on reference to some specific information that is not given in the poem itself. It presupposes a knowledge and interpretation of the Lucifer myth. Lucifer, the Archangel, rebelled against God, and as a result of his pride, which would not endure the divine dominion over him, was hurled out of heaven. But the subject not only carries with it the bare facts of the myth, but also associations derived from a treatment such as that in Milton's epic, *Paradise Lost,* which involves the rebellion of the angels, and his temptation of Man as a revenge against God. From the myth and its different treatments the reader knows that Lucifer may be taken as the incarnation of pride, and therefore as the principle of anarchy and disorder, in conflict with the principle of order in the universe.

Essentially, Meredith presents this same theme in his poem, but he has put his theme into a new set of terms, and though depending on the body of information and associations which the reader brings to the poem, has succeeded in creating a new poem. Meredith has made, as it were, a new myth, a kind of sequel to the more traditional treatments of the idea. Lucifer, who, as in Milton's *Paradise Lost,* maintains his pride even in the depth of Hell, is shown rising through the starry universe, above the sphere of the earth which is partially concealed from him by clouds. He is not now interested in the sinners on earth through whom, since the Fall of Man, he has been striking at God in revenge; apparently, in his "hot fit of pride" he is aiming at nothing less than a return to his old estate.

Meredith attempts to give as vivid a picture as possible of the enormous bulk of the Fiend, like a planet, flying so near the "rolling ball" of the earth that he shadows it, presumably, from the moon. One may notice that in giving this picture Meredith casts the mythical figure of the Fiend into the universe as we now conceive it, describing the earth revolving in its orbit, and does not use the fixed, central earth of the Ptolemaic conception, which Milton, for instance, used. This detail, though small in itself, gives a certain novelty to Meredith's treatment. It seems to imply, perhaps as a kind of undertone to the poem, that the old force of anarchy is still operating, despite changes in human conceptions, and trying to reach out, even beyond human affairs, to the very center of the universe.

But the real novelty in the new "myth" lies in the reason given by Meredith for Lucifer's failure to proceed with his present rebellion. He does not sink again because he encounters the divine force that once hurled him down. It is definitely stated in the poem that he passes through.

wider zones that pricked his scars
With memory of the old revolt from Awe.

But this does not deter him, for the reader will observe that he goes on, fearless, to another height, where, simply, he regards the stars, and then quietly sinks to his proper place. The stars, the poet says, are "the brain of heaven." Apparently, the recognition of this fact is what conquers the impulse of the Fiend. The order of the stars demonstrates the reasonable nature of the universe, against which it is useless to rebel. One need not call on an exhibition of the divine powers, the poet is saying, to conquer the impulse of anarchy and rebellion; the slightest understanding of the construction of the universe is enough. The perception of the stars, or of any other item of the ordered universe, not only may comfort man by assuring him that the universe in which he lives is a reasonable one, but may at the same time rebuke his pride, as it rebukes Lucifer, and may teach man humility.

We cannot know very certainly the stages through which the poet's mind passed in writing "Lucifer in Starlight," but we can try to define the logical steps (see "How Poems Come About," p. 591). Let us assume that he starts with the general idea, the theme, that rebellion against the reasonable order of the universe is futile. He decides, on reflection, that the orderly procedure of the constellations most majestically exemplifies this order. He might write a poem describing, to a certain extent, the organization of the constellations and stating his conclusion in general terms. The chances are strong that such a poem, even if many of the individual lines and passages were beautiful, would be dull. It would have no real principle of poetic organization, would give no device for suspense, and would actually give little scope for the play of the imagination except in so far as the poet might develop details. Presumably, the poet would not long entertain the notion of writing his poem in this way. He would probably want to present his idea more sharply, more concretely. It might next occur to him that he could put an observer in the poem, say a man looking at the stars and musing, as in the Bible (Job 38:4–8), on the order of the firmament. In this way the stars might be made to take a symbolic meaning. But such a poem would tend to be undramatic, for not much would happen in it unless the personal situation of the man were so developed that the reader would feel that the fact that he has grasped the meaning of the firmament would have some effect on the man's life. The poet might discard such a solution for his problem on the ground that to build up such a situation for the man would take too much effort and space and would throw the poem out of proportion; in fact, if attempted at all, it would probably develop into a very different piece from the first conception, perhaps a character study. Then the poet might strike upon the subject of Lucifer, who decides on a new revolt and is deterred by a recognition of the meaning of the firmament. This solves the poet's problem. First, it is a dramatic situation. Second, the character of the personage involved, Lucifer, is already established in the reader's mind to give a basis for the poet's new twist of interpretation: that, not the intervention of divine power, but a recognition of the natural order of things, is sufficient to conquer the impulse toward anarchy. Fourth, the use of Lucifer enables the poet to make the same dramatic incident present both of the points involved: the natural order is both a comfort and a rebuke to man.

The process outlined above, as has already been said, is not to be taken as a true account of the working of Meredith's mind in composing the poem. It is far more probable that a poet works from some sudden suggestion of detail, perhaps his stumbling on such a little clause such as "which are the brain of heaven," or his suddenly expressing to himself the idea of the order of the firmament with the line, "the army of unalterable law." Or perhaps he visualized to himself Lucifer moving through the firmament, and asked himself, "Well, what *would* happen?" Almost anything may provide the germ of a poem to the poet, and until he starts developing the poem, exploring in the actual composition the possibilities of the subject, he may not be quite sure where he is going and may not quite know all he intends to say or mean. Writing the poem is for the poet a process of discovery just as reading it is a process of discovery for the reader (see pp. 335–36).

It is perhaps easier to understand this when one remembers that the total meaning of a poem is not communicated by any single element of a poem—by the statements, connotations, symbols, or rhythms. We may say that the meaning of a poem is the total result of all of these. We have seen earlier that a poet, for instance, does not merely put an idea into a verse form; he expects the verse to serve as part of the expression of the poem, for, otherwise, there would be no purpose in using verse at all. In this particular poem one can indicate some of the features of the verse that contribute to the total expression of the theme. The poem may be scanned as follows:

1. On a | starred night | Prince Lu | cifer | uprose.
2. Tired of | his dark | domin | ion swung | the fiend
3. Above | the rol | ling ball | in cloud | part screened,
4. Where sin | ners hug | their spec | ter of | repose.
5. Poor prey | to his | hot fit | of pride | were those.
6. And now | upon | his wes | tern wing | he leaned,
7. Now his | huge bulk | o'er Af | ric's sands | careened,
8. Now the | black plan | et shad | owed Arc | tic snows.
9. Soaring | through wi | der zones | that pricked | his scars
10. With mem | ories of | the old | revolt | from Awe,
11. He reached | a mid | dle height, | and at | the stars,
12. Which are | the brain | of heav | en, he looked, | and sank.
13. Around | the an | cient track | marched, rank | on rank,
14. The ar | my of | unal | tera | ble law.

One can observe that the relatively regular and heavy beat of the verse, the preponderance of monosyllables and hovering accents making for a retarded movement, and the many end-stop lines with light caesura, help give the impression of ponderous, sullen majesty which the image of Lucifer inspires.[1] But there are some more special details that are worthy of notice. The relative absence of heavy internal pauses in the lines makes such pauses come, by contrast, with a special emphasis. The first one appears in line 11 to give an emphatic preparation for the "stars," the word that raises the fundamental idea of the poem. In line 12 the pauses set off "he looked," and "and sank" so that the pauses contribute to the impression of Lucifer's taking a long and thoughtful inspection of the firmament and then slowly descending. In line 13 the fourth foot of the line is composed of the words *marched, rank,* but the foot gives a spondaic effect, because of the hovering accent, which occurs elsewhere as in the second foot, *black plan-* of line 8. This fact and the preparatory pause before *rank* give a powerful emphasis. In line 14 the most important idea, in fact, the most important idea of the poem, is contained in the word *unalterable.* This word is composed of five syllables. It is two syllables longer than any other in the poem, standing in contrast to the prevailing use of monosyllables. It is divided *un-al-ter-a-ble.* The accent falls on the second syllable, *al,* and the last three syllables tend to be slurred together. But in the iambic pentameter line in which the word appears in the poem, two of the regular metrical beats fall on syllables of the word:

un-ál-ter-á-ble.

This means that the entire word is given more force than is usual; and this is effective, because of the importance of the word in relation to the subject of the poem.

Concerning another technical factor Chard Powers Smith writes:

> Spoken sounds fall naturally into certain groups, the members of each group arising from approximately the same location in the vocal apparatus. In utterance, even in the silent utterance of reading to one's self, the sounds within any one group *feel* alike because the same vocal muscles come into play. It is upon this kinetic basis that assonance rests, quite as much as upon the actual auditory quality

[1] Of the 111 words in the poem 86 are monosyllables, 3 are trisyllables, and the rest, with the exception of one word, *unalterable,* are disyllables. There are only two run-on lines, and only four cases of internal punctuation.

of words; it is upon this basis that the sensed similarity of sounds may be most easily explained. Intuitively we feel, for instance, that such a line as this is musically all of a piece:

The army of unalterable law.

The reason is that the principal vowel sounds—the *a* in "army," the first *a* in "unalterable" and the *a* in "law," along with the unimportant vowel sound in "of," all arise in the same region of the throat, while the *u,* second *a* and terminal *e* of "unalterable" arise from an adjoining region; and the dominant consonants—*r, m, n,* and *l*—are likewise all members of a single assonance group.

It will be observed in the line quoted, as in all cases, that it is the stressed syllables that dominate phonetically in any passage, those syllables that receive emphasis in normal prose utterance—quite independent of prosodic scansion. . . . In the line just quoted we may capitalize these stressed syllables, as follows:

the ARMy of UNALterable LAW.

These are the sounds which, made emphatic by the sense, are most intrusive and which, consequently, give the line its phonetic flavor. According as they do or do not fall into the same assonance group, according, that is, as they are or are not repetitions and variations in the same rhythms of sound, the passage is or is not musical in the present sense. Compared to these syllables, all the rest are of secondary importance.[1]

Exercise:

1. What is the effect of metrical accent on the preposition *at* in line 11?

2. Compare Meredith's use of the stars as a symbol of order here with Eliot's use of them as a symbol of wearisome routine in "Preludes" (p. 102).

1887

A. E. HOUSMAN [1859–1936]

From Clee to heaven the beacon burns,
The shires have seen it plain,

[1] *Pattern and Variation in Poetry,* New York: Scribner's, pp. 57–58.

From north and south the sign returns
  And beacons burn again.

Look left, look right, the hills are bright, 5
  The dales are light between,
Because 'tis fifty years tonight
  That God has saved the Queen.

Now, when the flame they watch not towers
  About the soil they trod, 10
Lads, we'll remember friends of ours
  Who shared the work with God.

To skies that knit their heartstrings right,
  To fields that bred them brave,
The saviors come not home tonight: 15
  Themselves they could not save.

It dawns in Asia, tombstones show
  And Shropshire names are read;
And the Nile spills his overflow
  Beside the Severn's dead. 20

We pledge in peace by farm and town
  The Queen they served in war,
And fire the beacons up and down
  The land they perished for.

"God save the Queen" we living sing, 25
  From height to height 'tis heard;
And with the rest your voices ring,
  Lads of the Fifty-third.

Oh, God will save her, fear you not:
  Be you the men you've been, 30
Get you the sons your fathers got,
  And God will save the Queen.

EXERCISE:

1. This poem concerns the celebration of the fiftieth year of Queen Victoria's reign. How does the poet develop his attitude toward the patriotic occasion?

2. In the foregoing connection notice the shift in tone at the beginning of the third stanza, and discuss the technical features involved in this shift.

3. Notice the Biblical allusion in the fourth stanza. What is its effect?

4. How does the last stanza serve to summarize the effect of the poem? How has it been prepared for?

Elegy

WRITTEN IN A COUNTRY CHURCHYARD

THOMAS GRAY [1716–1771]

The Curfew tolls the knell of parting day,
  The lowing herd wind slowly o'er the lea,
The plowman homeward plods his weary way,
  And leaves the world to darkness and to me.

Now fades the glimmering landscape on the sight, 5
  And all the air a solemn stillness holds,
Save where the beetle wheels his droning flight,
  And drowsy tinklings lull the distant folds;

Save that from yonder ivy-mantled tower
  The moping owl does to the moon complain 10
Of such, as wandering near her secret bower,
  Molest her ancient solitary reign.

Beneath those rugged elms, that yew-tree's shade,
  Where heaves the turf in many a mould'ring heap,
Each in his narrow cell for ever laid, 15
  The rude Forefathers of the hamlet sleep.

The breezy call of incense-breathing Morn,
  The swallow twitt'ring from the straw-built shed,
The cock's shrill clarion, or the echoing horn,
  No more shall rouse them from their lowly bed. 20

For them no more the blazing hearth shall burn,
  Or busy housewife ply her evening care:

No children run to lisp their sire's return,
  Or climb his knees the envied kiss to share.

Oft did the harvest to their sickle yield, 25
  Their furrow oft the stubborn glebe has broke;
How jocund did they drive their team afield!
  How bowed the woods beneath their sturdy stroke!

Let not Ambition mock their useful toil,
  Their homely joys, and destiny obscure; 30
Nor Grandeur hear with a disdainful smile
  The short and simple annals of the poor.

The boast of heraldry, the pomp of power,
  And all that beauty, all that wealth e'er gave,
Awaits alike th' inevitable hour. 35
  The paths of glory lead but to the grave.

Nor you, ye Proud, impute to These the fault,
  If Memory o'er their Tomb no Trophies raise,
Where through the long-drawn aisle and fretted vault
  The pealing anthem swells the note of praise. 40

Can storied urn or animated bust
  Back to its mansion call the fleeting breath?
Can Honor's voice provoke the silent dust,
  Or Flattery sooth the dull cold ear of Death?

Perhaps in this neglected spot is laid 45
  Some heart once pregnant with celestial fire;
Hands, that the rod of empire might have swayed,
  Or waked to ecstasy the living lyre.

But Knowledge to their eyes her ample page
  Rich with the spoils of time did ne'er unroll; 50
Chill Penury repressed their noble rage,
  And froze the genial current of the soul.

Full many a gem of purest ray serene,
  The dark unfathomed caves of ocean bear:
Full many a flower is born to blush unseen, 55
  And waste its sweetness on the desert air.

Some village-Hampden, that with dauntless breast
The little Tyrant of his fields withstood;
Some mute inglorious Milton here may rest,
Some Cromwell guiltless of his country's blood. 60

Th' applause of list'ning senates to command,
The threats of pain and ruin to despise,
To scatter plenty o'er a smiling land,
And read their history in a nation's eyes,

Their lot forbade: nor circumscribed alone 65
Their growing virtues, but their crimes confined;
Forbade to wade through slaughter to a throne,
And shut the gates of mercy on mankind,

The struggling pangs of conscious truth to hide,
To quench the blushes of ingenuous shame, 70
Or heap the shrine of Luxury and Pride
With incense kindled at the Muse's flame.

Far from the madding crowd's ignoble strife,
Their sober wishes never learned to stray;
Along the cool sequestered vale of life 75
They kept the noiseless tenor of their way.

Yet ev'n these bones from insult to protect,
Some frail memorial still erected nigh,
With uncouth rhymes and shapeless sculpture decked,
Implores the passing tribute of a sigh. 80

Their name, their years, spelt by th' unlettered muse,
The place of fame and elegy supply:
And many a holy text around she strews,
That teach the rustic moralist to die.

For who to dumb Forgetfulness a prey, 85
This pleasing anxious being e'er resigned,
Left the warm precincts of the cheerful day,
Nor cast one longing ling'ring look behind?

On some fond breast the parting soul relies,
Some pious drops the closing eye requires; 90

Ev'n from the tomb the voice of Nature cries,
  Ev'n in our Ashes live their wonted Fires.

For thee, who mindful of th' unhonored Dead
  Dost in these lines their artless tale relate,
If chance, by lonely contemplation led, 95
  Some kindred Spirit shall inquire thy fate,

Haply some hoary-headed Swain may say,
  "Oft have we seen him at the peep of dawn
Brushing with hasty steps the dews away
  To meet the sun upon the upland lawn. 100

"There at the foot of yonder nodding beech
  That wreathes its old fantastic roots so high,
His listless length at noontide would he stretch,
  And pore upon the brook that babbles by.

"Hard by yon wood, now smiling as in scorn, 105
  Mutt'ring his wayward fancies he would rove,
Now drooping, woeful wan, like one forlorn,
  Or crazed with care, or crossed in hopeless love.

"One morn I missed him on the customed hill,
  Along the heath and near his favorite tree; 110
Another came; nor yet beside the rill,
  Nor up the lawn, nor at the wood was he;

"The next with dirges due in sad array
  Slow through the church-way path we saw him borne.
Approach and read (for thou can'st read) the lay, 115
  Graved on the stone beneath yon agèd thorn."

THE EPITAPH

Here rests his head upon the lap of earth
  A youth to fortune and to fame unknown.
Fair Science frowned not on his humble birth,
  And Melancholy marked him for her own. 120

Large was his bounty, and his soul sincere,
  Heaven did a recompense as largely send:

He gave to Misery all he had, a tear,
He gained from Heaven ('twas all he wished) a friend.

No farther seek his merits to disclose, 125
Or draw his frailties from their dread abode,
(There they alike in trembling hope repose)
The bosom of his Father and his God.

EXERCISE:

This poem may be said to be, among other things, a speculation upon the proper place to be buried. The speaker contemplates the country churchyard where those are buried whose fortune entitled them to no more glorious grave. He compares with these humble graves the tombs of the rich and the famous as he imagines them standing in some great abbey church. As for himself, though "Fair Science frowned not on his humble birth," and he might have aspired to the rich abbey tomb, he chooses to be buried among "th' unhonored Dead."

1. Is the speaker saying that the villagers lack all vanity? Does he sentimentalize their innocence? Is he patronizing in his attitude toward them? If you are inclined to answer no, indicate your reasons with specific reference to the text of the poem.

2. How well, or how poorly, does Gray use the device of personification in this poem?

3. What is the nature of the irony in lines 33–36? In lines 41–44? Define it as precisely as you can.

4. In line 74 the poet writes, "Their sober wishes never learned to stray." Why does he use the word *learned?*

5. This poem makes a number of general statements about life. Are these statements insisted upon in isolation? Or do they grow out of the dramatic context of the poem?

If Poisonous Minerals

JOHN DONNE [1573–1631]

If poisonous minerals, and if that tree
Whose fruit threw death on else immortal us,

If lecherous goats, if serpents envious
Cannot be damned, Alas! why should I be?
Why should intent or reason, born in me, 5
Make sins, else equal, in me more heinous?
And mercy being easy, and glorious
To God, in his stern wrath why threatens he?
But who am I, that dare dispute with thee,
O God? O! of thine only worthy blood, 10
And my tears, make a heavenly Lethean flood,
And drown in it my sin's black memory;
That thou remember them, some claim as debt,
I think it mercy, if thou wilt forget.

The theme of this poem may be put as a question: What should be the attitude of sinful man toward God's justice? The theme is presented by a method quite different from that employed in "Lucifer in Starlight," in which the idea appears in terms of an obvious dramatic incident. Here no incident, no narrative element, appears directly. But this poem is, in one sense, dramatic in that, being a prayer, it is addressed by a sin-convicted man to God, and has therefore a special speaker and a special listener and is not merely a general thought or speculation. Being dramatic, it involves a special instance. But the handling of the idea is direct, in the form of argument. The question, then, is: How does the poet invest this argument with the emotional force necessary to poetic effect?

The argument may be briefly summarized as follows: Although it appears unjust that man, merely because he possesses the faculty of reason, should be damned for actions common to lower Nature and unpunished there, man should realize that God's treatment is not to be understood by human reason, and should therefore seek the remission of his sins through the double force of Christ's blood and his own repentance. This is a flat prose statement using none of the imaginative resources that can vivify language with poetic force. This statement, as prose, has an interest, not because of the form in which it is put, but because the idea it involves is a serious one in human experience. But as it stands, the reader must supply, by such application as his own imagination affords, the emotional force. One cannot say, however, that the seriousness of the theme of this poem permits the poet to employ successfully a more direct presentation through argument than is characteristic of most poems; for the theme of all effective poetry has, in some degree, a serious reference to human experience. Even such poems as Herrick's "Delight in Disorder" (p. 187) or Corbet's "The Fairies' Farewell" (p. 250), both of which show a playful or fanciful surface effect, have a concealed bearing on important elements of human life. In Donne's poem, then, the success of the more direct presentation of the idea is still dependent upon the way in which it is handled, on the total organization and structure of the poem, and not on the mere seriousness or importance of the idea as such.

We should study, then, the way in which the idea is handled and try to define some of the devices.

In the first paragraph, in comparing the poem with "Lucifer in Starlight," we said that it has a certain dramatic context because of the form of a prayer, an address from man to God. This dramatic effect is heightened in various incidental ways. First, the *octave* (*Glossary*) is composed of three questions, each one leading to the next. A question is more provocative than a statement. This is especially true when the linking, as in this case, creates a kind of suspense, rising to a climax with

> . . . in his stern wrath why threatens he?

Then this is answered in the beginning of the sestet, not by a statement, but by another question:

> But who am I, that dare dispute with thee?

Second, the exclamatory effects, which occur twice in the poem, serve to heighten the dramatic quality. A poet must be very careful in using exclamation, for it frequently strikes the reader as an arbitrary attempt to force him to respond; the poet must, that is, be careful of the context and of preparation for his use of exclamation. But observe in this poem how the preparation has been made. The first case occurs in the fourth line with the word "Alas!" Let us shift the use to see what change would follow:

> Alas! if poisonous minerals and that tree.

Or, perhaps a better version:

> Alas! if poisonous minerals, if that tree.

In such cases the exclamation merely serves as a signal to the reader that the poet intends something important, and unless what does follow fulfills that promise the reader feels cheated. Even if the reader feels that the exclamation is justified by what follows, such a use is essentially undramatic because unprepared for. By contrast observe how Donne introduces the exclamatory word just after the idea of damnation has been given, and just before that idea receives a personal application:

> . . . if serpents envious
> Cannot be damned, Alas! why should I be?

It is as though the cry were wrung from some one by the sudden full awareness of the meaning of damnation. The same principle is applied in the second instance. The cry "O God, O!" occurs at the point where the thought of the sonnet turns. The first line of the sestet has just stated that human reason cannot question God. It marks the moment when the man ceases to reason about God's justice and question it, and pleads that the memory of his sin be drowned in Christ's blood and the tears of repentance. In both cases, the use of the exclamation is psychologically justified, and is therefore dramatic.

Third, the idea is worked out in a series of contrasts, a device that, as we have seen, is often used to heighten interest. In the first four lines the lower creation is contrasted with man on the grounds of guilt—the mineral, vegetable, and animal kingdoms as distinguished from man. In the fifth and sixth lines the contrast is made on the grounds of the possession of reason. But these lines also imply a paradox: reason, which presumably is given man to raise him from the brute, is the source of his damnation, which even the brute cannot suffer. In the seventh and eighth lines there is the opposition of God's mercy and God's wrath. In the ninth line, human reason is contrasted with divine justice. In the tenth, eleventh, and twelfth lines, the climax, the method of argument is abandoned, and the man throws himself on the promise of redemption. But in the concluding couplet the whole poem is again summarized with a contrast: though some men, the poet says, have hoped for salvation by praying that God remember them, he himself, reflecting on his sinful state, hopes for salvation by a divine forgetfulness.

All of these devices for heightening the effect of the poem depend on the detailed working out of the idea, that is, on the relating of the logical structure to the psychological and emotional effect desired by the poet. (We can see that such devices are somewhat different from devices such as narrative incident, symbol, simile, and metaphor. This poem makes no use, in fact, of narrative incident to embody its theme, as does "Johnie Armstrong" or "Patterns"; and it seems peculiarly bare of simile and metaphor, which are so important in most poetry). But there are still other ways in which the poet has heightened his statement of the idea. He does not give his contrast between man and the lower creation in general terms, but introduces the idea with concrete instances, "poisonous minerals," "that tree whose fruit threw death," "lecherous goats," and "serpents envious." By taking this approach he has put the reader's imagination to work; the objects named serve to symbolize the idea to a certain extent. Though, as we have said, the poem is peculiarly bare of metaphor, the major metaphor in the poem is very violent and powerful. It seems that the poet, feeling the effectiveness of such a device, has reserved it for his climax, introducing it to focus the idea just stated. The image of the blood of Christ and the tears of the penitent combining to make a flood is very bold, and especially bold in contrast with the more direct method characteristic of the octave.

Let us return now to consider the versification. We may scan the poem as follows:

> If poi | sonous min | erals, | and if | that tree
> Whose fruit | threw death | on else | immor | tal us,
> If lech | erous goats, | if ser | pents en | vious
> Cannot | be damned, | Alas! | why should | I be?
> Why should | intent | or rea | son, born | in me, 5

Make sins, | else e | qual, in | me more | heinous?
And mer | cy be | ing eas | y, and glo | rious
To God, | in his | stern wrath | why threat | ens he?
But who | am I | that dare | dispute | with thee,
O God? | O! of | thine on | ly wor | thy blood 10
And my | tears, make | a heav | enly Le | thean flood,
And drown | in it | my sin's | black mem | ory;
That thou | remem | ber them, | some claim | as debt,
I think | it mer | cy, if | thou wilt | forget.

The poem opens with a calm, logical tone; that is, not with a burst of feeling or excitement, but with the conditional "if," which sets up a logical expectation. The meter of the first four feet of the first line is, appropriately, regular,[1] and the unaccented syllables are very light and at about the same level. But with the last foot of the first line,

that tree,

we have a sudden emphasis with the accentuation of *that.*

In the first two feet of the second line we find the same kind of emphasis, and in addition, the three forced pauses between *whose* and *fruit, fruit* and *threw,* and *threw* and *death.* In other words, the realization of the terrible event in the Garden is supported by the heavy retardation of rhythm and the general cacophony. However, as the thought turns from the terror of the Fall to the wistful "on else immortal us," the meter slips into an easy regularity, with the light syllables very light and even. We have, as it were, a tension and a release, a retardation and a flow.

In the third line the thin, tight texture and the hissing ejective *s*'s associate with the serpent (see comment on "No More Be Grieved," pp. 152–53). The clipped meter of the line is changed to the

[1] We may say that the second foot, -sonous min- is an anapaest, but it is a very light one, readily slurred or absorbed.

spondaic, retarded rhythm of line 4. We may glance particularly at the last two feet:

why should I be?

Here rhetorical consideration would accent *why* and *I,* but meter would accent *should* and *be*. Since *be* is a rhyme word, it must have an accent, and we can't resolve the matter by a trochee. This tension and uncertainty in the accentuation points up the agonized question on which the quatrain concludes.

With the beginning of the second quatrain there is a return to the calm, logical tone, and to a regular meter, but with line 6, as the urgency of the problem begins to return, the spondaic distortions again appear. We may notice also how the meter "spreads" and emphasizes *heinous,* the meter forcing an accent on the normally unaccented second syllable (see the discussion of the word *consecrate* in "Rose Aylmer," p. 147). The first three feet of the next line are regular; then with the last two feet we get a strong, lifting effect. The anapaest

-y, and glo-

cuts across the units of phrasing,[1] the word *glorious* is spread and receives two metrical accents, and the last phrase runs over the end of the line to fulfill itself in the first foot of the next line. Then the triumphant thrust of the phrase "and glorious || To God," is broken, as it were, against the heavy, spondaic passage,

in his stern wrath why threatens he?

The first line of the sestet falls again into a regular movement, as the tension is resolved momentarily into the speaker's resignation.

[1] We may indicate the phrasing by the loops above the line, and the foot grouping by the loops below:

And mercy being easy, and glorious || To God,

The metrical pull has to re-establish itself by absorbing the *y* of easy and the pause at the end of the phrase, and the overcoming of this resistance increases the emphasis. (See the comment on the word *young* in line 7 of "Speech After Long Silence," p. 121.)

This resignation, however, is interrupted by the cry,

O God? O!

with its massed accentuation, which falls away then into regularity. In the last three lines the regularity is interrupted only three times,

with tears, make,

black mem-,

some claim,

and I think.

The logic of the emphasis is, in each instance, obvious. Throughout the passage, as the poem subsides to its conclusion in resignation to God's will, the meter is regular with an even level of accentuation.

We can see that in general, part of line against part of line, or line against line, the poem shows the principle of contrast between acceleration and retardation, lightness and weight, release and tension, and that the contrasts are associated with and emphasize the content. That is, the technical features of the poem help to dramatize the idea and give depth to the feeling.

Death

JOHN DONNE [1573–1631]

Death, be not proud, though some have callèd thee
Mighty and dreadful, for thou art not so;
For those whom thou think'st thou dost overthrow
Die not, poor Death; nor yet canst thou kill me.
From rest and sleep, which but thy picture be, 5
Much pleasure, then from thee much more must flow;
And soonest our best men with thee do go—
Rest of their bones and souls' delivery!
Thou'rt slave to Fate, chance, kings and desperate men,
And dost with poison, war, and sickness dwell, 10
And poppy or charms can make us sleep as well,
And better than thy stroke; why swell'st thou then?
One short sleep past, we wake eternally,
And death shall be no more: Death, thou shalt die!

EXERCISE:

Using the analysis of "If Poisonous Minerals" for a model, write an analysis of this sonnet. In writing your analysis, take into account the following: (1) the personality of death implied by the nature of the poet's argument with him; (2) the variations in the meter; (3) the use of paradox.

Prospice

ROBERT BROWNING [1812–1889]

Fear death? to feel the fog in my throat,
The mist in my face,
When the snows begin, and the blasts denote
I am nearing the place,
The power of the night, the press of the storm, 5
The post of the foe;
Where he stands, the Arch Fear in a visible form,
Yet the strong man must go:
For the journey is done and the summit attained,
And the barriers fall, 10
Though a battle's to fight ere the guerdon be gained,
The reward of it all.
I was ever a fighter, so—one fight more,
The best and the last!
I would hate that death bandaged my eyes, and forbore, 15
And bade me creep past.
No! let me taste the whole of it, fare like my peers
The heroes of old,
Bear the brunt, in a minute pay glad life's arrears
Of pain, darkness and cold. 20
For sudden the worst turns the best to the brave,
The black minute's at end,
And the elements' rage, the fiend-voices that rave,
Shall dwindle, shall blend,
Shall change, shall become first a peace out of pain, 25
Then a light, then thy breast,
O thou soul of my soul! I shall clasp thee again,
And with God be the rest!

EXERCISE:

1. What basic metaphor underlies this poem?

2. Does the poet seem boastful? Does he seem to be talking bravely to counterbalance his own fear? If not, how has he avoided this note? What is the tone of the poem?

3. Discuss the management of the metrical pattern from line 21 to the end of the poem.

4. To whom is the poem addressed?

After Apple-Picking

ROBERT FROST [1875–]

My long two-pointed ladder's sticking through a tree
Toward heaven still,
And there's a barrel that I didn't fill
Beside it, and there may be two or three
Apples I didn't pick upon some bough. 5
But I am done with apple-picking now.
Essence of winter sleep is on the night,
The scent of apples: I am drowsing off.
I cannot rub the strangeness from my sight
I got from looking through a pane of glass 10
I skimmed this morning from the drinking trough
And held against the world of hoary grass.
It melted, and I let it fall and break.
But I was well
Upon my way to sleep before it fell, 15
And I could tell
What form my dreaming was about to take.
Magnified apples appear and disappear,
Stemend and blossomend,
And every fleck of russet showing clear. 20
My instep arch not only keeps the ache,
It keeps the pressure of a ladder-round.
I feel the ladder sway as the boughs bend.
And I keep hearing from the cellar bin
The rumbling sound 25
Of load on load of apples coming in.
For I have had too much

Of apple-picking: I am overtired
Of the great harvest I myself desired.
There were ten thousand thousand fruit to touch, 30
Cherish in hand, lift down, and not let fall.
For all
That struck the earth,
No matter if not bruised or spiked with stubble,
Went surely to the cider-apple heap 35
As of no worth.
One can see what will trouble
This sleep of mine, whatever sleep it is.
Were he not gone,
The woodchuck could say whether it's like his 40
Long sleep, as I describe its coming on,
Or just some human sleep.

The student has already read this poem in Section II where it was placed among a group of descriptive poems. As a realistic account of apple-picking in New England, the poem yields a great deal. The student may well feel that there is little to be gained by going beyond that reading. The poem is an admirable piece of description; the farmer who speaks the poem is simply "overtired" and turns away with a bit of whimsical humor and with an honest weariness to thoughts of sleep.

But as we have already found, a really fine piece of even "realistic" description—a piece of description that engages our feelings and stirs our imaginations—tends to generate symbolic overtones. Such a description is more than an account of physical objects: it suggests, if only vaguely, further experiences. All of this is true of "After Apple-Picking." Furthermore, a second glance at the poem reveals—or should at least now reveal to the student—elements that cannot be readily accommodated to a merely realistic reading of the poem. The first of these elements obtrudes itself in line 7. Up to that point everything *may* be taken at the literal descriptive level.

With line 7 we are forced to consider nonrealistic readings. For one thing, and merely as a kind of preliminary, the word *essence* comes strangely into the poem. It is not the kind of everyday, ordinary word characteristic of the vocabulary of the previous part of the poem. We may have observed how sometimes in poetry the unusual word, unusual in the context if not absolutely, may be a signal, a sign-post.[1] But what of the word here? Here the word *essence* most readily brings in the notion of some sort of perfume, some sort of distillate; but it also involves the philosophical meaning of something permanent and eternal, of some necessary element or substance. The word scent (as contrasted with synonyms such as odor or smell) supports the first idea in *essence,* but the other meanings are there, too, with their philosophical weighting. The scent of apples is a valuable perfume, as it were, but it is also to be associated in some significant way with the "winter sleep." Does the poet merely mean to say that the odor of apples, in a quite literal way, is a characteristic of the harvest season? It *is* a characteristic odor, but the word *essence* hints at something more fundamental.

We notice that a colon comes after the phrase "scent of apples" to introduce the statement, "I am drowsing off." The scent of apples puts to sleep, as it were, the harvester. The next line implies that this is scarcely a normal, literal sleep. The sleep, in fact, had begun that morning with a "strangeness" got from looking through the pane of ice. So somehow the scent of apples and the strangeness of the ice-view combine to produce the "winter sleep."

Then comes the dream. It is true that when we are overtired we tend to repeat in dream the activity that has caused the fatigue, as when after driving all day you see the road still coming at you. There is such a realistic psychological basis for the nature of this dream, but at the same time we must remember that the dream had been previsioned that morning, and dreams that are literal in a literal world don't begin that way.

[1] In "Preludes," by T. S. Eliot (p. 102), we find a good example of this. In Part II, the word *masquerades* stands out in contrast to the very ordinary vocabulary of the preceding and surrounding parts of the poem. It stands out even more when regarded in its phrase—"the other masquerades / That time resumes," an arresting metaphor coming suddenly in a poem that thus far had presented no obviously metaphorical elements. And so in Part III with the metaphor involving the "sordid images" of which the woman's soul is "constituted." In the same section the word *vision* comes with a certain shock. And it, too, is a key word: we must understand the nature of the woman's "vision" in order to understand the poem.

So even before we have got through the poem we are forewarned that it is not to be taken literally, even in the way that Frost's "Desert Places" (p. 86) can be taken literally. In that poem, for example, all the details are in their own right directly descriptive of nature; the snow falling into the dark field does become a kind of metaphorical rendering of the observer's loneliness in the world, but it also remains literal. But the details of "After Apple-Picking" are not like this: they are constantly implying a kind of fantasy.

To go back and take a fresh start with the poem, we see a set of contrasts gradually developing: the world of summer and the world of winter; the world of labor and the world of rest; the world of effort and the world of reward; the world of wakefulness and the world of sleep; the world of ordinary vision and the world distorted by the ice-view; the world of fact and the world of dream. And we understand that these various pairs are various aspects of a single contrast. But a contrast of what? A contrast of two views of experience, of the world in general, of life, if you will. In other words, we take a broad, simple, generalized view of apple-picking and harvest—the end of some human effort in the real world, which is followed by reward, rest, dream. To go one step further, we may say that the contrast is between the actual and the ideal. Now we can look back at the very beginning of the poem and see that what appeared to be but a casual, literal detail—the ladder sticking through a tree—initiates this line of meaning. The ladder is pointing "Toward heaven still." It points, not toward the sky or even the heavens, words that carry merely a literal meaning and in this context would merely say that the ladder was pointing upward; but toward *heaven,* the place of man's rewards, the home of his aspirations, the deposit of perfection and ideal values.

At this point it may be objected that to associate the dream in the poem with the ideal is a peculiar thing, for the dream seems to be a bad dream, a nightmare of the day's labor. But is the dream a nightmare? The poet, it is true, says that he has had too much of apple-picking and is "overtired," and says that his sleep will be "troubled," and says that the instep arch will keep the ache of the ladder-round. Over against these explicit statements, however, we must put the quality of the passage taken as a whole.

We start with the description of the apples:

> Magnified apples appear and disappear,
> Stemend and blossomend,
> And every fleck of russet showing clear.

The apples of reality had been a "good"; now in dream the apples become magnified. Furthermore, though the apples of reality had been a good, they had been a good in a practical sense; now in the dream they come as a good for contemplation—we see them bigger than life, every aspect, stemend and blossomend, every tiny fleck of russet. In the dream there is emancipation from the pressure of work; there can be appreciation of the object as object. Let us consider the words *russet* and *clear*. They are smuggling some kind of plus-value into the dream. *Russet* carries an agreeable, decorative, poetical flavor, and *clear* has all sorts of vague connotations of the desirable, opposed to the turgid, the murky, the dirty, the impure, the confused, etc. Suppose we paraphrase the line,

> And every spot of brown now visible.

We have lost the plus-quality, the sense of the desirable in the apples.

To proceed with the passage, if the ache of the instep arch remains, there is also the line,

> I feel the ladder sway as the boughs bend.

The experience described may be taken in itself as an agreeable one, and in addition the line is euphonius and delicately expressive. Notice the swoop of the anapaest "as the boughs" caught by the solid monosyllabic foot "bend," and brought, as it were, safely to rest. Also notice that though the first three feet are regularly iambic,

> Ĭ féel | thĕ lád | dĕr swáy |,

the phrase "the ladder" gives a kind of sweeping, then falling, movement across the iambic structure, a movement which, again, is brought to rest by an accented monosyllable, "sway." So the rhythmic structure of the line falls into two parts, each with a sweep brought to rest.

Then we have the sound of apples rumbling into the cellar bin. Is this part of a nightmare or of a good dream? We can say that the sound may "trouble" the sleep, but at the same time we must remember that the sound was the signal of the completion of labor, the accomplishing of the harvest. So it brings over into the dream the plus-value of reality. This is not to deny, necessarily, the negative aspect, the troubling effect. It is merely to affirm that both elements are present.

Immediately after the poet has said that he is overtired because there were ten thousand fruit to handle, he uses the word *cherish*. This word, too, smuggles a plus-value into the dream. If the picking was labor, it was a loving labor, not a labor simply for practical reward. It is true that the word is applied to the work in the real world and not to the dream, but it appears in the context of the dream and colors the dream.

We may conclude, then, that though the dream does carry over the fatigue of the real world it also carries over its satisfactions in a magnified form, satisfactions now freed from the urgencies of practical effort—the apples may now be contemplated in their fullness of being. The ideal—if we have accepted the whole cluster of notions on one side of the contrast to amount to that—is not to be understood as something distinct from the actual, from man's literal, experience in the literal world. Rather, it is to be understood as a projection, a development, of the literal experience. When the poet picks his apples he gets his practical reward of apples and gets the satisfaction of a job well done, the fulfilment of his energies and ambitions. But the rest, the reward, the heaven, the dream that come after labor, all repeat, on a grander scale, the nature of the labor. This is not to be taken as a curse, but as a blessing. The dream, as we have seen, is not a nightmare.

We have not yet finished the poem. We still must account for the woodchuck. We notice that here the poet is still working with a contrast, the contrast between the woodchuck's sleep and "just some human sleep." The woodchuck's sleep will be dreamless and untroubled. The woodchuck is simply a part of the nature from which man is set apart. The woodchuck toils not, neither does he dream. Man does work and does dream. He is "troubled," but the trouble is exactly what makes him human and superior to the woodchuck. The word *just,* in the phrase "just some human sleep," gives a faintly ironical understatement to the notion of man's superiority, but this is merely whimsical, a way, not of denying the fact of man's superiority, but of avoiding the embarrassment of making a grandiose claim. It is appropriate that a poem which states the real as the necessary context for the ideal, should not end by making a grandiose claim; the whimsical understatement is a way of indicating a continuing awareness of the real as context of the ideal—of the natural as context of the human.

Some readers may be inclined to say that we have pushed matters too far. They are willing, perhaps, to admit that the poem is not to be taken with absolute literalness. They say that the poem is not merely about apple-picking, but is about life and death as imaged in a set of contrasts: summer-winter; labor-rest; ordinary view and the view seen through the pane of ice. They go on to say that the dream is an image for life-after-death, and indicates the kind of immortality the poet expects and/or wants. They support this notion by reference to the word *heaven* in the second line, and perhaps to the contrast between man and woodchuck (the woodchuck does not dream, i.e., is not immortal).

This reading is still too literal. It takes the ideas of heaven and immortality at their face value, and does not comprehend the broad basic theme. It is true that *if* the poet did believe in immortality, he would by the logic of this poem want an immortality like the dream, and would recognize a continuity between this world and the next. It is conceivable, to be sure, that the poet does accept the idea of immortality, but there is no evidence in the poem that he does (nor, as a matter of fact, elsewhere in Frost's work). And even if the poet did accept the idea of immortality, that fact would not limit the theme; it would in itself be but *one application of the theme,* one illustration of it. All sorts of other applications of the basic idea which is the theme would still exist in relation to the human life of the here and now, a life involving both the real and the ideal.

What would be some of the other and more secular applications of the root-idea or fundamental attitude of the poem? The idea would apply to any ideal that man sets up for himself. An ideal to be valid must stem from the real world, and must not violate it or deny it. For instance, a certain theory of poetry, or of any of the other arts, is implied here. By this theory, poetry should develop from, and treat of, ordinary experience; it should reflect life and the needs and activities of life—it should present the apples magnified, but yet as apples. Or a theory of morality is implied: the ideal of conduct should not deny the human but should fulfil the human. Or a theory of labor and reward is there: reward and labor should not be distinct, the reward coming after, and distinct from, the labor; the reward should be in fulfilment through the labor.

These examples are intended merely to point us back into the poem, to the central impulse and root-idea of the poem. It is a root-idea that we can find developed in certain other poems by Frost, and lying behind many more. For instance, let us take "Mowing":

> There was never a sound beside the wood but one,
> And that was my long scythe whispering to the ground.
> What was it it whispered? I knew not well myself;
> Perhaps it was something about the heat of the sun,
> Something, perhaps, about the lack of sound— 5
> And that was why it whispered and did not speak.
> It was no dream of the gift of idle hours,
> Or easy gold at the hand of fay or elf:
> Anything more than the truth would have seemed too weak
> To the earnest love that laid the swale in rows, 10
> Not without feeble-pointed spikes of flowers
> (Pale orchises), and scared a bright green snake.
> The fact is the sweetest dream that labor knows.
> My long scythe whispered and left the hay to make.

Here the line, "The fact is the sweetest dream that labor knows," might almost be taken as a kind of summing up of "After Apple-Picking." Or we can refer to the last stanza of "Two Tramps in Mud-Time" (p. 566) where "need" and "love," and "work" and "play" take the place of the contrast between "fact" and "dream":

But yield who will to their separation,
My object in living is to unite
My avocation and my vocation
As my two eyes make one in sight.
Only where love and need are one, 5
And the work is play for mortal stakes,
Is the deed ever really done
For Heaven and the future's sakes.

And the same theme appears in "Stopping by Woods on a Snowy Evening" (p. 169), "Come In" (p. 568), and "Birches" (p. 397).

We see here how one poem may help to interpret other poems by the same poet. We recognize a kind of continuity in the poet's work, the presence of a basic idea which can have various formulations.[1] With Frost, however, we have more than the interrelations among the various poems to help us toward interpretations. We have also some prose statements by the author. For instance, we can see the pertinence of the following passage to the discussion of the theme of "After Apple-Picking." Here Frost is comparing his own basic attitudes to those of E. A. Robinson:

I am not the Platonist Robinson was. By Platonist[2] I mean one who believes what we have here is an imperfect copy of what is in heaven. The woman you have is an imperfect copy of some woman in heaven or in somebody else's bed. Many of the world's greatest—maybe all of them—have been ranged on that romantic side. I am philosophically opposed to having one Iseult for my vocation and another for my avocation. . . . Let me not sound the least bit smug. I define a difference with proper humility. A truly gallant Platonist will remain a bachelor as Robinson did from unwillingness to reduce any woman to the condition of being used without being idealized.

To summarize Frost's attitude, we may try something like this: Man is set off from nature because he is capable of the "dream," because he is an ideal-creating being (the woodchuck has no dream). But man is also of nature, he fulfills himself in the world

[1] See the discussion of Wordsworth, pp. 631–45.

[2] Plato held that everything in the world about us was simply an imperfect copy of the perfect "Idea" of the thing, a kind of pattern, which existed in another realm.

of labor and his ideals develop from the real world; he does not get his ideals from some Platonic realm of perfect "Ideas," but must create them from his experience and imagination.

EXERCISE:

1. What is the tone of the poem? The poem, as we have seen, is very rich, and deals with very serious issues. Does the poem ever become oversolemn or pompously philosophical? How has the poet avoided this? What is the function of the whimsical reference to the woodchuck in this connection?

2. Return to the poem "Mowing" quoted above and try to see how the various details are related to the theme. That is, how does the line we have taken as summarizing the poem really develop from the poem?

3. What is the significance of the word *still* in the second line of "After Apple-Picking"?

4. Turn to "Stopping by Woods on a Snowy Evening" (p. 169) and "Come In" (p. 568) and compare the use of the little horse and the bird in those poems with that made of the woodchuck in "After Apple-Picking."

Birches

ROBERT FROST [1875–]

When I see birches bend to left and right
Across the lines of straighter darker trees,
I like to think some boy's been swinging them.
But swinging doesn't bend them down to stay.
Ice-storms do that. Often you must have seen them 5
Loaded with ice a sunny winter morning
After a rain. They click upon themselves
As the breeze rises, and turn many-colored
As the stir cracks and crazes their enamel.
Soon the sun's warmth makes them shed crystal shells 10
Shattering and avalanching on the snow-crust—
Such heaps of broken glass to sweep away
You'd think the inner dome of heaven had fallen.
They are dragged to the withered bracken by the load,

And they seem not to break; though once they are bowed 15
So low for long, they never right themselves:
You may see their trunks arching in the woods
Years afterwards, trailing their leaves on the ground
Like girls on hands and knees that throw their hair
Before them over their heads to dry in the sun. 20
But I was going to say when Truth broke in
With all her matter-of-fact about the ice-storm
I should prefer to have some boy bend them
As he went out and in to fetch the cows—
Some boy too far from town to learn baseball, 25
Whose only play was what he found himself,
Summer or winter, and could play alone.
One by one he subdued his father's trees
By riding them down over and over again
Until he took the stiffness out of them, 30
And not one but hung limp, not one was left
For him to conquer. He learned all there was
To learn about not launching out too soon
And so not carrying the tree away
Clear to the ground. He always kept his poise 35
To the top branches, climbing carefully
With the same pains you use to fill a cup
Up to the brim, and even above the brim.
Then he flung outward, feet first, with a swish,
Kicking his way down through the air to the ground. 40
So was I once myself a swinger of birches.
And so I dream of going back to be.
It's when I'm weary of considerations,
And life is too much like a pathless wood
Where your face burns and tickles with the cobwebs 45
Broken across it, and one eye is weeping
From a twig's having lashed across it open.
I'd like to get away from earth awhile
And then come back to it and begin over.
May no fate willfully misunderstand me 50
And half grant what I wish and snatch me away
Not to return. Earth's the right place for love:
I don't know where it's likely to go better.
I'd like to go by climbing a birch tree,
And climb black branches up a snow-white trunk 55

Toward heaven, till the tree could bear no more,
But dipped its top and set me down again.
That would be good both going and coming back.
One could do worse than be a swinger of birches.

Exercise:

1. Does this poem have a structure? It begins with description (lines 1–20); then goes on to sketch the life of the boy who swings on the birches (lines 21–40); then it proceeds to make some comments on "life." What is the poem about?

2. Compare this poem with "After Apple-Picking" in theme and method. Are the first 40 lines necessary to the statement that this poem makes? What do these lines do specifically?

3. Why has the poet had the word *toward* (line 56) printed in italic? In what senses does the speaker insist upon this word?

4. What is the tone of this poem? Does it contain humor, whimsy, serious comment?

The Vanity of Human Wishes

The Tenth Satire of Juvenal Imitated

SAMUEL JOHNSON [1709–1784]

Let observation with extensive view,
Survey mankind, from China to Peru;
Remark each anxious toil, each eager strife,
And watch the busy scenes of crowded life;
Then say how hope and fear, desire and hate, 5
O'erspread with snares the clouded maze of fate,
Where wav'ring man, betrayed by vent'rous pride,
To tread the dreary paths without a guide;
As treach'rous phantoms in the mist delude,
Shuns fancied ills, or chases airy good. 10
How rarely reason guides the stubborn choice,
Rules the bold hand, or prompts the suppliant voice,
How nations sink, by darling schemes oppress'd,
When vengeance listens to the fool's request.
Fate wings with ev'ry wish th' afflictive dart, 15
Each gift of nature, and each grace of art,

With fatal heat impetuous courage glows,
With fatal sweetness elocution flows,
Impeachment stops the speaker's pow'rful breath,
And restless fire precipitates on death. 20
But scarce observ'd, the knowing and the bold
Fall in the gen'ral massacre of gold;
Wide-wasting pest! that rages unconfin'd,
And crowds with crimes the records of mankind;
For gold his sword the hireling ruffian draws, 25
For gold the hireling judge distorts the laws;
Wealth heap'd on wealth, nor trust nor safety buys,
The dangers gather as the treasures rise.
Let hist'ry tell where rival kings command,
And dubious title shakes the madded land, 30
When statutes glean the refuse of the sword,
How much more safe the vassal than the lord;
Low skulks the hind beneath the rage of pow'r,
And leaves the wealthy traitor in the Tow'r,
Untouch'd his cottage, and his slumbers sound, 35
Tho' confiscation's vultures hover round.
The needy traveller, serene and gay,
Walks the wild heath, and sings his toil away.
Does envy seize thee? crush th' upbraiding joy,
Increase his riches and his peace destroy; 40
Now fears in dire vicissitude invade,
The rustling brake alarms, and quiv'ring shade,
Nor light nor darkness bring his pain relief,
One shows the plunder, and one hides the thief.
Yet still one gen'ral cry the skies assails, 45
And gain and grandeur load the tainted gales;
Few know the toiling statesman's fear or care,
Th' insidious rival and the gaping heir.
Once more, Democritus, arise on earth,
With cheerful wisdom and instructive mirth, 50
See motley life in modern trappings dress'd,
And feed with varied fools th' eternal jest:
Thou who couldst laugh where want enchain'd caprice,
Toil crush'd conceit, and man was of a piece;
Where wealth unlov'd without a mourner died. 55
And scarce a sycophant was fed by pride;

Where ne'er was known the form of mock debate,
Or seen a new-made mayor's unwieldy state;
Where change of fav'rites made no change of laws,
And senates heard before they judg'd a cause; 60
How wouldst thou shake at Britain's modish tribe,
Dart the quick taunt, and edge the piercing gibe?
Attentive truth and nature to descry,
And pierce each scene with philosophic eye.
To thee were solemn toys or empty show, 65
The robes of pleasure and the veils of woe:
All aid the farce, and all thy mirth maintain,
Whose joys are causeless, or whose griefs are vain.
 Such was the scorn that fill'd the sage's mind,
Renew'd at ev'ry glance on humankind; 70
How just that scorn ere yet thy voice declare,
Search every state, and canvass ev'ry pray'r.
 Unnumber'd suppliants crowd Preferment's gate,
Athirst for wealth, and burning to be great;
Delusive Fortune hears th' incessant call, 75
They mount, they shine, evaporate, and fall.
On ev'ry stage the foes of peace attend,
Hate dogs their flight, and insult mocks their end.
Love ends with hope, the sinking statesman's door
Pours in the morning worshiper no more; 80
For growing names the weekly scribbler lies,
To growing wealth the dedicator flies,
From every room descends the painted face,
That hung the bright Palladium of the place,
And smok'd in kitchens, or in auctions sold, 85
To better features yields the frame of gold;
For now no more we trace in ev'ry line
Heroic worth, benevolence divine:
The form distorted justifies the fall,
And detestation rids th' indignant wall. 90
 But will not Britain hear the last appeal,
Sign her foes doom, or guard her fav'rites zeal?
Through Freedom's sons no more remonstrance rings,
Degrading nobles and controlling kings;
Our supple tribes repress their patriot throats, 95
And ask no questions but the price of votes;

With weekly libels and septennial ale,
Their wish is full to riot and to rail.
In full-blown dignity, see Wolsey stand,
Law in his voice, and fortune in his hand: 100
To him the church, the realm, their pow'rs consign,
Thro' him the rays of regal bounty shine,
Turn'd by his nod the stream of honor flows,
His smile alone security bestows:
Still to new heights his restless wishes tow'r, 105
Claim leads to claim, and pow'r advances pow'r;
Till conquest unresisted ceas'd to please,
And rights submitted, left him none to seize.
At length his sov'reign frowns—the train of state
Mark the keen glance, and watch the sign to hate. 110
Where-e'er he turns he meets a stranger's eye,
His suppliants scorn him, and his followers fly;
At once is lost the pride of awful state,
The golden canopy, the glitt'ring plate,
The regal palace, the luxurious board, 115
The liv'ried army, and the menial lord.
With age, with cares, with maladies oppress'd,
He seeks the refuge of monastic rest.
Grief aids disease, remember'd folly stings,
And his last sighs reproach the faith of kings. 120
Speak thou, whose thoughts at humble peace repine,
Shall Wolsey's wealth, with Wolsey's end be thine?
Or liv'st thou now, with safer pride content,
The wisest justice on the banks of Trent?
For why did Wolsey near the steeps of fate, 125
On weak foundations raise th' enormous weight?
Why but to sink beneath misfortune's blow,
With louder ruin to the gulfs below?
What gave great Villiers to th' assassin's knife,
And fixed disease on Harley's closing life? 130
What murder'd Wentworth, and what exil'd Hyde,
By kings protected, and to kings ally'd?
What but their wish indulg'd in courts to shine,
And pow'r too great to keep, or to resign?
When first the college rolls receive his name, 135
The young enthusiast quits his ease for fame;

Through all his veins the fever of renown
Burns from the strong contagion of the gown;
O'er Bodley's dome his future labors spread,
And Bacon's mansion trembles o'er his head. 140
Are these thy views? proceed, illustrious youth,
And virtue guard thee to the throne of Truth!
Yet should thy soul indulge the gen'rous heat,
Till captive Science yields her last retreat;
Should Reason guide thee with her brightest ray, 145
And pour on misty Doubt resistless day;
Should no false Kindness lure to loose delight,
Nor Praise relax, nor Difficulty fright;
Should tempting Novelty thy cell refrain,
And Sloth effuse her opiate fumes in vain; 150
Should Beauty blunt on fops her fatal dart,
Nor claim the triumph of a letter'd heart;
Should no Disease thy torpid veins invade,
Nor Melancholy's phantoms haunt thy shade;
Yet hope not life from grief or danger free, 155
Nor think the doom of man revers'd for thee:
Deign on the passing world to turn thine eyes,
And pause awhile from letters, to be wise;
There mark what ills the scholar's life assail,
Toil, envy, want, the patron, and the jail. 160
See nations slowly wise, and meanly just,
To buried merit raise the tardy bust.
If dreams yet flatter, once again attend,
Hear Lydiat's life,[1] and Galileo's end.
Nor deem, when learning her last prize bestows, 165
The glitt'ring eminence exempt from foes;
See when the vulgar 'scape, despis'd or aw'd,
Rebellion's vengeful talons seize on Laud.
From meaner minds, tho' smaller fines content,
The plunder'd palace or sequester'd rent; 170
Mark'd out by dangerous parts he meets the shock,
And fatal Learning leads him to the block:
Around his tomb let Art and Genius weep,
But hear his death, ye blockheads, hear and sleep.

[1] A mathematician and Biblical scholar of the seventeenth century who died in poverty.

The festal blazes, the triumphal show, 175
The ravish'd standard, and the captive foe,
The senate's thanks, the gazette's pompous tale,
With force resistless o'er the brave prevail.
Such bribes the rapid Greek o'er Asia whirl'd,
For such the steady Romans shook the world; 180
For such in distant lands the Britons shine,
And stain with blood the Danube or the Rhine;
This pow'r has praise, that virtue scarce can warm,
Till fame supplies the universal charm.
Yet Reason frowns on War's unequal game, 185
Where wasted nations raise a single name,
And mortgag'd states their grandsires' wreaths regret,
From age to age in everlasting debt;
Wreaths which at last the dear-bought right convey
To rust on medals, or on stones decay. 190
On what foundation stands the warrior's pride,
How just his hopes let Swedish Charles decide;
A frame of adamant, a soul of fire,
No dangers fright him, and no labors tire;
O'er love, o'er fear, extends his wide domain, 195
Unconquer'd lord of pleasure and of pain;
No joys to him pacific scepters yield,
War sounds the trump, he rushes to the field;
Behold surrounding kings their pow'r combine,
And one capitulate, and one resign; 200
Peace courts his hand, but spreads her charms in vain;
"Think nothing gain'd," he cries, "till nought remain,
On Moscow's walls till Gothic standards fly,
And all be mine beneath the polar sky."
The march begins in military state, 205
And nations on his eye suspended wait;
Stern Famine guards the solitary coast,
And Winter barricades the realms of Frost;
He comes, not want and cold his course delay;—
Hide, blushing Glory, hide Pultowa's day: 210
The vanquish'd hero leaves his broken bands,
And shows his miseries in distant lands;
Condemn'd a needy supplicant to wait,
While ladies interpose, and slaves debate.

But did not Chance at length her error mend? 215
Did no subverted empire mark his end?
Did rival monarchs give the fatal wound?
Or hostile millions press him to the ground?
His fall was destin'd to a barren strand,
A petty fortress, and a dubious hand; 220
He left the name, at which the world grew pale,
To point a moral, or adorn a tale.
All times their scenes of pompous woes afford,
From Persia's tyrant to Bavaria's lord.
In gay hostility, and barb'rous pride, 225
With half mankind embattled at his side,
Great Xerxes comes to seize the certain prey,
And starves exhausted regions in his way;
Attendant Flatt'ry counts his myriads o'er,
Till counted myriads soothe his pride no more; 230
Fresh praise is try'd till madness fires his mind,
The waves he lashes, and enchains the wind;
New pow'rs are claim'd, new pow'rs are still bestow'd,
Till rude resistance lops the spreading god;
The daring Greeks deride the martial show, 235
And heap their valleys with the gaudy foe;
Th' insulted sea with humbler thoughts he gains,
A single skiff to speed his flight remains;
Th' encumber'd oar scarce leaves the dreaded coast
Through purple billows and a floating host. 240
The bold Bavarian, in a luckless hour,
Tries the dread summits of Caesarean pow'r,
With unexpected legions bursts away,
And sees defenseless realms receive his sway;
Short sway! fair Austria spreads her mournful charms, 245
The queen, the beauty, sets the world in arms;
From hill to hill the beacons rousing blaze
Spreads wide the hope of plunder and of praise;
The fierce Croatian, and the wild Hussar,
And all the sons of ravage crowd the war; 250
The baffled prince in honor's flatt'ring bloom
Of hasty greatness finds the fatal doom,
His foes' derision, and his subjects' blame,
And steals to death from anguish and from shame.

Enlarge my life with multitude of days, 255
In health, in sickness, thus the suppliant prays;
Hides from himself his state, and shuns to know,
That life protracted is protracted woe.
Time hovers o'er, impatient to destroy,
And shuts up all the passages of joy: 260
In vain their gifts the bounteous seasons pour,
The fruit autumnal, and the vernal flow'r,
With listless eyes the dotard views the store,
He views, and wonders that they please no more;
Now pall the tasteless meats, and joyless wines, 265
And Luxury with sighs her slave resigns.
Approach, ye minstrels, try the soothing strain,
Diffuse the tuneful lenitives of pain:
No sounds, alas, would touch th' impervious ear,
Though dancing mountains witness'd Orpheus near; 270
Nor lute nor lyre his feeble pow'rs attend,
Nor sweeter music of a virtuous friend,
But everlasting dictates crowd his tongue,
Perversely grave, or positively wrong.
The still returning tale, and ling'ring jest, 275
Perplex the fawning niece and pamper'd guest,
While growing hopes scarce awe the gath'ring sneer,
And scarce a legacy can bribe to hear;
The watchful guests still hint the last offense,
The daughter's petulance, the son's expense, 280
Improve his heady rage with treach'rous skill,
And mould his passions till they make his will.
Unnumbered maladies his joints invade,
Lay siege to life and press the dire blockade;
But unextinguish'd Avarice still remains, 285
And dreaded losses aggravate his pains;
He turns, with anxious heart and crippled hands,
His bonds of debt, and mortgages of lands;
Or views his coffers with suspicious eyes,
Unlocks his gold, and counts it till he dies. 290
But grant, the virtues of a temp'rate prime
Bless with an age exempt from scorn or crime;
An age that melts with unperceiv'd decay,
And glides in modest Innocence away;

Whose peaceful day Benevolence endears, 295
Whose night congratulating Conscience cheers;
The gen'ral fav'rite as the gen'ral friend:
Such age there is, and who shall wish its end?
  Yet ev'n on this her load Misfortune flings,
To press the weary minutes' flagging wings: 300
New sorrow rises as the day returns,
A sister sickens, or a daughter mourns.
Now kindred Merit fills the sable bier,
Now lacerated Friendship claims a tear.
Year chases year, decay pursues decay, 305
Still drops some joy from with'ring life away;
New forms arise, and diff'rent views engage,
Superfluous lags the vet'ran on the stage,
Till pitying Nature signs the last release,
And bids afflicted worth retire to peace. 310
  But few there are whom hours like these await,
Who set unclouded in the gulfs of fate.
From Lydia's monarch should the search descend,
By Solon caution'd to regard his end,
In life's last scene what prodigies surprise, 315
Fears of the brave, and follies of the wise?
From Marlb'rough's eyes the streams of dotage flow,
And Swift expires a driv'ler and a show.
  The teeming mother, anxious for her race,
Begs for each birth the fortune of a face: 320
Yet Vane could tell what ills from beauty spring;
And Sedley curs'd the form that pleas'd a king.
Ye nymphs of rosy lips and radiant eyes,
Whom Pleasure keeps too busy to be wise,
Whom Joys with soft varieties invite, 325
By day the frolic, and the dance by night,
Who frown with vanity, who smile with art,
And ask the latest fashion of the heart,
What care, what rules your heedless charms shall save,
Each nymph your rival, and each youth your slave? 330
Against your fame with fondness hate combines,
The rival batters, and the lover mines.
With distant voice neglected Virtue calls,
Less heard and less, the faint remonstrance falls;

Tir'd with contempt, she quits the slipp'ry reign, 335
And Pride and Prudence take her seat in vain.
In crowd at once, where none the pass defend,
The harmless Freedom, and the private Friend.
The guardians yield, by force superior ply'd;
By Int'rest, Prudence; and by Flatt'ry, Pride. 340
Now beauty falls betray'd, despis'd, distress'd,
And hissing Infamy proclaims the rest.
  Where then shall Hope and Fear their objects find?
Must dull Suspense corrupt the stagnant mind?
Must helpless man, in ignorance sedate, 345
Roll darkling down the torrent of his fate?
Must no dislike alarm, no wishes rise,
No cries attempt the mercies of the skies?
Inquirer, cease, petitions yet remain,
Which heav'n may hear, nor deem religion vain. 350
Still raise for good the supplicating voice,
But leave to heav'n the measure and the choice,
Safe in his pow'r, whose eyes discern afar
The secret ambush of a specious pray'r.
Implore his aid, in his decisions rest, 355
Secure whate'er he gives, he gives the best.
Yet when the sense of sacred presence fires,
And strong devotion to the skies aspires,
Pour forth thy fervors for a healthful mind,
Obedient passions, and a will resign'd; 360
For love, which scarce collective man can fill;
For patient sov'reign o'er transmuted ill;
For faith, that panting for a happier seat,
Counts death kind Nature's signal of retreat:
These goods for man the laws of heav'n ordain, 365
These goods he grants, who grants the pow'r to gain;
With these celestial Wisdom calms the mind,
And makes the happiness she does not find.

EXERCISE:

1. Does this poem present its ideas directly? Is the "form" merely the adornment of a moral "content"? Or are form and content inextricably interwoven? Is the poem rich and dramatic—or is it versified prose? Compare it in this regard with "The Elegy in a Country Churchyard" (p. 375).

2. The poet says that the great career of Charles XII of Sweden serves merely "To point a moral, or adorn a tale" (line 222). Is Johnson merely "pointing a moral" with it? (Does the line suggest that Johnson is quite conscious of what he is doing in this poem?) Does Johnson actually "point" the moral—focusing dramatically the significance of Charles's story? Or does he merely present it as illustration?

3. Compare lines 323–42 with Pope's various treatments of the young beauty in *The Rape of the Lock* (p. 223). Are there any resemblances? What are the differences?

4. What is the tone of this poem? Is it sanctimonious? Pompous? Morally indignant? Cynical? Mockingly scornful? Or what? In this connection discuss the use of paradox, antithesis, and ironical contrasts.

5. Does the poet avoid monotony? How? Discuss his use of personifications. Are they empty and awkward? If not, why not?

6. Make a careful analysis of lines 146 and 354, dealing with imagery, metrics, and the relation of these lines to the lines that precede them.

The Scholar Gipsy

MATTHEW ARNOLD [1822–1888]

"There was very lately a lad in the University of Oxford, who was by his poverty forced to leave his studies there; and at last to join himself to a company of vagabond gipsies. Among these extravagant people, by the insinuating subtilty of his carriage, he quickly got so much of their love and esteem as that they discovered to him their mystery. After he had been a pretty while well exercised in the trade, there chanced to ride by a couple of scholars, who had formerly been of his acquaintance. They quickly spied out their old friend among the gipsies; and he gave them an account of the necessity which drove him to that kind of life, and told them that the people he went with were not such impostors as they were taken for, but that they had a traditional kind of learning among them, and could do wonders by the power of imagination, their fancy binding that of others: that himself had learned much of their art, and when he had compassed the whole secret, he intended, he said, to leave their company, and give the world an account of what he had learned."—Glanvil's *Vanity of Dogmatising,* 1661.

Go, for they call you, Shepherd, from the hill;
Go, Shepherd, and untie the wattled cotes:
No longer leave thy wistful flock unfed,
Nor let thy bawling fellows rack their throats,
Nor the cropped grasses shoot another head. 5
But when the fields are still,
And the tired men and dogs all gone to rest,
And only the white sheep are sometimes seen
Cross and recross the strips of moon-blanched green;
Come, Shepherd, and again begin the quest. 10

Here, where the reaper was at work of late,
In this high field's dark corner, where he leaves
His coat, his basket, and his earthen cruse,
And in the sun all morning binds the sheaves,
Then here, at noon, comes back his stores to use; 15
Here will I sit and wait,
While to my ear from uplands far away
The bleating of the folded flocks is borne,
With distant cries of reapers in the corn—
All the live murmur of a summer's day. 20

Screened is this nook o'er the high, half-reaped field,
And here till sun-down, Shepherd, will I be.
Through the thick corn the scarlet poppies peep,
And round green roots and yellowing stalks I see
Pale pink convolvulus in tendrils creep: 25
And air-swept lindens yield
Their scent, and rustle down their perfumed showers
Of bloom on the bent grass where I am laid,
And bower me from the August sun with shade;
And the eye travels down to Oxford's towers: 30

And near me on the grass lies Glanvil's book—
Come, let me read the oft-read tale again,
The story of that Oxford scholar poor,
Of pregnant parts and quick inventive brain,
Who, tired of knocking at Preferment's door, 35
One summer morn forsook

His friends, and went to learn the Gipsy-lore,
And roamed the world with that wild brotherhood,
And came, as most men deemed, to little good,
But came to Oxford and his friends no more. 40

But once, years after, in the country lanes,
Two scholars whom at college erst he knew
Met him, and of his way of life inquired.
Whereat he answered, that the Gipsy crew,
His mates, had arts to rule as they desired 45
The workings of men's brains;
And they can bind them to what thoughts they will:
"And I," he said, "the secret of their art,
When fully learned, will to the world impart:
But it needs Heaven-sent moments for this skill." 50

This said, he left them, and returned no more,
But rumors hung about the country side
That the lost Scholar long was seen to stray,
Seen by rare glimpses, pensive and tongue-tied,
In hat of antique shape, and cloak of gray, 55
The same the Gipsies wore.
Shepherds had met him on the Hurst in spring;
At some lone alehouse in the Berkshire moors,
On the warm ingle bench, the smock-frocked boors
Had found him seated at their entering. 60

But, mid their drink and clatter, he would fly:
And I myself seem half to know thy looks,
And put the shepherds, Wanderer, on thy trace;
And boys who in lone wheatfields scare the rooks
I ask if thou hast passed their quiet place; 65
Or in my boat I lie
Moored to the cool bank in the summer heats,
'Mid wide grass meadows which the sunshine fills,
And watch the warm green-muffled Cumner hills,
And wonder if thou haunt'st their shy retreats. 70

For most, I know, thou lov'st retired ground.
Thee, at the ferry, Oxford riders blithe
Returning home on summer nights have met

Crossing the stripling Thames at Bablock-hithe,
Trailing in the cool stream thy fingers wet, 75
As the slow punt swings round:
And leaning backwards in a pensive dream,
And fostering in thy lap a heap of flowers
Plucked in shy fields and distant Wychwood bowers,
And thine eyes resting on the moonlit stream: 80

And then they land, and thou art seen no more.
Maidens who from the distant hamlets come
To dance around the Fyfield elm in May,
Oft through the darkening fields have seen thee roam,
Or cross a stile into the public way. 85
Oft thou hast given them store
Of flowers—the frail-leafed, white anemone—
Dark bluebells drenched with dews of summer eves—
And purple orchises with spotted leaves—
But none has words she can report of thee. 90

And, above Godstow Bridge, when hay-time's here
In June, and many a scythe in sunshine flames,
Men who through those wide fields of breezy grass
Where black-winged swallows haunt the glittering Thames,
To bathe in the abandoned lasher pass, 95
Have often passed thee near
Sitting upon the river bank o'ergrown:
Marked thine outlandish garb, thy figure spare,
Thy dark vague eyes, and soft abstracted air;
But, when they came from bathing, thou wert gone. 100

At some lone homestead in the Cumner hills,
Where at her open door the housewife darns,
Thou hast been seen, or hanging on a gate
To watch the threshers in the mossy barns.
Children, who early range these slopes and late 105
For cresses from the rills,
Have known thee watching, all an April day,
The springing pastures and the feeding kine;
And marked thee, when the stars come out and shine,
Through the long dewy grass move slow away. 110

In autumn, on the skirts of Bagley Wood,
Where most the gipsies by the turf-edged way
Pitch their smoked tents, and every bush you see
With scarlet patches tagged and shreds of gray,
Above the forest ground called Thessaly— 115
The blackbird picking food
Sees thee, nor stops his meal, nor fears at all;
So often has he known thee past him stray
Rapt, twirling in thy hand a withered spray,
And waiting for the spark from Heaven to fall. 120

And once, in winter, on the causeway chill
Where home through flooded fields foot-travellers go,
Have I not passed thee on the wooden bridge
Wrapt in thy cloak and battling with the snow,
Thy face towards Hinksey and its wintry ridge? 125
And thou hast climbed the hill
And gained the white brow of the Cumner range,
Turned once to watch, while thick the snow-flakes fall,
The line of festal light in Christ-Church hall—
Then sought thy straw in some sequestered grange. 130

But what—I dream! Two hundred years are flown
Since first thy story ran through Oxford halls,
And the grave Glanvil did the tale inscribe
That thou wert wandered from the studious walls
To learn strange arts, and join a Gipsy tribe: 135
And thou from earth art gone
Long since, and in some quiet churchyard laid;
Some country nook, where o'er thy unknown grave
Tall grasses and white flowering nettles wave—
Under a dark red-fruited yew-tree's shade. 140

—No, no, thou hast not felt the lapse of hours.
For what wears out the life of mortal men?
'Tis that from change to change their being rolls:
'Tis that repeated shocks, again, again,
Exhaust the energy of strongest souls, 145
And numb the elastic powers.

Till having used our nerves with bliss and teen,
And tired upon a thousand schemes our wit,
To the just-pausing Genius we remit
Our worn-out life, and are—what we have been. 150

Thou hast not lived, why should'st thou perish, so?
Thou hadst *one* aim, *one* business, *one* desire:
Else wert thou long since numbered with the dead—
Else hadst thou spent, like other men, thy fire!
The generations of thy peers are fled, 155
And we ourselves shall go;
But thou possessest an immortal lot,
And we imagine thee exempt from age
And living as thou liv'st on Glanvil's page,
Because thou hadst—what we, alas, have not! 160

For early didst thou leave the world, with powers
Fresh, undiverted to the world without,
Firm to their mark, not spent on other things;
Free from the sick fatigue, the languid doubt,
Which much to have tried, in much been baffled, brings.
O life unlike to ours! 166
Who fluctuate idly without term or scope,
Of whom each strives, nor knows for what he strives,
And each half lives a hundred different lives;
Who wait like thee, but not, like thee, in hope. 170

Thou waitest for the spark from Heaven: and we,
Vague half-believers of our casual creeds,
Who never deeply felt, nor clearly will'd,
Whose insight never has borne fruit in deeds,
Whose weak resolves never have been fulfilled; 175
For whom each year we see
Breeds new beginnings, disappointments new;
Who hesitate and falter life away,
And lose to-morrow the ground won to-day—
Ah, do not we, Wanderer, await it too? 180

Yes, we await it, but it still delays,
And then we suffer; and amongst us One,
Who most has suffered, takes dejectedly

His seat upon the intellectual throne;
And all his store of sad experience he 185
Lays bare of wretched days;
Tells us his misery's birth and growth and signs,
And how the dying spark of hope was fed,
And how the breast was sooth'd, and how the head,
And all his hourly varied anodynes. 190

This for our wisest: and we others pine,
And wish the long unhappy dream would end,
And waive all claim to bliss, and try to bear,
With close-lipped Patience for our only friend,
Sad Patience, too near neighbor to Despair: 195
But none has hope like thine.
Thou through the fields and through the woods dost stray,
Roaming the country-side, a truant boy,
Nursing thy project in unclouded joy,
And every doubt long blown by time away. 200

O born in days when wits were fresh and clear,
And life ran gaily as the sparkling Thames;
Before this strange disease of modern life,
With its sick hurry, its divided aims,
Its heads o'ertaxed, its palsied hearts, was rife— 205
Fly hence, our contact fear!
Still fly, plunge deeper in the bowering wood!
Averse, as Dido did with gesture stern
From her false friend's approach in Hades turn,
Wave us away, and keep thy solitude. 210

Still nursing the unconquerable hope,
Still clutching the inviolable shade,
With a free onward impulse brushing through,
By night, the silvered branches of the glade—
Far on the forest-skirts, where none pursue, 215
On some mild pastoral slope
Emerge, and resting on the moonlit pales,
Freshen thy flowers, as in former years,
With dew, or listen with enchanted ears,
From the dark dingles, to the nightingales. 220

But fly our paths, our feverish contact fly!
For strong the infection of our mental strife,
Which, though it gives no bliss, yet spoils for rest;
And we should win thee from thy own fair life,
Like us distracted, and like us unblest. 225
Soon, soon thy cheer would die,
Thy hopes grow timorous, and unfixed thy powers,
And thy clear aims be cross and shifting made:
And then thy glad perennial youth would fade,
Fade, and grow old at last, and die like ours. 230

Then fly our greetings, fly our speech and smiles!
—As some grave Tyrian trader, from the sea,
Descried at sunrise an emerging prow
Lifting the cool-haired creepers stealthily,
The fringes of a southward-facing brow 235
Among the Aegean isles;
And saw the merry Grecian coaster come,
Freighted with amber grapes, and Chian wine,
Green bursting figs, and tunnies steeped in brine;
And knew the intruders on his ancient home, 240

The young light-hearted Masters of the waves;
And snatched his rudder, and shook out more sail,
And day and night held on indignantly
O'er the blue Midland waters with the gale,
Betwixt the Syrtes and soft Sicily, 245
To where the Atlantic raves
Outside the Western Straits, and unbent sails
There, where down cloudy cliffs, through sheets of foam,
Shy traffickers, the dark Iberians come;
And on the beach undid his corded bales. 250

This poem has four sections. The first ends with the third stanza of the poem. The second may be said, perhaps arbitrarily, to end with the fourteenth stanza (line 140). The third section ends with the twenty-third stanza (line 230). The last two stanzas of the poem compose the fourth section. The first of these sections gives a kind of setting, or frame, for the poem. The second section gives the story of the scholar. The third section contrasts the faith and simplicity of the scholar with the doubts and divided aims of Arnold and his age. The fourth summarizes this contrast by an image of the Tyrian and Grecian traders.

In some discussions of this poem the third section (or some part of the third section, for these divisions are somewhat arbitrary) is said to give the "heart of the poem" or to make the "point of the poem." It is perfectly true that in the third section one finds the most explicit statement of the theme of the poem. The poet says that his own age is confused by doubts and lacks the powers which are, like those of the scholar, "Fresh, undiverted to the world without," that it suffers from the "strange disease of modern life," which is full of "sick hurry" and "divided aims." He says that the scholar, as contrasted with the modern world, at least has the "unconquerable hope" of a fulfillment, and should avoid contact with the "strong . . . infection of our mental strife," which destroys faith and purpose. In these matters the statement is absolutely definite, and although the poem does not, appropriately enough, support the statement by a series of arguments, the opinion is as definitely put as in Arnold's various prose statements on the same general subject.

But in comparing any general prose statement of this view with the third section of this poem, we may see certain matters that make for decided differences of effect—meter, rime, the dramatic framework, and the use of incidental comparisons, such as the reference to Dido and Aeneas. These devices tend to make the statement from the poem more imaginatively compelling, and perhaps more memorable, than the prose statement. But these devices do not differentiate the third section of the poem from other sections; what differentiates it from those sections, and gives rise to the statement that it is the "heart of the poem," is the explicitness of statement. But if this explicitness of statement is taken in itself to be the central poetic fact, a great error has been made. If that were true, then a prose paraphrase would have a similar poetic effect.

The question, then, is how the third section is related to the other sections. How do the other sections affect this one and how does this one affect the others in the reader's mind?

Let us assume that the poem were treated entirely in the explicit method characteristic of lines 171–200. If we eliminated from these lines the references to the scholar, and the dramatic framework depending on them, even these lines would be considerably weakened, for there would be no point of focus for the indictment the poet is making, and no symbol or object on which the imagination of the reader could seize. That is, the element of statement is only one factor in giving the effect, even in this section that seems to contain the most explicit statement; only in so far as the statement acts on, and is acted on by, the preceding section, the section of the poem which makes us accept the scholar imaginatively, do we get the full force of the poem. The statement, as a statement, lacks a context until we discover a dramatic form for it: the poet's musing over Glanvil's book that contains the story of the scholar, the series of imagined meetings with the scholar, the address to the scholar and the warning to him to fly, etc. These elements prevent the idea from coming to us as an abstraction. But at the same time, the preceding section has been prevented from being merely a presentation of a quaint character and a curious incident. The character of the gipsy and the incidents woven about him by the poet are interesting, but if the poem should end with that, we would probably have some confusion of mind mixed with our pleasure in Arnold's method of presentation. *The basic imaginative fact of the poem is the making of the scholar into a symbol of a way of life.* Therefore, either the second or the third section of the poem would be greatly impoverished if the other were omitted.

But what of the last section of the poem, the concluding two stanzas? The point, as it were, of the poem has already been made, and made, as we have said, in terms of the symbolic and dramatic reference to the scholar. What, then, does the last section add? The poem could end, and remain a very good poem, with the third stanza from the end, with

> And then thy glad perennial youth would fade,
> Fade, and grow old at last, and die like ours.

But if the poem should end there, it would tend to fall into two long sections (exclusive of the short introductory section) that are closely related poetically, each supporting the other, but which, nevertheless, do not give the poem a final effect of unity. To give the poem this unity the poet has concluded with a rather short, brilliantly presented image that serves as a symbolic summary of the entire poem. This image is introduced by a repetition of the injunction to the scholar to flee contact with modern men: The Tyrian trader, because of the coming of the "merry Grecian coaster," leaves the small and safe Aegean Sea and ventures out into the open Atlantic. So the scholar should avoid the trivial contact and pursue independently his own lonely attempt at truth.

The poet, one might suspect, felt that the poem without these last two stanzas concluded too flatly, with too great a proportion of generalization and statement, and preferred, instead, to leave the reader with a symbol that had absorbed the meaning of these generalizations but, at the same time, directly stimulated the imagination. Many excellent poems do conclude with general statements, for instance Keats's "Ode on a Grecian Urn" and many of Shakespeare's sonnets. But one can observe that in these cases the general statement grows intimately out of a special context—Keats's description of the urn, for instance—and does not come merely as a kind of disconnected comment on life or as an adage. We accept such a general statement, not because we promptly decide that it is true or false, but because we feel that it is justified and interpreted by the more directly imaginative elements to be found in the rest of the poem. A poem, then, may give very good advice to us, or may state what we regard as important truths, but may remain a very bad poem because the writer has been unable to give his statement any imaginative appeal—because, for example, he lacks dramatic force, a strong sense of imagery, or a good ear for the rhythm of verse (pp. 181–83). The mere fact of the abstract truth of a poem, does not make it a good poem, any more surely than does the fact of the writer's personal sincerity (pp. 299–302, 470–71). An example of a poor poem that we know was composed in full personal sincerity is Lowell's "After the Burial" (p. 183).

The opposite line of reasoning may also be taken. It is possible for a reader to derive great pleasure from a poem that does not conform in the opinions stated with the reader's own view. For example, it would be possible for a person who did not share the opinion expressed in Arnold's poem that the nineteenth century was spiritually poorer than the seventeenth century to appreciate

"The Scholar Gipsy." He could do this because Arnold has dramatized the poem so that it may strike him as more than a mere general commentary.

Dover Beach

MATTHEW ARNOLD [1822–1888]

The sea is calm tonight,
The tide is full, the moon lies fair
Upon the straits;—on the French coast the light
Gleams and is gone; the cliffs of England stand,
Glimmering and vast, out in the tranquil bay. 5
Come to the window, sweet is the night-air!
Only, from the long line of spray
Where the sea meets the moon-blanched land,
Listen! you hear the grating roar
Of pebbles which the waves draw back, and fling, 10
At their return, up the high strand,
Begin, and cease, and then again begin,
With tremulous cadence slow, and bring
The eternal note of sadness in.

Sophocles long ago 15
Heard it on the Aegean, and it brought
Into his mind the turbid ebb and flow
Of human misery; we
Find also in the sound a thought,
Hearing it by this distant northern sea. 20

The Sea of Faith
Was once, too, at the full, and round earth's shore
Lay like the folds of a bright girdle furled.
But now I only hear
Its melancholy, long, withdrawing roar, 25
Retreating, to the breath
Of the night-wind, down the vast edges drear
And naked shingles of the world.

Ah, love, let us be true
To one another! for the world, which seems 30

To lie before us like a land of dreams,
So various, so beautiful, so new,
Hath really neither joy, nor love, nor light,
Nor certitude, nor peace, nor help for pain;
And we are here as on a darkling plain 35
Swept with confused alarms of struggle and flight,
Where ignorant armies clash by night.

EXERCISE:

1. The theme of this poem is very similar to the basic theme of "The Scholar Gipsy." Is there any similarity between the two poems in method of presentation and in poetic structure?

2. To whom is the poem addressed?

3. By using the last figure (lines 35–37) does the poet make an abrupt and unjustified shift in imagery? If not, how do you justify the figure?

4. The importance of the sea imagery in this poem is perfectly obvious. How important is it for the meaning of the poem that the scene be flooded with moonlight?

A Poet's Epitaph

WILLIAM WORDSWORTH [1770–1850]

Art thou a Statist in the van
Of public conflicts trained and bred?
—First learn to love one living man;
Then may'st thou think upon the dead.

A lawyer art thou?—draw not nigh! 5
Go, carry to some fitter place
The keenness of that practiced eye,
The hardness of that sallow face.

Art thou a man of purple cheer?
A rosy man, right plump to see? 10
Approach; yet, doctor, not too near,
This grave no cushion is for thee.

Or art thou one of gallant pride,
A soldier and no man of chaff?

Welcome!—but lay thy sword aside, 15
And lean upon a peasant's staff.

Physician art thou?—one, all eyes,
Philosopher!—a fingering slave,
One that would peep and botanize
Upon his mother's grave? 20

Wrapped closely in thy sensual fleece,
O turn aside,—and take, I pray,
That he below may rest in peace,
Thy ever-dwindling soul, away!

A moralist perchance appears; 25
Led, Heaven knows how! to this poor sod:
And he has neither eyes nor ears;
Himself his world, and his own God;

One to whose smooth-rubbed soul can cling
Nor form, nor feeling great or small; 30
A reasoning, self-sufficing thing,
An intellectual all-in-all!

Shut close the door; press down the latch;
Sleep in thy intellectual crust;
Nor lose ten tickings of thy watch 35
Near this unprofitable dust.

But who is he, with modest looks,
And clad in homely russet brown?
He murmurs near the running brooks
A music sweeter than their own. 40

He is retired as noontide dew,
Or fountain in a noon-day grove;
And you must love him ere to you
He will seem worthy of your love.

The outward shows of sky and earth, 45
Of hill and valley, he has viewed;
And impulses of deeper birth
Have come to him in solitude.

In common things that round us lie
Some random truths he can impart,— 50
The harvest of a quiet eye
That broods and sleeps on his own heart.

But he is weak; both man and boy,
Hath been an idler in the land;
Contented if he might enjoy 55
The things which others understand.

—Come hither in thy hour of strength;
Come, weak as is a breaking wave!
Here stretch thy body at full length;
Or build thy house upon this grave. 60

The Scoffers

WILLIAM BLAKE [1757–1827]

Mock on, mock on, Voltaire, Rousseau,
  Mock on, mock on; 'tis all in vain;
You throw the sand against the wind
  And the wind blows it back again.

And every sand becomes a gem 5
  Reflected in the beams divine;
Blown back, they blind the mocking eye,
  But still in Israel's paths they shine.

The atoms of Democritus
  And Newton's particles of light 10
Are sands upon the Red Sea shore,
  Where Israel's tents do shine so bright.

Blake's "Scoffers" and Wordsworth's "A Poet's Epitaph" have similar themes. Both poets are protesting against the supremacy of intellectual abstraction, and place over against it what is usually referred to as "appreciation of spiritual values." They are protesting against the habit of breaking life up into neat and unrelated fragments instead of perceiving it as a whole, and against the habit of conceiving of it exclusively in terms of the intellect rather than in terms of the imagination.

The theme is one on which a good poem may be based, and the theme emerges with sufficient clarity in both poems. A comparison of the two poems, however, will remind us that poems with similar themes may be vastly different.

How does Wordsworth go about making us share with him the theme, not as mere intellectual statement, but as an imaginative experience? He constructs a little framework into which to cast his statement. He states what he has to say as a poet might state it in his epitaph, warning away from his grave those who lack interest in spiritual qualities: thus he warns away the statesman, the lawyer, the scholar, the physicist (physician), and the moralist. On the other hand, he welcomes the soldier, a man of honor and warm feeling, provided he exchanges his sword for a peasant's staff and lays aside his pride; and most of all he welcomes the person who has lived simply and close to nature and who is content if he may enjoy "the things which others understand." Indeed, in his adverse characterizations of the men of intellect and in his favorable description of the lover of nature, he states the basic theme of the poem. With the first class, the poet can feel no kinship; to the second class, he wishes to bequeath his strength and help. And from the form which the statement of the theme takes, there results a subsidiary theme: namely, that poetry is based not on the observation of rules—not on nice calculations—but on warm and loving appreciation of nature.

Now such a framework *may* support a very fine poem; the framework at least indicates an attempt to make an otherwise abstract point concretely and with some dramatic force. Is this particular poem successful? It may be best to defer a consideration of this point until we have examined the structure of Blake's "Scoffers."

Blake also has constructed a dramatic framework to support his theme, and it seems, at least at first glance, to be a far less elaborate and dramatic framework than that which Wordsworth uses. Blake begins abruptly by addressing two of the Scoffers, Voltaire and Rousseau. (It does not matter, in so far as the poem is concerned, whether or not we think that the historical Voltaire and Rousseau, or for that matter Newton and Democritus, are really scoffers against the things of the spirit. The important thing is that Blake felt them so, and should have made out of his indignation against them a fine poem. The poem is to be judged good or bad in terms of itself —not in terms of what we think today is the essential truth with regard to either Voltaire or Rousseau. "Foreword," Section VI, pp. 363–64, and analysis of "The Scholar Gipsy," pp. 416–20.)

Blake taunts the Scoffers with the futility of their mockery. He uses a vivid figure to make his point: they are throwing sand against the wind. The action is that of a madman: though endlessly repeated, it is in vain.

The second stanza gives a further extension of meaning (though the development of the idea is made in terms of the development of the figure). "To throw dust into a person's eyes" is a proverbial image for an attempt at deception. Blake freshens and sharpens the conventional figure by having the wind blow the sand back into the eyes of the would-be deceivers. Blake makes further extensions of the meaning by stating that every "sand" (that is, grain of sand) becomes a gem, and by making the momentarily puzzling statement that the grains of sand shine in *Israel's* path.

The third stanza develops and extends the reference to Israel. Here the sand thrown by the mockers seems to be equated with the sand along the Red Sea shore where Israel camped on the way out of Egypt.

Blake, one sees at once, is not building his poem in terms of a logical chain of ideas, as Wordsworth does. And for this reason, Wordsworth's poem is much clearer for the casual reader. One gets the "prose" meaning of Wordsworth's poem almost at once. But Blake's poem contributes a much sharper shock of emotion, even at a first reading. He gains in force and intensity by pointing to some real people as mockers, Voltaire and Rousseau (though he may lose in clarity, since his reader is compelled to know these characters and to define their meaning in this context). Consider also the opening of the poem. The statement, "Mock on, mock on," is much more powerful than Wordsworth's question, "Art thou a Statist . . . ?" The fact that the various persons in Wordsworth's poem are, after all, only general types and not particular people, makes the irony diffuse and weakens the dramatic effect of the poet's indignation.

Wordsworth's poem, then, is less concentrated in effect than Blake's, though his theme *as a statement* is more easily found. We have then what may seem an odd contrast: at a first reading we understand Wordsworth's poem more easily, but we feel Blake's more intensely. We have already found that poetry insists on more than abstract statement. Blake's poem, if we accept this view of poetry, scores higher than Wordsworth's even on a first reading. But a closer examination will reveal that Blake's poem makes an much more intricate and rich statement than does Wordsworth's.

We have already remarked on the fact that Blake's poem is knit together by its *imagery,* and we have already noted that the image of throwing sand has been made to carry a complex idea.

It is important to notice that the development of the theme is made *through a development of the figure.* The poet implies that nature itself opposes the mocker: the sand blown back, ironically enough, blinds the "mocking eye." And since the sand in reality is performing the service of nature ("Reflected in the beams *divine*"), the poet says that the grains of sand shine like gems. Here, one may notice that Blake keeps hold on the concrete figure. Particles of sand shining in the light do seem to gleam like points of light, and thus give the poet some sort of physical basis for his characterization of the grains as *gems.* This makes his treatment of them as "Reflected in the beams divine," not a mere extravagance of statement, but part of a definite symbolism.

The last stanza picks up and summarizes the meanings already developed. The analytic attitude, the exclusive preoccupation with abstractions, which Blake is protesting against, is represented by the various atomic theories which seem to break up the universe into little separate entities—separate entities which are like the small particles of sand. Blake refers to the founder of the atomic theory in ancient times, Democritus, and to an exponent of the theory in modern times, Newton. Democritus's atoms and Newton's particles of light are seen finally as mere grains of sand on the seashore by which God's chosen people encamp in triumph on their way to the Land of Promise. The sands lying on the shore are a strong image of the inert and worthless and meaningless matter in contrast to Israel's tents shining with God's favoring light. Moreover, far from being a stop or impediment, the sands form the roadway across which they will travel.

Blake has done his thinking in terms of his concrete images; and yet his thinking is much more intricate than is Wordsworth's; but it is also more concentrated and gives a sharper and more forceful experience.

London

WILLIAM BLAKE [1757–1827]

I wander through each chartered street,
Near where the chartered Thames does flow
And mark in every face I meet
Marks of weakness, marks of woe.

In every cry of every man, 5
In every infant's cry of fear,
In every voice; in every ban,
The mind-forged manacles I hear:

How the chimney-sweeper's cry
Every blackening church appalls, 10
And the hapless soldier's sigh
Runs in blood down palace-walls.

But most, through midnight streets I hear
How the youthful harlot's curse
Blasts the new-born infant's tear, 15
And blights with plagues the marriage-hearse.

EXERCISE:

1. What is the meaning of *chartered* in lines 1 and 2? What does the poet gain by repeating *mark* in lines 3 and 4? Does it have the effect of childish repetition? Or what?

2. In the eighteenth century, children were employed as chimney-sweepers. Does this help account for the fact that the chimney-sweeper's cry appalls the church?

3. The speaker says that he hears the "mind-forged manacles" in every cry. In what sense do the various cries mentioned come under

this description? Does the youthful harlot's voice serve as a climax to these cries? How?

Brahma

RALPH WALDO EMERSON [1803–1882]

If the red slayer think he slays,
Or if the slain think he is slain,
They know not well the subtle ways
I keep, and pass, and turn again.

Far or forgot to me is near; 5
Shadow and sunlight are the same;
The vanished gods to me appear;
And one to me are shame and fame.

They reckon ill who leave me out;
When me they fly, I am the wings; 10
I am the doubter and the doubt,
And I the hymn the Brahmin sings.

The strong gods pine for my abode,
And pine in vain the sacred Seven;
But thou, meek lover of the good! 15
Find me, and turn thy back on heaven.

EXERCISE:

Brahma, in philosophic Hinduism, is the impersonal supreme being, the primal source and the ultimate goal of all that exists.

1. Does the poem give vitality and power to this concept?

2. Does the poem state meaningless contradictions or meaningful paradoxes?

And Did Those Feet

WILLIAM BLAKE [1757–1827]

And did those feet in ancient time
Walk upon England's mountains green?
And was the holy Lamb of God
On England's pleasant pastures seen?

And did the countenance divine 5
  Shine forth upon our clouded hills?
And was Jerusalem builded here
  Among these dark Satanic mills?

Bring me my bow of burning gold!
  Bring me my arrows of desire! 10
Bring me my spear! O clouds, unfold!
  Bring me my chariot of fire!

I will not cease from mental fight,
  Nor shall my sword sleep in my hand,
Till we have built Jerusalem 15
  In England's green and pleasant land.

(From *Milton*)

EXERCISE:

1. What are the "dark Satanic mills" in line 8? Has the poet left purposely vague that thing which he proposes to overthrow? Or do other details in the poem ("pleasant pastures," "Jerusalem") serve sufficiently to indicate what the evil is which he proposes to attack?

2. What details has the poet used to dramatize his theme? In particular consider the details of stanza three.

3. How has the poet managed to give the sense of abrupt and impassioned utterance?

The Love Song of J. Alfred Prufrock

T. S. ELIOT [1888–]

S'io credesse che mia risposta fosse
A persona che mai tornasse al mondo,
Questa fiamma staria senza piu scosse.
Ma perciocche giammai di questo fondo
Non torno vivo alcun, s'i'odo il vero,
Senza tema d'infamia ti rispondo.

Let us go then, you and I,
When the evening is spread out against the sky
Like a patient etherized upon a table;

Let us go, through certain half-deserted streets,
The muttering retreats 5
Of restless nights in one-night cheap hotels
And sawdust restaurants with oyster-shells:
Streets that follow like a tedious argument
Of insidious intent
To lead you to an overwhelming question. . . . 10
Oh, do not ask, "What is it?"
Let us go and make our visit.

In the room the women come and go
Talking of Michelangelo.

The yellow fog that rubs its back upon the windowpanes, 15
The yellow smoke that rubs its muzzle on the windowpanes
Licked its tongue into the corners of the evening,
Lingered upon the pools that stand in drains,
Let fall upon its back the soot that falls from chimneys,
Slipped by the terrace, made a sudden leap, 20
And seeing that it was a soft October night,
Curled once about the house, and fell asleep.

And indeed there will be time
For the yellow smoke that slides along the street,
Rubbing its back upon the windowpanes; 25
There will be time, there will be time
To prepare a face to meet the faces that you meet;
There will be time to murder and create,
And time for all the works and days of hands
That lift and drop a question on your plate; 30
Time for you and time for me,
And time yet for a hundred indecisions,
And for a hundred visions and revisions,
Before the taking of a toast and tea.

In the room the women come and go 35
Talking of Michelangelo.

And indeed there will be time
To wonder, "Do I dare?" and, "Do I dare?"
Time to turn back and descend the stair,
With a bald spot in the middle of my hair— 40

(They will say: "How his hair is growing thin!")
My morning coat, my collar mounting firmly to the chin,
My necktie rich and modest, but asserted by a simple pin—
(They will say: "But how his arms and legs are thin!")
Do I dare 45
Disturb the universe?
In a minute there is time
For decisions and revisions which a minute will reverse.

For I have known them all already, known them all:
Have known the evenings, mornings, afternoons, 50
I have measured out my life with coffee spoons;
I know the voices dying with a dying fall
Beneath the music from a farther room.
 So how should I presume?

And I have known the eyes already, known them all— 55
The eyes that fix you in a formulated phrase,
And when I am formulated, sprawling on a pin,
When I am pinned and wriggling on the wall,
Then how should I begin
To spit out all the butt-ends of my days and ways? 60
 And how should I presume?

And I have known the arms already, known them all—
Arms that are braceleted and white and bare
(But in the lamplight, downed with light brown hair!)
Is it perfume from a dress 65
That makes me so digress?
Arms that lie along a table, or wrap about a shawl.
 And should I then presume?
 And how should I begin?

. . .

Shall I say, I have gone at dusk through narrow streets 70
And watched the smoke that rises from the pipes
Of lonely men in shirt-sleeves, leaning out of windows? . . .

I should have been a pair of ragged claws
Scuttling across the floors of silent seas.

. . .

And the afternoon, the evening, sleeps so peacefully! 75
Smoothed by long fingers,
Asleep . . . tired . . . or it malingers,
Stretched on the floor, here beside you and me.
Should I, after tea and cakes and ices,
Have the strength to force the moment to its crisis? 80
But though I have wept and fasted, wept and prayed,
Though I have seen my head (grown slightly bald) brought in
upon a platter,
I am no prophet—and here's no great matter;
I have seen the moment of my greatness flicker,
And I have seen the eternal Footman hold my coat, and snicker,
And in short, I was afraid. 86

And would it have been worth it, after all,
After the cups, the marmalade, the tea,
Among the porcelain, among some talk of you and me,
Would it have been worth while, 90
To have bitten off the matter with a smile,
To have squeezed the universe into a ball
To roll it toward some overwhelming question,
To say: "I am Lazarus, come from the dead,
Come back to tell you all, I shall tell you all"— 95
If one, settling a pillow by her head,
Should say: "That is not what I meant at all;
That is not it, at all."

And would it have been worth it, after all,
Would it have been worth while, 100
After the sunsets and the dooryards and the sprinkled streets,
After the novels, after the teacups, after the skirts that trail along
the floor—
And this, and so much more?—
It is impossible to say just what I mean!
But as if a magic lantern threw the nerves in patterns on a screen:
Would it have been worth while 106
If one, settling a pillow or throwing off a shawl,
And turning toward the window, should say:
"That is not it at all,
That is not what I meant, at all." 110

. . .

No! I am not Prince Hamlet, nor was meant to be;
Am an attendant lord, one that will do
To swell a progress, start a scene or two,
Advise the prince; no doubt, an easy tool,
Deferential, glad to be of use, 115
Politic, cautious, and meticulous;
Full of high sentence, but a bit obtuse;
At times, indeed, almost ridiculous—
Almost, at times, the Fool.

I grow old . . . I grow old . . . 120
I shall wear the bottoms of my trousers rolled.

Shall I part my hair behind? Do I dare to eat a peach?
I shall wear white flannel trousers, and walk upon the beach.
I have heard the mermaids singing, each to each.

I do not think that they will sing to me. 125

I have seen them riding seaward on the waves
Combing the white hair of the waves blown back
When the wind blows the water white and black.

We have lingered in the chambers of the sea
By sea-girls wreathed with seaweed red and brown 130
Till human voices wake us, and we drown.

This poem is a dramatic monologue. As in Tennyson's "Ulysses" (p. 67) or Amy Lowell's "Patterns" (p. 55), a person utters a speech that implies his story and reveals his character. The implication of the story is fairly clear in the poems by Tennyson and Amy Lowell and the revelation is fairly simple, but in both the reader must depend to some extent upon his imagination to fill in what is unsaid. In "The Love Song of J. Alfred Prufrock" the reader must assume even more responsibility for filling in the unsaid. For one thing, the events are not as fully indicated in Eliot's poem as in the others, but for another and more important thing, the continuity is not as clear. In neither "Ulysses" nor "Patterns" are the transitions always strictly logical. Sometimes the speaker moves from one aspect of the subject to another by a process of association. One thing suggests another in the flow of consciousness. But the transitions in Prufrock's utterance are more violent, at first glance more unjustifiable. But can we make sense of them? Is the poem a mere jumble?

It is obviously not a mere jumble, for upon early reading a general impression of Prufrock comes through. He is a middle-aged man, somewhat over-sensitive and timid, yearning and procrastinating, fearful that life has passed him by and yet somehow resigned to the fact, very much a creature of his world of drawing rooms and yet feeling a vague dissatisfaction with that world. But only a closer inspection will give us the full significance of many details in the poem and permit us to realize the implications of the whole poem. To make this inspection, let us take up points in their order.

Who is the "you" of the poem? It is the same "you" who appears in many other poems, the generalized reader. But in this poem, the "you" is a little more—the person to whom Prufrock wishes to make his revelation, to tell his secret. In the end we shall return to this question.

The time is evening, when the "you" is invited to make the visit, and this evening world becomes more and more important as the poem proceeds. It is a world of neither night nor day. Twilight is the atmosphere of the poem. It is an evening "Like a patient etherized upon a table," and with this image the twilight world becomes also the world of twilight in another way, the realm between life and death. Here, too, enters the notion of a sick world, the atmosphere of the operating room: and we can say that, in one sense, Prufrock is performing an operation, or at least making a clinical examination. (The patient, however, is himself as well as his world.) He is seeking the answer to a question—the "overwhelming question," which the "you" must not ask about but can understand only by making his visit, by seeing Prufrock's world.

To reach Prufrock's proper world, the "you" must pass through a slum section of sinister streets. This provides the setting for Prufrock's world, a contrast that becomes more important later in the poem, but which for the moment points up the triviality of the conversation of the women upon whom we suddenly come. This is not to say that the subject of their conversation is trivial. On the contrary, the subject, Michelangelo, is in contrast with the triviality of the women, for he, a man of violent personality and an artist of epic grandeur, and furthermore an almost typical figure of the great creative period of the Renaissance, would scarcely be at home with the women of Prufrock's world.

With lines 15 to 22 we find more of the twilight atmosphere of the poem. But there is some development here, for the settling down of the smoke and fog tends to emphasize the isolation of the drawing room from the outside world. In addition, the image of the housecat falling asleep involves the relaxed, aimless quality of Prufrock's world.

In the next section (lines 23–34) two new motifs enter the poem, the motif of time and that of appearance-and-reality. For the first, there will be time for some great, as yet unnamed, decision to settle the "overwhelming question"—for the "visions and revisions." The word *vision* here is important, for it implies the possibility of some fundamental insight, a flash of truth, a glimpse of beauty. Mystics, saint, seers, poets have "visions." But this word is played off against *revision,* with its implication of the second thought, the calculated change, etc. For the second motif of this section, we see that Prufrock prepares a mask for the world. He cannot face the world directly, there is a need for disguise.

What this need is, does not yet emerge, but in the next section (lines 37–48) we see that the disguise is prompted by fear of the mocking, inimical eyes of the world that will avidly note all defects and failings. And here, too, the time motif changes its emphasis. In the section before, there was enough time to allow for postponement of vital decision, but now mixed with that idea is the idea of the closing in of time, of age. With this sense of the closing in of time, and with the fear, does Prufrock dare disturb the universe with the significant question?

The next three sections (lines 49–69) further explain why Prufrock may not disturb the universe. First, he himself belongs to that world, and therefore it would be a presumption for him to criticize it. On what grounds could he, the perfect product of that world, enervated by its sense of fatuity, offer a judgment against it? Second, he fears the world, and again the inimical eyes appear. This fear would prevent him from changing his "days and ways."

The last of these three sections (lines 62–69) has the same outline, as it were, as the other two: I have known this world, etc., therefore, how should I presume? But the content is new, the arms and the perfume, and cannot be accounted for as merely details of the Prufrock world. After all, the poem is called a "love song," and there has been no love story thus far. Now, not a woman, but women enter significantly. Prufrock is attracted by the sight of the bare arms, by the whiff of perfume, but in the midst of the lines recording the romantic attraction, we find the more realistic observation put as a parenthesis:

> But in the lamplight, downed with light brown hair!

Is this a mere observation, or does it indicate something about Prufrock? The fact that the observation of the "real" arms is put in contrast with the "romantic" arms, modifies the attraction: against the attraction there is a hint of revulsion, a hint of neurotic repudiation of the real, the physical. In the face of this situation, how should Prufrock "begin"?

The next five lines (70–74), which are a kind of interpolation, develop the "love" motif. Prufrock remembers having passed through the mean streets and slums, as in the opening of the poem, and having seen the lonely men there, the old derelicts and discards of society. Why is this recollection relevant here? Why does it come now into Prufrock's mind, and into the poem? Prufrock, too, is a lonely man, a derelict and a discard, and he suddenly feels an identification with those other lonely men. But at the same time his condition is in contrast to theirs. They are lonely because of poverty, bad luck, sickness, or age, while Prufrock is lonely because of some shrinking from, and repudiation of, life.

This reading is supported by the lines about the ragged claws. The claws come as a kind of embodiment of blind appetite, the opposite end of the scale from the over-refined and neurotic existence of Prufrock. But Prufrock, in his despair, would prefer that life of the claws, no matter how low and rudimentary, merely because it *is* life and is purposeful. Both the glimpse of the slum and of the primitive sea-floor are in contrast with the Prufrock world; and we may notice how, with line 70, a flat, prosaic rhythm appears, very different from the fluent, relaxed rhythm characteristic of the rest of the poem.

With line 75, we return to the drawing room and the etherized, peaceful twilight world in which Prufrock does not have the strength to force the "crisis," the overwhelming question. The motif that dominates the section is the time motif, the sense of physical decay and impending death, the sense of there being, not too much time, but not enough time. In this sense of time having run out Prufrock's agony now seems of no account; it has led to nothing. He admits that he is no prophet, no announcer of a new dispensation like John the Baptist. And in the reference to John the Baptist we catch also an allusion to the love story, for the prophet's death was demanded by Salome because he had rejected her love: Prufrock, too, has rejected love, but not because he is a prophet with a burning message and faith. He is merely a product of his world, where even Death is a kind of footman who holds the coat and snickers at the slightly ridiculous guest. Even Prufrock's death will lack dignity and meaning.

In the two sections from line 87 to line 110 Prufrock asks would it have been worth it, even if he had forced the crisis. But what would the crisis have been? It seems to involve the love story, it involves some understanding with a woman. We have an allusion to Marvell's love poem "To His Coy Mistress" (p. 320) in the line "To have squeezed the universe into a ball." Marvell's lovers would squeeze up their strength and sweetness into a supreme moment, but with Prufrock it is the universe which is to be rolled toward the "overwhelming question." In other words, with Prufrock it is not merely the personal relationship, but the meaning of the world, of life, that is involved. But the two are to be somehow related: the personal relationship cannot be significant if life is without significance.

Prufrock, if he had been able to force the crisis, would have seemed, he feels, like Lazarus come from the dead. Let us examine what is implied in the allusion. There are two characters by this name in the Bible. One is the beggar (*Luke,* 16) who lay at the rich man's gate, and the other is the brother of Mary and Martha who died and was raised by Jesus (*John,* 11). When the first Lazarus died he was carried by angels to Abraham's bosom, while the rich man was sent to hell. The rich man, seeing Lazarus happy, asked that Lazarus be sent to give him water. When Abraham replied that this was impossible, the rich man asked that at least Lazarus be sent to warn the rich man's five brothers that they might not come to hell for their lack of charity. Abraham replied that the brothers already had the prophets.

And he [the rich man] said, Nay, father Abraham: but if one went unto them from the dead, they will repent.

And he [Abraham] said unto him, If they hear not Moses and the prophets, neither will they be persuaded, though one rose from the dead.

So both references involve a return from the dead, and we may say that elements of both are suggested by the allusion. To return from the dead would be for Prufrock to awaken from his meaningless existence. To tell all, as related to the raising of Lazarus by Jesus, would be to tell what it is like to be dead, to report the horror. In relation to the other Lazarus story, to tell all would mean to utter the warning to repentance. The story of the beggar Lazarus seems to have a little more weight in the allusion than the story of the other Lazarus. The warning from Prufrock, like that given to the rich men by the beggar Lazarus, would not be heeded by the lady of the drawing room; she simply would not understand what Prufrock was talking about if he should raise the "overwhelming question." (Neither of the Biblical stories gives an exact parallel to Prufrock's situation, for in the one from the *Gospel of John* the importance of the risen Lazarus to the living is not stressed, and in the one from the *Gospel of Luke,* the dead man, unlike Prufrock, is called back from bliss to the world. But the general import of the allusion is clear, and that is what matters.)

With the realization that even if he had had the strength to raise the question the lady would not have understood him, Prufrock is struck again by his own inadequacy. He is not Prince Hamlet (lines 111–120). Hamlet suffered doubt and despair. Hamlet brought an "overwhelming question" to Ophelia, who could not understand what he meant. Hamlet postponed decisive action. But there the parallel ends. Hamlet struggled grandly and passionately with his problem. He was not a victim of neurotic shrinking and timidity. The world he confronted was evil and violent, it was not twilit and relaxed. The play *Hamlet,* like the work of Michelangelo, belongs to a great creative period in history, and the mere reference evokes that world in contrast to Prufrock's world. Prufrock, with sad self-irony, sees all this, and knows that if he corresponds to any character in the play it is to the sententious, empty, old Polonius, the sycophantic Rosenkranz, or the silly, foppish Osric. Perhaps—though there is no fool in *Hamlet*—to the fool, that stock character of many Elizabethan tragedies.

So with line 121 we see Prufrock resigned to his rôle, resigned to the fact that he will never raise the overwhelming question, resigned to the fact of age which has overtaken his postponements. With this reference to the motif of time, we see him as an aging man on the beach wistfully watching the girls, who have no attention to spare for him. Suddenly this scene is transformed into a vision of beauty and vitality, in contrast to the world Prufrock has inhabited. The girls become mermaids, as it were, riding triumphantly and effortlessly seaward into their natural creative element. (We may notice how this refers also to the sea of the ragged claws: the brute vitality and the vision of beauty are both aspects of the sea, the life-source.)

The concluding reference to the mermaids (lines 129–31) gives us a kind of odd reversion to Prufrock's original situation: he has "lingered," not in the drawing-room surrounded by the women talking of Michelangelo, but in the "chambers of the sea," surrounded by "sea-girls." But such an experience can occur only in dream: "human voices wake us. . . ." And to wake is to return to the human world—is to suffocate and die: ". . . and we drown."

The concluding image thus summarizes brilliantly Prufrock's character and his plight: he can immerse himself in the life-giving sea only in dream, and even in that dream, it is essentially his passive, negative self that is projected: *he* does not ride "seaward on the waves"; he lingers in the "chambers"—he is wreathed by the "sea-girls." Yet, though he cannot live in the sea, or in a romantic dream of the sea, his desiccated "human" world suffocates him. He is a fish out of water indeed.

Is this poem merely a character sketch, the ironical self-revelation of a neurotic "case"? Or does the poem carry more? And if it does carry more, how are we to get at it? For one thing, we notice the sudden use of "we" in the last three lines of the poem. Prufrock has generalized the situation; not only himself but others are in the same predicament. Further, much is made of Prufrock's world —it is a meaningless world of half-lights and shadows, the world of an ether dream, and it is set in another world, the defeated world of the slum. But there is another indication that a generalized application is involved. The epigraph with which Eliot introduces the poem, from Dante's *Divine Comedy,* is part of a speech by Guido da Montefeltro, who is one of the damned in the Inferno. He speaks from his flame: "If I believed that my answer were to someone who might ever go back to the world, this flame would shake no more.[1] But since, if I hear truth, no one ever returned alive from this pit, I respond to you without fear of infamy." Guido thinks that Dante, to whom the words are addressed, is damned too; therefore, since Dante cannot go back to the world to report it, Guido does not mind telling his own story, exposing his infamy. So the epigraph is but a way of saying that Prufrock is like Guido, the damned man who speaks from his flame; but he speaks to the "you" of the poem —the reader—only because he takes the reader to be damned too, to belong to the same world and to share the same disease. It is the disease of loss of conviction, of loss of faith in the meaning of life, of loss of creativity of all kinds, of feeble purpose, of neurotic self-absorption. So the poem, in the end, is not about poor Prufrock. He is merely a symbol for a general disease, the disease which Matthew Arnold has written about in "The Scholar Gipsy" (p. 409) and "Dover Beach" (p. 420).

The reference to Matthew Arnold's poems on the same general theme suggests an observation, the difference between Eliot and Arnold. Arnold is fairly direct, especially in "The Scholar Gipsy," where a large part reads almost like a versified essay, but Eliot is very indirect, very abrupt in his transitions, very chary of general

[1] In the circle in the Inferno reserved for counselors of fraud and deceit, each of the damned is closed within a great flame, and when the damned speaks the voice issues from the tip of the flame, which thereupon shakes and wavers like a tongue.

statements and applications. We might say that Arnold's poem consists of two large images, that of the Gipsy and that of the Tyrian trader, with the application or interpretation, and that Eliot's poem is all one image, all Prufrock as it were, and that we have to make the application from hints buried in the poem and in the epigraph. Eliot's method is more dramatic; we see the person revealing himself and gradually see the revelation of the person becoming the revelation of a world. Arnold is primarily concerned with the idea, while Eliot is concerned with the mutual relation of the idea and a personality. The difference in concern implies the difference in method.

Furthermore, "Prufrock" is an ironical poem. It is ironical that Prufrock should expose himself. There is an irony in that he can see his predicament but cannot act to remedy it. There is an irony in his self-deprecation. He cannot claim too much, even for his despair: he is not Prince Hamlet. Irony is an awareness of the limits of response, an understating of response, a refusal to make exaggerations. Sentimentality, as we have said, is the exaggeration of response. This sounds as if irony were a kind of automatic salvation from sentimentality, but things are not that easy and simple. Irony can become a mere mannerism, a mere mechanical juggling of opposites and contrasts. To judge the acceptable limits of response for any situation we must come back, on the one hand, to our own common sense experience of the world, and on the other hand, to the context in the poem or other literary work that we are discussing. When King Lear and Cordelia are reunited the effect is not sentimental because of the background of experience: Lear's remorse and his new attitude toward the world are merely finding here an appropriate expression. Wordsworth's "Michael" (p. 23) is not a sentimental poem because we have been led to understand the father's attachment to his land and his son. Marvell's "Definition of Love" (p. 293), though it makes very elaborate claims for the love celebrated, is not sentimental. The tone is, as we have indicated on p. 295, calm and reasoned. Large, direct, simple statements, not in the least "ironical" as we commonly use that term, may constitute fine poetry which avoids every trace of sentimentality. But in such instances we shall always find that these direct statements develop out of implied or presented contexts which justify them. There is no rule of thumb in such matters. Each instance must be studied independently. (See also the discussion of this matter on pp. 380–83.)

As for "Prufrock," first, the irony is in keeping with the character. Prufrock is intelligent; he does see around and beyond himself; he sees his own failure in a perspective. Furthermore, Eliot the poet, as distinguished from the dramatic character in the poem, wants to make the point that the modern damnation is not a grand damnation: Prufrock is not to be taken too seriously, he is comic as well as tragic. It is easy to be self-pitying and over-serious about one's damnation, and Eliot would deprive the modern "you" of that satisfaction.

There are many shades of irony, and sometimes the direct statement or presentation that is meant to be taken with full seriousness may be accompanied by some irony, perhaps the merest flicker, to indicate that the poet, in making his statement, is still aware of other possible attitudes toward the subject. Or the weight may be shifted heavily toward the negative aspect of the statement, so that we feel it merely as a bitter, sardonic jest. Between these extremes there are all sorts of intermediate shades, shadings as complex and various as those in Campion's "Blame Not My Cheeks" (p. 187), Ransom's "Winter Remembered" (p. 191), Hardy's "Channel Firing" (p. 163), Frost's "After Apple-Picking" (p. 388) or Robinson's "Mr. Flood's Party" (p. 171). Irony, in skillful hands is a very subtle and delicate instrument. It is not to be taken as indicating merely the negative and destructive attitudes, but as an indication of an awareness of the complication and depth of experience. The affirmative statement that comes out of the ironical context may shine all the more bright for that context.

One last question may be glanced at, that raised by the literary allusions in the poem. If we do not get the allusions, we miss things more or less important to the whole poem. But has the poet a right to expect this knowledge on the part of the reader? Perhaps the best way to answer this question is, for the moment, to look at what has been the practice of poets. For centuries we find that poets, or at least a great many of them, have used literary, historical, and mythological allusions. They have felt themselves to belong to a certain broad cultural group in which certain things were common property. They felt that their society had a certain available inheritance. This is not to say that every reader would get every allusion but merely to say that certain kinds of references were available and significant. For instance, Milton's "Lycidas" (p. 465), as well as his epics, uses many allusions. So does Blake's "Scoffers" (p. 423). Housman's poetry, though seemingly so simple, is frequently packed with echoes of other literature, as, for example, in "The Immortal Part" (facing p. 617); if we miss them, the effect is poorer.

When we come to read traditional literature, we usually find that all the allusions have been cleared up for us, that generations of editors and scholars have prepared the texts and given us notes and comments. The fact that the poet originally used allusions therefore does not disturb us. We have been accustomed to it from school days. We tend, however, to take a different attitude when we confront a poem, like "Prufrock," by a contemporary poet. We feel that we ought to get it more easily and more immediately. If we do not have already at our disposal the necessary information, we are inclined to think that the poet is willful or perverse or proud of his learning. It is perfectly true that poets sometimes are willful and perverse and proud of their learning. But can we, on the other hand, take our own ignorance at any given moment to be the norm of poetry? If we are not willing to make that rather conceited assumption, then it is our responsibility to try to remedy our ignorance. The critics and scholars are there to help us. Then we can try to see if the allusions in a particular poem are really functional, if they really do something for the poem.

In "Prufrock," for instance, is the reference to Michelangelo a perverse parade of learning? We may not know much about him, but if we find out, we may be inclined to agree that by this reference Eliot has accomplished something not possible otherwise: he has quickly and dramatically introduced a significant contrast into the poem. Or with Lazarus he has implied a group of ideas immediately relevant but also useful by establishing a long perspective on the lady who does not understand: she is suddenly equated with the rich brothers who would not listen to Moses and the prophets. Furthermore, we may agree that the allusions are "in character" with the man Prufrock. He is a cultivated man, and one of the implied ironies is that he has lived only in the secondhand life of the past and not in the present on his own account. He sees himself in contrast with the force and creativity of the past.

We cannot lay down any fixed rule for the permissible number or difficulty of allusions. There are many kinds of poetry in this respect, ranging from folk ballads or the songs of Robert Burns to "The Waste Land," by T. S. Eliot (p. 506), in which allusion is made into a system. We can only try to see if the allusions in any particular poem really accomplish something for the poem and are not willful. And here we must remind ourselves that the reading of any poetry requires some preparation. We must be ready for it. All our life and education is the preparation we bring to the poem which we can understand and appreciate today. If today we can read Shakespeare with pleasure, it is only because we have educated ourselves to it.

The Return

JOHN PEALE BISHOP [1892–1944]

Night and we heard heavy and cadenced hoofbeats
Of troops departing: the last cohorts left
By the North Gate. That night some listened late
Leaning their eyelids toward Septentrion.

Morning flared and the young tore down the trophies 5
And warring ornaments: arches were strong
And in the sun but stone; no longer conquests
Circled our columns; all our state was down

In fragments. In the dust, old men with tufted
Eyebrows whiter than sunbaked faces gulped 10
As it fell. But they no more than we remembered
The old sea-fights, the soldiers' names and sculptors'.

We did not know the end was coming: nor why
It came; only that long before the end
Were many wanted to die. Then vultures starved 15
And sailed more slowly in the sky.

We still had taxes. Salt was high. The soldiers
Gone. Now there was much drinking and lewd
Houses all night loud with riot. But only
For a time. Soon the taverns had no roofs. 20

Strangely it was the young, the almost boys,
Who first abandoned hope; the old still lived
A little, at last a little lived in eyes.
It was the young whose child did not survive.

Some slept beneath the simulacra, until 25
The gods' faces froze. Then was fear.
Some had response in dreams, but morning restored
Interrogation. Then O then, O ruins!

Temples of Neptune invaded by the sea
And dolphins streaked like streams sportive 30
As sunlight rode and over the rushing floors
The sea unfurled and what was blue raced silver.

EXERCISE:

1. In this poem a Roman setting is suggested. But is the poem an account of the breakdown of Roman civilization? Or has the poet sought to give the poem a more general and wider reference? If so, how has he done this?

2. Investigate the details which the poet has chosen to give. On what principle have they been selected?

3. Why did the poet in line 29 write "Temples of Neptune" rather than, say, "Temples of Jupiter" or "Temples of Mars"? What is the meaning of this last stanza? Does it serve as a climactic summary of the poem?

The March into Virginia

ENDING IN THE FIRST MANASSAS
(July 1861)

HERMAN MELVILLE [1819–1891]

Did all the lets and bars appear
To every just or larger end,

Whence should come the trust and cheer?
  Youth must its ignorant impulse lend—
Age finds place in the rear. 5
  All wars are boyish, and are fought by boys,
The champions and enthusiasts of the state:
  Turbid ardours and vain joys
    Not barrenly abate—
  Stimulants to the power mature, 10
    Preparatives of fate.

Who here forecasteth the event?
What heart but spurns at precedent
And warnings of the wise,
Contemned foreclosures of surprise? 15
The banners play, the bugles call,
The air is blue and prodigal.
  No berrying party, pleasure-wooed,
No picnic party in the May,
Ever went less loth than they 20
  Into that leafy neighborhood.
In Bacchic glee they file toward Fate,
Moloch's uninitiate;
Expectancy, and glad surmise
Of battle's unknown mysteries. 25

All they feel is this: 'tis glory,
A rapture sharp, though transitory,
Yet lasting in belaurelled story.
So they gaily go to fight,
Chatting left and laughing right. 30

But some who this blithe mood present,
  As on in lightsome files they fare,
Shall die experienced ere three days are spent—
  Perish, enlightened by the volleyed glare;
Or shame survive, and, like to adamant, 35
  The throe of Second Manassas share.

EXERCISE:

1. What is the quality of irony in this poem? The speaker is not mocking the young soldiers, though he sees through their callowness. What, precisely, is his attitude toward them?

2. What shifts of tone occur in the poem? How are they indicated?

3. Note the change in rhythm in the third stanza. What effect does it have on the tone?

4. What weight does the poet place upon *Second* Manassas? How does this last line relate to the subtitle of the poem?

5. What does this poem "say" about war? About soldiers? About the human being in crisis?

Frescoes for Mr. Rockefeller's City

ARCHIBALD MACLEISH [1892–]

1. *Landscape as a Nude*

She lies on her left side her flank golden:
Her hair is burned black with the strong sun:
The scent of her hair is of rain in the dust on her shoulders:
She has brown breasts and the mouth of no other country:

Ah she is beautiful here in the sun where she lies: 5
She is not like the soft girls naked in vineyards
Nor the soft naked girls of the English islands
Where the rain comes in with the surf on an east wind:

Hers is the west wind and the sunlight: the west
Wind is the long clean wind of the continents— 10
The wind turning with earth: the wind descending
Steadily out of the evening and following on:

The wind here where she lies is west: the trees
Oak ironwood cottonwood hickory: standing in
Great groves they roll on the wind as the sea would: 15
The grasses of Iowa Illinois Indiana.

Run with the plunge of the wind as a wave tumbling:

Under her knees there is no green lawn of the Florentines:
Under her dusty knees is the corn stubble:
Her belly is flecked with the flickering light of the corn: 20

She lies on her left side her flank golden:
Her hair is burned black with the strong sun:
The scent of her hair is of dust and of smoke on her shoulders:
She has brown breasts and the mouth of no other country:

II. *Wildwest*

There were none of my blood in this battle: 25
There were Minneconjous: Sans Arcs: Brules:
Many nations of Sioux: they were few men galloping:

This would have been in the long days in June:
They were galloping well deployed under the plum-trees:
They were driving riderless horses: themselves they were few:

Crazy Horse had done it with few numbers: 31
Crazy Horse was small for a Lakota:
He was riding always alone thinking of something:

He was standing alone by the picket lines by the ropes:
He was young then: he was thirty when he died: 35
Unless there were children to talk he took no notice:

When the soldiers came for him there on the other side
On the Greasy Grass in the villages we were shouting
"Hoka Hey! Crazy Horse will be riding!"

They fought in the water: horses and men were drowning: 40
They rode on the butte: dust settled in sunlight:
Hoka Hey! they lay on the bloody ground:

No one could tell of the dead which man was Custer . . .
That was the end of his luck: by that river:
The soldiers beat him at Slim Buttes once: 45

They beat him at Willow Creek when the snow lifted:
The last time they beat him was the Tongue:
He had only the meat he had made and of that little:

Do you ask why he should fight? It was his country:
My God should he not fight? It was his: 50
But after the Tongue there were no herds to be hunting:

He cut the knots of the tails and he led them in:
He cried out "I am Crazy Horse! Do not touch me!"
There were many soldiers between and the gun glinting. . . .

And a Mister Josiah Perham of Maine had much of the 55
land Mister Perham was building the Northern Pacific
railroad that is Mister Perham was saying at lunch that

forty say fifty millions of acres in gift and
government grant outright ought to be worth a
wide price on the Board at two-fifty and 60

later a Mister Cooke had relieved Mister Perham and
later a Mister Morgan relieved Mister Cooke:
Mister Morgan converted at prices current:

It was all prices to them: they never looked at it: 64
why should they look at the land: they were Empire Builders:
it was all in the bid and the asked and the ink on their books . . .

When Crazy Horse was there by the Black Hills
His heart would be big with the love he had for that country
And all the game he had seen and the mares he had ridden

And how it went out from you wide and clean in the sunlight 70

III. *Burying Ground by the Ties*

Ayee! Ai! This is heavy earth on our shoulders:
There were none of us born to be buried in this earth:
Niggers we were Portuguese Magyars Polacks:

We were born to another look of the sky certainly:
Now we lie here in the river pastures: 75
We lie in the mowings under the thick turf:

We hear the earth and the all-day rasp of the grasshoppers:
It was we laid the steel on this land from ocean to ocean:
It was we (if you know) put the U. P. through the passes

Bringing her down into Laramie full load 80
Eighteen mile on the granite anticlinal
Forty-three foot to the mile and the grade holding:

It was we did it: hunkies of our kind:
It was we dug the caved-in holes for the cold water:
It was we built the gully spurs and the freight sidings: 85

Who would do it but we and the Irishmen bossing us?
It was all foreign-born men there were in this country:
It was Scotsmen Englishmen Chinese Squareheads Austrians. . . .

Ayee! but there's weight to the earth under it:
Not for this did we come out—to be lying here 90
Nameless under the ties in the clay cuts:

There's nothing good in the world but the rich will buy it:
Everything sticks to the grease of a gold note—
Even a continent—even a new sky!

Do not pity us much for the strange grass over us: 95
We laid the steel to the stone stock of these mountains:
The place of our graves is marked by the telegraph poles!

It was not to lie in the bottoms we came out
And the trains going over us here in the dry hollows. . . .

IV. *Oil Painting of the Artist as the Artist*

The plump Mr. Pl'f is washing his hands of America: 100
The plump Mr. Pl'f is in ochre with such hair:

America is in blue-black-grey-green-sandcolor:
America is a continent—many lands:

The plump Mr. Pl'f is washing his hands of America:
He is pictured at Pau on the *place* and his eyes glaring: 105

He thinks of himself as an exile from all this:
As an émigré from his own time into history—

(History being an empty house without owners
A practical man may get in by the privy stones—

The dead are excellent hosts: they have no objections— 110
And once in he can nail the knob on the next one

Living the life of a classic in bad air with
Himself for the Past and his face in the glass for Posterity)

The Cinquecento is nothing at all like Nome
Or Natchez or Wounded Knee or the Shenandoah: 115

Your vulgarity Tennessee: your violence Texas:
The rocks under your fields Ohio Connecticut:

Your clay Missouri your clay: you have driven him out:
You have shadowed his life Appalachians purple mountains:

There is much too much of your flowing Mississippi: 120
He prefers a tidier stream with a terrace for trippers and

Cypresses mentioned in Horace or Henry James:
He prefers a country where everything carries the name of a

Countess or real king or an actual palace or
Something in Prose and the stock prices all in Italian: 125

There is more shade for an artist under a fig
Than under the whole damn range (he finds) of the Big Horns.

v. *Empire Builders*

The Museum Attendant:

This is *The Making of America in Five Panels:*

This is Mister Harriman making America:
Mister-Harriman-is-buying-the-Union-Pacific-at-Seventy:
The Sante Fe is shining on his hair: 130

This is Commodore Vanderbilt making America:
Mister-Vanderbilt-is-eliminating-the-short-interest-in-Hudson:
Observe the carving on the rocking chair:

This is J. P. Morgan making America:
(The Tennessee Coal is behind to the left of the Steel Company:) 135
Those in mauve are braces he is wearing:

This is Mister Mellon making America:
Mister-Mellon-is-represented-as-a-symbolical-figure-in-aluminum-
Strewing-bank-stocks-on-a-burnished-stair:

This is the Bruce is the Barton making America: 140
Mister-Barton-is-selling-us-Doctor's-Deliciousest-Dentifrice:
This is he in beige with the canary:

You have just beheld the Makers making America:
This is *The Making of America in Five Panels:*
America lies to the west-southwest of the Switch-Tower: 145
There is nothing to see of America but land:

The Original Document under the Panel Paint:

"To Thos. Jefferson Esq. his obd't serv't
M. Lewis: captain: detached:
Sir:
Having in mind your repeated commands in this matter: 150
And the worst half of it done and the streams mapped:

And we here on the back of this beach beholding the
Other ocean—two years gone and the cold

Breaking with rain for the third spring since St. Louis:
The crows at the fishbones on the frozen dunes: 155

The first cranes going over from south north:
And the river down by a mark of the pole since the morning:

And time near to return, and a ship (Spanish)
Lying in for the salmon: and fearing chance or the 159

Drought or the Sioux should deprive you of these discoveries—
Therefore we send by sea in this writing:

Above the
Platte there were long plains and a clay country:
Rim of the sky far off: grass under it:

Dung for the cook fires by the sulphur licks:
After that there were low hills and the sycamores: 165

And we poled up by the Great Bend in the skiffs:
The honey bees left us after the Osage River:

The wind was west in the evenings and no dew and the
Morning Star larger and whiter than usual—

The winter rattling in the brittle haws: 170
The second year there was sage and the quail calling:

All that valley is good land by the river:
Three thousand miles and the clay cliffs and

Rue and beargrass by the water banks
And many birds and the brant going over and tracks of 175

Bear elk wolves marten: the buffalo
Numberless so that the cloud of their dust covers them:

The antelope fording the fall creeks: and the mountains and
Grazing lands and the meadow lands and the ground

Sweet and open and well-drained:
We advise you to 180
Settle troops at the forks and to issue licenses:

Many men will have living on these lands:
There is wealth in the earth for them all and the wood standing

And wild birds on the water where they sleep:
There is stone in the hills for the towns of a great people . . ."

You have just beheld the Makers making America: 186

They screwed her scrawny and gaunt with their seven-year
panics:

They bought her back on their mortgages old-whore-cheap:
They fattened their bonds at her breasts till the thin blood ran
  from them:

Men have forgotten how full clear and deep 190
The Yellowstone moved on the gravel and grass grew
When the land lay waiting for her westward people!

VI. *Background with Revolutionaries*

And the corn singing Millennium!
Lenin! Millennium! Lennium!

When they're shunting the cars on the Katy a mile off 195
When they're shunting the cars when they're shunting the cars
  on the Katy
You can hear the clank of the couplings riding away

Also Comrade Devine who writes of America
Most instructively having in 'Seventy-four
Crossed to the Hoboken side on the Barclay Street Ferry 200

She sits on a settle in the State of North Dakota
O she sits on a settle in the State of North Dakota
She can hear the engines whistle over Iowa and Idaho

Also Comrade Edward Remington Ridge
Who has prayed God since the April of 'Seventeen 205
To replace in his life his lost (M.E.) religion.

And The New York Daily Worker *goes a'blowing over Arkan-*
  sas
The New York Daily Worker *goes a'blowing over Arkansas*
The grasses let it go along the Ozarks over Arkansas

Even Comrade Grenadine Grilt who has tried since 210
August tenth for something to feel about strongly in
Verses—his personal passions having tired

I can tell my land by the jays in the apple-trees
Tell my land by the jays in the apple-trees
I can tell my people by the blue-jays in the apple-trees 215

Aindt you read in d'books you are all brudders?
D' glassic historic objective broves you are brudders!
You and d'Wops and d'Chinks you are all brudders!
Havend't you got it d' same ideology? Havend't you?

When it's yesterday in Oregon it's one A M in Maine 220
And she slides: and the day slides: and it runs: runs over us:
And the bells strike twelve strike twelve strike twelve
In Marblehead in Buffalo in Cheyenne in Cherokee
Yesterday runs on the states like a crow's shadow

For Marx has said to us Workers what do you need? 225
And Stalin has said to us Starvers what do you need?
You need the Dialectical Materialism!

She's a tough land under the corn mister:
She has changed the bone in the cheeks of many races:
She has winced the eyes of the soft Slavs with her sun on them:
She has tried the fat from the round rumps of Italians: 231
Even the voice of the English has gone dry
And hard on the tongue and alive in the throat speaking:

She's a tough land under the oak-trees mister:
It may be she can change the word in the book 235
As she changes the bone of a man's head in his children:
It may be that the earth and the men remain. . . .

There is too much sun on the lids of my eyes to be listening

Exercise:

1. What is the theme of this long poem? Is the poet attacking financiers? Artists? Radicals? What is he attacking?

2. What is the function of the various sections of the poem in developing the theme? How are the sections related to each other? Is the poem unified?

3. In "Wild West," lines 25–54, we are presented largely with a succession of concrete details. Is the poem thereby made incoherent? What does the poem gain by this kind of presentation?

4. In "Empire Builders," lines 147–192, the poet pretends to be

reproducing Lewis's letter to Jefferson. Again the manner of presentation is through a succession of concrete details. Is the method effective? Do some of the concrete particulars take on symbolic power (e.g., see line 155)?

5. Discuss the various verse forms used. How do they support the tone of the passage in question? Discuss shifts of tone, giving attention to the use of satirical and realistic elements.

Losses

RANDALL JARRELL [1914–]

It was not dying: everybody died.
It was not dying: we had died before
In the routine crashes—and our fields
Called up the papers, wrote home to our folks,
And the rates rose, all because of us. 5
We died on the wrong page of the almanac,
Scattered on mountains fifty miles away;
Diving on haystacks, fighting with a friend,
We blazed up on the lines we never saw.
We died like ants or pets or foreigners. 10
(When we left high school nothing else had died
For us to figure we had died like.)

In our new planes, with our new crews, we bombed
The ranges by the desert or the shore,
Fired at towed targets, waited for our scores— 15
And turned into replacements and woke up
One morning, over England, operational.
It wasn't different: but if we died
It was not an accident but a mistake
(But an easy one for anyone to make). 20
We read our mail and counted up our missions—
In bombers named for girls, we burned
The cities we had learned about in school—
Till our lives wore out; our bodies lay among
The people we had killed and never seen. 25
When we lasted long enough they gave us medals;

When we died they said, "Our casualties were low."
They said, "Here are the maps"; we burned the cities.

It was not dying—no, not ever dying;
But the night I died I dreamed that I was dead, 30
And the cities said to me: "Why are you dying?
We are satisfied, if you are; but why did I die?"

EXERCISE:

1. What is the purpose of the references to school (line 11 and line 23)?

2. What is meant by "the people we had killed and never seen" (line 25)? Is the speaker insisting upon the *abstractness* of modern war? Are there other suggestions of this sort in the poem?

3. What is the poem "about"? In trying to determine the answer to this question, consider again the descriptive details in the poem and, most of all, the tone of the poem.

Two Songs from a Play

WILLIAM BUTLER YEATS [1865–1939]

I

I saw a staring virgin stand
Where holy Dionysus died,
And tear the heart out of his side,
And lay the heart upon her hand
And bear that beating heart away; 5
And then did all the Muses sing
Of Magnus Annus at the spring,
As though God's death were but a play.

Another Troy must rise and set,
Another lineage feed the crow, 10
Another Argo's painted prow
Drive to a flashier bauble yet.
The Roman Empire stood appalled:
It dropped the reins of peace and war
When that fierce virgin and her Star 15
Out of the fabulous darkness called.

II

In pity for man's darkening thought
He walked that room and issued thence
In Galilean turbulence;
The Babylonian starlight brought 20
A fabulous, formless darkness in;
Odor of blood when Christ was slain
Made all Platonic tolerance vain
And vain all Doric discipline.

Everything that man esteems 25
Endures a moment or a day.
Love's pleasure drives his love away,
The painter's brush consumes his dreams;
The herald's cry, the soldier's tread
Exhaust his glory and his might: 30
Whatever flames upon the night
Man's own resinous heart has fed.

These songs may be considered as separate poems, although they have certain definite connections; and though they form the prologue and epilogue of a play, they are not integral parts of that play. Their obscurity, in so far as they are obscure poems, is not occasioned by their having been removed from the play.

Most readers would, in fact, admit to finding a certain obscurity in these poems. There are, however, really two types of obscurity involved. One type has been touched on in various connections in the discussion of previous poems, especially Blake's "The Scoffers" (p. 423), and Eliot's "The Love Song of J. Alfred Prufrock" (p. 429). This type of obscurity comes from the poet's allusions to history, literature, etc. The reader may miss part, or all, of the meaning of such a poet because he simply does not have the knowledge which the poet expects from his audience. The reader of the present poems, for example, must be able to grasp the references to Dionysus, Magnus Annus, Troy, the Argo, the Roman Empire, Galilee, Babylon, Plato, and the Dorians. Information of this sort may be said to belong to the common heritage of our civilization, and a poet who makes such general references assumes that he is addressing readers of a certain degree of education. No one reader, of course, possesses a complete body of information of this sort, but he knows that the information is available to him for the interpretation of any particular poem.

But a second type of obscurity met with in these poems seems to derive from the poet's own symbolism. Why, for example, "Babylonian starlight" (line 20)? The reader senses that it probably has to mean something more than "the starlight in Babylon," and yet dictionaries and encyclopedias may give him little direct help on this point. Does a poet have the right to use references and symbols that are not, as it were, in the public domain? If the poet insists upon using a private system of symbols, will he not render his work impenetrably obscure?

This is a difficult topic, all the more so since Yeats did have something of a private system of symbols which he set forth in *A Vision,* a book printed privately in 1925, and published in revised form in 1938. Yet every poet to some extent finds his own symbols or tends to modify the traditional symbols to his own use. How far does he have a right to go in doing this? Where does one draw the line? At this point, our best procedure will probably be to discuss the "Two Songs" with as much help as we can get from *A Vision.* Then, with the "Two Songs" as a concrete example, we may attempt a few comments on the general problem. (The general problem will be further discussed in Section X.)

The "Two Songs from a Play" deal with the moment of transition from the classical civilization to the Christian. In the first poem, the poet represents the birth of Christ, not only as marking a date in history, but as offering a new principle that was to change the nature of all human activity. But though emphasizing the contrast between the two civilizations ("The Roman Empire stood appalled"), the poet establishes, paradoxically, the continuity between them. The Virgin tears the heart from the slain Dionysus. (According to the rites of the Dionysiac cult, those who tasted sacramentally of the flesh of Dionysus might live again.) With her child (the "Star," which we may take as expressing the same principle as Dionysus) she then utters her challenge to the older civilization. The poet implies further that one cycle (according to *A Vision,* of roughly 2000 years) is merely ended and another is begun. (The Great Year, the period in which twelve such cycles run their course, begins, according to Yeats's system, approximately at the birth of Christ.) But this new cycle, the poet implies, will merely recapitulate that which has preceded it: it too will have Troys that rise to power and fall, races of heroes whose bodies feed the crows, and Argonauts who search for a Golden Fleece.

It is worth noting that a reader unacquainted with Yeats's special symbols and his special way of treating them might infer from the poem much of the foregoing account. He might even manage, lines 15–16, taking "Star" to be a vague poetic epithet for child (or to be the Star of Bethlehem), and the "fabulous darkness," the night through which the Star of Bethlehem shone.

As a matter of fact, we can find almost all the imagery of the first "Song," including the "Star," in a passage which Yeats wrote in another connection. The poet, contemplating the positions of the heavenly bodies as they were at the birth of Christ, comments as follows:

Three hundred years, two degrees of the Great Year, would but correspond to two days of the Sun's annual journey, and his transition from Pisces to Aries had for generations been associated with the ceremonial death and resurrection of Dionysus. Near that transition the women wailed him, and night showed the full moon separating from the constellation Virgo, with the star in the wheatsheaf, or in the child, for in the old maps she is represented carrying now one now the other. (*A Vision,* [Privately printed] London: Werner Laurie, Ltd., p. 156.)

Moreover, in another passage of the same work (p. 190), Yeats mentions the fact that a Roman philosopher of the fourth century described Christianity as "a fabulous formless darkness" which blotted out "every beautiful thing." To the reasonable, ordered thought of the Graeco-Roman civilization this new religion seemed to be a superstitious, irrational belief inimical to all clarity and good order and to all its achievements:

Meanwhile the irrational force that would create confusion and uproar as with the cry "The Babe, the Babe, is born"—the women speaking unknown tongues, the barbers and weavers expounding

Divine revelation with all the vulgarity of their servitude, the tables that move or resound with raps—still but creates a negligible sect. (*A Vision,* pp. 188–189.)

This points the paradox of the antagonism and continuity of the two cycles. Furthermore, it helps explain why the Virgin, usually portrayed as meek, appears here as a fierce, pitiless force at which the Roman Empire stands appalled.

In dealing with the first "Song," we have already stated that Yeats believes in a cyclic theory of history. He has a particular set of symbols for describing the stages of these cycles through which human events move. The beginning of such a cycle he compares, in his system of symbols, to the new moon, or the dark of the moon; the height of the civilization of such a cycle he compares to the full moon; and the various phases of the moon as it waxes from new to full, or wanes from full back to new, he uses to symbolize the stages in the development and decay of a civilization. Thus, the moment of transition from the classical to the Christian civilization he compares to the dark of the moon; and when the moon is dark one sees only the starlight. But why does he call it "Babylonian starlight"?

First, the Babylonians, from remote antiquity, have been associated with the study of the stars. Second, Yeats conceives of the motive power for the new Christian cycle as coming from Asia Minor, where, of course, Babylon had been situated. Yeats conceives of Christ as representing a "primary" force; by "primary" he means objective as opposed to subjective, physical as opposed to intellectual and rational, democratic as opposed to aristocratic. All of these "primary" attributes are associated with the dark of the moon as opposed to the full moon, which symbolizes the intellectual, the rational, the individual, the ordered. Moreover, Yeats associates the East with the "primary" and the West with its opposite, which he calls the "antithetical." Thus the lines

> The Babylonian starlight brought
> A fabulous, formless darkness in

indicate the impingement of a "primary" elemental force coming in from the East to put a close to the ordered, rational "antithetical" cycle of Greek civilization. Further, the two lines suggest a very powerful concrete image—a dark, mysterious cloud boiling up out of the ancient East to obscure all the distinctions that the rational Western mind had made.

We must not understand these opposed aspects, "primary" and "antithetical," to be absolute. They represent an emphasis in the temper of a civilization—not attitudes complete in themselves. The Greeks, for instance, had not been unaware of the supernatural and irrational aspect of life, but the temper of the Greek or Western mind had emphasized the search for rational explanations and systematic ordering, and the gradual development of Greek philosophy up through Aristotle was in the direction of rational explanation.

But the "odor of blood"—blood is another symbol Yeats uses in many of his poems for the "primary" force—renders vain the achievements of the "antithetical" civilization as represented here by Platonic tolerance and Doric discipline. Yeats, then, has used here three different symbols of the general "primary" force; first, "Babylonian starlight," as the symbol which indicates the history and the basic continuity of the force; second, the "fabulous, formless darkness" as the force as it appeared to men of the antithetical civilization; and third, blood as symbolizing the violent fact of the transition itself.

The last stanza of the second song seems to abandon the consideration of the particular matters involved in the first stanza of the second song, and, indeed, the matters involved in the whole of the first song. It makes a statement about the relation of a man to his various activities—love, art, politics, war. But we must assume that the content of this last stanza is determined by the content of the three preceding stanzas. The problem here is to define the particular nature of the relationship involved.

After presenting, in terms of his symbols, the recurrent cycles of history, the poet sums up by saying that

> Everything that man esteems
> Endures a moment or a day.

But the emphasis here is not merely upon the pathos of the transience of human achievements. Their very meaning, the last stanza implies, lies in the fact that they express man's deepest nature; that in expressing this nature, man's achievements fulfill his creative impulse in the act of consuming it.

Instead of the static idea of the vanity of all human glory—the fall of the mighty, the feebleness of man's might—the poem expresses a dynamic idea, an idea of development and fulfillment in this process. Most of all, we are to see the varied and constant pageant of man's life, either primary or antithetical in emphasis, as springing from man's own creative and imaginative force. This ties back to the idea of the repetition of the cycles as given in the first song—

> Another Troy must rise and set,
> Another lineage feed the crow.

The whole idea is brought to a climactic summary in the last figure which the poet uses, the figure of man's "resinous heart" feeding the flame, just as, on a larger scale, the last figure of "The Scholar Gipsy" (p. 409) summarizes that poem.

The "Two Songs," as we have seen, are enriched by a full acquaintance with Yeats's system of symbols. But before we leap to conclusions about the general problem of the poet's right to make up his own symbolism or to the specific problem of the relation of Yeats's poetry to his *Vision,* several comments are in order. In the first place, we should point out that the reader who had never seen *A Vision* might, by a careful reading of a large part of Yeats's poetry, come to an adequate understanding of his symbols. In this view, *A Vision* can be regarded primarily as a special kind of dictionary—a compendium of materials which may be found at large elsewhere in the body of his poetry. In the second place, whether *A Vision* is or is not to be regarded as a book of philosophy or a book on the meaning of history, our use of it in this analysis has been to throw light upon the meanings of the symbols employed in "Two Songs." Understanding of the poems does not demand our literal belief in Yeats's philosophy or in his view of history. The "Songs" must justify themselves in their own right and the symbols they employ must be brought to life within the context in which they are used: they cannot be validated by an appeal to their "truth" in *A Vision* or elsewhere.

To sum up: the general problem we have raised is an aspect of the relation between a single poem and the complete body of the poet's work. It is a problem by no means confined to Yeats. It could be argued, for example, that any one of Keats's odes requires, for full appreciation, a knowledge of the rest of Keats's poetry. There is an approach to the body of a poet's works as well as to single examples of it. In Section X (pp. 631–83) we shall consider the poem as seen in this wider perspective.

Shine, Perishing Republic

ROBINSON JEFFERS [1887–]

While this America settles in the mold of its vulgarity, heavily thickening to empire,
And protest, only a bubble in the molten mass, pops and sighs out, and the mass hardens,

I sadly smiling remember that the flower fades to make fruit, the fruit rots to make earth.
Out of the mother; and through the spring exultances, ripeness and decadence; and home to the mother.

You make haste on decay: not blameworthy; life is good, be it stubbornly long or suddenly 5
A mortal splendor: meteors are not needed less than mountains: shine, perishing republic.

But for my children, I would rather have them keep their distance from the thickening center; corruption
Never has been compulsory, when the cities lie at the monster's feet there are left the mountains.

And boys, be in nothing so moderate as in love of man, a clever servant, insufferable master.
There is the trap that catches noblest spirits, that caught—they say—God, when he walked on earth. 10

EXERCISE:

1. Does this poet hate America? Is he trying to admonish his country? What does he mean by asking it to "shine"? Is he saying

that America's course of action is "not blameworthy" (line 5)? Does he love the "perishing republic"?

2. To whom are the last 2 lines addressed? How do these lines relate to the first four stanzas of the poem?

3. Compare and contrast the theme of this poem with that of "The Return" (p. 444).

4. What theory of history is implied in this poem?

Lycidas

JOHN MILTON [1608–1674]

Yet once more, O ye Laurels, and once more,
Ye Myrtles brown, with Ivy never sear,
I come to pluck your berries harsh and crude,
And with forced fingers rude
Shatter your leaves before the mellowing year. 5
Bitter constraint and sad occasion dear
Compels me to disturb your season due;
For Lycidas is dead, dead ere his prime,
Young Lycidas, and hath not left his peer.
Who would not sing for Lycidas? he knew 10
Himself to sing, and build the lofty rhyme.
He must not float upon his wat'ry bier
Unwept, and welter to the parching wind,
Without the meed of some melodious tear.
  Begin, then, Sisters of the Sacred Well 15
That from beneath the seat of Jove doth spring,
Begin, and somewhat loudly sweep the string.
Hence with denial vain and coy excuse:
So may some gentle Muse
With lucky words favor my destined urn, 20
And, as he passes, turn,
And bid fair peace be to my sable shroud!
For we were nursed upon the self-same hill,
Fed the same flocks, by fountain, shade, and rill;
  Together both, ere the high lawns appeared 25
Under the opening eyelids of the Morn,
We drove a-field, and both together heard
What time the gray-fly winds her sultry horn,

Battening our flocks with the fresh dews of night,
Oft till the star that rose at evening bright 30
Towards Heaven's descent had sloped his westering wheel.
Meanwhile the rural ditties were not mute,
Tempered to the oaten flute,
Rough Satyrs danced, and Fauns with cloven heel
From the glad sound would not be absent long; 35
And old Damætas loved to hear our song.
But, O the heavy change, now thou art gone,
Now thou art gone, and never must return!
Thee, Shepherd, thee the woods and desert caves,
With wild thyme and the gadding vine o'ergrown, 40
And all their echoes mourn.
The willows, and the hazel copses green,
Shall now no more be seen
Fanning their joyous leaves to thy soft lays.
As killing as the canker to the rose, 45
Or taint-worm to the weanling herds that graze,
Or frost to flowers, that their gay wardrobe wear
When first the white thorn blows;
Such, Lycidas, thy loss to shepherd's ear.
Where were ye, Nymphs, when the remorseless deep 50
Closed o'er the head of your loved Lycidas?
For neither were ye playing on the steep
Where your old bards, the famous Druids, lie,
Nor yet on the shaggy top of Mona high,
Nor yet where Deva spreads her wizard stream. 55
Ay me! I fondly dream
"Had ye been there" . . . for what could that have done?
What could the Muse herself that Orpheus bore,
The Muse herself, for her enchanting son,
Whom universal Nature did lament, 60
When, by the rout that made the hideous roar,
His gory visage down the stream was sent,
Down the swift Hebrus to the Lesbian shore?
Alas! what boots it with uncessant care
To tend the homely, slighted, shepherd's trade, 65
And strictly meditate the thankless Muse?
Were it not better done, as others use,
To sport with Amaryllis in the shade,
Or with the tangles of Neæra's hair?

Fame is the spur that the clear spirit doth raise 70
(That last infirmity of noble mind)
To scorn delights and live laborious days;
But the fair guerdon when we hope to find,
And think to burst out into sudden blaze,
Comes the blind Fury with the abhorrèd shears, 75
And slits the thin-spun life. "But not the praise,"
Phœbus replied, and touched my trembling ears:
"Fame is no plant that grows on mortal soil,
Nor in the glistering foil
Set off to the world, nor in broad Rumor lies, 80
But lives and spreads aloft by those pure eyes
And perfect witness of all-judging Jove;
As he pronounces lastly on each deed,
Of so much fame in Heav'n expect thy meed."
  O fountain Arethuse, and thou honored flood, 85
Smooth-sliding Mincius, crowned with vocal reeds,
That strain I heard was of a higher mood:
But now my oat proceeds,
And listens to the Herald of the Sea,
That came in Neptune's plea. 90
He asked the waves, and asked the felon winds,
What hard mishap hath doomed this gentle swain?
And questioned every gust of rugged wings
That blows from off each beakèd promontory:
They knew not of his story; 95
And sage Hippotadés their answer brings,
That not a blast was from his dungeon strayed:
The air was calm, and on the level brine
Sleek Panopé with all her sisters played.
It was that fatal and perfidious bark, 100
Built in the eclipse, and rigged with curses dark,
That sunk so low that sacred head of thine.
  Next, Camus, reverend sire, went footing slow,
His mantle hairy, and his bonnet sedge,
Inwrought with figures dim, and on the edge 105
Like to that sanguine flower inscribed with woe.
"Ah! who hath reft," quoth he, "my dearest pledge?"
Last came, and last did go,
The pilot of the Galilean lake;

Two massy keys he bore of metals twain 110
(The golden opes, the iron shuts amain).
He shook his mitered locks, and stern bespake:—
"How well could I have spared for thee, young Swain,
Enow of such, as for their bellies' sake,
Creep, and intrude, and climb into the fold! 115
Of other care they little reckoning make
Than how to scramble at the shearers' feast,
And shove away the worthy bidden guest.
Blind mouths! that scarce themselves know how to hold
A sheep-hook, or have learned aught else the least 120
That to the faithful herdsman's art belongs!
What recks it them? What need they? they are sped;
And, when they list, their lean and flashy songs
Grate on their scrannel pipes of wretched straw;
The hungry sheep look up, and are not fed, 125
But, swollen with wind and the rank mist they draw,
Rot inwardly, and foul contagion spread;
Besides what the grim wolf with privy paw
Daily devours apace, and nothing said;
But that two-handed engine at the door 130
Stands ready to smite once, and smite no more."
Return, Alphéus; the dread voice is past
That shrunk thy streams; return, Sicilian Muse,
And call the vales, and bid them hither cast
Their bells and flowerets of a thousand hues. 135
Ye valleys low, where the mild whispers use
Of shades, and wanton winds, and gushing brooks,
On whose fresh lap the swart star sparely looks,
Throw hither all your quaint enameled eyes,
That on the green turf suck the honied showers, 140
And purple all the ground with vernal flowers.
Bring the rathe primrose that forsaken dies,
The tufted crow-toe, and pale jessamine,
The white pink, and the pansy freaked with jet,
The glowing violet, 145
The musk-rose, and the well-attired woodbine,
With cowslips wan that hang the pensive head,
And every flower that sad embroidery wears;
Bid Amaranthus all his beauty shed,
And daffadillies fill their cups with tears, 150

To strew the laureate hearse where Lycid lies.
For so, to interpose a little ease,
Let our frail thoughts dally with false surmise,
Ay me! whilst thee the shores and sounding seas
Wash far away, where'er thy bones are hurled; 155
Whether beyond the stormy Hebrides,
Where thou, perhaps, under the whelming tide
Visit'st the bottom of the monstrous world;
Or whether thou, to our moist vows denied,
Sleep'st by the fable of Bellerus old, 160
Where the great Vision of the guarded mount
Looks toward Namancos and Bayona's hold:
Look homeward, angel, now, and melt with ruth;
And, O ye Dolphins, waft the hapless youth.
  Weep no more, woeful shepherds, weep no more, 165
For Lycidas, your sorrow, is not dead,
Sunk though he be beneath the watery floor:
So sinks the day-star in the ocean bed,
And yet anon repairs his drooping head,
And tricks his beams, and with new-spangled ore 170
Flames in the forehead of the morning sky:
So Lycidas sunk low, but mounted high,
Through the dear might of Him that walked the waves,
Where, other groves and other streams along,
With nectar pure his oozy locks he laves, 175
And hears the unexpressive nuptial song,
In the blest kingdoms meek of Joy and Love.
There entertain him all the Saints above,
In solemn troops, and sweet societies,
That sing, and singing in their glory move, 180
And wipe the tears forever from his eyes.
Now, Lycidas, the shepherds weep no more;
Henceforth thou art the Genius of the shore,
In thy large recompense, and shalt be good
To all that wander in that perilous flood. 185

  Thus sang the uncouth swain to the oaks and rills,
While the still Morn went out with sandals grey;
He touched the tender stops of various quills,
With eager thought warbling his Doric lay:

And now the sun had stretched out all the hills, 190
And now was dropped into the western bay.
At last he rose, and twitched his mantle blue:
Tomorrow to fresh woods and pastures new.

EXERCISE:

1. This is a pastoral elegy written at the death of one of Milton's friends, Edward King, a young scholar who was drowned in the Irish Sea. At this time Milton was a relatively young man already engaged in his pursuit of literary fame. Is the poem a mere compliment to King and a mere expression of grief at his death? What is the real theme of the poem? How is the theme related to the fact of the death of King? What is the relation of the apparently irrelevant passages (line 64 to line 84, line 103 to line 131) to the theme?

2. Dr. Samuel Johnson criticized this poem adversely in the following terms:

One of the poems on which much praise has been bestowed is *Lycidas* of which the diction is harsh, the rhymes uncertain, and the numbers unpleasing. What beauty there is we must therefore seek in the sentiments and images. It is not to be considered as the effusion of real passion; for passion runs not after remote allusions and obscure opinions. Passion plucks no berries from the myrtle and ivy, nor calls upon Arethuse and Mincius, nor tells of rough *satyrs* and *fauns with cloven heel.* Where there is leisure for fiction there is little grief.

In this poem there is no nature, for there is no truth; there is no art, for there is nothing new. Its form is that of a pastoral, easy, vulgar, and therefore disgusting; whatever images it can supply are long ago exhausted, and its inherent improbability always forces dissatisfaction on the mind. When Cowley [a poet who was the contemporary of Milton] tells of Hervey, that they studied together, it is easy to suppose how much he must miss the companion of his labors, and the partner of his discoveries; but what image of tenderness can be excited by these lines?—

We drove a-field, and both together heard
What time the gray-fly winds her sultry horn,
Batt'ning our flocks with the fresh dews of night.

We know that they never drove a-field, and that they had no flocks to batten; and though it be allowed that the representation may be allegorical, the true meaning is so uncertain and remote that it is never sought because it cannot be known when found. . . . He who thus grieves will excite no sympathy; he who thus praises will confer no honor.

("John Milton," in *Lives of the English Poets*)

In this book there is a selection from the poetry of Dr. Johnson himself. Judging from a comparison of his "The Vanity of Human Wishes" (p. 399) with "Lycidas," try to determine why Dr. Johnson did not approve of the versification of "Lycidas." How could the versification of "Lycidas," although it is not as regular as that of "The Vanity of Human Wishes," be justified? Dr. Johnson also attacked "Lycidas," because the pastoral imagery, having no basis in biographical fact, indicates insincerity on the part of the poet. Is not the question of insincerity approached by Johnson on false terms? For instance, does a poet in writing a poem about grief ever try to make the reader have an experience identical with that caused by a bereavement (*Introduction,* pp. xlvi–xlvii)? Is the pastoral machinery in itself any more artificial than the fiction indulged in by Yeats that his loved one is a "daughter of the swan" (p. 358)?

3. Note that the speaker acknowledges difficulty in maintaining a pastoral note. Apollo was one of the high gods, and his pronouncement is acknowledged as a strain of "higher mood" as the speaker tries to resume the humbler pastoral note (lines 85–87). After St. Peter's scathing comment on unworthy shepherds, the speaker calls back the Sicilian muse (the muse of pastoral poetry) as if she had been frightened away (lines 131–32). Do these admissions weaken the poem or strengthen it? How do they bear upon Dr. Johnson's charges that the pastoral was by Milton's time a worn-out and artificial form?

4. Discuss the shifts in tone in this poem. How are they marked? What do the last eight lines do for the tone of the whole? (Note that we have a third-person ending, though the poem begins in the first person, with the swain speaking. Can you justify this lack of symmetry?)

5. Dr. Johnson also objected to the mixture of pagan and Chris-

tian materials in this poem. Can you justify it? Is there evidence that the poet mixed them consciously and for a purpose?

6. Note the water imagery in this poem. Why is there so much of it? Does it develop into a symbolism?

7. For an interpretation of "Lycidas," see E. M. W. Tillyard, *Milton,* New York, 1930, pp. 80–85.

The Miracle

WALTER DE LA MARE [1873–]

Who beckons the green ivy up
  Its solitary tower of stone?
What spirit lures the bindweed's cup
    Unfaltering on?
Calls even the starry lichen to climb 5
By agelong inches endless Time?

Who bids the hollyhock uplift
  Her rod of fast-sealed buds on high;
Fling wide her petals—silent, swift,
    Lovely to the sky? 10
Since as she kindled, so she will fade,
Flower above flower in squalor laid.

Ever the heavy billow rears
  All its sea-length in green, hushed wall;
But totters as the shore it nears, 15
    Foams to its fall;
Where was its mark? on what vain quest
Rose that great water from its rest?

So creeps ambition on; so climb
  Man's vaunting thoughts. He, set on high, 20
Forgets his birth, small space, brief time,
    That he shall die;
Dreams blindly in his stagnant air;
Consumes his strength; strips himself bare;

Rejects delight, ease, pleasure, hope, 25
  Seeking in vain, but seeking yet,

Past earthly promise, earthly scope,
On one aim set:
As if, like Chaucer's child, he thought
All but "O Alma!" nought. 30

EXERCISE:

1. What does the poet gain by linking man's ambition with the force that exerts itself in lichen and plant and wave? Does he suggest that "Man's vaunting thoughts" are really akin to some blind irrational force?

2. How do the previous images qualify and inform the description of man in stanza four? For example, "Dreams blindly" would apply to the ivy and the hollyhocks. What are other instances?

3. What is the speaker's attitude toward the progress of the ivy or that of the bindweed? What is his attitude toward man? One of mockery, pity, or what?

4. Lines 29–30 refer to Chaucer's "Prioress' Tale." In her story, the little clergeon sings his hymn to the Virgin, "O Alma Redemptoris" in spite of threats, and, miraculously, even after his throat has been cut. How does this comparison qualify what the poet has to say about man's ambition? How does it contrast with (or perhaps support) the images drawn from the blind motion of the billow or of the blind life-force in plants?

5. Compare the theme of this poem with that of the second of the "Songs" by Yeats (p. 458).

The Force That through the Green Fuse

DYLAN THOMAS [1914–]

The force that through the green fuse drives the flower
Drives my green age; that blasts the roots of trees
Is my destroyer.
And I am dumb to tell the crooked rose
My youth is bent by the same wintry fever. 5

The force that drives the water through the rocks
Drives my red blood; that dries the mouthing streams
Turns mine to wax.
And I am dumb to mouth unto my veins
How at the mountain spring the same mouth sucks. 10

The hand that whirls the water in the pool
Stirs the quicksand; that ropes the blowing wind
Hauls my shroud sail.
And I am dumb to tell the hanging man
How of my clay is made the hangman's lime. 15

The lips of time leech to the fountain head;
Love drips and gathers, but the fallen blood
Shall calm her sores.
And I am dumb to tell a weather's wind
How time has ticked a heaven round the stars. 20

And I am dumb to tell the lover's tomb
How at my sheet goes the same crooked worm.

Exercise:

1. Compare and contrast the theme of this poem with that of "The Miracle" (p. 472).

2. What is the speaker's attitude toward his kinship with plant and water and wind? Does he exult in the kinship? Or commiserate, as with fellow victims? Or what? Compare and contrast the tone of this poem with that of "The Miracle."

3. How do the last two lines sum up the poem? How do they bear upon the tone of the poem?

Ode on a Grecian Urn

JOHN KEATS [1795–1821]

Thou still unravished bride of quietness,
  Thou foster-child of silence and slow time,
Sylvan historian, who canst thus express
  A flowery tale more sweetly than our rime:

What leaf-fringed legend haunts about thy shape 5
  Of dieties or mortals, or of both,
    In Tempe or the dales of Arcady?
What men or gods are these? What maidens loth?
  What mad pursuit? What struggle to escape?
    What pipes and timbrels? What wild ecstasy? 10

Heard melodies are sweet, but those unheard
  Are sweeter; therefore, ye soft pipes, play on;
Not to the sensual ear, but, more endeared,
  Pipe to the spirit ditties of no tone:
Fair youth, beneath the trees, thou canst not leave 15
  Thy song, nor ever can those trees be bare;
    Bold Lover, never, never canst thou kiss,
Though winning near the goal—yet, do not grieve;
  She cannot fade, though thou hast not thy bliss,
    Forever wilt thou love, and she be fair! 20

Ah, happy, happy boughs! That cannot shed
  Your leaves, nor ever bid the Spring adieu:
And, happy melodist, unweariѐd,
  Forever piping songs forever new;
More happy love! more happy, happy love! 25
  Forever warm and still to be enjoy'd,
    Forever panting, and forever young;
All breathing human passion far above,
  That leaves a heart high-sorrowful and cloyed,
    A burning forehead, and a parching tongue. 30

Who are these coming to the sacrifice?
  To what green altar, O mysterious priest,
Lead'st thou that heifer lowing at the skies,
  And all her silken flanks with garlands drest?
What little town by river or sea shore, 35
  Or mountain-built with peaceful citadel,
    Is emptied of this folk, this pious morn?
And, little town, thy streets for evermore
  Will silent be; and not a soul to tell
    Why thou art desolate, can e'er return. 40

O Attic shape! Fair Attitude! with brede
Of marble men and maidens overwrought,
With forest branches and the trodden weed;
Thou, silent form, dost tease us out of thought
As doth eternity: Cold Pastoral! 45
When old age shall this generation waste,
Thou shalt remain, in midst of other woe
Than ours, a friend to man, to whom thou sayst,
"Beauty is truth, truth beauty,"—that is all,
Ye know on earth, and all ye need to know. 50

EXERCISE:

1. In what sense is the urn a "sylvan historian" (line 3)? What are some of the "flowery tales" that it expresses to the observer?

2. How is the paradox of the speaking urn—the urn that can express tales "more sweetly than our rime"—related to some of the other paradoxes in the poem (e.g., the unheard pipes that play ditties)?

3. The ideal life expressed in the scenes wrought upon the urn avoids the disappointments of actual life. Has the poet played fair in presenting these scenes as being in a sense lifeless and cold? Is the ironic counterpoise maintained in the poem?

4. What is the force of the phrase "Cold Pastoral" (line 45)? How does it gather up and summarize the relation of the ideal to the actual?

5. Is the famous concluding passage (lines 49–50) insisted upon as a philosophic generalization in its own right? Or is it to be regarded as a dramatic utterance spoken by the urn? The poet has said that the urn "tease[s] us out of thought / As doth eternity." The timeless ideal world of the urn is as enigmatic as eternity. It bewilders our time-ridden human minds: it teases us. Are the last two lines a teasing utterance or not? What is their truth? Do the preceding 48 lines serve to define it?

VII

POEMS FOR STUDY: NEW AND OLD

The Rawk o' the Autumn

JOHN CLARE [1793–1864]

The rawk [1] o' the autumn hangs over the woodlands
  Like smoke from a city dismembered and pale;
The sun without beams burns dim o'er the floodlands
  Where white cawdy-mawdies [2] slow swiver [3] and sail;
The flood froths away like a fathomless ocean, 5
  The wind winnows chill like a breeze from the sea,
And thoughts of my Susan give my heart an emotion
  To think does she e'er waste a thought upon me.

Full oft I think so on the banks of the meadows,
  Where the pale cawdy-mawdy flies swopping [4] all day; 10
I think of our true love where grass and flowers hid us
  As by the dyke-side of the meadows we lay.
The seasons have changed since I sat wi' my true love;
  Now the flood roars and raves o'er the bed where we lay;
There the bees kissed the flowers. Has she got a new love? 15
  I feel like a wreck of the flood cast away.

The rawk of the autumn hangs o'er the woodland
  Like smoke from a city sulphurously grey;
The heronshaw lonely hangs over the floodland
  And cranks [5] its lone story throughout the dull day; 20
There's no green on the hedges, no leaves on the dark wood,
  No cows on the pasture or sheep on the lea;
The linnets chirp still, and how happy the lark would
  Sing songs to sweet Susan to remind her of me.

[1] mist [2] curlews [3] flutter [4] swooping [5] croaks

When First I Came Here

EDWARD THOMAS [1878–1917]

When first I came here I had hope,
Hope for I knew not what. Fast beat
My heart at sight of the tall slope
Or grass and yews, as if my feet

Only by scaling its steps of chalk 5
Would see something no other hill
Ever disclosed. And now I walk
Down it the last time. Never will

My heart beat so again at sight
Of any hill although as fair 10
And loftier. For infinite
The change, late unperceived, this year,

The twelfth, suddenly, shows me plain.
Hope now,—not health, nor cheerfulness,
Since they can come and go again, 15
As often one brief hour witnesses,—

Just hope has gone for ever. Perhaps
I may love other hills yet more
Than this: the future and the maps
Hide something I was waiting for. 20

One thing I know, that love with chance
And use and time and necessity
Will grow, and louder the heart's dance
At parting than at meeting be.

When Lovely Woman

OLIVER GOLDSMITH [1728–1774]

When lovely woman stoops to folly,
  And finds too late that men betray,

What charm can soothe her melancholy,
  What art can wash her guilt away?

The only art her guilt to cover, 5
  To hide her shame from every eye,
To give repentance to her lover,
  And wring his bosom—is to die.

Prothalamion

EDMUND SPENSER [1552–1599]

Calm was the day, and through the trembling air
Sweet-breathing Zephyrus did softly play,
A gentle spirit, that lightly did delay
Hot Titan's beams, which then did glister fair;
When I (whom sullen care, 5
Through discontent of my long fruitless stay
In princes' court, and expectation vain
Of idle hopes, which still do fly away,
Like empty shadows, did afflict my brain)
Walked forth to ease my pain 10
Along the shore of silver streaming Thames;
Whose rutty bank, the which his river hems,
Was painted all with variable flowers,
And all the meads adorned with dainty gems
Fit to deck maidens' bowers, 15
And crown their paramours,
Against the bridal day, which is not long.
  Sweet Thames, run softly, till I end my song.

There, in a meadow, by the river's side,
A flock of nymphs I chancëd to espy, 20
All lovely daughters of the flood thereby,
With goodly greenish locks, all loose untied,
As each had been a bride;
And each one had a little wicker basket,
Made of fine twigs entrailëd curiously, 25
In which they gathered flowers to fill their flasket,
And with fine fingers cropped full feateously
The tender stalks on high.

Of every sort which in that meadow grew
They gathered some; the violet pallid blue, 30
The little daisy, that at evening closes,
The virgin lily, and the primrose true,
With store of vermeil roses,
To deck their bridegroom's posies
Against the bridal day, which was not long. 35
Sweet Thames, run softly, till I end my song.

With that I saw two swans of goodly hue
Come softly swimming down along the Lee.
Two fairer birds I yet did never see;
The snow which doth the top of Pindus strew 40
Did never whiter shew,
Nor Jove himself, when he a swan would be
For love of Leda, whiter did appear;
Yet Leda was, they say, as white as he,
Yet not so white as these, nor nothing near; 45
So purely white they were
That even the gentle stream, the which them bare,
Seemed foul to them, and bade his billows spare
To wet their silken feathers, lest they might
Soil their fair plumes with water not so fair, 50
And mar their beauties bright,
That shone as heaven's light,
Against their bridal day, which was not long.
Sweet Thames, run softly, till I end my song.

Eftsoons the nymphs, which now had flowers their fill, 55
Ran all in haste to see that silver brood,
As they came floating on the crystal flood;
Whom when they saw, they stood amazëd still,
Their wondering eyes to fill;
Them seemed they never saw a sight so fair 60
Of fowls so lovely, that they sure did deem
Them heavenly born, or to be that same pair
Which through the sky draw Venus' silver team;
For sure they did not seem
To be begot of any earthly seed, 65
But rather angels, or of angels' breed;

Yet were they bred of summer's heat, they say,
In sweetest season, when each flower and weed
The earth did fresh array;
So fresh they seemed as day, 70
Even as their bridal day, which was not long.
  Sweet Thames, run softly, till I end my song.

Then forth they all out of their baskets drew
Great store of flowers, the honor of the field,
That to the sense did fragrant odors yield, 75
All which upon those goodly birds they threw,
And all the waves did strew,
That like old Peneus' waters they did seem,
When down along by pleasant Tempe's shore,
Scatt'rëd with flowers, through Thessaly they stream, 80
That they appear, through lilies' plenteous store,
Like a bride's chamber floor.
Two of those nymphs meanwhile two garlands bound
Of freshest flowers which in that mead they found,
The which presenting all in trim array, 85
Their snowy foreheads therewithal they crowned,
Whilst one did sing this lay,
Prepared against that day,
Against their bridal day, which was not long:
  Sweet Thames, run softly, till I end my song. 90

"Ye gentle birds, the world's fair ornament,
And heaven's glory, whom this happy hour
Doth lead unto your lovers' blissful bower,
Joy may you have, and gentle hearts' content
Of your love's couplement; 95
And let fair Venus, that is queen of love,
With her heart-quelling son, upon you smile,
Whose smile, they say, hath virtue to remove
All love's dislike, and friendship's faulty guile
For ever to assoil. 100
Let endless peace your steadfast hearts accord,
And blessëd plenty wait upon your board;
And let your bed with pleasures chaste abound,
That fruitful issue may to you afford,

Which may your foes confound, 105
And make your joys redound
Upon your bridal day, which is not long."
  Sweet Thames, run softly, till I end my song.

So ended she; and all the rest around
To her redoubled that her undersong, 110
Which said their bridal day should not be long;
And gentle Echo from the neighbor ground
Their accents did resound.
So forth those joyous birds did pass along,
Adown the Lee, that to them murmured low, 115
As he would speak, but that he lacked a tongue,
Yet did by signs his glad affection show,
Making his stream run slow.
And all the fowl which in his flood did dwell
'Gan flock about these twain, that did excel 120
The rest, so far as Cynthia doth shend
The lesser stars. So they, enrangëd well,
Did on those two attend,
And their best service lend,
Against their wedding day, which was not long. 125
  Sweet Thames, run softly, till I end my song.

At length they all to merry London came,
To merry London, my most kindly nurse,
That to me gave this life's first native source,
Though from another place I take my name, 130
An house of ancient fame.
There when they came, whereas those bricky towers
The which on Thames' broad, agëd back do ride,
Where now the studious lawyers have their bowers,
There whilom wont the Templar Knights to bide, 135
Till they decayed through pride;
Next whereunto there stands a stately place,
Where oft I gainëd gifts and goodly grace
Of that great lord which therein wont to dwell,
Whose want too well now feels my friendless case— 140
But ah! here fits not well
Old woes, but joys, to tell,

Against the bridal day, which is not long.
  Sweet Thames, run softly, till I end my song.

Yet therein now doth lodge a noble peer, 145
Great England's glory, and the world's wide wonder,
Whose dreadful name late through all Spain did thunder,
And Hercules' two pillars standing near
Did make to quake and fear.
Fair branch of honor, flower of chivalry, 150
That fillest England with thy triumph's fame,
Joy have thou of thy noble victory,
And endless happiness of thine own name,
That promiseth the same;
That through thy prowess and victorious arms 155
Thy country may be freed from foreign harms;
And great Eliza's glorious name may ring
Through all the world, filled with thy wide alarms,
Which some brave muse may sing
To ages following, 160
Upon the bridal day, which is not long.
  Sweet Thames, run softly, till I end my song.

From those high towers this noble lord issuing,
Like radiant Hesper, when his golden hair
In the ocean billows he hath bathëd fair, 165
Descended to the river's open viewing,
With a great train ensuing.
Above the rest were goodly to be seen
Two gentle knights of lovely face and feature,
Beseeming well the bower of any queen, 170
With gifts of wit, and ornaments of nature,
Fit for so goodly stature,
That like the twins of Jove they seemed in sight,
Which deck the baldrick of the heavens bright.
They two, forth pacing to the river's side 175
Received those two fair brides, their love's delight;
Which, at the appointed tide,
Each one did make his bride,
Against their bridal day, which is not long.
  Sweet Thames, run softly, till I end my song. 180

The Canonization

JOHN DONNE [1573–1631]

For God's sake hold your tongue, and let me love,
  Or chide my palsy, or my gout,
My five gray hairs, or ruined fortune flout,
  With wealth your state, your mind with arts improve,
    Take you a course, get you a place, 5
    Observe his honor, or his grace,
Or the king's real, or his stampèd face.
  Contemplate, what you will approve,
  So you will let me love.

Alas, alas, who's injured by my love? 10
  What merchant's ships have my sighs drowned?
Who says my tears have overflowed his ground?
  When did my colds a forward spring remove?
    When did the heats which my veins fill
    Add one more to the plaguey bill? 15
Soldiers find wars, and lawyers find out still
  Litigious men, which quarrels move,
  Though she and I do love.

Call us what you will, we are made such by love;
  Call her one, me another fly, 20
We are tapers too, and at our own cost die,
  And we in us find the eagle and the dove.
    The phoenix riddle hath more wit
    By us, we two being one, are it.
So to one neutral thing both sexes fit, 25
  We die and rise the same, and prove
  Mysterious by this love.

We can die by it, if not live by love,
  And if unfit for tombs and hearse
Our legend be, it will be fit for verse; 30
  And if no piece of chronicle we prove,
    We'll build in sonnets pretty rooms;
    As well a well-wrought urn becomes

The greatest ashes, as half-acre tombs,
  And by these hymns, all shall approve 35
  Us *canonized* for love;

And thus invoke us; you whom reverend love
  Made one another's hermitage;
You to whom love was peace, that now is rage;
  Who did the whole world's soul contract, and drove 40
    Into the glasses of your eyes
    (So made such mirrors, and such spies,
That they did all to you epitomize),
  Countries, towns, courts: beg from above
  A pattern of your love! 45

They Flee from Me

SIR THOMAS WYATT [1503?–1542]

They flee from me, that sometime did me seek
With naked foot, stalking in my chamber.
I have seen them gentle, tame, and meek,
That now are wild, and do not remember
That sometime they put themself in danger 5
To take bread at my hand; and now they range
Busily seeking with a continual change.

Thanked be fortune it hath been otherwise
Twenty times better; but once, in special,
In thin array, after a pleasant guise, 10
When her loose gown from her shoulders did fall,
And she me caught in her arms long and small,
Therewith all sweetly did me kiss,
And softly said: "Dear heart, how like you this?"

It was no dream: I lay broad waking 15
But all is turned, thorough my gentleness,
Into a strange fashion of forsaking;
And I have leave to go of her goodness:
And she also to use newfangleness.
But since that I so kindly am served, 20
I would fain know what she hath deserved.

To the Memory of Mr. Oldham

JOHN DRYDEN [1631–1700]

Farewell, too little and too lately known,
Whom I began to think and call my own:
For sure our souls were near allied, and thine
Cast in the same poetic mold with mine.
One common note on either lyre did strike, 5
And knaves and fools we both abhorred alike.
To the same goal did both our studies drive:
The last set out the soonest did arrive.
Thus Nisus fell upon the slippery place,
Whilst his young friend performed and won the race. 10
O early ripe! to thy abundant store
What could advancing age have added more?
It might (what nature never gives the young)
Have taught the numbers of thy native tongue.
But satire needs not those, and wit will shine 15
Through the harsh cadence of a rugged line.
A noble error, and but seldom made,
When poets are by too much force betrayed.
Thy generous fruits, though gathered ere their prime,
Still showed a quickness; and maturing time 20
But mellows what we write to the dull sweets of rhyme.
Once more, hail, and farewell! farewell, thou young,
But ah! too short, Marcellus of our tongue!
Thy brows with ivy and with laurels bound;
But Fate and gloomy night encompass thee around. 25

Upon a Dying Lady

W. B. YEATS [1865–1939]

1. *Her Courtesy*

With the old kindness, the old distinguished grace,
She lies, her lovely piteous head amid dull red hair
Propped upon pillows, rouge on the pallor of her face.
She would not have us sad because she is lying there,

And when she meets our gaze her eyes are laughter-lit, 5
Her speech a wicked tale that we may vie with her,
Matching our broken-hearted wit against her wit,
Thinking of saints and of Petronius Arbiter.

II. *Certain Artists Bring Her Dolls and Drawings*

Bring where our Beauty lies
A new modeled doll, or drawing, 10
With a friend's or an enemy's
Features, or maybe showing
Her features when a tress
Of dull red hair was flowing
Over some silken dress 15
Cut in the Turkish fashion,
Or, it may be, like a boy's.
We have given the world our passion,
We have naught for death but toys.

III. *She Turns the Dolls' Faces to the Wall*

Because to-day is some religious festival 20
They had a priest say Mass, and even the Japanese,
Heel up and weight on toe, must face the wall
—Pedant in passion, learned in old courtesies,
Vehement and witty she had seemed—; the Venetian lady
Who had seemed to glide to some intrigue in her red shoes, 25
Her domino, her panniered skirt copied from Longhi;
The meditative critic; all are on their toes,
Even our Beauty with her Turkish trousers on.
Because the priest must have like every dog his day
Or keep us all awake with baying at the moon, 30
We and our dolls being but the world were best away.

IV. *The End of Day*

She is playing like a child
And penance is the play,
Fantastical and wild
Because the end of day 35
Shows her that some one soon
Will come from the house, and say—

Though play is but half done—
"Come in and leave the play."

v. *Her Race*

She has not grown uncivil 40
As narrow natures would
And called the pleasures evil
Happier days thought good;
She knows herself a woman,
No red and white of a face, 45
Or rank, raised from a common
Unreckonable race;
And how should her heart fail her
Or sickness break her will
With her dead brother's valor 50
For an example still?

vi. *Her Courage*

When her soul flies to the predestined dancing-place
(I have no speech but symbol, the pagan speech I made
Amid the dreams of youth) let her come face to face,
Amid that first astonishment, with Grania's shade, 55
All but the terrors of the woodland flight forgot
That made her Diarmuid dear, and some old cardinal
Pacing with half-closed eyelids in a sunny spot
Who had murmured of Giorgione at his latest breath—
Aye, and Achilles, Timor, Babar, Barhaim, all 60
Who have lived in joy and laughed into the face of Death.

vii. *Her Friends Bring Her a Christmas Tree*

Pardon, great enemy,
Without an angry thought
We've carried in our tree,
And here and there have bought 65
Till all the boughs are gay,
And she may look from the bed
On pretty things that may

Please a fantastic head.
Give her a little grace, 70
What if a laughing eye
Have looked into your face?
It is about to die.

Praise for an Urn

HART CRANE [1899–1932]

It was a kind and northern face
That mingled in such exile guise
The everlasting eyes of Pierrot
And, of Gargantua, the laughter.

His thoughts, delivered to me 5
From the white coverlet and pillow,
I see now, were inheritances—
Delicate riders of the storm.

The slant moon on the slanting hill
Once moved us toward presentiments 10
Of what the dead keep, living still,
And such assessments of the soul

As, perched in the crematory lobby,
The insistent clock commented on,
Touching as well upon our praise 15
Of glories proper to the time.

Still, having in mind gold hair,
I cannot see that broken brow
And miss the dry sound of bees
Stretching across a lucid space. 20

Scatter these well-meant idioms
Into the smoky spring that fills
The suburbs, where they will be lost.
They are no trophies of the sun.

In Memory of W. B. Yeats

W. H. AUDEN [1907–]

I

He disappeared in the dead of winter:
The brooks were frozen, the airports almost deserted,
And snow disfigured the public statues;
The mercury sank in the mouth of the dying day.
O all the instruments agree 5
The day of his death was a dark cold day.

Far from his illness
The wolves ran on through the evergreen forests,
The peasant river was untempted by the fashionable quays;
By mourning tongues 10
The death of the poet was kept from his poems.

But for him it was his last afternoon as himself,
An afternoon of nurses and rumors;
The provinces of his body revolted,
The squares of his mind were empty, 15
Silence invaded the suburbs,
The current of his feeling failed: he became his admirers.

Now he is scattered among a hundred cities
And wholly given over to unfamiliar affections;
To find his happiness in another kind of wood 20
And be punished under a foreign code of conscience.
The words of a dead man
Are modified in the guts of the living.

But in the importance and noise of tomorrow 24
When the brokers are roaring like beasts on the floor of the Bourse,
And the poor have the sufferings to which they are fairly accustomed,
And each in the cell of himself is almost convinced of his freedom;
A few thousand will think of this day
As one thinks of a day when one did something slightly unusual.

O all the instruments agree 30
The day of his death was a dark cold day.

II

You were silly like us: your gift survived it all;
The parish of rich women, physical decay,
Yourself; mad Ireland hurt you into poetry.
Now Ireland has her madness and her weather still, 35
For poetry makes nothing happen: it survives
In the valley of its saying where executives
Would never want to tamper; it flows south
From ranches of isolation and the busy griefs,
Raw towns that we believe and die in; it survives, 40
A way of happening, a mouth.

III

Earth, receive an honored guest;
William Yeats is laid to rest:
Let the Irish vessel lie
Emptied of its poetry. 45

Time that is intolerant
Of the brave and innocent,
And indifferent in a week
To a beautiful physique,

Worships language and forgives 50
Everyone by whom it lives;
Pardons cowardice, conceit,
Lays its honors at their feet.

Time that with this strange excuse
Pardoned Kipling and his views, 55
And will pardon Paul Claudel,
Pardons him for writing well.

In the nightmare of the dark
All the dogs of Europe bark,
And the living nations wait, 60
Each sequestered in its hate;

Intellectual disgrace
Stares from every human face,
And the seas of pity lie
Locked and frozen in each eye. 65

Follow, poet, follow right
To the bottom of the night,
With your unconstraining voice
Still persuade us to rejoice;

With the farming of a verse 70
Make a vineyard of the curse,
Sing of human unsuccess
In a rapture of distress;

In the deserts of the heart
Let the healing fountain start, 75
In the prison of his days
Teach the free man how to praise.

The Quaker Graveyard in Nantucket

(*For* WARREN WINSLOW, *Dead at Sea*)

ROBERT LOWELL [1917–]

Let man have dominion over the fishes of the sea and the fowls of the air and the beasts and the whole earth, and every creeping creature that moveth upon the earth.

I

A brackish reach of shoal off Madaket,—
The sea was still breaking violently and night
Had steamed into our North Atlantic Fleet,
When the drowned sailor clutched the drag-net. Light
Flashed from his matted head and marble feet, 5
He grappled at the net
With the coiled, hurdling muscles of his thighs:
The corpse was bloodless, a botch of reds and whites,
Its open, staring eyes
Were lustreless dead-lights 10
Or cabin-windows on a stranded hulk

Heavy with sand. We weight the body, close
Its eyes and heave it seaward whence it came,
Where the heel-headed dogfish barks its nose
On Ahab's void and forehead; and the name 15
Is blocked in yellow chalk.
Sailors, who pitch this portent at the sea
Where dreadnaughts shall confess
Its hell-bent deity,
When you are powerless 20
To sand-bag this Atlantic bulwark, faced
By the earth-shaker, green, unwearied, chaste
In his steel scales: ask for no Orphean lute
To pluck life back. The guns of the steeled fleet
Recoil and then repeat 25
The hoarse salute.

II

Whenever winds are moving and their breath
Heaves at the roped-in bulwarks of this pier,
The terns and sea-gulls tremble at your death
In these home waters. Sailor, can you hear 30
The Pequod's sea wings, beating landward, fall
Headlong and break on our Atlantic wall
Off 'Sconset, where the yawing S-boats splash
The bellbuoy, with ballooning spinnakers,
As the entangled, screeching mainsheet clears 35
The blocks: off Madaket, where lubbers lash
The heavy surf and throw their long lead squids
For blue-fish? Sea-gulls blink their heavy lids
Seaward. The winds' wings beat upon the stones,
Cousin, and scream for you and the claws rush 40
At the sea's throat and wring it in the slush
Of this old Quaker graveyard where the bones
Cry out in the long night for the hurt beast
Bobbing by Ahab's whaleboats in the East.

III

All you recovered from Poseidon died 45
With you, my cousin, and the harrowed brine
Is fruitless on the blue beard of the god,
Stretching beyond us to the castles in Spain,

Nantucket's westward haven. To Cape Cod
Guns, cradled on the tide, 50
Blast the eelgrass about a waterclock
Of bilge and backwash, roil the salt and sand
Lashing earth's scaffold, rock
Our warships in the hand
Of the great God, where time's contrition blues 55
Whatever it was these Quaker sailors lost
In the mad scramble of their lives. They died
When time was open-eyed,
Wooden and childish; only bones abide
There, in the nowhere, where their boats were tossed 60
Sky-high, where mariners had fabled news
Of Is, the swashing castle. What it cost
Them is their secret. In the monster's slick
I see the Quakers drown and hear their cry:
"If God himself had not been on our side, 65
If God himself had not been on our side,
When the Atlantic rose against us, why
Then it had swallowed us up quick."

IV

This is the end of the whaleroad and the whale
Who spewed Nantucket bones on the thrashed swell 70
And stirred the troubled waters to whirlpools
To send the Pequod packing off to hell:
This is the end of them, three-quarters fools,
Snatching at straws to sail
Seaward and seaward on the turntail whale, 75
Spouting out blood and water as it rolls,
Sick as a dog to these Atlantic shoals:
Clamavimus, O depths. Let the sea-gulls wail

For water, for the deep where the high tide
Mutters to its hurt self, mutters and ebbs. 80
Waves wallow in their wash, go out and out,
Leave only the death-rattle of the crabs,
The beach increasing, its enormous snout
Sucking the ocean's side.
This is the end of running on the waves; 85
We are poured out like water. Who will dance

The mast-lashed master of Leviathans
Up from this field of Quakers in their unstoned graves?

V

When the whale's viscera go and the roll
Of its corruption overruns this world 90
Beyond tree-swept Nantucket and Woods Hole
And Martha's Vineyard, Sailor, will your sword
Whistle and fall and sink into the fat?
In the great ash-pit of Jehoshaphat
The bones cry for the blood of the white whale, 95
The fat flukes arch and whack about its ears,
The death-lance churns into the sanctuary, tears
The gun-blue swingle, heaving like a flail,
And hacks the coiling life out: it works and drags
And rips the sperm-whale's midriff into rags, 100
Gobbets of blubber spill to wind and weather,
Sailor, and gulls go round the stoven timbers
Where the morning stars sing out together
And thunder shakes the white surf and dismembers
The red flag hammered in the mast-head. Hide, 105
Our steel, Jonas Messias, in Thy side.

Ode to the Confederate Dead

ALLEN TATE [1899–]

Row after row with strict impunity
The headstones yield their names to the element,
The wind whirrs without recollection;
In the riven troughs the splayed leaves
Pile up, of nature the casual sacrament 5
To the seasonal eternity of death;
Then driven by the fierce scrutiny
Of heaven to their election in the vast breath,
They sough the rumor of mortality.

Autumn is desolation in the plot 10
Of a thousand acres where these memories grow

From the inexhaustible bodies that are not
Dead, but feed the grass row after rich row.
Think of the autumns that have come and gone!—
Ambitious November with the humors of the year, 15
With a particular zeal for every slab,
Staining the uncomfortable angels that rot
On the slabs, a wing chipped here, an arm there:
The brute curiosity of an angel's stare
Turns you, like them, to stone, 20
Transforms the heaving air
Till plunged to a heavier world below
You shift your sea-space blindly
Heaving, turning like the blind crab.

Dazed by the wind, only the wind 25
The leaves flying, plunge

You know who have waited by the wall
The twilight certainty of an animal,
Those midnight restitutions of the blood
You know—the immitigable pines, the smoky frieze 30
Of the sky, the sudden call: you know the rage,
The cold pool left by the mounting flood,
Of muted Zeno and Parmenides.
You who have waited for the angry resolution
Of those desires that should be yours tomorrow, 35
You know the unimportant shrift of death
And praise the vision
And praise the arrogant circumstance
Of those who fall
Rank upon rank, hurried beyond decision— 40
Here by the sagging gate, stopped by the wall.

Seeing, seeing only the leaves
Flying, plunge and expire

Turn your eyes to the immoderate past,
Turn to the inscrutable infantry rising 45
Demons out of the earth—they will not last.
Stonewall, Stonewall, and the sunken fields of hemp,
Shiloh, Antietam, Malvern Hill, Bull Run.

Lost in that orient of the thick-and-fast
You will curse the setting sun. 50

Cursing only the leaves crying
Like an old man in a storm

You hear the shout, the crazy hemlocks point
With troubled fingers to the silence which
Smothers you, a mummy, in time. 55

The hound bitch
Toothless and dying, in a musty cellar
Hears the wind only.

Now that the salt of their blood
Stiffens the saltier oblivion of the sea, 60
Seals the malignant purity of the flood,
What shall we who count our days and bow
Our heads with a commemorial woe
In the ribboned coats of grim felicity,
What shall we say of the bones, unclean, 65
Whose verdurous anonymity will grow?
The ragged arms, the ragged heads and eyes
Lost in these acres of the ínsane green?
The gray lean spiders come, they come and go;
In a tangle of willows without light 70
The singular screech-owl's tight
Invisible lyric seeds the mind
With the furious murmur of their chivalry.

We shall say only the leaves
Flying, plunge and expire 75

We shall say only the leaves whispering
In the improbable mist of nightfall
That flies on multiple wing:
Night is the beginning and the end
And in between the ends of distraction 80
Waits mute speculation, the patient curse
That stones the eyes, or like the jaguar leaps
For his own image in a jungle pool, his victim.

What shall we say who have knowledge
Carried to the heart? Shall we take the act 85
To the grave? Shall we, more hopeful, set up the grave
In the house? The ravenous grave?

Leave now
The shut gate and the decomposing wall:
The gentle serpent, green in the mulberry bush, 90
Riots with his tongue through the hush—
Sentinel of the grave who counts us all!

The College Colonel

HERMAN MELVILLE [1819–1891]

He rides at their head;
A crutch by his saddle just slants in view,
One slung arm is in splints, you see,
Yet he guides his strong steed—how coldly too.

He brings his regiment home— 5
Not as they filed two years before,
But a remnant half-tattered, and battered, and worn,
Like castaway sailors, who—stunned
By the surf's loud roar,
Their mates dragged back and seen no more— 10
Again and again breast the surge,
And at last crawl, spent, to shore.

A still rigidity and pale—
An Indian aloofness lones his brow;
He has lived a thousand years 15
Compressed in battle's pains and prayers,
Marches and watches slow.
There are welcoming shouts, and flags;
Old men off hat to the Boy,
Wreaths from gay balconies fall at his feet, 20
But to *him*—there comes alloy.

It is not that a leg is lost,
It is not that an arm is maimed,

It is not that the fever has racked—
  Self he has long disclaimed. 25

But all through the Seven Days' Fight,
  And deep in the Wilderness grim,
And in the field-hospital tent,
  And Petersburg crater, and dim
Lean brooding in Libby, there came— 30
  Ah heaven!—what *truth* to him.

In Distrust of Merits

MARIANNE MOORE [1887–]

Strengthened to live, strengthened to die for
  medals and positioned victories?
They're fighting, fighting, fighting the blind
  man who thinks he sees,—
who cannot see that the enslaver is 5
enslaved; the hater, harmed. O shining O
    firm star, O tumultuous
      ocean lashed till small things go
    as they will, the mountainous
      wave makes us who look, know 10

depth. Lost at sea before they fought! O
  star of David, star of Bethlehem,
O black imperial lion
  of the Lord—emblem
of a risen world—be joined at last, be 15
joined. There is hate's crown beneath which all is
    death; there's love's without which none
      is king; the blessed deeds bless
    the halo. As contagion
      of sickness makes sickness, 20

contagion of trust can make trust. They're
  fighting in deserts and caves, one by
one, in battalions and squadrons;
  they're fighting that I

may yet recover from the disease, *my* 25
self; some have it lightly, some will die. "Man's
wolf to man?" And we devour
ourselves? The enemy could not
have made a greater breach in our
defenses. One pilot- 30

ing a blind man can escape him, but
Job disheartened by false comfort knew,
that nothing is so defeating
as a blind man who
can see. O alive who are dead, who are 35
proud not to see, O small dust of the earth
that walks so arrogantly,
trust begets power and faith is
an affectionate thing. We
vow, we make this promise 40

to the fighting—it's a promise—"We'll
never hate black, white, red, yellow, Jew,
Gentile, Untouchable." We are
not competent to
make our vows. With set jaw they are fighting, 45
fighting, fighting,—some we love whom we know,
some we love but know not—that
hearts may feel and not be numb.
It cures me; or am I what
I can't believe in? Some 50

in snow, some on crags, some in quicksands,
little by little, much by much, they
are fighting fighting fighting that where
there was death there may
be life. "When a man is prey to anger, 55
he is moved by outside things; when he holds
his ground in patience patience
patience, that is action or
beauty," the soldier's defense
and hardest armor for 60

the fight. The world's an orphans' home. Shall
we never have peace without sorrow?

without pleas of the dying for
  help that won't come? O
quiet form upon the dust, I cannot 65
look and yet I must. If these great patient
    dyings—all these agonies
      and woundbearings and blood shed—
    can teach us how to live, these
      dyings were not wasted. 70

Hate-hardened heart, O heart of iron,
  iron is iron till it is rust.
There never was a war that was
  not inward; I must
fight till I have conquered in myself what 75
causes war, but I would not believe it.
    I inwardly did nothing.
      O Iscariotlike crime!
    Beauty is everlasting
      and dust is for a time. 80

Lee in the Mountains

1865–1870

DONALD DAVIDSON [1893–]

Walking into the shadows, walking alone
Where the sun falls through the ruined boughs of locusts
Up to the president's office . . .
                                        Hearing the voices
Whisper, *Hush, it is General Lee!* And strangely
Hearing my own voice say, *Good morning, boys.* 5
(Don't get up. You are early. It is long
Before the bell. You will have long to wait
On these cold steps. . . .)
                                The young have time to wait.
But soldiers' faces under their tossing flags
Lift no more by any road or field, 10
And I am spent with old wars and new sorrow.
Walking the rocky path, where steps decay
And the paint cracks and grass eats on the stone.

It is not General Lee, young men . . .
It is Robert Lee in a dark civilian suit who walks, 15
An outlaw fumbling for the latch, a voice
Commanding in a dream where no flag flies.

My father's house is taken and his hearth
Left to the candle-drippings where the ashes
Whirl at a chimney-breath on the cold stone. 20
I can hardly remember my father's look, I cannot
Answer his voice as he calls farewell in the misty
Mounting where riders gather at gates.
He was old then—I was a child—his hand
Held out for mine, some daybreak snatched away, 25
And he rode out, a broken man. Now let
His lone grave keep, surer than cypress roots,
The vow I made beside him. God too late
Unseals to certain eyes the drift
Of time and the hopes of men and a sacred cause. 30
The fortune of the Lees goes with the land
Whose sons will keep it still. My mother
Told me much. She sat among the candles,
Fingering the *Memoirs,* now so long unread.
And as my pen moves on across the page 35
Her voice comes back, a murmuring distillation
Of old Virginia times now faint and gone,
The hurt of all that was and cannot be.

Why did my father write? I know he saw
History clutched as a wraith out of blowing mist 40
Where tongues are loud, and a glut of little souls
Laps at the too much blood and the burning house.
He would have his say, but I shall not have mine.
What I do is only a son's devoir
To a lost father. Let him only speak. 45
The rest must pass to men who never knew
(But on a written page) the strike of armies,
And never heard the long Confederate cry
Charge through the muzzling smoke or saw the bright
Eyes of the beardless boys go up to death. 50
It is Robert Lee who writes with his father's hand—
The rest must go unsaid and the lips be locked.

If all were told, as it cannot be told—
If all the dread opinion of the heart
Now could speak, now in the shame and torment 55
Lashing the bound and trampled States—

If a word were said, as it cannot be said—

I see clear waters run in Virginia's Valley
And in the house the weeping of young women
Rises no more. The waves of grain begin. 60
The Shenandoah is golden with new grain.
The Blue Ridge, crowned with a haze of light,
Thunders no more. The horse is at plow. The rifle
Returns to the chimney crotch and the hunter's hand.
And nothing else than this? Was it for this 65
That on an April day we stacked our arms
Obedient to a soldier's trust? To lie
Ground by heels of little men,
Forever maimed, defeated, lost, impugned?
And was I then betrayed? Did I betray? 70

If it were said, as still it might be said—
If it were said, and a word should run like fire,
Like living fire into the roots of grass,
The sunken flag would kindle on wild hills,
The brooding hearts would waken, and the dream 75
Stir like a crippled phantom under the pines,
And this torn earth would quicken into shouting
Beneath the feet of ragged bands—
The pen
Turns to the waiting page, the sword
Bows to the rust that cankers and the silence. 80

Among these boys whose eyes lift up to mine
Within gray walls where droning wasps repeat
A hollow reveillé, I still must face,
Day after day, the courier with his summons
Once more to surrender, now to surrender all. 85
Without arms or men I stand, but with knowledge only
I face what long I saw, before others knew,
When Pickett's men streamed back, and I heard the tangled
Cry of the Wilderness wounded, bloody with doom.

The mountains, once I said, in the little room 90
At Richmond, by the huddled fire, but still
The President shook his head. The mountains wait,
I said, in the long beat and rattle of siege
At cratered Petersburg. Too late
We sought the mountains and those people came. 95
And Lee is in mountains now, beyond Appomattox,
Listening long for voices that never will speak
Again; hearing the hoofbeats come and go and fade
Without a stop, without a brown hand lifting
The tent-flap, or a bugle call at dawn, 100
Or ever on the long white road the flag
Of Jackson's quick brigades. I am alone,
Trapped, consenting, taken at last in mountains.

It is not the bugle now, or the long roll beating.
The simple stroke of a chapel bell forbids 105
The hurtling dream, recalls the lonely mind.
Young men, the God of your fathers is a just
And merciful God Who in this blood once shed
On your green altars measures out all days,
And measures out the grace 110
Whereby alone we live;
And in His might He waits,
Brooding within the certitude of time,
To bring this lost forsaken valor
And the fierce faith undying 115
And the love quenchless
To flower among the hills to which we cleave,
To fruit upon the mountains whither we flee,
Never forsaking, never denying
His children and His children's children forever 120
Unto all generations of the faithful heart.

Good Friday, 1613. Riding Westward

JOHN DONNE [1573–1631]

Let man's soul be a sphere, and then in this
The intelligence that moves, devotion is;

And as the other spheres, by being grown
Subject to foreign motion, lose their own,
And being by others hurried every day, 5
Scarce in a year their natural form obey:
Pleasure or business, so, our souls admit
For their first mover, and are whirled by it.
Hence is 't that I am carried towards the west
This day, when my soul's form bends towards the east. 10
There I should see a sun, by rising set,
And by that setting, endless day beget;
But that Christ on this cross did rise and fall,
Sin had eternally benighted all.
Yet dare I'almost be glad I do not see 15
That spectacle of too much weight for me.
Who sees God's face, that is self life, must die;
What a death were it then to see God die!
It made his own lieutenant, nature, shrink;
It made his footstool crack, and the sun wink. 20
Could I behold those hands which span the poles
And tune all spheres at once, pierced with those holes?
Could I behold that endless height, which is
Zenith to us and our antipodes,
Humbled below us? or that blood which is 25
The seat of all our souls, if not of his,
Made dirt of dust, or that flesh which was worn
By God for his apparel, ragg'd and torn?
If on these things I durst not look, durst I
Upon his miserable mother cast mine eye, 30
Who was God's partner here, and furnished thus
Half of that sacrifice which ransomed us?
Though these things, as I ride, be from mine eye,
They'are present yet unto my memory,
For that looks towards them; and thou look'st towards me, 35
O Savior, as thou hang'st upon the tree;
I turn my back to thee but to receive
Corrections, till thy mercies bid thee leave.
Oh, think me worth thine anger, punish me,
Burn off my rusts, and my deformity; 40
Restore thine image, so much, by thy grace,
That thou mayst know me, and I'll turn my face.

The Second Coming

W. B. YEATS [1865–1939]

Turning and turning in the widening gyre
The falcon cannot hear the falconer;
Things fall apart; the centre cannot hold;
Mere anarchy is loosed upon the world,
The blood-dimmed tide is loosed, and everywhere 5
The ceremony of innocence is drowned;
The best lack all conviction, while the worst
Are full of passionate intensity.

Surely some revelation is at hand;
Surely the Second Coming is at hand. 10
The Second Coming! Hardly are those words out
When a vast image out of *Spiritus Mundi*
Troubles my sight: somewhere in sands of thc desert
A shape with lion body and the head of a man,
A gaze blank and pitiless as the sun, 15
Is moving its slow thighs, while all about it
Reel shadows of the indignant desert birds.
The darkness drops again; but now I know
That twenty centuries of stony sleep
Were vexed to nightmare by a rocking cradle, 20
And what rough beast, its hour come round at last,
Slouches towards Bethlehem to be born?

The Waste Land

T. S. ELIOT [1888–]

"Nam Sibyllam quidem Cumis ego ipse oculis meis vidi in ampulla pendere, et cum illi pueri dicerent: Σίβυλλα τι θέλεις; respondebat illa: ἀποθανεῖν θέλω."

I. *The Burial of the Dead*

allusion to Chaucer? (Kenner)

April is the cruelest month, breeding
Lilacs out of the dead land, mixing
Memory and desire, stirring
Dull roots with spring rain.

Winter kept us warm, covering 5
Earth in forgetful snow, feeding
A little life with dried tubers.
Summer surprised us, coming over the Starnbergersee
With a shower of rain; we stopped in the colonnade,
And went on in sunlight, into the Hofgarten, 10
And drank coffee, and talked for an hour.
Bin gar keine Russin, stamm' aus Litauen, echt deutsch.
And when we were children, staying at the archduke's,
My cousin's, he took me out on a sled,
And I was frightened. He said, Marie, 15
Marie, hold on tight. And down we went.
In the mountains, there you feel free.
I read, much of the night, and go south in the winter.

What are the roots that clutch, what branches grow
Out of this stony rubbish? Son of man, 20
You cannot say, or guess, for you know only
A heap of broken images, where the sun beats,
And the dead tree gives no shelter, the cricket no relief,
And the dry stone no sound of water. Only
There is shadow under this red rock, 25
(Come in under the shadow of this red rock),
And I will show you something different from either
Your shadow at morning striding behind you
Or your shadow at evening rising to meet you;
I will show you fear in a handful of dust. 30

Frisch weht der Wind
Der Heimat zu
Mein Irisch Kind,
Wo weilest du?

'You gave me hyacinths first a year ago; 35
'They called me the hyacinth girl.'
—Yet when we came back, late, from the hyacinth garden,
Your arms full, and your hair wet, I could not
Speak, and my eyes failed, I was neither
Living nor dead, and I knew nothing, 40
Looking into the heart of light, the silence.
Oed' und leer das Meer.

Madame Sosostris, famous clairvoyante,
Had a bad cold, nevertheless

Is known to be the wisest woman in Europe, 45
With a wicked pack of cards. Here, said she,
Is your card, the drowned Phoenician Sailor,
(Those are pearls that were his eyes. Look!)
Here is Belladonna, the Lady of the Rocks,
The lady of situations. 50
Here is the man with three staves, and here the Wheel,
And here is the one-eyed merchant, and this card,
Which is blank, is something he carries on his back,
Which I am forbidden to see. I do not find
The Hanged Man. Fear death by water. 55
I see crowds of people, walking round in a ring.
Thank you. If you see dear Mrs. Equitone,
Tell her I bring the horoscope myself:
One must be so careful these days.

Unreal City, 60
Under the brown fog of a winter dawn,
A crowd flowed over London Bridge, so many,
I had not thought death had undone so many.
Sighs, short and infrequent, were exhaled,
And each man fixed his eyes before his feet. 65
Flowed up the hill and down King William Street,
To where Saint Mary Woolnoth kept the hours
With a dead sound on the final stroke of nine.
There I saw one I knew, and stopped him, crying: 'Stetson!
'You who were with me in the ships at Mylae! 70
'That corpse you planted last year in your garden,
'Has it begun to sprout? Will it bloom this year?
'Or has the sudden frost disturbed its bed?
'Oh keep the Dog far hence, that's friend to men,
'Or with his nails he'll dig it up again! 75
'You! hypocrite lecteur!—mon semblable,—mon frère!'

II. *A Game of Chess*

The Chair she sat in, like a burnished throne,
Glowed on the marble, where the glass
Held up by standards wrought with fruited vines
From which a golden Cupidon peeped out 80
(Another hid his eyes behind his wing)

Doubled the flames of seven branched candelabra
Reflecting light upon the table as
The glitter of her jewels rose to meet it,
From satin cases poured in rich profusion; 85
In vials of ivory and colored glass
Unstoppered, lurked her strange synthetic perfumes,
Unguent, powdered, or liquid—troubled, confused
And drowned the sense in odors; stirred by the air
That freshened from the window, these ascended 90
In fattening the prolonged candle-flames,
Flung their smoke into the laquearia,
Stirring the pattern on the coffered ceiling.
Huge sea-wood fed with copper
Burned green and orange, framed by the colored stone, 95
In which sad light a carvèd dolphin swam.
Above the antique mantel was displayed
As though a window gave upon the sylvan scene
The change of Philomel, by the barbarous king
So rudely forced; yet there the nightingale 100
Filled all the desert with inviolable voice
And still she cried, and still the world pursues,
'Jug Jug' to dirty ears.
And other withered stumps of time
Were told upon the walls; staring forms 105
Leaned out, leaning, hushing the room enclosed.
Footsteps shuffled on the stair.
Under the firelight, under the brush, her hair
Spread out in fiery points
Glowed into words, then would be savagely still. 110

'My nerves are bad tonight. Yes, bad. Stay with me.
'Speak to me. Why do you never speak. Speak.
'What are you thinking of? What thinking? What?
'I never know what you are thinking. Think.'

I think we are in rats' alley 115
Where the dead men lost their bones.

'What is that noise?'
The wind under the door.

'What is that noise now? What is the wind doing?'
Nothing again nothing. 120
'Do
'You know nothing? Do you see nothing? Do you remember
'Nothing?'

I remember
Those are pearls that were his eyes. 125
'Are you alive or not? Is there nothing in your head?'
But
O O O O that Shakespeherian Rag—
It's so elegant
So intelligent 130
'What shall I do now? What shall I do?'
'I shall rush out as I am, and walk the street
'With my hair down, so. What shall we do tomorrow?
'What shall we ever do?'
The hot water at ten. 135
And if it rains, a closed car at four.
And we shall play a game of chess,
Pressing lidless eyes and waiting for a knock upon the door.

When Lil's husband got demobbed, I said—
I didn't mince my words, I said to her myself, 140
HURRY UP PLEASE ITS TIME
Now Albert's coming back, make yourself a bit smart.
He'll want to know what you done with that money he gave you
To get yourself some teeth. He did, I was there.
You have them all out, Lil, and get a nice set, 145
He said, I swear, I can't bear to look at you.
And no more can't I, I said, and think of poor Albert,
He's been in the army four years, he wants a good time,
And if you don't give it him, there's others will, I said.
Oh is there, she said. Something o'that, I said. 150
Then I'll know who to thank, she said, and give me a straight look.
HURRY UP PLEASE ITS TIME
If you don't like it you can get on with it, I said.
Others can pick and choose if you can't.
But if Albert makes off, it won't be for lack of telling. 155
You ought to be ashamed, I said, to look so antique.
(And her only thirty-one.)

I can't help it, she said, pulling a long face,
It's them pills I took, to bring it off, she said.
(She's had five already, and nearly died of young George.) 160
The chemist said it would be all right, but I've never been the same.
You *are* a proper fool, I said.
Well, if Albert won't leave you alone, there it is, I said,
What you get married for if you don't want children?
HURRY UP PLEASE ITS TIME 165
Well, that Sunday Albert was home, they had a hot gammon,
And they asked me in to dinner, to get the beauty of it hot—
HURRY UP PLEASE ITS TIME
HURRY UP PLEASE ITS TIME
Goonight Bill. Goonight Lou. Goonight May. Goonight. 170
Ta ta. Goonight. Goonight.
Good night, ladies, good night, sweet ladies, good night, good night.

III. *The Fire Sermon*

The river's tent is broken: the last fingers of leaf
Clutch and sink into the wet bank. The wind
Crosses the brown land, unheard. The nymphs are departed. 175
Sweet Thames, run softly, till I end my song.
The river bears no empty bottles, sandwich papers,
Silk handkerchiefs, cardboard boxes, cigarette ends
Or other testimony of summer nights. The nymphs are departed.
And their friends, the loitering heirs of city directors; 180
Departed, have left no addresses.
By the waters of Leman I sat down and wept . . .
Sweet Thames, run softly till I end my song,
Sweet Thames, run softly, for I speak not loud or long.
But at my back in a cold blast I hear 185
The rattle of the bones, and chuckle spread from ear to ear.
A rat crept softly through the vegetation
Dragging its slimy belly on the bank
While I was fishing in the dull canal
On a winter evening round behind the gashouse 190
Musing upon the king my brother's wreck
And on the king my father's death before him.
White bodies naked on the low damp ground
And bones cast in a little low dry garret,
Rattled by the rat's foot only, year to year. 195
But at my back from time to time I hear

The sound of horns and motors, which shall bring
Sweeney to Mrs. Porter in the spring.
O the moon shone bright on Mrs. Porter
And on her daughter 200
They wash their feet in soda water
Et O ces voix d'enfants, chantant dans la coupole!

Twit twit twit
Jug jug jug jug jug jug
So rudely forc'd. 205
Tereu

Unreal City
Under the brown fog of a winter noon
Mr. Eugenides, the Smyrna merchant
Unshaven, with a pocket full of currants 210
C. i. f. London: documents at sight,
Asked me in demotic French
To luncheon at the Cannon Street Hotel
Followed by a weekend at the Metropole.
At the violet hour, when the eyes and back 215
Turn upward from the desk, when the human engine waits
Like a taxi throbbing waiting,
I Tiresias, though blind, throbbing between two lives,
Old man with wrinkled female breasts, can see
At the violet hour, the evening hour that strives 220
Homeward, and brings the sailor home from sea,
The typist home at teatime, clears her breakfast, lights
Her stove, and lays out food in tins.
Out of the window perilously spread
Her drying combinations touched by the sun's last rays, 225
On the divan are piled (at night her bed)
Stockings, slippers, camisoles, and stays.
I Tiresias, old man with wrinkled dugs
Perceived the scene, and foretold the rest—
I too awaited the expected guest. 230
He, the young man carbuncular, arrives,
A small house agent's clerk, with one bold stare,
One of the low on whom assurance sits
As a silk hat on a Bradford millionaire.

The time is now propitious, as he guesses, 235
The meal is ended, she is bored and tired,
Endeavors to engage her in caresses
Which still are unreproved, if undesired.
Flushed and decided, he assaults at once;
Exploring hands encounter no defense; 240
His vanity requires no response,
And makes a welcome of indifference.
(And I Tiresias have foresuffered all
Enacted on this same divan or bed;
I who have sat by Thebes below the wall 245
And walked among the lowest of the dead.)
Bestows one final patronizing kiss,
And gropes his way, finding the stairs unlit . . .

She turns and looks a moment in the glass,
Hardly aware of her departed lover; 250
Her brain allows one half-formed thought to pass:
'Well now that's done: and I'm glad it's over.'
When lovely woman stoops to folly and Goldsmith p. 478
Paces about her room again, alone,
She smooths her hair with automatic hand, 255
And puts a record on the gramophone.

'This music crept by me upon the waters'
And along the Strand, up Queen Victoria Street.
O City city, I can sometimes hear
Beside a public bar in Lower Thames Street, 260
The pleasant whining of a mandolin
And a clatter and a chatter from within
Where fishmen lounge at noon: where the walls
Of Magnus Martyr hold
Inexplicable splendor of Ionian white and gold. 265

The river sweats
Oil and tar
The barges drift
With the turning tide
Red sails 270
Wide
To leeward, swing on the heavy spar.

The barges wash
Drifting logs
Down Greenwich reach 275
Past the Isle of Dogs.
        Weialala leia
        Wallala leialala

Elizabeth and Leicester
Beating oars 280
The stern was formed
A gilded shell
Red and gold
The brisk swell
Rippled both shores 285
Southwest wind
Carried down stream
The peal of bells
White towers
        Weialala leia 290
        Wallala leialala

'Trams and dusty trees.
Highbury bore me. Richmond and Kew
Undid me. By Richmond I raised my knees
Supine on the floor of a narrow canoe.' 295

'My feet are at Moorgate, and my heart
Under my feet. After the event
He wept. He promised "a new start."
I made no comment. What should I resent?'

'On Margate Sands. 300
I can connect
Nothing with nothing
The broken fingernails of dirty hands.
My people humble people who expect
Nothing.' 305
        la la

To Carthage then I came
Burning burning burning burning

O Lord Thou pluckest me out
O Lord Thou pluckest 310

burning

IV. *Death by Water*

Phlebas the Phoenician, a fortnight dead,
Forgot the cry of gulls, and the deep sea swell
And the profit and loss.
A current under sea 315
Picked his bones in whispers. As he rose and fell
He passed the stages of his age and youth
Entering the whirlpool.
Gentile or Jew
O you who turn the wheel and look to windward, 320
Consider Phlebas, who was once handsome and tall as you.

V. *What the Thunder Said*

After the torchlight red on sweaty faces
After the frosty silence in the gardens
After the agony in stony places
The shouting and the crying 325
Prison and palace and reverberation
Of thunder of spring over distant mountains
He who was living is now dead
We who were living are now dying
With a little patience 330

Here is no water but only rock
Rock and no water and the sandy road
The road winding above among the mountains
Which are mountains of rock without water
If there were water we should stop and drink 335
Amongst the rock one cannot stop or think
Sweat is dry and feet are in the sand
If there were only water amongst the rock
Dead mountain mouth of carious teeth that cannot spit
Here one can neither stand nor lie nor sit 340
There is not even silence in the mountains
But dry sterile thunder without rain

There is not even solitude in the mountains
But red sullen faces sneer and snarl
From doors of mudcracked houses
If there were water 345
And no rock
If there were rock
And also water
And water
A spring 350
A pool among the rock
If there were the sound of water only
Not the cicada
And dry grass singing
But sound of water over a rock 355
Where the hermit-thrush sings in the pine trees
Drip drop drip drop drop drop drop
But there is no water

Luke 24:13-31

Who is the third who walks always beside you?
When I count, there are only you and I together 360
But when I look ahead up the white road
There is always another one walking beside you
Gliding wrapped in a brown mantle, hooded
I do not know whether a man or a woman
—But who is that on the other side of you? 365

What is that sound high in the air
Murmur of maternal lamentation
Who are those hooded hordes swarming
Over endless plains, stumbling in cracked earth
Ringed by the flat horizon only 370
What is the city over the mountains
Cracks and reforms and bursts in the violet air
Falling towers
Jerusalem Athens Alexandria
Vienna London 375
Unreal

A woman drew her long black hair out tight
And fiddled whisper music on those strings

And bats with baby faces in the violet light
Whistled, and beat their wings 380
And crawled head downward down a blackened wall
And upside down in air were towers
Tolling reminiscent bells, that kept the hours
And voices singing out of empty cisterns and exhausted wells.

In this decayed hole among the mountains 385
In the faint moonlight, the grass is singing
Over the tumbled graves, about the chapel
There is the empty chapel, only the wind's home.
It has no windows, and the door swings,
Dry bones can harm no one. 390
Only a cock stood on the rooftree
Co co rico co co rico
In a flash of lightning. Then a damp gust
Bringing rain

Ganga was sunken, and the limp leaves 395
Waited for rain, while the black clouds
Gathered far distant, over Himavant.
The jungle crouched, humped in silence.
Then spoke the thunder
Da 400
Datta: what have we given?
My friend, blood shaking my heart
The awful daring of a moment's surrender
Which an age of prudence can never retract
By this, and this only, we have existed 405
Which is not to be found in our obituaries
Or in memories draped by the beneficent spider
Or under seals broken by the lean solicitor
In our empty rooms
Da 410
Dayadhvam: I have heard the key
Turn in the door once and turn once only
We think of the key, each in his prison
Thinking of the key, each confirms a prison
Only at nightfall, ethereal rumors 415
Revive for a moment a broken Coriolanus
Da

Damyata: The boat responded
Gaily, to the hand expert with sail and oar
The sea was calm, your heart would have responded 420
Gaily, when invited, beating obedient
To controlling hands

I sat upon the shore
Fishing, with the arid plain behind me
Shall I at least set my lands in order? 425
London Bridge is falling down falling down falling down
Poi s'ascose nel foco che gli affina
Quando fiam uti chelidon—O swallow swallow
Le Prince d'Aquitaine à la tour abolie
These fragments I have shored against my ruins 430
Why then Ile fit you. Hieronymo's mad againe.
Datta. Dayadhvam. Damyata.
Shantih shantih shantih

O Where Are You Going?

W. H. AUDEN [1907–]

"O where are you going?" said reader to rider,
"That valley is fatal when furnaces burn,
Yonder's the midden whose odors will madden,
That gap is the grave where the tall return."

"O do you imagine," said fearer to farer, 5
"That dusk will delay on your path to the pass,
Your diligent looking discover the lacking
Your footsteps feel from granite to grass?"

"O what was that bird," said horror to hearer,
"Did you see that shape in the twisted trees? 10
Behind you swiftly the figure comes softly,
The spot on your skin is a shocking disease?"

"Out of this house"—said rider to reader,
"Yours never will"—said farer to fearer,
"They're looking for you"—said hearer to horror, 15
As he left them there, as he left them there.

Just a Smack at Auden

WILLIAM EMPSON [1906–]

Waiting for the end, boys, waiting for the end.
What is there to be or do?
What's become of me or you?
Are we kind or are we true?
Sitting two and two, boys, waiting for the end. 5

Shall I build a tower, boys, knowing it will rend
Crack upon the hour, boys, waiting for the end?
Shall I pluck a flower, boys, shall I save or spend?
All turns sour, boys, waiting for the end.

Shall I send a wire, boys? Where is there to send? 10
All are under fire, boys, waiting for the end.
Shall I turn a sire, boys? Shall I choose a friend?
The fat is in the pyre, boys, waiting for the end.

Shall I make it clear, boys, for all to apprehend,
Those that will not hear, boys, waiting for the end, 15
Knowing it is near, boys, trying to pretend,
Sitting in cold fear, boys, waiting for the end?

Shall we send a cable, boys, accurately penned,
Knowing we are able, boys, waiting for the end,
Via the Tower of Babel, boys? Christ will not ascend, 20
He's hiding in his stable, boys, waiting for the end.

Shall we blow a bubble, boys, glittering to distend,
Hiding from our trouble, boys, waiting for the end?
When you build on rubble, boys, Nature will append
Double and re-double, boys, waiting for the end. 25

Shall we make a tale, boys, that things are sure to mend,
Playing bluff and hale, boys, waiting for the end?
It will be born stale, boys, stinking to offend,
Dying ere it fail, boys, waiting for the end.

Shall we go all wild, boys, waste and make them lend, 30
Playing at the child, boys, waiting for the end?

It has all been filed, boys, history has a trend,
Each of us enisled, boys, waiting for the end.

What was said by Marx, boys, what did he perpend?
No good being sparks, boys, waiting for the end. 35
Treason of the clerks, boys, curtains that descend,
Lights becoming darks, boys, waiting for the end.

Waiting for the end, boys, waiting for the end.
Not a chance of blend, boys, things have got to tend.
Think of those who vend, boys, think of how we wend, 40
Waiting for the end, boys, waiting for the end.

Journey of the Magi

T. S. ELIOT [1888–]

'A cold coming we had of it,
Just the worst time of the year
For a journey, and such a long journey:
The ways deep and the weather sharp,
The very dead of winter.' 5
And the camels galled, sore-footed, refractory,
Lying down in the melting snow,
There were times we regretted
The summer palaces on slopes, the terraces,
And the silken girls bringing sherbet. 10
Then the camel men cursing and grumbling
And running away, and wanting their liquor and women,
And the night-fires going out, and the lack of shelters,
And the cities hostile and the towns unfriendly
And the villages dirty and charging high prices: 15
A hard time we had of it.
At the end we preferred to travel all night,
Sleeping in snatches,
With the voices singing in our ears, saying
That this was all folly. 20

Then at dawn we came down to a temperate valley,
Wet, below the snow line, smelling of vegetation;
With a running stream and a water-mill beating the darkness,

And three trees on the low sky,
And an old white horse galloped away in the meadow. 25
Then we came to a tavern with vine-leaves over the lintel,
Six hands at an open door dicing for pieces of silver,
And feet kicking the empty wine-skins.
But there was no information, and so we continued
And arrived at evening, not a moment too soon 30
Finding the place; it was (you may say) satisfactory.

All this was a long time ago, I remember,
And I would do it again, but set down
This set down
This: were we led all that way for 35
Birth or Death? There was a Birth, certainly,
We had evidence and no doubt. I had seen birth and death,
But had thought they were different; this Birth was
Hard and bitter agony for us, like Death, our death.
We returned to our places, these Kingdoms, 40
But no longer at ease here, in the old dispensation,
With an alien people clutching their gods.
I should be glad of another death.

NOTE: The first lines of the poem are taken from a sermon preached by Lancelot Andrews (1555–1626) on Christmas Day, 1622. The relevant passage reads as follows:

It was no summer progress. A cold coming they had of it at this time of the year, just the worst time of the year to take a journey, and specially a long journey in. The ways deep, the weather sharp, the days short, the sun farthest off, *in solstitio brumali,* the very dead of winter.

Twelfth Night

JOHN PEALE BISHOP [1892–1944]

All night I thought on those wise men who took
A midnight leave of towers and came peering
Pyramidally down to the dark guards
And stared apart, each with a mad, hid look
Twitching his mummied beard 5
while the night swords

Conferred and chains fell and the unwieldy bar
Slid and swung back
then wandered out to name
The living demon of an unnamed star. 10

All night I followed them and came at last
On a low hutch propped in an alleyway
And stretched aside
while one by one they passed
Those stilted mages mitred in stiff blue 15
Under the sagging beams and through the stalls.

Following, through stench and misty fug I saw
And nothing were clearer in the scrupulous day
The rigid drooping of their ancient palls
Burnish with light, where on a toss of straw 20
Swaddled in rags, to their abashment, lay
Not the pedantic god whose name they knew
But a small child petulant with cries.
With courtesies unperturbed and slow
They laid their gifts down, unburnt scents and gold: 25
But gray evasions shamed their skeptic eyes
And the starved hands were suddenly boned with cold
As plucking their gorgeous skirts they shook to go.

The Windhover:

To Christ Our Lord

GERARD MANLEY HOPKINS [1844–1889]

I caught this morning morning's minion, king-
dom of daylight's dauphin, dapple-dawn-drawn Falcon, in his riding
Of the rolling level underneath him steady air, and striding
High there, how he rung upon the rein of a wimpling wing
In his ecstasy! then off, off forth on swing, 5
As a skate's heel sweeps smooth on a bow-bend: the hurl and gliding
Rebuffed the big wind. My heart in hiding
Stirred for a bird,—the achieve of, the mastery of the thing!

Brute beauty and valour and act, oh, air, pride, plume, here
Buckle! AND the fire that breaks from thee then, a billion 10
Times told lovelier, more dangerous, O my chevalier!

No wonder of it; shéer plód makes plough down sillion
Shine, and blue-bleak embers, ah my dear,
Fall, gall themselves, and gash gold-vermilion.

The Owl

EDWARD THOMAS [1878–1917]

Down hill I came, hungry, and yet not starved;
Cold, yet had heat within me that was proof
Against the North wind; tired, yet so that rest
Had seemed the sweetest thing under a roof.

Then at the inn I had food, fire, and rest, 5
Knowing how hungry, cold, and tired was I.
All of the night was quite barred out except
An owl's cry, a most melancholy cry

Shaken out long and clear upon the hill,
No merry note, nor cause of merriment, 10
But one telling me plain what I escaped
And others could not, that night, as in I went.

And salted was my food, and my repose,
Salted and sobered, too, by the bird's voice
Speaking for all who lay under the stars, 15
Soldiers and poor, unable to rejoice.

An Horatian Ode upon Cromwell's Return from Ireland

ANDREW MARVELL [1621–1678]

The forward youth that would appear
Must now forsake his muses dear,
Nor in the shadows sing
His numbers languishing:

'Tis time to leave the books in dust, 5
And oil the unused armor's rust,
Removing from the wall
The corselet of the hall.

So restless Cromwell could not cease
In the inglorious arts of peace, 10
But through adventurous war
Urgèd his active star;

And, like the three-forked lightning, first
Breaking the clouds where it was nursed,
Did thorough his own side 15
His fiery way divide;

For 'tis all one to courage high,
The emulous, or enemy,
And with such to inclose,
Is more than to oppose. 20

Then burning through the air he went,
And palaces and temples rent;
And Caesar's head at last
Did through his laurels blast.

'Tis madness to resist or blame 25
The face of angry heaven's flame;
And if we would speak true,
Much to the man is due,

Who from his private gardens, where
He lived reservèd and austere, 30
As if his highest plot
To plant the bergamot,

Could by industrious valor climb
To ruin the great work of Time,
And cast the kingdoms old, 35
Into another mould;

Though Justice against Fate complain,
And plead the ancient rights in vain;
  But those do hold or break,
  As men are strong or weak. 40

Nature, that hateth emptiness,
Allows of penetration less,
  And therefore must make room
  Where greater spirits come.

What field of all the civil war, 45
Where his were not the deepest scar?
  And Hampton shows what part
  He had of wiser art;

Where, twining subtle fears with hope,
He wove a net of such a scope 50
  That Charles himself might chase
  To Carisbrooke's narrow case.

That thence the royal actor borne
The tragic scaffold might adorn:
  While round the armèd bands 55
  Did clap their bloody hands.

He nothing common did or mean
Upon that memorable scene:
  But with his keener eye
  The ax's edge did try: 60

Nor called the gods with vulgar spite
To vindicate his helpless right,
  But bowed his comely head,
  Down as upon a bed.

This was that memorable hour 65
Which first assured the forcèd power.
  So when they did design
  The Capitol's first line,

A bleeding head where they begun,
Did fright the architects to run; 70
  And yet in that the state
  Foresaw its happy fate.

And now the Irish are ashamed
To see themselves in one year tamed:
  So much one man can do, 75
  That does both act and know.

They can affirm his praises best,
And have, though overcome, confessed
  How good he is, how just,
  And fit for highest trust: 80

Nor yet grown stiffer with command,
But still in the Republic's hand:
  How fit he is to sway
  That can so well obey.

He to the Commons' feet presents 85
A kingdom, for his first year's rents;
  And what he may, forbears
  His fame to make it theirs:

And has his sword and spoils ungirt,
To lay them at the public's skirt. 90
  So when the falcon high
  Falls heavy from the sky,

She, having killed, no more does search,
But on the next green bough to perch;
  Where, when he first does lure, 95
  The falconer has her sure.

What may not then our isle presume
While victory his crest does plume!
  What may not others fear
  If thus he crowns each year! 100

A Caesar he ere long to Gaul,
To Italy a Hannibal,
  And to all states not free
  Shall climacteric be.

The Pict no shelter now shall find 105
Within his parti-colored mind;
  But from this valor sad
  Shrink underneath the plaid:

Happy if in the tufted brake
The English hunter him mistake; 110
  Nor lay his hounds in near
  The Caledonian deer.

But thou, the War's and Fortune's son
March indefatigably on;
  And for the last effect 115
  Still keep thy sword erect:

Besides the force it has to fright
The spirits of the shady night,
  The same arts that did gain
  A power must it maintain. 120

The Rime of the Ancient Mariner

IN SEVEN PARTS

SAMUEL TAYLOR COLERIDGE [1772–1834]

Facile credo, plures esse Naturas invisibiles quam visibiles in rerum universitate. Sed horum omnium familiam quis nobis enarrabit? et gradus et cognationes et discrimina et singulorum munera? Quid agunt? quæ loca habitant? Harum rerum notitiam semper ambivit ingenium humanum, nunquam attigit. Juvat, interea, non diffiteor, quandoque in animo, tanquam in Tabulâ, majoris et melioris mundi imaginem contemplari: ne mens assuefecta hodiernæ vitæ minutiis se contrahat nimis, & tota subsidat in pusillas cogitationes. Sed veritati interea invigilandum est, modusque servandus, ut certa ab incertis, diem a nocte, distinguamus.

(T. Burnet: Archæol. Phil., p. 68 [1])

[1] I readily believe that in the universe are more invisible beings than visible. But who will expound to us the nature of them all, and their ranks

PART I

An ancient Mariner meeteth three Gallants bidden to a wedding-feast and detaineth one.

It is an ancient Mariner,
And he stoppeth one of three.
"By thy long gray beard and glittering eye,
Now wherefore stopp'st thou me?

"The Bridegroom's doors are opened wide, 5
And I am next of kin;
The guests are met, the feast is set:
May'st hear the merry din."

He holds him with his skinny hand,
"There was a ship," quoth he. 10
"Hold off! unhand me, graybeard loon!"
Eftsoons his hand dropt he.

The Wedding-Guest is spellbound by the eye of the old seafaring man, and constrained to hear his tale.

He holds him with his glittering eye—
The wedding-guest stood still,
And listens like a three years' child: 15
The Mariner hath his will.

The wedding-guest sat on a stone:
He cannot choose but hear;
And thus spake on that ancient man,
The bright-eyed Mariner. 20

"The ship was cheered, the harbor cleared,
Merrily did we drop
Below the kirk, below the hill,
Below the lighthouse top.

and relationships and distinguishing characteristics and the function of each? What is it they perform? What regions do they inhabit? Ever about the knowledge of these things circles the thought of man, never reaching it. Meanwhile, it is pleasant, I must confess, sometimes to contemplate in the mind, as in a picture, the image of this greater and better world: that the mind, accustomed to the little things of daily life, may not be narrowed overmuch and lose itself in trivial reflections. But meanwhile must we diligently seek after truth, maintaining just measure, that we may distinguish things certain from uncertain, day from night.

(From edition by Carleton Noyes, New York, 1900)

The Mariner tells how the ship sailed southward with a good wind and fair weather till it reached the Line.

"The sun came up upon the left, 25
Out of the sea came he!
And he shone bright, and on the right
Went down into the sea.

"Higher and higher every day,
Till over the mast at noon—" 30
The wedding-guest here beat his breast,
For he heard the loud bassoon.

The Wedding-Guest heareth the bridal music; but the Mariner continueth his tale.

The bride hath paced into the hall,
Red as a rose is she;
Nodding their heads before her goes 35
The merry minstrelsy.

The wedding-guest he beat his breast,
Yet he cannot choose but hear;
And thus spake on that ancient man,
The bright-eyed Mariner: 40

The ship driven by a storm toward the south pole.

"And now the storm-blast came, and he
Was tyrannous and strong:
He struck with his o'ertaking wings,
And chased us south along.

"With sloping masts and dipping prow, 45
As who pursued with yell and blow
Still treads the shadow of his foe,
And forward bends his head,
The ship drove fast, loud roared the blast,
And southward aye we fled. 50

"And now there came both mist and snow,
And it grew wondrous cold;
And ice, mast-high, came floating by,
As green as emerald;

The land of ice, and of fearful sounds where no living thing was to be seen.

"And through the drifts the snowy clifts 55
Did send a dismal sheen:
Nor shapes of men nor beasts we ken—
The ice was all between.

"The ice was here, the ice was there,
The ice was all around: 60
It cracked and growled, and roared and howled,
Like noises in a swound!

Till a great sea-bird, called the Albatross, came through the snow-fog, and was received with great joy and hospitality.

"At length did cross an Albatross:
Thorough the fog it came:
As if it had been a Christian soul, 65
We hailed it in God's name.

"It ate the food it ne'er had eat,
And round and round it flew.
The ice did split with a thunder-fit;
The helmsman steered us through! 70

And lo! the Albatross proveth a bird of good omen, and followeth the ship as it returned northward through fog and floating ice.

"And a good south wind sprung up behind;
The Albatross did follow,
And every day, for food or play,
Came to the mariners' hollo!

"In mist or cloud, on mast or shroud, 75
It perched for vespers nine;
Whiles all the night, through fog-smoke white,
Glimmered the white moon-shine."

The ancient Mariner inhospitably killeth the pious bird of good omen.

"God save thee, ancient Mariner!
From the fiends, that plague thee thus!— 80
Why look'st thou so?"—"With my cross-bow
I shot the Albatross!

PART II

"The sun now rose upon the right:
Out of the sea came he,
Still hid in mist, and on the left 85
Went down into the sea.

"And the good south wind still blew behind,
But no sweet bird did follow,
Nor any day, for food or play,
Came to the mariners' hollo! 90

His shipmates cry out against the ancient Mariner for killing the bird of good luck.

"And I had done a hellish thing,
And it would work 'em woe;
For all averred, I had killed the bird
That made the breeze to blow.
Ah wretch! said they, the bird to slay 95
That made the breeze to blow!

But when the fog cleared off, they justify the same, and thus make themselves accomplices in the crime.

"Nor dim nor red, like God's own head,
The glorious sun uprist:
Then all averred, I had killed the bird
That brought the fog and mist. 100
'Twas right, said they, such birds to slay,
That bring the fog and mist.

The fair breeze continues; the ship enters the Pacific Ocean, and sails northward, even till it reaches the Line.

"The fair breeze blew, the white foam flew,
The furrow followed free:
We were the first that ever burst 105
Into that silent sea.

The ship hath been suddenly becalmed.

"Down dropt the breeze, the sails dropt down,
'Twas sad as sad could be;
And we did speak only to break
The silence of the sea! 110

"All in a hot and copper sky,
The bloody sun, at noon,
Right up above the mast did stand,
No bigger than the moon.

"Day after day, day after day, 115
We stuck, nor breath nor motion;
As idle as a painted ship
Upon a painted ocean.

And the Albatross begins to be avenged.

"Water, water, everywhere,
And all the boards did shrink; 120
Water, water, everywhere,
Nor any drop to drink.

"The very deep did rot: O Christ!
That ever this should be!

A Spirit had followed them; one of the invisible inhabitants of this planet, neither departed souls nor angels; concerning whom the learned Jew, Josephus, and the Platonic Constantinopolitan, Michael Psellus, may be consulted. They are very numerous, and there is no climate or element without one or more.

Yea, slimy things did crawl with legs 125
Upon the slimy sea.

"About, about, in reel and rout,
The death-fires danced at night;
The water, like a witch's oils,
Burnt green, and blue, and white. 130

"And some in dreams assurèd were
Of the spirit that plagued us so:
Nine fathom deep he had followed us,
From the land of mist and snow.

"And every tongue, through utter drought, 135
Was withered at the root;
We could not speak, no more than if
We had been choked with soot.

The shipmates, in their sore distress, would fain throw the whole guilt on the ancient Mariner: in sign whereof they hang the dead sea-bird round his neck.

"Ah! well-a-day! what evil looks
Had I from old and young! 140
Instead of the cross, the Albatross
About my neck was hung.

PART III

The ancient Mariner beholdeth a sign in the element afar off.

"There passed a weary time. Each throat
Was parched, and glazed each eye.
A weary time! A weary time! 145
How glazed each weary eye!
When looking westward I beheld
A something in the sky.

"At first it seemed a little speck,
And then it seemed a mist: 150
It moved and moved, and took at last
A certain shape, I wist.

"A speck, a mist, a shape, I wist!
And still it neared and neared:
As if it dodged a water-sprite, 155
It plunged and tacked and veered.

At its nearer approach, it seemeth him to be a ship; and at a dear ransom he freeth his speech from the bonds of thirst.

"With throats unslaked, with black lips baked,
We could nor laugh nor wail;
Through utter drought all dumb we stood!
I bit my arm, I sucked the blood, 160
And cried, 'A sail! a sail!'

A flash of joy;

"With throats unslaked, with black lips baked,
Agape they heard me call:
Gramercy! they for joy did grin,
And all at once their breath drew in, 165
As they were drinking all.

And horror follows. For can it be a ship that comes onward without wind or tide?

" 'See! see (I cried) she tacks no more!
Hither to work us weal;
Without a breeze, without a tide,
She steadies with upright keel!' 170

"The western wave was all a-flame:
The day was well nigh done:
Almost upon the western wave
Rested the broad bright sun;
When that strange shape drove suddenly 175
Betwixt us and the sun.

It seemeth him but the skeleton of a ship.

"And straight the sun was flecked with bars,
(Heaven's Mother send us grace!)
As if through a dungeon grate he peered,
With broad and burning face. 180

"Alas! (thought I, and my heart beat loud)
How fast she nears and nears!
Are those her sails that glance in the sun,
Like restless gossameres?

And its ribs are seen as bars on the face of the setting sun.

"Are those her ribs through which the sun 185
Did peer, as through a grate?
And is that Woman all her crew?

The Spectre-Woman and her Death-mate, and no other on board the skeleton-ship.

Is that a Death? and are there two?
Is Death that woman's mate?

"Her lips were red, her looks were free, 190
Her locks were yellow as gold:

Like vessel, like crew!

Her skin was as white as leprosy,
The nightmare Life-in-Death was she,
Who thicks man's blood with cold.

Death and Life-in-Death have diced for the ship's crew, and she (the latter) winneth the ancient Mariner.

"The naked hulk alongside came, 195
And the twain were casting dice;
'The game is done! I've won, I've won!'
Quoth she, and whistles thrice.

No twilight within the courts of the sun.

"The sun's rim dips; the stars rush out:
At one stride comes the dark; 200
With far-heard whisper, o'er the sea,
Off shot the spectre-bark.

"We listened and looked sideways up!
Fear at my heart, as at a cup,
My life-blood seemed to sip! 205
The stars were dim, and thick the night,
The steersman's face by his lamp gleamed white;
From the sails the dew did drip—

At the rising of the moon,

Till clomb above the eastern bar
The hornèd moon, with one bright star 210
Within the nether tip.

One after another,

"One after one, by the star-dogged moon,
Too quick for groan or sigh,
Each turned his face with a ghastly pang,
And cursed me with his eye. 215

His shipmates drop down dead.

"Four times fifty living men,
(And I heard nor sigh nor groan)
With heavy thump, a lifeless lump,
They dropped down one by one.

But Life-in-Death begins her work on the ancient Mariner.

"The souls did from their bodies fly,— 220
They fled to bliss or woe!
And every soul, it passed me by,
Like the whizz of my cross-bow!"

PART IV

The Wedding-Guest feareth that a spirit is talking to him;

"I fear thee, ancient Mariner!
I fear thy skinny hand! 225
And thou art long, and lank, and brown,
As is the ribbed sea-sand.

But the ancient Mariner assureth him of his bodily life, and proceedeth to relate his horrible penance.

"I fear thee and thy glittering eye,
And thy skinny hand, so brown."—
"Fear not, fear not, thou wedding-guest! 230
This body dropt not down.

"Alone, alone, all, all alone,
Alone on a wide, wide sea!
And never a saint took pity on
My soul in agony. 235

He despiseth the creatures of the calm,

"The many men, so beautiful!
And they all dead did lie:
And a thousand thousand slimy things
Lived on; and so did I.

And envieth that they should live, and so many be dead.

"I looked upon the rotting sea, 240
And drew my eyes away;
I looked upon the rotting deck,
And there the dead men lay.

"I looked to heaven, and tried to pray;
But or ever a prayer had gushed, 245
A wicked whisper came, and made
My heart as dry as dust.

"I closed my lids, and kept them close,
And the balls like pulses beat;
For the sky and the sea, and the sea and the
  sky, 250
Lay like a load on my weary eye,
And the dead were at my feet.

But the curse liveth for him in the eye of the dead men.

"The cold sweat melted from their limbs,
Nor rot nor reek did they:
The look with which they looked on me 255
Had never passed away.

"An orphan's curse would drag to hell
A spirit from on high;
But oh! more horrible than that
Is the curse in a dead man's eye! 260
Seven days, seven nights, I saw that curse,
And yet I could not die.

In his loneliness and fixedness he yearneth towards the journeying moon, and the stars that still sojourn, yet still move onward; and everywhere the blue sky belongs to them, and is their appointed rest, and their native country and their own natural homes, which they enter unannounced, as lords that are certainly expected; and yet there is a silent joy at their arrival.

"The moving moon went up the sky,
And nowhere did abide:
Softly she was going up, 265
And a star or two beside—

"Her beams bemocked the sultry main,
Like April hoar-frost spread;
But where the ship's huge shadow lay,
The charmèd water burnt alway 270
A still and awful red.

By the light of the moon he beholdeth God's creatures of the great calm.

"Beyond the shadow of the ship,
I watched the water-snakes:
They moved in tracks of shining white,
And when they reared, the elfish light 275
Fell off in hoary flakes.

"Within the shadow of the ship
I watched their rich attire:
Blue, glossy green, and velvet black,
They coiled and swam; and every track 280
Was a flash of golden fire.

Their beauty and their happiness.

"O happy living things! no tongue
Their beauty might declare:
A spring of love gushed from my heart,

He blesseth them in his heart.

And I blessed them unaware! 285
Sure my kind saint took pity on me,
And I blessed them unaware.

The spell begins to break.

"The selfsame moment I could pray;
And from my neck so free
The Albatross fell off, and sank 290
Like lead into the sea.

PART V

"O sleep! it is a gentle thing,
Beloved from pole to pole!
To Mary Queen the praise be given!
She sent the gentle sleep from Heaven, 295
That slid into my soul.

By grace of the Holy Mother, the ancient Mariner is refreshed with rain.

"The silly buckets on the deck,
That had so long remained,
I dreamt that they were filled with dew;
And when I awoke, it rained. 300

"My lips were wet, my throat was cold,
My garments all were dank;
Sure I had drunken in my dreams,
And still my body drank.

"I moved, and could not feel my limbs: 305
I was so light—almost
I thought that I had died in sleep,
And was a blessèd ghost.

He heareth sounds and seeth strange sights and commotions in the sky and the element.

"And soon I heard a roaring wind:
It did not come anear; 310
But with its sound it shook the sails,
That were so thin and sere.

"The upper air burst into life!
And a hundred fire-flags sheen,
To and fro they were hurried about; 315
And to and fro, and in and out,
The wan stars danced between.

"And the coming wind did roar more loud,
And the sails did sigh like sedge;
And the rain poured down from one black
cloud; 320
The moon was at its edge.

"The thick black cloud was cleft, and still
The moon was at its side:

Like waters shot from some high crag,
The lightning fell with never a jag, 325
A river steep and wide.

The bodies of the ship's crew are inspired, and the ship moves on;

"The loud wind never reached the ship,
Yet now the ship moved on!
Beneath the lightning and the moon
The dead men gave a groan. 330

"They groaned, they stirred, they all uprose,
Nor spake, nor moved their eyes;
It had been strange, even in a dream,
To have seen those dead men rise.

"The helmsman steered, the ship moved on;
Yet never a breeze up-blew; 336
The mariners all 'gan work the ropes,
Where they were wont to do:
They raised their limbs like lifeless tools—
We were a ghastly crew. 340

"The body of my brother's son
Stood by me, knee to knee:
The body and I pulled at one rope,
But he said nought to me."

But not by the souls of the men, nor by demons of earth or middle air, but by a blessed troop of angelic spirits, sent down by the invocation of the guardian saint.

"I fear thee, ancient Mariner!" 345
"Be calm, thou Wedding-Guest!
'Twas not those souls that fled in pain,
Which to their corses came again,
But a troop of spirits blest:

"For when it dawned—they dropped their arms,
And clustered round the mast; 351
Sweet sounds rose slowly through their mouths,
And from their bodies passed.

"Around, around, flew each sweet sound,
Then darted to the sun; 355
Slowly the sounds came back again,
Now mixed, now one by one.

"Sometimes a-dropping from the sky
I heard the skylark sing;
Sometimes all little birds that are, 360
How they seemed to fill the sea and air
With their sweet jargoning!

"And now 'twas like all instruments,
Now like a lonely flute;
And now it is an angel's song, 365
That makes the heavens be mute.

"It ceased; yet still the sails made on
A pleasant noise till noon,
A noise like of a hidden brook
In the leafy month of June, 370
That to the sleeping woods all night
Singeth a quiet tune.

"Till noon we quietly sailed on,
Yet never a breeze did breathe:
Slowly and smoothly went the ship, 375
Moved onward from beneath.

The lonesome Spirit from the south pole carries on the ship as far as the Line, in obedience to the angelic troop, but still requireth vengeance.

"Under the keel nine fathom deep,
From the land of mist and snow,
The spirit slid; and it was he
That made the ship to go. 380
The sails at noon left off their tune,
And the ship stood still also.

"The sun, right up above the mast,
Had fixed her to the ocean;
But in a minute she 'gan stir, 385
With a short uneasy motion—
Backwards and forwards half her length,
With a short uneasy motion.

"Then like a pawing horse let go,
She made a sudden bound: 390
It flung the blood into my head,
And I fell down in a swound.

The Polar Spirit's fellow-demons, the invisible inhabitants of the element, take part in his wrong, and two of them relate, one to the other, that penance long and heavy for the ancient Mariner hath been accorded to the Polar Spirit, who returneth southward.

"How long in that same fit I lay,
I have not to declare;
But ere my living life returned, 395
I heard, and in my soul discerned
Two voices in the air.

" 'Is it he?' quoth one, 'is this the man?
By Him who died on cross,
With his cruel bow he laid full low 400
The harmless Albatross.

" 'The spirit who bideth by himself
In the land of mist and snow,
He loved the bird that loved the man
Who shot him with his bow.' 405

"The other was a softer voice,
As soft as honey-dew:
Quoth he, 'The man hath penance done,
And penance more will do.'

PART VI

First Voice

" 'But tell me, tell me! speak again, 410
Thy soft response renewing—
What makes that ship drive on so fast?
What is the ocean doing?'

Second Voice

" 'Still as a slave before his lord,
The ocean hath no blast; 415
His great bright eye most silently
Up to the moon is cast—

" 'If he may know which way to go;
For she guides him, smooth or grim.
See, brother, see! how graciously 420
She looketh down on him.'

First Voice

The Mariner hath been cast into a trance; for the angelic power causeth the vessel to drive northward faster than human life could endure.

"'But why drives on that ship so fast,
Without or wave or wind?'

Second Voice

"'The air is cut away before,
And closes from behind. 425

"'Fly, brother, fly! more high, more high!
Or we shall be belated:
For slow and slow that ship will go,
When the Mariner's trance is abated.'

The supernatural motion is retarded; the Mariner awakes, and his penance begins anew.

"I woke, and we were sailing on, 430
As in a gentle weather:
'Twas night, calm night, the moon was high;
The dead men stood together.

"All stood together on the deck,
For a charnel-dungeon fitter: 435
All fixed on me their stony eyes,
That in the moon did glitter.

"The pang, the curse, with which they died,
Had never passed away:
I could not draw my eyes from theirs, 440
Nor turn them up to pray.

The curse is finally expiated.

"And now this spell was snapt: once more
I viewed the ocean green,
And looked far forth, yet little saw
Of what had else been seen— 445

"Like one, that on a lonesome road
Doth walk in fear and dread,
And having once turned round, walks on,
And turns no more his head;
Because he knows a frightful fiend 450
Doth close behind him tread.

"But soon there breathed a wind on me,
Nor sound nor motion made:
Its path was not upon the sea,
In ripple or in shade. 455

"It raised my hair, it fanned my cheek
Like a meadow-gale of spring—
It mingled strangely with my fears,
Yet it felt like a welcoming.

"Swiftly, swiftly flew the ship, 460
Yet she sailed softly too:
Sweetly, sweetly blew the breeze—
On me alone it blew.

And the ancient Mariner beholdeth his native country.

"Oh! dream of joy! is this indeed
The lighthouse top I see? 465
Is this the hill? is this the kirk?
Is this mine own countree?

"We drifted o'er the harbor-bar,
And I with sobs did pray—
'O let me be awake, my God! 470
Or let me sleep alway.'

"The harbor-bay was clear as glass,
So smoothly it was strewn!
And on the bay the moonlight lay,
And the shadow of the moon. 475

"The rock shone bright, the kirk no less,
That stands above the rock:
The moonlight steeped in silentness
The steady weathercock.

The angelic spirits leave the dead bodies.

"And the bay was white with silent light, 480
Till rising from the same,
Full many shapes, that shadows were,
In crimson colors came.

And appear in their own forms of light.

"A little distance from the prow
Those crimson shadows were: 485

I turned my eyes upon the deck—
Oh, Christ! what saw I there!

"Each corse lay flat, lifeless and flat,
And, by the holy rood!
A man all light, a seraph-man, 490
On every corse there stood.

"This seraph-band, each waved his hand:
It was a heavenly sight!
They stood as signals to the land,
Each one a lovely light: 495

"This seraph-band, each waved his hand,
No voice did they impart—
No voice; but oh! the silence sank
Like music on my heart.

"But soon I heard the dash of oars, 500
I heard the pilot's cheer;
My head was turned perforce away,
And I saw a boat appear.

"The pilot, and the pilot's boy,
I heard them coming fast: 505
Dear Lord in Heaven! it was a joy
The dead men could not blast.

"I saw a third—I heard his voice:
It is the Hermit good!
He singeth loud his godly hymns 510
That he makes in the wood.
He'll shrieve my soul, he'll wash away
The Albatross's blood.

PART VII

The Hermit of the wood,

"This Hermit good lives in that wood
Which slopes down to the sea. 515
How loudly his sweet voice he rears!
He loves to talk with marineres
That come from a far countree.

"He kneels at morn, and noon, and eve—
He hath a cushion plump: 520
It is the moss that wholly hides
The rotted old oak-stump.

"The skiff-boat neared: I heard them talk,
'Why, this is strange, I trow!
Where are those lights so many and fair, 525
That signal made but now?'

Approacheth the ship with wonder.

"'Strange, by my faith!' the Hermit said—
'And they answered not our cheer!
The planks look warped! and see those sails,
How thin they are and sere! 530
I never saw aught like to them,
Unless perchance it were

"'Brown skeletons of leaves that lag
My forest-brook along:
When the ivy-tod is heavy with snow, 535
And the owlet whoops to the wolf below,
That eats the she-wolf's young.'

"'Dear Lord! it hath a fiendish look'—
(The pilot made reply)
'I am a-feared'—'Push on, push on!' 540
Said the Hermit cheerily.

"The boat came closer to the ship,
But I nor spake nor stirred;
The boat came close beneath the ship,
And straight a sound was heard. 545

The ship suddenly sinketh.

"Under the water it rumbled on,
Still louder and more dread:
It reached the ship, it split the bay;
The ship went down like lead.

The ancient Mariner is saved in the Pilot's boat.

"Stunned by that loud and dreadful sound, 550
Which sky and ocean smote,
Like one that hath been seven days drowned,
My body lay afloat;

But swift as dreams, myself I found
Within the pilot's boat. 555

"Upon the whirl, where sank the ship,
The boat spun round and round;
And all was still, save that the hill
Was telling of the sound.

"I moved my lips—the pilot shrieked, 560
And fell down in a fit;
The Holy Hermit raised his eyes,
And prayed where he did sit.

"I took the oars: the pilot's boy,
Who now doth crazy go, 565
Laughing loud and long, and all the while
His eyes went to and fro.
'Ha! ha!' quoth he, 'full plain I see,
The Devil knows how to row.'

"And now, all in my own countree, 570
I stood on the firm land!
The Hermit stepped forth from the boat,
And scarcely he could stand.

The ancient Mariner earnestly entreateth the Hermit to shrieve him; and the penance of life falls on him.

" 'O shrieve me, shrieve me, holy man!'
The Hermit crossed his brow. 575
'Say quick,' quoth he, 'I bid thee say—
What manner of man art thou?'

"Forthwith this frame of mine was wrenched
With a woeful agony,
Which forced me to begin my tale; 580
And then it left me free.

And ever and anon throughout his future life an agony constraineth him to travel from land to land,

"Since then at an uncertain hour,
That agony returns;
And till my ghastly tale is told,
This heart within me burns. 585

"I pass, like night, from land to land;
I have strange power of speech;

That moment that his face I see,
I know the man that must hear me:
To him my tale I teach. 590

"What loud uproar bursts from that door:
The wedding-guests are there;
But in the garden-bower the bride
And bride-maids singing are;
And hark the little vesper bell, 595
Which biddeth me to prayer!

"O Wedding-Guest! this soul hath been
Alone on a wide, wide sea:
So lonely 'twas, that God himself
Scarce seemèd there to be. 600

"O sweeter than the marriage-feast,
'Tis sweeter far to me,
To walk together to the kirk
With a goodly company!—

"To walk together to the kirk, 605
And all together pray,
While each to his great Father bends,
Old men, and babes, and loving friends,
And youths and maidens gay!

And to teach, by his own example, love and reverence to all things that God made and loveth.

"Farewell, farewell! but this I tell 610
To thee, thou Wedding-Guest!
He prayeth well, who loveth well
Both man and bird and beast.

"He prayeth best, who loveth best
All things both great and small; 615
For the dear God who loveth us,
He made and loveth all."

The Mariner, whose eye is bright,
Whose beard with age is hoar,
Is gone; and now the Wedding-Guest 620
Turned from the bridegroom's door.

He went like one that hath been stunned,
And is of sense forlorn:

A sadder and a wiser man
He rose the morrow morn. 625

Ode

Intimations of Immortality from Recollections of Early Childhood

WILLIAM WORDSWORTH [1770–1850]

The Child is father of the Man;
And I could wish my days to be
Bound each to each by natural piety.

I

There was a time when meadow, grove, and stream,
The earth, and every common sight,
To me did seem
Apparelled in celestial light,
The glory and the freshness of a dream. 5
It is not now as it hath been of yore;—
Turn wheresoe'er I may,
By night or day,
The things which I have seen I now can see no more.

II

The Rainbow comes and goes, 10
And lovely is the Rose,
The Moon doth with delight
Look round her when the heavens are bare,
Waters on a starry night
Are beautiful and fair; 15
The sunshine is a glorious birth;
But yet I know, where'er I go,
That there hath past away a glory from the earth.

III

Now, while the birds thus sing a joyous song,
And while the young lambs bound 20
As to the tabor's sound,

To me alone there came a thought of grief:
A timely utterance gave that thought relief,
And I again am strong:
The cataracts blow their trumpets from the steep; 25
No more shall grief of mine the season wrong;
I hear the Echoes through the mountains throng,
The Winds come to me from the fields of sleep,
And all the earth is gay;
Land and sea 30
Give themselves up to jollity,
And with the heart of May
Doth every beast keep holiday;—
Thou Child of Joy,
Shout round me, let me hear thy shouts, thou happy Shepherd-boy! 35

IV

Ye blessèd Creatures, I have heard the call
Ye to each other make; I see
The heavens laugh with you in your jubilee;
My heart is at your festival,
My head hath its coronal, 40
The fullness of your bliss, I feel—I feel it all.
Oh evil day! if I were sullen
While Earth herself is adorning,
This sweet May-morning,
And the children are culling 45
On every side,
In a thousand valleys far and wide,
Fresh flowers; while the sun shines warm,
And the Babe leaps up on his mother's arm:—
I hear, I hear, with joy I hear! 50
—But there's a Tree, of many, one,
A single Field which I have looked upon,
Both of them speak of something that is gone:
The Pansy at my feet
Doth the same tale repeat: 55
Whither is fled the visionary gleam?
Where is it now, the glory and the dream?

V

Our birth is but a sleep and a forgetting:
The Soul that rises with us, our life's Star,
        Hath had elsewhere its setting, 60
           And cometh from afar:
        Not in entire forgetfulness,
        And not in utter nakedness,
But trailing clouds of glory do we come
        From God, who is our home: 65
Heaven lies about us in our infancy!
Shades of the prison-house begin to close
        Upon the growing Boy,
But he beholds the light, and whence it flows,
        He sees it in his joy; 70
The Youth, who daily farther from the east
        Must travel, still is Nature's priest,
        And by the vision splendid
        Is on his way attended;
At length the Man perceives it die away, 75
And fade into the light of common day.

VI

Earth fills her lap with pleasures of her own;
Yearnings she hath in her own natural kind,
And, even with something of a mother's mind,
           And no unworthy aim, 80
           The homely nurse doth all she can
   To make her Foster-child, her inmate Man,
           Forget the glories he hath known,
   And that imperial palace whence he came.

VII

Behold the Child among his new-born blisses, 85
A six years' darling of a pigmy size!
See, where 'mid work of his own hand he lies,
Fretted by sallies of his mother's kisses,
With light upon him from his father's eyes!
See, at his feet, some little plan or chart, 90

Some fragment from his dream of human life,
Shaped by himself with newly-learnèd art;
A wedding or a festival,
A mourning or a funeral;
And this hath now his heart, 95
And unto this he frames his song:
Then will he fit his tongue
To dialogues of business, love, or strife;
But it will not be long
Ere this be thrown aside, 100
And with new joy and pride
The little Actor cons another part;
Filling from time to time his 'humorous stage'
With all the Persons, down to palsied Age,
That Life brings with her in her equipage; 105
As if his whole vocation
Were endless imitation.

VIII

Thou, whose exterior semblance doth belie
Thy soul's immensity;
Thou best philosopher, who yet dost keep 110
Thy heritage, thou eye among the blind,
That, deaf and silent, read'st the Eternal Deep,
Haunted forever by the Eternal Mind,—
Mighty prophet! seer blest!
On whom those truths do rest, 115
Which we are toiling all our lives to find,
In darkness lost, the darkness of the grave;
Thou, over whom thy Immortality
Broods like the Day, a master o'er a slave,
A Presence which is not to be put by; 120
Thou little Child, yet glorious in the might
Of heaven-born freedom on thy being's height,
Why with such earnest pains dost thou provoke
The years to bring the inevitable yoke,
Thus blindly with thy blessedness at strife? 125
Full soon thy Soul shall have her earthly freight,
And custom lie upon thee with a weight,
Heavy as frost, and deep almost as life!

IX

O joy! that in our embers
Is something that doth live, 130
That nature yet remembers
What was so fugitive!
The thought of our past years in me doth breed
Perpetual benediction: not indeed
For that which is most worthy to be blest; 135
Delight and liberty, the simple creed
Of childhood, whether busy or at rest,
With new-fledged hope still fluttering in his breast:—
Not for these I raise
The song of thanks and praise; 140
But for those obstinate questionings
Of sense and outward things,
Fallings from us, vanishings;
Blank misgivings of a Creature
Moving about in worlds not realized, 145
High instincts before which our mortal nature
Did tremble like a guilty thing surprised:
But for those first affections,
Those shadowy recollections,
Which, be they what they may, 150
Are yet the fountain-light of all our day,
Are yet a master-light of all our seeing;
Uphold us, cherish, and have power to make
Our noisy years seem moments in the being
Of the Eternal Silence: truths that wake, 155
To perish never:
Which neither listlessness, nor mad endeavor,
Nor man nor boy,
Nor all that is at enmity with joy,
Can utterly abolish or destroy! 160
Hence in a season of calm weather
Though inland far we be,
Our souls have sight of that immortal sea
Which brought us hither,
Can in a moment travel thither, 165
And see the children sport upon the shore,
And hear the mighty waters rolling evermore.

X

Then sing, ye Birds, sing, sing a joyous song!
And let the young Lambs bound
As to the tabor's sound! 170
We in thought will join your throng,
Ye that pipe and ye that play,
Ye that through your hearts to-day
Feel the gladness of the May!
What though the radiance which was once so bright 175
Be now forever taken from my sight,
Though nothing can bring back the hour
Of splendor in the grass, of glory in the flower;
We will grieve not, rather find
Strength in what remains behind; 180
In the primal sympathy
Which having been must ever be;
In the soothing thoughts that spring
Out of human suffering;
In the faith that looks through death, 185
In years that bring the philosophic mind.

XI

And O, ye Fountains, Meadows, Hills, and Groves,
Forebode not any severing of our loves!
Yet in my heart of hearts I feel your might;
I only have relinquished one delight 190
To live beneath your more habitual sway.
I love the Brooks which down their channels fret,
Even more than when I tripped lightly as they;
The innocent brightness of a new-born Day
Is lovely yet; 195
The Clouds that gather round the setting sun
Do take a sober coloring from an eye
That hath kept watch o'er man's mortality;
Another race hath been, and other palms are won.
Thanks to the human heart by which we live, 200
Thanks to its tenderness, its joys, and fears,
To me the meanest flower that blows can give
Thoughts that do often lie too deep for tears.

Ode on Indolence

JOHN KEATS [1795–1821]

They toil not, neither do they spin.

One morn before me were three figures seen,
With bowed necks, and joined hands, side-fac'd;
And one behind the other stepp'd serene,
In placid sandals, and in white robes grac'd;
They pass'd, like figures on a marble urn, 5
When shifted round to see the other side;
They came again; as when the urn once more
Is shifted round, the first seen shades return;
And they were strange to me, as may betide
With vases, to one deep in Phidian lore. 10

How is it, shadows! that I knew ye not?
How came ye muffled in so hush a mask?
Was it a silent deep-disguisèd plot
To steal away, and leave without a task
My idle days? Ripe was the drowsy hour; 15
The blissful cloud of summer-indolence
Benumb'd my eyes; my pulse grew less and less;
Pain had no sting, and pleasure's wreath no flower:
O, why did ye not melt, and leave my sense
Unhaunted quite of all but—nothingness? 20

A third time pass'd they by, and, passing, turn'd
Each one the face a moment whiles to me;
Then faded, and to follow them I burn'd
And ach'd for wings because I knew the three;
The first was a fair maid, and Love her name; 25
The second was Ambition, pale of cheek,
And ever watchful with fatiguèd eye;
The last, whom I love more, the more of blame
Is heap'd upon her, maiden most unmeek,—
I knew to be my demon Poesy. 30

They faded, and, forsooth! I wanted wings:
O folly! What is Love? and where is it?

And for that poor Ambition! it springs
From a man's little heart's short fever-fit;
For Poesy!—no,—she has not a joy,— 35
At least for me,—so sweet as drowsy noons,
And evenings steep'd in honied indolence;
O, for an age so shelter'd from annoy,
That I may never know how change the moons,
Or hear the voice of busy common-sense! 40

And once more came they by;—alas! wherefore?
My sleep had been embroider'd with dim dreams;
My soul had been a lawn besprinkled o'er
With flowers, and stirring shades, and baffled beams:
The morn was clouded, but no shower fell, 45
Tho' in her lids hung the sweet tears of May;
The open casement press'd a new-leav'd vine,
Let in the budding warmth and throstle's lay;
O shadows! 'twas a time to bid farewell!
Upon your skirts had fallen no tears of mine. 50

So, ye three ghosts, adieu! Ye cannot raise
My head cool-bedded in the flowery grass;
For I would not be dieted with praise,
A pet-lamb in a sentimental farce!
Fade softly from my eyes, and be once more 55
In masque-like figures on the dreamy urn;
Farewell! I yet have visions for the night,
And for the day faint visions there is store;
Vanish, ye phantoms! from my idle spright,
Into the clouds, and nevermore return! 60

Sailing to Byzantium

WILLIAM BUTLER YEATS [1865–1939]

That is no country for old men. The young
In one another's arms, birds in the trees
—Those dying generations—at their song,
The salmon-falls, the mackerel-crowded seas,
Fish, flesh, or fowl, commend all summer long 5
Whatever is begotten, born, and dies.

Caught in that sensual music all neglect
Monuments of unaging intellect.

An aged man is but a paltry thing,
A tattered coat upon a stick, unless 10
Soul clap its hands and sing, and louder sing
For every tatter in its mortal dress,
Nor is there singing school but studying
Monuments of its own magnificence;
And therefore I have sailed the seas and come 15
To the holy city of Byzantium.

O sages standing in God's holy fire
As in the gold mosaic of a wall,
Come from the holy fire, perne in a gyre,
And be the singing-masters of my soul. 20
Consume my heart away; sick with desire
And fastened to a dying animal
It knows not what it is; and gather me
Into the artifice of eternity.

Once out of nature I shall never take 25
My bodily form from any natural thing,
But such a form as Grecian goldsmiths make
Of hammered gold and gold enameling
To keep a drowsy Emperor awake;
Or set upon a golden bough to sing 30
To lords and ladies of Byzantium
Of what is past, or passing, or to come.

Peter Quince at the Clavier

WALLACE STEVENS [1879–]

I

Just as my fingers on these keys
Make music, so the self-same sounds
On my spirit make a music too.

Music is feeling, then, not sound;
And thus it is that what I feel, 5
Here in this room, desiring you,

Thinking of your blue-shadowed silk,
Is music. It is like the strain
Waked in the elders by Susanna:

Of a green evening, clear and warm, 10
She bathed in her still garden, while
The red-eyed elders, watching, felt

The basses of their being throb
In witching chords, and their thin blood
Pulse pizzicati of Hosanna. 15

II

In the green evening, clear and warm,
Susanna lay.
She searched
The touch of springs,
And found 20
Concealed imaginings.
She sighed
For so much melody.

Upon the bank she stood
In the cool 25
Of spent emotions.
She felt, among the leaves,
The dew
Of old devotions.

She walked upon the grass, 30
Still quavering.
The winds were like her maids,
On timid feet,
Fetching her woven scarves,
Yet wavering. 35

A breath upon her hand
Muted the night.
She turned—
A cymbal clashed,
And roaring horns. 40

III

Soon, with a noise like tambourines,
Came her attendant Byzantines.

They wondered why Susanna cried
Against the elders by her side:

And as they whispered, the refrain 45
Was like a willow swept by rain.

Anon their lamps' uplifted flame
Revealed Susanna and her shame.

And then the simpering Byzantines
Fled, with a noise like tambourines. 50

IV

Beauty is momentary in the mind—
The fitful tracing of a portal;
But in the flesh it is immortal.

The body dies; the body's beauty lives.
So evenings die, in their green going, 55
A wave, interminably flowing.

So gardens die, their meek breath scenting
The cowl of Winter, done repenting.
So maidens die to the auroral
Celebration of a maiden's choral. 60

Susanna's music touched the bawdy strings
Of those white elders; but, escaping,
Left only Death's ironic scraping.
Now in its immortality, it plays
On the clear viol of her memory, 65
And makes a constant sacrament of praise.

The Heavy Bear Who Goes with Me

DELMORE SCHWARTZ [1913–]

"the withness of the body"—WHITEHEAD

The heavy bear who goes with me,
A manifold honey to smear his face,
Clumsy and lumbering here and there,
The central ton of every place,
The hungry beating brutish one 5
In love with candy, anger, and sleep,
Crazy factotum, dishevelling all,
Climbs the building, kicks the football,
Boxes his brother in the hate-ridden city.

Breathing at my side, that heavy animal, 10
That heavy bear who sleeps with me,
Howls in his sleep for a world of sugar,
A sweetness intimate as the water's clasp,
Howls in his sleep because the tight-rope
Trembles and shows the darkness beneath. 15
—The strutting show-off is terrified,
Dressed in his dress-suit, bulging his pants,
Trembles to think that his quivering meat
Must finally wince to nothing at all.

That inescapable animal walks with me, 20
Has followed me since the black womb held,
Moves where I move, distorting my gesture,
A caricature, a swollen shadow,
A stupid clown of the spirit's motive,
Perplexes and affronts with his own darkness, 25
The secret life of belly and bone,
Opaque, too near, my private, yet unknown,
Stretches to embrace the very dear
With whom I would walk without him near,
Touches her grossly, although a word 30
Would bare my heart and make me clear,
Stumbles, flounders, and strives to be fed
Dragging me with him in his mouthing care,

Amid the hundred million of his kind,
The scrimmage of appetite everywhere. 35

Low Barometer

ROBERT BRIDGES [1844–1930]

The south-wind strengthens to a gale,
Across the moon the clouds fly fast,
The house is smitten as with a flail,
The chimney shudders to the blast.

On such a night, when Air has loosed 5
Its guardian grasp on blood and brain,
Old terrors then of god or ghost
Creep from their caves to life again;

And Reason kens he herits in
A haunted house. Tenants unknown 10
Assert their squalid lease of sin
With earlier title than his own.

Unbodied presences, the pack'd
Pollution and remorse of Time,
Slipp'd from oblivion reënact 15
The horrors of unhouseld crime.

Some men would quell the thing with prayer
Whose sightless footsteps pad the floor,
Whose fearful trespass mounts the stair
Or bursts the lock'd forbidden door. 20

Some have seen corpses long interr'd
Escape from hallowing control,
Pale charnel forms—nay ev'n have heard
The shrilling of a troubled soul,

That wanders till the dawn hath cross'd 25
The dolorous dark, or Earth hath wound
Closer her storm-spredd cloke, and thrust
The baleful phantoms under ground.

From Canto LXXXI

EZRA POUND [1885–]

What thou lovest well remains,
                    the rest is dross
What thou lov'st well shall not be reft from thee
What thou lov'st well is thy true heritage
Whose world, or mine or theirs   5
                    or is it of none?
First came the seen, then thus the palpable
        Elysium, though it were in the halls of hell,
What thou lovest well is thy true heritage

The ant's a centaur in his dragon world.   10
Pull down thy vanity, it is not man
Made courage, or made order, or made grace,
        Pull down thy vanity, I say pull down.
Learn of the green world what can be thy place
In scaled invention or true artistry,   15
Pull down thy vanity,
                    Paquin pull down!
The green casque has outdone your elegance.

"Master thyself, then others shall thee beare"
        Pull down thy vanity   20
Thou art a beaten dog beneath the hail,
A swollen magpie in a fitful sun,
Half black half white
Nor knowst'ou wing from tail
Pull down thy vanity   25
                    How mean thy hates
Fostered in falsity,
                    Pull down thy vanity,
Rathe to destroy, niggard in charity,
Pull down thy vanity,   30
                    I say pull down.

But to have done instead of not doing
                    this is not vanity

To have, with decency, knocked
That a Blunt should open 35
To have gathered from the air a live tradition
or from a fine old eye the unconquered flame
This is not vanity.
Here error is all in the not done,
all in the diffidence that faltered. . . . 40

The Goat Paths

JAMES STEPHENS [1882–]

The crooked paths go every way
Upon the hill—they wind about
Through the heather in and out
Of the quiet sunniness.
And there the goats, day after day, 5

Stray in sunny quietness,
Cropping here and cropping there,
As they pause and turn and pass,
Now a bit of heather spray,
Now a mouthful of the grass. 10

In the deeper sunniness,
In the place where nothing stirs,
Quietly in quietness,
In the quiet of the furze,
For a time they come and lie 15
Staring on the roving sky.

If you approach they run away,
They leap and stare, away they bound,
With a sudden angry sound,
To the sunny quietude; 20
Crouching down where nothing stirs
In the silence of the furze,
Crouching down again to brood
In the sunny solitude.

If I were as wise as they, 25
I would stray apart and brood,
I would beat a hidden way
Through the quiet heather spray
To a sunny solitude;

And should you come I'd run away, 30
I would make an angry sound,
I would stare and turn and bound
To the deeper quietude,
To the place where nothing stirs
In the silence of the furze. 35

In that airy quietness
I would think as long as they;
Through the quiet sunniness
I would stray away to brood
By a hidden, beaten way 40
In the sunny solitude,

I would think until I found
Something I can never find,
Something lying on the ground,
In the bottom of my mind. 45

Past Ruined Ilion

WALTER SAVAGE LANDOR [1775–1864]

Past ruined Ilion Helen lives,
Alcestis rises from the shades;
Verse calls them forth; 'tis verse that gives
Immortal youth to mortal maids.

Soon shall Oblivion's deepening veil 5
Hide all the peopled hills you see,
The gay, the proud, while lovers hail
These many summers you and me.

Because I Could Not Stop for Death

EMILY DICKINSON [1830–1886]

Because I could not stop for Death,
He kindly stopped for me;
The carriage held but just ourselves
And Immortality.

We slowly drove, he knew no haste, 5
And I had put away
My labor, and my leisure too,
For his civility.

We passed the school where children played,
Their lessons scarcely done; 10
We passed the fields of gazing grain,
We passed the setting sun.

We paused before a house that seemed
A swelling on the ground;
The roof was scarcely visible, 15
The cornice but a mound.

Since then 'tis centuries; but each
Feels shorter than the day
I first surmised the horses' heads
Were toward eternity. 20

The Gallows

EDWARD THOMAS [1878–1917]

There was a weasel lived in the sun
With all his family,
Till a keeper shot him with his gun
And hung him up on a tree,
Where he swings in the wind and rain, 5
In the sun and in the snow,
Without pleasure, without pain,
On the dead oak tree bough.

There was a crow who was no sleeper,
But a thief and a murderer 10
Till a very late hour; and this keeper
Made him one of the things that were,
To hang and flap in rain and wind
In the sun and in the snow.
There are no more sins to be sinned 15
On the dead oak tree bough.

There was a magpie, too,
Had a long tongue and a long tail;
He could both talk and do—
But what did that avail? 20
He, too, flaps in the wind and rain
Alongside weasel and crow,
Without pleasure, without pain,
On the dead oak tree bough.

And many other beasts 25
And birds, skin, bone, and feather,
Have been taken from their feasts
And hung up there together.
To swing and have endless leisure
In the sun and in the snow, 30
Without pain, without pleasure,
On the dead oak tree bough.

The Groundhog

RICHARD EBERHART [1904–]

In June, amid the golden fields,
I saw a groundhog lying dead.
Dead lay he; my senses shook,
And mind outshot our naked frailty.
There lowly in the vigorous summer 5
His form began its senseless change,
And made my senses waver dim
Seeing nature ferocious in him.
Inspecting close his maggots' might

And seething cauldron of his being, 10
Half with loathing, half with a strange love,
I poked him with an angry stick.
The fever arose, became a flame
And Vigour circumscribed the skies,
Immense energy in the sun, 15
And through my frame a sunless trembling.
My stick had done nor good nor harm.
Then stood I silent in the day
Watching the object, as before;
And kept my reverence for knowledge 20
Trying for control, to be still,
To quell the passion of the blood;
Until I had bent down on my knees
Praying for joy in the sight of decay.
And so I left; and I returned 25
In Autumn strict of eye, to see
The sap gone out of the groundhog,
But the bony sodden hulk remained.
But the year had lost its meaning,
And in intellectual chains 30
I lost both love and loathing,
Mured up in the wall of wisdom.
Another summer took the fields again
Massive and burning, full of life,
But when I chanced upon the spot 35
There was only a little hair left,
And bones bleaching in the sunlight
Beautiful as architecture;
I watched them like a geometer,
And cut a walking stick from a birch. 40
It has been three years, now.
There is no sign of the groundhog.
I stood there in the whirling summer,
My hand capped a withered heart,
And thought of China and of Greece, 45
Of Alexander in his tent;
Of Montaigne in his tower,
Of Saint Theresa in her wild lament.

Two Tramps in Mud Time

ROBERT FROST [1875–]

Out of the mud two strangers came
And caught me splitting wood in the yard.
And one of them put me off my aim
By hailing cheerily "Hit them hard!"
I knew pretty well why he dropped behind 5
And let the other go on a way.
I knew pretty well what he had in mind:
He wanted to take my job for pay.

Good blocks of beech it was I split,
As large around as the chopping block; 10
And every piece I squarely hit
Fell splinterless as a cloven rock.
The blows that a life of self-control
Spares to strike for the common good
That day, giving a loose to my soul, 15
I spent on the unimportant wood.

The sun was warm but the wind was chill.
You know how it is with an April day
When the sun is out and the wind is still,
You're one month on in the middle of May. 20
But if you so much as dare to speak,
A cloud comes over the sunlit arch,
A wind comes off a frozen peak,
And you're two months back in the middle of March.

A bluebird comes tenderly up to alight 25
And fronts the wind to unruffle a plume
His song so pitched as not to excite
A single flower as yet to bloom.
It is snowing a flake: and he half knew
Winter was only playing possum. 30
Except in color he isn't blue,
But he wouldn't advise a thing to blossom.

The water for which we may have to look
In summertime with a witching-wand,

In every wheelrut's now a brook, 35
In every print of a hoof a pond.
Be glad of water, but don't forget
The lurking frost in the earth beneath
That will steal forth after the sun is set
And show on the water its crystal teeth. 40

The time when most I loved my task
These two must make me love it more
By coming with what they came to ask.
You'd think I never had felt before
The weight of an ax-head poised aloft, 45
The grip on earth of outspread feet.
The life of muscles rocking soft
And smooth and moist in vernal heat.

Out of the woods two hulking tramps
(From sleeping God knows where last night, 50
But not long since in the lumber camps).
They thought all chopping was theirs of right.
Men of the woods and lumberjacks,
They judged me by their appropriate tool.
Except as a fellow handled an ax, 55
They had no way of knowing a fool.

Nothing on either side was said.
They knew they had but to stay their stay
And all their logic would fill my head:
As that I had no right to play 60
With what was another man's work for gain.
My right might be love but theirs was need.
And where the two exist in twain
Theirs was the better right—agreed.

But yield who will to their separation, 65
My object in living is to unite
My avocation and my vocation
As my two eyes make one in sight.
Only where love and need are one,
And the work is play for mortal stakes, 70
Is the deed ever really done
For Heaven and the future's sakes.

Come In

ROBERT FROST [1875–]

As I came to the edge of the woods,
Thrush music—hark!
Now if it was dusk outside,
Inside it was dark.

Too dark in the woods for a bird 5
By sleight of wing
To better its perch for the night,
Though it still could sing.

The last of the light of the sun
That had died in the west 10
Still lived for one song more
In a thrush's breast.

Far in the pillared dark
Thrush music went—
Almost like a call to come in 15
To the dark and lament.

But no, I was out for stars:
I would not come in.
I meant not even if asked,
And I hadn't been. 20

Poem

WILLIAM CARLOS WILLIAMS [1883–]

By the road to the contagious hospital,
under the surge of the blue
mottled clouds driven from the
northeast—a cold wind. Beyond, the
waste of broad, muddy fields, 5
brown with dried weeds, standing and fallen,

patches of standing water,
the scattering of tall trees.

All along the road the reddish,
purplish, forked, upstanding, twiggy 10
stuff of bushes and small trees
with dead, brown leaves under them
leafless vines—

Lifeless in appearance, sluggish,
dazed spring approaches— 15

They enter the new world naked,
cold, uncertain of all
save that they enter. All about them
the cold, familiar wind—

Now the grass, tomorrow 20
the stiff curl of wild-carrot leaf.

One by one objects are defined—
It quickens: clarity, outline of leaf,

But now the stark dignity of
entrance— Still, the profound change 25
has come upon them; rooted, they
grip down and begin to awaken.

VIII

AMBIGUITY, ADDED DIMENSION, AND SUBMERGED METAPHOR

We have already read enough poems to see that often the most powerful effect that a particular poem gives comes from the total impact of the poem, not from some special and overt reference. "After Apple-Picking" (p. 388), for example, is not about the relation between the real and the ideal—not ostensibly, that is. We say that it is in part a realistic, in part a whimsical, account of what it feels like to end a day's work in the apple orchard in the fall. But the poem, we have seen (p. 395), speaks for something a good deal wider that that: it suggests a commentary on a deeper experience, even though the poem is too modest to claim that it is making any solemn, philosophical statement.

We can put the matter of apparent subject and real subject in a slightly different way. We can say that a poem need not point directly toward its real subject. The movement of expository prose is, of course, direct; but poetry frequently—one is tempted to say usually—moves by indirection. It does not make a frontal attack: it outflanks its real subject. We can put the matter in still another way: a genuine poem, even a poem on some apparently trivial subject, possesses a richness, a massiveness, and a depth that is baffling if we try to account for it as the padding out (with meter and imagery) of what seems to be the overt and specific statement that the poem makes. This is why we get such a lame answer if we take a poem like "Proud Maisie" (p. 53) and reduce it to its plot: we have to say, "It's just a story about a bird's telling a girl that she is going to die." Or, if we take a lyric like Webster's "Dirge" (p. 83), we have to say, "This poem just says that nature is comforting and consoling as well as terrifying."

Moreover, it doesn't help much to say that the story in question is beautifully told or that the theme is eloquently stated; for "beautifully" and "eloquently" are primarily ways of indicating that we approve of the job that the poet has done. These terms do not help us very much in exploring the *how* of the doing or even the *what* that has been done.

Herrick's "Delight in Disorder" (p. 187) provides a rather simple instance of the indirection of poetry. On the surface the speaker is simply saying that he prefers in dress a certain kind of untidiness rather than preciseness. But, as Bateson argues (p. 188), the little poem says much more than this: it implies that the attractive untidiness is actually a reflection of a certain kind of personality; and in expressing a delight in that kind of personality it becomes a "plea for paganism." Bateson indicates that it is primarily through the adjectives which describe the pleasing untidiness that Herrick makes his point, the adjectives having larger implications, including moral implications.

What Herrick does here is, of course, not particularly abstruse. He is making use of an aspect of language which has full force in our day, an aspect of language with which we are all thoroughly familiar.

For example, we speak today of a person who is "strait-laced." Now "strait-laced" in its literal meaning applies to clothing: a strait-laced person is a person who wears tightly laced garments. But this literal sense is now archaic, and today we use it most often to describe matters of conduct. The person whom we censure as strait-laced may not wear garments that have to be laced at all—may, for that matter, be a man as well as a woman. We can go further: the dance-hall girl of the 1890's portrayed by a Mae West, though tightly corseted, is not "strait-laced"—as we have come to use the term. For nowadays we use the adjective (though it embodies a metaphor taken from dress) with a very definite reference to matters of conduct, and we use it in this transferred sense quite naturally and without any sense of being abstruse or indirect.

In speaking of the implications of the adjectives which Herrick has chosen to describe the girl's clothing, Bateson uses the term "ambiguous associations." The word "ambiguous," though quite justified, can cause difficulty. For we are accustomed to consider ambiguity in writing as a defect. We are cautioned to make our prose clear and "unambiguous." We are urged to say what we mean, and to make that meaning unmistakable. We want a set of road directions to be thoroughly unambiguous. We want a legal document to have one clear meaning—so clear indeed that any other meaning is ruled out of account.

Because, therefore, of our deep-settled language habits, praise of a poet for his use of "ambiguous associations," and emphasis upon indirection as a characteristic of poetry, can easily suggest that the poet is trying to be difficult or obscure. It can even suggest that reading poetry is primarily an exercise in detecting the hidden references and unraveling the problems that the poet has cunningly set for us. Nothing, of course, could be more absurd. But we may avoid falling into this absurdity if we see clearly how the method of poetry differs from that of expository prose, and why indirection is an essential part of the method of poetry. In this connection, it may help also to substitute for "indirection" and "ambiguity"—terms which insist upon the difference between poetic statement and prosaic statement—other terms that relate more positively to the effect that poetry aims to give.

Poetry, as we have said, does not lead *directly* to its subject: it encompasses its subject. What seems to be *indirection* when measured against the standard of two-dimensional expository prose, is really massiveness and density. By the same token, "ambiguity" is seen to be depth and richness. To return to Bateson's example: "Delight in Disorder" does give, as he says, "the impression of a surprising richness," and though we can say with him that this richness is primarily due "to the skill with which [Herrick] has exploited the ambiguous associations of the epithets," we can just as properly attribute it to the *richness and multiple* associations of the epithets. The poem has depth and fullness, slight though the ostensible subject is; for the three themes that Bateson mentions are woven tightly together, not as an abstract argument, but as the presentation of an attitude with some of the concentration and condensation that we associate with dramatic presentation. If the adjectives in this poem are doing double duty, that is quite in keeping with the concentration at which poetry aims.

To sum up: the poet is never to be praised for having succeeded in being obscure as if that were something in itself valuable. But we may well praise him for giving us depth and richness and dramatic concentration. Genuine poems, great and small, have this quality of richness and concentration.

Since words have connotations as well as denotations, and since the poet tends to exploit all the resources of language, even simple poems will yield examples of "ambiguity." A humble instance occurs in the last stanza of "The Demon Lover" (p. 22),

> And he brake that gallant ship in twain,
> And sank her in the sea.

Does "her" refer to the ship or to the woman? Most of us will answer "to the ship"—since "ship" is the nearest possible antecedent of "her." (We will probably go on to point out that it doesn't matter particularly. Both ship and woman are destroyed, the destruction of the ship involving that of the woman.) But the accident of language which allows us to refer to a ship with the feminine pronoun does give a special effect here and helps to enforce the suggestion that the gaily caparisoned ship and the fate that befalls it symbolize the woman and the fate that overwhelms her. The point is doubtless trivial: that it is not entirely so, however, is suggested by the difference of effect given if we alter the last line to read:

> And sank it in the sea.

A more interesting and important example of ambiguity occurs in line 9 of Marvell's "Horatian Ode" (p. 524) where Cromwell is called "restless." As we read the poem, we see that all its connotations come into play, the unfavorable as well as the favorable. If Marvell praises Cromwell for being unwilling to rest, *tireless* in his labors, he also suggests that Cromwell is restless in the sense that he chafes at inactivity—he cannot keep quiet—he cannot let things be. The term has been well chosen: the poem explores and exploits the implications of the various senses in which Cromwell may be said to be *restless.*

In this last instance, the different connotations of the word are developed in the context; and in the developing context, even the opposed connotations are shown to apply. But the poet may on occasion deliberately play one connotation against another, emphasizing the discrepancy for playfully ironic or humorous effect. A rather simple instance of this kind of ambiguity is to be found in the first stanza of Corbet's "The Fairies' Farewell" (p. 250), where "farewell" is used in the first line in the sense of "good-bye" as spoken in leave taking, but then, in the fourth line, is broken down into its original components: "Do *fare* as *well* as they." The effect is witty and playful.

This device can also be used for quite different and much more serious effects. For example, consider the second stanza of Housman's "1887" (p. 374): the beacons are lighted and people are singing

> Because 'tis fifty years tonight
> That God has saved the Queen.

The last line comes with some shock: "God save the Queen (or King)" is a ritualistic phrase, a phrase grammatically petrified, as it were; and we are momentarily disconcerted at its being fitted into a matter-of-fact statement, with the change of tense and the other normal syntactical adjustments. The poet wants the shock; but the effect of the shock here is not playful but sobering. The rest of the poem is devoted to working out the implications of this wrenching of the phrase from its conventional context. Indeed, the poem may be described as a realistic and ironic examination of the real meanings of a phrase, usually so glibly and unthinkingly uttered.

In a good poem the words are continually interacting with each other to qualify and specialize meanings. Consider, for example, the word *intrinsicate* in the following passage from Shakespeare's *Antony and Cleopatra* (V, 2):

> [Cleopatra, taking up the asp, says to it]
> Come, thou mortal wretch,
> With thy sharp teeth this knot intrinsicate

Of life at once untie; poor venomous fool,
Be angry and dispatch.

Professor I. A. Richards[1] comments as follows:

> . . . Edward Dowden, following the fashion of his time in making Shakespeare as simple as possible, gives "intricate" as the meaning here of *intrinsicate*. And the Oxford Dictionary, sad to say, does likewise. But Shakespeare is bringing together half a dozen meanings from *intrinsic* and *intrinse:* "Familiar," "intimate," "secret," "private," "innermost," "essential," "that which constitutes the very nature and being of a thing,"—all the medical and philosophic meanings of his time as well as "intricate" and "involved." What the word does is exhausted by no one of these meanings and its force comes from all of them and more. As the movement of my hand uses nearly the whole skeletal system of the muscles and is supported by them, so a phrase may take its powers from an immense system of supporting uses of other words in other contexts.

This interaction of words occurs constantly in poetry—even when it does not produce, as in the passage just discussed, a new word form. What, for example, is a "green thought" (Marvell's "The Garden," p. 356, line 48)? We shall not find out by merely looking in the dictionary (though that is a necessary part of the process of finding out). The relevant meanings of *green* have been developed for us in the context of the poem itself: a green thought is, among other things, a garden thought—a thought characterized by the coolness, solitude, innocence, and "natural" organic quality of the garden in which the speaker thinks the thought.

The enrichment of words by the exploitation of their associations is well illustrated by the word *underworld* as Tennyson uses it in "Tears, Idle Tears" (p. 351). Tennyson describes the sadness of the "days that are no more" in terms of a ship coming up over the horizon, a ship which "brings our friends up from the underworld." *Underworld* means here literally the world that lies below the curve of the earth—"under" as illustrated in old-fashioned books of geography which showed the distant ship below the line of vision of the observer on shore. But *underworld* has very rich asso-

[1] *The Philosophy of Rhetoric,* New York: Oxford University Press, 1936, pp. 64–65.

ciations. It meant, for example, in Greek mythology, the land of the dead. In this poem, which is concerned with the sadness and strangeness of the past, the word *underworld* takes on another dimension. The "days that are no more" bring our friends back from the underworld of the dead.

With the last examples we raise the problem of deeper references. These references may, of course, point to materials outside the poem—for example, history or literature or folklore. Unless we understand these references, the poem may not be fully comprehensible, or if comprehensible, impoverished and thin. But references of this sort constitute, on the whole, the easiest kind of problem for the student to deal with. Scholarship may provide the necessary information, and for a great many poems of the past it has done so.

A fairly obvious example of literary reference which adds powerfully to the poem occurs in lines 15–16 of Housman's "1887" (p. 374). The poet says of the dead soldiers who helped God save the Queen,

> The saviors come not home tonight:
>   Themselves they could not save.

For the reader who remembers *Matthew* 27:42 ("He saved others; himself he cannot save"), the lines become freighted with a powerful irony. Like Christ on the cross, these saviors have not been able to save themselves.

Another simple instance of literary reference occurs in Landor's poem "Past Ruined Ilion" (p. 562). In order to understand the poem we must know the story of Helen of Troy and that of Alcestis, the woman who voluntarily died for her husband and whom the hero Hercules brought back from the underworld. If we have this information, the metaphorical structure of the poem is enriched; for we see that the poet is saying that the true Hercules who rescues "mortal maids" from the oblivion of death is verse:

> Verse calls them forth; 'tis verse that gives
>   Immortal youth to mortal maids.

With this example of implied metaphor we return to the more typical and serious difficulty in reading poetry, which is not lack of information but inability to deal with metaphorical and symbolic structure. The various elements in a poem not only make their contribution to the full context of the poem: they are affected by that context—given special meaning—charged with special values. A rather simple though important instance of this charging of an element is the use of the dewdrop in "Corinna's Going a-Maying." As it is used in this poem it becomes a special symbol of youth. The dewdrops are the natural jewels of the dawn, flashing in the early light like gems; they are the appropriate adornment for the girl on this May morning; they are the free gift of nature which the trees will shower down upon the girl as she passes beneath them. But they last no more than an hour. They must be enjoyed now, for in a little while they will have disappeared completely.

Now the dewdrop is a kind of natural symbol, and Herrick may seem to do no more than exploit the dew's associations with dawn, freshness, and sparkling light. Granted that the symbolism seems an obvious one, still we must not underestimate the importance of the context in serving to focus attention on these meanings. Moreover, "natural" symbolism is much more plastic—much more subject to manipulation by the poet—than we may think. Darkness, for example, seems a "natural" symbol of evil, but darkness *can* be used in very different fashion. In Vaughan's "The Night" (p. 291), darkness is associated with the soul's humility before, and receptiveness to, the divine influence. The student should also, in this connection, compare and contrast the dewdrop as used by Herrick with the dewdrop as used by Marvell (p. 90).

The poet's ability to invest an object or incident with quasi-symbolic force is abundantly illustrated in Pope's "Rape of the Lock." For example, three times in the poem there is a reference to the breaking of a frail piece of china, each time associated with some dire event. The first two instances may be regarded as merely witty collocations of the important with the trivial. Ariel, in his charge to the sylphs who guard Belinda, cautions them that on this day dark omens threaten Belinda, but he does not know what the threatened disaster will be:

> Whether the nymph shall break Diana's law,
> Or some frail China jar receive a flaw (II, 105–06).

Later in the poem the same image is used to describe the ecstasy of grief. When Belinda's lock is clipped her shrieks of grief are as loud as those evoked by the death of a husband or of a favorite lap dog,

> Or when rich China vessels fall'n from high,
> In glitt'ring dust and painted fragments lie (III, 159–60).

The third instance occurs when Belinda describes the omens which warned her of impending disaster:

> Thrice from my trembling hand the patchbox fell;
> The tott'ring China shook without a wind (IV, 162–63).

The breaking of a piece of rich China becomes almost a measuring stick for disaster in the charmingly artificial world of this poem. The porcelain is brittle, precious, useless, overvalued, and easily shattered. But Belinda and her airy guardians, it is implied, cannot conceive a more dire event. But if staining her "new brocade" is as bad as staining her honor, and if breaking a "frail China jar" is as terrible as breaking "Diana's law," there is at least the suggestion that staining one's honor is perhaps not much worse than staining a new brocade, and that the infraction of the law of chastity is not much more terrible than shattering the jar. As Pope handles the figure in his poem, the deflation tends to work both ways.

If, however, this last example seems rather minute and special, consider Pope's association of the sylphs with "honor." Pope is quite explicit in associating the sylphs with honor (see I, 67–78). But Pope's treatment of the sylphs in the poem goes far to suggest that honor is something pretty, airy, fluid, and not really believed in. The devoted sylph who interposes himself between the lock and the closing shears is clipped in two, but suffers no permanent damage (III, 151–52):

> Fate urged the shears, and cut the sylph in twain,
> (But airy substance soon unites again).

One should not perhaps press these quasi-symbolic devices too far, but much of the richness of this charming poem depends upon the poet's cunning use of them.

Throughout this section we have touched upon a number of ideas which have already been discussed, particularly in Section V on Imagery. But in Section V, we were concerned primarily with imagery which operated in full view—on the surface of the poem, as it were. A great many of the most important kind of images, however, are more deeply embedded in the make-up of the poem. There are, for example, submerged metaphors, of which the reader may not be conscious, and yet which powerfully condition the effect of the poem upon him.

Blake's poem "To Spring" is a rather simple instance of such submerged imagery. We have already commented upon the way in which the coming of an oriental prince is suggested by "bright pavilions," "perfumed garments," "scatter thy pearls," "put Thy golden crown," and most of all by the general reminiscence of the diction used in the *Song of Solomon*.

Another rather simple and obvious instance of submerged imagery is that to be found in Dryden's "To the Memory of Mr. Oldham" (p. 486). In line 11 Dryden addresses the younger poet as "early ripe" and asks what advancing age could have added to "thy abundant store." Oldham's harvest has been gathered early. But Dryden does not stress the figure or develop it: both "ripe" and "abundant store" can be taken with a mere general reference. They need be no more than hints of a concrete image of ripening. But at line 19, Dryden returns to the figure and develops it. "Thy generous fruits," he says:

> Still showed a quickness; and maturing time
> But mellows what we write to the dull sweets of rhyme.[1]

[1] Dryden's awaking and using the dormant metaphor implicit in "early ripe" suggests a further comment upon dormant metaphor in general. Many a careless prose writer suffers the embarrassment of having dormant metaphor unexpectedly wake up, to the confusion of his meaning. Everyone knows the statement of the congressman: "I smell a rat, but I shall nip it in the bud." Here is an example from a more literate source: "As a literary historian I am reminded that in Alexandria scholars also went in for glosses, producing that hieratic library which paved the road to Byzantium."

Much modern jargon derives from a tired and careless use of what was once metaphoric language. As Robert Graves puts it: ". . . from the inability to think poetically—to resolve speech into its original images and

His own rhymes, Dryden implies, are like mellow fruit, not sharp to the taste ("dull sweets"), but sweet to the point of insipidity, whereas the young satirist's works have an acid astringency ("Still showed a quickness") like fruit which has not fully ripened. But more still is involved in this playing off of "dull" against "quickness." "Quickness" is the quality of being alive; the still sour fruit is capable of further growth. The "dull sweets" have exhausted themselves and are dead. Through his nice choice of image, the elder poet gracefully deprecates his own accomplishment and makes a virtue out of the younger poet's limitation.

Keats's "On First Looking into Chapman's Homer" is an instance of a whole poem based upon a submerged image. The first six lines develop a consistent figure: that of a man who has traveled through many realms though he has merely heard of what is the most important realm of all. Then there is a shift in image from that of the traveler to that of the astronomer; and then once more to that of Cortez gazing at the Pacific. But the various figures, for all their diversity, are related to each other; all three stem from, and point back to, the exciting period of exploration and rediscovery that came at the end of the Middle Ages. The poem, as we know, is a poem about discovery—Keats's discovery of Chapman's translation; and Chapman himself, as a poet of the English Renaissance, has a place in this great period of rediscovery.

How, more specifically, do the surface images suggest the Renaissance? The "realms of gold" coupled with "western islands" suggest the newly discovered Americas—that is, the lands of gold as they appeared to the men of the Renaissance; and the final image concerns one of the explorers of the new realms of gold, Cortez.

rhythms and re-combine these on several simultaneous levels of thought into a multiple sense—derives the failure to think clearly in prose. In prose one thinks on only one level at a time, and no combination of words needs to contain more than a single sense; nevertheless the images resident in words must be securely related if the passage is to have any bite. This simple need is forgotten: what passes for simple prose nowadays is a mechanical stringing together of stereotyped word-groups, without regard for the images contained in them. The mechanical style, which began in the counting-house, has now infiltrated into the university, some of its most zombiesque instances occurring in the works of eminent scholars and divines."

(*The White Goddess,* New York, Creative Age Press, 1948, p. 186.)

But even the astronomer image is cognate with the others, for it gives us Renaissance discovery in another dimension—the sort carried out by a man like Galileo, for example, whom Keats perhaps, though not necessarily, had in mind.

Did Keats, then, make a preliminary blueprint of his sonnet, deciding to make all of his basic images radiate from the theme of Renaissance discovery? No, he need not have been conscious of that at all. Is it necessary, in order to appreciate the sonnet fully, that the reader "work out" the theme of Renaissance discovery—that he become fully conscious of the submerged references? Again no; not at all. Many people have enjoyed the poem, fully and with understanding, who have not explored the interconnections of the images. Why, then, call attention to them? Why the discussion in the preceding paragraphs?

The reason for calling attention to the interconnections among images and for pointing to submerged metaphors is to have us understand a little more clearly how a poem is held together and how it works, and to remind us that a poem frequently does its work imperceptibly. Confronted with two poems, both of which make use of diverse imagery, we sometimes feel that one is a clutter—a jumble—of unrelated images, whereas the divergent images of the other poem seem "magically" to fit together—to have been chosen, in spite of their diversity, in accord with some principle of order. We can let the matter go at this, if we like: one poem is somehow bad, the other good; one poet has thrown his images together helter-skelter, the other possessed a harmonizing taste, or was "inspired." But we need not leave the matter a dark mystery. Though we shall probably never understand fully the workings of language, still we may get some inklings as to what is happening, and we shall not think less of the "happy inspiration" or the "lucky accident" if we see that it is not a blind violation of the principles of language but a further exploitation of those principles. (See also Coleridge's discussion of the imagery in Shakespeare's "Venus and Adonis," p. 265, and "How Poems Come About," p. 591.)

The added dimension that the full exploitation of the resources of language may give to a poem accounts for the fact that the really good poems do not wear thin after a few readings. They continue to yield meanings, and because they are rich, come to be understood fully only after the reader has come to know them intimately.

Marvell's "The Garden" (p. 354) is an admirable instance of such richness. It is obvious that we can read the poem at a rather simple level. Read at this level, the poem yields a great deal. There is appropriate description of the garden itself, and of the speaker's pleasure in the garden's cool solitude.

But as we have seen, the poem also comments upon the opposed values of the active life and the contemplative life—upon ambition and the proper objects of ambition, etc. In the first stanza the poet suggests that men can attempt to use nature, spending a lifetime attempting to win one bit of the tree of victory when they might, without effort, have all the trees. Men sweat for the meager shade cast by one small chaplet when they might possess, as nature's free gift, the over-arching shade woven by the entire grove.

The poem abounds in examples of witty ambiguity, deeper reference, ironical play of association against association, and all the other devices discussed in this chapter. Here, however, we shall limit our consideration to a basic image, one which the poet allows to emerge explicitly only at the end of the poem, and even there only casually. The image is that of the Garden of Eden in which the yet unfallen Adam lived. The speaker's joy as he walks in his garden gives him some sense of what the "happy Garden-state" in Eden was, and some premonition of what the harmony of heaven will be. His garden experience is thus a kind of foretaste of eternity, an experience of the timeless vouchsafed for a moment to one who has just stepped into the garden from a time-harried world.

Marvell does not treat his theme solemnly or pretentiously. He smiles at the labors of the ambitious soldier and the statesman, he teases the ladies and the "fond lovers," and though he goes on to express the spiritual delight that the garden affords (stanza seven), he returns to a tone of ironic urbanity. Yet the poem in its treatment of the timeless experience is thoroughly serious. Almost every quality of this earthly garden bears its relation to the terrestrial paradise: the repose of stanza one; the presence of innocence as in the Eden of unfallen Man (stanza two); a friendly nature which accepts man and presses its delights upon him (stanza five); the calm joy of the mind in stanza six; the soul untrammeled by the body in stanza seven. Even the teasing of the lovers (stanzas three and four) fits into this reference, for the "happy Garden-state" is that before the differentiation of man into male and female—while "man there walked without a mate." And in the last stanza, as in the terrestrial paradise, time exerts no harsh pressure. The only clock in this garden is a sun dial whose numerals are worked out in beds of flowers.

But what is accomplished by the implied comparison of this garden, in which the poet takes his ease, with Eden's Garden? Is the poet simply paying his garden a kind of hyperbolic compliment? Or does the comparison have a more complex and important function? Does it help to define the present garden experience? Does it give depth and stability to that experience? To see just how complex and yet stable the experience is, the student will need to read or reread the poem carefully, paying not least attention to the way in which the playfulness and the seriousness define and support each other. But the student who does this successfully will find that the "wondrous life" which the speaker leads in his walk through the garden is wondrous in several senses, and that "wondrous" is much more than an unthinking cry of delight.

Another beautiful example of the way in which the various devices discussed in this chapter are employed richly and meaningfully in a fine poem is illustrated by "Among School Children" (p. 357). On the simplest level this poem is about a sixty-year-old man's strolling through a schoolroom and the rather rambling meditation on youth and education and growing up which it provokes in him. A casual reader may be a little puzzled by the philosophical allusions and wonder whether the last three stanzas are really closely related to the schoolroom experience at all. Closer inspection will show that they are, and that the poem concerns itself with the very essence of the educational process: the imposition of ideal patterns upon living material. The imposition is not always easy: the imposition may hurt and bruise. Furthermore, the pattern can never be expressed fully in the living, and therefore shifting, material upon which it is imposed. To this problem nearly all the references in the poem are related: the mother and the ideal which she has for her child; the nun and the image to which she gives her devotion; Aristotle giving a spanking to his pupil, the young Alexander, fitting him for his destined rôle of king of kings; Plato with his vision of the relation of ideal and actual; Pythagoras with his theories of number and harmony as the structural basis for the universe; and not least, the little girls in the schoolroom, learning how "To cut and sew, be neat in everything / In the best modern way."

The last stanza with its vision of a harmony in which "body is not bruised to pleasure soul" and where consequently labor is not labor as we think of it, but a blossoming or dancing, reconciles this war between the ideal and the real. This vision of achieved harmony, however, suggests that we can state what the poem is "about" in still other terms: we can say that the poem deals with, among other things, the world of being and the world of becoming —the world of "Presences" that are absolute and do not change, and the world of becoming which passes from birth to decay and death. The poet does not choose between the two: he cannot, for this is the human predicament. Man cannot be man without his ideals even though he can never fully achieve them and is thus condemned to be bruised by them.

Now thus far we have sketched out some of the elements of the poem conceived in intellectual terms, but we have yet to consider how the poem embodies these ideas, develops them, qualifies them, in a dramatic context. And until we have done this we have merely dealt with the poem as an argument, not as realized experience. Let us consider the way in which some of the details are charged with meaning, developed as symbols, and used to express and link the various parts of the poem. Let us take the egg-bird-scarecrow group. The sight of the little school girls reminds the speaker of the youth of his beloved, a woman with a body like Leda's, beloved of Zeus in the form of a swan. Her story to him of some hurt suffered in childhood "blent" their two natures until they seemed in this access of sympathy to be one; and to describe this intimacy, the poet refers to Plato's parable of the egg. According to one of Plato's myths, love is to be accounted for as follows: Men were originally double, until Zeus split them apart "as you might divide an egg with a hair" and ever since these half-men have tried to find their partners.

The poet wonders whether his beloved, whose achieved beauty is like that of Helen of Troy, might once have looked like one of the schoolroom children. Helen, whose beauty caused the Trojan War, was a daughter of Leda, the bride of the swan, and

> . . . even daughters of the swan can share
> Something of every paddler's heritage. . . .

And here there is obviously a reference to the fairy story of the ugly duckling: even the woman of Ledaean body may have been a gangly-legged little girl, an "ugly duckling," once. The speaker, the "sixty-year-old smiling public man," ruefully remembers that he too "though never of Ledaean kind / Had pretty plumage once." But the plumage has been lost. He is now a comfortable kind of scarecrow—the angular body draped in old clothes calculated to scare away the birds—not to attract them.

At first glance, these various items of imagery may seem quite unrelated, images which the poet chose because of their momentary application to the reverie which the poem develops. Even at second glance, they may seem to reveal no more than arbitrary connections one with another. But in the light of the total poem, they are seen to body forth the theme of development: the egg, the fledgling, the full-grown bird, the tattered molting bird, the scarecrow. (Compare the scale set up by the human references: the babe at birth, the child, the schoolboy Alexander and the little girls in the schoolroom, Leda and the golden-thighed Pythagoras, and last the man with sixty winters on his head.) Seeing this, we may be willing to explore the poem as a carefully organized body of particulars related most cunningly to the various themes. The student may find it interesting to consider, for example, the way in which the casual reference to Plato in Stanza II helps prepare for Stanza VI; or how the nun and the mother balance and supplement each other; or the double sense of "labor" ("work" and "birth-throes") in Stanza VIII.

All the devices discussed in this section affirm the special kind of unity to which poetry aspires. These devices may all be considered as means by which the poet attempts to gain the fullest integration possible among the various elements of his poem. It is not enough that the denotations of words be fitted together; the connotations must be fitted together as well. It is not enough that the image give the particular picture which the poet needs at that moment; ideally, that image has to be related to the other images in the poem. As we look toward the integration of the whole poem, each word in the good poem seems the inevitable word, the just word, which makes its definite contribution to the total organization of the poem. On the other hand, if we look from the totality of the poem back to the individual word, the word seems to acknowledge the pressures of the whole context in which it has its place. It is charged with the special meaning by the context; it is warped a bit from its conventional meaning; it is qualified to some degree by the context of the whole. The various devices treated in this section may be described as special ways in which the word or phrase acknowledges the pressure of the context.

The term *irony* may be added to the number of these devices. In sarcasm the literal meaning of the word is actually reversed. In less extreme forms of irony it is modified so that it carries a special sense. We lack a term to indicate the less extreme kinds of modification of a word by its context. And in this book it is possible that we have sometimes overused the term *irony* by applying it to instances in which the warping of meaning by the context is only slight. But every word in a good poem acknowledges to some degree the pressure of the context.

The poet's task, as T. S. Eliot has remarked, is to "dislocate words into meaning." If "dislocate" seems too violent a term to apply generally, one can recur to Eliot for an alternate account of the situation. He refers elsewhere to "that perpetual slight alteration of language, words perpetually juxtaposed in new and sudden combinations." Even where the combinations are not to be described as "sudden," the poet is constantly sharpening or specializing or altering the meanings of words by controlling their relations to a governing context.

What we have described in these last paragraphs is an ideal, but in poetry it is a fundamental ideal. Unless we understand it, we shall hardly be able to see what the nature of poetic language is. Moreover, it is an ideal which in the great poems is much more nearly realized than we may be apt to think. Certainly the great poems continue to yield a sense of freshness and unforeseen meanings—a fact that seems to substantiate this general account of the matter.

In this section we have stressed the richness and further levels of meaning which poetry possesses. But there are two further important considerations which ought to be mentioned in this connection. The first is precision. Poetry is not a fuzzy, vague use of language. It is rather an extremely precise use of language. The poet, by means of the devices that we have discussed, gives us not a merely conventional set of word meanings but employs a language tailor-made to fit precisely what he is saying. This is not the precision of scientific language, granted. But it is not loose, vague language. For its special purpose it is thoroughly precise.

The second consideration is stability. The interplay of part against part in a good poem makes for the stability of the experience. The good poem is not an irresponsible letting loose of emotion. The great poems may move us intensely but they are not gushy. The stability of the experience is analogous to that achieved by the principle of the arch: the very downward drag of the individual stones holds the arch together. In a good poem, the very counterthrusts of the various elements play their parts in establishing the ordered structure of the poem.

EXERCISE:

1. Comment upon the words "blackening" and "appalls" in line 10 of Blake's "London" (p. 427). What do they mean literally or primarily? What further meanings do they take on in this context? Comment upon "youthful" and "curse" in line 14.

2. How can the poet say that the days that are no more are "deep as love, / Deep as first love, and wild with all regret" ("Tears, Idle Tears," p. 352, lines 18–19)? How can days be *deep* and *wild?* What do these words come to mean in the context of the poem? Has their application to "days" been prepared for? How?

3. Study carefully the use of sunlight and moonlight in "The Rime of the Ancient Mariner" (p. 527). With what events are the two kinds of light associated? Could it be said that sunlight and moonlight have a symbolic (or quasi-symbolic) function in this poem? What do they symbolize?

4. The killing of the albatross in "The Rime of the Ancient Mariner" is treated as if it were a kind of murder. How has the poet associated the albatross with human qualities?

5. In "The March into Virginia" (p. 445, line 34) the poet says that some of the young soldiers will "Perish, enlightened by the volleyed glare." *Enlightened* is obviously used ironically, but why is it not a glib or brittle irony? How is line 34 prepared for by the whole poem? How close does it come to summing up the poem?

6. Investigate the interplay between images of divine love and secular love in "The Canonization" (p. 484). How does the poet prove that the lovers are "saints"? What is the paradox developed in the last stanza?

7. In line 41 of Gray's "Elegy" (p. 376), "animated bust" means presumably a speaking likeness—a statue so like the subject that it seems to breathe. But what else does "animated bust" mean in this context? How are the various other submeanings pointed up by the context? Investigate the meanings of "homely joys" (line 30), "pleasing anxious being" (line 86), and "artless tale" (line 94).

IX

HOW POEMS COME ABOUT: INTENTION AND MEANING

Why are we, or why should we be, interested in how poems come about? A historian or biographer might be intensely interested in the materials that got into a poem—the personal experiences or observations of the poet, or ideas current in his time. Or a psychologist might equally well be interested in the mental process of creation that gave us the poem. But the historian or psychologist, strictly as historian or psychologist, would not be interested in the quality of the poem. For his interests the bad poem might be as useful as the good poem. But our present concern is different from that of the historian or psychologist. Now we are primarily interested in the nature of the poem and its quality: we are critics and appreciators of poetry.

If the poem itself is our primary interest, we may say that there is no good reason why we should investigate the origins of the poem, that the poem is what we want in the end and that a knowledge of the materials that went into the poem or of the process by which it came to be, cannot change the nature of the poem itself. Many people take the view that we have no proper concern with the private lives of writers even if the lives do provide material for the work. Wordsworth says in a letter to James Gray, a friend of Robert Burns:

> Our business is with their books,—to understand and to enjoy them. And, of poets more especially, it is true—that, if their works be good, they contain within themselves all that is necessary to their being comprehended and relished.

And Charles Lamb was shocked when he saw the manuscript of Milton's "Lycidas" and got an idea of the process of its creation. He reports his feeling in an essay on "Oxford in the Vacation":

> I had thought of the Lycidas as a full-grown beauty—as springing up with all its parts absolute—till, in an evil hour, I was shown the original copy of it, together with the other minor poems of the author, in the library of Trinity, kept like some treasure to be proud of. I wish they had thrown them in the Cam, or sent them after the latter Cantos of Spenser, into the Irish Channel. How it staggered me to see the fine things in their ore! interlined, corrected! as if their words were mortal, alterable, displaceable at pleasure! as if they might have been otherwise, and just as good! as if inspiration were made up of parts, and these fluctuating, successive, indifferent! I will never go into the workshop of any great artist again.

In one sense, Wordsworth is right. We must not confuse information about the life of a poet, or about his time, or about his materials, with the poem itself. And in one sense Lamb is right. What is important is the poem itself and not the psychological process whereby it was created. But in another sense both Wordsworth and Lamb are wrong. What we can learn about the origin of a poem may, if we do not confuse origin and poem, enlarge our understanding and deepen our appreciation.[1]

In thinking of the origin of a poem we may distinguish two general aspects of the question: first, the *materials* of the poem, and second, the *process* whereby the poem is made.

The materials of a poem are various. We can, for instance, say

[1] This gain in understanding and appreciation is not merely, in fact not primarily, of the poem whose development we can trace because early drafts or information about the poet's experience have been preserved to us. It is, rather, a gain in our understanding and appreciation of poetry in general; when we learn about the materials of poetry and about the poetic process, we also learn something about the nature of poetry. The value of this study of biographical and textual material is to be distinguished sharply, however, from the value of certain historical information which is necessary for the understanding of particular literary works from another age or another culture. For example, we can presumably understand *Hamlet* without knowing Shakespeare's private life or the steps in the composition of the play, but we cannot understand the play unless we know something of the heroic tradition that revenge is honorable.

that language itself is a material of poetry. It is one of the things the poet shapes and uses. We have to know something of the language a poet is using before we can appreciate his poem—before we can see how the poem came to be. This applies not only to poems in foreign languages but also to poems in our own tongue. The English of one time is not like the English of another. Words are born and die, and to make matters more complicated, the same word may change its meaning from one period to another. Furthermore, the poet himself may twist and wrench the language he uses so that words get new meanings. The material is plastic and he may mould it even as he uses it. But ordinarily, of course, the poet works with the language as it comes to him, exploring its possibilities, but not actually changing it.

To take another example, we may regard literary convention as a material for poetry. When Campion came to write "Blame Not My Cheeks" (p. 187) he used as one of the elements in his poem the Petrarchan convention of the lover who is abject and self-pitying before the cruel lady who despises him.[1] Actually in the course of the poem this convention is brought into contrast with other attitudes, and the almost whimsical irony of the last line, which yet remains serious, is anything but Petrarchan. But the convention provides the starting point. The same is true of the convention of the pastoral elegy in Milton's "Lycidas." Milton and Edward King, the drowned friend in whose honor the poem is written, had not been shepherds at all. They had been students at Cambridge University. Milton is simply using this conventional fiction which had persisted from classical times. It is a material which he adapts in his own way.[2]

Or let us consider the ideas that are available at a given time. Those, too, are materials. Tennyson uses a foreshadowing of the

[1] The poems which the Italian poet Petrarch (1304–1374) addressed to his lady Laura set a fashion in love poetry which persisted for nearly three centuries. Attitudes toward the beloved lady that were personal and meaningful in Petrarch became exaggerated into mere artificial posturings among many of his imitators. In the figure of Romeo as he appears in the beginning of the play, when he thinks he is in love with Rosaline, Shakespeare is poking fun at the Petrarchan convention as it had survived to his time.

[2] For a discussion of the meaning of this poem see E. M. W. Tillyard: *Milton*, New York, Dial Press, 1930, pp. 80–85.

theory of evolution in his *In Memoriam,* and Whitman expresses certain notions of democracy. These ideas were available in their time. On the contrary, it is nonsense to read "Sir Patrick Spence" as a statement of modern democratic ideas, for that poem came out of a feudal society. A poet may, of course, do something original with the ideas available to him. A poet is not a mere stenographer to his time. But his ideas are conditioned by his time.

So far we have been speaking of some of the materials of poetry that are generally available in a period: the language, the literary conventions, the ideas. But the personal experiences of the poet are also materials. This is not to say that a poet simply reports his personal experiences. Because Shakespeare wrote a play about Macbeth, who killed a king and stole a throne, we do not have to assume that Shakespeare ever committed murder or robbery. Sometimes, very often in fact, the events in a poem are fictitious, are products of imagination. But the imagination is not entirely free; it is conditioned, too, by the experience of the poet. It is true, as Robert Frost says, that the poet needs only samples for the imagination to work on, but it does not work in a vacuum.

The relation between the actual work of a poet and his personal experiences may be a very delicate and tenuous one, but sometimes we find a very close correlation between the actual events and the poetry. Dorothy Wordsworth, the sister of the poet, records in her journal for April 15, 1802, the episode that gave the material for the poem on the daffodils (p. 270):

It was a threatening, misty morning, but mild. . . . The wind was furious, and we thought we must have returned. We first rested in the large boat-house, then under a furze bush opposite Mr. Clarkson's. Saw the plough going in the field. The wind seized our breath. The Lake was rough. There was a boat by itself floating in the middle of the bay below Water Millock. . . . When we were in the woods beyond Gowbarrow Park we saw a few daffodils close to the water-side. We fancied that the lake had floated the seeds ashore, and that the little colony had so sprung up. But as we went along there were more and yet more; and at last, under the boughs of the trees, we saw that there was a long belt of them along the shore, about the breadth of a country turnpike road. I never saw daffodils so beautiful. They grew among the mossy stones about and about them; some rested their heads upon these stones as on a pillow for weariness; and the rest tossed and reeled and danced, and seemed as if they verily laughed with the wind, that blew upon them over the lake; they looked so gay, ever glancing, ever changing. This wind blew directly over the lake to them. There was here and there a little knot, and a few stragglers a few yards higher up; but they were so few as not to disturb the simplicity, unity, and life of that one busy highway.

It is true that in his poem Wordsworth does more than merely report the scene, but the scene is vividly there, a piece of material from his experience. And we are fairly safe in concluding that when he came to write the poem two years after the event, in 1804, the interpretation he gives the original event—the notion that experience grows in the imagination and the notion of the sympathetic relation between man and nature—is drawn also from personal experience. The real scene had really flashed upon his inward eye. That is, the whole poem, event and interpretation, presumably come as a presentation of real experience, *preceding* the act of composition.

To take another instance, we have an account by William Butler Yeats of a visit to a dying friend, the sister of the artist Aubrey Beardsley, who himself had died young and courageously. We also have a group of poems by Yeats called "Upon a Dying Lady." The prose account runs:

She was propped up on pillows with her cheeks I think a little rouged and looking very beautiful. Beside her an Xmas tree with little toys containing sweets, which she gave us. . . . I will keep the little toy she gave me and I dare say she knew that. On a table near were four dolls dressed like people out of her brother's drawings. . . . Ricketts had made them, modelling the faces and sewing the clothes. They must have taken him days. She had all her great lady airs and asked after my work and health as if they were the most important things in the world to her. "A palmist told me," she said, "that when I was forty-two my life would take a turn for the better and now I shall spend my forty-second year in heaven," and then emphatically pretending we were incredulous. "O yes, I shall go to heaven. Papists do." . . . Then she began telling improper stories and inciting us (there were two men besides myself) to do the like. At moments she shook with laughter. . . . I lay awake most of the night with a poem in my head. I cannot overstate her strange charm—the pathetic gaiety—It was her brother but her brother was not I think lovable, only astonishing and intrepid.[1]

If we compare this with the poems (pp. 486–89), we find that most of the details and attitudes of the poems are already here, either explicitly or implicitly.

The relation, however, between the personal experience and the poem is somewhat less definite in the following instance. In a letter to his brother, Keats describes his feelings as he lay late abed one morning:

This morning I am in a sort of temper, indolent and supremely careless—I long after a stanza or two of Thomson's *Castle of Indolence*—my passions are all asleep, from my having slumbered till nearly eleven, and weakened the animal fibre all over me, to a delightful sensation, about three degrees this side of faintness. If I had teeth of pearl and the breath of lilies I should call it languor, but as I am I must call it laziness. In this state of effeminacy the fibres of the brain are relaxed in common with the rest of the body, and to such a happy degree that pleasure has no show of enticement and pain no unbearable frown. Neither Poetry, nor Ambition, nor Love have any alertness of countenance as they pass by me; they seem rather like figures on a Greek vase—a man and two women whom no one but myself could distinguish in their disguisement.

If we compare this passage with Keats's "Ode on Indolence" (p. 553), we see that the poem and the letter are very similar. Both the letter and the poem use the same material, the experience of a strange and delightful lethargy in which one rejects the things ordinarily held dear in the world. Already, lying abed, Keats has let his imagination begin to work on the experience, to explore it, to find images and action to give it body, or, perhaps, as he writes the letter the process begins. We are not saying that Keats deliberately set himself the task of summoning up the figures to embody his feeling. They may have sprung to mind quite unexpectedly, well before Keats had the intention of writing a poem on "indolence."

When he comes to write the poem, he does a little more than de-

[1] Quoted by A. Norman Jeffares: *W. B. Yeats, Man and Poet.* New Haven: Yale University Press, 1949; London: Routledge and Kegan Paul Ltd., p. 166.

scribe the "drowsy hour" and the "blissful cloud of summer-indolence," and the three figures that pass mysteriously before him. He bids these "ghosts" farewell,

> For I would not be dieted with praise,
> A pet-lamb in a sentimental farce!

This reason for the rejection seems a strange and intrusive notion in the poem, but if we go back to the letter and read all of it we may find some explanation. In the letter Keats speculates in a rambling way about several topics. First, he comments on the rarity of true disinterestedness and unselfishness in men, then on the instinctiveness of human behavior and the "animal eagerness" in men. "The Hawk wants a Mate, so does the Man—look at them both, they set about it and procure one in the same manner. They want both a nest and they both set about one in the same manner—they get their food in the same manner." Then he modifies that notion: "There is an electric fire in human nature tending to purify—so that among these human creatures there is continually some birth of new heroism." Then he thinks of his own rôle as a poet, which he may be pursuing as instinctively and as interestedly as an animal, and wonders if, nevertheless, it may not have some value.

> May there not be superior beings amused with any graceful, though instinctive, attitude my mind may fall into, as I am entertained with the alertness of a Stoat or the anxiety of a Deer? Though a quarrel in the Streets is a thing to be hated, the energies displayed in it are fine; the commonest Man shows a grace in his quarrel. . . . This is the very thing in which consists Poetry, and if so it is not so fine a thing as philosophy—the same reason that an eagle is not so fine a thing as a truth. Give me this credit—Do you not think I strive—to know myself.

We do not find here anything that specifically accounts for the farewell to the mysterious figures, but we do find both here and in the poem that Keats is concerned with the nature and worth of human motivations—love, ambition, poetry. How far are they tainted with the instinctive interest?

Now in the poem he repudiates Love, Ambition, and Poetry, because to accept them would be somehow to make himself unworthy, would make him the "pet-lamb." So the indolence that in the beginning is a kind of languor or laziness, a merely "delightful sensation," becomes in the end a sort of disinterestedness, a sort of detachment from the "interested" and "instinctive" spurs to human action. The visions of indolence remain, but in so far as they save him from the taint of "interest" there is something almost noble about them; in them, at least, he will not be "dieted with praise" and take an ignoble part in a "sentimental farce." [1] This repudiation at the end of the ode is similar to that at the end of the following sonnet by Keats:

> When I have fears that I may cease to be
> Before my pen has glean'd my teeming brain,
> Before high-piled books in charact'ry,
> Hold like rich garners the full-ripen'd grain;
> When I behold, upon the night's starr'd face, 5
> Huge cloudy symbols of a high romance,
> And think that I may never live to trace
> Their shadows, with the magic hand of chance;
> And when I feel, fair creature of an hour,
> That I shall never look upon thee more, 10
> Never have relish in the faery power
> Of unreflecting love;—then on the shore
> Of the wide world I stand alone, and think
> Till love and fame to nothingness do sink.

Here, in the thought of death, in the thought of the smallness and the transience of the individual, there is the repudiation of love and fame.

In the journal of Dorothy Wordsworth and the letters of Yeats and Keats we have an account of personal experiences that later become the material of poetry. In these instances, the relation between the experience and the poem is close. We have the impression that the poet had the experience—the sight of the daffodils or the morning-indolence—and then did his thinking about its significance before he entered upon composition, before he had the impulse to make a poem.

[1] The fact that scholars may see in the pet lamb reference a repudiation of the literary group of Leigh Hunt, who had encouraged Keats as an aspiring young poet, does not argue against the notion given above. That would merely be a particular instance of Keats's new "disinterestedness."

We may, of course, be wrong about this. Wordsworth may have begun to turn around in his mind the idea of a poem on the daffodils even as he looked marveling at them, and Keats may have had the intention of writing a poem before he struck on the three muffled figures, and the letter itself may have been the first vague movement towards the composition of the poem. What is important is that the first simple experience is interpreted, is turned about and about, until it gets a meaning for the poet and until he finds words that develop the meaning.

It may be objected here that the thinking about the original experience is also *material,* that it is as much material as the sight of the daffodils, and that it is certainly to be regarded as material if the poet did his thinking and interpreting *before* he actually began the process of composition. Then the question arises as to what we mean by the process of composition. Does it begin when the poet first takes pen in hand, or when, without necessarily intending a poem, he begins to think about the material and try to interpret it?

But does it really matter which view we take? The important thing is to see some line of connection between the experience and the poem which in its finished form interprets the experience.

All poems, however, do not start directly from a personal experience of the poet. A poet may actually start from a general idea—a theme—and seek episodes and images to embody it. For example, Coleridge apparently intended to write a poem about guilt and atonement, and actually began a prose-poem on Cain, long before he struck on the story of the Ancient Mariner to embody his ideas. And Milton, too, was casting about for a story to embody his ideas on guilt and atonement before he settled on *Paradise Lost.* In the manuscript of Milton's minor poems, preserved in the library of Trinity College at Cambridge University, there are notes toward a drama on the Deluge as well as a drama on the Fall of Man. Or a poem may start from a story, an episode, or a situation heard about or read. It strikes the poet as interesting, and he begins to try to make a poem of that material, even before he is clear as to why it interests him or what it means to him. Or it may start with a casual phrase that pops into the poet's head or is picked up somewhere; or an image of some kind or a comparison may fire his imagination.

However the process may start, what is its nature?

At first glance, the accounts we have of the process seem contradictory and confusing. Some poets work very slowly and carefully. Some work by fits and starts, trusting to the suggestion of the moment. Some poems have been dreamed up in an instant. Some have required years of thought. There is Poe's famous account, in "The Philosophy of Composition," of the creation of "The Raven." After arguing that a poem must make its effect immediately, in a limited time, Poe says:

> Holding in view these considerations, as well as that degree of excitement which I deemed not above the popular, while not below the critical, taste, I reached at once what I conceived the proper *length* for my intended poem—a length of about one hundred lines. It is, in fact, a hundred and eight.
>
> My next thought concerned the choice of an impression, or effect, to be conveyed: and here I may as well observe that, throughout the construction, I kept steadily in view the design of rendering the work *universally* appreciable. . . . That pleasure which is at once the most intense, the most elevating, and the most pure, is, I believe, found in the contemplation of the beautiful. When, indeed, men speak of Beauty, they mean, precisely, not a quality, as is supposed, but an effect. . . . Now I designate Beauty as the province of the poem, merely because it is an obvious rule of Art that effects should be made to spring from direct causes. . . .
>
> Regarding, then, Beauty as my province, my next question referred to the *tone* of its highest manifestation—and all experience has shown that this tone is one of *sadness*. . . . Melancholy is thus the most legitimate of all the poetical tones. . . .
>
> The length, the province, and the tone, being thus determined, I betook myself to ordinary induction with the view of obtaining some artistic piquancy which might serve me as a key-note in the construction of the poem—some pivot upon which the whole structure might turn. In carefully thinking over all the usual artistic effects . . . I did not fail to perceive immediately that no one had been so universally employed as that of the *refrain*.

Poe continues in this fashion, as systematically as though working out a theorem in geometry. The refrain must be a single word, it must close each stanza, it must be sonorous, it must be melancholy, for that is the already determined tone. So he selects the word *never-*

more, as logically as a mechanic picks up the proper monkey-wrench. The selection of every detail of the poem is accounted for in the same fashion.

Over against this systematic, well-planned approach of Poe (which seems almost too systematic and well planned to be true) we can put the account given by Coleridge of the composition of "Kubla Khan."

In the summer of the year 1797, the author, then in ill health, had retired to a lonely farmhouse between Porlock and Linton, on the Exmoor confines of Somerset and Devonshire. In consequence of a slight indisposition, an anodyne had been prescribed, from the effects of which he fell asleep in his chair at the moment that he was reading the following sentence, or words of the same substance, in *Purchas's Pilgrimage:* "Here the Khan Kubla commanded a palace to be built, and a stately garden thereunto. And thus ten miles of fertile ground were inclosed with a wall." The author continued for about three hours in a profound sleep, at least of the external senses, during which time he has the most vivid confidence, that he could not have composed less than from two to three hundred lines; if that indeed can be called composition in which all the images rose up before him as *things,* with a parallel production of the correspondent expressions, without any sensation or consciousness of effort. On awaking he appeared to himself to have a distinct recollection of the whole, and taking his pen, ink, and paper, instantly and eagerly wrote down the lines that are here preserved. At this moment he was unfortunately called out by a person on business from Porlock, and detained by him above an hour, and on his return to his room, found, to his no small surprise and mortification, that though he still retained some vague and dim recollection of the general purport of the vision, yet, with the exception of some eight or ten scattered lines and images, all the rest has passed away like the images on the surface of a stream into which a stone has been cast, but, alas! without the after restoration of the latter.

In between these two extremes there are all sorts of ways of composition. Though Shakespeare never, as far as we know, dreamed up a poem, he apparently did compose with great speed and fluency, and did little revision. Dryden, too, came to have more and more readiness so that, as he says, the thoughts outran the pen. The

French poet Bonnard[1] records that when he composed, all the words seemed to crowd in at the same time so that he had the impression of having a thousand voices. But one part of the same poem may be composed in almost a flash and another part may require long and tedious effort. A. E. Housman provides us with such a poem. He tells us, in *The Name and Nature of Poetry,* how he was accustomed to compose on his afternoon walk, when he was a little drowsy from lunch and beer and his mind was relaxed and free for the movement of association. Under these circumstances, sometimes stanzas, or even whole poems, came almost in a flash, sometimes merely the germs of poems which had to be developed later. He tells us, for example, that of the poem given below two stanzas came immediately while he was walking along, that another stanza came that same afternoon during tea time, but that another took a year and went through thirteen versions. Unfortunately, Housman did not specify the stanzas, but one critic[2] has argued that the first and second stanzas must have come spontaneously on the walk, for they make a finished thought, and that the last most probably came at tea time, separate from the first two. Then the problem was to get something that would carry over from the second to the fourth stanza to give balance to the repetition and return of the poem.

I hoed and trenched and weeded,
  And took the flowers to fair:
I brought them home unheeded;
  The hue was not the wear.

So up and down I sow them 5
  For lads like me to find,
When I shall lie below them,
  A dead man out of mind.

Some seed the birds devour,
  And some the season mars, 10

[1] N. Kostyleff: *Le Mécanisme Cérébral de la Pensée,* Paris: Librairie Félix Alcan, 1914, p. 187.

[2] Donald A. Stauffer, *Poets at Work,* New York: Harcourt, Brace and Company, 1948, pp. 42–43.

But here and there will flower
  The solitary stars,

And fields will yearly bear them
  As light-leaved spring comes on,
And luckless lads will wear them 15
  When I am dead and gone.

Robert Frost says that many of his best poems came spontaneously, without effort:

I won't deny I have worried quite a number of my poems into existence. But my sneaking preference remains for the ones I carried through like the stroke of a raquet, club, or headsman's ax. It is only under pressure from friends that I can consent to come out into the open and expose myself in a weakness so sacred and in the present trend of criticism so damaging. When I look into myself for the agony I am supposed to lay claim to as an artist it has to be over the poems that went wrong and came to grief without coming to an end; and they made me less miserable than I deserved when I discovered that though lost they were not entirely lost: I could and did quite freely quote lines and phrases of them from memory. I never wrote a poem for practice: I am always extended for the best yet. But what I failed with I learned to charge up to practice after the fact. Now if I had only treasured my first drafts along with my baby shoes to bear me out in all this I should be more comfortably off in a world of suspicion. My word will be more or less taken for it that I played certain poems through without fumbling a sentence: such as for example November Days, The Mountain, After Apple-Picking, The Wood-Pile, Desert Places, The Gift Outright, The Lovely Shall Be Choosers, Directive. With what pleasure I remember their tractability. They have been the experience I couldn't help returning for more of—I trust I may say without seeming to put on inspired airs.[1]

[1] From a letter to Charles Madison, February 26, 1950. The letter continues: "Then for a small chaser of the low-down under the head perhaps of curiosa I might confess the trade secret that I wrote the third line of the last stanza of Stopping by Woods in such a way as to call for another stanza when I didn't want another stanza and didn't have another stanza in me, but with great presence of mind and a sense of what a good boy I was I instantly struck the line out and made my exit with a repeat end. I left the Ingenuities of Debt lying round nameless for forty years because I couldn't

As Housman spontaneously caught little or much of a poem on his walks, so Hart Crane tried to evoke the creative process by drink and jazz music, which might hypnotically start trains of verbal association; and so Schiller is reported to have kept a rotting apple in his desk because he found the odor stimulating. And many poets have had little tricks and habits which seem to make the process easier, more automatic, more like Coleridge's dream.[1]

What are we to make of all this? Is there one kind of poetry that comes from calculation and another kind that comes from inspiration? Is the poetry composed slowly and by calculation more reasonable than that composed rapidly and by inspiration? Or are the differences in the process of composition really accidental?

Perhaps the best way to approach the question is to ask how the composition of poetry compares with other kinds of creative activity, for instance, the discovery of a scientific principle. We find parallels here to the poetic activity. Some scientific discoveries have been made as the result of elaborate calculation, but some have been dreamed up as was "Kubla Khan."

find a fourth line for it to suit me. A friend, a famous poet, saw it in 1913 and wasn't so much disturbed by my bad fourth line as he was by the word "terrelation" further on. The same famous poet did persuade me to omit a line or two from the Death of the Hired Man and wanted me to omit the lines Home is the place where when you have to go there they have to take you in. The last three lines of Nothing Gold Can Stay were once entirely different. A lady in Rochester, N. Y., has, I think, the earlier version. I haven't. Birches is two fragments soldered together so long ago I have forgotten where the joint is."

[1] Here is Charlie Chaplin's account of how he provokes the unconscious: "There's no use just sitting down and waiting for an inspiration, though. You've got to play along. The main thing you've got to do is preserve your vitality. A couple of days of complete rest and solitude helps. Not seeing anybody. I even conserve my emotions. 'I'm not going to get excited about anybody or anything,' I say, 'until I get this gag worked out.' I go along that way, living a quiet and righteous life, and then I stay out late one night, and have a couple of drinks—perhaps all night—and the next morning the reserve pours out. But you've got to have the reserve. Dissipation is no use except as a release. You've been damming it up inside of you, and all of a sudden you say: 'Oh, here it is!' And then you go to work." (From Max Eastman: *Heroes I Have Known,* New York: Simon and Schuster, 1942, p. 177.)

The great German chemist Kekulé quite literally dreamed up his two most important discoveries, dealing with the structure of the molecule. He describes his discovery of the structure of benzene, which came to him one night as he sat at his desk trying to write a section of a text book on chemistry. "But it did not go well; my spirit was with other things. I turned my chair to the fireplace and sank into a half-sleep. Again the atoms flitted before my eyes." The atoms took the pattern of rings:

Long rows, variously, more closely, united; all in movement, wriggling and turning like snakes. And see, what was that? One of the snakes seized its own tail and the image whirled scornfully before my eyes. As though from a flash of lightning I awoke; this time again I occupied the rest of the night in working out the consequences of the hypothesis.[1]

There is the account, too, of William Oughtred, the seventeenth-century mathematician who introduced the multiplication and proportion signs, as given in Aubrey's *Brief Lives:*

He has told Bishop Ward, and Mr. Elias Ashmole . . . that on this spott of ground (or leaning against this Oake, or that ashe) the Solution of such or such a Probleme came into my head, as if infused by a Divine Genius, after I had thought on it without Successe for a yeare, two, or three.[2]

The German scientist von Helmholtz almost made a method of getting solutions for his problems from the intuitive flash. Kekulé even went so far as to say to his fellow-scientists: "Let us learn to dream, gentlemen; then perhaps we shall find the truth."

Are we prepared to say that there is a difference between scientific discoveries arrived at by calculation and those dreamed up in a flash? No, we judge them in exactly the same way, by the same

[1] Quoted by John R. Baker: *The Scientific Life,* New York: The Macmillan Company, 1943, p. 14.

[2] Henry D. Smyth, an important physicist, says: ". . . the outstanding mathematicians quite frequently are able to guess at the truth of a theorem. Their problem is then to fill in the proof by a series of logical steps. . . . Thus we have a paradox in the method of science. The research man may often think and work like an artist but he has to talk like a bookkeeper, in terms of precise facts, figures, and logical sequences of thought." (Address at Amherst College, March 23, 1950.)

standards. The fact that in one instance the scientist had the conscious intention of getting the solution and in the other instance did not have it does not affect the solution.

But people ask: "If poets sometimes write poems in such a crazy way, how can we know what the poet intended? Isn't any interpretation we put on it just what we personally happen to make of the poem?"

But what does the word *intend* mean in such a connection?

It is true that sometimes the poet has a pretty clear idea of what he wants his poem to be. He may be able to state a theme and describe the sort of atmosphere or feeling he wants the whole thing to have. But even in such circumstances, is the process of creation analogous to that of building a house by a blueprint? An architect intends a certain kind of house and he can predict it down to the last nail. The carpenter simply follows the blueprint. But at the best the poet cannot envisage the poem as the architect can envisage the house; and in so far as the poet can envisage the poem, he cannot transfer it into words in a mechanical fashion corresponding to the builder's work on the house. As he begins to work with the poem he is never simply following a plan; he is also exploring the possibilities of imagination and language. Until the poem is actually written down to the last word, the poet cannot be sure *exactly* what it will mean—for we know that the meaning of a poem is fuller than the paraphrasable idea, that the rhythms, the verbal texture, the associations of words, the atmosphere, all the elements, enter into and modify the meaning.

Sometimes, as we have said above, the poet may not have a very clear idea, perhaps not any idea, to start with. He may start with a personal experience as yet uninterpreted, a general, vague feeling, an episode, a metaphor, a phrase—anything that comes along to excite the imagination. Then as he composes, he moves toward his idea—toward his general conception of the poem. At the same time that he is trying to envisage the poem as a whole, he is trying to relate the individual items to that whole. He cannot assemble them in a merely arbitrary fashion; they must bear some relation to each other. So he develops his sense of the whole, the anticipation of the finished poem, as he works with the parts, and moves from one part to another. Then, as the sense of the whole develops, it modifies the process by which the poet selects and relates the parts, the words, images, rhythms, local ideas, events, etc. As the sense of the poem develops, as the idea becomes clearer, the poet may have to go back and change his beginnings, revise them or drop them entirely. It is a process in which one thing leads to another, then to a whole, and the whole leads back to single things. It is an infinitely complicated process of establishing interrelations.[1]

We can trace something of this process in certain passages of Shakespeare. When Shakespeare came to compose a particular passage in one of his plays, he had some notion of the relations of the characters and of the over-all business of the scene, but the local composition often seems to move by a fairly free process of association and suggestion.[2] In the following passage from *Henry V,* the oration of Henry V to his army before the battle of Agincourt, the italicized words indicate the links of thoughts: how a word used in one connection prompts its use in another connection and suggests a new idea:

> We few, we happy few, we band of *brothers:*
> For he to-day that sheds his blood with me
> Shall be *my brother;* be he ne'er so vile,

[1] One of the best accounts of the creative process, of the way in which the parts become related to each other and to an envisaged whole, is in Mozart's description: "My ideas come as they will, I don't know how, all in a stream. If I like them I keep them in my head, and people say that I often hum them over to myself. Well, if I can hold on to them, they begin to join on to one another, as if they were bits that a pastry cook should joint together in his pantry. And now my soul gets heated, and if nothing disturbs me the piece grows larger and brighter until, however long it is, it is all finished at once in my mind, so that I can see it at a glance, as if it were a pretty picture or a pleasing person. Then I don't hear the notes one after another, as they are hereafter to be played, but it is as if in my fancy they were all at once. And that *is* a revel (*das ist nun ein Schmaus*). While I'm inventing, it all seems to me like a fine vivid dream; but that hearing it all at once (when the invention is done), that's the best. What I have once so heard I forget not again, and perhaps this is the best gift that God has granted me." (Quoted by Josiah Royce: *The Spirit of Modern Philosophy,* p. 457.)

[2] The examples here are drawn from E. E. Kellett's "Some Notes on a Feature of Shakespeare's Style" in *Suggestions,* Cambridge: Cambridge University Press, 1923, pp. 57–78.

This day shall *gentle* his *condition:*
And *gentlemen* in England now abed 5
Shall think themselves accurst they were not here,
And hold their *manhoods* cheap whiles any speaks
That fought with us upon St. Crispin's Day.

Again, let us take the speech of Antony, in *Antony and Cleopatra,* when he sees his followers deserting him for Octavius Caesar:

The hearts
That *spanieled* me at heels, to whom I gave
Their wishes, do *discandy, melt* their *sweets,*
On *blossoming* Caesar; and this *pine* is *barked*
That overtopped them all.

The word *discandy* combines the notions of melting and of sweetness; *spanieled* leads to *barked,* but in another sense than that of a dog barking; *barked* leads to *pine* (perhaps with some notion of languishing away or losing strength also leading to the word), and to *blossoming* (though this pine is barked and dies, another, i.e., Caesar, is blossoming).

Here, in a limited way, by verbal suggestion, we can see something of the process that sometimes works more generally.

In these instances, however, the drift is established by the dramatic situation. There is a predetermined direction, more or less general, for the development of a passage. But what of poems that, like "Kubla Khan," spring fully formed, or almost fully formed, without any predetermining intention? Can they be said to express a poet's meaning?

They can be said to embody meaning in exactly the same way as any other poem: by the relations among the various elements that constitute the poem. The validity of the scientific discoveries of Kekulé or Oughtred is not prejudiced by the fact that they were dreamed up; they are to be judged as any other scientific theories are judged. In the same way, it is the nature of the poem that counts.

But, granting this, it may still be asked how the dreamed-up poem, the poem that comes by a kind of inspiration, is related to the poet himself. Is the poem that is dreamed up irrelevant to the kind of man the poet is? Can it be said to express him? Or are we to regard it, as the ancients sometimes did, as the words of a god coming through the mouth of a man? Or as a kind of accident? Does it just happen, and might it equally well happen to somebody else?

It is the last question that gives us our clue. Only poets dream up poems, and only scientists dream up scientific discoveries. That is, the thing dreamed up is the product of the kind of mind and the kind of training possessed by the dreamer. As Louis Pasteur said: "Chance favors only the prepared spirits." So with inspiration: it only comes to those who are ready for it. Coleridge could dream up "Kubla Khan" because he had thought long and deeply about poetry, because his mind was stocked with certain materials, images and rhythms and ideas. Kekulé could dream up the benzene ring because he had devoted years of conscious and rigorously logical effort to the study of chemistry, and the dream of the benzene ring was the fruit of his training. The effortlessness was the result of long effort.[1]

To sum up this last matter, we may turn to Wordsworth's famous Preface to the second edition (1800) of the *Lyrical Ballads,* the volume of poems that he and Coleridge published together. He says that his poems will be distinguished by a "worthy *purpose,*" and *purpose* we can interpret as theme, meaning, or idea. He continues:

> Not that I always began to write with a distinct purpose formally conceived: but habits of meditation have, I trust, so prompted and regulated my feelings, that my descriptions of such objects as strongly excite those feelings, will be found to carry along with them a *purpose*. If this opinion be erroneous, I can have little right to the name of a Poet. For all good poetry is the spontaneous overflow of powerful feelings: and though this be true, Poems to which any value can be attached were never produced on any variety of subjects but by a man who, being possessed of more than usual organic sensibility, had also thought long and deeply.

We find a parallel to Wordsworth's account of how ideas get into poetry, or may get into poetry, in a letter from T. S. Eliot concerning an essay on the themes of one of his poems:

[1] The relation of "Kubla Khan" to the background of Coleridge's reading and experience is investigated by John Livingston Lowes: *The Road to Xanadu,* Boston: Houghton Mifflin, 1927.

I think that this kind of analysis is perfectly justified so long as it does not profess to be a reconstruction of the author's method of writing. Reading your essay made me feel, for instance, that I had been a great deal more ingenious than I had been aware of, because the conscious problems with which one is concerned in the actual writing are more those of a quasi musical nature, in the arrangement of metric and pattern, than of a conscious exposition of ideas.[1]

What is important here for our purpose is that Wordsworth took the most spontaneous poem, which might begin in a burst of feeling and with no preconceived notion of its "purpose" or meaning, to be the fruit of his serious thinking at some earlier time. He took the poem to represent him, and accepted the full responsibility for it. The "objects" that excited the feelings carried along with them the "purpose" without the poet's conscious concern with the purpose. And Eliot, also, emphasized the poet's conscious concern with the immediate problems of the poem, with the problems of the medium, rather than with the ideas as such. But if the unconscious is, as Coleridge says, the genius in the man of genius, it is still far from independent of the conscious; both the conscious and the unconscious are of the same man.

For better or for worse, the poet is responsible for his poem. He can always reject any ideas, images, phrases, etc., that come into his head. He cannot guarantee to himself that the right thing for his poem will come along out of his unconscious, but he can certainly refrain from putting the wrong one down on paper. As the poem grows during the process of composition, as he more clearly senses the kind of poem it is to be, he can more consciously criticize and reject elements that are not adequate or coherent, or do not express him. Some years ago a young scholar who greatly admires Housman's work wrote to the poet and asked him how he managed always to select the right word. Housman replied that he didn't bother about trying to get the right word, he simply bothered about getting rid of the wrong one.[2] That is, the conscious activity was critical, and the unconscious was productive. But the conscious ac-

[1] Letter to Cleanth Brooks, March 15, 1937.

[2] Letter to Arnold Stein, August 22, 1935.

tivity is extremely important. It lays down, as it were, the limits for the activity of the unconscious. And in the end, if a poet feels that a poem doesn't represent him, that it does violence to his ideas, etc., he can always burn the poem instead of publishing it. His veto is absolute.

All this is not to say that the process of rejection and revision is carried on at a fully conscious level, that the poet gives himself the reasons for every rejection he makes. He may simply "feel" that the line isn't right, that the image does not fulfill the idea, that the rhythm is awkward. The rejection, that is, may be spontaneous, too. On the other hand, the poet may be fully aware of the issues, and may argue out each step with himself. But it doesn't matter which line he pursues. His act finally represents him. And if the poem is a good poem we can say that the act, whether the poet consciously reasoned about it or not, is a reasonable act.

The manuscripts and work-sheets of a number of poets have been preserved. Sometimes from these we can get a fairly good notion of how the poet composed a poem, how the first notion and first lines came, how these were developed, how revisions were made. We can sometimes trace the line of reasoning implied in the process—whether or not the poet bothered to state the reason to himself—and when we do this we participate in the creative act and sharpen our own capacity for appreciation.

Here is Karl Shapiro's account of how he composed "The Minute." [1]

What gave rise to the idea of the poem was some reading I was doing at the time about time religions and eternity religions. My thinking ran along these lines: When Christianity became militant it lost its mysticism of the eternal and became a mundane force to prompt man to practice a temporal goodness on earth, rather than sacrifice the material world for the timeless worlds of the spirit. The material kingdom of man was reflected in the industrial revolution, etc. I thought of the remark the Lilliputians made about Gulliver's watch: they said it must be his god because he never did anything without consulting it. And I recalled Baudelaire's sinister

[1] "Case History of 'The Minute,'" *Hopkins Review,* Vol. 3, number 2.

frightening clock, and Hopkins' lines, "the telling time our task is, time's some part, not all, but we were framed to fail and die." I wished to write a poem about a clock (time) which should be a thing used by the dark forces to engage us in wasteful material ends. And at this point my interest flagged and I abandoned the project and closed my notebook. The idea persisted, however, and a few days later I found myself reading scientific articles about chronology, watch-making, and the like. Some rather curious things turned up: a Pope had reputedly invented the clock; clocks were never really on time but had to be corrected periodically to imitate the rotation of the earth. One sidereal day equalled 24 hours, three minutes, and 55.9095 seconds solar. I learned also some beautiful things such as one always finds buried in encyclopedias and dictionaries. A clock is a train of wheels that pull each other through space. Our real timekeeper is the stars, said the *Encyclopedia Britannica* in a burst of poetry. Early watches were called Nuremberg eggs, an idea which suggested high explosives. My notes for the poem began to look something like this.

> Round little timekeeps set with crystal eye.
> The crooked ray of tricky sidereal day.
> Sometimes it gave forth music or a wooden bird leaped
>   from a lock. Sometimes it was a dancing ship.
> Each watch has its exploding point, each tick stabs
>   at an angel.
> A chime is a false note struck by a mistake. 5
> Our real timekeeper is the stars.
> Sun dial and hour glass lose us in shadow
> We drink and love to lose time
> Under the fatherly dome of the universe and the town
> Beside the golden and maternal dial. 10

These last two lines were the first effort at a verse opening. But they didn't please me very much and I tried a new beginning.

> So say the watchmen: time is a tremulous egg
> Laid in the city at midnight under the dome
> Of zero, and beside the golden maternal dial.

This offered possibilities and I tried to work it out thus:

> So say the watchmen. Time is a tremulous (or perilous
>   or delicate) egg
> Laid (or hatched) in the city at midnight under the dome

Beside the golden dial
On a million bureaus of the home
Under the dome, beside the golden dial. 5

But something was not right, and no rhythm had come up. In the next version, which sought after the meter, the result was better.

What shall we say of time, the tremulous egg
Laid in the city at midnight, under the dome
Of sidereal dark, beside the golden dial,
The man's face with the maternal smile.
The earliest minute protrudes a leg 5
Upon a million bureaus of the home.
O time, O tremulous egg
Hatched in the town at midnight, under the dome
Of sidereal dark, beneath the golden dial.

In the middle of the stanza I had begun to re-write the beginning, and I knew therefore that I did not like the beginning. A better attack was needed, or one with more animation of the symbols, or some fresher dramatization of the elements. So I began once again in this fashion:

At zero of sidereal night
Now while the towers pace the sidereal corridors
Pace the gloomy corridors of night
Pace in the corridors of sidereal dark.

Wrong again. This time I went back to the watchmen, pretty much discouraged but with a feeling that something was about to happen.

So say the watchmen. Time is a tremulous egg
Laid in the city at midnight under the dome
Of sidereal dark, beside the golden dial.
The town clock creaks into a maternal smile
As time puts forth a whir, a hair-like leg 5
On all the million bureau-tops of town.

It was finally apparent, after so much trial and error, that what was needed was a central or main clock, the great clock that keeps time for the city, the one that would give birth to all the minutes in the town at the same time. The father of time would be the skyscraper, the mother the town clock, the city hall clock, the symbolic clock.

> When the office building paces
> The gloomy sidereal halls of night
> The suffering clock with golden dial
> Births

This was the idea but not the verse or the image.

> The office buildings pace the corridors of cloud
> While all the clocks with wide and golden dials
> Suffer and glow.
> The office buildings pace the marble aisles

Giving the idea of a maternity ward, which I hardly wanted—

> While the chief clock with dark and golden dial
> Suffers and glows
> Now through the marble halls of night

But this sounded frightfully like Thomas Moore.

Then came the penultimate version:

> The office buildings pace the marble dark
> While all the clocks with dark and golden dials
> Suffer and glow.

Now, by changing the word "pace" to the word "tread," I had what I wanted: the building must be singular. As the word "pace" in the third person singular develops an extra syllable, it would throw the rhythm off:

> The office building paces the marble dark

"Tread" in the third person singular remains a monosyllable, though a nice long one. And so I completed the first stanza.

> The office building treads the marble dark,
> The mother clock with wide and golden dial
> Suffers and glows. Now is the hour of birth
> Of the tremulous egg. Now is the time of correction.
> O midnight, zero of eternity, 5
> Soon on a million bureaus of the city
> Will lie the new born minute.

Stanzas two and three came rapidly and all jumbled together. I knew that the scene must change without preparation to the personal, or to the man living in time somewhere in the town. So

> Then far off in the distant bed I turn
> Titanically, expelling from my lungs
> The bitter gas of life
> Meanwhile all about the atmosphere
> Range the clean angels, stabbed by the ticking 5
> Somewhere in ether, somewhere in atmosphere.
> Clean angels ranging round the atmosphere
> Are studying that noise like a strange dirt
> But will not pick it up
> Nor carry it gingerly out of harm's way 10
> Thousands had gathered at a jewel to hear
> The crude beat, yet admiring the balance
> While the loathsome minute grows in length and strength.

Then the stanza formed itself:

> The new born minute on the bureau lies
> Scratching the glass with happy kick, cutting (etching)
> With diamond foot, with diamond cry the crystal gaze
> With evil frost of timelessness, etching with evil frost

The work here was purely linguistic, getting rid of the less accurate and less pertinent images and keeping the more useful. This was not difficult. From the notes of stanzas two and three, which came quite easily, I took a line about the loathsome minute growing like a metal worm, and began the third section. This version was almost final as it arrived. The fourth stanza required a return to the original idea of the evil of time, and having already involved myself in a kind of Hieronymus Bosch drama, I introduced the devils as the timekeepers and workers of timepieces. The seed of this stanza was also in the notes of two and three which I have just read. The stanza appeared:

> An angel is stabbed and is carried aloft howling
> For devils have gathered on a ruby jewel
> Like red mites on a berry; others arrive
> To tend the points with oil and smooth the heat.
> See how their vicious faces lit with sweat 5
> Worship the train of wheels; see how they pull

The tapeworm tongue that hangs from time.
The time tape measure lolling from the face.
The tapeworm time from nothing into thing.

The fifth stanza I knew would be the last one. The climax of the poem, as far as I was concerned, was the stabbed angel. The denouement would be my indifference to or my involvement in the watch, the timepiece of time. The work of this stanza came all jumbled together and the work of writing the stanza was again editing, rather than finding the flow.

I with my hot heart lie awake, away,
Smiling at that Swiss perfect engine room
Driven by tiny evils. The crashing gongs of clocks
The crashing gongs of mammoth clocks in towers
Even of metal hands the size of masts 5
And gongs that crash around in towers
And hands as high as iron masts. I sleep
While the departing angels in one covey
Rise and sweep past my ear with frightening farewells
Sweep 10
Shrill
Which at a sign the angels in a flock
Sweep past my hearing with melodious fear
At which sad sign the angels in a flock
Rise and sweep past me with melodious fear. 15

The editing resulted in this:

I with my distant heart lie wide awake
Smiling at that Swiss perfect engine room
Driven by tiny evils. Knowing no harm
Even of gongs that loom and move in towers
And hands as high as iron masts, I sleep, 5
At which sad sign the angels in a flock
Rose and sweep past me, querulous with fear.

And here is the finished poem:

The Minute

The office building treads the marble dark,
The mother-clock with wide and golden dial

The Immortal Part

(1) ~~Every night and day~~

(2) I hear my bones within me say (2a) ~~This betray~~

night day,

(3) "Another ~~eve,~~ another ~~morn~~ (3a) ~~xxxx~~

(4) ~~It's long~~ (4a) ~~It's born~~

(5) When shall this slough of flesh be cast

life

(6) This dust of ~~thought~~ ^ be laid at last

life

This flame past

(7) The immortal bones obey control

(8) Of dying flesh and dying soul

(9) This tongue that talks, these lungs that shout,

(10) These thews that hustle us about

morn eve

(11) When will ~~nights~~ and ~~days~~ be gone

(12) And the endless night come on?

(13) Another night, another day,

(14) So my bones within me say

they shall do

(15) Therefore ~~I shall have~~ my will

(16) Today while I am master still,

(17) And flesh and soul, now both are strong,

haul

(18) Shall ~~lug~~ the sullen slaves along,

this sense

(19) Before ~~these~~ fires of ~~flesh~~ decay,

thoughts

(20) This smoke of ~~soul~~ blow clean away,

(21) And leave with ancient night alone

(22) The ~~immortal~~ and enduring bone.

~~senseless~~

stedfast

The immortal part.

...ear my soul within me say 2a

...ther night another day 3a

When shall this slough of flesh be cast,

The dust of thoughts be laid at last

The immortal bones obey control

Of dying flesh and dying soul

...his tongue that talks, these lungs that shout,

These thews that hustle us about

When will more nights and days be gone

And the endless night come on?

Another night, another day.

So my bones within me say

...efore they shall do my will

...ay while I am master still,

...d flesh and soul, now both are strong,

...hall haul the sullen slaves along,

Before this fire of sense decay,

This smoke of thoughts blow clean away,

And leave with ancient night alone

The [illegible] and enduring bone.

steadfast

The Immortal Part

When I meet the morning beam
Or lay me down at night to dream,
I hear my bones within me say,
"Another night, another day.

"When shall this slough of sense be cast, 5
This dust of thoughts be laid at last,
The man of flesh and soul be slain
And the man of bone remain?

"This tongue that talks, these lungs that shout,
These thews that hustle us about, 10
This brain that fills the skull with schemes,
And its humming hive of dreams,—

"These to-day are proud in power
And lord it in their little hour:
The immortal bones obey control 15
Of dying flesh and dying soul.

" 'Tis long till eve and morn are gone:
Slow the endless night comes on,
And late to fulness grows the birth
That shall last as long as earth. 20

"Wanderers eastward, wanderers west,
Know you why you cannot rest?
'Tis that every mother's son
Travails with a skeleton.

"Lie down in the bed of dust; 25
Bear the fruit that bear you must;
Bring the eternal seed to light,
And morn is all the same as night.

"Rest you so from trouble sore,
Fear the heat o' the sun no more, 30
Nor the snowing winter wild,
Now you labor not with child.

"Empty vessel, garment cast,
We that wore you long shall last.
—Another night, another day." 35
So my bones within me say.

Therefore they shall do my will
To-day while I am master still,
And flesh and soul, now both are strong,
Shall hale the sullen slaves along, 40

Before this fire of sense decay,
This smoke of thought blow clean away,
And leave with ancient night alone
The steadfast and enduring bone.

Suffers and glows. Now is the hour of birth
Of the tremulous egg. Now is the time of correction.
O midnight, zero of eternity, 5
Soon on a million bureaus of the city
Will lie the new-born minute.

The new-born minute on the bureau lies,
Scratching the glass with infant kick, cutting
With diamond cry the crystal and expanse 10
Of timelessness. This pretty tick of death
Etches its name upon the air. I turn
Titanically in distant sleep, expelling
From my lungs the bitter gas of life.

The loathsome minute grows in length and strength, 15
Bending its spring to forge an iron hour
That rusts from link to link, the last one bright,
The late one dead. Between the shining works
Range the clean angels, studying that tick
Like a strange dirt, but will not pick it up. 20
Nor move it gingerly out of harm's way.

An angel is stabbed and is carried aloft howling,
For devils have gathered on a ruby jewel
Like red mites on a berry; others arrive
To tend the points with oil and smooth the heat. 25
See how their vicious faces, lit with sweat,
Worship the train of wheels; see how they pull
The tape-worm Time from nothing into thing.

I with my distant heart lie wide awake
Smiling at that Swiss-perfect engine room 30
Driven by tiny evils. Knowing no harm
Even of gongs that loom and move in towers,
And hands as high as iron masts, I sleep,
At which sad sign the angels in a flock
Rise and sweep past me, spinning threads of fear. 35

Let us take an example from A. E. Housman (see insert opposite). Here the poet has left no record of his reasoning. We must, then, try to reconstruct the stages by which the poet moved from his original idea to the finished poem. Our poem is "The Immortal Part," by Housman. In its finished form the poem has forty-four lines, but the version given here is much shorter and is very early. It is clearly not the first version, however; on the manuscript we can see erasures beneath the first visible text. Let us try to reconstruct the stages of the poem.

First we notice that the manuscript has a title, "The Immortal Part." Very rarely does Housman give a title to a poem, and so we can hazard that the title was the start of the poem, that the germ is the ironical idea that the bones are the immortal part of man.

The first line has been erased, but as far as we can now tell it ran

Every —— night and day.

And was followed by

(2) I hear my bones within me say
(3) "Another eve another morn

The next line, (4), intended to rhyme with (3), had two versions, both of which are erased, but we can make out that the second version ended with *born*. But the stanza was unsatisfactory. For one thing, "Every —— night and day" is a rather flat line. And for another thing, it doesn't seem to be enough preparation for line (2). Furthermore, the sharp, succinct effect of what the bones say would be weakened by the addition of another line, and the line ending in *born* was, in all likelihood, but a descriptive elaboration. So Housman began again on the right margin, lines (2a) and (3a). The erasure here leaves little legible, but line (2a) seems to end with *betray*. We may guess that Housman was with his new rhyme trying to get a new preparation for line (2). In any case, this couplet did not work out. So Housman came back to lines (2) and (3), and by changing *eve* and *morn* in line (3) to *night* and *day,* got the sharp, epigrammatic couplet to embody his key idea, where before the idea had been split between the last line of one couplet and the first of another. So we have what, except for punctuation, is the final version:

I hear my bones within me say
"Another night another day,

The next line (5) came fairly well:

When shall this slough of flesh be cast,

But line (6) caused more trouble. Under the erasure we see something that looks like:

This flame —— be past.

And above the erasure the word *life,* which seems to have been a revision of the rejected line, perhaps something like, "flame of life." Another try gives us:

This dust of thought be laid at last.

But the word *thought* is not satisfactory to Housman, probably because it does not somehow associate with *flesh,* the key word of the above line. So he cancels *thought* and substitutes *life* (suggested perhaps by the revision of the earlier version of the same line), a word that pairs more readily with *flesh.* Neither line is now in its final form, but the poet, as we shall see, probably did not touch them again until he had worked out his last stanza.

Now we face a question. We see that the next two lines on the manuscript, (7) and (8), though in their final form, are not in their final place. Did Housman jot them down here, as they came into his mind, realizing that they were to be placed later, or did he first think of them as coming after line (6) and leading up to line (11)? Under any circumstances, lines (7) and (8) could not lead up to lines (9) and (10).

So far in the poem, Housman is thinking in couplets, not in stanzas, and he is not establishing a very clear progression from one couplet to the next. It is true that we do get a progression from lines (2–3) to lines (5–6), but otherwise what we seem to find are germinal bits, points of focus, pegs on which the poem is to be hung as it develops.

In the next four lines, however, Housman composes a rounded stanza, one that is clearly intended to end the speech of the bones. In line (11) he repeats the night-day motif, which starts the speech of the bones, but after he has struck on the phrase "endless night" in the next line, he comes back and changes *nights* to *morn* and *days* to *eve,* to avoid repetition. But this stanza is not to survive.

After the speech of the bones, the turn of the poem comes, the consequence of the speech:

> (15) Therefore I shall have my will
> (16) Today while I am master still,
> (17) And flesh and soul, now both are strong,
> (18) Shall lug the sullen slaves along,

The form of statement in line (15) throws the emphasis off the bones, the key word; and so "I shall have my will" is altered to "they shall do my will." And in the last line of the stanza *lug* becomes *haul,* which, in the final version, becomes *hale.*

The first change in line (18) may be argued like this: the word *lug* sets up too positive an alliteration on *l* in the line, and a nonfunctional forced pause between *shall* and *lug.* Housman uses alliteration very freely but rather discreetly. As for the forced pause, the general notion of the line is that flesh and soul get their will done effortlessly, masterfully, and freely, and the impediment of the pause destroys this impression. Furthermore, the word *lug* means carrying an absolutely dead weight—and that is not what a man does to his bones, which are active, or what a master does to his slaves. So Housman tries *haul.* This does avoid the forced pause and the obvious alliteration; the *l* sound is not initial and is lightly absorbed into the texture of the line. Also the word doesn't imply as much dead weight as *lug,* it is not quite as chunky a word, as it were. But it still fails on this general score: the bones are still passive. But sometime between this version and the last, Housman strikes on *hale,* an easy sound association from *haul.* The new word fulfills all the requirements indicated above, and brings, besides, a new element. The *a*-sound in *hale* provides an assonantal binder with the *a*-sound in *slaves,* and emphasizes the flow and unity of the line, but discreetly.

This brings us to the last stanza. In line (19) the first version "these fires of flesh" becomes "this fire of sense," and in line (20) "smoke of soul" becomes "smoke of thoughts." But it seems unlikely that these changes were made until Housman had written the last two lines. We might argue in this way: Line (21) with "ancient night" is really an echo of line (12). Then in line (22) Housman first put down "immortal and enduring," the word *im-*

mortal coming almost automatically from the title, which, as we have said, probably contained the germ of the poem. But the word didn't suit. Perhaps it is too closely associated with *soul,* used above, carrying some notion of lightness, of delicacy, of an aspiring quality, of a continuity in life. So *senseless* comes next. This try indicates something of Housman's objection to *immortal.* The new word covers part of the objection, but it does not retain the idea of permanence in *immortal.* Then he finds what he in the manuscript spells as "stedfast." This word avoids the objections to *immortal* and yet carries the idea of permanence, but permanence by solidity, by weight, by massive indestructibility, with the faint hint of some sort of moral victory in its permanence. We may notice, too, that *enduring* carries a sort of double meaning, mere durability as its primary sense and a capacity for surviving suffering as its secondary sense. But to return to *steadfast,* the word introduces a new rhythm, a *spondaic effect* (*Glossary*) that adds appropriately to the solidity and heaviness of the line, and to the final stoical temper of the poem.

It is the revision of this last line, further, that may react on the poem to instigate other revision. Perhaps the try at *senseless* for *immortal* suggested *sense* for *flesh* in line (19): if the bones are "senseless," then the flesh is "senseful," and the contrast between flesh and bone becomes more precise. But once having struck on *sense* in (19), Housman cannot let *soul* stand in the next line. In traditional psychology, the aspects of consciousness to be associated are sensation and thought, and thought was supposed to derive from sensation; so the "fire of sense," which, by the way, is a good image for man's appetite for the immediate experience of the world, leads to the "smoke of thought," the evanescent, useless thing that comes from man's experience.

Of course, Housman may have arrived at the sense-thought notion before he wrote the last line. He may have simply objected to *soul* because it did carry the idea of immortality, and he wished to imply that the only immortality was in the bone. Thus, having rejected *soul* he would have to start on a new train of thinking; and then he may have picked up the rejected *thought* of line (6). But in any case, having set up the last stanza, he went back at some point, as we know from the final version, and changed the *flesh* in line (5) to *sense,* and the *life* in line (6) back to *thoughts.* It is even possible that the version of line (6) as we have it in the manuscript was not written at all until after the last stanza, that Housman came back and erased his earlier line (6) which may very well have had *soul* in it to pair with *flesh* above, and then got his "dust of thought" idea and changed *thought* to *life* on a bad hunch that he later had to revoke. The precise order of events here is not what is important. What is important is a kind of relation among them.

To sum up, we may say that Housman probably struck on the idea of man's bones as being his immortal part. That gave the germ of the poem, and the title. Next he struck on the idea that the bones would speak in pitying protest against their enslavement to flesh. After jotting down several almost unrelated couplets, which served as notes, as it were for the speech of the bones, Housman worked seriously at what was to be the climax of his poem, the response to the bones. Even in this first manuscript these last two stanzas, with the exception of one word in line (18), come out in final form. This much may have come on a walk and at an hour at tea time, but the actual time involved here is not very significant. It *is* significant that we have here the germ of a poem, the development of its plan (introduction, speech of bones, reply), the establishing of its theme and tonality. What the poet had to do later was to get a satisfactory introduction to the speech of the bones, and then fill in the speech. This meant finding a principle of continuity for the speech, and, in fact, the splitting of the one stanza (lines 11–14) already set up in this section. The process may have required a long time, but the control by which it would take place already existed.

Let us take another example, from another poet, the second stanza of Keats's "Ode to Autumn" (p. 92). In the original draft it began:

> Who hath not seen thee? for thy haunts are many
> Sometimes whoever seeks for thee may find

Keats, according to one critic,[1] sees that *many* is going to be a difficult rhyme, and so starts over again, "feeling also no doubt a kind

[1] M. R. Ridley: *Keats' Craftsmanship*. Oxford: Clarendon Press, 1933, pp. 285–286.

of thin abruptness in the half-line question, and a certain feebleness both of sound and sense in *for thee.*" Almost immediately, for the manuscript shows signs of haste, Keats composes the first four lines of the stanza:

> Who hath not seen thee oft amid thy stores?
> Sometimes whoever seeks abroad may find
> Thee sitting careless on a granary floor
> Thy hair soft lifted by the winnowing wing

Then Keats strikes off the final *s* of *stores* to make his rhyme with *floor,* and changes *wing* to *wind.*

Ridley continues the analysis:

However, whatever small points there may have been in the first four lines, they were soon and easily solved. Now the real troubles begin.

> husky
> While bright the Sun slants through the / barn;
> Or sound asleep in a half reaped field
> Dosed with read poppies; while thy reeping hook
> Spares form Some slumbrous

At this point the lines, which have clearly been going from bad to worse, have petered out altogether, and no rhyme for *field* is in sight anyway. The next stage is some minor tinkering. The line about the sun, and the next line, are deleted altogether, and the second rewritten as

> on on a half reap'd furrow sound asleep

(i.e., intending not to delete the *Or* and to write *on* once only), then *Some slumbrous* is deleted, and under it written

> minutes while wam slumpers creep

So that now he has in front of him

> ~~husky~~,
> ~~While bright the Sun slants through the barn~~
> on on a half reap'd furrow sound asleep
> ~~Or sound asleep in a half reaped field~~
> Dosed with re~~a~~d poppies; while thy reeping hook
> Spares form ~~Some slumbrous~~
> minutes while wam slumpers creep

That has at least achieved a rhyme; but if the line about the sun is to disappear altogether the rhyme is in the wrong place; none of it is very satisfactory; and the *eep* sound has got out of hand. So Keats cancels the whole passage with some vigorous cross-hatching, and begins all over again, using the rewritten sixth line as the fifth, and improving the old seventh for use as the new sixth.

Or on a half reap'd furrow sound asleep
  Dos'd with the fume of poppies, while thy hook
Spares for ~~one~~some slumbrous minutes the next swath;

So far, so good; and as any troubles about a rhyme for the unpromising *swath* are still four lines off he goes on his way rejoicing:

And sometimes like a gleans thost dost keep
  Steady thy laden head across the brook
  Or by a Cyder-press with patent look
Thou . . .

Well, and now what about the swath, waiting four lines above for its rhyme. But the Cyder-press is going as well as can be, so for the moment confound the swath, and finish

watchest the last oozing hours by hours

and now go back and get the rhyme, even if we have to sacrifice in the process the idea of the tenacious *slumpers* which has hung onto existence through two corrections.

Spares the next swath and all its twined flowers;

The copy in the Woodhouse letter omits to notice the cancellation of the *s* of *stores;* corrects some spellings, but writes *Stready* for *Steady;* does some punctuating; reads *a brook* for *the brook,* and *Dased* for *Dos'd,* either an easy misreading of a word so written that it might be either, or a deliberate alteration; and greatly accentuates the opiate *z* sound of the last line by reading *oozings* for *oozing.*[1]

[1] For instructive accounts by two contemporary poets of methods of revision, see Allen Tate: "Narcissus as Narcissus," in *On the Limits of Poetry,* New York: The Swallow Press and William Morrow and Company, 1948; and Stephen Spender: "The Making of a Poem," in *The Partisan Review,* Vol. xiii, pp. 294–308.

EXERCISE:

1. Below are two versions of Housman's "To an Athlete Dying Young" (p. 266). Version A is very early, but Version B is approaching the finished form. Study both versions in comparison with the finished poem. On the basis of this evidence write an account of the development of the poem. Try to define the reasons for the changes in text.

(To an Athlete Dying Young: no title on manuscript)

Version: (A)

your
(1) The day you won ~~the~~ town the race
through
(2) We chaired you ~~in~~ the market place,
——— ~~folk~~
(3) ——— stood cheering by, xxxxxxxxxxxxxxx
And home xxxxxxxxxxxxxxx
(4) ~~Home~~ we brought you shoulder-high. xxxxxxxxxxxxxxx
(5) So ——— fade (5a) ——— betrayed (?)
~~feet~~ (?) So set, before its echoes fade,
(6) ——— ~~race~~, sill of shade, (6a) ~~Set foot upon~~ the sill of shade
low The fleet foot on
(7) And hold to the ~~dark~~ lintel up
(8) The still defended challenge cup.
(9) Wise lad, to steal betimes away
(10) From fields where victory will not stay
xxxxxxxxxxxxx
(11) A garland briefer than a girl's A garland briefer than a ———
(12) ~~xxxxxxxx~~xxxxx ——— that night has shut
(13) ——— see your record cut
that young
(14) And round your early laurelled head
(15) Will throng to gaze the strengthless dead
find unwithered on
(16) And ~~yet unfaded round~~ its curls
(17) ~~The xx~~ The garland briefer than a girl's,
(18) Of runners whom renown outran
~~Or~~
(19) And the name died before the man

VERSION B.

time
(1) The ~~day~~ you won your town the race
(2) We chaired you through the market place;
(3) Man and boy stood cheering by,
(4) And home we brought you shoulder-high.
(5) Today, the road all runners come,
(6) Shoulder-high we bring you home,
(7) And set you at your threshold down,
(8) Townsman of a stiller town.
Well done,
(9) Wise lad, to slip betimes away   Smart lad,
glory
(10) From fields where ~~victory~~ will not stay.
(11) ~~And glory for the runner braids~~   And early though the laurel grows
lasts no ~~longer~~ better a
(12) ~~A chaplet briefer than a maid's~~   It withers sooner than ~~the~~ rose.
The man   cloudy
(13) ~~He~~ whose eye the night has shut   Eyes the shady night has shut
~~Will never~~
(14) ~~Never sees his record cut~~   ~~never see the record cut~~
sounds no worse than
(15) And silence ~~is the same as~~ cheers
~~his~~
(16) After earth has stopped the ears.
~~have~~ ~~swelled~~
(17) ~~And~~ Now you will not ~~join~~ the throng   swell   No fear you now should join the throng.
stayed spell
(18) Of lads that lived a ~~day~~ too long,
(19) Runners whom renown outran
(20) And the name died before the man.
(21) So set before its echoes fade,
(22) The fleet foot on the sill of shade,
(23) And hold to the low lintel up
(24) The still defended challenge-cup
~~that your~~
(25) And round ~~that~~ early-laurelled head
(26) Will flock to gaze the strengthless dead
(27) And find unwithered on its curls
(28) The garland briefer than a girl's.
Eyes the cloudy
(29) ~~Now the eye that~~ night has shut

(30) Will never see the record cut,
(31) And silence sounds no worse than cheers
After
(32) ~~Now that~~ earth has stopped the ears.
(33) Cannot see the record cut
Now you'll never
(34) ~~xxxxxxxxx~~ swell the rout
(35) Of lads that wore their honours out.

2. Here is a second version of the poem by Sir Thomas Wyatt, "They Flee from Me," which appears earlier in this book (p. 485). The present version, which was printed in an anthology called *Tottel's Miscellany,* in 1557, some years after Wyatt's death, probably represents an attempt, among other things, to correct Wyatt's meter. Does the increased regularity improve or impair the poem? Discuss each change individually. Aside from questions of meter, what idea motivated changes? Do you approve of them? (The lines with important changes are italicized.)

They flee from me, that sometime did me seek
With naked foot stalking within my chamber.
Once have I seen them gentle, tame, and meek,
That now are wild, and do not once remember
That sometime they have put themselves in danger, 5
To take bread at my hand, and now they range,
Busily seeking in continual change.
Thanked be fortune, it hath been otherwise
Twenty times better: but once especial,
In thin array, after a pleasant guise, 10
When her loose gowne did from her shoulders fall,
And she me caught in her arms long and small,
And therewithal so sweetly did me kiss,
And softly said: "Dear heart, how like you this?"
It was no dream: for I lay broad awaking. 15
But all is turned now through my gentleness
Into a bitter fashion of forsaking:
And I have leave to go of her goodness,
And she also to use newfangleness.
But since that I unkindly so am served, 20
How like you this, what hath she now deserved?

3. Below is a section rejected by Yeats for his "Upon a Dying Lady." Study it carefully and compare it with the sections which he published (pp. 486–89). What grounds can you give for his rejection of this? Are there elements here better developed in the poem as we finally have it?

Although she has turned away
The pretty waxen faces
And hid their silk and laces
For mass was said today
She has not begun denying 5
Now that she is dying
The pleasures she loved well
The strong milk of her mother
The valour of her brother
Are in her body still 10
She will not die weeping
May God be with her sleeping.[1]

4. In some of her manuscripts Emily Dickinson did not indicate her final choice among various possibilities indicated, as in the poem below. An editor working to prepare an edition of the poems would have to take the responsibility of a choice. What choices would you make if you were editing this poem? Try to explain your reasons for each. After you have done so, compare your choices with those of Emily Dickinson's most recent editor (p. 161).

STANZA I

(1) Two butterflies went out at noon

(2) And waltzed upon a farm,

(3) And then espied circumference
Then overtook circumference

(4) And caught a ride with him;
And took a bout with him

[1] Quoted in A. Norman Jeffares: *W. B. Yeats: Man and Poet.* New Haven: Yale University Press, 1949, pp. 166–167.

STANZA II

(5) Then lost themselves and found themselves
Then staked themselves and lost themselves
Then chased themselves and caught themselves

(6) In eddies of the sun
In fathoms in the sun
In rapids of the sun
In gambols with (of) the sun
In frenzies with (of) the sun
For frenzy of the sun
In antics (gambols) in (with) the sun

(7) Till rapture missed her footing
Till gravitation missed (chased) them
Till gravitation humbled (ejected) them
Till gravitation foundered (grumbled)
Until a zephyr pushed (chased) (flung) (spurned) them
Until a zephyr scourged them

(8) And both were wrecked in noon.
And both were drowned (quenched) (whelmed) in noon
And they were hurled from noon

STANZA III

(9) To all surviving butterflies

(10) Be this fatuity
Be this biography,

(11) Example, and monition

(12) To entomology.[1]

[1] From *Bolts of Melody, New Poems of Emily Dickinson.* Edited by Mabel Loomis Todd and Millicent Todd Bingham, New York: Harper and Brothers, 1945, p. xxiii.

X

THE POEM VIEWED IN WIDER PERSPECTIVE

1: WORDSWORTH

In this volume we have emphasized the reading of poems as poems; that is, we have been concerned with the poem as a poem rather than with the poem as a reflection of the poet's private life. In a reading manual, this emphasis is surely the proper one. Moreover, the most important aspect of a poet is usually his production of poetry, outweighing his rôle as lover, husband, father, statesman, or philosopher. We are interested in Wordsworth's ideas, for instance, primarily because he was a poet. His status as poet makes us want to read his biography—to find out all that we can about him.

Granted, however, that we are interested in a poet, and want to know all that we can about him, we go not merely to his poems in order to satisfy this interest: we read his prose works, his letters, his journals and diaries (and those of his friends), and we may find on occasion that records of lawsuits and even laundry-bills may have something of importance in telling us what sort of man the poet was.

We have already touched upon (in Section IX, pp. 591–99) the relation to each other of our various possible interests in the poet and his work. As we have indicated in that discussion, when our interest is strictly in history or biography, we may derive knowledge not only from his best poems (in which as biographers we are certain to be interested) but sometimes from the poet's worst poems as well, and often from documents that fall outside the category of poetry altogether. An interest in biography may take us beyond the poems themselves; moreover, it can conceivably distort our reading of the poem. Professor Douglas Bush has recently pointed out that prevalent conceptions and misconceptions of the personality of Milton, for instance, have warped his poems for many people.[1]

But to say this is certainly not to deny that the study of the poet's mind and personality may be a fascinating and valuable activity; nor is it to deny that, since a poet tends to use over and over again the same themes and techniques, one of his poems tends to throw light upon another. In fact, it is sometimes said that a poet's work is really one long poem of which the individual poems are but parts. The work of a serious and able poet springs from certain basic ideas and attitudes that give it unity and continuity even in the midst of variety and change.

It may be clearer, however, to make these points very concretely, illustrating from a poet, William Wordsworth, represented by eight poems in this text. Eight poems represent only a tiny fraction of the corpus of his work. Even so, they may serve to illustrate how one goes about studying the work of the poet as a whole.

Let us begin with "A Poet's Epitaph" (p. 421). The poem tells us a great deal about some of Wordsworth's beliefs and makes some very clear suggestions as to what Wordsworth felt the poet's function to be. On this score, it might well be the most important of the eight Wordsworth poems with which we have to deal. As a poem, however, it is probably the least important of the eight, for reasons already given (pp. 423–27).

In contrast to the abstract intellect, Wordsworth here exalts the life of the emotions; over against the politician, the lawyer, the "physician" (physicist), and the moralist, he sets such men of feeling as the soldier and the man "clad in homely russet brown" who has gathered the "harvest of a quiet eye."

What have "The outward shows of sky and earth" to teach a man? What are these "impulses of deeper birth" that come "in solitude"? Evidently, for Wordsworth, they are of the highest importance and yield a wisdom to which "reasoning" and "understanding" do not give access. The poem "Expostulation and Reply" (p. xliv) can tell us more about Wordsworth's conception of this wisdom. Wisdom is acquired in a "wise passiveness"—it may come

[1] "The Critical Significance of Biographical Evidence: John Milton," *English Institute Essays, 1946,* New York, 1947.

unbidden, by *not* being actively sought for. It is associated with feeling as opposed to mere intellection, and with a sense of the whole of being ("this mighty sum / Of things") rather than with analysis which breaks the world of things down into their separate parts. The acquisition of this wisdom can easily be despised because confused with sloth and idle dreaming. The William of this poem is obviously very closely akin to the man "clad in homely russet brown."

The two poems, then, tell us something of what "Nature" means to Wordsworth: it is not merely a mechanism to be analyzed by the intellect, and then manipulated by man to his own benefit. It is no mere machine, but is alive; it is not merely operated on by man, but moulds and influences man ("there are Powers / Which of themselves our minds impress"). Men who habituate themselves to manipulating the world or who are preoccupied with mere analysis of it, miss this wisdom. Men of affairs and men of "learning" as the world conceives of learning are then precisely those most likely to be debarred from true wisdom. Such wisdom, we are more likely to find in the child or the peasant or, as here, in the impractical dreamer and poet.

Why in such types as these? Because they are not divorced from sympathy and emotion; because they tend to look at the world concretely and as a whole; because they lack intellectual pride, and do not live in realms of barren intellection. The poet does not merely analyze, but synthesizes; he cannot strip away emotion from ideas, but must include in his account of the world idea *and* emotion. As for the peasant, he lives too close to the elemental realities to be able to afford the luxury of a specialized world. Life for him has to have a concrete wholeness.

For Wordsworth, however, this concrete wholeness is to be found pre-eminently in the life of the child. In this connection, it will be interesting to consider Wordsworth's testimony as to how he viewed the world about him when he himself was a child. He writes that nothing "was more difficult for me in childhood than to admit the notion of death as a state applicable to my own being." He goes on to say: "I was often unable to think of external things as having external existence, and I communed with all that I saw as something not apart from, but inherent in, my own immaterial nature. Many times while going to school have I grasped at a wall or tree to recall myself from this abyss of idealism to the reality" (from Wordsworth's note on the "Intimations Ode").

This difficulty in admitting the separateness of the world from his own perceiving spirit is not attributed by Wordsworth to a unique mystical experience to which he had access as other men do not have. Wordsworth clearly thinks of his experience, not as special but as general and normal, and rooted in basic human psychology. In the same note from which we have quoted, Wordsworth goes on to say: "To that dreamlike vividness and splendor which invest objects of sight in childhood, every one, I believe, if he would look back, could bear testimony, and I need not dwell upon it here. . . ." These comments by Wordsworth have a special bearing on the "Intimations Ode," which we are to consider a little later in this section. But the child's insight into his world is of great general importance to Wordsworth, and is given special significance in many of his poems. Moreover, it can throw light upon the whole problem of truth and wisdom as Wordsworth deals with it: the man of learning who comes to treat nature as a mere mechanism has, in his pride, lost a basic insight with which every human being at birth is endowed.

Now the foregoing paragraphs do not pretend to give an adequate summary of Wordsworth's view of nature or his definition of truth. That is a large and complicated matter, and a full discussion of Wordsworth's conception of nature, how he came to it, and of how his conception was developed and modified, lies quite outside the province of this volume. (There is a large and interesting body of scholarship on this subject to which your instructor can direct you.) But what has been said even so briefly will suggest that the theme of man's attitude toward nature was an important one for Wordsworth, and it may help to explain why so many of his poems deal with simple people—children, peasants, and villagers. The two poems that we have been discussing are not, in the editors' opinion, altogether successful as poems. The poet, though he has tried to dramatize his theme, has in these two poems actually tended to state it abstractly. We may ask: Has Wordsworth managed to dramatize the wise passiveness and the harvest of a quiet eye? Does he ever make his peasant or his child come alive for us in a poem, convincing us dramatically of the sense of wholeness which springs from solitude?

"I Wandered Lonely as a Cloud" provides a simple instance. (See also p. 270.) The speaker, wandering "lonely," finds that he is not alone: the daffodils provide a "jocund company." They not only fill him with pleasure; they seem themselves to participate in the pleasure. Both they and the sparkling waves are treated as if they had a life of their own, and felt a joy which links them with the human observer. And the experience is lasting: later the scene flashes "upon that inward eye / Which is the bliss of solitude." The daffodils, long after they have faded, have a kind of immortality in his imagination; the recollection of them fortifies and sustains the man.

"Lucy Gray; or, Solitude" (p. 65) provides a somewhat more complex instance. The poem, as we have seen, describes the life of a "solitary" child, and one whose death comes while she is alone. But, the poem suggests, she is not alone—not lost—any more than the hare or the mountain roe is lost when it is on the moors. She has the natural grace and natural fearlessness which we associate with animals; but she is also "at home" on the moors; and her last footsteps in the snow have the confidence of her setting out.

The poem goes further in its suggestion: she is still alive. She still walks the moors, for she is part of the spirit of the moors. Notice that the poet does not *say* this: nor does he say that he himself has glimpsed her. But the simple folk of the country "maintain" that she is still alive. For them she is still alive—and still fearless and "at home." For the poet does not present us at the end of the poem with a little wailing, frightened ghost. She still "trips along, / And never looks behind."

"The Solitary Reaper" (p. 272) also illustrates the importance of Wordsworth's basic theme. The girl's song is like the bird's song: the hearer cannot get the words, and it is evident that the words ultimately do not matter. Like the bird, the girl is not singing for effect, does not know that she is overheard, and sings "As if her song could have no ending." Her song, again like that of the bird, wells up out of her daily activity. For that very reason it seems to the speaker as if he had been permitted to overhear the music of humanity itself. If he has succeeded in dramatizing the experience for us, we overhear it with him.

The two poems just discussed are obviously not expositions of a thesis or preachments to the effect that we ought to look at nature in a certain way. They are indirect in their approach to the theme; they are concrete and independent embodiments of the theme.[1] But they are easily related to Wordsworth's abiding concern with nature and its effect upon people who are simple enough and innocent enough to let that effect operate upon them.

"Michael" (p. 23) provides another dramatization of Wordsworth's conception of nature and its effect upon human nature. It is a story, as we have seen, about a man's love for the land. Luke is sent to the city in the hope that he will be able to pay off the debt for which Michael has gone surety so that the patrimonial lands will not have to be sold but may pass intact to Luke. In Michael's mind, there is no thought that Luke, if he prospers, will stay in the city: Luke is to return, to live on his lands, and carry on the family heritage.

The plan fails, and Michael loses not only his hope of redeeming the debt, but loses his son as well. What the poem emphasizes, however, is not Michael's crushing disappointment, but his ability to endure sorrow. The pathos is actually rendered more acute by the fact that the now old man does not fall under it, but is able to carry on.

The poem is related, we have said, to Wordsworth's basic theme, but it is much more than a "statement" of the theme. It is certainly not a simple expression of the theme. If Michael's closeness to nature and his desire to hold on to his life on the land comforts him in sorrow, it has, nevertheless, in a sense, been a cause of the sorrow. If the influence of nature has given Michael strength, that same influence to which Luke was exposed for eighteen years has not saved Luke. But these considerations are properly irrelevant to the poem, for Wordsworth is not preaching a pet dogma. He does not claim too much. What he does is to tell a very simple story, to tell it with full concrete detail, and to tell it with very little explicit comment of his own. If he has been successful, Michael's

[1] See Wordsworth's comment on how ideas get into poetry (p. 609).

character has become dramatically convincing to the reader. The reader believes in that character, and senses what has shaped it and what has given it its fortitude and dignity.

In "Michael," Wordsworth alludes almost casually to the "dissolute city" as if its dissoluteness was common knowledge and could be assumed. In "Composed upon Westminster Bridge" (p. 101) he gives us a vision of such a dissolute city, but sees it as something very different. Is there any contradiction here? No, for this sonnet is actually very closely related to Wordsworth's conception of beauty and truth. The silent city at dawn reveals itself to him as something that is not merely dead and mechanical. Asleep, it shows itself alive; with the pall of smoke lifted, it reveals itself as truly a part of nature as any "valley, rock, or hill" of Cumberland. At this moment of the day (and of insight), the distracting activity which ordinarily reduces the city to jarring atoms has not begun, and the observer is able to see the city as a whole and as an entity—as an organic thing, not cut off from nature, but a part of it, related to the world above it and about it ("Open unto the fields, and to the sky").

We are not then to apply Wordsworth's love of nature mechanically and superficially as if he were only interested in rural scenes and natural objects: he can feel the beauty of London. And conversely, we must remember that he can sometimes use natural objects to suggest mechanism. "A Slumber Did My Spirit Seal" (p. 54) is a case in point. The body of the dead girl is said to be "Rolled round in earth's diurnal course, / With rocks, and stones, and trees." We may argue that at least some of the things with which she is associated are alive—the trees, for instance—and that she is pictured here as merged with "nature"; but the effect given by this poem is far different from that at the end of "Lucy Gray" where the child seems to live on as part of the spirit of the place. In this poem, it is as if the earth itself were seen as a mighty wheel, mechanically spinning, and carrying with it, along with other objects lacking motion, the inert body of the girl.

Wordsworth's interest in "nature," then, is much more than a sentimental interest in country scenes. Interested in them he was, and a consideration of his biography will suggest how much he relied upon his experiences in the Lake District of England for the material which went into his poetry and for the inspiration which wove that material into poetry. But the poems show a certain flexibility in his treatment of man's attitude toward natural objects and natural scenes. They show common sense in the management of his basic theme; they show artistic sense as well.

Thus far we have been primarily concerned with theme; it may be well to glance at some of Wordsworth's typical devices for treating his themes. In the poems thus far discussed, Wordsworth's method is to tell a story or to sketch an incident, sometimes commenting upon it, but frequently merely framing it—giving it a setting which will allow the reader to draw the proper inference. ("Michael" is a tale provided with such a framework; so is "Lucy Gray.") The folk ballad—a song that tells a story—would obviously suggest such methods of treatment, and we will not be surprised to find that Wordsworth admired the folk ballad very much, or that his first important volume of poetry (done in collaboration with Coleridge) was entitled *Lyrical Ballads.*

Some of his poems show the condensation of the folk ballad and its use of shock and dramatic contrast: "A Slumber Did My Spirit Seal" is an example. But the situations that interested Wordsworth often do not allow for this kind of effect. What Wordsworth tends to take over from the folk ballad, therefore, is the use of concrete imagery and an apparently straightforward treatment of simple and even homely details. The shock is rarely that of some violent or untoward happening in the action or plot (as in "Sir Patrick Spence"): the shock occurs in the reader's mind in the contrast between the conventional expectancy and the actual effect—between the simple unimportance of the event and the emotional charge that it carries. The speaker in "The Solitary Reaper" is evidently surprised at the effect of the song upon himself—though he does not comment overtly on why it has that effect. The observer in "Upon Westminster Bridge" is evidently surprised—even shocked—at the effect of the vision of the familiar, smoky, "unpoetic" city.

Both poems, it is true, provide the reason for the effect: the poem is so constructed that we can participate in the experience with the speaker; but in these poems, as nearly always in Wordsworth's best poems, we are not told what the effect ought to be: it is generated out of the poem itself; e.g., out of the imagery as in "The Solitary Reaper."

We can get at this matter of Wordsworth's technique in another way. Since Wordsworth was so much concerned with the influence of natural scenes upon the human mind—with the unconscious molding of the mind by nature—and since the people so influenced are children or peasants or thinkers who cultivate a wise passiveness, it will not do for the poems themselves to make use of self-conscious rhetorical devices. Such rhetorical techniques will seem to contradict the doctrine of the quiet and unconscious influence of nature, and dramatically they will be out of keeping with the kinds of people who figure in the poems. The form of the poem will have to show a surface simplicity, and will have to work upon the reader quietly and almost unconsciously.

The same considerations will in part account for Wordsworth's emphasis upon a "language really used by men" as opposed to "gaudiness and inane phraseology." In his Preface to the second edition of the *Lyrical Ballads,* Wordsworth insists upon this point, and some of the claims which he makes for the language of humble, rustic men who "convey their feelings and notions in simple and unelaborate expressions" are somewhat extravagant, as his friend S. T. Coleridge was to show later in his *Biographia Literaria.* But Wordsworth's basic emphasis is sound: he rightly distrusts a special "poetic" language and any "mechanical device of style." Poetry, as he clearly saw, does not reside in the glitter and shimmer of external ornament: it is an effect of the poem as a whole.

We have remarked that the typical Wordsworth lyric works on the reader quietly and almost unconsciously. At Wordsworth's best, this is precisely what we find. But we can more clearly define this best by pointing up the typical kinds of failure that are likely to occur with such a conception of poetry: (1) in his desire to shun all rhetorical tricks—all that smacks of the considered effect, the poet sometimes cuts it too fine and we get a simplicity that is doctrinaire: nothing happens; there is no effect; e.g., Wordsworth's "Idiot Boy." Or (2) the poet tells us about the effect—states it abstractly rather than realizing it for us dramatically; e.g., "A Poet's Epitaph."

Wordsworth's "Intimations Ode" (p. 547) provides a fitting culmination to these notes. Many of Wordsworth's dominant themes come together in this poem. Moreover, Wordsworth's notes on the poem (which the student should consult) make clear how important the poem is as a document on Wordsworth's own development as a man and as a poet. But study of the poem in these terms does not preclude our going on to view it in other terms. Moreover, the more nearly that we succeed in mastering it as a poem—and it is a very rich poem—the more light will it shed for us on Wordsworth's life and ideas.

The student might well begin with a study of the poem in its larger outline: (I) the speaker laments the loss of a special radiance in nature which it once possessed for him though (II) he finds the world still beautiful. (III) He tries to join in the joy of the spring scene but (IV) he cannot recover the vision which he once had, and he comes back to the question: Where has the radiance fled? Stanzas V, VI, and VII attempt an explanation: we come to earth "trailing clouds of glory," but the glory is lost in the process of growing up, of education, of becoming involved in the affairs of earth. In Stanza VIII, the speaker addresses the child as the "best philosopher," able to see truths which the adult cannot see, but in his eagerness to grow up, striving to become blind like the adult. The "rally" begins in Stanza IX; what the gleam implies has not been lost; "shadowy recollections" from the childhood state remain; in these recollections, whatever they are, our deepest insights are rooted, and we can still, on occasion, have a glimpse of the eternal truth. Therefore in Stanza (X), though the radiance is lost, the speaker joins in the spring-time joy. He refuses to grieve over his loss: there are compensations in the "years that bring the philosophic mind." Stanza XI closes the poem with a renewed avowal of his love for the objects of nature, and a testimony to the influence which they have exerted, and continue to exert, upon him.

Perhaps the next step is to develop some of the "problems" that emerge as one becomes closer acquainted with the poem. One of these problems has to do with the relation between the natural and the supernatural. The source of the radiance as given in Stanza V is supernatural. How far are we to press this explanation of the source? Wordsworth in a note on the poem disclaims any attempt to "inculcate" a literal belief in the Platonic notion of the soul's pre-existence before birth. Moreover, there are passages in the poem which imply that animals and even inanimate objects share in the child's vision of an earth clad in celestial splendor. Certainly Wordsworth's phrase "Ye blessèd Creatures" (line 36) is meant to include birds and lambs as well as the "happy Shepherd-boy."

This question touches upon the problem which Wordsworth's friend Coleridge raised with regard to Stanza VII of the poem.

> In what sense is a child of that age a *philosopher?* . . . In what sense is he declared to be *forever haunted* by the Supreme Being? or so inspired as to deserve the splendid titles of a *mighty prophet,* a *blessed seer?* By reflection? by knowledge? by conscious intuition? or by *any* form or modification of consciousness? These would be tidings indeed; but such as would presuppose an immediate revelation to the inspired communicator, and require miracles to authenticate his inspiration. . . ."

In the same chapter, Coleridge goes on to say, a few paragraphs later:

> In what sense can the magnificent attributes, above quoted, be appropriated to a *child,* which would not make them equally suitable to a *bee,* or a *dog,* or a *field of corn;* or even to a ship, or to the wind and waves that propel it? The omnipresent Spirit works equally in them, as in the child; and the child is equally unconscious of it as they.[1]

Are the "magnificent attributes" indeed applicable to the birds and lambs—creatures which may hardly be thought to come into this world "trailing clouds of glory"? Has Wordsworth in his poem defined the sense in which the child reads "the Eternal Deep"? Does the child see the world clad in radiance because he is still close to the *supernatural,* or because, like the lamb, he is so utterly *natural?*

This problem of natural and supernatural shows itself further in the various associations which "earth" and "earthly" take on in the poem. The earth and its natural creatures in many parts of the poem seem appropriately to wear the garments of celestial light (see Stanzas II and III), and yet the earth is also associated with "every common sight" (line 2); and in Stanza VI the earth is the "homely nurse" attempting to make man "forget the glories he hath known." In other words, it is immersion in earthly life that dims

[1] *Biographia Literaria,* Chap. XXII.

man's perception of the visionary gleam, it would appear; and yet the poet turns again and again to natural earthly scenes for illustrations of the heavenly radiance.

If "earth" and "earthly" are, in this poem, somewhat ambiguous, is there any ambiguity in Wordsworth's use of the imagery of light? For example, in Stanza II the sunshine is a "glorious birth"; in Stanza V it becomes the "light of common day." In the same way, "shades" and "shadowy" seem to point two ways. "Shades of the prison-house" as used in line 67 suggests something opposed to the celestial radiance. The implied metaphor is that of a darkening prison in which the adult man will find himself shut up. Yet, the "shadowy recollections" of line 149 are called "the fountain light of all our day" (line 151). Even if we take "shadowy" to mean here "dim" or "faint" or "apparently illusory," the word still stands in rather shocking contrast to "fountain light," for "fountain light" suggests an intense radiance.

The point in raising these problems is not to raise doubts about the goodness of the poem. It is rather to let us see difficulties inherent in Wordsworth's theme, and therefore better understand the magnitude of his accomplishment. How did Wordsworth solve these problems?

Here we are obviously dealing with a philosophical question of some complexity. We are dealing, among other things, with the problem of how man knows his world and the relative truth of each of his various ways of perceiving it. One way in which to deal with this question is to consult the scholars who have studied the development of Wordsworth's philosophical ideas, and who can define them with some precision in their various stages of development. If we want to know what Wordsworth, the man, thought, it is imperative that we have recourse to this scholarship.[1]

[1] Moreover, it can be argued that this scholarship is necessary for an understanding of the poetry. Every poet alters, if ever so little, the meanings of the words that he uses (see p. 587). To read the "Ode," we need to know precisely what Wordsworth's terms mean—what concepts they denote, what world view they imply. Insofar as knowledge of Wordsworth's other poems and of his life can help us understand his language, we are the better equipped to read his poetry with understanding. Though in theory it is a nice question as to how far a poet may be allowed to use a special vocabulary and to lean upon a set of private references, nothing smacking of a

But we are dealing here also, it should be plain, with a poetic problem of some complexity—a problem primarily of mixed and contradictory images. Has Wordsworth used his images of light successfully? Has he managed to make them a concrete embodiment of his ideas? Do they define those ideas with subtlety and precision?

Wordsworth, it would seem, has chosen to represent man's varying perceptions of his world by the various kinds of light by which he sees it. We have on the one hand dawn light, moonlight, starlight, the light of the setting sun, and we have on the other hand, "the light of common day." We have the child's intuitive vision of the world and we have the man's more analytic and prosaic way of looking at it. The perception of the child imperceptively becomes that of the man; the celestial gleam disappears—not into darkness—but into another kind of light—the "light of common day."

Wordsworth quite properly employs a contrast between two kinds of light, for both kinds of perception are ways of seeing, and they are closely related to each other. The more "poetic" light is easily lost in the prosaic light by which we do the necessary work of the world. In this poem the progress of the sun through the sky with the altering quality of its light seems to parallel closely man's progress from childhood to age. The sun at his rising is not explicitly compared to the child, but "The Soul that rises with us . . . / . . . not in utter nakedness, / But trailing clouds of glory" (lines 59–64) is an image taken from the sunrise, and the "sunshine is a glorious birth" (line 16) suggests the same image. Like the growing boy, however, the sun as it mounts the sky, loses his clouds of glory, and his light becomes that of common day. Near the end of the poem, Wordsworth writes: "The Clouds that gather round the setting sun / Do take a sober coloring from an eye / That hath kept watch o'er man's mortality" (lines 196–98). The fact that the light is that of sunset is significant. Is it the "eye" of the man or is it the eye of day, the sun, that gives a sober coloring to the clouds?

doctrinaire solution to this problem is offered in this text. The more that the student knows about Wordsworth, the better. As we have already remarked, the other Wordsworth poems in this text may be used, and should be used, to throw light upon the "Ode."

Which eye has "kept watch o'er man's mortality"? Both sun and the poet may be said to have kept such a watch.

We need not insist, however, that Wordsworth has consciously elaborated his light images in this fashion. It will be enough to make a more modest suggestion: that it may be worth exploring the light imagery in order to see whether Wordsworth found in this imagery a means to express his ideas about the way in which man apprehends his world.

Exercise:

1. Does Wordsworth's handling of the light imagery help solve the problem of the source of the celestial gleam? Note that the soul is likened to a celestial light-bearer, a star (line 59). Do lines 12–13 have any bearing on this question? Is it implied that the moon looking round her with delight is like the other "blessèd Creatures" which see the world bathed in celestial light?

2. In line 197, the poet says that the sunset clouds "take a sober coloring *from* an eye"; in line 202, he says that the flower can give thoughts *to* the observer. Is this a meaningless reversal? Does it relate to Wordsworth's view that "there are Powers / Which of themselves our minds impress" (see p. xlv)?

3. With reference to Coleridge's objection (see p. 641): suppose that one admitted for the sake of argument that the attributes which Wordsworth claims for the child could, so far as the poem is concerned, be claimed for a "bee" or a "dog"; would this admission destroy the poem? Note that if the child "sees" he cannot any more than the bee tell us what he sees. Wordsworth admits that "this eye among the blind" is "deaf and silent." May the child be a "seer blest," for all of that?

4. How does the child read "the Eternal Deep" (line 112)? How are the children who are portrayed in line 166 reading the deep? Does their innocent joy in the presence of the sea—their being happy and unterrified—involve a perception into reality which the mature philosopher wins with difficulty?

5. What is the underlying metaphor in Stanza VI? How does Stanza VII carry the poem forward? Some readers have felt that Stanza VII represents a relative weakness in the power of the poem. Would you agree or not?

6. According to the poem, is (1) the gleam subjective, an effect of the child's *way* of looking at the world; or is (2) the gleam objective, a light that exists in the world but which escapes the adult's bleared vision? Can these views be reconciled? Is there a third possibility: that the eye and the light by which it sees are interrelated, one modifying the other? Can you relate this last statement to the concluding lines of this poem? Where does this poem find its center? What is it finallv "about"?

2: T. S. ELIOT: "THE WASTE LAND"

"The Waste Land" has the reputation of being a most difficult poem, and it has its difficulties to be sure, though the most formidable of these are not necessarily the number of literary allusions, nor the many quotations in foreign languages. The allusions can be pointed out; the foreign languages, translated. (See p. 577.) The discussion that follows will occupy itself in part with this kind of elucidation. The danger is that the student may take the elucidation to *be* the poem, and assume that having understood the one, he has grasped the other. But the discussion that follows is to be considered as a means to an end: the imaginative apprehension of the poem itself. The student would do well, therefore, to begin by reading the poem and "listening" to it before worrying too much with the meaning of specific parts. This is good advice for understanding any poem. It applies fully to "The Waste Land." The student may, by doing this, learn sufficient respect for the poem as poem to resist being overwhelmed by the commentary. For the commentary, however necessary, is useless if it substitutes itself for the poem itself.

The title of the poem is taken from a medieval legend about a parched land ruled over by the maimed and impotent Fisher King whose castle stands on the banks of a river. The fate of the land is bound up with the fate of its lord. Until he is healed, the land remains under a curse: the cattle do not breed; the crops do not grow. The curse may be removed only when a knight makes his way to the castle of the Fisher King and asks the meanings of the various objects that will be shown him there.

In her book, *From Ritual to Romance,*[1] Miss Jessie Weston argues that the Fisher King was originally the vegetation god whose death was mourned in the dying year, but whose triumphant return as expressed in the renewed life of nature was celebrated in the spring. According to Miss Weston this fertility cult was widely disseminated, particularly by soldiers and Syrian merchants. This story was later Christianized in the Grail legends as the reminiscence of an initiation rite. The candidate's courage was tested by making a journey to the Perilous Chapel, around which demons seemed to howl. Moreover, when he arrived at the Castle of the Fisher King, the candidate must actively seek truth—must demand the meaning of the various symbols, if the secret doctrine was to be revealed to him and he was to be shown that death and birth are interrelated and that the way into life was through death.

The student has already become acquainted with this theme in reading Eliot's "Preludes" (p. 102) and more particularly in "The Love Song of J. Alfred Prufrock." Indeed, the best preparation that the student of this text may have for reading "The Waste Land" is to reread the analysis of "Prufrock" (p. 433), for the poems have a similar theme and in "The Waste Land" Eliot merely extends and develops techniques of presentation which he had already used in the earlier poem. The student may well begin by assuming that in "The Waste Land" the world of Prufrock is seen under a metaphor derived from the cursed land of the medieval legend.

The waste-land symbolism is echoed in a number of the incidents in the poem. It accounts for the fortune-telling scene (lines 43–59) where Madame Sosostris uses the Tarot pack. The symbols used on the Tarot cards are traced by Miss Weston back to the symbolism of the fertility cult. The cards were probably used in ancient Egypt to predict the rise of the waters upon which the prosperity of a whole people depended. (We may also see the fortune-telling scene as the presentation to the knight of the symbols whose meaning he is to ask in order that the curse may be lifted.)

[1] In his notes on the poem, Eliot writes: "Not only the title, but the plan and a good deal of the symbolism of the poem were suggested by" this book. Eliot's principal notes have been incorporated in this discussion of the poem.

The waste-land symbolism is reflected also in the reference to Mr. Eugenides (line 209). He is a modern descendant of the Syrian merchants who, like Phlebas the Phoenician (Section IV), once brought the mysteries to faraway Britain. *Eugenides* means "son of the well born," but his function is now degraded. His invitation to a "week end at the Metropole" does not promise initiation into the secret of life but into a cult of empty, and perhaps perverted, pleasure. The agonized journey to the chapel (Section V) alludes to the journey to the Perilous Chapel, part of the initiation ceremony of the seekers after knowledge.

The waste-land symbolism, however, will not in itself account for all things in the poem. (As we shall see, many other analogies are used to suggest the nature of the modern world.) We may be disposed to question the poet's adopting so remote an analogy and so complex a set of references. But the centrality of the problem with which the fertility cult deals makes it appropriate here. Some such cult has appeared in every culture that we know of: man, in trying to assign a meaning to life, has had to deal with the facts of birth and death. Moreover, any high culture, having grown out of a more primitive culture, is bound to be saturated with references to, and modifications of, fertility cult symbols.

The treatment of the legend based upon such symbols gives a powerful and flexible device for dealing with the meaning or lack of meaning of modern civilization. The Tarot cards will illustrate: the importance of the use to which they were once put is contrasted with the use to which they are put by the shabby fortune-teller; the teaching that the hanged god died in order to renew life for his people is contrasted here with Madame Sosostris' warning against death.

If we feel that the contrasts simply show up a sordid present by contrasting it with a glorious and meaningful past, we miss the point just as we miss it if we reverse the debunking and say that the passage implies that all priests of the past were merely charlatans like Madame Sosostris. The contrasts used throughout the poem are not so simple in their import as that. They have to do with the fundamental questions that persist through all cultures though in some cultures men are impelled to answer them and in others they may listlessly refrain.

But for the reader of this poem, the employment of the waste-land legend has a special relevance. The poet is attempting to dramatize for us what it feels like to live in a secularized world—a world emptied of religious meaning. But the prime difficulty for the modern reader is that he is himself too thoroughly secularized to see what the poet is talking about. The poet has in effect, therefore, adopted the device of putting the reader into something of the position of the knight in the Grail legends. The knight in the story was able to remove the curse only if he questioned what he saw—only if he demanded meanings of the symbols shown to him. If he merely wondered at them, the truth was not revealed to him. If we are to experience the poem—as opposed to being merely "told" about the theme—we must be alert for the significance of what we see. Otherwise we shall find a mere jumble of fragments that can be tied together in terms of an abstract and arbitrary scheme, but which never unite in felt significance.

We have said that this poem employs other symbols by which to describe the modern world and makes much use of literary allusion. In the following account (which may be regarded as a preliminary sketch) we shall restrict ourselves largely to the following works: the Bible, Shakespeare, and Dante, all documents central to our culture. (They are certainly not esoteric documents, though one today can scarcely count on any given reader's knowing them.) To these we shall add for this preliminary account only [1] the poems with which the student is presumably already familiar: Spenser's "Prothalamion" (p. 479), Webster's "Dirge" (p. 83), Goldsmith's "When Lovely Woman Stoops to Folly" (p. 478), and Marvell's "To His Coy Mistress" (p. 320). These will not suffice to give a full account of the poem, but they may serve to acquaint us with the basic themes. What Eliot describes as the character of the modern world has occurred before. The second chapter of *Ezekiel* (from which Eliot takes the phrase "Son of man" (line 20) pictures a world thoroughly secularized:

1. And he said unto me, Son of man, stand upon thy feet, and I will speak unto thee.

[1] An exception will be made in our discussion of the last forty lines of the poem. In dealing with the conclusion, even a preliminary account should be as full as possible.

2. And the spirit entered into me when he spake unto me and set me upon my feet, that I heard him that spake unto me.

3. And he said unto me, Son of man, I send thee to the children of Israel, to a rebellious nation that hath rebelled against me: they and their fathers have transgressed against me, even unto this very day.

The thirty-seventh chapter of *Ezekiel* describes the prophet's vision of a waste land—a valley of dry bones. He is asked (v. 3), "Son of man, can these bones live? And I answered, O Lord God, thou knowest (v. 4). Again he said unto me, Prophesy over these bones, and say unto them, O ye dry bones, hear the word of the Lord."

The twelfth chapter of *Ecclesiastes* (to which Eliot's note refers, line 23 of our poem) also describes a parched and nightmare world:

1. Remember now thy Creator in the days of thy youth, while the evil days come not, nor the years draw nigh, when thou shalt say, I have no pleasure in them;

2. While the sun, or the light, or the moon, or the stars, be not darkened, nor the clouds return after the rain;

3. In the day when the keepers of the house shall tremble, and the strong men shall bow themselves, and the grinders cease because they are few, and those that look out of the windows be darkened,

4. And the doors shall be shut in the streets, when the sound of the grinding is low, and he shall rise up at the voice of the bird, and all the daughters of music shall be brought low;

5. Also when they shall be afraid of that which is high, and fears shall be in the way, and the almond tree shall flourish, and the grasshopper shall be a burden, and desire shall fail: because man goeth to his long home, and the mourners go about the streets;

6. Or ever the silver cord be loosed, or the golden bowl be broken, or the pitcher be broken at the fountain, or the wheel broken at the cistern.

7. Then shall the dust return to the earth as it was: and the spirit shall return unto God who gave it.

8. Vanity of vanities, saith the preacher; all is vanity.

This vision is suggested also in the landscape described in Section V of our poem.

The modern waste land also resembles Dante's hell. Eliot's notes on line 63 refer us to the Third Canto of the *Inferno;* his note on line 64, to the Fourth Canto. The Third Canto describes the place of those who on earth had "lived without praise or blame." They share this antechamber of hell with the angels "who were not rebels, nor were faithful to God, but were for themselves." These then are the "trimmers," those who make no commitment. They bewail the fact that they "have no hope of death." But though they may not hope for death,[1] Dante scornfully calls them "these unfortunate who never were alive." To have real life demands a kind of commitment which men too fearful of death can never make. The souls described in the Fourth Canto of the Inferno are those who lived virtuously but died before the proclamation of the Gospel. They are the unbaptized. They form the second of the two classes of people who inhabit the modern waste land: those who are thoroughly secularized and those who have no knowledge of the faith.

Having in mind these three realms of negation and sterility (as described in the Grail legend, the Bible, and Dante), let us see how the poem is developed. In Section I, there pass through the speaker's mind glimpses of a world that is tired and timid, bored and yet uneasy, preferring the half life of winter to the violent renewal of the energies of spring. It is a world that fears death as the greatest evil but is disturbed by the idea of birth, and certainly sees birth and death as utterly distinct. We have reflections on the quality of this world (lines 1–7, 20–30) intermingled with memories of specific scenes (lines 8–18 and lines 35–41). These are interspersed with scraps of song or remembered bits of poetry.

It is a world apprehensive of the future and eager for signs and portents, even though it cannot believe in them. The hero has his fortune told, and in contrast to the almost prophetic injunction of line 30, "I will show you fear in a handful of dust," is admonished by the fortune-teller to "Fear death by water."

[1] This is the hopeless wish of the Sibyl in the epigraph at the beginning of the poem. The passage is from the *Satyricon* of Petronius. "For I saw with my own eyes the Sibyl at Cumae, hanging in a cage, and when the boys said to her, 'Sibyl, what do you want'; she would answer, 'I want to die.'" The Sibyl was a prophetess to whom the god Apollo had granted a thousand years of life, but she had forgotten to ask for youth as well.

As he sees the crowds going to work over London Bridge in the foggy winter dawn, he is reminded of the multitude of the dead whom Dante saw in his vision of hell. These people in their meaningless activity are dead, not really alive. The ritual burial of the fertility god was carried out in the confidence that his energies, like those of the world of nature, would revive again. Now the burial of the dead is without hope. The reference to Webster's "Dirge" (p. 83) describes a burial as conceived in an earlier age. It should be a scene of horror: the corpse, unfriended, left to the ant, the field mouse, and the mole; but as conceived in the Webster poem, the scene is not horrible at all. In spite of the wolf, nature is presented as more than friendly to man. But the beauty generated in Webster's "Dirge" is turned to a special horror here, and the horror arises, in part, from the "domestication" of the scene: not wild nature but the suburban garden; not the abandoned body, but the "corpse you planted"; not the wolf that's "foe to men," but the domesticated wolf, the dog, who will scratch up the body out of pure friendliness. The taming of nature, the robbing it of its terror (the wolf that's foe transformed to the friendly dog) is part of the process of secularization.

The one scene of ecstasy and beauty in this first section is the memory of the incident outside the hyacinth garden. It recalls a moment not of half life but of full life; and yet the protagonist has to say that in that moment "I was neither / Living nor dead." But this phrasing, though it seems to take the moment out of "life," does so by equating the moment with the moment of the mystic's vision, and thus distinguishes it sharply from the death-in-life in the waste land. Compare "I could not / Speak . . . and I knew nothing" in this passage with "Do / You know nothing? Do you see nothing?" (lines 121–22) in the next section. The passages register with entirely different effect.

Section II is in a sense the easiest section of the poem. We have two vignettes of life in the waste land, having to do with two women from opposite ends of the social scale: the woman in the rich room, and Lil, who is discussed by her two Cockney friends in the pub. But both women are frustrated and unhappy; for both, "love" is a problem—for the one whose nerves are bad and who threatens to rush out into the street, and for the other who has had an abortion and dreads the return to childbearing now that her husband has been demobilized. Both, as sterile women, are symbols of the spiritual sterility of the modern secular world. Furthermore they represent two aspects of the modern world: the degradation of the slum and the neuroticism of the drawing room, though superficially so different, are both embodiments of the spiritual failures of the modern world.

Lines 77–78 associate the first woman with Cleopatra as she first appeared to Antony on the River Cydnus (see Shakespeare, *Antony and Cleopatra,* II, 2, 190). But the richness of the room simply comments ironically upon the essential emptiness of the woman's life. The decoration of the room reflects the richness of the cultural heritage; but the symbols are meaningless to her and the past is dead; so that the poem suddenly dismisses the rest of the décor of the room at line 104 as "other withered stumps of time." There is no real communication between her and her lover or husband who sits in the room with her. She finally demands desperately, "Are you alive, or not? Is there nothing in your head?" She can see in her life no purpose—only a monotonous round of activities: "The hot water at ten. / And if it rains, a closed car at four." The meaning of her life is as arbitrary as that of a game of chess.

The pathetic sordidness of Lil's life comes out as her friends discuss her over their beer. The barman's notice that it is closing time is heard more and more urgently, until finally he manages to hustle the women out of the pub.

The river dominates the third section of the poem: the modern river, its banks littered with debris, and the Elizabethan river as described by Spenser in the "Prothalamion" (p. 479), the scene of stately bridals. The protagonist walks through the city down to the river front, and the river is seen again, the modern river, sweating "oil and tar," the river on which Queen Elizabeth rode in her barge of state, and the modern river, once more, the scene of sordid love affairs.

The love theme suggested in the river scenes finds explicit development in the central episode of this section. This is the meeting of the typist and the carbuncular young man, whose love affair has no meaning beyond the action of biological mechanism. The automatism is reflected even in the verse. The young woman "stoops to folly," but she is not betrayed because she is not deluded, expects nothing, and thus loses nothing. The poet's rewriting of Goldsmith's poem (p. 478), with the alteration of theme, mood, and even the quality of rhythm, conveys brilliantly the contrast between two radically different conceptions of the same act. She is not stricken with horror and remorse. She doesn't feel anything at all. Her automatic gesture of smoothing her hair as she puts a record on the gramophone signifies that the act for her is meaningless.

Philomela achieved her music through suffering (see pp. 95–96); through her violation comes the "inviolable voice" (line 101). The typist, of course, is not violated, but there is no inviolable music either—simply the automatic music of the gramophone.

One other allusion of considerable importance figures in this third section. It is the song from Shakespeare's *Tempest,* "Full fathom five thy father lies." Here, as in the Philomela story, the song promises that hurt and loss will be transmitted to richness and beauty. In the fertility cult, death was transformed into life: the seed was buried to flourish again as a plant; the god died to rise again. In Shakespeare's play, the young Prince Ferdinand wanders disconsolately along the shores of Prospero's island after the shipwreck, sorrowing over his father's death (see line 192). As he wanders there, he hears Ariel's song, "Full fathom five thy father lies," music which seems to him to come from no mortal source. Led on by the music, he finds Miranda and love, and later will find his father alive and transformed by his experience on the island.

Fragments of this song have haunted the speaker through the day. At the fortune-teller's, mention of the card of the drowned "Phoenician sailor" brings into his head the line "Those are pearls that were his eyes" (line 48); and in Section II, when he is asked "Do you see nothing? Do you remember / Nothing?" he remembers unaccountably "Those are pearls that were his eyes (line 125). Now, as he walks behind the gashouse, he remembers Prince Ferdinand's sorrowful wandering, but death presents to his mind no bones turned to coral or eyes to pearls. There has been no transformation "into something rich and strange," only dry bones "Rattled by the rat's foot, year to year" (line 195). And the music that creeps by him on the waters (line 257) is that from the typist's gramophone.

In the monotonous world of the waste land, even time has a different character. Consciousness of time is not felt as an insistent urgency to action as in "To His Coy Mistress" (p. 320). Marvell, at his back, "always" hears "Time's winged Chariot"; the protagonist hears "from time to time" (line 196), not "Time's winged Chariot" but the sound of "horns and motors" (line 197), the noise of the London traffic.

Perhaps in this section the one modern scene that possesses vitality and beauty is that described in lines 260–65. The magnificent church built by Wren is now surrounded by squalid buildings; but the whining mandolin is "pleasant," and the fishmen are alive ("a clatter and a chatter from within"), and the church still holds "Inexplicable splendour of Ionian white and gold." There is here the sense of life quite other than the half-life that dominates the other scenes. At the literal level, these poor fishmen have vitality; at the symbolic level, they are associated with the fish, symbol of fertility. Section III ends with the word "burning" and the world portrayed in this section is depicted as burning with sterile lust. The brief lyric interlude furnished by Section IV presents a contrast: not sterile burning, but drowning; not half death, but actual death; and not the dry bones in the low dry garret, but bones picked by the sea currents in whispers. The student may be tempted to take this passage as merely a simple contrast—a shift in tone and mood. But the passage is heavily "charged" by the three sections that precede it. Phlebas is one of the Syrian merchants. This is a "death by water" that Madame Sosostris has admonished the hero to fear. Whether or not Phlebas here suffers a "sea change / Into something rich and strange," there is at least a sense of peace and forgetfulness. Profit and loss no longer disturb him. He has returned to the source of all life, the sea, and there is even the sense of regression—"passed the stages of his age and youth"—as if he were now retracing his journey from the womb.

This section, like Section I, ends in an address to all men: "O you who turn the wheel and look to windward"—that is, you who like Phlebas steer your ship and watch the weather signs—you who think that you direct your own course and are confident that you are not merely turning helplessly on the "wheel," moving in meaningless circles—do not forget that Phlebas, once as strong as you, could not avoid the whirlpool. Death is a fact that cannot be evaded.

The last section of the poem gives the sense of a painful journey through a landscape of nightmare. The god has died. Lines 322–23 suggests Christ's agony in the Garden of Gethsemane; lines 324–25, his trial before Pilate. "He who was living is now dead." But for those who cannot believe in him, he is now in a special sense dead; and the unbelievers, being the people of the waste land, are themselves not really alive: "We who were living are now dying / With a little patience" (lines 329–30).

The lines that follow suggest an experience in which the drought-tormented traveler suffers from delirium. The speaker is haunted by the sense of an unseen presence. The two apostles on the road to Emmaus (*Luke* 24:13–31) after the crucifixion found themselves walking beside a stranger who later revealed himself to them as the risen Christ. Here no revelation is made, and the sense of hallucination is extended into a nightmare vision of a topsy-turvy world. The city, like a city seen inverted as in a mirage, "Cracks and reforms and bursts in the violet air." The towers are "upside down in air," the bells which ring from them are "reminiscent," and voices sing out of "exhausted wells."

The civilization is breaking up; reality and unreality seem to mix. The woman who exclaimed "I shall rush out as I am, and walk the street / With my hair down, so" (line 132–33) reappears, and having drawn "her long black hair out tight / . . . [fiddles] whisper music from those strings" (lines 377–78). The bats with "baby faces" and the voices "singing out of empty cisterns and exhausted wells" point to a nightmare of sterile longing.

The nightmare journey is made to take on the character of the initiate's journey to the Perilous Chapel. The Chapel is deserted and apparently abandoned, and made the more ominous thereby. But the cock upon the rooftree, as the lightning flashes, crows: and there is "a damp gust / Bringing rain," the promise of relief.

The lightning flash is followed by the clap of thunder. The sound of the thunder is represented by the onomatopoeic syllable "da." But the poet takes advantage of its occurrence as the first syllable of the Sanskrit words *datta* (give), *dayadhvam* (sympathize), and *damyata* (control).[1] What the thunder says contains the secret for removing the curse. The unwillingness to give of oneself—to make a positive commitment—is bound up with the sense of isolation and with the paralysis of action which are the special characteristics of the waste land. "Give," "sympathize," and "control" answer to the situation, point by point.

The passages that follow each of these words comment upon them and relate them to situations presented earlier in the poem. Man cannot be absolutely self-regarding. Even the propagation of the race calls for a commitment and surrender. To live demands belief in something more than "life."

The surrender to something outside the self is an attempt (whether on the sexual level or some other) to transcend one's essential isolation. We are each of us shut up within the private world of our thoughts and sensations just as Count Ugolino was locked within his tower (see *Inferno,* Canto XXXIII). Only "for a moment" can the "broken Coriolanus" be revived. (For Coriolanus as a figure of pride, see Shakespeare's play of that name.)

The comment on the thunder's third command echoes, and contrasts with, "Death by Water." Instead of the passivity of the drowned sailor, Phlebas, rising and falling with the sea currents, here the sailor dominates the boat so thoroughly that it seems an extension of his own will. It responds "gaily." To say "your heart would have responded gaily" implies that the heart has not. The speaker's condition has been negative. (The command to give prompts in him the question: "what have we given?" the command to sympathize reminds him that he has heard the key turn "once only." There must be a second turning of the key if his prison is to be unlocked.)

By interpreting the rumbling of the thunder in terms of Sanskrit words, the poet extends his reference back to the earliest history of the race. The fable of the meaning of the thunder is found in one of the Upanishads and thus the ancient wisdom can be found couched in the primordial language from which most of the modern European languages are finally derived.

[1] The onomatopoeic effect is not, of course, limited to the syllable *da. Dayadhvam,* for example, admirably suggests the rolling thunder peal.

The poem does not end, however, with the falling of the reviving rain. This poem undertakes to embody the experience of the modern waste land, and the waste land remains. The speaker's perception of the ancient wisdom cannot in itself lift the general curse. Yet if secularization has destroyed or is likely to destroy modern civilization, the speaker has his own private obligations to fulfill. Even if London Bridge is falling down, "Shall I at least set my lands in order?"

"The fragments" which the protagonist has "shored against [his] ruins" may seem to furnish a difficult and unsatisfactory ending for the poem. But if we know from what they are taken and of what they are fragments, we shall find that though they measure the desperate plight of the protagonist, they are more than a jumble: they shore up his ruins to some purpose. Line 427, to be translated "Then he hid him in the fire which refines them," is spoken in Dante's *Purgatorio* by the poet Arnaut who says to Dante, "I am Arnaut that weep and go a-singing; in thought I see my past madness, and I see with joy the day which I await before me." His is no meaningless suffering and he steps back into the refining fire with joy.[1]

Line 428 ("When shall I be like the swallow") is taken from the *Pervigilium Veneris,* a late Latin poem. That poem too ends on a note of hope with the refrain "Tomorrow may he who has never loved and he who has loved, make love."

Line 429 ("The Prince of Aquitaine at the ruined tower") is taken from "El Desdichado" (The Disinherited), a sonnet by Gerard de Nerval. The poem ends with lines that may be translated: "I have twice crossed Acheron [the river of Hell] victorious: modulating upon the lyre of Orpheus, by turns, the sighs of the saints and the cries of the fay." Like him, the protagonist in "The Waste Land" has come back from hell. The ruined tower is the Perilous Chapel, and it is also the whole tradition in decay. The

[1] The third of the Thames daughters (lines 293–94) also echoes a passage from the *Purgatorio,* the speech of Pia, Canto V, but here the reference to the *Purgatorio* provides an ironical contrast. For like Arnaut's, Pia's suffering is a purgation; she has hope, whereas the first of the Thames daughters speaks in dejected hopelessness.

protagonist resolves to claim his tradition and rehabilitate it. "Why then Ile fit you" in line 431 comes from an Elizabethan play, *The Spanish Tragedy,* the subtitle of which is "Hieronymo's mad againe." In order to avenge the murder of his son, Hieronymo feigns madness. When he is asked to write a play for the court's entertainment, he replies:

> Why then, I'll fit you; say no more.
> When I was young, I gave my mind
> And plied myself to fruitless poetry;
> Which though it profit the professor naught,
> Yet it is passing pleasing to the world. 5

He sees that the play will give him the opportunity he has been seeking to avenge his son's murder. Like Hieronymo (and like Arnaut and El Desdichado), the protagonist has now found his theme; what he is about to perform is not "fruitless."

The various parts in Hieronymo's play are written in various foreign tongues (*cf.* the cluster of quotations with which this poem ends). When the courtiers protest that this device will make the play "a mere confusion," Hieronymo persists; and his odd scheme is accepted, presumably in order to humor his madness.

The poet's manner of proceeding here may seem mad in the same way, the poem ending in a "mere confusion." But if we understand that the poem is about the breakup of a culture and if we have seen the importance of the fact of convergence of many cultures upon a common theme, then the method makes sense. There is a further justification for this ending: the protagonist is conscious that the words with which the poem closes will seem to many to be a meaningless babbling, though they contain the oldest and most permanent truth of the race:[1] "Datta. Dayadhvam. Damyata." There is one more roll of the thunder: "Shantih Shantih Shantih." Eliot's note tells us that these Sanskrit words repeated as here are equivalent to our "The Peace that passeth understanding."

[1] Compare in a later work by Eliot, *The Family Reunion,* the speech made by Harry toward the end of the play: "It is very hard, when one has just recovered sanity, / And not yet assured of its possession, that is when / One begins to seem the maddest to other people."

In the preceding account of the poem we have neglected many incidental allusions and special references. These will be identified in the notes that conclude this section. It is better, however, to make out as briefly as can be done the thematic progression of the poem, and to allow the student himself to fit in, as a special exercise or exercises, the other symbols and allusions.

It is even more important for the student to see as clearly as possible how the poem works as a poem, rather than to get merely an elaborate paraphrase of the poem. To that end it may be best to illustrate the typical cross connections and contrasts before the student attempts to work out in detail the precise purpose served by some of the subsidiary allusions.

The basic method used in "The Waste Land" may be described as follows: The poet works in terms of surface parallelisms which in reality make ironical contrasts, and in terms of surface contrasts which in reality constitute parallelisms. The two aspects taken together give the effect of chaotic experience ordered into a new whole, though the realistic surface of experience is faithfully retained. The complexity of the experience is not violated by the apparent forcing upon it of a pre-determined scheme.

The fortune-telling of "The Burial of the Dead" will illustrate the general method very satisfactorily. On the surface of the poem the poet reproduces the patter of the charlatan, Madame Sosostris, and there is the surface irony: that is, the contrast between the original use of the Tarot cards and the use made by Madame Sosostris. But each of the details (justified realistically in the palaver of the fortune-teller) assumes a new meaning in the general context of the poem. The "fortune-telling," which is taken *ironically* by a twentieth-century audience, becomes *true* as the poem develops—true in a sense in which Madame Sosostris herself does not think them true. The surface irony is thus reversed and becomes an irony on a deeper level. The items of her speech have only one reference in terms of the context of her speech: the "man with three staves," the "one-eyed merchant," the "crowds of people, walking round in a ring," etc. But transferred to other contexts they become loaded with special meanings. To sum up, all the central symbols of the poem head up here; but here, in the only section in which they are explicitly bound together, the binding is slight and accidental. The deeper lines of association emerge only in terms of the total context as the poem develops—and this is, of course, exactly the effect to be sought.

This transference of items from an "innocent" context into a context in which they become charged and transformed in meaning will account for many of the literary allusions in the poem. For example, the "change of Philomel" is merely one of the items in the decorative detail of the room in the opening of "A Game of Chess." But the violent change of tense—"And still she cried, and still the world pursues"—make it a comment upon, and a symbol of, the modern world. And further allusions to it through the course of the poem gradually equate it with the general theme of the poem. The allusions to *The Tempest* display the same method. The parallelism between Dante's Hell and the waste land of the Grail legends is fairly close. But the first allusion to Ariel's song is merely an irrelevant and random association of the stream-of-consciousness: "Is your card, the drowned Phoenician Sailor, / (Those are pearls that were his eyes. Look!)." And on its second appearance in "A Game of Chess" it is still only an item in the protaganist's abstracted reverie. Even the association of *The Tempest* symbol with the Grail legends in the lines "While I was fishing in the dull canal, / Musing upon the king my brother's wreck," and in the passage which follows, is ironical merely. But the associations have been established, even though they may seem to be made in ironic mockery, and when we come to the passage, "Death by Water," with its change of tone, they assert themselves positively. We have a sense of revelation out of material apparently accidentally thrown together.

The melting of the characters into each other is, of course, an aspect of this general process. Queen Elizabeth and the girl born at Highbury both ride on the Thames, one in the barge of state, the other supine in a narrow canoe. The girl is a Thames-nymph, who has been violated and thus is like the Rhine-nymphs (see p. 665) who have also been violated. With the characters as with the other symbols, the surface relationships may be accidental and apparently trivial and they may be made either ironically or through random association or in hallucination, but in the total context of the poem the deeper relationships are revealed. The effect is a sense of the oneness of experience, and of the unity of all periods, and with this, a sense that the general theme is being generated out of the poem, that the theme has not been imposed, but has been revealed.

This complication of parallelisms and contrasts makes, of course, for ambiguity, but the ambiguity, in part, resides in the poet's fidelity to the complexity of experience. The symbols resist complete equation with a simple meaning. To take an example, "rock" throughout the poem seems to be one of the "desert" symbols. The "dry stone" gives "no sound of water"; woman in the waste land is "the Lady of the Rocks," and most pointed of all, there is the long delirium passage in "What the Thunder Said": "Here is no water but only rock." So much for its general meaning, but in "The Burial of the Dead" occur the lines: "Only / There is shadow under this red rock, / (Come in under the shadow of this red rock)." Rock here is a place of refuge. The paradox, life through death, penetrates the symbol itself.

For a more striking instance of this ambiguous use of symbols, consider the lines which occur in the hyacinth girl passage. The vision gives obviously a sense of the richness and beauty of life. It is a moment of ecstasy (the basic imagery is obviously sexual); but the moment in its intensity is like death. The protagonist looks in that moment into the "heart of light, the silence," and so looks into—not richness—but blankness: he is neither "living nor dead." The symbol of life stands also for a kind of death. This duality of function may, of course, extend to a whole passage. For example, consider: "Where fishmen lounge at noon: where the walls / Of Magnus Martyr hold / Inexplicable splendour of Ionian white and gold." The function of the passage is to indicate the poverty into which religion has fallen: the splendid church now surrounded by the poorer districts. But the passage has an opposed effect also: the fishmen in the "public bar in Lower Thames Street" next to the church have a meaningful life which has been largely lost to the secularized upper and middle classes.

The poem would undoubtedly be "clearer" if every symbol had a single, unequivocal meaning; but the poem would be thinner, and less honest. For the poet has not been content to develop a didactic allegory in which the symbols are two-dimensional items adding up directly to the sum of the general scheme. They represent dramatized instances of the theme, embodying in their own nature the fundamental paradox of the theme.

We have been speaking as if the poet were a strategist trying to win acceptance from a hostile audience. But of course this is true only in a sense. The poet himself is audience as well as speaker; we state the problem more exactly if we state it in terms of the poet's integrity rather than in terms of his strategy. He is so much a man of his own age that he can indicate his attitude toward the Christian tradition without falsity only in terms of the difficulties of a rehabilitation; and he is so much a poet and so little a propagandist that he can be sincere only as he presents his theme concretely and dramatically.

To put the matter in still other terms: the Christian terminology is for the poet a mass of clichés. However "true" he may feel the terms to be, he is still sensitive to the fact that they must operate superficially as clichés, and his method of necessity must be a process of bringing them to life again. The method adopted in "The Waste Land" is thus violent and radical, but thoroughly necessary. For the renewing and revitalizing of symbols which have been crusted over with the film of familiarity demands the type of organization which we have already commented on in discussing particular passages: the statement of surface similarities which are ironically revealed to be dissimilarities, and the association of apparently obvious dissimilarities which culminates in a later realization that the dissimilarities are only superficial—that the chains of likeness are in reality fundamental. In this way the statement of beliefs emerges *through* confusion and cynicism—not in spite of them.

In making a more detailed examination of the poem, the student will want to take into account the following notes:

L. 31–34. *Fresh blows the wind to the homeland. My Irish child, where dost thou tarry.* From *Tristan und Isolde,* Act I, verses 5–8. It is a song sung by a young sailor aboard the ship which is bringing Isolde to Cornwall.

L. 42. *Empty and wide the sea.* From *Tristan und Isolde,* III, verse 24. The reply of the watcher to the wounded Tristan, who hopes that Isolde will come to him, and who has asked whether there is any sight of a ship that may be bearing her to him. Note that these two quotations from the opera frame the hyacinth-garden passage.

L. 49. *Belladonna,* literally "beautiful lady."

L. 51. *The man with three staves,* a card in the Tarot pack, with which Eliot says that he quite arbitrarily associates the Fisher King.

L. 50. *The wheel,* a symbol throughout the poem of purposeless activity—the monotonous round of aimless life.

L. 52. *The one-eyed merchant.* Literally a card with the face presented in profile. But as associated with Mr. Eugenides (line 209), "one-eyed" suggests the function of the *seer* in decay. *Cf.* with the fortune-teller's bad cold.

L. 53. *Which is blank,* etc. The secret that the merchant is supposed to carry.

L. 55. *The Hanged Man.* A type of the god who dies for his people; the hanged god of Frazer's *Golden Bough* including Christ.

L. 60. Eliot adds the note: "Cf. Baudelaire: 'Fourmillante cité, cité plein de rêves, / Où le spectre en plein jour raccroche le passant' " (Swarming city, city full of dreams, where the specter in broad daylight seizes on the passer-by).

L. 66. *King William Street* runs north from London Bridge to the heart of the "City" of London.

L. 67. *Saint Mary Woolnoth,* a church on the corner of King William and Lombard streets.

L. 70. *Mylae,* 200 B.C., a naval battle fought between the Romans and the Carthaginians in the first Punic War. We expect the protagonist to hail his friend as a comrade in some battle of World War I, but the souls in hell are gathered from every age. All the pasts mingle there, ancient and recent; and in the modern waste land, all wars seem to be essentially the same.

L. 76. *You! hypocritical reader!—my likeness,—my brother!* from Baudelaire's Preface to *Fleurs de Mal.* Here the reader is suddenly addressed directly. Compare the "you" in "Prufrock," and note in particular p. 434.

L. 92. *Laquearia,* the hollow spaces between the intersecting cross beams of a ceiling. Eliot takes the word from the *Aeneid,* I, 726, where it is used in the description of the scene in which Dido entertains Aeneas at a great feast. The setting for this interview is thus meant to suggest not only the meeting of Antony and Cleopatra, but that of Dido and Aeneas, another great tragic love story of the past.

L. 98. *Sylvan scene.* Eliot's note indicates that the phrase is taken from Milton's description in *Paradise Lost* (IV, 140) of the mountain on which the Garden of Eden was located.

L. 103. *Jug Jug.* The Elizabethans sometimes represented bird songs by these—to our ears—outlandish syllables.

L. 110. Note that it is the hair here that speaks. The hair is an immemorial fertility symbol.

L. 138. Eliot gives a note: "Cf. the game of chess in Middleton's *Women beware Women.*" In that play the chess game is used as a device to keep the widow occupied while her daughter-in-law is being seduced. The seduction, in a *double-entendre,* is actually described in terms of the game.

L. 172. From *Hamlet,* Act IV, sc. v. Ophelia, driven mad by her sorrow, sings her pathetic song, and then speaks this line as she takes her leave of the company in the room. Like Philomela, her music has come from her suffering. Here the line counterpoints ironically the goodnights of the company in the pub.

L. 180. *City directors;* i.e., directors of corporations. The "City" in London is the financial district.

L. 182. From Psalm 137. It is a song of mourning for Zion, sung by those carried away into Babylonian captivity. The waste land is such a Babylonian captivity.

L. 191. Compare the lines spoken by Prince Ferdinand ("Weeping again the king my father's wreck") in Shakespeare's *The Tempest,* I, 2, just after he has heard Ariel's first song.

L. 195. See line 115.

L. 197. Eliot gives the note: "Cf. Day, *Parliament of Bees,* 'When of a sudden, listening you shall hear, / A noise of horns and hunting, which shall bring / Actaeon to Diana in the spring, / Where all shall see her naked skin. . . .'" Actaeon, a hunter, caught a glimpse of Diana, goddess of chastity, bathing. For this sacrilege he was turned into a stag and killed by his own hunting dogs. But here nakedness is put upon exhibition. Actaeon becomes Sweeney, and Diana, the hardly chaste Mrs. Porter.

L. 199. From a ballad reported to Eliot from Sydney, Australia.

L. 202. *And O the voices of children singing in the cupola,* from Verlaine's *Parsifal.* The story of Parsifal is one of the Grail legends. Just before the healing of Amfortas (the Fisher King) by Parsifal there is heard the clear song of the children in the choirloft of the Grail Chapel.

L. 204. See line 103.

L. 205. See line 100.

L. 207. See line 60.

L. 211. *C.i.f. London: documents at sight* means carriage and insurance free to London, and the Bill of Lading, etc., were to be handed to the buyer upon payment of the sight draft.

L. 214. *The Metropole,* a luxury hotel in the resort town of Brighton.

L. 218. *Tiresias,* the blind Greek prophet who is one of the characters in Sophocles' *Oedipus Rex.* When the land of Thebes lay under a curse—another "waste land" parallel—it was Tiresias who discerned the cause of the curse. Eliot's note states that "What Tiresias *sees* . . . is the substance of the poem." He sees here the life-giving act turned into something meaningless. The allusion to his "wrinkled female breasts" refers to the legend that he had been changed by the gods into a woman and then, after seven years, turned back into a man.

L. 221. This line is an alteration of lines by Sappho: "Hesperus [the evening star], you bring home all things bright morning scattered; you bring the sheep, you bring the goat, you bring the child to the mother."

L. 234. *Bradford,* an industrial town in north England.

L. 257. Spoken by Prince Ferdinand (*The Tempest,* I, 2) just after he has heard Ariel's first song. See also line 191.

L. 258. *The Strand* is one of the great shopping streets of London; *Queen Victoria Street* connects the "City" to Victoria wharf.

L. 260. *Lower Thames Street* runs alongside Billingsgate Market, the central fish market of London.

L. 266. From here through line 306 we have the songs of the three Thames daughters. The songs are patterned upon those of the Rhine daughters in Wagner's *Götterdämmerung,* III, 1. These were the nymphs of the Rhine, whose treasure, the Rhine gold, was stolen from them. Like the Rhine daughters, the Thames daughters here sing of the violation of the river, and as they sing in turn (lines 292–306), they tell of other violations.

L. 279. Leicester was one of Queen Elizabeth's great favorites, and Eliot's note quotes from a letter which describes her dalliance with Leicester on the Queen's barge.

L. 293. *Highbury, Richmond,* and *Kew* are suburbs of London.

L. 296. *Moorgate* is a slum district in the heart of the "City."

L. 300. *Margate* is a popular, unfashionable resort town in Kent at the end of the Thames estuary.

L. 307. From St. Augustine's *Confessions:* "To Carthage then I came, where a cauldron of unholy loves sang all about my ears."

L. 308. From Buddha's *Fire Sermon.* The following excerpts will suggest its nature: "Everything, O priests, is burning. . . . The eye, O priests, is burning; visible things are burning. . . . I declare unto you that it is burning with the fire of lust, with the fire of anger. . . . The ear is burning. . . . The tongue is burning. . . ." Etc.

L. 309. From St. Augustine's *Confessions* (according to Eliot's note). *Cf.* also *Zechariah,* 3:2; *Psalms,* 25:15; and *Amos,* 4:11.

L. 368. For this and the lines that immediately follow, *cf.* these lines from Eliot's play, *The Family Reunion:* "The sudden solitude in a crowded desert / In a thick smoke, many creatures moving / Without direction, for no direction / Leads anywhere but round and round that vapor. . . ."

L. 377. One of the "daughters of music"; see p. 649 for the quotation from *Ecclesiastes.*

L. 379. Violet is the liturgical color for repentance. See also line 220 and line 372.

L. 382. *Cf.* the towers and the bells (in the next line) with lines 288–89.

L. 392. The cock was believed to scare away evil spirits. Ariel's first song in *The Tempest,* I, 2, ends with the lines, "O hear / The strain of strutting chanticleer / Cry, cock-a-doodle-do."

L. 407. Eliot gives a note: "Cf. Webster, *The White Devil,* V, vi: '. . . they'll remarry / Ere the worm pierce your winding-sheet, ere the spider / Make a thin curtain for your epitaphs.'"

L. 411. In connection with this passage Eliot quotes from F. H. Bradley's *Appearance and Reality,* p. 346: "My external sensations are no less private to myself than are my thoughts or my feelings. In either case my experience falls within my own circle, a circle closed on the outside; and, with all its elements alike, every sphere is opaque to the others which surround it. . . . In brief, regarded as an existence which appears in a soul, the whole world for each is peculiar and private to that soul."

L. 428. The swallow is the bird of summer. Philomela's sister Procne was transformed into a swallow. See line 100 and the later references to Philomela.

3: MARVELL'S "HORATIAN ODE"

The relationship of poetry to history is, needless to say, a most important one, though it is a relationship frequently confused. We know that poems arise out of the process of history—that they are written by men who live in that process—and the temptation is strong to see the poem merely as a historical document or to allow our reading of it as a historical document to settle for us the whole question of the failure or success of the poem. Moreover, if one protests against so simple a view, he may seem to be denying the importance of history and historical contexts altogether.

The editors are confident that it is necessary to distinguish between the poem as poem and the poem as historical document. For example, it may be an extremely useful historical document and yet have no value at all as a poem, or the reverse may be true. We promptly get into trouble if we say: "This is sound history, *therefore* it is good poetry." But the editors would be the last to deny the intimacy of the relationship between specifically critical studies and historical studies, and they would agree that for a great many poems, a knowledge of the historical references is a fundamental requirement.

But these problems are best discussed with reference to concrete examples. Marvell's "Horatian Ode" (p. 523) provides an excellent example. The title itself, "An Horatian Ode upon Cromwell's Return from Ireland," warns us that this poem deals with historical figures and comments on a historical occasion. The poem welcomes Cromwell home from his subjugation of Ireland and looks forward (see lines 105–112) to his campaign against the Scots. Since Cromwell returned from Ireland in May 1650 and entered Scotland on July 22 of that year, the poem was probably written in the early summer of 1650. The student may consult a life of Cromwell or a history of the English civil war for a full account of these campaigns and of the other events alluded to in the "Ode." But it may be serviceable to present a very brief summary here.

The long-standing quarrel between Charles I and the Parliamentarians or Roundheads—a quarrel involving religious, political, and constitutional matters—broke out into open hostilities in August 1642. In the battles that followed, Oliver Cromwell soon proved himself to be the most vigorous and powerful general that the Roundheads had. He organized the New Model army which inflicted a crushing defeat upon the royal army at Naseby in 1645. Charles surrendered to his Scottish subjects, who later turned him over to the English in 1647.

Charles was kept in protective custody at Hampton Court, from which he fled to Carisbrooke Castle in November 1647. Many Englishmen, including many who fought against Charles, shrank from the prospect of executing him. They held the person of the king sacred and acknowledged him as the legal head of the state. But Charles kept dickering with the Scots and attempting to regain his lost power. Finally, a strong-minded group of men in the Parliamentary party, led by Cromwell, drove forcibly out of Parliament the members opposed to extreme measures, tried Charles for treason, condemned him, and executed him on the scaffold on January 30, 1649. In the next year, Cromwell crushed Ireland and, as Marvell predicted he would in the "Ode," speedily broke the Royalist forces in Scotland. As Lord Protector, Cromwell ruled England until his death in 1658. Today we would call him a "dictator," though he was in many ways a beneficent dictator, and though he attempted several times to find a parliamentary basis for his government. The year before his death he was offered the crown and refused it.

What was Marvell's attitude toward Cromwell in 1650? A few years later he was to write several poems full of eloquent praise of Cromwell, and he was to become the assistant of John Milton in his post as Latin Secretary to Cromwell. But two of Marvell's earlier poems (published in 1649) seem definitely pro-Royalist in sentiment, and the "Elegy upon the Death of Lord Villiers," which has been quite plausibly attributed to Marvell, is quite explicit in its Royalist bias. As H. M. Margoliouth puts it: "If [the 'Elegy on Villiers'] is Marvell's, it is his one unequivocal royalist utterance; it throws into strong relief the transitional character of *An Horatian*

Ode where royalist principles and admiration for Cromwell the Great Man exist side by side. . . ."[1]

The puzzle of Marvell's attitude becomes more complicated still if we take into account two more facts having to do with Marvell's life in the year after he wrote the "Ode." Sometime after November 1650 (the date of May's death), he wrote "Tom May's Death," in which he slurs at the Commander of the Parliamentary armies—either Essex or Fairfax is meant—as "Spartacus," and he lashes May as a partisan of the parliamentary party. Yet within a few months—Margoliouth suggests early in 1651—Marvell was actually living under Fairfax's roof, acting as tutor to his little daughter Mary.

The poem, "Tom May's Death," suggests a further complication. It is the curious fact that the "Horatian Ode" in which Marvell seems to affirm the ancient rights of the monarchy—

> Though Justice against Fate complain,
> And plead the ancient rights in vain—
> (lines 37–38)

is full of echoes of the poetry of Tom May, the poet whom Marvell was to denounce a few months later for having failed poetry in the hour of crisis:

> When the sword glitters o'er the judge's head,
> And fear the coward churchman silencèd,
> Then is the poet's time, 'tis then he draws,
> And single fights forsaken Virtue's cause.
> He, when the wheel of empire, whirleth back, 5
> And though the world's disjointed axle crack,
> Sings still of ancient rights and better times,
> Seeks wretched good, arraigns successful crimes.

The echoes of May's poetry, of course, may well have been unconscious: but it seems significant that they are from May's translation of Lucan's poem on the Roman civil wars.[2] One is tempted to suppose that in the year or so that followed the execution of Charles,

[1] *The Poems and Letters of Andrew Marvell,* Oxford: The Clarendon Press, 1927, 2 vols., I, 334.

[2] See Margoliouth, I, 237. In one short passage, May uses the phrases "restless valor," "forward sword," "lightning from a cloud breaks" (*cf.* lines 9, 1, 13–14 of Marvell's poem).

Marvell was obsessed with the problem of the poet's function in such a crisis; that the poet May was frequently in his mind through a double connection—(1) through the parallels between the English and the Roman civil wars, Lucan's poem on which May had translated, and (2) through May's conduct as a partisan of the Commonwealth; and that the "Horatian Ode" and "Tom May's Death," though so different in tone, are closely related and came out of the same general state of mind.

If Marvell censures May's attitude in this crisis of the English state, what is his own attitude? Marvell's biographer, Pierre Legouis, finds in the "Ode" a complete impartiality between the contestants and even an indifference as to forms of government. But Marvell, as we shall see, is far from indifferent.

Margoliouth, Marvell's editor, is much more specific and much nearer the point. He sums up as follows: "The ode is the utterance of a constitutional monarchist, whose sympathies have been with the King, but who yet believes more in men than in parties or principles, and whose hopes are fixed now on Cromwell, seeing in him both the civic ideal of a ruler without personal ambition, and the man of destiny moved by and yet himself driving a power which is above justice." But what sort of constitutional monarchist is it who "believes more in men than in . . . principles"? Or who can accept a "power which is above justice"? Margoliouth's statement raises as many problems as it solves. We have already referred to Margoliouth's description of the "Ode" as a poem "where royalist principles and admiration for Cromwell the Great Man exist side by side." The Royalist principles and admiration for Cromwell do exist side by side, but how are they related to each other? Do they exist in separate, contradictory layers; or are they somehow unified? Unified, in some sense, they must be if the "Ode" is a *poem* and not a heap of contradictory fragments.

With this last statement we raise the specific problem that we must try to solve: it is a problem of poetic organization, and it addresses itself properly to the critic. For important as the historical evidence is—and as concerned as we have been to assemble all the data that is relevant—this question is one that cannot be settled by historical evidence. We must try to read the poem as fully, as richly as possible. But if we do succeed in mastering the poem, we shall have the poem; and we *may* have gained some insight into the attitude of Marvell the man. For the poem was fashioned by him.

We may well begin our examination of the "Ode" by considering the ambiguity of the first compliments that the speaker pays to Cromwell. The ambiguity reveals itself as early as the second word of the poem. It is the "forward" youth whose attention the speaker directs to Cromwell's example. "Forward" may mean no more than "high-spirited," "ardent," "properly ambitious"; but the *Oxford Dictionary* sanctions the possibility that there lurks in the word the sense of "presumptuous," "pushing." The forward youth can no longer now "in the shadows sing / His numbers languishing." In the light of Cromwell's career, he must forsake the shadows and the Muses and become a man of action.

The speaker, one observes, does not identify Cromwell himself as the "forward youth," or say directly that Cromwell's career has been motivated by a striving for fame. But the implications of the first two stanzas do carry over to Cromwell. There is, for example, the important word "so" to relate Cromwell to these stanzas: "So restless Cromwell could not cease. . . ." And "restless" is as ambiguous in its meanings as "forward," and in its darker connotations even more damning. For, though "restless" can mean "scorning indolence," "willing to forego ease," it can also suggest the man with a maggot in the brain. "To cease," used intransitively, is "to take rest, to be or remain at rest," and the *Oxford Dictionary* gives instances as late as 1701. Cromwell's "courage high" will not allow him to rest "in the inglorious arts of peace."[1] And this thirst for glory, merely hinted at here by negatives, is developed further in the ninth stanza (lines 33–34). "Climb" certainly connotes a kind of aggressiveness. In saying this we need not be afraid that we are reading into the word some smack of such modern phrases as "social climber." Marvell's translation of the second chorus of

[1] For a very different treatment of the "inglorious arts of peace" see Marvell's "The Garden" (p. 354). It makes the comparison more interesting if one recalls that Marvell sees Cromwell as once pursuing such arts in "his private gardens" (line 29), and leaving them to "Win the palm, the oak, or bays" (line 2).

Seneca's *Thyestes* sufficiently attests that the work could have such associations for him:

> Climb, at Court, for me, that will,
> Tottering favor's pinnacle;
> All I seek is to lie still.

Cromwell, on the other hand, does not seek to lie still—has sought something quite other than this. His valor is called—strange collocation—an "industrious valor," and his courage is too high to brook a rival (lines 17–20). The implied metaphor is that of some explosive which does more violence to that which encloses it—the powder to its magazine, for instance—than to some wall which merely opposes it—against which the charge is fired.

But, as we have already remarked, the speaker has been careful to indicate that Cromwell's motivation must be conceived of as more complex than any mere thirst for glory. The poet has even pointed this up. The forward youth is referred to as one who "would appear"—that is, as one who wills to leave the shadows of obscurity. But restless Cromwell "could not cease"—for Cromwell it is not a question of will at all, but of a deeper compulsion. Restless Cromwell could not cease, if he would.

Indeed, the lines that follow extend the suggestion that Cromwell is like an elemental force—with as little will as the lightning bolt, and with as little conscience (lines 13–16). We are told that the last two lines refer to Cromwell's struggles after the Battle of Marston Moor with the leaders of the Parliamentary party. Doubtless they do, and the point is important for our knowledge of the poem. But what is more important is that we be fully alive to the force of the metaphor. The clouds have bred the lightning bolt, but the bolt tears its way through the clouds, and goes on to blast the head of Caesar himself. As Margoliouth puts it: "The lightning is conceived as tearing through the side of its own body the cloud." In terms of the metaphor, then, Cromwell has not spared his own body: there is no reason therefore to be surprised that he has not spared his own party or the body of Charles.

The treatment of Cromwell as a natural force is emphasized in the lines that follow (lines 21–26). A few lines later the point is reinforced with another naturalistic figure, an analogy taken from physics (lines 41–44). The question of right, the imagery insists, is beside the point. If nature will not tolerate a power vacuum, no more will it allow two bodies to occupy the same space.

What, by the way, are the implications for Charles? Does the poet mean to imply that Charles has angered heaven—that he has merited his destruction? There is no suggestion that Cromwell is a thunderbolt hurled by an angry Jehovah—or even by an angry Jove. The general emphasis on Cromwell as an elemental force is thoroughly relevant here to counter this possible misreading. Certainly, in the lines that follow, there is nothing to suggest that Charles has angered heaven, or that the Justice which complains against his fate is anything less than justice.

We began this examination of the imagery with the question: What is the speaker's attitude toward Cromwell? We have seen that the speaker more than once hints at his thirst for glory: "Restless Cromwell could not cease . . . ," "Could by industrious valor climb. . . ." But we have also seen that the imagery tends to view Cromwell as the product of historical necessity—as a kind of natural phenomenon like the bolt bred in the cloud. Is there a contradiction? No, for if the driving force has been a desire for glory, it is a glory of that kind which allows a man to become dedicated and, in a sense, even selfless in his pursuit of it. Moreover, the desire for such glory can become so much a compulsive force that the man does not appear to act by an exercise of his personal will but seems to become the will of some great force outside himself. There is in the poem at least one specific suggestion of this sort: "But through adventurous war / Urgèd his active star. . . ." Cromwell is the marked man, the man of destiny, but he is not merely the man governed by his star. Active though it be, he cannot remain passive, even in relation to it: he is not merely urged by it, but himself urges it on.

Yet if thus far Cromwell has been treated as naked force, something almost too awesome to be considered as a man, the poet does not forget that after all he is a man too—that "the force of angry Heaven's flame" is embodied in a human being: "And, if we would speak true, / Much to the man is due." The stanzas that follow proceed to define and praise that manliness—the strength, the industrious valor, the cunning. (The student must guard against taking the lines to mean "After all, Cromwell has accomplished much that is good." Such an interpretation could sort well enough with the view that sees Marvell as the cool and detached honest broker between the factions: unfortunately it will not survive a close scrutiny of the grammar and of the general context in which the passage is placed.)

One notices that among the virtues comprising Cromwell's manliness, the speaker mentions his possession of the "wiser art" of cunning and intrigue (lines 49–52). On this point Cromwell has been cleared by modern historians. Charles's flight to Carisbrooke Castle, as it turned out, aided Cromwell; but Cromwell could hardly have known that it would; and there is no evidence that he cunningly induced the king to flee to Carisbrooke. Royalist pamphleteers, of course, believed that Cromwell did, and used the item in their general bill of damnation against Cromwell. How does the speaker use it here—to damn or to praise? We tend to answer "to praise." But then it behooves us to notice what is being praised. The things praised are Cromwell's talents as such—the tremendous disciplined powers which Cromwell brought to bear against the king.

For the end served by those powers, the speaker has no praise at all. Rather he has gone out of his way to insist that Cromwell was deaf to the complaint of Justice and its pleading of the "ancient rights." The power achieved by Cromwell is a "forcèd power"—a usurped power. On this point the speaker is unequivocal. One must question therefore Margoliouth's statement that Marvell sees in Cromwell "the man of destiny moved by . . . a power that is above justice." Above justice, yes, in the sense that power can enforce decisions that are unjust. Charles has no way to vindicate his "helpless right"; but it is no less right because it is helpless. But the speaker, though he is not a cynic, is a realist. A kingdom cannot be held by mere pleading of the "ancient rights": "For those do hold or break / As men are strong or weak."

In short, the more closely we look at the "Ode," the more clearly apparent it becomes that the speaker has chosen to emphasize Cromwell's virtues as a man, and likewise, those of Charles as a man. The poem does not debate which of the two was right, for that issue is here not even in question. In his treatment of Charles, then, the speaker no more than Charles himself attempts to vindicate his "helpless right." Instead, he emphasizes his dignity, his fortitude, and what has finally to be called his consummate good taste. The portraits of the two men beautifully supplement each other. Cromwell is—to use Aristotle's distinction—the man of character, the man of action, who "does both act and know." Charles, on the other hand, is the man of passion, the man who is acted upon, the man who knows how to suffer. The contrast is pointed up in half a dozen ways.

Cromwell, acted upon by his star, is not passive but actually urges his star. Charles in "acting"—in chasing away to Carisbrooke—actually is passive—performs the part assigned to him by Cromwell. (True, we can read "chase" as an intransitive verb—the *Oxford Dictionary* sanctions this use for the period: "that Charles himself might hurry to Carisbrooke." But the primary meaning asserts itself in the context: "that Charles might chase himself to Carisbrooke's narrow case." For this hunter, now preparing to "lay his hounds in near / The *Caledonian* deer," the royal quarry has dutifully chased itself.)

Even in the celebrated stanzas on the execution, there is ironic realism as well as admiration. In this fullest presentation of Charles as king, he is the player king, the king acting in a play. He is the "royal actor" who knows his assigned part and performs it with dignity. He truly adorned the scaffold like a stage "While round the armèd bands / Did clap their bloody hands." The soldiers are said to have clapped in order to drown out the king's speech from the scaffold, but Marvell, drawing the incident into his theater metaphor, interprets the clapping as applause. Did Charles's enemies applaud Cromwell's resolution in bringing the king to a deserved death? Or did they applaud Charles's resolution on the scaffold as he suffered that death? Marvell does not resolve the ambiguity. It is enough that he makes the armed bands applaud.

With line 65, what may be regarded as the second part of the "Ode" begins. Cromwell is now the *de facto* head of the state, and the speaker, as a realist, recognizes that fact. Cromwell is seen henceforth, not primarily in his character as the destroyer of the monarchy, but as the agent of the new state that has been erected upon the dead body of the king. The thunderbolt simile of the first part of the poem gives way here to the falcon simile in this second part of the poem. The latter figure revises and qualifies the former: it repeats the suggestion of ruthless energy and power, but Cromwell falls from the sky now, not as the thunderbolt, but as the hunting hawk. The trained falcon is not a wanton destroyer, nor an irresponsible one. It knows its master: it is perfectly disciplined (lines 93–94).

The speaker's admiration for Cromwell the man culminates here. Cromwell might make Fame his own; he *need* not present kingdoms to the state. He might assume the crown rather than "crowning" each year. Yet he forbears: "Nor yet grown stiffer with command, / But still in the *Republic's* hand. . . ." Does the emphasis on "still" mean that the speaker is surprised that Cromwell has continued to pay homage to the republic? Does he imply that Cromwell may not always do so? Perhaps not: the emphasis is upon the fact that he need not obey and yet does obey. Yet the compliment derives its full force from the fact that the homage is not forced, but voluntary and even unexpected.

And now what of the republic which Cromwell so ruthlessly and efficiently serves? What is the speaker's attitude toward it? To begin with, the speaker recognizes that its foundations rest upon the bleeding head of Charles. The speaker is aware, it is true, of the Roman analogy, and the English state is allowed the benefit of that analogy. But it is well to notice that the speaker does not commit himself to the opinion that the bleeding head is a happy augury (lines 71–72). The Roman state was able to take it as a favorable omen, and was justified by the event. But here it seems more to the point to notice what prophecy the speaker is willing to commit himself to. He does not prophesy peace. He is willing to predict that England, under Cromwell's leadership, will be powerful in war, and will strike fear into the surrounding states (lines 97–100). Specifically, he predicts a smashing victory over the Scots.

But what of the compliments to Cromwell on his ruthlessly effective campaign against the Irish? Does not the speaker succumb, for once, to a bitter and biased patriotism, and does this not constitute a blemish upon the poem? (See lines 73–80.) Margoliouth glosses the word "confessed" as follows: "Irish testimony in favour of Cromwell at this moment is highly improbable. Possibly there is a reference to the voluntary submission of part of Munster with its English colony." But the most intense partisan of Cromwell would have had some difficulty in taking the lines without some undertone of grim irony. The final appeal in this matter, however, is not to what Marvell the Englishman must have thought, or even to what Marvell the author must have intended, but rather to the full context of the poem itself. In that context, the lines in question can be read ironically, and the earlier stanzas sanction that reading. Cromwell's energy, activity, bravery, resolution—even what may be called his "efficiency"—are the qualities that have come in for praise, not his gentleness or his mercy.

The Irish, indeed, are best able to affirm such praise as has been accorded to Cromwell; and they know from experience "how good he is, how just," for they have been blasted by the force of angry Heaven's flame, even as Charles has been. But it is not necessary to turn the passage into sarcasm. The third quality which the speaker couples with goodness and justice is fitness for "highest trust," and the goodness and justice of Cromwell culminate in this fitness. But the recommendation to trust is not to the Irish, but to the English state. The Irish are quite proper authorities on Cromwell's trustworthiness in this regard, for they have come to know him as the completely dedicated instrument of the English state.

To say all this is not to suggest that Marvell shed any unnecessary tears over the plight of the Irish, or even to imply that he was not happy, as one assumes most Englishmen were, to have the Irish rebellion crushed promptly and efficiently. It is to say that the passage fits into the poem—a poem which reveals itself to be no panegyric on Cromwell but an unflinching analysis of the Cromwellian character.

The wild Irish have been tamed, and now the Pict will no longer be able to shelter under his particolored mind. It is the hour of decision, and the particolored mind affords no protection against the man who "does both act and know." In Cromwell's mind there are no conflicts, no teasing mixture of judgments. Cromwell's is not only an "industrious valor," but a "sad" valor. Margoliouth glosses "sad" as "steadfast," and no doubt he is right. But sad can mean "sober" also, and there may be, in this context, an implied reference to Scottish plaids, for "sad" means also "drab of hue."

Thus far the speaker has been content to view Cromwell from a distance, as it were, against the background of recent history. He has referred to him consistently in the third person. But in the last two stanzas, he addresses Cromwell directly. He salutes him as "The War's and Fortune's son." It is a great compliment: Cromwell is the son of the war in that he is the master of battles, and he seems fortune's own son in the success that has constantly waited upon him. But we do not wrench the lines if we take them to say also that Cromwell is the creature of the war and the product of fortune. The imagery of the early stanzas which treats Cromwell as a natural phenomenon certainly supports this reading. Cromwell can claim no sanction for his power in "ancient rights." His power has come out of the wars and the troubled times. Note that we do not have to choose between readings: the readings do not mutually exclude each other: they support each other, and this double interpretation has the whole poem behind it.

Cromwell is urged to march "indefatigably on." The advice is good advice; but it partakes of quiet commentary as much as of exhortation. If "restless" Cromwell could not cease "in the inglorious arts of peace" when his "highest plot" was "To plant the bergamot," one cannot conceive of his ceasing now in the hour of danger. The speaker goes on to say: "And for the last effect / Still keep thy sword erect." Once more the advice carries with it as much of warning as it does of approval. Those who take up the sword shall perish by the sword: those who by the sword have achieved their power in contravention of ancient rights can expect to maintain their power only by the sword.

What kind of sword is it that is able to "fright / The spirits of the shady night"? Margoliouth writes: "The cross hilt of the sword would avert the spirits. . . ." But the speaker has made it quite plain that it is not merely the spirits of the shady night that Cromwell will have to fright as he marches indefatigably on. It will not be enough to hold the sword aloft as a ritual sword, an emblematic sword. The naked steel will still have to be used against bodies less diaphanous than spirits. If there is any doubt as to this point, Marvell's concluding lines put the matter as explicitly as it can be put: "The same arts that did gain / A power must it maintain."

What, then, is the final attitude toward Cromwell? Is it ultimately one of approval or disapproval? Does admiration overbalance condemnation? Or is the "Ode," after all, merely a varied Scottish plaid, the reflection of Marvell's own particolored mind—a mind which had not been finally "made up" with regard to Cromwell? Enough has been said to make it plain that there is no easy, pat answer to such questions. There is a unified total attitude, but it is so complex that we may oversimplify and distort its complexity by the way in which we ask the question. For a really full answer, of course, one must refer the questioner to the poem itself; but one can at least try to suggest some aspects of the total attitude.

We might begin by re-emphasizing the dramatic character of the poem. It is not a statement—an essay on "Why I cannot support Cromwell" or on "Why I now am ready to support Cromwell." It is a poem, essentially dramatic in its presentation, which means that it is diagnostic rather than remedial, and eventuates, not in a course of action, but in contemplation. Perhaps the best way therefore in which to approach it is to conceive of it as, say, one conceives of a Shakespearian tragedy. Cromwell is the usurper who demands and commands admiration. What, for example, is our attitude toward Macbeth? We assume his guilt, but there are qualities which emerge from his guilt which properly excite admiration. The point is not that the qualities palliate his guilt or that they compensate for his guilt. They actually come into being through his guilt, but they force us to exalt him even as we condemn him.

We do not mean to imply that in writing the "Ode" Marvell had Shakespeare's tragedy in mind. Not at all, but the kinds of honesty and insight and whole-mindedness which we associate with tragedy are to be found to some degree in all great poetry and they are to be found in this poem. Moreover, though Marvell does not have Shakespeare's tragedy in mind, it is obvious that he is thoroughly conscious of the drama, and in this poem consciously makes use of dramatic perspective. Charles, as we have seen, becomes the "royal actor," playing his part on the "tragic scaffold." But the tragedy of Charles is merely glanced at. The poem is Cromwell's—Cromwell's tragedy, the first three acts of it, as it were, which is not a tragedy of failure but of success.

Cromwell is the truly kingly man who is not king—whose very virtues conduce to kingly power and seem to force kingly power upon him. It is not any fumbling on the poet's part which causes him, before the poem ends, to call Cromwell "a Caesar," even though he has earlier appropriated that name to Charles. *Both* men are Caesar, Charles the wearer of the purple, and Cromwell the invincible general, the inveterate campaigner, the man "That does both act and know." Cromwell is the Caesar who must refuse the crown—whose glory it is that he is willing to refuse the crown—but who cannot enjoy the reward and the security that a crown affords. The tension between the speaker's admiration for the kingliness that has won Cromwell his power and his awareness that such power can be maintained only by a continual exertion of these kingly powers—this tension is never relaxed. Cromwell is not of royal blood—he boasts a higher and a baser pedigree: he is the "War's and Fortune's son." He cannot rest because he is restless Cromwell. He must march indefatigably on, for he cannot afford to become fatigued. These implications enrich and qualify an insight into Cromwell which is as heavily freighted with admiration as it is with a great condemnation. But the admiration and the condemnation do not cancel each other out. They define each other; and because there is responsible definition, they reinforce each other.

Was this, then, the attitude of Andrew Marvell, born 1621, sometime student of Cambridge, returned traveler and prospective tutor, toward Oliver Cromwell in the summer of 1650? The honest answer must be: we do not know. We have tried to read the poem, not Andrew Marvell's mind. That seems sensible in view of the fact that we have the poem, whereas the attitude held by Marvell at any particular time must be a matter of inference, even though we grant that the poem may be put in as part of the evidence from which we are to draw inferences. True, we do know that Marvell was capable of composing the "Ode" and one must concede that that very fact *may* tell us a great deal about Marvell's attitude toward Cromwell. We think it probably does. But we shall not claim that it tells us everything: there is the problem of the rôle of the unconscious in the process of composition, there is the possibility of the poet's having written better than he knew, there is even the matter of the happy accident. It is wise to maintain the distinction between the total attitude as manifested in the poem and the attitude of the author as man and private citizen. Yet the total attitude realized in the "Ode" does not have to be regarded as monstrously inhuman in its complexity. It could be held by human beings. Something very like it apparently was held. Here, for example, is the Earl of Clarendon's judgment on Cromwell:

He was one of those men, quos vituperare ne inimici quidem possunt, nisi ut simul laudent [whom not even their enemies can inveigh against without at the same time praising them], for he could never have done halfe that mischieve, without great partes of courage and industry and judgement, and he must have had a wounderful understandinge in the natures and humours of men, and as greate a dexterity in the applyinge them, who from a private and obscure birth, (though of a good family) without interest of estate, allyance or frendshipps, could rayse himselfe to such a height, and compounde and kneade such opposite and contradictory humour and interests, into a consistence, that contributed to his designes and to ther owne distruction, whilst himselfe grew insensibly powerfull enough, to cutt off those by whome he had climed, in the instant, that they projected to demolish ther owne buildinge. . . . In a worde, as he had all the wickednesses against which damnation is denounced and for which Hell frye is prepared, so he had some virtues, which have caused the memory of some men in all ages to be celebrated, and he will be looked upon by posterity, as a brave badd man.

The resemblance between the judgment of Clarendon, who lived at this time, and that reflected in the "Ode" is so remarkable that one wonders whether Clarendon had not seen and been impressed by some now lost MS. of the "Ode." Compare "who from a private and obscure birth"—"Who from his private gardens, where / He lived reservèd and austere"; "could rayse himselfe to such a height . . . by whome he had climed"—"Could by industrious valor climb," etc. But we do not mean to suggest that Clarendon was influenced by Marvell's "Ode." Our point in quoting from Clarendon is rather to show that the attitude of the "Ode" is not inhuman in its Olympian detachment, that something like it could be held by a human being, and by a human being of pronounced Royalist sympathies.[1]

[1] That Marvell in 1650 was Royalist in sympathy is suggested by two bits of evidence turned up recently by one of the editors. Robert Wild evidently is borrowing two lines from the "Ode" ("But with his keener eye / The ax's

EXERCISE (AND TOPICS FOR PAPERS):

1. Attempt to define Corbet's attitude toward the Reformation in England as indicated in his poem "The Fairies' Farewell" (p. 250). Find out what you can about the Reformation—its causes and its consequences. Remember that Corbet was later to become a bishop in the Church of England. Is his attitude as reflected in the poem consonant with the attitude you would expect an Anglican bishop to hold?

2. What historical and biographical events shed light upon "Lycidas" (p. 465)? Does a knowledge of literary history (particularly of the conventions of the pastoral elegy) contribute to your appreciation of this poem? Which kind of knowledge is the more important in appreciating this poem?

3. How much knowledge of the American Civil War is required for full appreciation of "The March into Virginia" (p. 445)? "Lee in the Mountains" (p. 501)? What do these poems contribute, if anything, to your insights into this period of American history?

4. Other poems which may profitably be investigated with relation to biography and history are:

(a) "On the Late Massacre in Piedmont" (p. 143).

(b) "Frescoes for Mr. Rockefeller's City" (p. 447).

(c) "Twelfth Night" (p. 521).

edge did try") in his poem on "The Death of Mr. Christopher Love," which includes the line "His keener words did their sharp ax exceed." Love was beheaded by Cromwell on August 22, 1651, and the poem would seem to have been composed shortly after the execution. Wild was definitely Royalist in sympathies.

Marvell did not invent the stanza form of his "Ode," as has been supposed, but apparently borrowed it from Sir Richard Fanshawe. Fanshawe uses the stanza several times in translating Horace's Odes in his *Selected Parts of Horace . . . Now newly put into English,* London, 1652. Mr. William Simeone, of the University of Pennsylvania, has found a MS. copy of one of these translations dated as early as 1625. The borrowing was probably made by Marvell from Fanshawe, not the reverse. Like Wild, Fanshawe was an ardent Royalist. Marvell was evidently associating with the Royalist party and perhaps his "Ode" was circulating among Royalist sympathizers soon after its composition.

GLOSSARY

Abstract: General statements, or purely theoretical statements, are called abstract. (The word is derived from the Latin *abstractus,* which means literally "drawn away from": thus an abstraction is a quality or idea considered apart from the thing or situation in which it inheres. *Sweetness, whiteness, roughness* are abstract, but *sugar* is concrete: *concrete* is derived from the Latin *concretus* which means "grown together.") The fundamental method of literature is to present a subject concretely—not abstractly. It depends, therefore, rather heavily upon implication rather than upon explicit statement. For instance, a novel or a play tells a particular story of particular people and does not merely give general comments on human nature. It presents individual human beings and presents them in action (p. 12). Poetry, even more than other literary forms, makes use of particular images and incidents for presenting its ideas (pp. 16–17).

Accent: See "Note on Versification and Metrics," p. 696.

Alexandrine: A line consisting of six feet. See "Note on Versification and Metrics," p. 696.

Allegory: See **Imagery.**

Alliteration: See "Note on Versification and Metrics," p. 696.

Allusion: A reference to some event, person, or place of literary or historical significance. For example, Keats in his "Ode to a Nightingale" alludes to Bacchus, to Provence, to an incident related in the Book of Ruth in the Bible, etc.

Ambiguity: Multiplicity of meaning. In expository prose, ambiguity is a defect, for what is wanted is one clear, unequivocal meaning. An ambiguous statement is one which is doubtful or obscure. A better term for poetic ambiguity is *richness.* See pp. 573–74.

Anapaest: A metrical foot consisting of two unaccented syllables followed by an accented syllable. See "Note on Versification and Metrics," p. 696.

Anticlimactic: Characterized by a flatness and falling off in intensity. See **Climax.**

Archaic Diction: See **Diction.**

Assonance: See "Note on Versification and Metrics," p. 696.

Atmosphere: This term is obviously a metaphor in itself. It refers to the general pervasive feeling which may be said to condition the treatment of the subject of any literary work. It is a mistake to connect atmosphere exclusively with the setting or background, even though the setting usually does contribute heavily to the establishing of the atmosphere of a particular piece. Rhythm and imagery, for instance, may also contribute to the establishing of the atmosphere (pp. 11, 19, 174, 176, 197–200).

Attitude: The author's way of regarding his materials, especially as it reflects his understanding and interpretation of them. See the Foreword to Section IV, pp. 157–58.

Ballad: (1) Folk ballad (pp. 6–7). (2) literary ballad (pp. 6, 54).

Ballad Stanza: See "Note on Versification and Metrics," p. 696.

Blank Verse: See "Note on Versification and Metrics," p. 696.

Cacophony: Harshness or dissonance. See "Note on Versification and Metrics," p. 696.

Caesura: The main pause within a line of verse. See p. 132 and "Note on Versification and Metrics," p. 696.

Cliché: This term is really a metaphor, for in French a *cliché* is a stereotype plate. It is applied to any expression which has lost all freshness and vitality because of continued use—that is, an expression which has become trite (pp. 182, 208, 299, 661–62). "Strong as an ox," "last but not least," "the cradle of the deep" are typical clichés.

Climax (Climactic): The peak of interest or intensity (p. 45).

Closed Couplet: See "Note on Versification and Metrics," p. 696.

Compensation: See "Note on Versification and Metrics," p. 696.

Concentration: An effect of compactness and intensity. In addition to what has already been said on this topic (p. 71), it may be pointed out that the concentration characteristic of poetry is a result of its highly organized form. This concentration does not depend on logical succinctness. Rather, it depends on the functional relationships existing among a number of complex factors—rhythm, imagery, theme, etc. See also pp. 573–74.

Concrete: See **Abstract.**

Connotation: See **Denotation.**

Consonance: See "Note on Versification and Metrics," p. 696.

Conventional: See **Conventions, Form.**

Conventions: Techniques and modes of treatment that are accepted by common agreement. For example, there are the conventions of the *pastoral* (which see) or the conventions that govern verse. But though conventions are necessary, the term *conventional* is frequently used in an adverse sense to indicate a merely dead and mechanical reliance upon past models. See **Form** and p. 593.

Couplet: Two consecutive lines of verse riming together. See "Note on Versification and Metrics," p. 696.

Dactyl: A metrical foot consisting of an accented syllable followed by two unaccented syllables. See "Note on Versification and Metrics," p. 696.

Denotation: The denotation of a word is its specific signification. For instance, the denotation of the word *hound* is "one of a class of carnivorous mammals (*Canis familiaris*) of the family *Canidae,* etc." But the word also has a large number of **Connotations,** or implied meanings and associations. The connotations of a word may vary considerably from person to person and from context to context. For instance, in the discussion of the poem "The Three Ravens" (p. 45), it is pointed out that the hounds symbolize fidelity. That is, certain connotations of the word *hound* are emphasized in the poem. But the word also has other connotations which, in another context, might appear. For instance, the word *hound* can be used as an insult. (For another discussion of connotation, see p. 88.)

Diction: Diction is simply the choice of words in poetry or in any other form of discourse. Critics sometimes refer to **Poetic Diction** as if certain words were especially poetic without regard to context. But the choice of words in any given poem must be determined by the needs of that specific case in terms of the whole context (pp. xlix–liv). The term **Archaic Diction** is used to indicate the use of words which are no longer current. For example, some of the words which Coleridge used in "The Rime of the Ancient Mariner" (p. 527) were no longer current in his day.

Dimeter: A line consisting of two feet. See "Note on Versification and Metrics," p. 696.

Double Rime: See "Note on Versification and Metrics," p. 696.

Dramatic: In earlier discussions frequent reference has been made to the means by which a poet may dramatize his theme. This term is, of course, metaphorical. It must not be taken to mean that a given poem represents in any detail the structure and circumstance of a play except in the sense which has been discussed (pp. liv–lv). But the fact that a drama presents its materials concretely and through action justifies the use of the term, for poetry tends to present its themes in the same manner, not abstractly. See **Abstract.**

Elegy: The term is used loosely for any poem of subjective and meditative nature, but more specially for a poem of grief, such as "Lycidas" (p. 465).

End-stopped Lines: See "Note on Versification and Metrics," p. 696.

Enjambment: See **Run-on** under "Note on Versification and Metrics," p. 696.

Epic: An epic is a long narrative poem dealing with persons of heroic proportions and actions of great significance. The general type includes poems as different as Homer's *Iliad,* Spenser's *Faerie Queene,* and Milton's *Paradise Lost.* The *Mock Epic,* or the *Mock Heroic* poem, adopts for ironical or comic purposes the manner of the true epic. It presents trivial materials in a grandiose style. See Pope's *Rape of the Lock,* p. 223.

Euphony: Agreeableness of sound. See "Note on Versification and Metrics," p. 696.

Exposition: The process of giving the information necessary for the understanding of an action (p. 10).

Feminine Ending: See "Note on Versification and Metrics," p. 696.

Feminine Rime: See "Note on Versification and Metrics," p. 696.

Figurative Language: See **Imagery.**

Focus: This term is metaphorical. Just as a burning glass concentrates and unifies the rays of the sun, so a poet may, by various means, concentrate and unify various elements of a poem. This concentration may be accomplished in many different ways. For instance, the farewell spoken by the youngest brother in "The Wife of Usher's Well" may be said to provide a focus for the poem (pp. 18–19). Or the image developed in the last two stanzas of "The Scholar Gipsy" may be said to serve the same purpose (pp. 418–19).

Foot: See "Note on Versification and Metrics," p. 696.

Form: This term is used in various senses. Usually when people use the term they mean **Metrical Form** or **Stanza Form** (see "Note on Versification and Metrics," p. 696, and also p. 142). But since metrical form, or stanza form, describes an organization of the rhythm of a poem, and since rhythm is only one element contributing to the poetic effect, it is obvious that the consideration of the form of a poem must, finally, involve the discussion of the organization of other elements in relation to the total effect. In "Lord Randal," for example, both the sequence of questions and answers and the use of refrain build toward the effect in the last stanza (p. 49). In the same way, the use of imagery contributes to the forming of a poem. For example, one may consider the functional interrelations among the images in "The Definition of Love" (pp. 294–97) or in "After Great Pain" (pp. 325–27). In brief, the form of a poem is the organization of the material (rhythm, imagery, idea, etc.) for the creation of the total effect. Though the poet must finally work out a form for each particular poem, this does not mean that he may not make use of elements of form handed down from other poets—elements such as metrical patterns, symbols, and ways of relating images to a theme, etc. Such elements, when their use has become fixed and recognized, are called **Conventions.** For instance, the sonnet in respect to its stanza pattern is a conventional form; or the pastoral elegy, such as "Lycidas," is a conventional form in regard to the "fictions" and symbols it employs in treating the subject of bereavement. A poet may properly make use of conventional patterns of all sorts, but, in so far as he is successful, he must relate the conventional elements to the total form of the individual poem. In this connection one might compare the use made of pastoral conventions in Milton's "Lycidas" (p. 465) and in Crashaw's "In the Holy Nativity" (p. 309). But the term *conventional* is sometimes used in an adverse sense to indicate that the poet has merely imitated his models and has failed to adapt the conventional elements to the general form of the individual poem (pp. 182, 208).

Free Verse: See "Note on Versification and Metrics," p. 696.

Heptameter: A line consisting of seven feet. See "Note on Versification and Metrics," p. 696.

Heroic Couplet: Two consecutive lines of iambic pentameter riming together. See "Note on Versification and Metrics," p. 696.

Hexameter: A line consisting of six feet. See "Note on Versification and Metrics," p. 696.

Hovering Accent: See "Note on Versification and Metrics," p. 696.

Iamb: A metrical foot consisting of an unaccented syllable followed by an accented syllable. See "Note on Versification and Metrics," p. 696.

Imagery: The representation in poetry of any sense experience is called imagery. Imagery does not consist merely of "mental pictures," but may make an appeal to any of the senses. Poetry characteristically appeals continually to the senses; this is another way of saying that poetry is concrete. But frequently the poet does not use imagery merely in an obviously descriptive fashion; the poet characteristically makes his statements and conveys his ideas through comparisons, that is, through what is called **Figurative Language.** The most common types of figurative language are **Simile** and **Metaphor.** The first is usually defined as a stated comparison (generally announced by *like* or *as*); the second as an implied comparison (in which the two things compared are identified with each other). The following comparison is a simile:

> This city now doth like a garment wear
> The beauty of the morning. . . .

The following comparison is a metaphor:

> So the soul, that drop, that ray
> Of the clear fountain of eternal day. . . .

As for the functions of imagery, it has been pointed out (pp. xlviii–xlix) that imagery is important, not as decoration, but for the presentation of essential meaning. The particular ways in which imagery functions are too numerous to be dealt with summarily here; indeed, every poem involves imagery in some respect, and in this book two sections (Section II and Section V) have been devoted to studying a number of special instances. Even in so brief a statement as this, however, one fact should be insisted upon: *The function of imagery in poetry is never, as is sometimes said, that of mere illustration.* Closely related to the metaphorical process is the process by which a poet creates or makes use of a **Symbol.** The symbol may be regarded as a metaphor from which the first term has been omitted. For example,

> Queen rose of the rosebud garden of girls

is a metaphor, but if the poet simply refers to the rose in order to suggest the qualities of love which he is treating, and does not indicate the metaphorical framework, he has turned the rose into a symbol. To take another example, the poet in "Patterns" does not say, "Life is a cruel pattern," but deals successively with various sorts of patterns—those of the woman's dress, of the beds of flowers and formal walks in the garden, of social codes and manners—so that the theme may be stated dramatically in terms of a symbol at the end of the poem:

> Christ! what are patterns for?

We use the term *metaphor* when we are emphasizing the metaphorical transfer: for example, the girl is a rose—that is, the qualities of the rose are transferred to the girl. We use the term *symbol* when we are thinking of the object or action as standing for something else: for example, the pattern becomes a symbol of the woman's life. Symbols, then, are "signs" pointing to meanings. Certain symbols are conventional, that is, arbitrary, and we agree upon what they are to signify. For instance, the cross is by convention a symbol of the Christian religion and the flag is the symbol of a nation. The important use of symbol which the poet makes, however, is not a conventional one: he must frequently create his own symbols (pp. li–lii, 578–80). The poems toward the end of Section II will indicate instances of objects which have been given symbolic force. More specialized instances appear later in the book (Section V and Section VI). The student should also consult the general discussion of metaphor and symbol in Section VIII, pp. 580–88.

Allegory, also, is a development of the metaphorical process. Allegory is often defined as an extended metaphor, and, in regard to the matter of structure, this is an adequate description, for an allegory, strictly speaking, is a narrative in which the objects and persons are equated with meanings lying outside the narrative itself. For example, *The Pilgrim's Progress* is on the surface the story of the journey which one of the characters, Christian, makes from his home to the Heavenly City; but, as the name implies, Christian really stands for any Christian man, and the various adventures which befall him stand for the perils and temptation which beset any Christian man in his progress through life. But most allegories are much less obvious than this. Allegory is bad when the system of equivalents used seems to be mechanical and arbitrary, or when it seems to be confused (pp. 299–302).

Allegorical personages are frequently **Personifications,** that is, abstract qualities treated in the narrative as though they were real persons. For instance, the Giant Despair in *The Pilgrim's Progress* is a personification. But the device of personification is not confined to formal allegory. "An Elegy Written in a Country Churchyard" (p. 375) is not an allegory, yet in such a line as the following it employs personification:

Let not Ambition mock their useful toil. . . .

Imagist: A group of poets in England and America who, about 1912, attempted to re-emphasize certain qualities of poetry which they felt had been ignored in the work of their immediate predecessors. Their manifesto reads as follows:

1. To use the language of common speech, but to employ always the *exact* word, not the merely decorative word.

2. To create new rhythms—as the expression of new moods. We do not insist upon "free-verse" as the only method of writing poetry. . . .

We do believe that the individuality of a poet may often be better expressed in free verse than in conventional forms.

3. To allow absolute freedom in the choice of subject.

4. To present an image (hence the name *Imagist*). We are not a school of painters, but we believe that poetry should render particulars exactly, and not deal in vague generalities, however magnificent and sonorous.

5. To produce poetry that is hard and clear, never blurred or indefinite.

6. Finally, most of us believe that concentration is the very essence of poetry.

To sum up, one may say that the Imagists revolted against the tendency toward vague abstractions and preachments in much of nineteenth-century poetry (see p. 78).

Indirect Method: See pp. 571–74 and **Irony.**

Intensity: It has been said previously (p. 71) that intensity is a result of the highly organized form of poetry. This implies, not simply a loose emotionalism or a preoccupation with thrilling subject matter (pp. xlvi–xlvii, 174–76), but a meaningful relationship among all the factors involved in a poem.

Internal Rime: Rime occurring within a line unit. See "Note on Versification and Metrics," p. 696.

Interpretation: See pp. xxxvii–xxxviii, 11–13, 74–76, 78–79, 571–74.

Irony: An ironical statement indicates a meaning contrary to the one it professes to give; an ironical event or situation is one in which there is a contrast between expectation and fulfilment or desert and reward. In the irony of both statement and event there is an element of contrast. Either form of irony, or both, may appear in a poem. For instance, the irony of situation appears in "Johnie Armstrong" (p. 11). But the irony of statement, and of tone and attitude, are more important for poetry. The successful management of ironical effects is one of the most difficult problems of a poet. In actual speech, gesture, tone of voice, and expression all serve to indicate an ironical intention, but poetry must indicate an ironical interpretation in other ways (p. 157).

There are many shades of irony and many functions which irony may perform. Certainly, the term is not to be limited to an obvious and heavy sarcasm. For instance, one may observe the different uses of irony in "Portrait" (pp. 158–60), "Channel Firing" (pp. 164–66), "A Litany" (pp. 206–10), "The Blossom" (pp. 248–50), "Ode to a Nightingale" (pp. 340–45), and "The Love Song of J. Alfred Prufrock" (pp. 433–44). See also pp. 586–88.

Obviously, irony, along with **Understatement** (in which there is a discrepancy, great or small, between what is *actually* said and what *might* be said), is a device of **Indirect Method.** (See pp. 571–74.) That is, the poet does not present his meaning abstractly and explicitly, but depends on the reader's capacity to develop implications imaginatively.

Italian Sonnet: See "Note on Versification and Metrics," p. 696.

Lyric: Originally a poem to be sung, but now much more loosely applied to any short poem of which the verse seems to be especially musical, for instance, "All But Blind" (p. 84). In a more special sense, the term is applied to poems having a marked subjective element, for instance, "Tears, Idle Tears," by Tennyson (p. 351), "In Tenebris, I," by Hardy (p. 153), or "Rose Alymer," by Landor (p. 144).

Masculine Ending: See "Note on Versification and Metrics," p. 696.

Masculine Rime: See "Note on Versification and Metrics," p. 696.

Metaphor: See **Imagery.**

Meter: See "Note on Versification and Metrics," p. 696.

Mock Epic: See **Epic.**

Mock Heroic: See **Epic.**

Monometer: A line consisting of one foot. See "Note on Versification and Metrics," p. 696.

Objective: See **Subjective.**

Octave: See "Note on Versification and Metrics," p. 696.

Ode: A rather extended poem, usually complicated in metrical and stanzaic form, dealing with a serious theme. Examples are: Shelley's "Ode to the West Wind" (p. 98), Keats's "Ode to a Nightingale" (p. 336), and Wordsworth's "Ode on Intimations of Immortality" (p. 547).

Onomatopoeia: See "Note on Versification and Metrics," p. 696.

Ottava Rima: See "Note on Versification and Metrics," p. 696.

Paradox: A statement which seems on the surface contradictory, but which involves an element of truth. Since there is an element of contrast between the form of the statement and its real implications, paradox is closely related to **Irony** (pp. 267–69, 294–97).

Pastoral: A term loosely used in application to any sympathetic literary treatment of simple rural life. In this sense, "Michael" (p. 23) is a pastoral poem. But more specially used, the term applies to a poetry which is based on the conventions descended from the classic poetry of shepherd life. The persons involved are presented as shepherds, although, as in

"Lycidas" (p. 465), they may be poets, scholars, and churchmen; and the subjects treated, such as ecclesiastical abuses (as in "Lycidas") may have no reference to rural life.

Pentameter: A line consisting of five feet. See "Note on Versification and Metrics," p. 696.

Personification: Representation of an idea or thing as a person. See **Imagery.**

Petrarchan: The Petrarchan conventions stem from the love sonnets of the Italian poet Petrarch. His sonnets represented his mistress as more than humanly beautiful, but cold and disdainful, and himself as completely abased before her. The imagery is frequently elaborate and far-fetched (pp. 208, 249–50, 593).

Poetic Diction: See **Diction.**

Quantitative Variation: See pp. 134–35, and "Note on Versification and Metrics," p. 696.

Quantity: See "Note on Versification and Metrics," p. 696.

Quatrain: A stanza consisting of four lines. See "Note on Versification and Metrics," p. 696.

Realistic: The term is used throughout this book with reference to the presentation of ordinary, easily observable details, which give an impression of fidelity to the facts of ordinary life (pp. 17, 36). It is to be contrasted with *romantic,* which implies the remote, the exotic, the uncontrolled, and the exaggerated. The special senses in which such terms as *realistic, romantic,* and *classic* are used by many critics do not appear in this book.

Rhetorical Variation: See pp. 129–31, and "Note on Versification and Metrics," p. 696.

Rhythmical Movement: A movement with recurrent beat or stress. See "Note on Versification and Metrics," p. 696.

Rime: See "Note on Versification and Metrics," p. 696.

Rime Royal: See "Note on Versification and Metrics," p. 696.

Rime Scheme: The pattern of rime occurring in a stanza. See "Note on Versification and Metrics," p. 696.

Romantic: See **Realistic.**

Run-on Line: See "Note on Versification and Metrics," p. 696.

Sentimentality: Emotional response in excess of the occasion; emotional response not prepared for nor justified by the poem in question (pp. 37, 146–47, 174–76, 181–83, 209–10, 294–97, 299–302).

Sestet: See "Note on Versification and Metrics," p. 696.

Shakespearian Sonnet: See "Note on Versification and Metrics," p. 696.

Simile: See **Imagery.**

Sincerity: This term is often used in two senses which are not clearly discriminated. The first sense refers to the poet's attitude, in his private life, toward a subject which he treats in a poem. This sense *may* have no reference to the critical judgment to be passed on a poem, for a poet may be thoroughly sincere in this personal sense and yet produce a very bad and sentimental piece of work (pp. 181–83, 185, 299). The second sense in which the term is used really refers to the degree of success which the poet has achieved in integrating the various elements of a poem. When one says that a poem is "sincere," one is actually saying, consciously or unconsciously, that it does not overreach itself, that it is not sentimental. Such a judgment is irrelevant to any biographical information concerning the poet.

Slant Rime: See "Note on Versification and Metrics," p. 696.

Sonnet: See "Note on Versification and Metrics," p. 696.

Spenserian Stanza: See "Note on Versification and Metrics," p. 696.

Spondee: See "Note on Versification and Metrics," p. 696.

Stanza: See "Note on Versification and Metrics," p. 696.

Stock Response: The general uncritical response made on conventional or habitual grounds to a situation, subject, phrase, or word. Advertisers frequently attempt to appeal to stock responses by arbitrarily associating a product with patriotism, mother love, etc. (pp. xl–xli). The good poet tries to provide in his work the grounds for the responses he seeks from his audience, but the bad poet, like the writer of advertising copy, merely appeals to the already established attitudes, however crude or general they may be (pp. 181–83, 198–99).

Stream of Consciousness: When a writer presents his material, not in the systematic order of narrative or logical argument, but in an apparently unorganized succession of items connected on grounds of association, he is said to employ the stream-of-consciousness method. In other words, he suggests the sequence of idea and image in the mind (pp. 433–34, 585–86, 659–60).

Structure: In its fullest sense the structure of a poem may be said to be synonymous with the form, but in practice there is a tendency to use the term with special reference to the arrangement of, and the relationships among, episodes, statements, scenes, and details of action, as contrasted with the arrangement of words, for which the term *style* is usually employed (p. 19).

Style: This term is usually used with reference to the poet's manner of choosing, ordering, and arranging his words. But when one asks on what grounds certain words are chosen and ordered, one is raising, of course, the whole problem of form. Style, in its larger sense, is essentially the same thing as form (see **Form** and **Structure**).

Subjective: The ordinary terms used to denote the person who perceives or experiences a thing and the thing perceived or experienced, are *subject* and *object*. Of course, there is a sense in which all poetry is subjective, that is, it represents the response of a person, the poet, to an object or to a body of objects (p. 75). But we shall use the term at another level: we shall apply it to the "speaker" in the poem and his manner of presentation, and here we shall find widely differing degrees of subjectivity. One may properly say, for example, that the "Ode to a Nightingale" (p. 336) or "The Love Song of J. Alfred Prufrock" (p. 429) is highly subjective, and that "The Main-Deep" (p. 73) or "Pear Tree" (p. 77) is objective.

Substitution: See "Note on Versification and Metrics," p. 696.

Symbol: See **Imagery.**

Terza Rima: See "Note on Versification and Metrics," p. 696.

Tetrameter: A line consisting of four feet. See "Note on Versification and Metrics," p. 696.

Thematic Development: The structure of a poem as related to the presentation of the theme.

Theme: The basic idea or attitude which is presented in a poem (pp. 12, 47, 157, 363–64, 571–74).

Tone: See Foreword (pp. 157–58) and pp. 586–87.

Trimeter: A line consisting of three feet. See "Note on Versification and Metrics," p. 696.

Triple Rime: See "Note on Versification and Metrics," p. 696.

Trochee: A metrical foot consisting of an accented syllable followed by an unaccented syllable. See "Note on Versification and Metrics," p. 696.

Understatement: Saying less than might be expected. See **Irony.**

Unity: The unity of a poem, like that of any work of art, is a unity of final meaning. This does not imply simplicity (in the sense of poverty of idea or emotion) or merely logical congruity or sequence. Poetry that is *merely* simple (or which strikes the sensitive reader as "simplified") achieves its effect by eliminating all elements that might prove discordant; but all really good poetry attains its unity by establishing meaningful relationships among its apparently discordant elements. This is why critics sometimes say of a successful poem that it gives a sense of revelation, or gives a new insight. For—far from trimming our view of a subject down to a single, neatly ordered category—the poet ties together the items of ordinarily disordered experience into a new, and perhaps unsuspected, pattern. For example, the sort of imaginative unity which is analyzed in Coleridge's discussion of Shakespeare's *Venus and Adonis* (pp. 265–66). Poems like "Lycidas" (p. 465), "Among School Children" (p. 357), "Frescoes for Mr. Rockefeller's City" (p. 447), and "Ode to a Nightingale" (p. 336) offer examples of the unification of apparently discordant materials. Moreover, many poems, like some of the folk ballads or "The Rime of the Ancient Mariner" (p. 527), which are praised for their "fine simplicity," reveal, on examination, a very complicated structure underlying the effect of simplicity which they achieve. A student should be careful to make the distinction between poems that are *apparently* simple because the poet has unified his materials, and poems that are simple because the poet has avoided using all recalcitrant or difficult materials.

Variation: See "Note on Versification and Metrics," p. 696.

Vers de Société: A term applied to light verse, usually occasional and complimentary, which deals in a witty and polished fashion with subjects that, on the surface at least, are not very serious (see pp. 189, 190). But there is no sharp line of demarcation between *vers de société* and serious poetry. For instance, "To His Coy Mistress" by Andrew Marvell (p. 320) opens with the tone and manner of *vers de société*.

Verse: This term is sometimes used to mean a single line of a poem. But the more usual and more important meaning of the term, and the one which will be discussed here, is that form of literary composition in which the rhythms are regularized and systematized. See "Note on Versification and Metrics," p. 696.

Verse Texture: The general relationship among the sounds in verse, of which euphony and cacophony are aspects. See "Note on Versification and Metrics," p. 696.

Weak Rime: See "Note on Versification and Metrics," p. 696.

NOTE ON VERSIFICATION AND METRICS

All language, as has been pointed out, has the quality of rhythm (pp. 105–08). It has also been pointed out that there are varying degrees of formalization of rhythm and that between the clear extremes of ordinary prose and strict verse there are many intermediary types (pp. 106–07).

Meter, in English verse, is the systematization of rhythm in so far as this systematization is determined by the relationships between **accented** or stressed and **unaccented** or unstressed syllables. (This relationship between accented and unaccented syllables is a fundamental factor, but not the only factor, in determining the **rhythm.** Other factors involved—pause and emphasis conditioned by the length of syllables, consideration of sense, rime, etc., which will be treated below—contribute to the total rhythmical effect.) The following set of terms is conventionally accepted to describe meter:

Foot: The metrical unit, a combination of one accented and one or more unaccented syllables. The following types of feet will describe most metrical situations which occur in English verse:

- **Iamb:** An unaccented followed by an accented syllable (ăvóid).
- **Anapaest:** Two unaccented syllables followed by an accented syllable (ĭntĕrvéne).
- **Trochee:** One accented followed by one unaccented syllable (ónlў).
- **Dactyl:** One accented syllable followed by two unaccented syllables (háppĭlў).

The **Line** of verse is composed of one or more feet. The following names are used to denominate various line lengths:

Monometer: One foot	**Pentameter:** Five feet
Dimeter: Two feet	**Hexameter:** Six feet (or **Alexandrine**)
Trimeter: Three feet	**Heptameter:** Seven feet
Tetrameter: Four feet	

(Since a line is really a unit of attention, lines composed of more than six feet tend to break up into smaller units. Thus a heptameter line tends to break up into a tetrameter and a trimeter line.) There are two items involved in the metrical description of a line: the kind of foot and the number of feet. Thus, a line containing five iambic feet would be described as *iambic pentameter*.

Even in a single poem a poet does not necessarily adhere to a single type of foot. For various reasons, he may make a **substitution** of one type of foot for another (p. 118). For instance, in the opening of the following line a trochaic foot has been substituted for an iambic foot:

Crówned fròm | sòme sín | glè hérb | òr trée

Thus far in discussing a scheme for indicating the scansion of verse, all accented syllables have been assumed to have equal value; and in an abstract schematic sense this is true. But obviously, in the rhythm as one actually experiences it in a particular line, accented syllables may be of very unequal emphasis (pp. 129–31). By the same token, unaccented syllables are not on the level as an abstract scheme would seem to indicate (p. 131, n.1). Sometimes a syllable which, according to the abstract metrical pattern, would be unaccented, receives, because of rhetorical considerations, what appears to be an additional accent in its own right. For instance, consider the first foot of the following line:

Ah, whát | ăváils | thĕ scép | trĕd ráce (p. 145)

The syllable *Ah* may be said to receive a **Secondary Accent** (indicated as above). When we consider the relationship between the two syllables of such a foot as *Ah, what,* we may describe the situation by saying that there is a **Hovering Effect**, or a **Hovering Accent** (indicated as follows: *Ah, what*). A similar situation is created when by substitution, or by the use of an **imperfect foot** (a foot from which the unaccented syllable or syllables are missing,[1] indicated thus ^), two regularly accented

[1] Such a defect may be **compensated** for in either or both of two ways. First, by the addition of an unaccented syllable elsewhere in the line, or second, by a pause before the accented syllable. As an example of the first:

Ŭpón | thĕ sŭpréme | théme | ŏf Árt | ănd Sóng (p. 120)

Of the second:

^ Spéech | ăftĕr lóng | sílĕnce; | ^ ít | ĭs ríght (p. 118)

In the first instance, there is **compensation** for the imperfect foot *theme* by the preceding anapaest, *the supreme;* in the second, there is compensation for the imperfect foot *it* by the caesural pause. (The second example also shows how an imperfect foot, *Speech,* may be compensated for by a following anapaest, *after long.*)

feet are thrown into juxtaposition (p. 119). When a hovering accent occurs, or when two regular accents are forced together, there is said to exist a **Spondaic Movement.** (This term is derived from one of the feet in classical metrics, the **Spondee,** which is composed of long syllables, for classical verse is founded on **quantity.** But the term is frequently used with reference to English verse, which is founded on accent, to describe any situation in which two accents appear in succession—either when the two accents are not in the same foot, or when one is a secondary accent.)

Though English metrics is founded on accent, the factor of quantity has an importance in determining the final rhythmical result of a piece of verse as actually experienced. But quantity never appears in systematic form; it works, merely, to condition and modify the rhythmical pattern defined by accent (pp. 134–35).

Another factor which influences the total rhythmical effect of a particular line is the location of pauses defined by sense units. Although the line may be abstractly considered as a metrical unit, it is obvious that the sense unit does not always coincide with the line unit. In practice, sense divisions—phrase, clause, sentence, etc.—often terminate within the line; and conversely, the end of a line unit may divide a sense unit. The pauses within the line, their number and their emphasis, are extremely important in determining the tempo of the rhythm. The main pause is called the **Caesura,** but obviously there may be other pauses, which may be called **Secondary Pauses.** Variety, from line to line, in the location of the caesura and of secondary pauses is extremely important in versification. But mere variety is not the only consideration, for in good verse there is usually a connection between the handling of pauses and the rhetorical (and other) devices employed in the poem (pp. 129–31, 143–44). Just as sense units may divide a line, so the end of a line, conversely, may divide sense units. This interplay between sense units and metrical units becomes extremely important when considered, not in relation to a single line, but in relation to a group of lines. When the end of the line does not coincide with a normal speech pause of any kind, it is called **Run-on;** when it does coincide with such a pause, the line is said to be **End-stopped.**

But sound as well as sense may condition the rhythm of verse. For example, the presence of certain groups of consonants may create a **Forced Pause.** Such combinations, which cause a sense of strain in pronunciation and a slowing of rhythmical tempo, are said to be **Cacophonous** (p. 154). Conversely, consonant combinations easily pronounced give a sense of ease and tend to speed up the rhythmical tempo. Such combinations are said to be **Euphonious.** Euphonious effects are pleasant, but euphony in itself is never a primary objective of any good poem—that is, poetry, even lyrical poetry, is not *merely* "verbal music."

Thus far we have spoken of relationships among consonants. The term euphony in its largest sense is used also to designate agreeable relationships among vowel sounds. Obviously, some vowels are closely related to each other; others are much more distantly related. For example, the vowel sounds *oh* and *ah* are formed far back in the voice chamber; the vowel sounds *ee* and *ay* far to the front. Obviously, a line dominated by closely related vowels gives—provided other factors support this effect—a sense of ease and fluency. Some lines may achieve a sense of vitality by the fact that the vowels in them are not closely related—involve shifts in position, which may be either violent or modulated. The combinations in this matter are, of course, infinite. One may be tempted to associate certain effects with certain vowels—an effect of heaviness with the sonority of the long back vowel sounds (*oh, ah, aw, oo*)—but this element is effective only in so far as it operates in conjunction with other factors.

Certain words have been developed, as a matter of fact, in imitation of the sounds which they designate. Words like *hiss* and *bang* are called **Onomatopoeic** words. But the relation of sound to sense, in onomatopoeia, and the relation of mood to specific vowel sounds, are not fundamental factors in poetic effects (pp. 135–36).

Euphony, like cacophony, is to be considered in its functional relation to the total effect of a poem. This general relationship among the sounds in verse, of which cacophony, euphony, and onomatopoeia are aspects, is sometimes called **Verse Texture.** Other aspects of this relationship are **Assonance, Consonance,** and **Alliteration.** Assonance may be defined as identity of vowel sounds, as in the words *scream* and *beach* (pp. 139–40); consonance as the identity of the pattern of consonants, as in the words *leaves* and *lives* (pp. 139–40); alliteration as the repetition of consonants, particularly initial consonants, as in the words *lovely* and *lullaby* (pp. 139–40). But assonance, consonance, and alliteration may also be considered as forms of **Rime** because they involve degrees of identity of sound combinations. The term *rime,* however, is ordinarily used in the sense of **End Rime,** which is the identity in the riming words of the accented *vowels* and of all consonants and vowels following. (This is sometimes called *rime suffisante* in distinction from *rime riche,* or identical rime, in which there is identity of the accented *syllables* of the words rimed. For instance: *incline* and *decline.*) The forms of end rime may be classified as follows:

MASCULINE RIME: The rimed syllables are the last syllables of the words in question, as in *surmount* and *discount.*

FEMININE RIME: The rimed syllables are followed by identical unaccented syllables, as in *delightful* and *frightful*. When only one unaccented syllable occurs after the accented syllable, there is an instance of DOUBLE RIME, as in the above example. When two unaccented syllables, identical in the rimed words, follow the accented syllable, there is an instance of TRIPLE RIME. For example: *regretfully* and *forgetfully*.

WEAK RIME: The rimed syllables are unstressed or only lightly stressed. For examples, see "In Distrust of Merits," p. 499.

In addition to the above forms of rime there are approximate rimes, sometimes called **Slant Rimes.** For instance, *rover* and *lover,* or *steel* and *chill*. Such rimes are not necessarily indications of a poet's carelessness, but may be used for various special effects. When the student discovers examples of slant rime, he should try to determine what the effect would have been with the emphasis of full rime. Many rimes that now are apparently slant rimes were, in the past, full rimes; therefore, a student should try to determine the pronunciation used by the poet before passing judgment on a poem of the past.

Although there is a pleasure in rime itself, and rime may serve as a decoration to verse, the fundamental function of rime is that of a binder. It is this function which makes rime so important as a device of emphasis and as a means of defining a pattern of lines, or a **Stanza.** Indeed, most stanzas involve not only a fixed pattern of lines, but also a pattern of rimes, or a **Rime Scheme.** An unrimed stanza is to be defined by the prevailing type of foot, the number of feet in each line, and the number of lines. That is, a poem might be written in iambic tetrameter quatrains. The definition of a rimed stanza would add to such items the description of the rime scheme. For instance, the rime scheme of the envelope quatrain, in which the first and fourth lines and the second and third lines rime, would be described as follows: *abba*. The most ordinary stanzas and line patterns are:

Couplet: (1) **Tetrameter** couplet, sometimes called the octosyllabic couplet; iambic tetrameter, *aa*. (2) **Heroic** couplet; iambic pentameter, *aa*. (A couplet is **closed** when the sense is completed within its compass.)

Terza Rima: iambic pentameter **Tercets** in **linked** rime: *aba-bcb-cdc,* etc.

Quatrain: (1) **Ballad Measure:** iambic, first and fourth lines tetrameter, second and fourth lines trimeter, with second and fourth lines riming. (This may be indicated as follows: iambic, 4,3,4,3, *xaxa*.)

A very common variant of this pattern rimes *abab*. (2) **Envelope,** or **"In Memoriam"** quatrain; iambic tetrameter, *abba*. (3) **"Rubaiyat"** quatrain; iambic pentameter, *aaxa*. (4) Several other types of quatrains are commonly used but have no specific names (see Index of Stanza Forms).

Rime Royal: iambic pentameter, *ababbcc*.

Ottava Rima: iambic pentameter, *abababcc*.

Spenserian Stanza: iambic pentameter, *ababbcbcc*. The last line is an alexandrine.

Sonnet: An iambic pentameter poem in fourteen lines. There are two general types: (1) **Italian** sonnet: iambic pentameter, *abbaabbacdedde*. The first eight lines, in which the general theme of the sonnet is usually presented, is called the **Octave.** The last six lines, in which the poet presents the conclusion he has drawn from the theme, is called the **Sestet.** Common variants on the rime scheme of the sestet are *cdeedc, cdedce*. (2) **Shakespearian** sonnet: iambic pentameter, *ababcdcdefefgg*. In its typical form this sonnet presents and develops its theme in the three quatrains, and states a conclusion in the couplet. But there are many variations of this method of handling the idea. For instance, the first two quatrains may be used as the octave of the Italian sonnet is used and the last quatrain and couplet as the sestet. (3) Irregular sonnets: in addition to various slight departures from the strict rime scheme of the Italian and Shakespearian sonnet, there occur rime schemes which are highly irregular.

Although **Blank Verse** is not a form of stanza it may be considered here. Blank verse is unrimed iambic pentameter not broken into formal units. This is not to say that a poem written in blank verse (or for that matter, in other verse forms not employing the stanza) may not be broken up into **Verse Paragraphs,** which may be defined as large rhetorical units. "Lycidas" (p. 465) is divided into verse paragraphs.

The definitions given above present various elements of **Versification** in an abstract and schematic form. In studying such definitions one should realize that they are merely terms conventionally accepted to describe certain verbal situations which occur in poetry and are not to be taken as "laws" for the making of poetry. When they are applied to the criticism of particular poems, it should be remembered that the degree of excellence achieved by any poet in his management of such technical factors is to be determined by answering the following question: *How has he adapted these technical factors to the other elements in the poem?*

We have given above in schematic form the conventions which apply to most modern English verse, a verse which is based on the patterned relationship between the number of syllables in a line and the disposition of accents. But there are two general types of verse represented in this book to which these conventions do not apply.

The first is **Free Verse.** Free verse, as the term implies, does not conform to any fixed pattern. This is not to say that none of the individual metrical situations previously discussed here may not appear, incidentally, in a free verse poem. But it is to say that such situations occur only incidentally. There is, obviously, in free verse a much looser organization of rhythm than there is in ordinary accentual-syllabic verse. In reading a free verse poem, the student should ask himself whether there is an appropriate relationship between the rhythm and the other elements in the poem.[1]

The second, **Old Native Meter,** is a verse derived originally from the Old English four-beat alliterative verse (p. 139). In the modern survivals of this verse, the alliteration may or may not appear, but the verse is still usually characterized by the presence of four heavily accented syllables and of a varying number of unaccented syllables, the line being usually broken between the second and third accents by an emphatic caesura.[2] For example:

> Síng a song of síxpence, póćketful of rýe,
> Fóur and twenty bláckbirds báked within a píe

or:

> For our héarts are grown héavy, and whére shall we túrn to,
> If thús the king's glóry, our gaín and salvátion. . . .
>
> (William Morris)

There are three poems in this book which seem to make systematic use of this or of a related measure: "Rocky Acres" (p. 93), "Just a Smack at Auden" (p. 519), and "The Windhover" (p. 522).[3]

[1] For a discussion of free verse, see Yvor Winters, *Primitivism and Decadence,* New York: Arrows Editions, 1937, pp. 102–21.

[2] For a discussion of some of the modern developments of the old alliterative meter, the student may consult Harold Whitehall's "Sprung Rhythm," in *Gerard Manley Hopkins,* Norfolk, Conn.: New Directions, 1944, pp. 28–54. For the historical development, he should consult Jakob Schipper, *A History of English Versification,* Oxford, England: Oxford University Press, pp. 85–125.

[3] For the meter of "The Windhover," see the Whitehall essay cited in the last footnote.

In some of the modern developments of the old native meter, there may be more than four beats to the line or fewer than four beats to the line. Parts of "Journey of the Magi" (p. 520) seem to be written in the old native meter.[1] "Doom Is Dark" (p. 330) gives a definite suggestion of the native meter, including the alliteration. Other poems in this book show perceptible traces of this metric, but such poems as can be scanned in terms of the standard system—for example, Auden's "O Where Are You Going?" (p. 518)—are so scanned in the Index of Stanza Forms.

A PRACTICAL NOTE ON SCANSION

Meter does not make rhythm. The rhythm is already there. Indication of the meter (scansion) is merely a *description* of the rhythm in schematic form. In scanning a poem, the student should read the poem, preferably aloud, in what seems the most normal way possible. When he has caught in this instinctive way what he feels to be the basic movement, he should note the distribution and number of the accents; that is, he should determine what is the normal foot and the number of such feet in the normal line. (Reading a number of lines will prove the best way to apprehend the normal foot and the normal line. The reading of one or two lines may not give these—least of all a reading of the first line, frequently the most irregular line in a poem.)

Having determined the norm—that the normal foot, say, is an iamb, and that the normal line is, say, pentameter—the student is ready to mark the syllables as unaccented and accented and to mark off the lines into feet, taking due account of variations from the norm such as substitutions, secondary accents, hovering accents, and defective feet.

The student should remember that the ear, not the eye, determines in scansion: *-ble* in *humble* is a syllable, and must be counted as such; *bead* is a word of one syllable, not two. He should remember that a foot is a metrical measure, not a sense measure, and that the foot divisions may cut across words, and that a foot may incorporate syllables from different words, thus:

Thĕ cúr | tăins dráwn | ŭpón | ŭnfriénd | lў níght.

The student may find useful these three simple rules of thumb: (1)

[1] For this poem and the metric of Eliot's later poetry in general, see Helen Gardner, *The Art of T. S. Eliot,* London, 1949, pp. 19–35.

Each pronounced syllable must be marked ᴗ , //, or /. (2) Each foot must have one main accent. (3) Each foot must contain no more than one main accent. (If the student uses the mark ⌒ to indicate a hovering accent, he should remember that this mark indicates that each of the two syllables so marked gets equal stress. This mark does *not* represent a slurred accent; moreover, it never designates light accents; i.e., two unaccented syllables. If the student finds the mark confusing, let him simply use a secondary accent and a primary accent, marking a hovering accent thus // / .)

Most of all, the student should bear in mind that the system of scansion suggested in this book represents the barest minimum of terms: three grades of accent and only four kinds of feet.[1] The secondary accent (//) must serve to mark everything from the lightest additional accent on a normally unaccented syllable up to a stress as heavy as that of the primary accent itself. The gain in simplicity is great, but the student must recognize the price paid for this simplicity: the system that he will be using will often give only the roughest approximation to what is actually going on, and at points it will be quite arbitrary. If, however, the student will use it with full awareness of its limitations, prepared to supplement its sketchiness by a full and detailed examination of the variation in question, it may serve well enough. For scansion is a means to an end: and the end is appreciation of the poem in its entirety.

[1] Many metrical systems include such feet as the pyrrhic (ᴗ ᴗ), the spondee (/ /), the amphibrach (ᴗ / ᴗ), and many others. But no system of metrics—not even the most elaborate—can give a complete description of what "goes on" in a poem. The editors have preferred to adopt a very simple system, urging the student to relate it to a full analysis of the poem in all its aspects, rather than to adopt a more elaborate system which must, even though quite elaborate, fall short of a full description of the actual metrical situation.

INDEX OF AUTHORS, TITLES, AND FIRST LINES

Names of authors are in capitals, titles of poems in bold face, and first lines in light face; asterisks (*) indicate poems that are analysed.

INDEX OF AUTHORS, TITLES, AND FIRST LINES

INDEX OF AUTHORS, TITLES, AND FIRST LINES

INDEX OF AUTHORS, TITLES, AND FIRST LINES

INDEX OF STANZA FORMS

Any stanza index must be arbitrary at certain points. For instance, some poems which might be regarded as written in couplets or as written in an irregular form, have been classified under stanzas. Some poems placed under the irregular forms might be regarded as exemplifying a regular stanza pattern. The following points should be noted: All poems are in iambic meter unless otherwise specified. Variations are not indicated unless very numerous. The use of repetition is not necessarily pointed out, but in some cases, where it seems particularly important, the repeated syllables are marked as follows: a^1,a^1.

INDEX OF STANZA FORMS

INDEX OF STANZA FORMS

INDEX OF STANZA FORMS

FIVE-LINE STANZAS

SIX-LINE STANZAS

SEVEN-LINE STANZAS

RIME ROYAL (pentameter, ababbcc)

OTHER SEVEN-LINE STANZAS

EIGHT-LINE STANZAS

FREE VERSE

OLD NATIVE METER

(Poems in this meter have also been entered under the proper *stanza forms* above.)